MCSA Guide to
Networking with
Windows Server® 2016

MCSE/MCSA

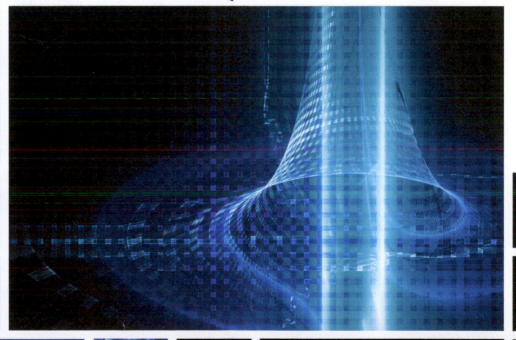

Exam #70-741

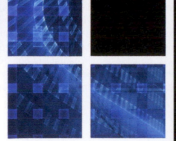

CENGAGE

Australia • Brazil • Mexico • Singapore • United Kingdom • United States

Greg Tomsho

MCSA Guide to Networking with Windows Server 2016, Exam 70-741
Greg Tomsho

SVP, GM Science, Technology & Math: Balraj S. Kalsi

Senior Product Director: Kathleen McMahon

Product Team Manager: Kristin McNary

Associate Product Manager: Amy Savino

Senior Director, Development: Julia Caballero

Senior Product Development Manager: Leigh Hefferon

Senior Content Developer: Michelle Ruelos Cannistraci

Product Assistant: Jake Toth

Marketing Director: Michele McTighe

Production Director: Patty Stephan

Senior Content Project Manager: Brooke Greenhouse

Art Director: Diana Graham

Cover image: iStockPhoto.com/Emelyanov

Production Service/Composition: SPi Global

For product information and technology assistance, contact us at
Cengage Customer & Sales Support, 1-800-354-9706

For permission to use material from this text or product, submit all requests online at **www.cengage.com/permissions**.
Further permissions questions can be e-mailed to
permissionrequest@cengage.com

Library of Congress Control Number: 2017947406

Student Edition ISBN: 978-1-337-40078-7
Loose-leaf Edition ISBN: 978-1-337-68579-5

Cengage
20 Channel Center Street
Boston, MA 02210
USA

Cengage is a leading provider of customized learning solutions with employees residing in nearly 40 different countries and sales in more than 125 countries around the world. Find your local representative at **www.cengage.com**.

Cengage products are represented in Canada by Nelson Education, Ltd.

To learn more about Cengage platforms and services, visit **www.cengage.com**

Purchase any of our products at your local college store or at our preferred online store **www.cengagebrain.com**

Printed in the United States of America
Print Number: 01   Print Year: 2017

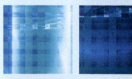

Brief Contents

Table of Contents

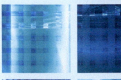
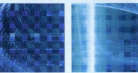

Introduction

MCSA Guide to Networking with Windows Server® 2016, Exam 70-741, gives you in-depth coverage of the 70-741 certification exam objectives and focuses on the skills you need to configure network services with Windows Server 2016. With dozens of hands-on activities and skill-reinforcing case projects, you'll be well prepared for the certification exam and learn valuable skills to perform on the job.

After you finish this book, you'll have an in-depth knowledge of Windows Server 2016 networking, including TCP/IP addressing, DNS configuration, DHCP configuration, remote access, distributed file-sharing solutions, and advanced network features configuration. This book is written from a teaching and learning point of view, not simply as an exam study guide. The chapters guide readers through the technologies they need to master to perform on the job, not just to pass an exam.

Intended Audience

MCSA Guide to Networking with Windows Server® 2016, Exam 70-741 is intended for people who want to learn how to configure and manage a Windows Server 2016 network and earn the Microsoft Certified Solutions Associate (MCSA) certification. This book covers in full the objectives of Exam 70-741, one of three required for the MCSA: Windows Server 2016 certification. Exam 70-741 is also one of four exams needed for the MCSE: Cloud Platform and Infrastructure certification. This book serves as an excellent tool for classroom teaching, but self-paced learners will also find that the clear explanations, challenging activities, and case projects serve them equally well.

For those readers who start their study of Windows Server 2016 with this book (instead of the 70-740 book), *MCSA Guide to Installation, Storage, and Compute with Windows Server® 2016* (Cengage, 2018), Chapter 1 of that text, which serves as an introduction to Windows Server 2016, is available as a free download from the Cengage website. That chapter introduces you to Windows Server 2016 core technologies, such as Active Directory and the file system, and provides a brief overview of new features found in Windows Server 2016 compared to earlier server versions.

What This Book Includes

- A lab setup guide is included in the "Before You Begin" section of this Introduction to help you configure a physical or virtual (recommended) lab environment for doing the hands-on activities.
- Step-by-step hands-on activities walk you through tasks ranging from configuring IP addressing to advanced network configurations with DNS and DHCP. All activities have been tested by a technical editor.

- Extensive review and end-of-chapter materials reinforce your learning.
- Critical thinking case projects require you to apply the concepts and technologies learned throughout the book.
- Abundant screen captures and diagrams visually reinforce the text and hands-on activities.
- A list of 70-741 exam objectives is cross-referenced with chapters and sections that cover each objective (inside cover and Appendix A).

Note

This text does not include Windows Server 2016 software. However, 180-day evaluation versions of Windows Server 2016 are available at no cost from *https://www.microsoft.com/en-us/evalcenter/evaluate-windows-server-2016*. More specific instruction can be found in "Using an Evaluation Version of Windows Server 2016" in the "Before You Begin" section of this Introduction.

About Microsoft Certification: MCSA

This book prepares you to take one of three exams in the Microsoft Certified Solutions Associate (MCSA) Windows Server 2016 certification. The MCSA Windows Server 2016 certification is made up of three exams, which can be taken in any order:

- Exam 70-740: Installation, Storage, and Compute with Windows Server 2016
- Exam 70-741: Networking with Windows Server 2016
- Exam 70-742: Identity with Windows Server 2016

Note

This text focuses on Exam 70-741. Companion texts focus on Exam 740 and Exam 742, respectively: *MCSA Guide to Installation, Storage, and Compute with Windows Server 2016* (Cengage, 2018) and *MCSA Guide to Identity with Windows Server 2016* (Cengage, 2018).

Microsoft Certified Solutions Expert (MCSE): The Next Step

After achieving the MCSA Windows Server 2016 certification, you can move on to the MCSE certification. For the MCSE: Cloud Platform and Infrastructure certification, the MCSA Windows Server 2016 certification is a prerequisite. You then have the option of taking one of ten exams to complete the MCSE. To see the list of exams you can take to complete the MCSE, see *https://www.microsoft.com/en-us/learning/mcse-cloud-platform-infrastructure.aspx*.

Chapter Descriptions

This book is organized to cover the 70-741 exam objectives in a pedagogical sequence, not in the sequence presented by the list of 70-741 exam objectives. Chapter 1 starts you off with an overview of the TCP/IP protocol and its various components and emphasizes configuration of IPv4 and IPv6 addressing and subnetting. It wraps up by discussing advanced network solutions found in Windows Server 2016. The 70-741 exam objectives are covered throughout the book, and you can find a map of objectives and the chapters in which they're covered on the inside front cover with a more detailed mapping in Appendix A. The following list describes this book's chapters:

> **Note** 📎
>
> Chapter 1 of the 70-740 book, *MCSA Guide to Installation, Storage, and Compute with Windows Server® 2016* (Cengage, 2018), is available as a PDF for free download by students and instructors from the Cengage website. If you start studying Windows Server 2016 with this 741 book, you may want to read Chapter 1 of the 70-740 book first as it provides an introduction to Windows Server 2016 and describes some of the core technologies you may need to understand while studying this book.

- **Chapter 1**, "Configuring TCP/IP," describes the components of the TCP/IP protocol suite and how to subnet IPv4 addresses. You learn how to configure IPv4 addresses on Windows computers with both GUI and command-line tools. Finally, you learn about the structure of IPv6 addresses, how to subnet an IPv6 address, a variety of methods for configuring IPv6 addresses on host computers, and ways to transition from an IPv4 network to an IPv6 network.
- **Chapter 2**, "Configuring DNS Servers," describes the structure of the worldwide DNS system and explains how to configure and maintain DNS in a Windows domain environment.
- **Chapter 3**, "Configuring Advanced DNS," explains how to manage DNS zones, the main structural component of DNS. Because DNS in an Active Directory environment can be stored in a traditional text file or in an Active Directory partition, you learn the advantages of using an Active Directory–integrated zone and how to tune replication between DNS servers. Next, you explore several methods to secure and protect DNS. In addition, you learn about managing DNS with DNS policies, delegated administration, and performance monitoring and tuning.
- **Chapter 4**, "Implementing DHCP," discusses how DHCP works. You learn how to install and configure DHCP, including server authorization, scopes, and DHCP options. You also learn about some advanced features, such as reservations, exclusions, server policies, and filters. In addition, you learn how DHCPv6 works and how to configure a DHCPv6 scope and options. In addition, you learn how to configure DHCP to work with DNS, DHCP relay, and DHCP high availability.
- **Chapter 5**, "Implementing IPAM," describes how to use a DHCP management tool called Internet Protocol Address Management (IPAM) to centrally manage DHCP servers and IP address spaces and DNS servers and zones. You learn how to install and provision an IPAM server and to select servers to manage and collect server data.
- **Chapter 6**, "Implementing Remote Access," discusses how to install and configure the Remote Access server role and its three role services. This chapter also focuses on configuring virtual private networks and the DirectAccess role service.
- **Chapter 7**, "Implementing Network Policy Server," covers how to configure centralized authentication and authentication policies using Network Policy Server and RADIUS. Incorporating industry standards for authentication and authorization, Windows Server 2016 includes ways to protect a network at the gate. With Network Policy Server, for example, you can create policies to determine who can access your network and how they can connect.
- **Chapter 8**, "Configuring Distributed File System and BranchCache," discusses how to configure DFS namespaces and replication, two of the main components of the DFS role service. You also learn about BranchCache, a file-sharing technology that allows computers at a branch office to cache files retrieved from a central server across a WAN link. Using BranchCache improves file-sharing performance for branch office users and reduces WAN link usage. This chapter also discusses the requirements and configuration steps for deploying BranchCache in a multisite network.

- **Chapter 9**, "Implementing Advanced Network Solutions," introduces you to several high-performance networking features that can be implemented on physical computers and virtual machines (VMs). Features such as QoS, RDMA, Data Center Bridging, and Virtual Machine Queue keep network traffic moving through your servers to keep up with today's demand for high-bandwidth network services. Next, in keeping with Windows Server 2016's focus on the software-defined datacenter (SDDC), you learn about software-defined networking (SDN) features available in Windows Server 2016, including Hyper-V Network Virtualization, Software Load Balancer, and Windows Server Gateways.
- **Appendix A**, "MCSA Exam 70-741 Objectives," maps each 70-741 exam objective to the chapter and section where you can find information on that objective.

Features

This book includes the following learning features to help you master the topics in this book and the 70-741 exam objectives:

- *Chapter objectives*—Each chapter begins with a detailed list of the concepts to be mastered. This list is a quick reference to the chapter's contents and a useful study aid.
- *Hands-on activities*—Several dozen hands-on activities are incorporated into this book, giving you practice in setting up, configuring, and managing Windows Server 2016 networks. Much of the learning about Windows Server 2016 comes from completing the hands-on activities, and much effort has been devoted to making the activities relevant and challenging.
- *Requirements for hands-on activities*—A table at the beginning of each chapter lists the hands-on activities and what you need for each activity.
- *Screen captures, illustrations, and tables*—Numerous screen captures and illustrations of concepts help you visualize theories and concepts and see how to use tools and desktop features. In addition, tables often are used to give you details and comparisons of practical and theoretical information and can be used for a quick review.
- *Chapter summary*—Each chapter ends with a summary of the concepts introduced in the chapter. These summaries are a helpful way to recap and revisit the material covered in the chapter.
- *Key terms*—All terms in the chapter introduced in bold text are gathered together in the Key Terms list at the end of the chapter. This list gives you a way to check your understanding of all important terms. All key term definitions are listed in the Glossary at the end of the book.
- *Review questions*—The end-of-chapter assessment begins with review questions that reinforce the concepts and techniques covered in each chapter. Answering these questions helps to ensure that you have mastered important topics.
- *Critical thinking*—Each chapter closes with one or more case projects to provide critical thinking exercises. Many of the case projects build on one another, as you take a small startup company to a flourishing enterprise.
- *Exam objectives*—Major sections in each chapter show the exam objective or objectives covered in that section, making it easier to find the material you need when studying for the MCSA exam.

Text and Graphics Conventions

Additional information and exercises have been added to this book to help you better understand what's being discussed in the chapter. Icons throughout the book alert you to these additional materials:

> **Tip** ⓘ
>
> Tips offer extra information on resources, how to solve problems, and time-saving shortcuts.

Note

Notes present additional helpful material related to the subject being discussed.

Caution

Caution icons identify important information about potential mistakes or hazards.

Activity

Each hands-on activity in this book is preceded by the Activity icon.

Critical Thinking

Critical Thinking icons mark the end-of-chapter case projects, which are scenario-based assignments that ask you to apply what you have learned in the chapter.

 **Certification**

- Certification icons under chapter headings list exam objectives covered in that section.

Instructor Companion Site

Everything you need for your course in one place! This collection of book-specific lecture and class tools is available online via *www.cengage.com/login*. Access and download PowerPoint presentations, images, the Instructor's Manual, and more.

- *Electronic Instructor's Manual*—The Instructor's Manual that accompanies this book includes additional instructional material to assist in class preparation, including suggestions for classroom activities, discussion topics, and additional quiz questions.
- *Solutions Manual*—The instructor's resources include solutions to all end-of-chapter material, including review questions and case projects.
- *Cengage Testing Powered by Cognero*—This flexible, online system allows you to do the following:
  - Author, edit, and manage test bank content from multiple Cengage solutions.
  - Create multiple test versions in an instant.
  - Deliver tests from your LMS, your classroom, or anywhere you want.
- *PowerPoint presentations*—This book comes with Microsoft PowerPoint slides for each chapter. They're included as a teaching aid for classroom presentation, to make available to students on the network for chapter review, or to be printed for classroom distribution. Instructors, please feel free to add your own slides for additional topics that you introduce to the class.
- *Figure files*—All the figures and tables in the book are reproduced in bitmap format. Similar to the PowerPoint presentations, they're included as a teaching aid for classroom presentation, to make available to students for review, or to be printed for classroom distribution.

MindTap

MindTap for Tomsho/*MCSA Guide to Networking with Windows Server 2016, Exam 70-741* is a personalized, fully online digital learning platform of content, assignments, and services that engages students and encourages them to think critically while allowing you to easily set your course through simple customization options.

MindTap is designed to help students master the skills they need in today's workforce. Research shows that employers need critical thinkers, troubleshooters, and creative problem solvers to stay relevant in our fast-paced, technology-driven world. MindTap helps you achieve this with assignments and activities that provide hands-on practice, real-life relevance, and certification test prep. Students are guided through assignments that help them master basic knowledge and understanding before moving on to more challenging problems.

The live virtual machine labs provide real-life application and practice. Based on the textbook's Hands-On Activities, the live virtual machine labs provide more advanced learning. Students work in a live environment via the Cloud with real servers and networks that they can explore. The IQ certification test prep engine allows students to quiz themselves on specific exam domains, and the pre- and post-course assessments are mock exams that measure exactly how much they have learned. Readings, labs, and whiteboard videos support the lecture, while "In the News" assignments encourage students to stay current.

MindTap is designed around learning objectives and provides the analytics and reporting to easily see where the class stands in terms of progress, engagement, and completion rates. Use the content and learning path as is or pick and choose how our materials will wrap around yours. You control what the students see and when they see it.

Students can access eBook content in the MindTap Reader, which offers highlighting, note-taking, search, and audio (students can listen to text), as well as mobile, access.

Learn more at *http://www.cengage.com/mindtap/*.

Instant Access Code: 9781337400800

Printed Access Code: 9781337400817

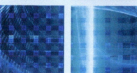

Acknowledgments

I would like to thank Cengage Product Team Manager Kristin McNary and Associate Product Manager Amy Savino for their confidence in asking me to undertake this challenging project. In addition, thanks go out to Michelle Ruelos Cannistraci, Senior Content Developer, who assembled an outstanding team to support this project. A special word of gratitude goes to Deb Kaufmann, Development Editor, who took an unrefined product and turned it into a polished manuscript. Danielle Shaw, Technical Editor, tested chapter activities diligently to ensure that labs work as they were intended, and for that, I am grateful. I also want to include a shout-out to a former student of mine, Shaun Stallard, who was instrumental in the creation of the end-of-chapter material including Chapter Summary, Key Terms, and Review Questions.

Finally, my family: my beautiful wife Julie, lovely daughters Camille and Sophia, and son Michael, deserve special thanks and praise for going husbandless and fatherless 7 days a week, 14 hours a day, for the better part of a year. Without their patience and understanding and happy greetings when I did make an appearance, I could not have accomplished this.

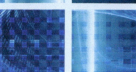

About the Author

Greg Tomsho has more than 30 years of computer and networking experience and has earned the CCNA, MCTS, MCSA, Network+, A+, Security+, and Linux+ certifications. Greg is the director of the Computer Networking Technology Department and Cisco Academy at Yavapai College in Prescott, Arizona. His other books include *MCSA Guide to Installation, Storage, and Compute with Windows Server 2016, Exam 70-740; MCSA Guide to Identity with Windows Server 2016, Exam 70-742; Guide to Operating Systems; MCSA Guide to Installing and Configuring Windows Server 2012/R2, Exam 70-410; MCSA Guide to Administering Windows Server 2012/R2, Exam 70-411; MCSA Guide to Configuring Advanced Windows Server 2012/R2 Services, Exam 70-412; MCTS Guide to Microsoft Windows Server 2008 Active Directory Configuration; MCTS Guide to Microsoft Windows Server 2008 Applications Infrastructure Configuration; Guide to Networking Essentials; Guide to Network Support and Troubleshooting;* and *A+ CoursePrep ExamGuide.*

Contact the Author

I would like to hear from you. Please email me at *w2k16@tomsho.com* with any problems, questions, suggestions, or corrections. I even accept compliments! Your comments and suggestions are invaluable for shaping the content of future books. You can also submit errata, lab suggestions, and comments via email. I have set up a website to support my books at *http://books.tomsho.com*, where you'll find lab notes, errata, web links, and helpful hints for using my books. If you're an instructor, you can register on the site to contribute articles and comment on articles.

Before You Begin

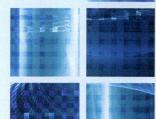

Windows Server has become more complex as Microsoft strives to satisfy the needs of enterprise networks. In years past, you could learn what you needed to manage a Windows Server-based network and pass the Microsoft certification exams with a single server, some good lab instructions, and a network connection. Today, as you work with advanced technologies—such as highly available DHCP, IPAM, and RADIUS, just to name a few—your lab environment must be more complex, requiring several servers. Setting up this lab environment can be challenging, and this section was written to help you meet this challenge. Using virtual machines in Hyper-V on Windows 10 or Windows Server 2016 is highly recommended; other virtual environments work, too, but you'll want to choose one that allows nested virtualization, which means running a virtual machine within a virtual machine so you can perform some of the Hyper-V activities that require it. Using virtual machines is also highly recommended because it allows you to easily change the storage and network configuration of your servers and to revert your lab to its original state for each chapter.

> **Note**
>
> The MindTap digital online learning platform for this text includes access to live virtual machine labs based on the textbook's hands-on activities without the need to set up your own lab environment.

Lab Setup Guide

> **Note**
>
> If you can't set up a lab environment exactly as described in this section, you might be able to configure a partial lab with just one Windows Server 2016 server and still do many of the hands-on activities. Having two servers is even better, and having three enables you to do the majority of the book's activities. If you can't do an activity, it's important to read the activity steps to learn important information about Windows Server 2016.

Because of the flexibility and availability of using a virtual environment, the lab setup guide is designed with the assumption that virtualization is used, whether Hyper-V, VMware, VirtualBox, or some other product. The lab environment is designed so that the initial configuration of the virtual machines will take you through any chapter. Each chapter starts with an activity that instructs the reader to revert the virtual machines (VMs) used in the chapter to the initial configuration using a saved snapshot/checkpoint.

A total of four VMs with Windows Server 2016 installed are used throughout the book. However, they are not all used at the same time; some activities use as many as three VMs while some require only one or two. No client OS is used. This decision was made primarily on the basis that many readers will be using evaluation versions of Windows on their VMs and the evaluation period for Windows client OSs such as Windows 10 is very short compared to the Windows Server 2016 evaluation period. In addition, Windows 10 is continually being upgraded, and the upgrades may affect the outcome of some of the activities. Therefore, any activities that require a client will use a VM that has Windows Server 2016 installed. Readers should see little to no difference between using Windows Server 2016 as a client OS and using Windows 10.

The activities use four VMs running Windows Server 2016 in which one server is a domain controller (DC) and two servers are domain members. The fourth server is configured as a stand-alone server that is operating in workgroup mode. Some activities require your VMs to access the Internet. An easy way to accommodate this is to install the Remote Access role on your Hyper-V host (if you're using Hyper-V and Windows Server 2016 for your host computer) and configure NAT so that your Hyper-V host can route packets to the physical network and the Internet. After installing the Remote Access role with the Routing role service, configure NAT and select the interface connected to the physical network as the public interface and the interface connected to the Hyper-V internal switch as the private interface. The interface connected to the Hyper-V internal switch should be configured with address 192.168.0.250/24. Figure 1 shows a diagram of this network.

A few words about the Figure 1 diagram:

- The router address is an example; you can use a different address. You can do most activities except those requiring Internet access without a router to the Internet.
- ServerDC1 is a domain controller for domain MCSA2016.local and has both the Active Directory Domain Services (AD DS) and DNS server roles installed.
- Specific installation requirements for each server are explained in the following sections.

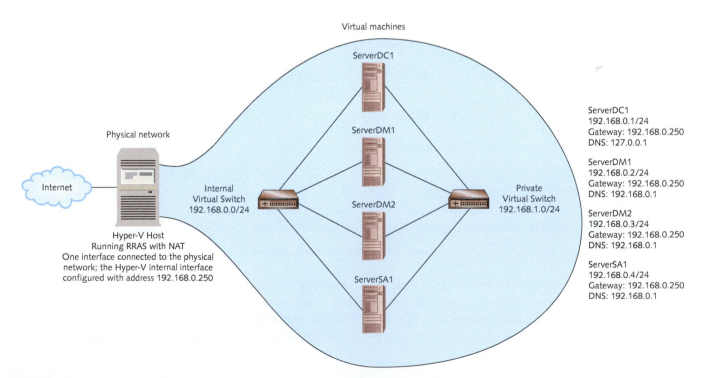

Figure 1   A diagram of the lab configuration used in this book

Host Computer Configuration

The following are recommendations for the host computer when you're using virtualization:

- Dual-core or quad-core CPU with Intel-VT-x/EPT support. You can see a list of supported Intel processors at *http://ark.intel.com/Search/Advanced* (click Processors, then select the "Intel-VT-x with Extended Page Tables (EPT)" filter).

Note

Most activities can be done without a CPU that supports EPT, but you can't install Hyper-V on a VM if the host doesn't support EPT for Intel CPUs.

- 8 GB RAM; more is better.
- 200 GB free disk space.
- Windows Server 2016 or Windows 10 if you're using Hyper-V.
- Windows 10 or Windows 8.1 if you're using VMware Workstation or VirtualBox.

Server Configuration Details

ServerDC1

This VM should be configured as follows:

- Windows Server 2016 Datacenter—Desktop Experience
- Server name: ServerDC1
- Administrator password: Password01
- Memory: 2 GB or more
- Hard disk 1: 60 GB or more
- Ethernet connection – connected to Internal Virtual Switch
  - IP address: 192.168.0.1/24
  - Default gateway: 192.168.0.250 (or an address supplied by the instructor)
  - DNS: 127.0.0.1
- Ethernet 2 connection—connected to Private Virtual Switch
  - IP address: 192.168.1.1/24
  - Default gateway: Not configured
  - DNS: Not configured
- Active Directory Domain Services and DNS installed:
  - Domain Name: MCSA2016.local
- Windows Update: Configured with most recent updates
- Power Setting: Never turn off display
- Internet Explorer Enhanced Security Configuration: Turned off for Administrator
- User Account Control: Lowest setting
- After ServerDC1 is fully configured, create a checkpoint/snapshot named InitialConfig that will be applied at the beginning of each chapter's activities where this VM is used. Turn off the VM before you create a checkpoint/snapshot.

ServerDM1

This VM should be configured as follows:

- Windows Server 2016 Datacenter—Desktop Experience
- Server name: ServerDM1

- Administrator password: Password01
- Memory: 2 GB or more
- Hard disk 1: 60 GB or more
- Hard disk 2: 20 GB
- Hard disk 3: 15 GB
- Hard disk 4: 10 GB
- Ethernet connection—connected to Internal Virtual Switch
  - IP address: 192.168.0.2/24
  - Default gateway: 192.168.0.250 (or an address supplied by the instructor)
  - DNS: 192.168.0.1 (the address of ServerDC1)
- Ethernet 2 connection—connected to Private Virtual Switch
  - IP address: 192.168.1.2/24
  - Default gateway: Not configured
  - DNS: Not configured
- Member of domain: MCSA2016.local
- Windows Update: Configured with most recent updates
- Power Setting: Never turn off display
- Internet Explorer Enhanced Security Configuration: Turned off for Administrator
- User Account Control: Lowest setting
- After Server DM1 is fully configured, create a checkpoint/snapshot named InitialConfig that will be applied at the beginning of each chapter's activities where this VM is used.

ServerDM2

This VM should be configured as follows:

- Windows Server 2016 Datacenter—Server Core
- Server name: ServerDM2
- Administrator password: Password01
- Memory: 2 GB or more
- Hard disk 1: 60 GB or more
- Hard disk 2: 20 GB
- Hard disk 3: 15 GB
- Hard disk 4: 10 GB
- Ethernet connection—connected to Internal Virtual Switch
  - IP address: 192.168.0.3/24
  - Default gateway: 192.168.0.250 (or an address supplied by the instructor)
  - DNS: 192.168.0.1 (the address of ServerDC1)
- Ethernet 2 connection—connected to Private Virtual Switch
  - IP address: 192.168.1.3/24
  - Default gateway: Not configured
  - DNS: Not configured
- Member of domain: MCSA2016.local
- Windows Update: Configured with most recent updates
- Power Setting: Never turn off display
- Internet Explorer Enhanced Security Configuration: Turned off for Administrator
- User Account Control: Lowest setting
- After Server DM2 is fully configured, create a checkpoint/snapshot named InitialConfig that will be applied at the beginning of each chapter's activities where this VM is used.

ServerSA1

This VM should be configured as follows:

- Windows Server 2016 Datacenter—Desktop Experience

- Server name: ServerSA1
- Administrator password: Password01
- Memory: 2 GB or more
- Hard disk 1: 60 GB or more
- Hard disk 2: 20 GB
- Hard disk 3: 15 GB
- Hard disk 4: 10 GB
- Ethernet connection—connected to Internal Virtual Switch
  - IP address: 192.168.0.4/24
  - Default gateway: 192.168.0.250 (or an address supplied by the instructor)
  - DNS: 192.168.0.1 (the address of ServerDC1)
- Ethernet 2 connection—connected to Private Virtual Switch
  - IP address: 192.168.1.4/24
  - Default gateway: Not configured
  - DNS: Not configured
- Workgroup: MCSA2016 (The workgroup name doesn't matter.)
- Windows Update: Configured with most recent updates
- Power Setting: Never turn off display
- Internet Explorer Enhanced Security Configuration: Turned off for Administrator
- User Account Control: Lowest setting
- After ServerSA1 is fully configured, create a checkpoint/snapshot named InitialConfig that will be applied at the beginning of each chapter's activities where this VM is used.

Using an Evaluation Version of Windows Server 2016

You can get a 180-day evaluation copy of Windows Server 2016 from the Microsoft Evaluation Center at *https://www.microsoft.com/en-us/evalcenter/evaluate-windows-server-2016/*. You will need to sign in with your Microsoft account or create a new account. You can download an ISO file that can then be attached to your VM's DVD drive to install Windows Server 2016.

If your evaluation version of Windows Server 2016 gets close to expiration, you can extend the evaluation period (180 days) up to five times. To do so, follow these steps:

1. Open a command prompt window as Administrator.
2. Type **slmgr -xpr** and press **Enter** to see the current status of your license. It shows how many days are left in the evaluation. If it says you're in notification mode, you need to rearm the evaluation immediately.
3. To extend the evaluation for another 180 days, type **slmgr -rearm** and press **Enter**. You see a message telling you to restart the system for the changes to take effect. Click **OK** and restart the system.
4. After you have extended the evaluation period, you should take a new checkpoint/snapshot and replace the InitialConfig checkpoint/snapshot.

Where to Go for Help

Configuring a lab and keeping everything running correctly can be challenging. Even small configuration changes can prevent activities from running correctly. The author maintains a website that includes lab notes, suggestions, errata, and help articles that might be useful if you're having trouble, and you can contact the author at these addresses:

- Website: *htttp://books.tomsho.com*
- Email: *w2k16@tomsho.com*

CHAPTER 1

CONFIGURING TCP/IP

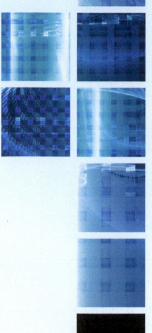

After reading this chapter and completing the exercises, you will be able to:

Describe the TCP/IP protocol and its components

Define IPv4 addresses and calculate subnet masks

Configure IPv4 addresses

Describe IPv6

Define IPv6 address types

Autoconfigure IPv6 addresses

Transition from IPv4 to IPv6

The TCP/IP protocol suite has been used to facilitate communication between computers for more than 40 years. From the smallest local area network to the worldwide Internet, computers use this enduring protocol because of its reliability, flexibility, and scalability. Although it has undergone changes throughout the years, the underlying protocol remains. In this chapter, you learn about some components of the TCP/IP protocol suite and how to subnet IPv4 addresses. Next, you learn how to configure IPv4 addresses on Windows computers with both GUI and command-line tools.

Although TCP/IP is scalable, developing a replacement for IPv4 has become necessary with the explosion of the Internet that started in the 1990s. This replacement, IPv6, provides a nearly unimaginable number of IP addresses with its 128-bit address space. You learn about the structure of IPv6 addresses, how to subnet an IPv6 address, a variety of methods for configuring IPv6 addresses on host computers, and ways to transition from an IPv4 network to an IPv6 network.

An Overview of TCP/IP

Certification

- **70-741 – Implement core and distributed network solutions:**
  Implement IPv4 and IPv6 addressing

Table 1-1 summarizes what you need for the hands-on activities in this chapter.

Table 1-1   Activity requirements

Activity	Requirements	Notes
Activity 1-1: Converting Decimal Numbers to Binary	Paper and pencil	
Activity 1-2: Converting Binary Numbers to Decimal	Paper and pencil	
Activity 1-3: Working with CIDR Notation	Paper and pencil	
Activity 1-4: Determining the Correct Prefix	Paper and pencil	
Activity 1-5: Using the `arp` Command	ServerDC1, ServerDM1	Internet access needed
Activity 1-6: Using the `tracert` Command	ServerDC1, ServerDM1	Internet access needed
Activity 1-7: Configuring a Server to Advertise an IPv6 Prefix	ServerDC1, ServerDM1	
Activity 1-8: Working with IPv6	ServerDC1, ServerDM1	

Transmission Control Protocol/Internet Protocol (TCP/IP) is a network protocol designed to deliver data packets to computers on any scale of network from a small two-computer LAN to the worldwide Internet. TCP/IP is a suite of protocols, meaning it's composed of several protocols performing different functions but working together. The name comes from two of these protocols: Transmission Control Protocol (TCP) and Internet Protocol (IP).

Network operating systems now include two versions of IP, so you see TCP/IPv4 and TCP/IPv6 when examining a network interface's properties in Windows Server 2016. The TCP part stays the same whether you're using IPv4 or IPv6 as do most other protocols in the suite, but the IP part of the suite is where big changes have occurred between versions. IP (both v4 and v6) is the focus of this chapter; later chapters discuss other components of the TCP/IP suite such as Domain Name System (DNS) and Dynamic Host Configuration Protocol (DHCP).

So why is a suite of protocols needed instead of just one protocol? The reason is that networking is a complex process, and all the components of TCP/IP have a specific job so that a single component doesn't become too big and unwieldy. It's because of this partitioning of responsibilities among protocols in the suite that TCP/IPv4 and TCP/IPv6 can run on the same system with the changes mostly isolated to the functions IP performs. Just so you have an idea of the multitude of tasks a suite of networking protocols handles, here's a partial list, in no particular order:

- Logical addressing
- Logical to physical address resolution
- Name resolution
- Dynamic address assignment
- Efficient packet delivery
- Reliable packet delivery
- Packet sequencing
- Status messages
- File transfer
- Webpage transfer
- Security

IP performs some of these functions alone, some are performed with a combination of IP and TCP, and others are performed by other protocols in the suite. So if you need to make a change to logical addressing, for example, which is handled by IP, you just need to change IP and leave the other protocols alone. In fact, the logical addressing shortcomings in IPv4 were the impetus for the development of IPv6. The next section lists some specific protocols in TCP/IP and their function.

> **Note** 🖉
>
> This chapter refers to layers of the Open Systems Interconnect (OSI) model when discussing TCP/IP protocols, so make sure you understand the OSI model before studying the material in this chapter.

TCP/IP Components

TCP/IP is the default network protocol installed on Windows computers. Both Internet Protocol version 4 (TCP/IPv4) and Internet Protocol version 6 (TCP/IPv6) are installed on Windows computers starting with Windows Vista and Windows Server 2008. As mentioned, TCP/IP is a suite of protocols, so when it's installed on a computer, a number of protocols, services, and programs are usually installed with it. Some of the more common TCP/IP-related protocols are listed here with a brief description. Most of these protocols operate in a similar fashion in both IPv4 and IPv6; any differences are noted:

- *Domain Name System (DNS)*—DNS is an Application-layer protocol that resolves domain names to addresses. When a network resource is requested by its name, such as \\server1\SharedFolder or *www.microsoft.com*, DNS client software queries a DNS server to resolve the name of the server hosting the resource to its IP address. The DNS client protocol is installed automatically on Windows computers running TCP/IP. A DNS server, which is required in a Windows domain, can be added as a server role in Windows Server 2016 (discussed in Chapter 2).
- *Dynamic Host Configuration Protocol (DHCP)*—DHCP provides automatic IP address configuration and operates at the Application layer. By default, Windows computers are configured to request their IP address configuration from a DHCP server. The client portion of DHCP is installed by default on all computers with TCP/IP installed. IPv6 uses DHCPv6 and requires separate configuration from DHCPv4. The DHCP server role can be installed in Windows Server 2016 and is discussed in Chapter 4.
- *Transmission Control Protocol (TCP)*—TCP is a Transport-layer component of the TCP/IP suite that provides reliable data transfer between applications on computers. It handles flow control, packet sequencing, and data acknowledgments to help ensure that data transfers are completed without error. TCP is used by applications that require reliable transfer of large amounts of data. Because it's used to communicate between applications, it allows a single computer to run many applications that use TCP/IP and keep track of all the conversations.
- *User Datagram Protocol (UDP)*—UDP is also a Transport-layer protocol used to communicate between applications, but it's a lightweight Transport-layer protocol, meaning it lacks many of the reliability and flow control features of TCP. It's used by applications transferring only small amounts of data that don't require the reliability features offered by TCP.
- *Internet Protocol version 4*—IPv4, operating at the Network layer, is the TCP/IPv4 component that provides logical network addressing, efficient packet delivery, and routing. It's still the most commonly used version of IP, but the trend is moving toward IPv6.
- *Internet Protocol version 6*—IPv6 offers the same functions as IPv4, but it addresses some shortcomings of IPv4, as you learn in this chapter. Like IPv4, IPv6 is a Network-layer protocol and is installed by default on Windows Server 2016. It's becoming more important in networking, especially in large networks and ISPs.
- *Address Resolution Protocol (ARP)*—ARP resolves a computer's IPv4 address to its physical, or Media Access Control (MAC), address. When a computer or router must deliver a packet of data to another

computer or router in the same network, ARP can be used to request the destination device's MAC address. ARP operates at the Network layer and is used only by IPv4.

- *Internet Control Message Protocol (ICMP)*—ICMP is a Network-layer protocol the `ping` program uses to test whether a computer can communicate with another computer. ICMP is also used by computers and network devices to send status messages to one another.
- *Internet Control Message Protocol (ICMPv6)*—ICMPv6 also operates at the Network layer and can be used to test connectivity. It's used for a host of other functions in an IPv6 network, including neighbor discovery, which replaces the function of ARP in an IPv4 network and performs router discovery and address autoconfiguration functions.

The TCP/IP suite has several other protocols, and not all of them are discussed at length in this book. This chapter focuses on IPv4 and IPv6 and some ancillary protocols, such as ICMP and ARP. Chapters 2 and 3 discuss DNS in detail, and Chapters 4 and 5 discuss DHCP in detail.

TCP/IP Communication

Before you get into the details of IP, you should make sure you have a solid understanding of the basic process of communication between two computers. Communication between two computers using TCP/IP often begins when one computer (the client) requires access to a resource or service on another computer (the server). When a user initiates the communication, the server's name is usually used. For example, a user wants to view the home page for *books.tomsho.com*. The user opens a web browser and types "books.tomsho.com" in the address bar. For communication to proceed, the web server's name (*books.tomsho.com*) must be resolved to its IP address, which involves a request to a DNS server.

After the client has the web server's IP address, it must determine whether the web server is on the same network or a different network. The client finds this information by comparing its own IP address with the web server's IP address. If the client and web server are on the same network, the client must get the web server's MAC address before the request can be sent. If they're on different networks, the client sends the request to its default gateway, or router. The router forwards the request until it gets to a router connected to the Web server's network. Understanding the basics of TCP/IP communication helps you better understand IP configuration and addressing, discussed throughout this chapter.

Before continuing, review the following general network terms:

- *MAC address*—The **MAC address** is the Physical-layer address that's an integral part of a network interface card (NIC). A NIC processes data it receives on the network only if the destination MAC address indicates the data is intended for that computer.
- *Frame*—A **frame** is a formatted unit of data that's ready to be transferred to the network medium. It contains a destination and source MAC address and an error-checking code called the frame check sequence (FCS). A frame is the unit of data used by the Data Link layer.
- *Packet*—A **packet** is the Network-layer unit of data used by IPv4 and IPv6. Its header contains the destination and source IP addresses along with other flags and parameters.
- *Segment*—A **segment** is the Transport-layer unit of data and is used by TCP and UDP. Among several other fields, it contains the destination and source port numbers used to identify Application-layer protocols.

The Role of TCP and UDP

TCP and UDP have a substantial role in most communication sessions between two computers. Have you ever wondered how your computer keeps track of the myriad network applications you run? At any time, you might be running a web browser, an email application, and a chat program and have a file open on a file server. When a computer receives data from the network, a frame is received by the NIC, which sends it as a packet up to the IP protocol, which then sends a segment to TCP or UDP. Now what? Eventually, data that's received usually goes to an application or a network service.

The TCP or UDP header provides the information needed to determine which application the received data should be sent to. TCP and UDP use port numbers to specify the source and destination

Application-layer protocols. Using the analogy of sending a letter via the post office, if the IP address is the zip code and the street number is the MAC address, the port number specifies the person in the house who should read the letter. In other words, the MAC address and IP address get network data to the computer, and the port number gets the data to the application or service.

The Internet Assigned Numbers Authority (IANA), a nonprofit agency responsible for Internet addressing and address management, assigns a dedicated port number to every well-known network service. For example, the Hypertext Transfer Protocol (HTTP) used by web servers is assigned port 80, so when your computer formats a message to a web server, the destination port number in the TCP header is 80. Similarly, when your email application requests messages from your mail server, it sends the request to port 110, the Post Office Protocol (POP3) port number. Most client applications are assigned a random port number when they make a request to a server. So when you start a web browser, for example, the web browser window is assigned a port number. When the request for a webpage goes out, the source port number in the TCP header contains the number assigned to that web browser window so that the web server knows which port the reply should be sent to. If you open another web browser window or tab, another port number is assigned, and so forth. The port number is a 16-bit value, so theoretically, you can open more than 65,000 windows!

Tip ⓘ

You can see the list of well-known port numbers at *www.iana.org/assignments/port-numbers*.

Some applications use TCP and some use UDP, depending on the requirements of the data being transmitted. If an application tends to send large amounts of data, such as a file transfer or web browsing, TCP is usually used for reliability. If only small amounts of data are transferred, as with DNS queries and DHCP requests, UDP is usually used for its speed and low overhead. Table 1-2 lists common TCP/IP applications and the related port numbers and protocols.

Table 1-2   Common TCP and UDP port numbers

Application	TCP or UDP	Port number
FTP data transfer	TCP	20
FTP control	TCP	21
Telnet	TCP	23
SMTP	TCP	25
HTTP	TCP	80
POP3	TCP	110
LDAP	TCP	389
HTTPS	TCP	443
DNS	UDP	53
DHCP server	UDP	67
DHCP client	UDP	68
TFTP	UDP	69
SNMP	UDP	161

IP Operation

Before you get into the details of IP addressing and configuration, you need to look more closely at the functions of IP:

- Performs logical addressing
- Ensures efficient packet delivery
- Provides the information needed for packet routing

> **Note**
>
> In this section, the term *IP* is used when the discussion refers to both IPv4 and IPv6. The version number is used when discussing features and functions that are specific to a version.

Logical Addressing

You might wonder why the term *logical address* is used. It's different from the MAC address, which is burned into a computer's NIC. A MAC address is called a *physical address* because it's actually part of the physical hardware and not easily changed.

Computers running TCP/IP use both a logical (IP) and physical (MAC) address to communicate. The MAC address is used to deliver data to a computer after data gets to the network the computer is connected to. The IP address is used mainly to find the network a computer is connected to and get data to that network. When an IP packet is constructed for delivery on the network, it always contains a source address and a destination address. The **source IP address** is the IP address of the computer that's sending the packet, and the **destination IP address** is the IP address of the computer the packet is being sent to. If the destination is a particular device, the destination address is called a **unicast address**, which simply means that one (uni) device is the intended recipient. As you see later in the section "IPv4 Addresses," there are also multicast and broadcast addresses.

Efficient Packet Delivery

IP is designed to deliver packets efficiently, so it doesn't have a lot of features for guaranteeing delivery of large amounts of data on a complex network. Its main job is to get data to the correct network and deliver it to the destination computer. If a large file consisting of hundreds or thousands of packets is transferred across the network, IP's only concern is delivering each packet making up the file, not delivering the file as a whole. If a packet gets lost or arrives at the destination out of order, fixing it isn't IP's job.

Returning to the mail delivery analogy, after you drop an envelope in a mailbox, you really have no way of knowing whether it made it safely to its destination. Certainly the mailman doesn't tell you. This process is like what happens with IP. If you want to know whether the letter arrived safely, you have to pay extra for certified mail, which is like using TCP as the Transport-layer protocol. With certified mail, an extra layer of complexity is added to send you an acknowledgment that your letter was delivered. The same is true of IP packets using TCP. IP just delivers packets, and TCP supplies the acknowledgment that a packet arrived at its destination. TCP can also assemble packets in the correct sequence if they arrive out of order. Most Internet data transfers use IP with TCP to ensure reliability.

Packet Routing

Routing packets is a key responsibility of IP. Routers use the destination IP address in each packet to determine which network the packet should be sent to and the best way (the route) to get it there. For example, in Figure 1-1, the networks are labeled Network 1 through Network 5, and the routers are labeled A to E. If Host 5.1 sends a packet to Host 2.1, the packet is first sent to Router C. Router C then determines the fastest way to get the packet to Network 2, which might mean sending it to Router A or Router B. Like traveling in a car, the shortest way isn't always the fastest way. For example, the link between Router C and Router B could be congested or a slow-bandwidth link, whereas the links from Router C to Router A to Router B might be fast and smooth sailing. It's the job of routers and the specialized IP-related protocols they run to make these decisions.

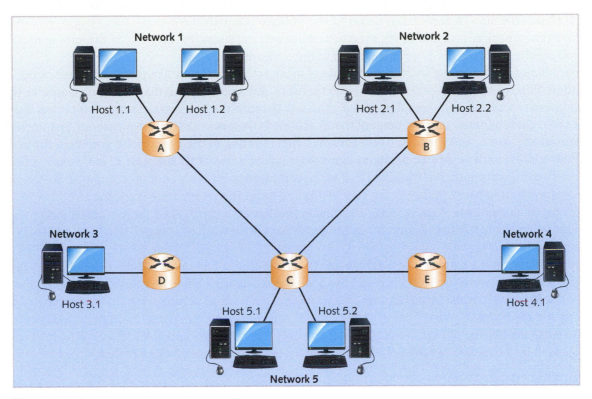

Figure 1-1   Routers in an IP network

IPv4 Addresses

Certification

- **70-741 – Implement core and distributed network solutions:**
  Implement IPv4 and IPv6 addressing

An IPv4 address is a 32-bit number divided into four 8-bit values called **octets**. Each octet can have a value from 0 to 255. IPv4 addresses are written in dotted decimal notation, yielding an address consisting of four decimal numbers, each in the range 0 to 255, separated by a period. For example, in the IPv4 address 10.255.0.100, 10 is the first octet and 100 is the fourth octet.

Every IP address contains a network ID, which specifies the network on which the computer is found, and a host ID, which uniquely identifies the computer on that network. Determining which part of the IP address is the network ID and which part is the host ID depends on the **subnet mask**, another 32-bit dotted decimal number that consists of a contiguous series of binary 1 values followed by a contiguous series of binary 0 values. A contiguous series of eight binary 1s equals the decimal value 255. For example, a typical subnet mask is 255.0.0.0 or 255.255.0.0. In these two examples, for each 255 in the subnet mask, the corresponding octet of the IP address is part of the network ID.

Take a look at an example. In binary, the subnet mask 255.255.0.0 looks like 11111111.11111111.00000000 .00000000. (Binary math is discussed in the next section.) Say you configured a Windows computer with the IP address 10.1.221.101 and the subnet mask 255.0.0.0. Because the first octet of the subnet mask is 255 (a series of eight binary 1s), the first octet of the IP address is the network ID, in this case, 10. The network ID is written as 10.0.0.0, and the host ID is 1.221.101. When referring to the network ID, you fill in the host part of the address with zeroes. Understand, however, that the network ID and host ID are used together when configuring a computer's IP address and when communicating with another computer. So, the source address in a network packet being sent by the computer in this example is 10.1.221.101.

Now say the IP address is 172.31.100.6, and subnet mask is 255.255.0.0. The first two octets of the subnet mask are 255 (a total of 16 contiguous binary 1s), so the network ID is 172.31, which is written as 172.31.0.0. The host ID is 100.6.

Continuing with this pattern, say you have the IP address and subnet mask 192.168.14.250 and 255.255.255.0. They give you the network ID 192.168.14.0 and the host ID 250. You can't have the subnet mask 255.0.255.0 because the network ID must be contiguous. However, you can have an IP address and a subnet mask such as 172.16.67.5 and 255.255.192.0. What's going on in the third octet of this subnet mask? Even though this subnet mask doesn't look like the other examples, which had only the values 255 and 0, it's still a contiguous series of ones followed by a contiguous series of zeroes. In binary, this subnet mask looks like this:

        11111111.11111111.11000000.00000000

In binary, the value 11000000 is the decimal number 192. The network ID in the previous example is 172.16.64.0, and the host ID is 3.5. How is this information determined? Before you go any further, it helps to understand a little about binary math and how to convert between binary and decimal.

Binary Math

An important part of IP addressing is how the subnet mask is used to determine the network ID. As you've seen, it's not as simple as stating that "Anywhere there's a 255 in the subnet mask, the corresponding octet in the IP address is part of the network ID." In addition, computers don't reason that way; they perform calculations using binary values. To determine the network ID of an IP address, computers use a **logical AND operation**, which is an operation between two binary values that you can think of as binary multiplication. Because there are only two unique digits in binary numbers, the multiplication is easy. There are only four possible results when you combine two binary numbers with AND, and three of these results are 0.

```
0 AND 0 = 0
1 AND 0 = 0
0 AND 1 = 0
1 AND 1 = 1
```

To determine the network ID based on the IP address and subnet mask, a computer simply performs a logical AND between the binary digits in the IP address and the binary digits in the subnet mask, which looks something like this:

```
10101100.00011111.01100100.00000110  (binary for 172.31.100.6)
                  AND
11111111.11111111.00000000.00000000  (binary for 255.255.0.0)
_____
10101100.00011111.00101110.00000000  (binary for 172.31.0.0)
```

You simply take the binary digit from the IP address (top number) and perform a logical AND with the corresponding digit in the subnet mask (bottom number). The result is the network ID 172.31.0.0. Take a look at the last example in the previous section:

```
10101100.00010000.01000011.00000101 (binary for 172.16.67.5)
                  AND
11111111.11111111.11000000.00000000 (binary for 255.255.192.0)
         _____
10101100.00010000.01000000.00000000 (binary for 172.16.64.0)
```

After you do the AND operation, you can see the network ID 172.16.64.0 (that is, if you know how to convert binary to decimal, discussed next). The remaining bits in the IP address that are not part of the network ID are the host ID, in this case 3.5. So, essentially, what you can say is that anywhere there is a 1 bit in the subnet mask, the corresponding bits in the IP address are part of the network ID and anywhere there are 0 bits in the subnet mask, the corresponding bits are part of the host ID. This sure would be easier if you knew how to convert from decimal to binary and back, wouldn't it?

Converting Binary to Decimal

Before you start converting from binary to decimal and back, you need to review how the decimal number system works. It's based on powers of 10 (which is where the word *decimal* comes from, with *dec* meaning "ten"). Ten different symbols, 0 through 9, are used to represent any possible number. Each place in a decimal number can have one of 10 possible values: again, 0 through 9. Furthermore, each place in a decimal number can be expressed as a power of 10. The ones place can be expressed as a number, 0 through 9, multiplied by 10 raised to the 0 power, or 10^0. (Any number raised to the 0 power equals 1.) The tens place can be expressed as a number multiplied by 10 to the 1 power, or 10^1. The hundreds place can be expressed as a number multiplied by 10^2, and so on. For example, the decimal number 249 can be expressed as either of the following:

```
2 * 10² + 4 * 10¹ + 9 * 10⁰ = 249
2 * 100 + 4 * 10  + 9 * 1    = 249
```

When you see the number 249, you don't think of it in these terms because you grew up using the decimal number system, and recognizing the hundreds place, tens place, and ones place happens without conscious effort, as does the multiplication and addition that occurs. However, take a look at this number:

```
379420841249
```

A little more thought has to go into recognizing that the 3 represents 300 billion, the 7 represents 70 billion, and so forth. The binary number system works the same way except that everything is governed by twos. Two digits, 0 and 1, represent every possible number, and each place in a binary number is 0 or 1 multiplied by a power of 2. So, instead of having the ones place, the tens place, the hundreds place, and so on, you have the ones place, the twos place, the fours place, and so on, based on 2^0, 2^1, 2^2, and so forth. For example, using the same method as for the decimal example, you can express the binary number 101 as either of the following. The numbers in bold are the binary digits.

```
1 * 2² + 0 * 2¹ + 1 * 2⁰ = 5
1 * 4  + 0 * 2  + 1 * 1  = 5
```

Converting Decimal to Binary

One way to convert from decimal to binary is shown in Table 1-3. The first two rows are the binary and exponent values of each bit position of an 8-bit number. You use 8 bits because in subnetting, most work can be done 8 bits at time. The third row is what you complete to determine the decimal number's binary representation.

Table 1-3   Decimal-to-binary conversion table: Converting 125 to 01111101

128	64	32	16	8	4	2	1
2^7	2^6	2^5	2^4	2^3	2^2	2^1	2^0
0	1	1	1	1	1	0	1

To use this method, start with the number you're trying to convert to binary: in this case, 125, which is referred to as the *test number*. You compare the test number with the leftmost number in the preceding table (128). If it's equal to or greater than this number, you place a 1 in the column and subtract the number in the column from your test number; otherwise, place a 0 in the column. Remember: Eight binary places or 8 bits can represent only a value up to 255. If you're converting a number greater than 255, simply extend the table to the left (256, 512, and so on). Here's the sequence of steps to convert 125 to binary:

1. 125 is less than 128, so you place a **0** in the column under the 128. The test number remains 125.
2. 125 is greater than 64, so you place a **1** in the column under the 64 and subtract 64 from 125, leaving your new test number as 61.
3. 61 is greater than 32, so you place a **1** in the column under the 32 and subtract 32 from 61, leaving your new test number as 29.
4. 29 is greater than 16, so you place a **1** in the column under the 16 and subtract 16 from 29, leaving your new test number as 13.
5. 13 is greater than 8, so you place a **1** in the column under the 8 and subtract 8 from 13, leaving your new test number as 5.
6. 5 is greater than 4, so you place a **1** in the column under the 4 and subtract 4 from 5, leaving your new test number as 1.
7. 1 is less than 2, so you place a **0** in the column under the 2.
8. 1 is equal to 1, so you place a **1** in the column under the 1 and subtract 1 from 1, leaving your new test number as 0. When your test number is 0, you're done.

Now try this with 199, 221, and 24. You should get the following results:

```
199 = 11000111
221 = 11011101
 24 = 00011000
```

Converting Binary to Decimal

The easiest way to convert an 8-digit binary number (octet) to decimal is to use Table 1-3, as you did for the decimal-to-binary conversion. Of course, if your binary number is more than 8 bits, you can simply extend the table to the left as many places as necessary. Here's how to do it: Write your binary number in the third row of the table as shown in Table 1-4. For every column with a 1 bit, write down the corresponding decimal number from the first row. For columns with a 0 bit, you can simply skip them or write down a 0. Using the binary number 11010011, you get the following:

```
128 + 64 + 0 + 16 + 0 + 0 + 1 + 1 = 211
```

Table 1-4   Binary-to-decimal conversion table: Converting 11010011 to 211

128	64	32	16	8	4	2	1
2^7	2^6	2^5	2^4	2^3	2^2	2^1	2^0
1	1	0	1	0	0	1	1

Plug in the binary values for 199, 221, and 24 whose binary equivalents are shown above, to make sure you get the correct results.

IP Address Classes

When you enter an IP address in the Internet Protocol Version 4 (TCP/IPv4) Properties dialog box shown in Figure 1-2, Windows fills in a subnet mask automatically, which you can change if needed. Windows bases the suggested subnet mask on the class of the IP address you enter.

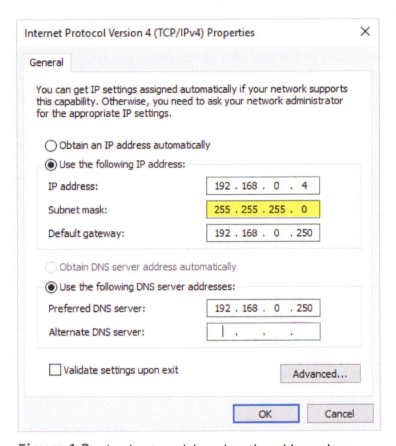

Figure 1-2   A subnet mask based on the address class

IP addresses are categorized in ranges referred to as *Classes A, B, C, D,* or *E*. Only IP addresses in the A, B, and C classes can be assigned to a network device (host). Although the IP address class system has been somewhat superseded by a more flexible way to manage IP addresses, called *Classless Interdomain Routing (CIDR)*, which is discussed later in this chapter in the section "Classless Interdomain Routing." The class system is a basis for determining which part of an IP address is the network ID and which part is the host ID. The first octet of an address denotes its class. Review the following facts about IP address classes:

- The value of the first octet for Class A addresses is between 1 and 127. Class A addresses were intended for use by large corporations and governments. An IP address registry assigns the first octet, leaving the last three octets for network administrators to assign to hosts. This allows 24 bits of address space or 16,777,214 hosts per network address. In a Class A IP address such as 10.159.44.201, for example, the network address is 10.0.0.0. So the first address in the 10.0.0.0 network is 10.0.0.1, and the last address is 10.255.255.254.
- Class B addresses begin with network IDs between 128 and 191 and were intended for use in medium-to-large networks. An IP address registry assigns the first two octets, leaving the third and fourth octets available for administrators to assign as host addresses. In the Class B address 172.17.11.4, for example, the network address is 172.17.0.0. Having two octets in the host ID allows 65,534 hosts per network address.

- Class C addresses were intended for small networks. An IP address registry assigns the first three octets, ranging from 192 to 223. In the Class C address 203.0.113.254, for example, the network address is 203.0.113.0. These networks are limited to 254 hosts per network.
- Class D addresses are reserved for **multicasting** in which a packet is addressed so that more than one destination can receive it. Applications using this feature include videoconferencing and live streaming media. In a Class D address, the first octet is in the range 224 to 239. Class D addresses can't be used to assign IP addresses to host computers.
- Class E addresses have a value from 240 to 255 in the first octet. This range of addresses is reserved for experimental use and can't be used for address assignment.

A couple of notes about this list: First, if you did your math, you would see that a Class C address provides 8 bits of address space, which yields 256 addresses (2^8), not 254. The number of addresses specified for Classes A and B are also two fewer than the address space suggests. This discrepancy happens because each network has two reserved addresses: the address in which all host ID bits are binary 0s and the address in which all host ID bits are binary 1s. For example, all the host bits in address 203.0.113.0 are binary 0s, and this address represents the network number and can't be assigned to a computer. The host bits in address 203.0.113.255 are binary 1s; this address is the broadcast address for the 203.0.113.0 network and can't be assigned to a computer.

The other note concerns the 127.0.0.0 network. Although technically a Class A address, it's reserved for the **loopback address**, which always refers to the local computer and is used to test the functioning of TCP/IP. A packet with a destination address starting with 127 is sent to the local device without reaching the network medium. Likewise, the reserved name **localhost** always corresponds to the IP address 127.0.0.1 so that a local machine can always be referenced by this name.

> **Note** ✐
>
> Even though localhost and the loopback address are usually associated with the address 127.0.0.1, any address in the 127.0.0.0 network (except 127.0.0.0 and 127.255.255.255) references the local machine in most OSs.

Table 1-5 summarizes address classes A, B, and C and the default subnet masks.

Table 1-5   IPv4 address class summary

Class	A	B	C
Value of first octet	0–127	128–191	192–223
Default subnet mask	255.0.0.0	255.255.0.0	255.255.255.0
Number of network ID bits	8	16	24
Maximum number of hosts/network	16,777,214	65,534	254
Number of host bits	24	16	8

Private IP Addresses

Each device that accesses the Internet must do so by using a public IP address. Because of the popularity of TCP/IP and the Internet, unique IP addresses to assign to Internet-accessible devices are almost exhausted. To help alleviate this problem, TCP/IP's technical governing body reserved a series of addresses for private networks—that is, networks whose hosts can't be accessed directly through the Internet. The reserved addresses are as follows:

- Class A addresses beginning with 10 (one Class A network address)
- Class B addresses from 172.16 to 172.31 (16 Class B network addresses)
- Class C addresses from 192.168.0 to 192.168.255 (256 Class C network addresses)

The addresses in these ranges can't be routed across the Internet, which is why any organization can use them to assign IP addresses to their internal hosts. If access to the Internet is necessary, a process called *Network Address Translation (NAT)* is used. It is explained next in the section "Network Address Translation."

Another type of private IP address is a link-local address. It's not assigned manually or through DHCP; it's assigned automatically when a computer is configured to receive an IP address through DHCP but no DHCP service is available. Another term for this type of addressing is **Automatic Private IP Addressing (APIPA)**. APIPA addresses are assigned in the range 169.254.1.0 through 169.254.254.255 with a subnet mask of 255.255.0.0. Computers that are assigned a **link-local** address can communicate only on the local LAN as packets containing these addresses aren't forwarded by routers.

Note

Link-local IPv4 addresses don't use the first and last subnets in the 169.254.0.0/16 range because these addresses are reserved for future use, according to RFC 3927 (*https://tools.ietf.org/html/rfc3927*).

Network Address Translation

Network Address Translation (NAT) helps alleviate the shortage of public IP addresses by allowing an organization to use private IP addresses while connected to the Internet. As you learned, the three ranges of private IP addresses (one range for each class) can't be used as the source or destination address in a packet that is routed on the Internet.

Anyone can use private IP addresses for address assignment to internal computers and devices, and because the addresses aren't sent to the Internet, there's no address conflict. What if you want your computers to have access to the Internet, however? That's where NAT comes in. An organization can, for example, assign all its computers' addresses in the 10.x.x.x private network. Say an organization has 1000 computers. Although these addresses can't be used on the Internet, the NAT process translates a private address (as a packet leaves the network) into a valid public Internet address. When data returns to the private network, the address is translated back to the original 10.x.x.x address before it is delivered to the destination computer. NAT is usually handled by a network device that connects the organization to the Internet, such as a router. As shown in Figure 1-3, when computer 10.0.0.1 sends a packet to the Internet, the NAT router intercepts the packet and replaces its source address with 198.60.123.101 (a public Internet

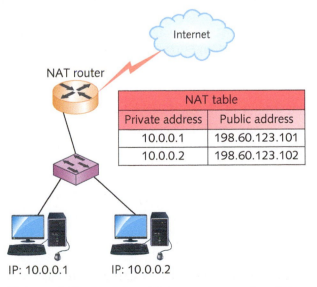

Figure 1-3   **Private addresses are translated to public addresses with NAT**

address). When a reply comes back addressed to 198.60.123.101, the NAT router replaces the destination address with 10.0.0.1 before delivering it to the computer.

This process allows any company to use private IP addresses in its own network, requiring a public IP address only when a workstation attempts to access the Internet. An extension of NAT, called *Port Address Translation (PAT)*, allows several hundred workstations to access the Internet with a single public Internet address. You'll learn how to configure Windows Server 2016 to be a NAT router in Chapter 6.

> **Tip** (i)
>
> For an excellent tutorial on NAT, see *computer.howstuffworks.com/nat.htm*.

Classless Interdomain Routing

If IP addresses have a default subnet mask assigned based on the value of the IP address's first octet, why do you even need to specify the subnet mask? The reason is that the default subnet mask doesn't always suit the needs of your network. Address classes and default subnet masks were designed when TCP/IP was in its infancy, and computer networks and the Internet were almost unheard of. These address classes and default subnet masks met the needs of the few government agencies and universities using TCP/IP in the late 1970s and 1980s. The use of IP addresses with their default subnet masks is referred to as **classful addressing**.

After computer networks were being installed in every business, and users wanted access to the new information source called the *Internet*, classful addressing clearly needed some flexibility—hence, subnet masks that could be configured regardless of the address class. This type of IP address configuration became what's known as **Classless Interdomain Routing (CIDR)**. For example, assigning the IP address 172.31.210.10 with a subnet mask of 255.255.255.0 (instead of the default of 255.255.0.0) is perfectly acceptable. In this case, the network ID is 172.31.210, and the host ID is 10. Why would you want to assign a subnet mask that is different from the default? Aren't the default subnet masks good enough? In some cases, they are, but not in others.

Take, for instance, the address 172.31.0.0 with the default subnet mask 255.255.0.0. As Table 1-5 showed, this subnet mask allows a 16-bit host ID, making it possible to assign more than 65,000 host addresses, starting with 172.31.0.1 and ending with 172.31.255.254. (Remember that you can't assign an address with all 0 bits or all 1 bits in the host ID, so you have to exclude 172.31.0.0 and 172.31.255.255 from the possible IP addresses you can assign to a host.) The exact calculation for the number of hosts is $2^n - 2$; n is the number of bits in the host ID. Being able to assign this many addresses might seem like an advantage if you have a large network. However, having such a large address space assigned to a single network has two distinct disadvantages: If you're actually using the number of computers that the address space affords (in this case, more than 65,000 computers), communication efficiency suffers, and if you aren't using the addresses, address space is wasted.

CIDR Notation

Writing IP addresses with their subnet masks can be tedious and takes up a lot of space. What's important is how many bits of the IP address constitute the network ID. To that end, you can specify an IP address and its subnet mask with CIDR notation. **CIDR notation** uses the format A.B.C.D/n; n is the number of 1 bits in the subnet mask, or expressed another way, the number of bits in the network ID. It's referred to as the "IP prefix" (or just "prefix"). For example, 172.31.210.10 with a 255.255.255.0 subnet mask is expressed as 172.31.210.10/24 in CIDR notation. The network ID is 24 bits, leaving 8 bits for the host ID. As another example, 10.25.106.12 with the subnet mask 255.255.240.0 is expressed as 10.25.106.12/20. In this case, the network ID is 20 bits, leaving 12 bits for the host ID.

Broadcast Domains

All computers and devices that share the same network ID in their IP address are said to be in the same broadcast domain. A **broadcast domain** defines which devices must receive a packet that's broadcast by any other device. A **broadcast** is a packet addressed to all computers on the network. TCP/IP communication relies heavily on broadcast packets to perform a variety of functions. For example, DHCP and ARP use broadcasts to perform their tasks. Every time a computer receives a broadcast packet, the NIC generates an interrupt, causing the CPU to stop what it's doing to read the packet. If the broadcast isn't relevant to the computer, the packet is usually discarded.

Now imagine 65,000 computers on the same broadcast domain; at any moment, probably several thousand are sending broadcast packets. The amount of traffic generated and the additional CPU utilization would likely bring the network to a screeching halt. Preventing this problem is where subnetting comes in.

Subnetting

If you do have 65,000 computers in your organization, instead of creating one large network with the network address 172.31.0.0/16, you can divide this very large network into many smaller subnetworks. For example, you can use 172.31.0.0/24, 172.31.1.0/24, and so forth up to 172.31.255.0/24. This strategy, called **subnetting**, makes 256 smaller subnetworks with a maximum of $2^8 - 2$, or 254, devices per subnetwork. If a computer on one subnetwork needs to communicate with a computer on another subnetwork, the packets are sent to a router that locates the subnetwork and forwards the data. Now the maximum size of your broadcast domain is only 254 computers, which is more manageable.

> **Note** 🖉
>
> When a classful network has been divided or subnetted into multiple smaller networks, the resulting networks are called *subnetworks*. Functionally, however, there's no difference between a classful network and a subnetwork.

Another reason to subnet is to conserve IP addresses. Companies that maintain Internet-connected devices need public Internet addresses, which must be unique in the world—meaning a public address can be assigned to only one device on the Internet. In the past, if a company had four web servers and two routers that needed public addresses, the only recourse an ISP had was to assign a Class C network address consisting of 254 possible host addresses, thereby wasting 248 addresses. By subnetting a network, the ISP can assign an address such as 198.60.123.0/29 that uses only addresses 198.60.123.0 through 198.60.123.7, which satisfies the company's needs and still makes addresses 198.60.123.8 through 198.60.123.254 available for other customers.

Calculating a Subnet Mask

There are usually two approaches to subnetting, and they depend on the answers to these questions: Am I subnetting to provide a network with a certain number of host addresses? Or am I subnetting to provide a network with a certain number of subnets? If you're working for an ISP, the answer is usually yes to the first question, and if you're a network administrator for an organization, the answer is more likely to be yes to the second question. Sometimes the answer is a combination of both.

Say you have a large internetwork and need to break an IP address space into several subnets. Follow this process:

1. First, decide how many subnets you need. You can figure out the number of subnets needed by seeing how many network cable segments are or will be connected to router interfaces. Each router interface connection indicates a required subnet.

2. Next, decide how many bits you need to meet or exceed the number of required subnets. To calculate this value, use the formula 2^n, with *n* representing the number of bits you must reallocate from the host ID to the network ID. For example, if your starting network number is the Class B address 172.20.0.0, its default subnet mask is 255.255.0.0, which is your starting point. The number of subnets you create is always a power of 2, so if you need 20 subnets, you must reallocate 5 bits ($2^5 = 32$) because reallocating 4 bits gives you only 2^4, or 16, subnets.

3. Reallocate bits from the host ID, starting from the most significant host bit (that is, from the left side of the host ID).

4. You must also make sure you have enough host bits available to assign to computers on each subnet. To determine the number of host addresses available, use the formula discussed previously: $2^n - 2$, with n representing the number of host (0) bits in the subnet mask.

Here's an example to help you put this formula to work: CSM Tech Publishing wants 60 subnets for its Class B address: 172.20.0.0/16. The nearest power of 2 to 60 is 64, which equals 2^6. This means you must reallocate 6 bits from the host portion of the original subnet mask (255.255.0.0) and make them subnet bits.

Reallocating 6 bits, starting from the leftmost bit of the third octet, creates a subnet mask with the bit pattern 11111100. The decimal value for this number is 252. This reallocating of bits changes the subnet mask from 255.255.0.0 to 255.255.**252**.0. Expressing it in CIDR notation gives you 172.20.0.0/22.

To calculate the number of host addresses for each subnet, just subtract the number of network ID bits from the total number of bits in an IP address: 32-22. The result is the number of bits left for the host ID. In this case, the number is 10. Again, the formula for determining the number of host addresses is $2^n - 2$, so you have $2^{10} - 2 = 1022$ addresses per subnet, which should be more than enough for most networks.

Now that you have a correct subnet mask, you need to determine what network numbers can be derived from using it. To do this, take the reallocated 6 bits, place them in the network number, and cycle the 6 bits through the possible combinations of values they represent. Table 1-6 shows the first 16 subnetwork numbers resulting from the preceding steps with the third octet written in binary on the left and the resulting subnetwork address written in decimal on the right. The bits shown in bold are the 6 bits used to create the subnets. If you convert the third octet on the left side from binary to decimal, you'll see that it equals the third octet on the right.

Table 1-6   Subnetwork numbers and addresses

Subnetwork number in binary	Subnetwork address
172.20.**000000**00.0	172.20.0.0
172.20.**000001**00.0	172.20.4.0
172.20.**000010**00.0	172.20.8.0
172.20.**000011**00.0	172.20.12.0
172.20.**000100**00.0	172.20.16.0
172.20.**000101**00.0	172.20.20.0
172.20.**000110**00.0	172.20.24.0
172.20.**000111**00.0	172.20.28.0
172.20.**001000**00.0	172.20.32.0
172.20.**001001**00.0	172.20.36.0
172.20.**001010**00.0	172.20.40.0
172.20.**001011**00.0	172.20.44.0
172.20.**001100**00.0	172.20.48.0
172.20.**001101**00.0	172.20.52.0
172.20.**001110**00.0	172.20.56.0
172.20.**001111**00.0	172.20.60.0
. . .	. . .
172.20.**111111**00.0	172.20.252.0

A Pattern Emerges

Table 1-6 shows the first 16 of the possible 64 subnets and the last subnet created for network 172.20.0.0. As you can see, there's a pattern to the subnetwork numbers—they go in increments of 4. You can derive this pattern without having to list the subnets, however. Look at the octet where the subnet bits are reallocated, and then look at the rightmost reallocated bit. The subnet increment is determined by the binary place value of this bit: in this case, the 4s place.

You know when to stop counting subnets when all the subnet bits are binary 1s, as in the last entry in the table. You also know to stop counting when the subnet number equals the value of the changed octet in the subnet mask. In this case, the subnet mask 255.255.0.0 was changed to 255.255.**252**.0 after the bit reallocation. The 252 in the third octet of the subnet mask is the same value as the last subnet number.

Determining Host Addresses

Similarly, the host addresses in each subnet can be determined by cycling through the host bits. Therefore, the subnetwork 172.20.32.0 would have host addresses from 172.20.32.1 through 172.20.35.255. However, you can't use the IP address in which all host bits are 1s because it's the broadcast address for that network, so the actual range is 172.20.32.1 through 172.20.35.254, giving you 1022 host addresses. Table 1-7 shows this for the first five subnets and the last subnet.

Table 1-7   Host addresses per subnet

Subnetwork number	Beginning and ending host addresses in binary	Beginning and ending host addresses in decimal
172.20.0.0	172.20.00000000.00000001–172.20.00000011.11111110	172.20.0.1–172.20.3.254
172.20.4.0	172.20.00000100.00000001–172.20.00000111.11111110	172.20.4.1–172.20.7.254
172.20.8.0	172.20.00001000.00000001–172.20.00001011.11111110	172.20.8.1–172.20.11.254
172.20.12.0	172.20.00001100.00000001–172.20.00001111.11111110	172.20.12.1–172.20.15.254
172.20.16.0	172.20.00010000.00000001–172.20.00010011.11111110	172.20.16.1–172.20.19.254
. . .		. . .
172.20.252.0	172.20.11111100.00000001–172.20.11111111.11111110	172.20.252.1–172.20.255.254

Another Subnet Mask Example

In Figure 1-4, the network number is 192.168.100.0, which is a Class C network address with the default subnet mask 255.255.255.0.

The following steps show how to calculate a new subnet mask:

1. In this example, you can see that four cable segments are connected to router interfaces. The wide area network (WAN) cable segment between the two routers counts as a single cable segment and, therefore, a single subnet. You have to account for the WAN subnet even if the network has no hosts because the router interfaces require an IP address. As you can see, there are four subnetworks: Subnet A requires 43 IP addresses (40 for the Windows 7 hosts, 2 for the servers, and 1 for the router interface). Subnet B requires 53 IP addresses, subnet C requires 43 IP addresses, and subnet D requires only 2 IP addresses.

2. To accommodate the required number of subnets (4), you need a power of 2 that's equal to or greater than 4. Because $2^2 = 4$, you need to reallocate 2 bits from the host ID to the network ID.

3. Reallocating 2 bits from the leftmost part of the host portion of the original subnet mask (255.255.255.0) gives the last octet of your new subnet mask the bit pattern 11000000. Converting to decimal and putting the entire subnet mask together yields 255.255.255.192.

4. To be sure you have enough host bits per subnet, use the formula $2^n - 2$, where n is the number of 0 bits in the new subnet mask. The result is $2^6 - 2 = 62$. This number of host addresses satisfies your requirement of a maximum of 53 hosts per subnet.

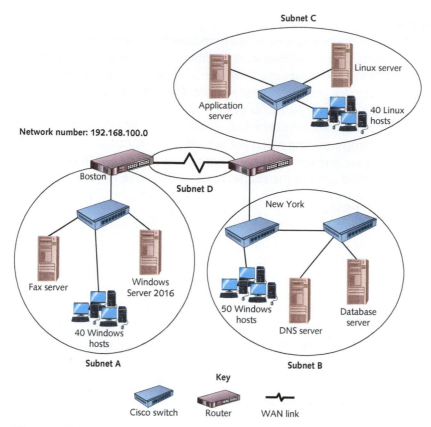

Figure 1-4 A sample network for calculating subnet mask requirements

Calculating a Subnet Mask Based on Needed Host Addresses

Sometimes you need to know what prefix to assign an IP network based on the number of host addresses required for the network. This process is fairly straightforward. Suppose you're told that you need to determine the subnet mask to use with network ID 172.16.16.0, and the network will support 60 hosts. In this problem, simply determine how many host bits are needed to support the number of hosts specified, and subtract this number from 32, giving you the number of bits in the network ID. For this example of 60 hosts, you need 6 bits for the host ID because $2^6 = 64$, which is the closest power of 2 to 60. Therefore, the prefix is 26, so in CIDR notation, the network ID is 172.16.16.0/26. Examine the examples in Table 1-8 to become more comfortable with this process.

Table 1-8 Examples for determining the correct CIDR notation

Network ID	Required hosts	Host bits required	Network ID bits	CIDR notation
10.19.32.0	900	10 ($2^{10} = 1024$)	22	10.19.32.0/22
172.25.110.0	505	9 ($2^9 = 512$)	23	172.25.110.0/23
192.168.100.32	28	5 ($2^5 = 32$)	27	192.168.100.32/27

Tip ⓘ

To learn more about this topic and get plenty of subnetting practice problems, go to *www.subnetting.net*.

Supernetting

Although not practiced as commonly as subnetting, **supernetting** is sometimes necessary to solve certain network configuration problems and to make routing tables more streamlined. When talking about routing tables, supernetting is usually referred to as *route aggregation* or *route summarization*.

Supernetting reallocates bits from the network portion of an IP address to the host portion, effectively making two or more smaller subnets a larger supernet. Supernets allow combining two or more consecutive IP network addresses and make them function as a single logical network. Here's how it works:

1. Suppose that you have four Class C network addresses—192.168.0.0, 192.168.1.0, 192.168.2.0, and 192.168.3.0—available for your network design. You have a total of 900 hosts on your proposed network. You don't have four router interfaces that can use the four different network numbers, however. You can combine the four networks into one by reallocating 2 bits ($2^2 = 4$) from the network portion of the address and adding them to the host portion. You then have a network address of 192.168.0.0 with the subnet mask 255.255.252.0. The 252 in the third octet is derived from setting the last 2 bits of the original Class C subnet mask (255.255.255.0) to 0, thereby making them part of the host portion.

2. Instead of supporting only 8 bits for the host address portion, the supernet now supports 10 bits (8 + 2) for host addresses. This number of bits provides $2^{10} - 2$ host addresses on this supernet, or 1022, which satisfies your requirement for 900 hosts and allows you to assign all host addresses in a single network.

As mentioned, combining two or more small networks into one larger network is only one reason to supernet. Routers on the Internet can have enormous routing tables. The larger the routing table, the more work the router must do to determine where to send a packet. Route aggregation or summarization can combine multiple routing table entries into a single entry, which can drastically decrease the table's size on Internet routers. This reduction in routing table size increases routers' speed and efficiency. The procedure is similar to supernetting except that you configure routers.

Routing tables grow partly because routers communicate with one another by sending information about their routing tables to one another. If several networks can be represented by a single routing table entry, the routing tables are more efficient. Taking the previous example, suppose that RouterA in a company network has the network addresses 192.168.0.0, 192.168.1.0, 192.168.2.0, and 192.168.3.0 in its routing table, and it communicates with RouterB (see Figure 1-5). Without supernetting/route summarization,

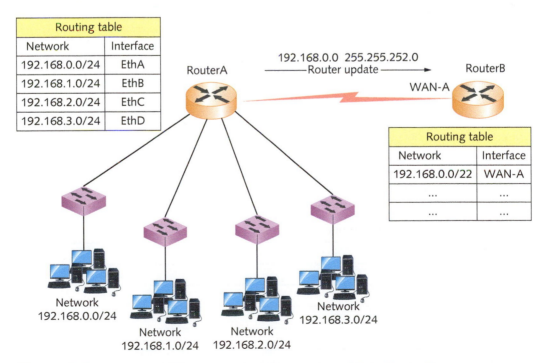

Figure 1-5   RouterA sends a summary of its routing table to RouterB

RouterA sends all four network addresses to RouterB, each with its 255.255.255.0 subnet mask. Consequently, RouterB's routing table expands with these four additional routes. However, because all four routes lead to the same place (RouterA), these routes can be represented by a single entry. RouterA can summarize these routes by simply sending RouterB the address 192.168.0.0 with subnet mask 255.255.252.0, which tells RouterB that all networks from 192.168.0.0 through 192.168.3.0 can be reached through RouterA.

Activity 1-1: Converting Decimal Numbers to Binary

Time Required: 20 minutes

Objective: Convert decimal numbers to binary.

Required Tools and Equipment: Paper and pencil

Description: Convert the following list of decimal numbers to binary without using a calculator. You can use Table 1-3 to help with the conversions or create your own table.

Decimal number	Binary number
167	
149	
252	
128	
64	
240	
255	
14	
15	
63	
188	
224	

Activity 1-2: Converting Binary Numbers to Decimal

Time Required: 20 minutes

Objective: Convert binary numbers to decimal.

Required Tools and Equipment: Paper and pencil

Description: Convert the following list of binary numbers to decimal without using a calculator. You can use Table 1-3 to help with the conversions or create your own table.

Binary number	Decimal number
00110101	
11111000	
00011111	
10101010	
01010101	
11111110	

Binary number	Decimal number
11111100	
00111011	
11001100	
00110011	
00000111	
00111100	

Activity 1-3: Working with CIDR Notation

Time Required: 20 minutes
Objective: Determine the subnet mask, number of host bits, and number of hosts for network numbers in CIDR notation.
Required Tools and Equipment: Paper and pencil
Description: Examine the IP addresses/prefixes specified in CIDR notation, and fill in the resulting subnet mask, number of host bits, and number of hosts possible in the network. The first row is completed for you. The next two rows include some of the information.

Network/prefix	Subnet mask	Host bits	Number of hosts
172.16.1.0/24	255.255.255.0	8	254
10.1.100.128/26	255.255.255.192	6	
10.1.96.0/19	255.255.224		8190
192.168.1.0/24			
172.31.0.0/16			
10.255.255.252/30			
172.28.240.0/20			
10.44.108.0/22			
192.168.100.24/21			
172.23.64.0/18			
192.168.5.128/25			

Activity 1-4: Determining the Correct Prefix

Time Required: 20 minutes
Objective: Determine the correct prefix given the required number of hosts per network.
Required Tools and Equipment: Paper and pencil
Description: Given the IP address and number of hosts in the first two columns, determine the number of host bits required and write the network number with the correct prefix. The first one is completed for you, and the next two are partially completed.

Network ID	Required hosts	Host bits needed	Network ID/prefix
172.16.1.0	254	8	172.16.1.0/24
10.1.100.128	62	6	
10.1.96.0	8190		10.1.96.0/19
192.168.1.0	200		
172.31.0.0	65000		
10.255.255.252	2		
172.28.240.0	4000		
10.44.108.0	900		
192.168.240.0	2200		
172.23.64.0	16000		
192.168.5.128	110		

Configuring IPv4 Addresses

 **Certification**

- **70-741 – Implement core and distributed network solutions:**
  Implement IPv4 and IPv6 addressing

When you assign a computer an IP address, there are some rules to remember:
- Every IP address configuration must have a subnet mask.
- All hosts on the same network must share the same network ID in their IP addresses. The word *network* in this case means a grouping of computers connected to one or more switches (or access points) not separated by a router. Put another way, all computers are in the same broadcast domain.
- All host IDs on the same network must be unique.
- You can't assign an IP address in which all the host ID bits are binary 0. This type of IP address is reserved as the network ID. For example, IP address 10.1.0.0 with subnet mask 255.255.0.0 is reserved to identify network 10.1.
- You can't assign an IP address in which all the host ID bits are binary 1. This type of IP address is reserved as the network broadcast address. For example, IP address 10.1.255.255 with subnet mask 255.255.0.0 has all host ID bits set to binary 1 and is reserved as the broadcast address for the 10.1 network.
- Computers assigned different network IDs can communicate only by sending network packets to a router, which forwards the packets to the correct network.

Configuring Multiple IP Addresses

Windows OSs allow assigning multiple IP addresses to a single network connection in the Advanced TCP/IP Settings dialog box shown in Figure 1-6. As long as the address isn't assigned via DHCP, you can click the Add button and enter a new IP address and subnet mask. Multiple IP addresses can be useful in these situations:
- The computer is hosting a service that must be accessed by using different addresses. For example, a web server can host multiple websites, each assigned a different IP address and domain name.
- The computer is connected to a physical network that hosts multiple IP networks. This situation can occur if your network addressing scheme is transitioning from one network ID to another, and you need a server to be available to both the old and the new IP networks until the transition is completed. It can also occur when you have multiple groups of computers (or hosts and virtual

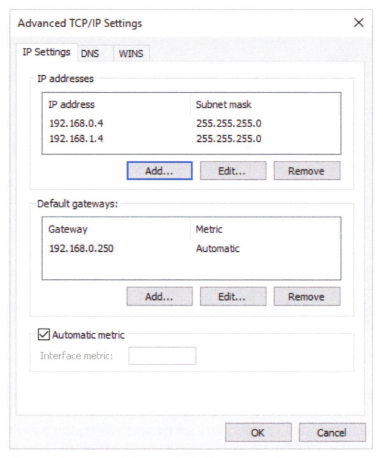

Figure 1-6   The Advanced TCP/IP Settings dialog box

machines) connected to the same physical network but with different network addresses. If all the computers need access to server resources, the servers can be configured with IP addresses to serve all the IP networks.

> **Note**
>
> When multiple IP addresses are assigned to a Windows computer that uses a Windows DNS server supporting Dynamic DNS (the default DNS server configuration), the DNS server has a host entry for each IP address assigned to the computer.

You also have to configure more than one IP address on servers with multiple NICs, which are called *multihomed servers*. They're discussed in the next section.

Configuring the Default Gateway

Almost all IP address configurations require a default gateway address. The **default gateway**, which is usually a router or a computer configured to act as a router, tells the computer where packets destined for another network should be sent. By definition, the default gateway's address must have the same network ID as the host's network ID.

You can configure multiple default gateways in the Advanced TCP/IP Settings dialog box, and then Windows attempts to select the gateway with the best metric automatically. A **metric** is a value assigned to the gateway based on the speed of the interface used to access the gateway. Multiple gateways provide fault tolerance to a computer, so if the primary default gateway is no longer responding, Windows switches to another gateway. By using a feature called *fail-back*, Windows attempts periodically to communicate with the original default gateway. If the original gateway comes back online, Windows switches back to it.

Using Multihomed Servers

A multihomed server has two or more NICs, each attached to a different IP network. Each NIC is assigned a network connection and requires its own IP address for the network it's connected to. This type of configuration can be used in the following situations:

- A server is accessed by internal clients (clients on the network) and external clients (clients on the Internet or an extranet). For example, you have a server for services such as file and printer sharing, DHCP, and DNS that also acts as a public web server.
- A server provides resources for computers on multiple subnets of the network. Interfaces can be configured for each subnet, which provides more throughput than is possible with a single NIC.
- A server is configured as a router or virtual private network (VPN) server. Both functions often use multiple NICs.

For network connections to a LAN, Windows uses names such as Ethernet, Ethernet2, and so forth, which aren't very descriptive. Renaming each network connection to describe the network it connects to is recommended. For example, if a server is connected to internal and external networks, you might name one connection LAN-Internal and the other LAN-External. If the server is connected to two internal networks, you could use the network address in the names, such as LAN-172.31 and LAN-172.16. To rename a connection, right-click it in the Network Connections window and click Rename.

When a server is multihomed, it's usually connected to two physical as well as logical networks. Each physical network likely has a router. Simply configuring a default gateway for each interface might be tempting. However, Windows always chooses only one default gateway for sending packets to remote networks. For example, a server could receive a packet through an interface connected to the internal network and send the reply to the default gateway on the external network. You probably don't want this to happen. To solve this problem, you can use the `route` command, explained in the next section.

Using the `route` Command

Windows computers maintain a routing table that dictates where a packet should be sent based on the packet's destination address. The `route.exe` command-line program enables you to display and alter the routing table's contents. Figure 1-7 shows partial results of the `route print` command, which displays the contents of the routing table.

These results are displayed in five columns. The first column, Network Destination, is a network number compared against an IP packet's destination address. The Netmask column displays the subnet mask associated with the network destination. The Gateway column is the address of the router where packets with a destination address matching the network destination should be forwarded. The Interface column is the address of the NIC through which the packet should be sent to reach the gateway. The Metric column is the value assigned to the route. If the routing table contains two or more entries that can reach the same destination, the one with the lowest metric is chosen.

In Figure 1-7, notice the network destination of 0.0.0.0 with a netmask of 0.0.0.0. This entry indicates the default route or default gateway. A packet with a destination address that doesn't match any entries in the routing table is forwarded to the gateway address in the default route entry—in this case, 192.168.0.250. A gateway specified as "On-link" simply means the network destination is a network connected directly to one of the computer's interfaces. All Network Destination entries beginning with 127 indicate the computer's loopback address, which means "this computer." The Network Destination entries starting with 224 are multicast addresses, and entries starting with 255 are broadcast addresses. All packets with a multicast or broadcast destination address are sent to the local network, not to a router.

The `route` command can be used to change the routing table. For instance, a multihomed computer might have two or more possibilities for a default gateway. Best practices dictate configuring only one interface with a default gateway. However, suppose you have a server connected to two networks: 192.168.1.0/24 and 172.16.208.0/24 as shown in Figure 1-8. The 192.168.1.0 network connects to the Internet, and the 172.16.208.0 network is part of the internal network and is connected to networks 172.16.200.0/24 through 172.16.207.0/24. In addition, the 192.168.1.0 network has no possible way to get to the 172.16 networks.

```
IPv4 Route Table
===========================================================================
Active Routes:
Network Destination        Netmask          Gateway         Interface  Metric
          0.0.0.0          0.0.0.0    192.168.0.250       192.168.0.4    271
        127.0.0.0        255.0.0.0         On-link         127.0.0.1    331
        127.0.0.1  255.255.255.255         On-link         127.0.0.1    331
  127.255.255.255  255.255.255.255         On-link         127.0.0.1    331
      169.254.0.0      255.255.0.0         On-link     169.254.23.25    271
    169.254.23.25  255.255.255.255         On-link     169.254.23.25    271
  169.254.255.255  255.255.255.255         On-link     169.254.23.25    271
      192.168.0.0    255.255.255.0         On-link       192.168.0.4    271
      192.168.0.4  255.255.255.255         On-link       192.168.0.4    271
    192.168.0.255  255.255.255.255         On-link       192.168.0.4    271
        224.0.0.0        240.0.0.0         On-link         127.0.0.1    331
        224.0.0.0        240.0.0.0         On-link       192.168.0.4    271
        224.0.0.0        240.0.0.0         On-link     169.254.23.25    271
  255.255.255.255  255.255.255.255         On-link         127.0.0.1    331
  255.255.255.255  255.255.255.255         On-link       192.168.0.4    271
  255.255.255.255  255.255.255.255         On-link     169.254.23.25    271
===========================================================================
Persistent Routes:
  Network Address          Netmask  Gateway Address  Metric
          0.0.0.0          0.0.0.0    192.168.0.250  Default
===========================================================================
```

Figure 1-7   Results of the `route print` command

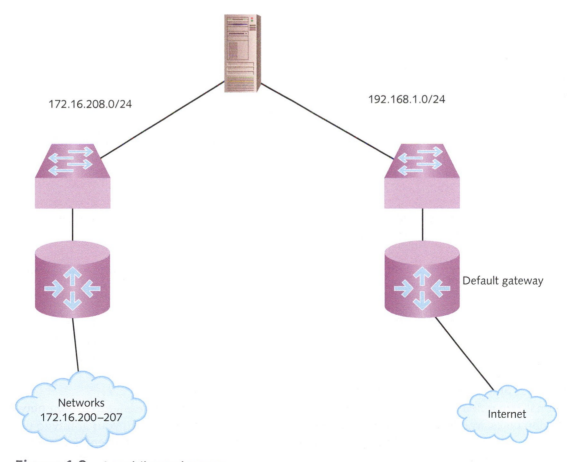

172.16.208.0/24

192.168.1.0/24

Default gateway

Networks
172.16.200–207

Internet

Figure 1-8   A multihomed server

If your default gateway is configured on the 192.168.1.0 network (as it should be, because it's connected to the Internet), when your server replies to a packet from the 172.16.200.0 to 172.16.207.0 networks, it sends the reply out the 192.168.1.0 interface because that's where the default gateway is. Remember that by default, the routing table contains entries only for networks the computer is directly connected to plus the default route. So the server doesn't have an entry for the 172.16 networks except 172.16.208.0. Any packets sent to these networks go to the default gateway, which can't deliver them to the destination network. To solve this problem, you can add routes to the routing table by using the following command:

```
route add 172.16.200.0 mask 255.255.255.0 172.16.208.250
```

This command creates a routing table entry for the 172.16.200.0 network with the subnet mask 255.255.255.0 and the gateway 172.16.208.250, which is the router on your server's network. You could make eight entries, one for each remote network, or a single entry, as shown:

```
route add 172.16.200.0 mask 255.255.248.0 172.16.208.250
```

This entry consolidates networks 172.16.200.0 through 172.16.207.0 into a single entry by using a modified subnet mask (the supernetting technique discussed earlier).

IP Configuration Command-Line Tools

Several command-line tools are available to help you troubleshoot, display, and configure IP addresses and related TCP/IP settings on a Windows computer. This section examines the following tools:

- `netsh`
- PowerShell cmdlets
- `ipconfig`
- `ping`
- `arp`
- `tracert`
- `nslookup`

Other network configuration and troubleshooting tools are available, but they're typically used to verify correct IP configuration settings and connectivity.

Using `netsh`

You can use the `netsh.exe` command to perform a wide variety of network configuration tasks, such as firewall configuration and IP address configuration. To see a list of `netsh` commands, type `netsh /?` at the command prompt. To configure the IP address of an interface named Ethernet to 10.1.1.1/16, use this command:

```
netsh interface ipv4 set address "Ethernet" static 10.1.1.1 255.255.0.0
```

You can include the default gateway by adding the address to the end of the command:

```
netsh interface ipv4 set address "Ethernet" static 10.1.1.1 255.255.0.0 10.1.1.250
```

To set the primary DNS server for the computer to 10.1.1.100, use the following command:

```
netsh interface ipv4 set dns "Ethernet" static 10.1.1.100 primary
```

The `netsh` command has many options that are useful for network configuration tasks. You should spend some time with this command so that you have an understanding of what you can do with it.

Using PowerShell Cmdlets

Microsoft has expanded the number of cmdlets in PowerShell and made them easier to use for network configuration tasks. Microsoft certification exams place considerable emphasis on your ability to use PowerShell for everyday configuration tasks. This section describes some PowerShell cmdlets for viewing and configuring IP address settings.

The `Get-NetIPConfiguration` cmdlet displays IP configuration information about your network's interfaces. You use it to get the interface name you need for other commands. Figure 1-9 shows the output this command produces.

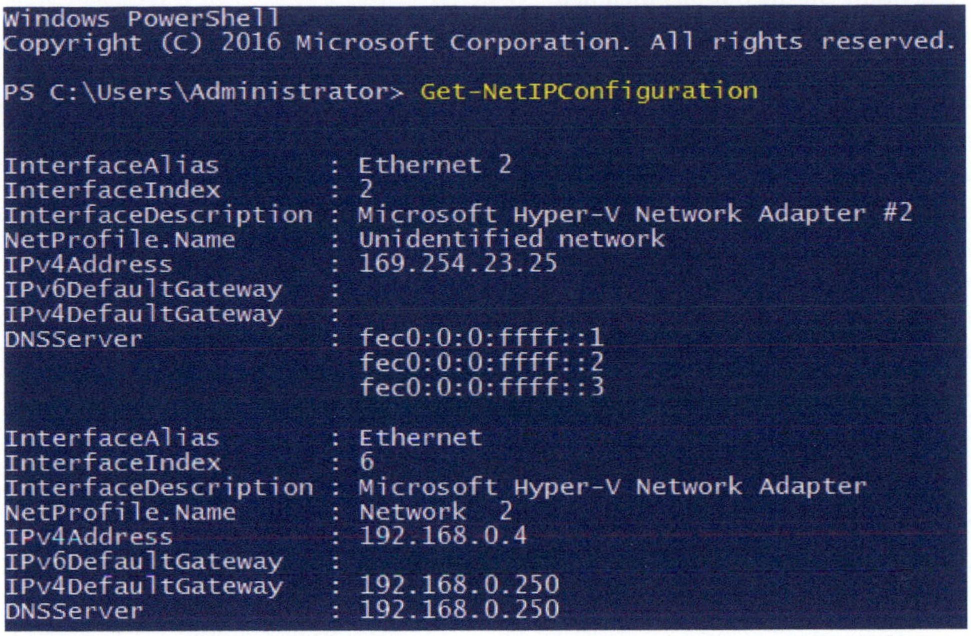

Figure 1-9   The `Get-NetIPConfiguration` cmdlet

You use the `Get-NetIPAddress` cmdlet to see detailed IP address configuration information on a specified interface. If no interface is specified, configuration information is shown for all interfaces.

The `Set-NetIPInterface` cmdlet is used to configure DHCP client settings, "wake on LAN" settings, and router settings. If it's used without specifying an interface, the settings apply to all interfaces. The first example disables DHCP on all interfaces, and the second example enables DHCP on the interface named Ethernet:

```
Set-NetIPInterface -DHCP disabled
Set-NetIPInterface -InterfaceAlias Ethernet -DHCP enabled
```

To get detailed help on this command, use `Get-Help Set-NetIPInterface -detailed`.

Use the `New-NetIPAddress` cmdlet to set new IP address configuration settings for an interface. You can also set the default gateway. To set the IP address to 172.16.1.10 with a subnet mask of 255.255.0.0 on the Ethernet interface, use the following command:

```
New-NetIPAddress -InterfaceAlias Ethernet -IPAddress 172.16.1.10
  -PrefixLength 16 -DefaultGateway 172.16.1.250
```

To modify the settings of an existing IP address, you use the `Set-NetIPAddress` cmdlet. For example, to change the prefix length (subnet mask) of the interface with IP addresses 172.16.1.10 to 24, use the following command:

```
Set-NetIPAddress -IPAddress 172.16.1.10 -PrefixLength24
```

The `Set-DnsClientServerAddress` cmdlet sets the DNS server addresses used by the DNS client on the specified interface, as shown in this example:

```
Set-DnsClientServerAddress -InterfaceAlias Ethernet
  -ServerAddress 172.16.1.100
```

There are many more options for these cmdlets. To get detailed help and see examples of using them, just use `Get-Help`.

Using `ipconfig`

As you've learned, `ipconfig` is usually used to display a computer's IP address settings but can perform other tasks, depending on the options included:

- *No options*—Displays the basic IP configuration, including the IP address, subnet mask, and default gateway.
- `/all`—Displays extended IP configuration information, such as the computer name, domain name, network adapter description, physical (MAC) address, whether DHCP is used, and DNS address.
- `/release`—Releases its IP address back to the DHCP server if DHCP is used. If the address is released, the computer is assigned the invalid address of 0.0.0.0.
- `/renew`—Renews the IP address configuration lease.
- `/displaydns`—Windows caches the most recent DNS lookup request results, and this option displays the contents of the local DNS cache. If a computer recently did a DNS lookup for *www.yahoo.com*, for example, it keeps that information in local memory so that the next time the address is needed, a DNS query is unnecessary.
- `/flushdns`—Deletes cached DNS information from memory. This option can be useful if a computer's IP address or hostname was changed recently, and the cache contains obsolete information.
- `/registerdns`—Requests new DHCP leases and registers these names again with a DNS server.

Using `ping`

You have used `ping` to test connectivity between two computers. It sends an ICMP Echo Request packet to the destination IP address specified in the command. If the destination computer receives the ICMP Echo Request, it replies with an ICMP Echo Reply packet. When the computer receives the reply packet, the `ping` program displays a message similar to this one:

```
reply from 192.168.100.201 bytes=32 time=1ms TTL=128
```

In this output, the IP address is the address of the computer that sent the reply. The `bytes=32` parameter specifies how many data bytes are in the ICMP message. You can change the number of data bytes with options in the `ping` command. The `time=>1ms` parameter indicates that the reply took less than a millisecond from the time the ICMP Echo Request was sent. The `TTL=128` indicates the message's time to live, which specifies how many routers a packet can go through before the packet should be expired and discarded. At each router, the time to live (TTL)is decremented. If the TTL reaches 0, the router sends the source computer a message indicating that the TTL expired before reaching its destination.

To see the options available with this command, type `ping /?` at a command prompt. Some of the options are as follows:

- `-t`—Sends ICMP Echo Request packets continually until you press Ctrl+C to stop. By default, `ping` sends four packets.
- `-a`—Tries to resolve the IP address to a hostname. If the name can be resolved, it's printed in the first line of the `ping` output.
- `-n count`—The *count* parameter is the number of Echo Request packets to send.
- `-l size`—The *size* parameter is the number of data bytes to send in each Echo Request packet. The default is 32 bytes.
- `-i TTL`—Time to live is the number of routers the packet can go through on the way to the destination before the packet should be expired.

Using `arp`

The `arp` command displays or makes changes to the ARP cache, which contains IP address–MAC address pairs. As discussed, when an IP packet is sent to a destination on the local network, the sending device must have the destination's MAC address. The source computer retrieves the MAC address by sending a broadcast ARP request packet to the local network. The ARP request packet essentially asks "Who has IP address A.B.C.D?" The computer on the local network that's assigned the IP address sends an ARP reply message containing its MAC address. When a computer learns another computer's MAC address, it keeps the address in its ARP cache temporarily so that it doesn't have to send another ARP request packet to communicate with that computer again. Entries in the ARP cache are kept for only a few minutes to prevent them from becoming obsolete. Some options for the `arp` command are as follows:

- `-a` or `-g`—Displays the contents of the ARP cache. These options perform the same function.
- `-d`—Deletes the entire contents of the ARP cache or a single entry specified by IP address. This option can be useful if a computer's NIC has changed recently and the cache contains obsolete information.
- `-s`—Adds a permanent entry to the ARP cache by specifying a host's IP address and MAC address. This option should be used only if the address of a frequently accessed computer is unlikely to change. Remember: If the NIC is changed on a computer, its MAC address changes, too.

Using `tracert`

The `tracert` command is usually called *trace route* because it displays the route packets take between two computers. It displays the address or DNS name of each router a packet travels through to reach the specified destination. It then sends a series of three ICMP Echo Request packets with a TTL value starting at 1 and increases the value until the destination is reached. Each router a packet encounters along the way to the destination decrements the TTL value by 1. If the TTL value reaches 0, the router sends a TTL-expired message back to the sending computer and drops the packet. When `tracert` receives the TTL-expired message, it records the sending router's IP address and the time to receive a reply and displays this information. Next, a new series of three ICMP Echo Request packets are sent with an incremented TTL value. This procedure continues until all routers between the source and destination have been recorded.

`Tracert` is useful for troubleshooting the routing topology of a complex network and finding the bottleneck between a computer and a destination network. Because `tracert` displays the time it took to receive a reply from each router, a router (or the link to this router) showing an inordinately long delay might be where the bottleneck lies.

Using `nslookup`

The `nslookup` command is used to test and troubleshoot DNS operation and can be used in command mode or interactive mode. In command mode, you type `nslookup host`; *host* is the name of a computer in the local domain or a fully qualified domain name. `Nslookup` replies with the specified host's IP address. By default, `nslookup` uses the DNS server address configured in the IP address settings. Following are some examples of using `Nslookup` in command mode:

```
nslookup serverDM2
nslookup www.yahoo.com
nslookup www.google.com 192.168.0.250
```

The first two commands query the default DNS server. The last command queries a DNS server at address 192.168.0.250. Because you can specify a different DNS server, you can compare the results of different DNS servers to verify correct DNS operation.

To use interactive mode, type `nslookup` at the command prompt, and the output shows which server it's using to perform lookups. You can type a question mark at the interactive mode prompt to get a list of available options and commands.

Activity 1-5: Using the `arp` Command

Time Required: 10 minutes

Objective: Use the `arp` command to display and delete ARP entries.

Required Tools and Equipment: ServerDC1, ServerDM1; Internet access

Description: You want to see how the `arp` command works, so you display the ARP cache, and then delete its contents. Next, you use the `ping` and `arp` commands to see the difference between pinging a computer on a local and a remote network.

1. Start ServerDC1. Start and sign in to ServerDM1 as the domain **Administrator**. Open a command prompt window by right-clicking **Start** and clicking **Command Prompt**.

2. Type **arp -a** and press **Enter**. You should see a few entries. Those listed as "static" in the Type column are created automatically by Windows. The dynamic entries are a result of your computer having recently sent an `arp` request message for the specified IP address. Note that these `arp` messages are sent automatically by your computer whenever it needs to get another computer's MAC address, such as when ServerDM1 needs to contact ServerDC1 when you signed in.

3. Type **arp -d** and press **Enter**. Type **arp -a** and press **Enter**. The `-d` option deletes the ARP cache. After the second command, you will probably see a few static entries, but no dynamic entries unless your computer contacted another computer between commands.

4. Type **arp -d** and press **Enter** to clear any recently acquired entries, and then immediately type **ping ServerDC1** and press **Enter**. Type **arp -a** and press **Enter** again. You should see an ARP entry for ServerDC1, which should be address 192.168.0.1.

5. (*Note:* This step requires access to the Internet. If your lab does not have access to the Internet, you can substitute another device name or address that is on a different network from your servers.) Type **arp -d** and press **Enter**, and then type **ping www.tomsho.com** and press **Enter**. Type **arp -a** and press **Enter**. The ARP cache should have at least two dynamic entries: One is ServerDC1's IP address, and the other should be for your default gateway address. Notice that there's no ARP entry for the address of *www.yahoo.com*. The entry for ServerDC1 exists because your computer had to do a DNS lookup for *www.yahoo.com* and, therefore, had to get ServerDC1's MAC address because ServerDC1 is also the DNS server. The entry for your default gateway exists because the `ping` packet had to be sent to your router to reach the network where *www.yahoo.com* is located. Remember that the MAC address is used to deliver a packet to a device only on the local network whether the device is a computer or a router.

6. Stay signed in to ServerDM1, leave the command prompt window open, and leave ServerDC1 running and continue to the next activity.

Activity 1-6: Using the `tracert` Command

Time Required: 10 minutes

Objective: Use the `tracert` command.

Required Tools and Equipment: ServerDC1 and ServerDM1; Internet access

Description: In this activity, you want to troubleshoot a slow Internet connection, so you use the `tracert` command to try to determine where the bottleneck is.

1. On ServerDM1 at the command prompt, type **tracert ServerDC1** and press **Enter**. Because there are no routers between ServerDM1 and ServerDC1, you should get only one response line of output. Notice that three different response times are displayed because `tracert` sends three packets for each TTL value it uses. By sending three packets, you can average the times to get a more accurate picture of the response time.

2. Type **tracert www.tomsho.com** and press **Enter**. Some router hops include a name with the router's address, and you can sometimes use this name to get an idea of the router's geographical location or the name of the ISP that operates the router.

3. To speed up `tracert` results, you can tell it not to do router name lookups. Type **tracert -d www.tomsho. com** and press **Enter**. The results are displayed much faster, especially if you're several router hops away from *www.cengage.com*.

4. If the connection to *www.tomsho.com* is slow, you may be able to see if there is a bottleneck between your network and the destination network. Look for time values of 100 ms or more in each router hop. Also, try the `tracert` command more than once to be sure slow response times are consistent.

5. Stay signed in and continue to the next activity.

Internet Protocol Version 6 Overview

 Certification

- **70-741 – Implement core and distributed network solutions:**
  Implement IPv4 and IPv6 addressing

IPv4 has been the driving force on the Internet for decades and continues to be the dominant protocol in use. However, it's starting to show its age as its address space becomes used up, and workarounds for security and quality of service must be put in place. IPv4 was developed more than 40 years ago, so it seems natural that as all other aspects of technology slowly get replaced, so will IPv4. This section discusses that replacement: IPv6. IPv6 addresses look very different from IPv4 addresses, and unlike IPv4, IPv6 addresses have a built-in hierarchy and fields with a distinct purpose. Configuring an IPv6 address is distinctly different from doing so for an IPv4 address. The transition from IPv4 to IPv6 is not going to happen overnight, so methods have been developed to allow IPv4 and IPv6 networks to coexist and communicate with one another.

This section doesn't attempt to give you a full explanation of IPv6 and its many complexities; there are entire books written on this topic. However, it addresses the key aspects of the IPv6 protocol and what you need to know to configure and support a Windows Server 2016 server using IPv6.

IPv6 Overview

The Internet Engineering Task Force (IETF) started development on IPng (IP next generation) in 1994, and it was later named IPv6. IPv6 was developed to address IPv4's shortcomings. Some improvements and changes in IPv6 include the following:

- *Larger address space*—IPv4 addresses are 32 bits, which provide a theoretical four billion addresses. IPv6 addresses are 128 bits, so the number of possible addresses can be expressed as 34 followed by 37 0s, or 340 trillion trillion trillion. It's probably safe to say that running out of IPv6 addresses is unlikely.
- *Hierarchical address space*—Unlike IPv4, in which numbers in the address have little meaning other than the address class and the network ID and host ID, IPv6 addresses have a more defined structure. For example, the first part of an address can indicate a particular organization or site.
- *Autoconfiguration*—IPv6 can be self-configuring or autoconfigured from a router or server running IPv6 or through DHCPv6.
- *Built-in Quality of Service (QoS) support*—IPv6 includes built-in fields in packet headers to support QoS strategies (used to prioritize data packets based on the type or urgency of information they contain) without having to install additional protocol components as IPv4 does.
- *Built-in support for security*—From the ground-up, IPv6 is built to support secure protocols, such as Internet Protocol Security (IPSec), whereas IPv4's support for IPSec is an add-on feature.

- *Support for mobility*—With built-in support for mobility, routing IPv6 packets generated by mobile devices over the Internet is more efficient than with IPv4.
- *Extensibility*—IPv6 uses extension headers instead of IPv4's fixed-size 40-byte header. Extension headers allow adding features to IPv6 simply by adding a new header.

IPv6 Address Structure

The good news with IPv6 is that subnetting as it's done in IPv4 will be a thing of the past. The bad news is that you still need to work with binary numbers, and with 128 bits in the address, there are quite a few new things to learn. IPv6 addresses are written as eight 16-bit hexadecimal numbers separated by colons. There's no official name for each part of the address, so each 16-bit value is simply called a *field*. A valid IPv6 address looks like this:

```
fe80:0:0:0:18ff:0024:8e5a:60
```

There are a few things to note in this address:

- IPv6 addresses often have several 0 values. One or more consecutive 0 values can be written as a double colon (::), so the preceding address can be written as `fe80::18ff:0024:8e5a:60`. However, you can have only one double colon in an IPv6 address.
- Leading 0s are optional. The value 0024 in the previous example could just as easily have been written as 24, and the value 60 could have been written as 0060.
- The hexadecimal numbering system was chosen to represent IPv6 addresses largely because it's much easier to convert to binary than decimal is. Each hexadecimal digit represents 4 bits, so to convert an IPv6 address to binary, simply convert each hexadecimal digit (accounting for leading 0s) to its binary equivalent. For example, the first field in the preceding address (`fe80`) can be written as follows:

```
1111 1110 1000 0000
  f    e    8    0
```

In Windows, when you view an IPv6 address in the network connection's Status dialog box or after using `ipconfig`, you see a percent sign (%) followed by a number at the end of the address. The number following the percent sign is the interface index used to identify the interface in some `netsh` and PowerShell commands. You don't see a subnet mask or even the prefix length as you do with an IPv4 address. However, IPv6 addresses have a prefix length; it's just that it's always 64 when discussing a host address. This is because in IPv6 host addresses, all IPv6 network IDs are 64 bits, so a typical IPv6 address can be written as follows:

```
fe80:0:0:0:18ff:0024:8e5a:60/64
```

However, because the prefix is always 64 for an IPv6 host address, the prefix is often omitted.

The IPv6 Interface ID

Because the prefix length (network ID) of an IPv6 address is 64 bits, the interface ID (the host ID in IPv4) of an IPv6 address is 64 bits, too. So you can easily identify the network ID of an IPv6 address by looking at the first 64 bits (16 hex digits or four fields) and the interface ID by looking at the last 64 bits. For example, in the following address, the network ID is `fe80:0:0:0` and the interface ID is `18ff:0024:8e5a:60`:

```
fe80:0:0:0:18ff:0024:8e5a:60
```

Because the prefix isn't a variable length, working with IPv6 addresses is somewhat easier because you don't have to do a binary calculation with a subnet mask to determine the network and interface IDs.

An IPv6 interface ID can be assigned to a host in these ways:

- *Using the 48-bit MAC address*—Because a MAC address is only 48 bits, the other 16 bits come from the value `fffe` inserted after the first 24 bits of the MAC address. In addition, the first two zeros that compose most MAC addresses are replaced with 02. For example, given the MAC address 00-0C-29-7C-F9-C4, the host ID of an IPv6 address is **02**0c:29**ff:fe**7c:f9c4. This autoconfigured

64-bit host ID is called an **Extended Unique Identifier (EUI)-64 interface ID**. This method is defined in RFC 4291.

- *A randomly generated permanent interface identifier*—The interface ID is generated randomly but is a permanent assignment maintained through system restarts. Windows Server 2008 and later use this method by default for permanent interfaces, such as Ethernet ports. However, you can have Windows use EUI-64 addresses with this `netsh` command or PowerShell cmdlet:

```
netsh interface ipv6 set global randomizeidentifiers=disabled
```

or

```
Set-NetIPv6Protocol -RandomizeIdentifiers Disabled
```

- *A temporary interface identifier*—Some connections, such as dial-up Point-to-Point Protocol (PPP) connections, might use this method for interface IPv6 address assignment, defined in RFC 4941, whereby the interface ID is assigned randomly and changes each time IPv6 is initialized to maintain anonymity.
- *Via DHCPv6*—Addresses are assigned via a DHCPv6 server to IPv6 interfaces when they're initialized.
- *Manually*—Similar to IPv4 configuration, the IPv6 address is entered manually in the interface's Properties dialog box.

IPv6 Address Types

- **70-741 – Implement core and distributed network solutions:**
  Implement IPv4 and IPv6 addressing

IPv4 defines unicast, multicast, and broadcast addresses, and IPv6 defines unicast, multicast, and anycast addresses. Unicast and multicast addresses in IPv6 perform much like their IPv4 counterparts with a few exceptions. Anycast addresses are an altogether different animal.

IPv6 Unicast Addresses

A unicast address specifies a single interface on a device. To participate in an IPv6 network, every device must have at least one network interface that has been assigned a unicast IPv6 address. In most cases, each interface on a device is assigned a separate unicast address, but for load-balancing purposes, multiple interfaces on a device can share the same IPv6 unicast address. In the realm of IPv6 unicast addresses, there are three primary types: link-local, unique local, and global. In addition, there are addresses reserved for special purposes and transition addresses, which were developed to help with the transition from IPv4 to IPv6.

Link-Local Addresses

Addresses starting with `fe80` are called **link-local IPv6 addresses** and are automatically configured on each interface on which IPv6 is enabled. Link-local addresses can't be routed and are somewhat equivalent to APIPA in IPv4. Link-local addresses are used only for device-to-device communication within the same subnet because a router doesn't forward packets with a link-local destination or source address. They are used, for example, for devices to communicate with DHCP servers or routers for the purpose of configuring the interface with a unique local or global address. However, IPv6 interfaces always retain their link-local address, even if they are assigned a unique local or global address.

Since each IPv6 interface is assigned a link-local address in which the network identifier is `fe80::`, there must be a way to distinguish which outbound interface link-local communication should use. To this end, a number called a **zone id** is used to distinguish which interface an IPv6 link-local address is bound to. If you look at the IP configuration of a computer using ipconfig, for example, you will see a percent sign followed by a number at the end of each address. For example, if a computer has two IPv6 interfaces, they are both assigned a link-local address with a prefix of `fe80::`. If you ping another computer's link-local address, you must add the zone id of the source interface (for example, %4) at the end of the address so Windows knows which interface the ping packet should originate from. The zone id on Windows computers is the same as the interface index and is only locally significant, meaning you don't use the zone id of the destination interface, only of the source interface.

Tip ⓘ

Link-local addresses are defined by RFC 4291, which you can read about at *http://tools.ietf.org/html/rfc4291*.

Unique Local Addresses

Unique local IPv6 addresses are analogous to the familiar private IPv4 addresses (refer back to the section "Private IP Addresses") that most companies use behind the network's firewall and are preconfigured on routers for use in small and medium networks. Unique local addresses, like private IPv4 addresses, can't be routed on the Internet (but can be routed inside the private network).

Tip ⓘ

RFC 4193 at *http://tools.ietf.org/html/rfc4193* defines unique local addresses.

Unique local addresses begin with `fc` or `fd` and are usually expressed as `fc00::/7`. The format for a unique local address is as follows:

`fdgg:gggg:gggg:ssss:iiii:iiii:iiii:iiii`

In this example, the string of g characters after the `fd` represents a 40-bit global ID, which identifies a specific site in an organization. The string of four s characters represents the subnet ID field, giving each site 16 bits for subnetting its unique local address. The string of i characters represents the 64-bit interface ID. This address format allows a whopping 65,536 subnets, each with a 64-bit interface ID field. With more than 65,000 subnets per site and more than 18 quintillion hosts per subnet, you can see that IPv6 solves the address space problem with IPv4.

This global ID is supposed to be set to a pseudo-random 40-bit value. RFC 4193 provides an algorithm for generating the pseudo-random global ID. It's set to a random number to ensure that organizations whose networks are connected still have unique IPv6 address prefixes. In practice, you can assign the 40-bit global ID manually if you aren't concerned about a future conflict with another network.

As mentioned, unique local addresses can begin with `fc` or `fd`. The global IDs of unique local addresses beginning with `fd` are called *locally assigned* and are the only type RFC 4193 defines. Those starting with `fc` aren't defined as of this writing but might be used later with an address registrar assigning the 40-bit global ID. For now, you should use `fd` when assigning unique local IPv6 addresses.

Note 📎

Unique local addresses effectively replace an older addressing format called *site-local addresses*, which have the format `fec0::/10`. Site-local addresses were defined by RFC 3879 but have been deprecated, and the IETF considers them reserved addresses.

Global Addresses

Global unicast IPv6 addresses, defined by RFC 4291, are analogous to public IPv4 addresses. They are accessible on the public Internet and can be routed. Essentially, an IPv6 address is global if it doesn't fall into one of the other categories of address (special use, link-local, unique local, loopback, transition, and so forth).

IPv6 addresses have one sizable advantage over IPv4 addresses aside from the much larger address space; a structure, or a hierarchy, can be built into IPv6 addresses that allows more efficient routing on the Internet. Global addresses have the following formats:

```
2ggg:gggg:gggg:ssss:iiii:iiii:iiii:iiii
```

or

```
3ggg:gggg:gggg:ssss:iiii:iiii:iiii:iiii
```

> **Note** 🖉
>
> In early specifications of the IPv6 standard, IPv6 addresses had a defined hierarchy built into the global ID. A top-level aggregator (TLA) was a 13-bit field allocated to Internet registries by the IANA, and a next-level aggregator was a 24-bit field to be used by ISPs to allocate addresses to its customers. These identifiers have been deprecated as specified by RFC 4147 and are no longer used. It's expected, however, that large ISPs and Internet registries will use the 45 bits of available global ID to form an address hierarchy for efficient routing.

As in the previous example, the g characters are the global ID or global routing prefix, the s characters are the subnet ID, and the i characters are the interface ID. As of this writing, only IPv6 addresses beginning with the binary bit pattern 0010 (decimal 2) or 0011 (decimal 3) are allocated for Internet use, which represent only one-eighth the total available address space. The rest of the address space is reserved. So, the global unicast address space is often specified as 2000::/3, which means that only the first three bits are a fixed value; the remaining part of the address is variable. Even with this constraint on the IPv6 address space, the 45 variable bits in the global ID allow more than 35 trillion different address prefixes, each with more than 65,000 subnets.

The global ID is typically 48 bits, and the subnet ID 16 bits; however, this allocation is not fixed. A larger global ID with a smaller subnet ID (or vice versa) is possible but not likely to be common. The interface ID is fixed at 64 bits.

> **Note** 🖉
>
> RFC 4147 lists IPv6 prefixes and their use. The table in that document shows that most of the address space is reserved by the IETF. The IPv6 address space has a tremendous amount of room to grow.

IPv6 Special-Purpose Addresses

There are a few IPv6 addresses and prefixes that have a special purpose:

- *Loopback address*—The loopback address in IPv6 is equivalent to 127.0.0.1 used in IPv4 and is written as ::1. Like its IPv4 counterpart, the IPv6 loopback is used only for testing local IPv6 protocol operation; no packets actually leave the local computer.
- *Zero address*—The zero (or unspecified) address, which can be written simply as ::, is used as a placeholder in the source address field of an outgoing IPv6 packet when the sending computer doesn't yet have an IPv6 address assigned.

- *Documentation*—The global unicast address `2001:db8::/32` has been reserved for use in books and other documentation discussing IPv6. This address prefix can also be used for test labs, but it shouldn't be routed on a company network or the Internet.
- *IPv4-to-IPv6 transition*—A number of address prefixes are used for transitioning from IPv4 to IPv6 and to support both IPv4 and IPv6 on the same network. These addresses are discussed later in the section "Transitioning from IPv4 to IPv6".

Subnetting with IPv6

Although subnetting as done in IPv4 will be a thing of the past, it doesn't mean subnetting won't be used at all in IPv6 networks. Typically, ISPs allocated IPv4 addresses to businesses in groups specified by a network address and IP prefix. ISPs try to give a business only the number of addresses it requires. However, with IPv6 having such a large address space, most address allocations will have a /48 prefix, even for small home networks. This means that the network ID is 48 bits, and the network administrator has 80 bits for assigning subnets and host IDs. Because the host ID is 64 bits, 16 bits are left for creating subnets. This number of bits allows for 65,536 subnets, more than enough for all but the largest organizations. Large conglomerates can get multiple /48 prefix addresses or /47 prefix addresses, which provide more than 130,000 subnets. A typical IPv6 address assigned by an ISP looks like Figure 1-10.

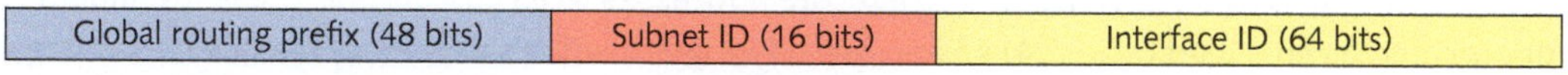

Global routing prefix (48 bits)	Subnet ID (16 bits)	Interface ID (64 bits)

Figure 1-10   Structure of a typical IPv6 address

With 16 bits available to subnet, there are many strategies you can use. A small network that doesn't have multiple subnets can simply leave the subnet ID as all zeroes, for example, and an address in this situation might look like this:

`2001:DB8:A00:0000:020C:29FF:FE7C:F9C4/64`

The first two fields (`2001:DB8`) of this address use the reserved documentation prefix mentioned previously. The A00 in the address is the last 16 bits of the network prefix and was randomly chosen for this example. The 0s following the A00 are the subnet ID, and the last 64 bits are the computer's interface ID. The `/64` just indicates that the network portion of the address is the first 64 bits (network prefix plus subnet ID), although the prefix for an interface ID is unnecessary.

A network that does need to subnet could just take the 16 bits for the subnet ID and start counting. For example, a company could make the first three subnets as follows; the bold part of the address is the subnet ID, and the 64-bit interface ID has been omitted.

`2001:DB8:A00:`**`0000`**
`2001:DB8:A00:`**`0001`**
`2001:DB8:A00:`**`0002`**

Large organizations with multiple locations could take a more structured approach and assign each location a bank of subnets as in the following:

- `2001:DB8:A00:0000`—Assigned to New York location
- `2001:DB8:A00:4000`—Assigned to London location
- `2001:DB8:A00:8000`—Assigned to Shanghai location

With this strategy, each location has 4000 hexadecimal subnet IDs to work with. For example, New York can make subnets `2001:DB8:A00:0000`, `2001:DB8:A00:0001`, `2001:DB8:A00:0002`, and so forth, up to

`2001:DB8:A00:3FFF`. Put another way, each location can configure up to 16,384 subnets. As you can see, subnetting does still exist in IPv6, but it's a more straightforward process than in IPv4.

Multicast Addresses

A multicast address in IPv6 performs the same function as its IPv4 counterpart. A multicast address isn't assigned to an interface, but a host can listen for packets with multicast addresses to participate in a multicast application. Multicast addresses are easily identified because they begin with `ff` (first 8 bits of the address set to 1). Beyond that, multicast addresses have the following structure:

`ffxy:zzzz:zzzz:zzzz:zzzz:zzzz:zzzz:zzzz`

- *Flags*—The 4-bit flags field, indicated by the `x`, uses the three low-order bits. The high-order bit is reserved and must be 0. The next high-order bit is the R (rendezvous point) flag; when set, it indicates that the address contains a rendezvous point. The next high-order bit is the P (prefix) flag; when set, it indicates that the multicast address is based on the network prefix. The last bit, called the T (transient) bit, indicates a permanently assigned or well-known address assigned by IANA when it's 0. If the T bit is 1, the multicast address isn't permanently assigned—in other words, "transient." If the R flag is set to 1, the P and T flags must also be set to 1. If the P flag is set to 1, the T bit must also be set. Common values for this field, therefore, are 0, 1, 3, and 7.
- *Scope*—The scope field, indicated by the `y`, specifies whether and where the multicast packet can be routed. Common values and scopes for this field are as follows:
  - 1: Interface-local scope, which is essentially a multicast loopback address because the packet can't be sent across the network; it must stay with the current host.
  - 2: Link-local scope, which means that the packet must stay on the current network and can't be routed.
  - 5: Site-local scope, meaning that this scope can be targeted at specific devices on the network, such as routers and DHCP servers.
  - 8: Organization-local, which means the packet can't be routed beyond the organization's network.
  - E: Global scope, meaning these multicast packets can be routed on the public Internet.
- *Group ID*—This field identifies a multicast group, which is the group of computers listening to the stream of multicast packets. In essence, this 112-bit field identifies the unique multicast application that's transmitting the multicast packets. RFC 2375 lists the well-known multicast address assignments.

Anycast Addresses

Anycast addresses are unique in that they can be assigned to multiple interfaces on different hosts and are recognized as anycast addresses only by the devices that use them. Specifically, anycast addresses are assigned to routers and are used to allow other IPv6 devices to deliver internetwork packets to the nearest router on a subnet. They're typically used when more than one router exists on a subnet. Each router interface on the subnet can be assigned the anycast address. When a device sends a packet to the anycast address, the packet is delivered to the "nearest" router as defined by the routing protocols. It's often defined as a one-to-one-of-many association because there are potentially many destinations, but the packet is delivered to only one.

Anycast addresses don't have a special format because they're just unicast addresses used in a special way. Just assigning an address to multiple interfaces makes a unicast address an anycast address. However, the device that's assigned the anycast address must be configured to recognize these addresses. Currently, only router interfaces should be assigned an anycast address, and the router must be configured to recognize that the interface has been assigned this type of address.

IPv6 Autoconfiguration

 **Certification**

- 70-741 – Implement core and distributed network solutions:
  Implement IPv4 and IPv6 addressing

IPv6 autoconfiguration occurs by two methods: stateless and stateful. With Windows Vista/Windows Server 2008 and later computers, these methods can actually be used together.

- *Stateless autoconfiguration*—The host listens for router advertisement messages from a local router. If the Autonomous (A) flag in the router advertisement message is set, the host uses the prefix information contained in the message. In this case, the host uses the advertised prefix and its 64-bit interface ID to generate the IPv6 address. If the A flag isn't set, the prefix information is ignored, and the host can attempt to use DHCPv6 for address configuration or an automatically generated link-local address. A variation of stateless autoconfiguration is DHCPv6 stateless autoconfiguration in which the host autoconfigures its IPV6 address, usually using the prefix advertised by a router, but uses DHCPv6 to get other IPv6 configuration information.
- *Stateful autoconfiguration*—The host uses an autoconfiguration protocol, such as DHCPv6, to obtain its IPv6 address and other configuration information. A host uses stateful autoconfiguration to get IPv6 address configuration information if there are no routers on the network providing router advertisements or if the router advertisement indicates through flags (discussed later) that the host should contact a DHCPv6 server.

Autoconfiguration on Windows Hosts

The Windows autoconfiguration process involves the following steps:

1. At initialization, a link-local address is determined.
2. The link-local address is verified as unique by using duplicate address detection.
3. If the address is verified as unique, the address is assigned to the interface; otherwise, a new address is generated and Step 2 is repeated.
4. The host transmits a router solicitation message. This message is addressed to the `all-routers` multicast address.
5. There are two possible results when the host transmits a router solicitation message:

   a. No router advertisement messages are received in response to the solicitation message, the host attempts to use DHCPv6 to get an address.

   b. A router advertisement message is received. The router advertisement contains two flags, the Managed address configuration (M) flag and the Other stateful configuration (O) flag that instruct the host how to proceed with autoconfiguration:

      - Both flags are 0: The host will not use DHCPv6 for configuration; it will use the prefix in the router solicitation message only to construct its IPv6 address as long as the Autoconfiguration (A) flag in the prefix option field is set.
      - The M flag is 1 and the O flag is 0: The host will use DHCPv6 to get its IPv6 address but not for any other configuration options. This is a type of stateful autoconfiguration but it is uncommon since other configuration settings are usually provided by a DHCPv6 server.
      - The M flag is 0 and the O flag is 1: DHCPv6 is not used to construct the IPv6 address but is used for other configuration options. This is sometimes called *DHCPv6 stateless autoconfiguration*.
      - Both flags are 1: The host will use DHCPv6 for its address and other configuration options. This is stateful autoconfiguration.

Note

These steps are for Windows 8/8.1/10 and Windows Server 2012/2016 hosts. Windows Server 2008 and Windows 7 hosts don't attempt to use DHCPv6 if no router advertisements are received; otherwise, the process is the same.

Note that the IPv6 host maintains its link-local address even if it successfully gets an address via stateful or stateless autoconfiguration. Also, it's possible for the router advertisement to have the Autonomous flag in the prefix options even if the M and O flags indicate that the host should use DHCPv6 to obtain an address. When this occurs, the host will autoconfigure an address using the prefix *and* use DHCPv6 to get an address. In this case, the host will have two addresses bound to its interface (along with the link-local address). It's also possible for more than one router to advertise an IPv6 prefix, causing the host to autoconfigure multiple addresses.

Note

One other big difference between DHCPv4 and DHCPv6 is the assignment of the default gateway to DHCP clients. The default gateway configuration is usually one of the configuration options supplied by a DHCPv4 server, but DHCPv6 servers don't assign the default gateway. Instead, the link-local address of the router that sent the router advertisement is used by the host as its default gateway.

Configuring IPv6 Autoconfiguration

You can manually configure IPv6 autoconfiguration using PowerShell cmdlets or the `netsh` command from the command prompt. In the following examples, the name of the interface being configured is Ethernet. For each type of configuration, first the PowerShell cmdlet and then the `netsh` command is shown. Where the keyword *enabled* is used, you can use the keyword *disabled* to disable the option.

- Enable router discovery on the interface. By default, router discovery is enabled on IPv6 interfaces, so you need to run this command only if it has been disabled.

```
Set-NetIPInterface -InterfaceAlias Ethernet -AddressFamily IPv6
  -RouterDiscovery Enabled
netsh interface ipv6 set interface Ethernet routerdiscovery=enabled
```

- Enable Managed address configuration (set the M flag to 1). The default value for the M flag is 0. Note that this command is relevant only if router discovery is disabled on the interface. If router discovery is enabled, the interface receives its M flag configuration from the router advertisement.

```
Set-NetIPInterface -InterfaceAlias Ethernet -AddressFamily IPv6
  -ManagedAddressConfiguration Enabled
netsh interface ipv6 set interface Ethernet managedaddress=enabled
```

- Enable Other stateful configuration (set the O flag to 1). The default value for the O flag is 0. Note that this command is relevant only if router discovery is disabled on the interface. If router discovery is enabled, the interface receives its O flag configuration from the router advertisement.

```
Set-NetIPInterface -InterfaceAlias Ethernet -AddressFamily IPv6
  -OtherStatefulConfiguration Enabled
netsh interface ipv6 set interface Ethernet otherstateful=enabled
```

> **Note**
>
> You can configure all three of the preceding options in the same command, if desired.

Configuring Windows to Send Router Advertisements

Windows Server 2016 can be configured to send router advertisements, so you don't need to configure a router to do so. You can use the following commands to make Windows Server 2016 send out router advertisements so that IPv6 hosts can autoconfigure their IPv6 addresses. These examples use the IPv6 prefix `2001:db8:1234:1::/64`, and the network interface is named Ethernet. Be sure the interface you are configuring has an IPv6 address set with the specified prefix. You replace the prefix with your own and Ethernet with the name of your network interface if it's different.

- Configure Windows Server 2016 to send router advertisements. When you configure router advertising, the M and O flags in the router advertisement will be the same as the interface that you are configuring, so set the M and O flags on the interface according to how you want hosts that receive the advertisements to autoconfigure their IPv6 interface.

```
Set-NetIPInterface -InterfaceAlias Ethernet -AddressFamily IPv6
  -Advertising Enabled
netsh interface ipv6 set interface Ethernet advertise=enabled
```

- Specify the address prefix you wish to advertise. The publish keyword indicates that the prefix should be advertised if advertising has been enabled.

```
Set-NetRoute -InterfaceAlias Ethernet -AddressFamily IPv6
  -DestinationPrefix 2001:db8:1234:1::/64 -Publish Yes
netsh interface ipv6 add route interface=Ethernet
prefix=2001:db8:1234:1::/64 publish=yes
```

Figure 1-11 shows the series of PowerShell cmdlets to configure the M and O flags on an interface named Ethernet 2 and then configure advertising and an address prefix. The M flag is disabled but the O flag is enabled, so IPv6 clients will use DHCPv6 stateless autoconfiguration, meaning they will get the IPv6 prefix from the router advertisement but use DHCPv6 for other configuration options.

```
PS C:\Users\administrator.MCSA2016> Set-NetIPInterface -InterfaceAlias "Ethernet 2" -AddressFamily IPv6
-ManagedAddressConfiguration Disabled -OtherStatefulConfiguration Enabled
PS C:\Users\administrator.MCSA2016> Set-NetIPInterface -InterfaceAlias "Ethernet 2" -AddressFamily IPv6
-Advertising Enabled
PS C:\Users\administrator.MCSA2016> Set-NetRoute -InterfaceAlias "Ethernet 2" -AddressFamily IPv6
-DestinationPrefix 2001:db8:1234:1::/64 -Publish Yes
PS C:\Users\administrator.MCSA2016> _
```

Figure 1-11   PowerShell cmdlets to configure the M and O flags and router advertising

Figure 1-12 shows the output of the `Get-NetIPInterface` cmdlet showing the results of the `Set-NetIPInterface` cmdlets on the server that will send the router advertisements. Relevant parts out of the output are highlighted, and some of the output has been omitted.

Figure 1-13 shows the output of the `ipconfig` command on an IPv6 host that has configured its interface with the advertised prefix.

```
PS C:\Users\administrator.MCSA2016> Get-NetIPInterface -InterfaceAlias "Ethernet 2" -AddressFamily IPv6
| fl


InterfaceIndex                  : 3
InterfaceAlias                  : Ethernet 2
CompartmentId                   : 1
AddressFamily                   : IPv6
Forwarding                      : Disabled
ClampMss                        : Disabled
Advertising                     : Enabled
NlMtu(Bytes)                    : 1500
AutomaticMetric                 : Enabled
RouterDiscovery                 : Enabled
ManagedAddressConfiguration     : Disabled
OtherStatefulConfiguration      : Enabled
WeakHostSend                    : Disabled
WeakHostReceive                 : Disabled
```

Figure 1-12   Results of the `Get-NetIPInterface` cmdlet

```
Ethernet adapter Ethernet 2:

   Connection-specific DNS Suffix  . :
   IPv6 Address. . . . . . . . . . . : 2001:db8:1234:1:fdfa:c7ff:c80d:c957
   Link-local IPv6 Address . . . . . : fe80::fdfa:c7ff:c80d:c957%2
   Autoconfiguration IPv4 Address. . : 169.254.201.87
   Subnet Mask . . . . . . . . . . . : 255.255.0.0
   Default Gateway . . . . . . . . . :
```

Figure 1-13   Results of the `ipconfig` command after receiving the router advertisement

Activity 1-7: Configuring a Server to Advertise an IPv6 Prefix

Time Required: 10 minutes

Objective: Configure a server to advertise an IPv6 prefix.

Required Tools and Equipment: ServerDC1, ServerDM1

Description: In this activity, you set a static IPv6 address on ServerDC1 and then configure the server to advertise its IPv6 address prefix so it can be used by other IPv6 hosts on the network. In this activity, you'll use the second interface on the servers, which should be named Ethernet 2.

1. Sign in to ServerDC1 as **Administrator**, if necessary. Open a PowerShell prompt window.

2. When you configure network interfaces with PowerShell, you can use the interface name or index number. In this activity, you'll use the index number. Type **Get-NetIPInterface** and press **Enter** to list the interfaces and their index numbers. Look for the interface named Ethernet 2 and note the number in the `ifIndex` column, which in the figure is 2 (see Figure 1-14).

```
PS C:\Users\Administrator> Get-NetIPInterface

ifIndex InterfaceAlias                     AddressFamily NlMtu(Bytes) InterfaceMetric Dhcp
------- --------------                     ------------- ------------ --------------- ----
7       isatap.{378B8A0A-6CC6-488B-8...    IPv6                  1280              75 Disabled
2       Ethernet 2                         IPv6                  1500              15 Enabled
16      Teredo Tunneling Pseudo-Inte...    IPv6                  1280              75 Enabled
15      Ethernet                           IPv6                  1500              15 Enabled
8       isatap.{DA6F31E1-5B51-44D3-B...    IPv6                  1280              75 Disabled
1       Loopback Pseudo-Interface 1        IPv6            4294967295              75 Disabled
2       Ethernet 2                         IPv4                  1500              15 Enabled
15      Ethernet                           IPv4                  1500              15 Disabled
1       Loopback Pseudo-Interface 1        IPv4            4294967295              75 Disabled
```

Figure 1-14   Finding the interface index number

3. Type **New-NetIPAddress -InterfaceIndex 2 -IpAddress 2001:db8:10::1 -PrefixLength 64** and press **Enter** (being sure to replace the `InterfaceIndex` number with the number you found in the previous step). You will see information displayed that is similar to what you would see if you used the `Get-NetIPAddress` cmdlet.

4. Next, you'll configure ServerDC1 to advertise the IPv6 address prefix. First, display the current configuration of the interface. Type **Get-NetIPInterface -InterfaceIndex 2 -AddressFamily IPv6 | fl** and press **Enter** (see Figure 1-15; some of the output has been omitted). The `-AddressFamily` parameter displays only IPv6 information and the `| fl` parameter displays detailed information in a list format (`fl` means format-list). Notice that Advertising and the M and O flag parameters are currently disabled. RouterDiscovery is enabled by default.

```
PS C:\Users\Administrator> Get-NetIPInterface -InterfaceIndex 2 -AddressFamily IPv6 | fl

InterfaceIndex                   : 2
InterfaceAlias                   : Ethernet 2
CompartmentId                    : 1
AddressFamily                    : IPv6
Forwarding                       : Disabled
ClampMss                         : Disabled
Advertising                      : Disabled
NlMtu(Bytes)                     : 1500
AutomaticMetric                  : Enabled
InterfaceMetric                  : 15
NeighborDiscoverySupported       : Yes
NeighborUnreachabilityDetection  : Enabled
BaseReachableTime(ms)            : 30000
ReachableTime(ms)                : 37500
RetransmitTime(ms)               : 1000
DadTransmits                     : 1
DadRetransmitTime(ms)            : 1000
RouterDiscovery                  : Enabled
ManagedAddressConfiguration      : Disabled
OtherStatefulConfiguration       : Disabled
```

Figure 1-15 Displaying IPv6 interface information

5. Type **Set-NetIPInterface -InterfaceIndex 2 -AddressFamily IPv6 -Advertising Enabled OtherStatefulConfiguration Enabled** and press **Enter**. This configures ServerDC1 to advertise its prefix and set the O flag to 1. We'll leave the M flag disabled.

6. Now, create a route and publish it so it is included in the advertisement. Type **Set-NetRoute -InterfaceIndex 2 -AddressFamily IPv6 -DestinationPrefix 2001:db8::/64 -Publish Yes** and press **Enter**.

7. Sign in to ServerDM1, if necessary, and open a PowerShell prompt. Type **ipconfig** and press **Enter**. Notice that the Ethernet 2 interface has an IPv6 address with the advertised prefix (see Figure 1-16). Type **Get-NetIPInterface -InterfaceAlias "Ethernet 2" -AddressFamily IPv6 | fl** and press **Enter**. Notice that the OtherStatefulConfiguration (the O flag) parameter is now enabled.

```
Ethernet adapter Ethernet 2:

   Connection-specific DNS Suffix  . :
   IPv6 Address. . . . . . . . . . . : 2001:db8::90b3:4ed7:b601:a3ed
   Link-local IPv6 Address . . . . . : fe80::90b3:4ed7:b601:a3ed%3
   IPv4 Address. . . . . . . . . . . : 192.168.1.2
   Subnet Mask . . . . . . . . . . . : 255.255.255.0
   Default Gateway . . . . . . . . . :
```

Figure 1-16 Results of the `ipconfig` command

8. Type **ping 2001:db8::1** and press **Enter**. You are pinging the IPv6 address of ServerDC1 and it should be successful.

9. Leave both servers running and continue to the next activity.

Activity 1-8: Working with IPv6

Time Required: 15 minutes

Objective: Use `ipconfig` and `ping` with IPv6 and change an IPv6 interface address to use the EUI-64 format.

Required Tools and Equipment: ServerDC1 and ServerDM1

Description: In this activity, you use common tools, such as `ipconfig` and `ping`, to work with IPv6.

1. Sign in to ServerDM1 as **Administrator** and open a PowerShell window, if necessary. Make sure ServerDC1 is running.
2. Type **ipconfig** and press **Enter**. Under both Ethernet interfaces, find the output line starting with "Link-local IPv6 Address." Notice that the assigned address starts with `fe80::`. The `fe80` indicates a link-local IPv6 address, and the `::` indicates a string of 0 values—in this case, a string of three consecutive 0 values. The rest of the address (64 bits) has been randomly assigned by Windows. (Also note that on Ethernet 2, there is a link-local address and the address assigned from the advertised prefix).
3. Type **ping ::1** and press **Enter**. Windows replies because you just pinged the IPv6 loopback address, your own computer. Type **ping -a ::1** and press **Enter**. The `-a` option tells Windows to display the hostname for the `::1` address, which is the name of your ServerDM1 computer.
4. Type **ping -6 ServerDC1** and press **Enter**. The `-6` option tells `ping` to use IPv6 addresses. You should receive a reply from ServerDC1 with an address that uses the 2001:db8:: prefix. (ServerDC1 actually has two addresses with the 2001:db8:: prefix, the one you statically assigned and one that was autoconfigured by Windows).
5. Type **getmac** and press **Enter** to display your computer's MAC addresses. Make a note of them.
6. Type **netsh interface ipv6 set global randomizeidentifiers=disabled** and press **Enter**. Your interface is now using the EUI-64 format to assign the link-local IPv6 address.
7. Type **ipconfig** and press **Enter**. Notice that the last 64 bits of the IPv6 link-local addresses now look like your MAC addresses with the addition of `fffe` after the first 24 bits and `02` instead of the first `00` of your MAC address.
8. Close the command prompt window, and sign out.

Transitioning from IPv4 to IPv6

 **Certification**

- 70-741 – Implement core and distributed network solutions:
  Implement IPv4 and IPv6 addressing

The move from IPv4 to IPv6 isn't happening on a particular date worldwide; rather, the transition is under way and will continue over several years. However, whether it's a small business with just a few Internet-connected computers or a 100,000-computer global enterprise, the switch to IPv6 is inevitable. Thankfully, both protocols can coexist easily on the same computer and the same network, allowing network administrators to ease into the transition instead of having to change from IPv4 to IPv6 instantly.

Starting with Windows Server 2008 and Vista, the Windows OS has maintained a **dual IP layer architecture** by default, meaning that both IPv4 and IPv6 are installed and enabled by default in current Windows OSs as you probably noticed when you examined the network connection properties earlier. So in one sense, Windows is IPv6 ready with no additional configuration required. However, transitioning an entire network from IPv4 to IPv6 successfully while maintaining compatibility with IPv4 requires a variety of transition technologies. Most of these technologies are built into Windows, but some you configure as needed. These technologies and special address types, discussed in the following sections, help ease the transition to IPv6 while maintaining compatibility with IPv4:

- Dual IP layer architecture
- IPv6-over-IPv4 tunneling
- Intra-Site Automatic Tunnel Addressing Protocol (ISATAP)
- 6to4
- Teredo

Dual IP Layer Architecture

A dual IP layer architecture means that both IPv4 and IPv6 are running, and the computer can communicate directly with both IPv4 and IPv6 devices by using the native packet types. A variation of dual IP layer architecture is dual-stack architecture. With dual IP layer architecture, there are two versions of the IP component of the TCP/IP stack and only one version of all the other components (TCP, UDP, and Application-layer protocols). With the dual-stack architecture, there are two versions of the entire TCP/IP protocol suite: one for IPv4 and one for IPv6. Windows XP and Windows Server 2003 use this architecture. The dual IP layer is slightly more efficient, but both architectures achieve the same objective: the capability to communicate with both IPv4 and IPv6 devices. In addition, computers running either architecture can encapsulate IPv6 packets in an IPv4 header, a process called *tunneling*.

IPv6-over-IPv4 Tunneling

Tunneling is a network protocol technique that allows transmitting a packet in a format that's otherwise incompatible with the network architecture by encapsulating the packet in a compatible header format. For example, VPNs use tunneling to send encrypted data across the Internet by encapsulating an encrypted packet in a standard unencrypted IP header (see Figure 1-17).

| IPv4 header | IPv6 headers and extensions | Upper-layer protocol data unit (PDU) |

Figure 1-17   IPv6 packet encapsulated in an IPv4 header

IPv6-over-IPv4 tunneling allows a host to send an IPv6 packet over an IPv4 network to an IPv6 device. How is this feature useful? Suppose your network runs a dual IP layer architecture and you need to access a server across the Internet that's running an IPv6-only application. Unfortunately, your ISP is still using IPv4-only routers. The only way to get IPv6 packets to the IPv6 application is to encapsulate them in IPv4 headers, allowing them to traverse the Internet as IPv4 packets. At the destination network, the packets are de-encapsulated and delivered to the server as IPv6 packets. Figure 1-18 illustrates this process.

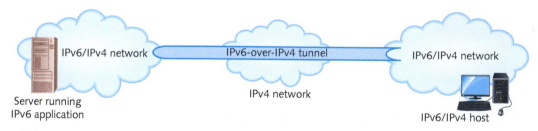

Figure 1-18   IPv6-over-IPv4 tunneling

Some details are left out of Figure 1-18 because a variety of methods are used to create tunnels. A common method is creating the tunnel from router to router so that the IPv6 packet is encapsulated when it gets to a router in the source network and de-encapsulated at the router connected to the destination network. Tunnels can also be created between two hosts and between a host and a router.

Manually Creating an IPv6-over-IPv4 Tunnel

An IPv6-over-IPv4 tunnel can be created in Windows Server 2016 when it's configured as a router by using the following command:

```
netsh interface ipv6 add v6v4tunnel tunnelToNet1 192.168.2.250 192.168.1.250
```

Figure 1-19 shows a network in which Windows Server 2016 is used as a router on both sides of the tunnel. In the preceding command, the parameter *tunnelToNet1* represents the name of the tunnel interface you're creating. The two IPv4 addresses are the addresses on the servers connected to the Internet. The first IP address is the address of the local server, and the second address is the address of the remote server interface that's connected to the Internet. This command runs on the server in the `2001:db8:2::/64` network. You repeat the command on the server on both sides of the tunnel, interchanging the IP addresses and changing the tunnel name, if you like.

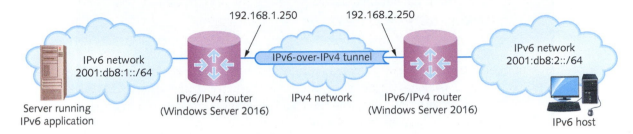

Figure 1-19   A router-to-router IPv6-over-IPv4 tunnel

Next, you need to create a route to the remote IPv6 network, specifying the tunnel as the interface to use to reach the IPv6 network:

```
netsh interface ipv6 add route 2001:db8:1::/64 tunnelToNet1
```

This command runs on the server in the `2001:db8:2::/64` network. You use the same command on the other server but change the destination IPv6 network and tunnel name, if necessary.

Intra-Site Automatic Tunnel Addressing Protocol

Intra-Site Automatic Tunnel Addressing Protocol (ISATAP) is used to transmit IPv6 packets between dual IP layer hosts across an IPv4 network. This automatic tunneling protocol doesn't require manual configuration as IPv6-over-IPv4 tunneling does. ISATAP is enabled by default on Windows Server 2016 as well as earlier versions of Windows through Windows Vista. ISATAP-enabled hosts can communicate over an IPv4 network, or to an IPv6 host through an ISATAP router. ISATAP addresses are composed of a prefix and the IPv4 address of the interface.

The prefix varies depending on whether the IPV4 address is a public or private address. For public IPv4 addresses, the prefix of an ISATAP link-local address is fe80::200:5efe and for private IPv4 addresses, fe80::0:5efe. For example, given the IPv4 address 192.168.0.1, the ISATAP link-local address would be:

```
fe80::5efe:192.168.0.1
```

For the IPV4 address 198.60.123.101 (a public IPv4 address), the ISATAP address would be:

```
fe80::200:5efe:198.60.123.101
```

Even though ISATAP is enabled by default in Windows Server 2016, the media state is disconnected, effectively disabling the interface. You can enable ISATAP interfaces using one of three methods:

- Create a DNS host record in the computer's DNS zone with the host name `isatap` mapped to the address of the ISATAP router. By adding a DNS record, ISATAP is enabled for all computers in the domain. Alternatively, add an entry to the computer's hosts file, which enables ISATAP on only that computer. For example, if the computer is a member of the mcsa2016.local domain and the ISATAP router's address is 192.168.0.250, create a hosts file entry that looks like the following:

```
192.168.0.250 isatap.mcsa2016.local
```

- Use the PowerShell cmdlet `Set-NetIsatapConfiguration -Router` *IPv4Address* where *IPv4Address* is the IPv4 address of the ISATAP router. An example is `Set-NetIsatapConfiguration -Router 192.168.0.250`. This method enables ISATAP on only the local computer.
- Use the `netsh` command. An example is `netsh interface IPv6 ISATAP set router 192.168.0.250`. Again, this method enables ISATAP only on the local computer.
- Use Group Policy. Configure the `Set ISATAP Router Name` policy with the name or address of the ISATAP router. This method enables ISATAP for all computer accounts in the scope of the policy.

After ISATAP is enabled using one of the above methods, the ISATAP interface name can be resolved, and the address is assigned as shown in Figure 1-20.

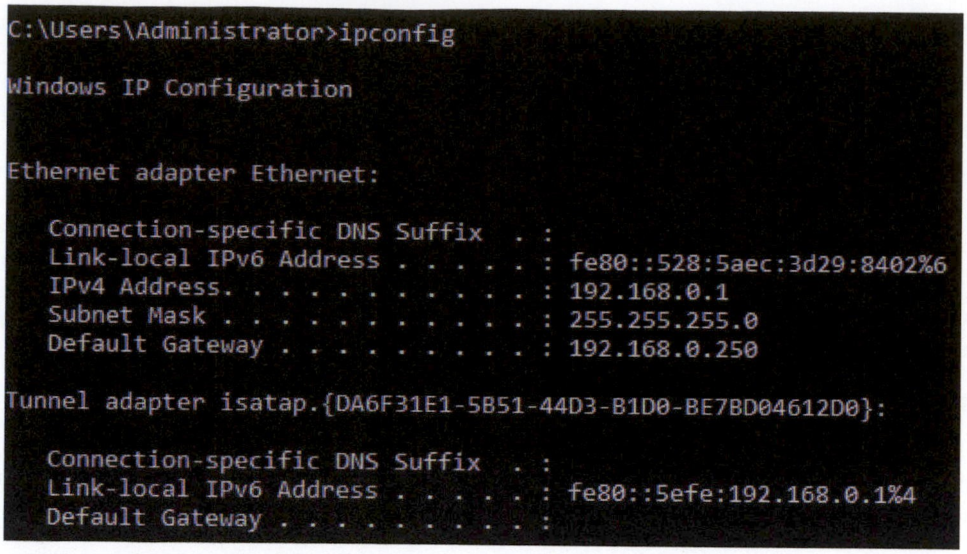

```
C:\Users\Administrator>ipconfig

Windows IP Configuration


Ethernet adapter Ethernet:

   Connection-specific DNS Suffix  . :
   Link-local IPv6 Address . . . . . : fe80::528:5aec:3d29:8402%6
   IPv4 Address. . . . . . . . . . . : 192.168.0.1
   Subnet Mask . . . . . . . . . . . : 255.255.255.0
   Default Gateway . . . . . . . . . : 192.168.0.250

Tunnel adapter isatap.{DA6F31E1-5B51-44D3-B1D0-BE7BD04612D0}:

   Connection-specific DNS Suffix  . :
   Link-local IPv6 Address . . . . . : fe80::5efe:192.168.0.1%4
   Default Gateway . . . . . . . . . :
```

Figure 1-20   The ISATAP interface

You can test an ISATAP interface by using `ping`. Suppose you have two computers with the IPv4 addresses 192.168.0.2 and 192.168.02 configured. Their ISATAP addresses are `fe80::5efe:192.168.0.1` and `fe80::5efe:192.168.0.2`. You must include the interface index of the source computer's ISATAP address in the `ping` command so that it knows the ISATAP address should be used as the source address. For example, to `ping` from fe80::5efe:192.168.0.1%4, use the following command:

```
ping fe80::5efe:192.168.0.2%4
```

You use the interface index of the source computer—the one you're sending the `ping` from, not the destination computer's. Figure 1-21 shows the results of this command.

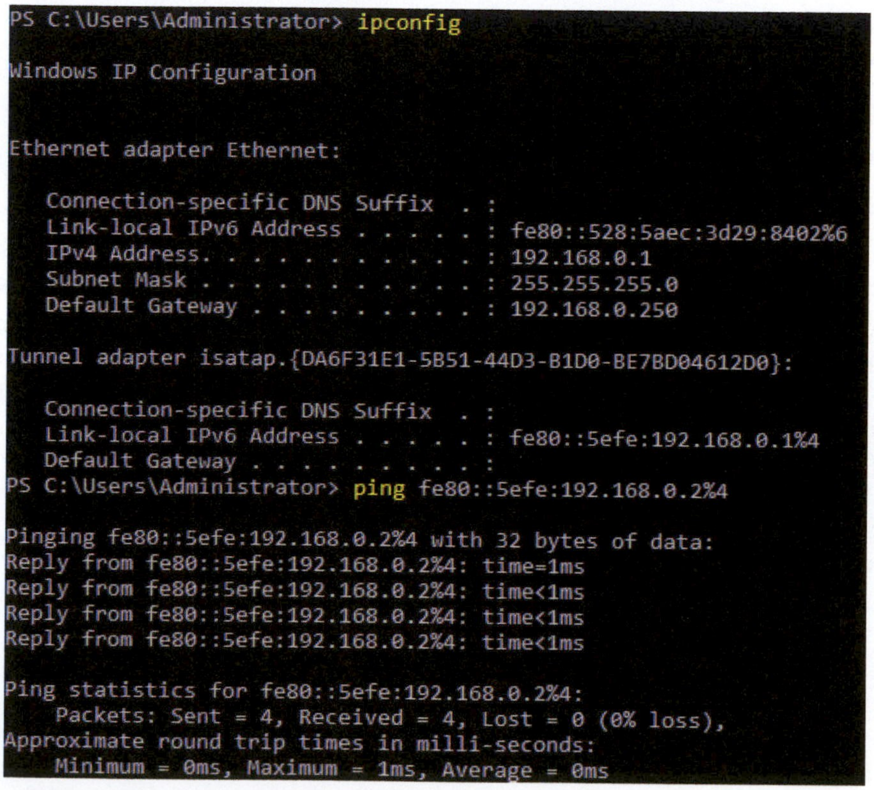

```
PS C:\Users\Administrator> ipconfig

Windows IP Configuration


Ethernet adapter Ethernet:

   Connection-specific DNS Suffix  . :
   Link-local IPv6 Address . . . . . : fe80::528:5aec:3d29:8402%6
   IPv4 Address. . . . . . . . . . . : 192.168.0.1
   Subnet Mask . . . . . . . . . . . : 255.255.255.0
   Default Gateway . . . . . . . . . : 192.168.0.250

Tunnel adapter isatap.{DA6F31E1-5B51-44D3-B1D0-BE7BD04612D0}:

   Connection-specific DNS Suffix  . :
   Link-local IPv6 Address . . . . . : fe80::5efe:192.168.0.1%4
   Default Gateway . . . . . . . . . :
PS C:\Users\Administrator> ping fe80::5efe:192.168.0.2%4

Pinging fe80::5efe:192.168.0.2%4 with 32 bytes of data:
Reply from fe80::5efe:192.168.0.2%4: time=1ms
Reply from fe80::5efe:192.168.0.2%4: time<1ms
Reply from fe80::5efe:192.168.0.2%4: time<1ms
Reply from fe80::5efe:192.168.0.2%4: time<1ms

Ping statistics for fe80::5efe:192.168.0.2%4:
    Packets: Sent = 4, Received = 4, Lost = 0 (0% loss),
Approximate round trip times in milli-seconds:
    Minimum = 0ms, Maximum = 1ms, Average = 0ms
```

Figure 1-21   Using `ping` to test ISATAP interfaces

Even though the ISATAP address begins with `fe80`, making it a link-local address, the packets get tunneled inside an IPv4 header, making the packets capable of traversing an IPv4-only routed network. Although ISATAP is an effective tunneling interface to carry IPv6 traffic across IPv4 networks, Microsoft recommends using it for testing while transitioning to a native IPv6 environment for a production network.

6to4 Tunneling

6to4 provides automatic tunneling of IPv6 traffic over an IPv4 network. It can provide host-to-router or router-to-host tunneling but is most often used to create a router-to-router tunnel. The key to 6to4 tunneling is the `2002::/16` prefix. Routers configured to perform 6to4 tunneling recognize the `2002` prefix as a 6to4 address, just as `fe80::5efe` is recognized as an ISATAP address. When an IPv6 packet with addresses using the `2002` prefix arrives at a 6to4 configured router, the router knows to encapsulate the packet in an IPv4 header. A 6to4 address has the following format:

`2002:xxxx:xxxx::/48`

The first 16 bits are always `2002`, and the next 32 bits, represented by the x characters, are the hexadecimal representation of the 32-bit IPv4 address. The remaining bits are the subnet ID and 64-bit interface ID. The IPv4 address embedded in the 6to4 address must be a public address, which limits the use of this tunneling technology because it can't traverse a router interface that uses NAT.

Teredo Tunneling

Teredo is an automatic IPv6-over-IPv4 tunneling protocol that solves the problem of 6to4's requirement of a public IPv4 address and the inability to traverse NAT routers. Teredo allows the tunnel endpoints to exist behind a NAT firewall by tunneling IPv6 packets between hosts instead of requiring a router as an endpoint.

Teredo achieves NAT traversal by encapsulating IPv6 packets in IPv4 UDP messages, which can traverse most NAT routers. It has the added benefit of allowing IPv4 applications to communicate through a NAT router that otherwise might not be able to. Teredo has three components:

- *Teredo client*—A **Teredo client** is a host device behind a NAT router that's running IPv4 and IPv6 and wants to use Teredo tunneling to access IPv6 devices or other Teredo clients across an IPv4 network. Windows versions starting with Windows 7 include the Teredo client.
- *Teredo server*—A **Teredo server** is a host on the Internet running IPv4 and IPv6 that's connected to both IPv4 and IPv6 networks. A Teredo server facilitates communication between Teredo clients. Teredo servers are most useful for an ISP that wants to provide Teredo services for its customers. Windows versions starting with Windows 7 include the Teredo server.
- *Teredo relay*—A **Teredo relay** is a router running IPv6 and IPv4 that forwards packets between Teredo clients and hosts on IPv6 networks. A Teredo relay advertises the `2001::/32` network (discussed next) to let hosts know that it provides Teredo relay services. Teredo relays are most useful for IPv6 content providers so that IPv4/IPv6 hosts can access their services across the IPv4 Internet.

A Teredo address can be identified by the Teredo prefix `2001::/32` and has the following format:

`2001:tttt:tttt:gggg:pppp:xxxx:xxxx`

The first 16 bits are always the Teredo prefix `2001`. The next 32 bits, represented by t characters, are the Teredo server's IPv4 public address. The next 16 bits, shown as g characters, are Teredo flags that specify processing options. The p characters represent an obscured UDP port the client uses for Teredo traffic. The port is obscured to prevent certain types of NATs from attempting to translate the port. The last 32 bits are the obscured IPv4 address the client uses for Teredo traffic.

Tip ⓘ

For more information on IPv6 transition technologies, see *http://technet.microsoft.com/en-us/library/ dd379548(v=ws.10).aspx*.

Chapter Summary

- TCP/IP is a network protocol designed to deliver data packets to computers on any scale of network, from a small two-computer LAN to the worldwide Internet. TCP/IP is a suite of protocols, meaning it's composed of several protocols performing different functions but working together.

- Both Internet Protocol Version 4 (TCP/IPv4) and Internet Protocol Version 6 (TCP/IPv6) are installed on Windows Server 2016. IP provides logical addressing, efficient packet delivery, and the information needed for packet routing.

- An IPv4 address is a 32-bit dotted decimal number broken into four octets. Every IP address must have a subnet mask to indicate which part of the IP address is the network ID and which part is the host ID. There are three IP address classes—A, B, and C—each with a default subnet mask.

- CIDR notation uses the format A.B.C.D/n; n is the number of 1 bits in the subnet mask.

- Subnetting uses a modified subnet mask to divide a large network into two or more smaller, more manageable networks. It's used to reduce the adverse effect of the many broadcast messages found in a large broadcast domain (another name for an IP network) and to conserve IP addresses by assigning to a company only the number of public IP addresses it requires.

- Supernetting reallocates bits from the network portion of an IP address to the host portion,

effectively combining two or more smaller subnets into a larger supernet.

- When you assign a computer an IP address, there are some rules to remember: Every IP address configuration must have a subnet mask, all hosts on the same network must share the same network ID in their IP addresses, and all host IDs on the same network must be unique.

- Several command-line tools are available for checking the status of and troubleshooting IP configuration, including `ping`, `ipconfig`, `arp`, `tracert`, and `nslookup`.

- IPv6 uses a 128-bit address expressed by eight 16-bit hexadecimal numbers separated by a colon. Some new features of this new IP version are a larger address space, a hierarchical address space, autoconfiguration, built-in QoS, and built-in security.

- IPv6 defines unicast, multicast, and anycast addresses. IPv6 autoconfiguration occurs by two methods: stateless and stateful. With current Windows versions, both methods can be used together.

- Several transition technologies and special address types are available to help ease the transition to IPv6 yet maintain compatibility with IPv4: dual IP layer architecture, IPv6-over-IPv4 tunneling, Intra-Site Automatic Tunnel Addressing Protocol, 6to4, and Teredo.

Key Terms

6to4
Automatic Private IP Addressing (APIPA)
broadcast
broadcast domain
CIDR notation
classful addressing
Classless Interdomain Routing (CIDR)
default gateway
destination IP address
dual IP layer architecture
Extended Unique Identifier (EUI)-64 interface ID
frame

Intra-Site Automatic Tunnel Addressing Protocol (ISATAP)
link-local
link-local IPv6 addresses
localhost
logical AND operation
loopback address
MAC address
metric
multicasting
Network Address Translation (NAT)
octet
packet
segment

source IP address
subnet mask
subnetting
supernetting
Teredo
Teredo client
Teredo relay
Teredo server
Transmission Control Protocol/ Internet Protocol (TCP/IP)
tunneling
unicast address
Unique local IPv6 addresses
zone id

Review Questions

1. Which of the following is needed if a computer with the IP address 172.31.210.10/24 wants to communicate with a computer with the IP address 172.31.209.122/24?
   a. Hub
   b. Router
   c. Switch
   d. Server

2. You have just typed the commands `ipconfig /flushdns` and `ping server1`. Which of the following protocols is used first as a result of these commands?
   a. TCP
   b. DNS
   c. ICMP
   d. DHCP

3. Which command should you use with a dual-homed server to make sure the server sends packets out to the correct interface?
   a. `ipconfig`
   b. `ping`
   c. `tracert`
   d. `route`

4. Which command should you use to determine whether there's a bottleneck between your computer and a computer on another network?
   a. `ipconfig`
   b. `ping`
   c. `tracert`
   d. `route`

5. Which command should you use to configure the primary DNS server on your computer?
   a. `ipconfig`
   b. `netsh`
   c. `nslookup`
   d. `arp`

6. Which IP address expressed in CIDR notation has the subnet mask 255.255.255.0?
   a. 10.100.44.123/24
   b. 172.16.88.222/16
   c. 192.168.100.1/26
   d. 172.29.111.201/18

7. Which IP network address expressed in CIDR notation can support a maximum of 1022 hosts?
   a. 10.100.44.0/24
   b. 172.16.4.0/22
   c. 192.168.100.64/26
   d. 172.29.128.0/18

8. You have just finished a default installation of Windows Server 2016. You know that TCP/IP is installed. How does your new server receive an assigned an IP address?
   a. TCP
   b. DNS
   c. ARP
   d. DHCP

9. Your DNS server is on the same network as the computer where you enter the following commands:
   ```
   arp -d
   ipconfig /flushdns
   nslookup server1
   ```
   Which of the following protocols is used first as a result of these commands?
   a. TCP
   b. DNS
   c. ARP
   d. DHCP

10. Which of the following IP addresses will be delivered to all the computers on the local network?
    a. 10.255.150.255/8
    b. 10.1.254.255/16
    c. 10.1.240.255/24
    d. 175.16.1.1/16

11. Which of the following is a good reason to subnet an IPv4 network? (Choose all that apply.)
    a. Eliminate the need for ARP requests.
    b. Decrease the size of the broadcast domain.
    c. Allow broadcasts to reach more computers.
    d. Conserve IP addresses.

12. Which of the following IP addresses has 12 bits in the host ID?
    a. 172.31.21.12/16
    b. 172.31.89.100/12
    c. 12.49.127.88/8
    d. 12.156.109.252/20

13. You have set up an email server that needs to respond to email requests by using *mail.coolgadgets.com* and *mail.niftytools.com* in the request URL. How can you do this?
    a. Install two NICs, and assign the same IP address to both NICs. Configure DNS to map one MAC address to *mail.coolgadgets.com* and the other MAC address to *mail.niftytools.com*.
    b. Configure two IP addresses on one NIC. Configure DNS to map one IP address to *mail.coolgadgets.com* and the other IP address to *mail.niftytools.com*.
    c. Install two NICs, and connect each one to a different network. Set up the router on each network to forward mail packets to the NIC bound to the correct URL.
    d. Install two NICs, and assign different IP addresses to each NIC, but make sure that both IP addresses use the same network ID. Configure the NICs to use default gateways on different networks.

14. You have a server with two NICs, each attached to a different IP network. You're having problems communicating with devices on remote networks that send packets to one of the interfaces. The server receives the packets fine, but the server's replies never reach the intended destination network. Replies to packets that come in through the other interface seem to reach their destination without any problems. What can you do that will most likely solve the problem?

    a. Configure a second default gateway on the interface exhibiting problems.

    b. Change the default gateway to use the router that's on the network of the interface exhibiting problems.

    c. Use the `route` command to add routes to the networks that aren't receiving replies.

    d. Replace the NIC that's having problems replying to packets.

15. You have just changed the IP address on a computer named computer5 in your domain from 172.31.1.10/24 to 172.31.1.110/24. You were communicating with this computer from your workstation with no problems right before you changed the address. Now when you try the command `ping computer5` from your workstation, you don't get a successful reply. Other computers on the network aren't having a problem communicating with the computer. Which command might help solve the problem?

    a. `arp -d`

    b. `ipconfig /flushdns`

    c. `tracert computer5`

    d. `ping -6 172.31.1.110`

16. Which command can cause an address of 0.0.0.0 to be assigned to a host?

    a. `nslookup 0.0.0.0`

    b. `netsh set IPv4 address=Null`

    c. `Set-NetIPInterface -InterfaceAlias Ethernet -DHCP enabled`

    d. `ipconfig /release`

17. Which IP address can 't be assigned to a host computer?

    a. 10.100.44.16/24   c. 192.168.100.66/26

    b. 172.16.7.255/22   d. 172.29.132.0/18

18. Which of the following is a benefit of using IPv6 rather than IPv4? (Choose all that apply.)

    a. You can assign four times the number of addresses in IPv6.

    b. Subnetting to conserve IP addresses is less of a concern.

    c. Features to improve communication security and quality are built into IPv6.

    d. IPv6 addresses are expressed as 16 8-bit numbers separated by colons, which are easier to read than dotted decimal notation.

19. Which of the following is a valid IPv6 address? (Choose all that apply.)

    a. `fe80:0:0:FEED::1`

    b. `2001:DB8:00AB:11:3344`

    c. `fe80:DB8::EE::8901`

    d. `2001:DB8:BAD:F00D:0020:3344:0:e4`

20. Which IPv6 transition technology can be used with NAT routers and has the address prefix `2001::/32`?

    a. Teredo   c. 6to4

    b. ISATAP   d. IPv6-over-IPv4

21. Which IPv6 transition technology requires the `netsh` command to manually create the tunnel to carry IPv6 traffic over the IPv4 Internet?

    a. Teredo   c. IPv6-over-IPv4

    b. ISATAP   d. 6to4

22. Which of the following IPv6 transition technologies is enabled by default in Windows Server 2016 and embeds an IPv4 address in a link-local IPv6 address?

    a. Teredo   c. IPv6-over-IPv4

    b. ISATAP   d. 6to4

23. How many bits are in the interface ID of an IPv6 address?

    a. 32   c. 16

    b. 64   d. 48

24. What type of IPv6 address should you use when you have multiple routers on a subnet and want hosts to use the nearest router for packets that should be delivered to remote networks?

    a. Multicast   c. Anycast

    b. Broadcast   d. Unicast

25. What address should you ping if you want to test local IPv6 operation but don't want to actually send any packets on the network?

    a. `1::f`   c. `fe80::ffff`

    b. `2001::db8`   d. `::1`

26. Which of the following IPv6 autoconfiguration methods utilizes an autoconfiguration protocol, such as DHCPv6, to acquire an IPv6 address?

    a. Static IPv6 configuration

    b. Stateful autoconfiguration

    c. Prefixed IPv6 autoconfiguration

    d. Stateless autoconfiguration

Critical Thinking

The following activities give you critical thinking challenges. Case Projects offer a scenario with a problem to solve for which you supply a written solution.

Case Project 1-1: Creating a List of MAC Addresses

You have been asked to create a list of all MAC addresses and corresponding IP addresses and computer names in your network. Propose at least two methods for performing this task. Your network has almost 100 computers in a Windows Server 2016 domain network with statically assigned IP addresses. Using the tools available in Windows Server 2016, carry out the procedure you think will work best. Write a short report of your results and submit it to your instructor.

Case Project 1-2: Calculating a Subnet Mask

You're the network administrator for a growing ISP. One of the networks the IANA assigned to you is 198.60.123.0/24. You have decided to use this address to satisfy the requirements of 16 corporate customers, each needing between 10 and 14 public addresses. Without using a subnet calculator, calculate a subnet mask that meets the requirements. In the following chart, write the subnet mask along with the 16 subnetworks in CIDR notation, and list the range of host addresses each subnetwork will have available:

Subnet mask:	
Subnetwork	Range of host addresses

Case Project 1-3: Using IPv6 Subnetting

You're the head network administrator for a large manufacturing enterprise that's completing its support for IPv6. The company has six major locations with several thousand users in each location. You have network administrators in each location. You're using a base IPv6 address of `2001:DB8:FAB/48` and want network administrators to be able to subnet their networks however they see fit. You want to maintain a reserve of address spaces for a possible 6 to 10 additional locations in the future. Each network administrator should be able to construct at least 200 subnets from the address you supply, and each location should have the same amount of available address space. What IPv6 addresses should you assign to each location? When constructing your answer, list each location as Location 1, Location 2, and so forth.

CHAPTER 2

CONFIGURING DNS SERVERS

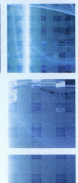

After reading this chapter and completing the exercises, you will be able to:

Describe the structure of Domain Name System (DNS)

Install DNS

Configure DNS

Create DNS resource records

Configure DNS zones

Configure DNS server settings

Monitor and troubleshoot DNS

To function correctly, most applications and services that use TCP/IP depend on a service to resolve computer names to addresses and to find computers that offer specific services. In fact, most network systems today would be almost unusable without a name-to-address translation system; without one, users and computers would need to know the address of each computer they communicate with. Because the TCP/IP suite is the default protocol for Windows, Domain Name System (DNS) is the default name resolution protocol for Windows computers. For Windows domain networks, DNS is required for operation because Active Directory depends on it. This chapter describes the structure of the worldwide DNS system and explains how to configure and maintain DNS in a Windows domain environment.

Introduction to Domain Name System

Table 2-1 describes what you need for the hands-on activities in this chapter.

Table 2-1	Activity requirements		
Activity	**Requirements**	**Notes**	
Activity 2-1: Resetting Your Virtual Environment	ServerDC1, ServerSA1		
Activity 2-2: Exploring DNS with DNS Manager	ServerDC1		
Activity 2-3: Installing DNS and Creating a New Zone	ServerSA1		
Activity 2-4: Working with Reverse Lookup Zones	ServerSA1		
Activity 2-5: Creating Static DNS Entries	ServerSA1		
Activity 2-6: Creating a Secondary Zone and Configuring Zone Transfers	ServerDC1, ServerSA1		
Activity 2-7: Configuring and Testing Forwarders	ServerDC1, ServerSA1		
Activity 2-8: Working with Root Hints	ServerDC1, ServerSA1	Internet connection required	

Domain Name System (DNS) is a distributed hierarchical database composed mainly of computer name and IP address pairs. A distributed database means no single database contains all data; instead, data is spread out among many different servers. In the worldwide DNS system, data is distributed among thousands of servers throughout the world. A hierarchical database, in this case, means there's a structure to how information is stored and accessed in the database. In other words, unless you're resolving a local domain name for which you have a local server, DNS lookups often require a series of queries to a hierarchy of DNS servers before the name can be resolved.

The Structure of DNS

To better understand the DNS lookup process, reviewing the structure of a computer name on the Internet or in a Windows domain is helpful. Computer names are typically expressed as *host.domain.top-level-domain*; the *top-level-domain* can be com, net, org, us, edu, and so forth. This naming structure is called the **fully qualified domain name (FQDN)**. The DNS naming hierarchy can be described as an inverted tree with the root at the top (named simply "dot," which is represented with a period "."), top-level domains branching out from the root, and domains and subdomains branching off the top-level domains (see Figure 2-1).

The entire DNS tree is called the **DNS namespace**. When a domain name is registered, the domain is added to the DNS hierarchy and becomes part of the worldwide DNS namespace. Every domain has one or more servers that are authoritative for the domain, meaning that the servers contain a master copy of all DNS records for that domain. A single server can be authoritative for multiple domains.

Each shape in Figure 2-1 has one or more DNS servers managing the names associated with it. For example, the root of the tree has 13 DNS servers called **root servers** scattered about the world that keep a database of addresses of other DNS servers managing top-level domain names. These other servers, aptly named, are called **top-level domain (TLD) servers**. Each top-level domain has servers that maintain addresses of other DNS servers. For example, the .com TLD servers maintain a database containing addresses of DNS servers for each domain name ending with .com, such as *tomsho.com* and *cengage.com*. Each second-level DNS server can contain hostnames, such as www, mail, or server1. **Hostnames** are associated

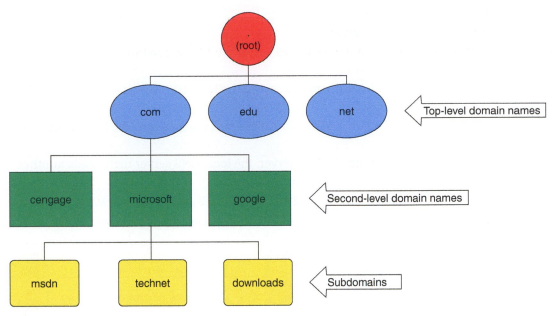

Figure 2-1   A partial view of the DNS naming hierarchy

with an IP address, so when a client looks up the name *www.microsoft.com*, the DNS server returns an IP address. Second-level domains can also have subdomains, such as the technet in *technet.microsoft.com*.

The DNS Database

DNS servers maintain a database of information that contains zones. A **zone** is a grouping of DNS information that belongs to a contiguous portion of the DNS namespace, usually a domain and possibly one or more subdomains. Each zone contains a variety of record types called **resource records** containing information about network resources, such as hostnames, other DNS servers, domain controllers, and so forth. Resource records are identified by letter codes. DNS resource records are discussed in more detail later in the section "Creating DNS Resource Records."

The DNS Lookup Process

When a computer needs to acquire information from a DNS server, such as looking up the IP address for host *www.tomsho.com*, it sends a lookup or query to the server. A computer making a DNS query is called a **DNS client** or **DNS resolver**. Two types of DNS queries can be made:

- *Iterative query*—When a DNS server gets an **iterative query**, it responds with the best information it currently has in its local database to satisfy the query, such as the IP address of an A record it retrieves from a local zone file or cache. If the DNS server doesn't have the specific information, it might respond with the IP address of a name server that *can* satisfy the query; this type of response is called a **referral** because the server is referring the DNS client to another server. If the server has no information, it sends a negative response that essentially says "I can't help you." DNS servers usually query each other by using iterative queries.
- *Recursive query*—A **recursive query** instructs the DNS server to process the query until it responds with an address that satisfies the query or with an "I don't know" message. A recursive query might require a DNS server to contact several other DNS servers before it finally sends a response to the client. Most queries made by DNS clients are recursive queries, and DNS servers also use recursive queries when using a forwarder (discussed later in this chapter in the section "DNS Server Roles.")

A typical DNS lookup made by a DNS client can involve both recursive and iterative queries. A sample query demonstrating the hierarchical nature of DNS (see Figure 2-2) is outlined in the following steps:

1. A user types *www.microsoft.com* in the web browser's address bar. The computer running the web browser is the DNS client, which sends a recursive query to the DNS server. Typically, this DNS server, called the *local DNS server*, is maintained on the local network or at the client's ISP.

2. The local DNS server checks its local zone data and cache. If the name isn't found locally, it sends an iterative query to a DNS root server.

3. The root server sends a referral to the local DNS server with a list of addresses for the TLD servers handling the .com top-level domain.

4. Using the referral information from the rooter server, the local DNS server sends another iterative query to a .com TLD server.

5. The .com TLD server responds with a referral to DNS servers responsible for the microsoft.com domain.

6. Using the referral information from the TLD server, the local DNS server then sends another iterative query to a microsoft.com DNS server.

7. The microsoft.com DNS server replies with the host record IP address for *www.microsoft.com*.

8. The local DNS server responds to the client with the IP address for *www.microsoft.com*.

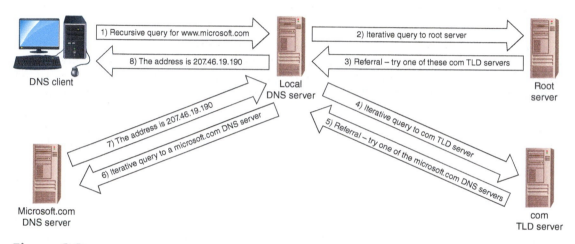

Figure 2-2   A DNS hierarchical lookup

Thankfully, the process shown in Figure 2-2 doesn't occur with every DNS lookup. Computers cache information they get from DNS and use the information in cache when possible instead of sending another query to a DNS server. Furthermore, the local DNS server also caches information from other DNS servers received as a result of recent lookups. So the entire eight-step process occurs only when neither the computer doing the lookup nor the local DNS server has a cached copy of the requested name resolution.

To add another wrinkle to the DNS lookup process, DNS clients maintain a text file called *Hosts* that can contain static DNS entries. On Windows, this file is stored in %*systemroot*%\System32\drivers\etc. By default, it contains only sample entries. In versions of Windows before Windows Server 2008 R2 and Windows 7, the Hosts file contained records for resolving the local loopback address for both IPv4 and IPv6. These records are now commented out with an explanation that the DNS service handles localhost name resolution. The file's format is simply IP address and hostname separated by one or more spaces. A typical Hosts file entry looks like this:

```
127.0.0.1 localhost

::1 localhost
```

Note

You see these two entries in the Hosts file in Windows Server 2016, but they have the # character in front of them, indicating that they're comments, which means they're ignored by the DNS client.

The entries in the Hosts file are cached at system startup and each time the file is changed. You can add as many entries as you like to this file. Usually, however, it's left as it is because in a dynamic network, static DNS entries are likely to cause more harm than good. Some people use the Hosts file as a sort of web filter. For example, you can add entries to this file for hosts on domains that create pop-up ads and fill your webpages with advertisements. For each entry, simply use the address 127.0.0.1. Unless your computer is also a web server, your browser won't get a response from this address, and the website supplying the ad will be blocked. You can even download a Hosts file that's already loaded with hundreds of entries for well-known web advertisers.

DNS Server Roles

DNS servers can perform one or more of the following roles for a zone:

- *Authoritative server*—An **authoritative server** for a domain holds a complete copy of a zone's resource records.
- *Forwarder*—A **forwarder** is a DNS server to which other DNS servers send requests they can't resolve themselves. It's commonly used when a DNS server on an internal private network receives a query for a domain on the public Internet. The internal DNS server forwards the request recursively to a DNS server connected to the public Internet. This method prevents the internal DNS server from having to contact root servers and TLD servers directly because the forwarder does that on its behalf.
- *Conditional forwarder*—A **conditional forwarder** is a DNS server to which other DNS servers send requests targeted for a specific domain. For example, computers in the csmtech.local domain might send a DNS query for a computer named server1.csmpub.local. The DNS server in the csmtech.local domain can be configured with a conditional forwarder that in effect says, "If you receive a query for csmpub.local, forward it to the DNS server handling the csmpub.local domain." Servers that are forwarders or conditional forwarders require no special configuration, but the servers using them as forwarders must be configured to do so.
- *Caching-only server*—A **caching-only DNS server** isn't configured with any zones. Its sole job is to field DNS queries, send iterative queries to upstream DNS servers, or send requests to forwarders and then cache the results. After the query results are cached, the caching server can respond to a similar query directly without having to contact other DNS servers. Caching servers are ideal for branch offices so that local computers' queries are forwarded to an authoritative server at a main office.

Activity 2-2: Exploring DNS with DNS Manager

Time Required: 15 minutes
Objective: Explore DNS with DNS Manager.
Required Tools and Equipment: ServerDC1
Description: In this activity, you familiarize yourself with the DNS Manager console on a domain controller.

1. Sign in to ServerDC1 as **Administrator**.
2. Open Server Manager, and click **Tools**, **DNS** to open the DNS Manager console.
3. Click **ServerDC1** in the left pane and double-click to expand **Forward Lookup Zones** in the right pane. Then click **Forward Lookup Zones**. You see a window similar to Figure 2-3

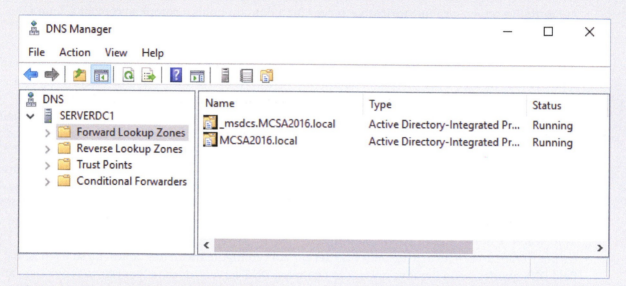

Figure 2-3   The DNS Manager console

4. In the right pane, double-click **MCSA2016.local** to see folders and resource records. Scroll to the right, if necessary, to see the Timestamp column. Records that were created dynamically have a time stamp; records created by an administrator or generated by the system are shown as static.
5. The first few entries show *(same as parent folder)* in the Name column, which means they take on the domain's name. If DNS gets a host record query for MCSA2016.local without a hostname, it returns the IP addresses shown for the *(same as parent folder)* Host (A) record entry. Double-click the **Start of Authority (SOA)** record. In the MCSA2016.local Properties dialog box, review the information available in all the tabs. (The SOA record is discussed in more detail later in the section "Start of Authority Records.") Click **Cancel**.
6. Double-click the **serverdc1** A record entry. Figure 2-4 shows the Properties dialog box for an A record. You can't change the Host or FQDN fields of an A record, but you can change the IP address. If you make a change, you can click the *Update associated pointer (PTR) record* check box to have the PTR record reflect the address change.
7. Click the **Security** tab. DNS records stored in Active Directory have the same type of permission settings as other Windows objects, including permission inheritance and special permissions. You can assign permissions to users to allow them to manage DNS records, if necessary. Click **Cancel**.
8. Click **View**, **Advanced** from the DNS Manager menu. The Advanced view shows additional information in DNS Manager, such as the folder Cached Lookups. Click to expand **Cached Lookups** and then the **.(root)** folder, which has subfolders named for TLDs (com, local, net, and so on). Click to expand the **com** folder. Domains you have visited with any computer using this DNS server for DNS lookups have a folder containing A, NS, and other resource records. Cached entries save time and bandwidth because the local DNS server can respond to queries for records it has in its cache.
9. Browse through the folders until you find an A or a CNAME record. (If you can't find one, start your web browser and go to *www.microsoft.com* to create a record in the microsoft folder. Close your browser and refresh DNS Manager.) Double-click the **A** or **CNAME** record. In the Properties dialog box, you see a time to

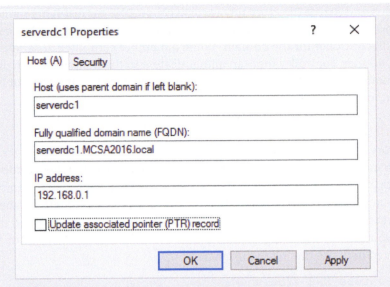

Figure 2-4   The Properties dialog box for an A record

live (TTL) value, which tells DNS how long to keep the cached entry. The referring DNS server (an authoritative DNS server for the domain the record came from) sends the TTL value, which prevents a DNS server from caching out-of-date information. Click **Cancel**.

10. Click the **com** folder. You should see several NS entries with names in the Data column, such as a.gtld-servers.net, b.gtld-servers.net, and so on, referred to as *generic top-level domain (GTLD) servers*. These servers are responsible for .com domains throughout the Internet. Double-click **a.gtld-servers.net**. Notice that no IP address is associated with the entry. When your DNS server needs to find the address of a .com name server, it must query to find a TLD server's address first. Click **Cancel**.

11. Right-click **Cached Lookups** and click **Clear Cache** to delete the cache. There are no entries in the cache now except for some folders and an entry for localhost. Clear the local DNS cache by opening a command prompt window, typing **ipconfig /flushdns**, and pressing **Enter**. Close the command prompt window.

12. Start your web browser, go to any .com domain, and then exit your web browser. Refresh the DNS Manager console. Under Cached Lookups, click to expand the **.(root)** folder, and then click the **com** folder. You should see the list of GTLD servers and a folder for the domain you visited (possibly more than one folder). Click the **net** folder, and then double-click the **gtld-servers** folder. You see several A records for the GTLD servers listed and perhaps some AAAA entries with IPv6 addresses.

13. Right-click **ServerDC1** in the left pane and click **Properties**. Click the **Forwarders** tab. If a forwarder is listed, it's because Windows installs the DNS server configured for this computer as a forwarder when DNS is installed. If there's a forwarder, click the **Edit** button, click the forwarder address, click **Delete**, and then click **OK**. Examine the other tabs in the Properties dialog box, and then click **Cancel**.

14. Shut down ServerDC1.

Installing DNS

 **Certification**

• 70-741 – Implement Domain Name System (DNS):
  Install and configure DNS servers

DNS is an integral part of most network communication sessions between computers. Each time an application or app (as it's called on mobile devices) communicates with the Internet or another device, it uses DNS to resolve a network device's name to an IP address. A correctly configured and efficiently functioning DNS service, therefore, is essential for a well-functioning network.

Windows domains and Active Directory rely exclusively on DNS for resolving names and locating services. When a workgroup computer attempts to join a domain, it contacts a DNS server to find records that identify a domain controller for the domain. When a member computer or server starts, it contacts a DNS server to find a domain controller that can authenticate it to the domain. When domain controllers replicate with one another and when trusts are created between domains in different forests, DNS is required to resolve names and services to IP addresses.

Installing DNS with Active Directory

During Active Directory installation, Windows attempts to find a DNS server and, if it's unsuccessful, asks whether you want to install DNS. When a new forest is created, it's best to have Windows install DNS during Active Directory installation because Windows automatically creates all the initial zone records that Active Directory needs. If DNS is installed later, you have to create the zone database manually.

You might need to install DNS manually on a domain controller, member server, or standalone server. In any case, you start by installing the DNS Server role with Server Manager or PowerShell. To install DNS with PowerShell, use the following cmdlet:

```
Install-WindowsFeature DNS -IncludeManagementTools
```

If the DNS server is intended to manage domain name services for Active Directory, you should install the DNS Server role on a domain controller so that you gain the benefits of Active Directory integration. If you're installing DNS on a domain controller, Windows detects the installation and informs you that DNS zones will be integrated with Active Directory.

Installing DNS on Nano Server

DNS is one of the roles that Nano Server is particularly well suited for. DNS is required on every Windows network, and most networks have several DNS servers for load sharing and fault tolerance. So, deploying DNS on Nano Server is ideal because of its small footprint and DNS can be managed remotely. Note that since the Active Directory role cannot be installed on Nano Server, DNS on Nano Server doesn't support Active Directory–integrated zones; only standard file-based zones are supported. Installing DNS on a new Nano Server image consists of four steps:

1. Create a Nano Server virtual disk image with the DNS server package by using the `-packages Microsoft-NanoServer-DNS-Package` option.

2. Once the Nano Server image is created, start Nano Server and from a remote PowerShell prompt (using PowerShell remoting or PowerShell Direct), use the `Enable-WindowsOptionalFeature -Online -FeatureName DNS-Server-Full-Role` cmdlet to extract the DNS server role and the associated PowerShell cmdlets.

3. Import the DNSserver module using the `Import-Module DNSServer` cmdlet.

4. Make the DNS management cmdlets operational using the `Get-Command -Module DNSServer` cmdlet.

Now, you are ready to create zones and add resource records to DNS on Nano Server. You can either use PowerShell or the DNS Manager from a remote computer to perform these tasks.

Note

For more information on deploying Nano Server, see *MCSA Guide to Installation, Storage, and Compute with Windows Server 2016, Exam 70–740* (Cengage, 2018).

Whether DNS is installed on Windows Server 2016 with Desktop Experience, Server Core, or Nano Server, after it's installed, your first step is usually to create a zone so it can be populated with resource records. In Activity 1-3, you install DNS, create a zone, and populate it with a host record.

Configuring DNS

- 70-741 – Implement Domain Name System (DNS):
  Create and configure DNS zones and records

After DNS is installed, it's ready to start resolving host and domain names to IP addresses. You don't even have to configure a zone if the DNS server will be a caching-only server. However, in most network environments that have an Internet presence or an Active Directory domain, there are a number of configuration tasks you'll want to undertake. There are three aspects of DNS configuration as discussed in the following sections:

- DNS zones
- DNS resource records
- DNS server settings

Creating DNS Zones

Although DNS zones are created automatically during Active Directory installation, you might need to create a zone manually in the following situations:

- When you don't install DNS at the time you install Active Directory
- When you install DNS on a server that's not a domain controller
- When you create a stub zone
- When you create a secondary zone for a primary zone
- When you create a primary or secondary zone for an Internet domain

When you create a zone in DNS Manager, you must answer the following questions about it:

- Will it be a forward or reverse lookup zone?
- What type of zone do you want to create: primary, secondary, or stub?
- Should the zone be Active Directory–integrated?
- What's the replication scope of the zone?
- What's the name of the zone?
- How should the zone handle dynamic updates?

Forward and Reverse Lookup Zones

There are two DNS zone categories that define what kind of information is stored in a zone:

- *Forward lookup zone*—A **forward lookup zone (FLZ)** contains ecords that translate names to IP addresses. The zone name is based on the domain of the resource records it contains. For example, the zone name might be csmtech.local, and it might contain resource records for www, mail, db-server, vpnserver, and so forth, which are hostnames of computers in the domain. FLZs can contain a variety of resource record types as discussed in Chapter 3. Forward lookup zones are used to perform forward lookups, which resolve computer names (FQDNs) to addresses. For example, the following `ping` command resolves the FQDN to an IP address before the `ping` program can send a packet to www.csmtech.local:

```
ping www.csmtech.local
```

- *Reverse lookup zone*—A **reverse lookup zone (RLZ)** contains records that map IP addresses to names and is named after the IP network address (IPv4 or IPv6) of the computers whose records it contains. For example, a typical name for an RLZ might be 1.10.in-addr.arpa, and it contains records for computers in the 10.1.0.0/16 subnet. An RLZ is queried when a network application has an IP address for a computer and needs the FQDN for that computer. A simple example of an application that queries an RLZ is `ping`, as in the following example:

```
ping -a 10.1.1.1
```

- The -a option in the command tells `ping` to do a reverse lookup query. If the query is successful, `ping` displays the FQDN of the computer with IP address 10.1.1.1. This option might be useful if you need to know where packets are coming from and all you have is the IP address of the packet's source. For example, your DNS server is sluggish, so you begin to monitor traffic to and from this server. You find that the server is receiving queries from an unknown source. To learn about the domain where these packets are originating, you can do a reverse lookup query with `ping -a`.

To create one of these zones, right-click the Forward Lookup Zones folder or the Reverse Lookup Zones folder in the DNS Manager console and click New Zone to start the New Zone Wizard.

Zone Type

After you have decided whether to install a FLZ or RLZ and started the New Zone Wizard, you select the type of zone you want to create as shown in Figure 2-5. As mentioned, a zone is a database containing resource and information records for a domain and possibly subdomains. There are three different zone types:

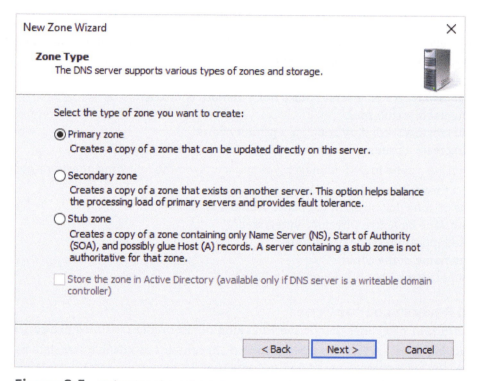

Figure 2-5   Selecting the zone type

- *Primary zone*—A **primary zone** contains a read/write master copy of all resource records for the zone. Updates to resource records can be made only on a server configured as a primary zone server. A primary DNS server is considered authoritative for the zone it manages. A primary zone can be an Active Directory–integrated or a standard zone. If a primary zone is a standard zone, there can be only one server that hosts the primary zone, referred to as the *primary DNS server*. If a primary zone is Active Directory integrated, each domain controller (DC) in the replication scope of the Active Directory partition in which the zone is stored gets a copy of the zone, and changes can be made on any DC that hosts the zone unless it's a read-only domain controller (RODC).
- *Secondary zone*— A **secondary zone** contains a read-only copy of all resource records for the zone. Changes can't be made directly on a secondary DNS server, but because it contains an exact copy of the primary zone, it's considered authoritative for the zone. A secondary zone can be only a

standard zone, not an Active Directory–integrated zone. However, a file-based secondary zone can be created on a standalone server or a DC. Secondary zones are sometimes used to resolve names for domain-based resources outside the domain. For example, if you have two Active Directory forests, Forest1 and Forest2, you can create secondary zones on servers in Forest2 to resolve names for domains in Forest1 and vice versa. Secondary zones are also used in environments without Active Directory, such as for Internet domains and networks that are Linux/UNIX or Mac OS based. When you're working with standard zones, a server that holds the primary zone is called the *master DNS server,* and servers that hold secondary zones are called *slave DNS servers.* You must configure zone transfer settings on the master DNS server that holds the primary zone to allow resource records to be transferred or copied to one or more slave DNS servers that hold secondary zones.

- *Stub zone*—A **stub zone** contains a read-only copy of only the SOA and NS records for a zone and the necessary A records to resolve NS records. A stub zone forwards queries to a primary DNS server for the zone for which it holds SOA and NS records and isn't authoritative for the zone. A stub zone can be an Active Directory–integrated or a standard zone.

Zone Name

The next step is to give the zone a name. For an FLZ, it's the FQDN, such as csmtech.local. For an RLZ, specify whether it's an IPv4 or IPv6 zone, and then enter the network ID portion of the zone. The zone name is created automatically by using the network ID's octets in reverse order and appending "in-addr.arpa" to the name. For example, if the IP network for which the RLZ is being created is 192.168.0.0/24, you enter 192.168.0 in the Zone Name window, and Windows creates a zone named 0.168.192.in-addr.arpa.

Zone File

If you're creating a standard zone, you specify the file name in which to store the zone data. The default name is *zonename*.dns where *zonename* is usually the FQDN. For example, for a zone named csmtech.local, the zone file name will be csmtech.local.dns (see Figure 2-6). You can change the name if desired, or you can specify an existing file. If you specify an existing file, DNS will load the zone data in that file.

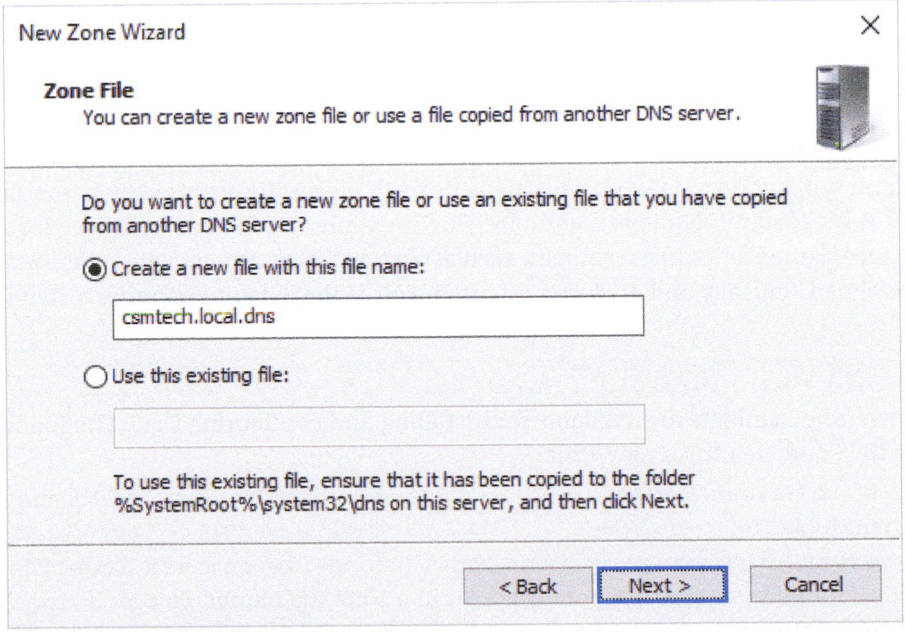

Figure 2-6   Specifying a zone file

Dynamic Updates

The final step in creating a new zone is to decide whether and how to use dynamic updates as shown in Figure 2-7. Dynamic updates can be configured in one of three ways:

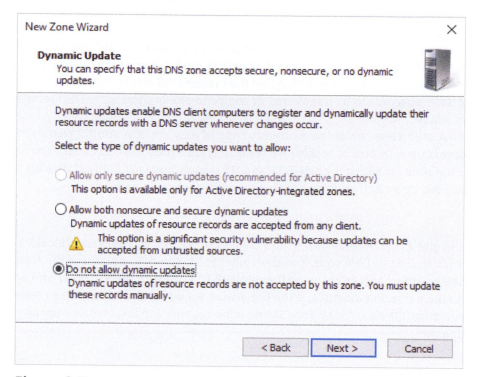

Figure 2-7 Configuring dynamic updates

- *Allow only secure dynamic updates*—Available only for Active Directory–integrated zones, this option ensures that the host initiating the record creation or update has been authenticated by Active Directory.
- *Allow both nonsecure and secure dynamic updates*—Both authenticated Active Directory clients and non-Active Directory clients can create and update DNS records. This option isn't recommended because it allows rogue clients to create DNS records with false information. A rogue DNS client can impersonate a server by updating the server's A record with its own IP address, thereby redirecting client computers to a fraudulent server.
- *Do not allow dynamic updates*—All DNS records must be entered manually. This option helps secure the environment, but on a network with many hosts that must be accessed by name and on networks using DHCP, it's an administrative nightmare. However, this option does work well for a DNS server that manages names for public resources, such as web and mail servers with addresses that are usually assigned statically and don't change often. This is the default option for a standard zone.

Configuring DNS with PowerShell

A number of PowerShell cmdlets are available for installing and configuring DNS. The following cmdlets cover installing DNS and creating a new zone:

- `Install-WindowsFeature DNS -IncludeManagementTools`—Installs DNS and the DNS management tools.
- `Add-DnsServerPrimaryZone csmtech.local -ZoneFile csmtech.local.dns`—Creates a standard FLZ named csmtech.local and stores it in a zone file named `csmtech.local.dns`.
- `Add-DnsServerPrimaryZone -NetworkID 10.10.0.0/16 -ZoneFile 10.10.in-addr.arpa.dns`—Creates a standard RLZ for network ID 10.10.0.0/16 and stores it in a zone file named `10.10.in-addr.arpa.dns`

To create secondary or stub zones, the relevant commands are `Add-DnsServerSecondaryZone` and `Add-DnsServerStubZone`. Remember that secondary zones can't be Active Directory integrated.

> **Note** 📎
>
> You can use the command-line tool `dnscmd.exe` to create zones and perform other DNS management tasks. However, this command might be deprecated in the future, and Microsoft recommends using PowerShell to manage DNS from the command line. Remember: To get help and examples for using PowerShell cmdlets, type `get-help CmdletName -detailed` at a PowerShell prompt.

Creating DNS Resource Records

 **Certification**

- 70-741 – Implement Domain Name System (DNS):
  Create and configure DNS zones and records

A DNS zone contains several types of resource records. Table 2-2 describes each record type briefly, and the following sections give you additional information. Resource records are added to a zone in one of two ways:

- *Static*—With this method, an administrator enters DNS record information manually. This method is reasonable with a small network of only a few resources accessed by name, but in a large network, creating and updating static records can be an administrative burden. Some records created by the system are also called *static records*, such as the SOA and NS records created automatically when a zone is created and records created automatically when Active Directory is installed.
- *Dynamic*—Referred to as **Dynamic DNS (DDNS)**, computers in the domain can register or update their own DNS records, or DHCP can update DNS on the clients' behalf when a computer leases a new IP address. Both the client computer and the DHCP server must be configured to use this feature.

Table 2-2   DNS resource record types

Record type (code)	Description
Host (A)	The most common resource record; consists of a computer name and an IPv4 address.
IPv6 Host (AAAA)	Like an A record but uses an IPv6 address.
Canonical Name (CNAME)	A record containing an alias for another record that enables you to refer to the same resource with different names yet maintain only one host record. For example, you could create an A record for a computer named "web" and a CNAME record that points to the A record but allows users to access the host with the name "www."
Pointer (PTR)	Used for reverse DNS lookups. Although DNS is used mainly to resolve a name to an address, it can also resolve an address to a name by using a reverse lookup. PTR records can be created automatically on Windows DNS servers.
Mail Exchanger (MX)	Contains the address of an email server for the domain. Because email addresses are typically specified as *user@domain*.com, the mail server's name is not part of the email address. To deliver a message to the mail server, an MX record query supplies the address of a mail server in the specified domain.

(continues)

Table 2-2   DNS resource record types *(continued)*

Record type (code)	Description
Service Location (SRV)	Allows DNS clients to request the address of a server that provides a specific service instead of querying the server by name. This type of record is useful when an application doesn't know the name of the server it needs but does know what service is required. For example, in Windows domains, DNS servers contain SRV records with the addresses of domain controllers so that clients can request the logon service to authenticate to the domain.
Start of Authority (SOA)	Less a resource than an informational record, an SOA identifies the name server that's authoritative for the domain and includes a variety of timers, dynamic update configuration, and zone transfer information.
Name Server (NS)	The FQDN of a name server that has authority over the domain. NS records are used by DNS servers to refer queries to another server that's authoritative for the requested domain.

Host (A and AAAA) Records

Host records are the most abundant type of record in a typical DNS primary or secondary zone. A **host record** is fairly simple; it consists of a hostname and an IP address. A host record can be an **A record**, meaning it contains an IPv4 address, or an **AAAA record**, which contains an IPv6 address. When you configure a host record, an A or AAAA record is selected automatically based on the IP address's format. When you create a host record, the only option by default is to update the associated PTR record in the RLZ if it exists.

There are additional options for host records, however, if you enable the advanced view setting in DNS Manager. In DNS Manager, click View and then Advanced. If you open the properties of a host record, you see a dialog box similar to Figure 2-8. The following list describes the options you see in this figure:

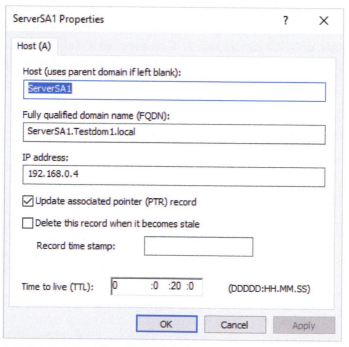

Figure 2-8   Properties of a host record with advanced view enabled

- *Update associated pointer (PTR) record*—If you enable this option, a PTR record is created or updated in the relevant RLZ if it's present.

- *Delete this record when it becomes stale*—A stale record hasn't been updated in a period longer than its TTL value. This option is set automatically on a dynamic record and can be set manually on a static record. If it's set, stale records are deleted (scavenged) from the database during aging and scavenging, a process discussed in Chapter 3.
- *Record time stamp*—For dynamic records, this field shows the date and time the record was created or updated. On static records, it's filled in automatically with the current date and time if the *Delete this record when it becomes stale* option is set and you click Apply in the Properties dialog box.
- *Time to live (TTL)*—The TTL tells the system how long the record should remain in the database after it was created or last updated. The default is 1 hour. This field is relevant only on zones that have scavenging enabled. It works with the *Record time stamp* option. If the actual time and date are past the Record time stamp value plus the TTL value, the record is eligible for scavenging.

Canonical Name (CNAME) Records

A **CNAME record** is an alias for another domain name record in the DNS database. It's often used when multiple services are running on the same server and you want users to be able to refer to each service with a different name. For example, you might have an FTP service and a web service hosted on the same server. You can set up DNS records as follows:

Record type	Name	Value
CNAME	www.csmtech.local	server1.csmtech.local
CNAME	ftp.csmtech.local	server1.csmtech.local
A	server1.csmtech.local	192.168.0.101

In this example, a reference to *www.csmtech.local* or *ftp.csmtech.local* returns server1.csmtech.local, which returns the IP address 192.168.0.101. A CNAME record must always point to another domain name; it can't point to an IP address. Although a CNAME record can point to another CNAME, it's not recommended because it can result in circular logic. For example, you could have CNAME record X point to CNAME record Y, which points back to CNAME record X, in an unresolvable loop.

You can also create CNAME records that point to records in other domains. For example, you can create a CNAME record with the alias ftp.csmpub.local that points to *www.csmtech.local* as long as the server on which you create the record has a way to resolve ftp.csmpub.local (from local zone data, a forwarder, or recursion).

Pointer (PTR) Records

As discussed, a **PTR record** is used to resolve a known IP address to a hostname. PTR records are used by some web-based applications that limit their use to specific domains. When the application is accessed, a reverse lookup is performed, and the domain name of the host attempting to access the application is verified against the list of permitted domains. PTR records are also useful for certain applications when only the IP address is known and you want to find the hostname. For example, when you use the `tracert` command to map the route between your computer and a destination, each router along the way replies with its IP address. The `tracert` command can then do a reverse lookup to determine the router's FQDN, which often contains information for determining where the router is located and which ISP it belongs to. PTR records are found only in RLZs.

PTR records have much the same information as a host record, including a time stamp and TTL. When you create a host record, you have the option to create the related PTR record for the host automatically as long as the RLZ already exists. In addition, you can edit an existing host record and select the *Update associated pointer (PTR) record* check box to create or update the PTR associated with the host.

Mail Exchanger (MX) Records

An **MX record** is used by mail services to find the mail server for a domain. When a user writes an email to mike@csmtech.local, for example, only what are known from the email address are the recipient name and domain name. However, the mail protocol needs the name of a host in the domain that provides mail services, which is where the MX record comes in. When an outgoing mail server, usually an SMTP server, needs to deliver an email message, it performs a DNS lookup for the MX record for the domain name contained in the email address. The MX record points to an A record (much as a CNAME record does). So in this example, there might be records in the csmtech.local zone that look like the following:

Record type	Name	Value
A	mail.csmtech.local	192.168.0.102
MX	csmtech.local	mail.csmtech.local

When a client queries for an MX record for the csmtech.local domain, the DNS server returns the name of the server (mail.csmtech.local) and its IP address. The outgoing mail server can then deliver the mail to address 192.168.0.102, which contains a mailbox for the user account mike.

To create an MX record, right-click the zone where you want to create the record and click New Mail Exchanger (MX). There's only one required field: the FQDN of the mail server, which can be a host or CNAME record (see Figure 2-9). The following list explains each option in this figure:

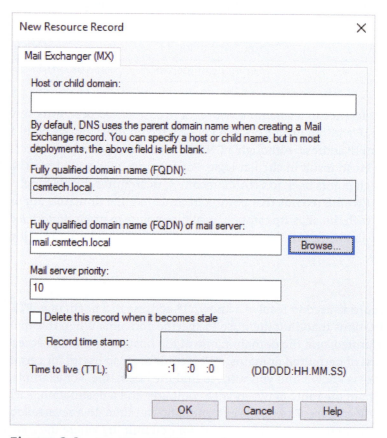

Figure 2-9   Creating an MX record

- *Host or child domain*—This field is usually left blank because the parent domain name is most often used. However, you can add a hostname or the name of a child domain. For example, if your primary domain name is csmtech.local but you also have mail accounts in a child domain, such as europe.csmtech.local, you could enter *europe* in this text box.

- *Fully qualified domain name (FQDN)*—This is the name of the domain where you're creating the record. If you enter a value in the *Host or child domain* text box, it's added to the beginning of the default value. For example, if you enter *europe* in the *Host or child domain* text box, this field changes to europe.csmtech.local. You can't change its contents manually.
- *Fully qualified domain name (FQDN) of mail server*—This is the FQDN of the actual mail server, which is usually a host or CNAME record in the zone. In this example, the mail server is mail.csmtech.local.
- *Mail server priority*—If you have multiple mail servers in the zone, you can set a priority in this text box. Lower values have higher precedence. When a client queries for an MX record, the DNS server returns all MX records defined in it database for the zone. The client first tries the MX record with the lowest priority value. If it gets no response, it tries the next one, and so on. You can set the same priority value on two or more servers for a round-robin type of load balancing because the equal-priority records are returned to the client in round-robin order. (Round-robin settings are discussed later in this chapter.)
- The last three fields are for scavenging stale records. Note that these fields can be seen only if Advanced view is turned on in DNA Manager. Scavenging is discussed in Chapter 3.

Service Location (SRV) Records

An SRV record specifies a hostname and port number for servers that supply specific services. For example, servers that provide Kerberos authentication or Lightweight Directory Access Protocol (LDAP) services can register an SRV record with a DNS server so that clients requiring these services can find them. SRV records are queried by client computers in the following format:

```
_ServiceName._Protocol.DomainName
```

For example, a client looking for an LDAP (Active Directory) server using the TCP protocol for the csmtech.local domain sends a query that looks like this:

```
_ldap._tcp.csmtech.local
```

In DNS Manager, several SRV records are in the _msdcs subdomain created for every Active Directory domain. Figure 2-10 shows DNS Manager with SRV records for the Kerberos, global catalog, and LDAP services in the MCSA2016.local domain.

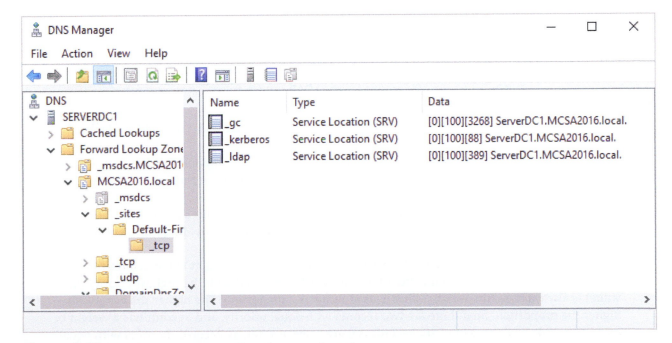

Figure 2-10   SRV records in an Active Directory domain

SRV records are critical to the operation of an Active Directory domain. Without the necessary SRV records, client computers couldn't find a domain controller or global catalog server to sign in or join a domain. SRV records for Active Directory are usually created automatically when Active Directory is installed. If for some reason these records aren't created or updated correctly, you can register them by stopping and starting the Netlogon service on the domain controller or by restarting the server. You can also create or edit an SRV record manually. To create an SRV record, right-click the zone and click Other New Records, and then click SRV in the list of options. Figure 2-11 shows an SRV record for the LDAP service. The following list explains each option:

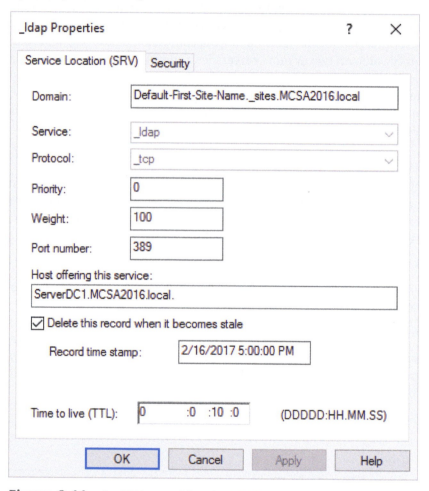

Figure 2-11 An SRV record for the LDAP service

- *Domain*—This is the name of the domain in which the service is located. This field is filled in for you, and you can't change it.
- *Service*—Choose a service in this list. The name is prefaced with an underscore character, so the Kerberos service, for example, is listed as _kerberos. Services you can choose from are finger, FTP, HTTP, Kerberos, LDAP, MSDCS, NNTP, Telnet, and Whois.
- *Protocol*—This is the Transport-layer protocol the service uses. The choices are TCP and UDP.
- *Priority*—This is the priority of this record if more than one server is providing the same service. Lower numbers are higher priority. The default value is 0.
- *Weight*—If two of the same service records have equal priority, the weight value determines which record the host should use. Unlike the priority in which the record with the highest priority (lowest value) is always used, the weight value is used more as a proportion. The higher the weight, the higher the proportion. So if there are two records with equal priority, and Record1 has a weight of 40 and Record2 has a weight of 20, Record1 is used twice as often as Record2. Records with equal weight are used equally. The default value is 0.

- *Port number*—This value is filled in automatically with the default port number for the selected service. However, you can change it if the service uses a nonstandard port number.
- *Host offering this service*—This is the FQDN of the host providing the service, ending with a dot.

Like all record types, if you have the Advanced View setting enabled, you can change the default TTL and select the option to delete the record when it becomes stale.

Note

The last two record types from Table 2-2, SOA and NS records, are discussed later in the chapter under "Configuring DNS Zones."

Creating Dynamic DNS Records

Dynamic DNS records are created and updated by a host computer or, when using DHCP to assign IP addresses, by the DHCP server when an IP address is leased or renewed. When a device is assigned an IP address, it registers its name with the DNS server configured in its IP address settings. If the device has an IPv4 address, an A record is created; if it has an IPv6 address, an AAAA record is created. If the device gets its IP address settings from a DHCP server, the DHCP server can be configured to register the computer's name and address on its behalf. Whenever a computer's IP address changes or it renews its IP address lease from the DHCP server, the DNS records are updated. Each time a dynamic record is created or updated, a TTL value and time stamp are added to the record. The TTL specifies how long the record should remain in the DNS database. If the record expires, it's deleted from the database.

Note

You can also force a Windows client to register its address by using the `ipconfig /registerdns` command.

If a reverse lookup zone exists for the host's IP address, PTR records are created dynamically in the same manner as host records. PTR records can also be created by opening a host record's properties and selecting the *Update associated pointer (PTR) record* check box.

Creating Static DNS Records

Static DNS records are called static because they don't expire. They stay in the DNS database until someone removes them. Unlike dynamically created records, which have a time stamp, static records have no time stamp by default. Static records are created manually by an administrator or automatically by Windows under some circumstances. To create a static record in DNS Manager, you right-click the zone and select the record type. In an FLZ, the most common type of record to create is a New Host record, which can be an IPv4 (A) record or an IPv6 (AAAA) record (see Figure 2-12). Enter a name in the Name text box to create the FQDN automatically. DNS Manager creates an A or AAAA record automatically, depending on whether an IPv4 or IPv6 address is entered. If you select the *Create associated pointer (PTR) record* check box, a PTR record is created if a suitable RLZ exists for the IP address entered.

To create a PTR record, right-click the RLZ and click New Pointer (PTR). Type the host IP address, and then type or browse for the hostname (see Figure 2-13).

As mentioned, Windows can create a static resource record automatically. When a new zone is created, SOA and NS static records are created for the zone, and in Active Directory–integrated zones, SRV, PTR, and A records are created automatically for domain controllers.

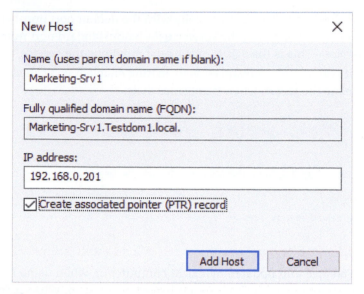

Figure 2-12   Creating a new host record

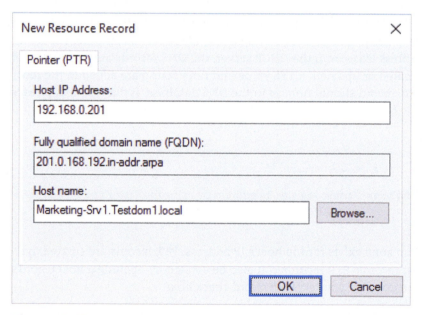

Figure 2-13   Creating a new PTR record

Note

This section has given you an overview of creating DNS records. This topic is covered in more detail in Chapter 3.

PowerShell Commands for Creating DNS Resource Records

The following PowerShell cmdlets are used to create DNS resource records:

- `Add-DnsServerResourceRecord -A -ZoneName csmtech.local -Name host1 -IPv4Address 192.168.0.11`—Adds an A record named host1 to the csmtech.local zone.
- `Add-DnsServerResourceRecord -AAAA -ZoneName csmtech.local -Name host1 -IPv6Address 2001:DB8::11`—Adds an AAAA record named host1 to the csmtech. local zone.

- `Add-DnsServerResourceRecord -CName -ZoneName csmtech.local -Name h1 -HostNameAlias host1.csmtech.local`—Adds a CNAME (alias) record named h1 with the target host1.csmtech.local.
- `Add-DnsServerResourceRecord -Ptr -ZoneName 0.168.192.in-addr.arpa Name 11 -PtrDomainName host1.csmtech.local`—Adds a PTR record named host1.csmtech.local with the IP address 192.168.0.11 to the 0.168.192.in-addr.arpa RLZ.

Activity 2-3: Installing DNS and Creating a New Zone

Time Required: 20 minutes

Objective: Install DNS on a standalone server.

Required Tools and Equipment: ServerSA1

Description: In this activity, you install DNS on a standalone server and create a test zone.

1. Start ServerSA1, sign in as **Administrator**, and open Server Manager.
2. Start the Add Roles and Features Wizard. In the Server Roles window, click to select **DNS Server**. Click **Add Features**, and accept the remaining default options. When the role is installed, close the wizard.
3. In Server Manager, click **Tools, DNS** from the menu to open DNS Manager. In the left pane, click to expand **ServerSA1** and then click **Forward Lookup Zones**. No zones are listed yet.
4. Right-click **Forward Lookup Zones** and click **New Zone** to start the New Zone Wizard. In the welcome window, click **Next**.
5. In the Zone Type window, notice that the option to store the zone in Active Directory is grayed out because the server isn't a DC. Accept the default **Primary zone setting**, and then click **Next**.
6. Type **Testdom1.local** in the Zone name text box, and then click **Next**. In the Zone File window, accept the default file name **Testdom1.local.dns**; this is the name of the file where the zone data is stored. Click **Next**.
7. In the Dynamic Update window, click the **Allow both nonsecure and secure dynamic updates** option, and then click **Next**. Click **Finish**.
8. In the DNS Manager console, double-click **Testdom1.local** in the right pane. You see two resource records: the SOA record that is created for every zone and an NS record. Double-click the SOA record to open the domain Properties dialog box to the Start of Authority (SOA) tab. Most of the settings for the SOA are discussed later in the section "Start of Authority Records." Click **Cancel**.
9. Double-click the NS record. The same Properties box is opened as for the SOA record, but it opens to the Name Servers tab. Click **Cancel**, and close the DNS Manager console.
10. Now that ServerSA1 is a DNS server, you're going to change its IP address configuration so that it uses itself for DNS lookups and DNS registration. Open a PowerShell window, and type **Set-DNSClientServerAddress Ethernet -ServerAddresses 127.0.0.1** and press **Enter**.
11. To set the DNS suffix search list for the Ethernet interface to testdom1.local so that the server registers its name with the zone you just created, type **Set-DnsClient Ethernet ConnectionSpecificSuffix testdom1. local -UseSuffixWhenRegistering $true** and press **Enter**.
12. Before you register the name with DNS, type **nslookup ServerSA1.testdom1.local** and press **Enter**. You see a message that localhost can't find ServerSA1, which means there's no A record yet for ServerSA1.
13. To register the server name with DNS, type **ipconfig /registerdns** and press **Enter**. Try the lookup again by typing **nslookup ServerSA1.testdom1.local** and pressing **Enter**. The lookup is successful this time (if it's not, wait a minute and try the command again).
14. Close the PowerShell window. Open the DNS Manager console, and click the **Testdom1.local** zone and click the **Refresh** icon to verify that the A record for ServerSA1 has been created (see Figure 2-14).

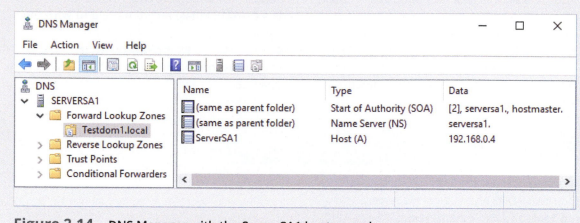

Figure 2-14   DNS Manager with the ServerSA1 host record

15. Stay signed in and continue to the next activity.

Activity 2-4: Working with Reverse Lookup Zones

Time Required: 15 minutes
Objective: Create an RLZ and view its properties.
Required Tools and Equipment: ServerSA1
Description: In this activity, you create an RLZ on ServerSA1 and add a PTR record to it.

1. Sign in to ServerSA1 as **Administrator**, if necessary.
2. Open a PowerShell window. Type **nslookup 192.168.0.4** (the address of ServerSA1) and press **Enter**. You see a response stating that the address can't be found. Note that `nslookup` is not a PowerShell cmdlet but can be run from a PowerShell window as well as from a command prompt.
3. To create an RLZ named 0.168.192.in-addr.arpa, type **Add-DnsServerPrimaryZone NetworkID 192.168.0.0/24 -ZoneFile 0.168.192.in-addr.arpa.dns** and press **Enter**.
4. Open the DNS Manager console, and click to expand **Reverse Lookup Zones** to verify that the zone has been created (if you don't see it, press the **Refresh** icon in DNS Manager). Click **0.168.192.in-addr.arpa**. You see the SOA and NS records.
5. You can use `ipconfig /registerdns` on each computer to create PTR records, but there's another method that can be done from the DNS Manager console. Click to expand **Forward Lookup Zones**, and then click **Testdom1.local**. Double-click **ServerSA1** in the right pane. Click to select the **Update associated pointer (PTR) record** check box, and then click **OK**.
6. Click the **0.168.192.in-addr.arpa** RLZ in the left pane again. If the PTR record isn't there, click the **Refresh** icon in DNS Manager to see the 192.168.0.4 PTR record.
7. In the PowerShell prompt, type **nslookup 192.168.0.4** and press **Enter** to verify that you can do a reverse lookup. You should get a response with the Name field shown as ServerSA1.testdom1.local.
8. Stay signed in to ServerSA1 for the next activity.

Activity 2-5: Creating Static DNS Entries

Time Required: 15 minutes
Objective: Create static A, CNAME, and PTR records.
Required Tools and Equipment: ServerSA1
Description: In this activity, you experiment with creating static DNS records using the test zone you created on ServerSA1.

1. On ServerSA1, open the DNS Manager console, if necessary, and click to expand **Forward Lookup Zones**. Right-click **Testdom1.local** and click **New Host (A or AAAA)**.

2. In the New Host dialog box, type **webserver1** in the Name text box and **192.168.0.101** in the IP address text box. Click the **Add Host** button. Click **OK** and then **Done**.

3. In PowerShell, type **nslookup webserver1.testdom1.local** and press **Enter**. The name is resolved. Type **nslookup 192.168.0.101** and press **Enter**. The IP address is resolved.

4. Now, you'll create a CNAME resource record using PowerShell. Type **Add-DnsServerResourceRecord -CName -Name www -HostNameAlias webserver1.testdom1.local ZoneName testdom1.local**, and then press **Enter**. This command creates an alias named www for the existing host record webserver1.

5. Type **nslookup www.testdom1.local** and press **Enter**. The command returns the address for webserver1. testdom1.local and lists the alias name www.testdom1.local.

6. Now, create a PTR record for the new alias. Type **Add-DnsServerResourceRecord -Ptr Name 101 ZoneName 0.168.192.in-addr.arpa -PtrDomainName www.testdom1.local** and press **Enter**.

7. At the command prompt, type **nslookup 192.168.0.101** and press **Enter**. Since webserver1 also has a PTR record with that address, either the www.testdom1.local or webserver1.testdom1.local record is returned. If you repeat the command, the other record will be returned.

8. Stay signed in to ServerSA1 and continue to the next activity.

Configuring DNS Zones

 **Certification**

- 70-741 – Implement Domain Name System (DNS):
  Create and configure DNS zones and records

After a zone is created, you can view and change its properties in DNS Manager by right-clicking the zone and clicking Properties. In the General tab (see Figure 2-15), you can view and change the following options:

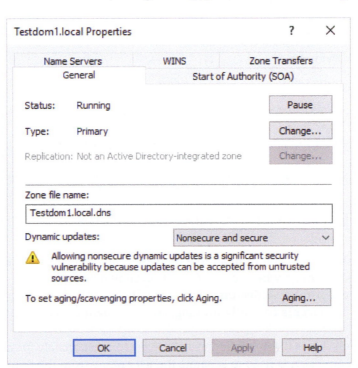

Figure 2-15   A zone's Properties dialog box

- *Status*—Pause a running DNS zone or start a paused DNS zone. When a zone is paused, queries made to it are refused.
- *Type*—Change the zone type (primary, secondary, or stub) and choose whether the zone should be Active Directory integrated.
- *Replication*—Change the replication scope (replication is discussed later). This button is grayed out for a standard zone.
- *Dynamic updates*—On an Active Directory–integrated zone, choose Secure only, Nonsecure and secure, or None. Standard zones don't have the Secure only option.
- *Aging*—Click this button to configure aging and scavenging options, which specify how often stale resource records are removed from the zone database. Aging and scavenging are covered in Chapter 3.

Start of Authority Records

The SOA record found in every zone contains information that identifies the server primarily responsible for the zone as well as some operational properties for the zone. You can edit the SOA record by double-clicking it in the right pane of DNS Manager after selecting the zone or by viewing the zone's properties and clicking the Start of Authority tab. Shown in Figure 2-16, the SOA record contains the following information:

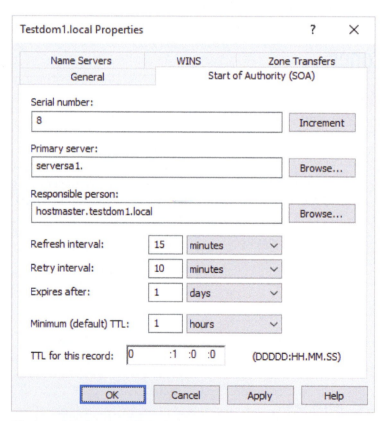

Figure 2-16   The Start of Authority (SOA) tab

- *Serial number*—This is a revision number that increases each time data in the zone changes. This number is used to determine when zone information should be replicated.
- *Primary server*—On a primary Active Directory–integrated zone, this field displays the name of the server where DNS Manager is currently running. For a standard zone, it displays the primary DNS server's name.
- *Responsible person*—This is the email address of the person responsible for managing the zone. A period rather than an @ sign is used to separate the user name from the domain name (according to RFC 1183, which defines DNS resource record types).

- *Minimum (default) TTL*—This setting specifies a default TTL value for zone data when a TTL isn't supplied. The TTL value tells other DNS servers from this zone how long to keep cached data; it should be adjusted according to how often data in the zone is likely to change. For example, a zone that maintains only static entries for resources that aren't changed, added, or removed can often specify a high TTL value. If a zone maintains dynamic records or records for resources that are going online and offline constantly, this value should be lower. If a redesign of your network will cause many changes to zone data, this value can be lowered temporarily. Then wait until the previous TTL time has elapsed before making the changes. This way, servers caching records that will be changed don't store them very long. The TTL set separately on resource records overrides this default value, which is 1 hour.

The other three fields—Refresh interval, Retry interval, and Expires after—control zone transfers and are discussed later in "Creating Secondary Zones and Configuring Zone Transfers."

Name Server Records

NS records specify FQDNs and IP addresses of authoritative servers for a zone. Each zone that's created has an NS record that points to an authoritative server for that zone. For example, when a primary zone is created, the NS record points to the server it's created on. A typical configuration with Active Directory–integrated zones has an NS record for each domain controller configured as a DNS server in the domain or forest, depending on the scope of zone replication.

NS records are also used to refer DNS queries to a name server that has been delegated authority for a subdomain. For example, .com TLD servers refer queries for resources in the technet.microsoft.com subdomain to a DNS server that's authoritative for the microsoft.com domain. The microsoft.com domain name server can then refer the query to another DNS server that has been delegated authority for the technet subdomain of microsoft.com. Subdomains need not be delegated; they can simply be created under the zone representing their parent domain. If the subdomain has many resources and traffic on it is heavy, however, zone delegation is a wise approach. Zone delegation is covered more in Chapter 3.

An NS record technically consists of just the name server's FQDN, but for the name to be useful, there must be a way to resolve it to an IP address. DNS does this with a **glue A record**, which is an A record containing the name server's IP address. On Windows DNS servers, glue records are created automatically, if possible, by a DNS lookup on the NS record's FQDN; they don't appear as an A record anywhere in the zone database. Figure 2-17 shows the interface for creating and editing NS records. If Windows fails to

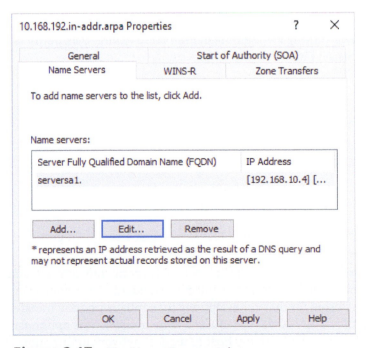

Figure 2-17   The Name Servers tab

resolve the name server's FQDN, you can edit the record and add an IP address manually. You can add a TTL value for the record that tells other servers caching the NS record during recursive lookups how long they should keep it in cache. If no value is specified, the default TTL for the domain is used.

Creating Secondary Zones and Configuring Zone Transfers

As mentioned, a secondary zone is a read-only copy of a primary zone. When a secondary zone is created, is must have the same name of an existing primary zone and zone transfers must be configured to load data from the primary zone to the secondary zone. Because secondary zones are read-only, all changes to the zone data occurs at the server hosting the primary zone and are subsequently transferred to all secondary zone servers. Whereas only one server can host a primary zone, multiple servers can host secondary zones.

> **Note** 🔗
>
> Only one server can host a *standard* primary zone. Active Directory–integrated primary zones can be hosted on as many servers as there are domain controllers.

Zone Transfer Settings

A **zone transfer** copies all or part of a zone from one DNS server to another and occurs as a result of a secondary server requesting the transfer from another server. The server requesting the zone transfer is sometimes called the *slave*, and the server providing the zone information is sometimes called the *master*. The master server can host a primary or secondary zone, but the slave server always hosts a secondary zone. Although Active Directory–integrated zones use Active Directory replication to transfer zone information, you can configure standard zone transfers if the target is a standard secondary zone. Zone transfers can be initiated in two ways:

- *Refresh interval*—The Refresh interface is found on the SOA tab of a zone's Properties window. As discussed, a secondary zone server requests zone information from another server (a primary or another secondary master) when the zone's refresh interval expires, which is every 15 minutes by default.
- *DNS notify*—A master server can be configured to send a DNS notify message to secondary servers when zone information changes. The secondary server can then request the zone transfer immediately without waiting for the refresh interval to expire. DNS notify is configured on the Zone Transfers tab, discussed next.

> **Tip:** ⓘ
>
> Zone transfers typically use TCP port 53, and most DNS queries from a client to a server use UDP port 53. If zone transfers must occur through a firewall, be sure to open TCP port 53 to allow master and slave servers to communicate.

Zone transfers are configured in the Zone Transfers tab of a zone's Properties dialog box, which has the following options (see Figure 2-18):

- *Allow zone transfers*—Selecting this check box enables zone transfers. By default, zone transfers in Active Directory–integrated zones are disabled. In standard zones, zone transfers are enabled for all other name servers listed for that zone. Options for configuring zone transfers are as follows:
  - To any server: Allows any server to request a zone transfer. This option isn't recommended for most environments because it allows any host to request network information, which is not secure.

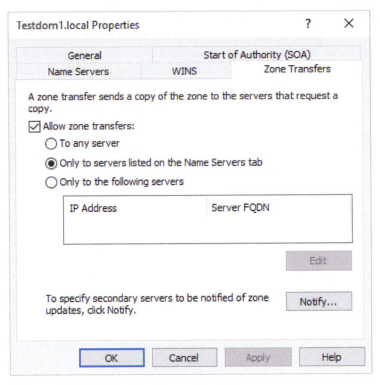

Figure 2-18   The Zone Transfers tab

- Only to servers listed on the Name Servers tab: This option is the default for standard zones. By default, no servers are listed on the Name Servers tab except the current server, so zone transfers are not allowed.
- Only to the following servers: You can specify servers to which zone information can be transferred.
- *Notify*—Clicking this button opens a dialog box where you can specify servers that should receive notifications of changed zone information. By default, the notify option is enabled in standard zones for servers listed in the Name Servers tab.

Note

If all zones are hosted on Windows domain controllers and are Active Directory integrated, there's no need to configure zone transfers because Active Directory replication handles this process.

You configure timing intervals of zone transfers in the Start of Authority tab. There are three timers related to zone transfers:

- *Refresh interval*—Specifies how often a secondary DNS server attempts to renew its zone information. When the interval expires, the server requests the SOA record from the primary DNS server. The serial number in the retrieved SOA record is then compared with the serial number in the secondary server's SOA record. If the serial number has changed, the secondary server requests a new copy of the zone data. After the transfer is completed, the refresh interval begins anew. The default value is 15 minutes. If notification is configured, the DNS server attempts to renew its zone information when it receives a notification and resets the Refresh interval timer.
- *Retry interval*—The amount of time a secondary server waits before retrying a zone transfer that has failed. This value should be less than the Refresh interval timer and defaults to 10 minutes. The Retry interval timer begins after the Refresh interval expires if the primary server can't be contacted or the zone transfer fails.

- *Expires after*—The amount of time before a secondary server considers its zone data obsolete if it can't contact the primary DNS server. If the Refresh interval timer expires without a successful zone transfer, this timer begins. If it expires without contacting the primary DNS server or without a successful zone transfer, the DNS server stops responding to queries. This value must be higher than the Refresh interval and Retry interval combined; the default is 1 day. This timer prevents a secondary server from responding to the DNS queries with data that might be stale.

Full versus Incremental Zone Transfers

There are two types of zone transfer: full zone transfers and incremental zone transfers. A full zone transfer was the only transfer method in DNS versions prior to Windows Server 2003. As DNS databases grew larger and zone files became more numerous and much bigger, incremental zone transfers were defined. Both the master and slave DNS servers must support incremental zone transfers to use them.

When a secondary server requests a zone transfer, it can request an incremental transfer. (If the secondary zone is newly configured on the server, it requests a full zone transfer.) If the serial number of the slave's zone is lower than the master's, the master determines the differences between its current zone data and the slave's zone data. The master then transfers only the resource records that have changed. For incremental zone transfers to work, the master must keep a record of incremental changes with each serial number change. For example, if a slave server requests an incremental zone transfer and its zone serial number is 500 and the master's zone serial number is 502, the master sends all changes that have occurred to the zone between serial number 500 and 502. Even if an incremental transfer is requested, the master can still respond with a full zone transfer if it doesn't support incremental transfers or have enough change history to respond accurately with an incremental transfer.

> **Note** 🔗
>
> A full zone transfer is often referred to as an AXFR because that's the query code used when the slave DNS server requests the transfer. An incremental zone transfer uses the code IXFR.

Using WINS with DNS

Windows Internet Name Service (WINS) is a legacy name service used to resolve NetBIOS names, sometimes referred to as *single-label names*. WINS has similarities to DDNS in that a central database of name-to-address mappings is maintained on a server where client computers update their own records dynamically. Windows clients do a WINS lookup by contacting the server with the name of the host whose IP address is required. WINS supports only IPv4 and is slowly becoming obsolete. You should configure your DNS server to use WINS only if you have older Windows clients, such as Windows 9x, and non-Windows clients that use only DNS. DNS/WINS integration allows non-Windows clients to resolve the names of older Windows clients that require NetBIOS name resolution. WINS might also be a part of your network if you're running older applications that depend on NetBIOS name resolution. The WINS tab in a zone's Properties dialog box has the following configuration options:

- *Use WINS forward lookup*—When this option is enabled for the zone, the DNS server attempts to contact a WINS server to resolve the name if it couldn't be resolved through DNS. WINS forward lookup is disabled by default.
- *Do not replicate this record*—If WINS forward lookups are enabled, selecting this check box prevents the WINS resource record from being replicated to other DNS servers. This option should be selected if you have non-Windows DNS servers in your environment because WINS resource records are Windows specific, and including them in a zone transfer could corrupt the zone or prevent its transfer.
- *IP address*—Enter the IP addresses of WINS servers that should be contacted for name resolution.
- *TTL*—This text box specifies how long a cached WINS resource record is kept.

Using the GlobalNames Zone

Although WINS is still supported in Windows, a feature to help IT administrators migrate away from WINS was introduced in Windows Server 2008. This feature, the **GlobalNames zone (GNZ)**, provides a method for IT administrators to add single-label names (computer names that don't use a domain suffix) to DNS, thereby allowing client computers to resolve these names without including a DNS suffix in the query. The GNZ is not a replacement for a dynamically created WINS database because records in this zone must be added manually. For important servers with names currently being resolved by WINS, however, a GNZ is an option worth considering, especially if only a few hosts are the sole reason for maintaining WINS.

The GNZ feature isn't just a partial replacement for WINS, however. If your network supports mobile users whose laptops and other mobile devices are unlikely to have the correct DNS suffixes configured, GNZ can make access to servers these users need more convenient. Instead of mobile users having to remember resource FQDNs, they can simply access them by using a single-label name, such as Web1.

You must enable the GNZ feature on servers hosting this zone before you create a GNZ. Use the following command to enable GNZ at a PowerShell prompt:

```
Set-DnsServerGlobalNameZone -Enable $true
```

The GNZ can also be enabled with the following command:

```
Dnscmd /config /enableglobalnamessupport 1
```

After GNZ support is enabled, you create a new primary zone that can be (but need not be) Active Directory integrated and named GlobalNames (not case sensitive). Dynamic updates should be disabled because GNZ doesn't support DDNS. For each host to be accessed with a single-label name, create a CNAME record in the GNZ that references the host's A record. You must enable GNZ support on each server the zone is replicated to.

Note

The GlobalNames Zone works only if the client making the query has either a primary DNS suffix or connection-specific DNS suffix configured that matches a zone on the DNS server.

Activity 2-6: Creating a Secondary Zone and Configuring Zone Transfers

Time Required: 15 minutes
Objective: Create a secondary zone and configure zone transfers.
Required Tools and Equipment: ServerDC1 and ServerSA1
Description: In this activity, you create a secondary zone for the Active Directory–integrated primary zone on ServerDC1 and configure zone transfers between ServerDC1 and ServerSA1.

1. Sign in to ServerSA1 as **Administrator** and open the DNS Manager console.
2. Right-click **Forward Lookup Zones** and click **New Zone**. In the New Zone Wizard's welcome window, click **Next**.
3. In the Zone Type window, click the **Secondary zone** option button, and then click **Next**. Type **MCSA2016.local** in the Zone name text box, and then click **Next**.
4. In the Master DNS Servers window, type **192.168.0.1** (the address of ServerDC1) in the Master Servers text box, and press **Enter**. You should see that the address is validated. Click **Next**, and then click **Finish**.
5. Sign in to ServerDC1 as **Administrator** and open the DNS Manager console.
6. Click to expand Forward Lookup Zones and right-click **MCSA2016.local** and click **Properties**. Click the **Name Servers** tab.

7. Click **Add** and type **ServerSA1** in the Server fully qualified domain name (FQDN) text box. In this case, you do not need the FQDN; the server name will suffice. In the IP Addresses of the NS record box, type **192.168.0.4** and press **Enter**, and then click **OK**.

8. Click the **Zone Transfers** tab. Click the **Allow zone transfers** check box, and then click the **Only to servers listed on the Name Servers tab** option button. Click **Notify** and then type **192.168.0.4** and press **Enter** in The Following servers box. Click **OK**. Click **OK** again.

9. On ServerSA1 in DNS Manager, click **MCSA2016.local** in the left pane of DNS Manager, and then click the **Refresh** icon in the toolbar. The zone data should have been transferred successfully, and you should see the resource records for MCSA2016.local. If you don't see the zone data, click **Refresh** again after a few moments. If you still don't see zone data, close DNS Manager and reopen it.

10. Test the zone by opening PowerShell and typing **nslookup serverdm1.mcsa2016.local** and pressing **Enter**. You should get a successful reply. Close the command prompt window.

11. Continue to the next activity.

Configuring DNS Server Settings

 Certification

- 70-741 – Implement Domain Name System (DNS):
  Install and configure DNS servers

So far, you have focused on DNS zone creation and configuration—and rightly so because zones are where all the data is and where most DNS configuration takes place. However, you should be familiar with several DNS server settings to configure an optimal DNS environment and solve DNS problems when they occur. These settings are discussed in the following sections:

- Forwarders
- Root hints
- Round robin
- Recursion
- Debug logging

DNS Forwarders

Forwarders were defined previously in the "DNS Server Roles" section, but this section goes into more detail on when to configure and use them. Recall how a typical DNS query is processed: A DNS server receives a lookup request from a client and, if it's unable to satisfy the request, a recursive query ensues, starting with a root server. This process works well, but in situations such as the following, referring the query to a forwarder is more efficient:

- *When the DNS server address for the target domain is known*—Suppose that a company has a department working on highly confidential research, and this department is segmented from the rest of the network by routers and firewalls. This department maintains its own domain controllers and DNS servers that aren't part of the organization's domain. However, department members often need access to resources on the network servers. In addition, the research department's DNS servers aren't permitted to contact the Internet. For computers in this department network to resolve names for company resources, a forwarder can be configured on its DNS server that points to a company DNS server. The company DNS server not only resolves queries for company domain resources but also performs recursive lookups for external domains on behalf of the research department's DNS server.
- *When only one DNS server in a network should make external queries*—A network consisting of several DNS servers might want to limit external queries to a single DNS server. This strategy has

several benefits. First, network security can be enhanced by limiting exposure to the Internet to only one server. Second, because a single server is making all the queries to Internet domains, overall DNS performance can be enhanced because the server builds an extensive cache of Internet names. To use this strategy, all DNS servers on the network except the actual forwarder should be configured with the forwarder.

- *When a forest trust is created*—Windows requires DNS name resolution between the two forests involved in a trust relationship. A good way to accomplish this is configuring conditional forwarders in the forest root name servers of both forests that point to each other.
- *When the target domain is external to the network and an external DNS server's address is known*—A company running a small network with limited bandwidth might find that the traffic caused by an internal DNS server's recursive lookups is excessive. The internal DNS server can provide name resolution for all internal resources and forward queries for external names to the DNS server of the company's ISP.

Another type of forwarding is called *conditional forwarding*. Whereas traditional forwarding means "If you can't resolve the query, forward it to this address," conditional forwarding enables administrators to forward queries for particular domains to particular name servers and all other unresolved queries to a different server.

Configuring Traditional Forwarders

Configuring a traditional forwarder is straightforward. Right-click the server node in DNS Manager, click Properties, and click the Forwarders tab (see Figure 2-19).

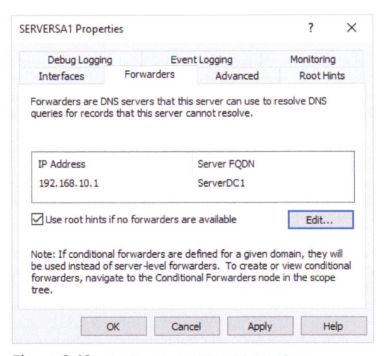

Figure 2-19   Configuring traditional forwarders

After clicking the Edit button, you can enter the IP address or FQDN of DNS servers that unresolved requests should be sent to. If more than one server is specified, they're queried in the order in which they're listed. Additional servers are queried only if no response is received from the first server. By default, the option to use root hints is enabled. If no response is received from any forwarder, the normal recursive lookup process is initiated, starting with a root server. If the *Use root hints if no forwarders are available* check box is cleared and no forwarders respond, the DNS server sends a failure reply to the client.

Configuring Conditional Forwarders

Conditional forwarders are configured in the Conditional Forwarders node in DNS Manager. To create a conditional forwarder, expand the Conditional Forwarders node, and then right-click Conditional Forwarders and click New Conditional Forwarder.

Enter the domain name for which you want to forward queries, and then add IP addresses for DNS servers that are authoritative for the domain. After you enter the IP address, Windows attempts to resolve the IP address to the server's FQDN. You can store the forwarder in Active Directory and have it replicated forestwide or domainwide. With forwarders and/or conditional forwarders configured, the DNS server attempts to resolve DNS queries in this order:

1. From locally stored zone resource records
2. From the DNS cache
3. From conditional forwarders (if configured and the domain name matches)
4. From traditional forwarders (if configured)
5. Recursively by using root hints (only if no traditional forwarder is configured)

Note

Root hints aren't used if a traditional forwarder is configured and responds because after the forwarder is queried, the recursive lookup process is complete.

Root Hints

Root hints consist of a list of name servers preconfigured on Windows DNS servers that point to Internet root servers, which are DNS servers located on the Internet and managed by the Internet Assigned Numbers Authority (IANA). These servers contain lists of name servers that are responsible for top-level domains. Root hints are configured in the Root Hints tab of a DNS server's Properties dialog box.

The root hints data comes from the Cache.dns file in the %*systemroot*%\System32\DNS folder on a DNS server. Why is this file called the root hints file? As you can imagine, if the file is loaded during DNS installation, its data (root server IP addresses, for the most part) can become obsolete quickly. Instead of using the addresses in Cache.dns to perform recursive lookups, Windows selects one of the addresses randomly to request an up-to-date list of root server addresses. Windows then caches this list to use for queries to TLD servers. The Cache.dns file is also updated with this list. The query for the list of root servers occurs each time the DNS server is started. The root hints file can also be copied from another DNS server by clicking the Copy from Server button in the Root Hints tab. In addition, root hints can be updated through the Windows Update service.

You can configure an internal DNS server as a root server if your network is isolated from the public Internet. You do this by creating an FLZ with the "." name. This server is then considered authoritative for all domains. After you create this root zone, your root hints file is disabled, and you can't create any forwarders. Next, configure your other DNS servers to point to your new root server by removing the existing root hints entries and adding an entry that points to your new root server. If you ever decide to remove the root server, simply delete the root FLZ, and Windows prompts you to reload the root hints file.

Round Robin

You can configure load sharing among servers running mirrored services. With a mirrored service, data for a service running on one server is duplicated on another server (or servers). For example, you can set up an FTP server or a web server on servers that synchronize their content with one another regularly. Then configure DNS with multiple A records using the server's name in both records but with each entry configured with a different IP address.

For example, suppose that you have a web server with the FQDN *www.csmtech.local* that's heavily used, responding slowly, and dropping connections. You can set up two additional web servers and configure a mechanism for synchronizing files between the servers. Next, you create two additional DNS A records (you already have one for the existing web server) in the csmtech.local domain that use the same hostname, www, but different IP addresses. The Windows DNS service responds to queries for the www host by sending all three IP addresses in the response but varying the order of IP addresses each time.

This process is called **round robin** because each IP address is placed first in the list an equal number of times. Hosts receiving the DNS response always attempt to use the first address listed. You can improve the results of round robin DNS by configuring a shorter TTL on the three A records so that remote DNS servers don't cache IP addresses for an extended period. By default, the round robin option is enabled on Windows DNS servers, but you can disable it in the Advanced tab of the DNS server's Properties dialog box (see Figure 2-20 in the next section).

> **Note**
>
> Unlike SRV records that have a weight parameter, you can't change the number of times a particular host record is used in round robin.

Recursive Queries

Recursive queries used in DNS queries were defined earlier in The DNS Lookup Process. Typically, resolving DNS queries involves iterative queries to a root server first, then to a TLD server, and finally to an authoritative server for the domain name being resolved. However, a recursive query might involve a forwarder instead in which the DNS server sends a recursive query to the forwarder. The forwarder resolves the query and responds to the DNS server or performs a recursive query starting with a root server. Recursion is enabled on Windows DNS servers by default, but there are two ways to change this setting. The first involves configuring forwarders. As shown previously in Figure 2-14, there's the check box *Use root hints if no forwarders are available*. If this check box isn't selected, recursion is disabled but only if forwarders don't respond. The second is the *Disable recursion (also disables forwarders)* option in the Advanced tab of the DNS server's Properties dialog box (see Figure 2-20). If this check box is selected, the DNS server doesn't attempt to contact any other DNS servers, including forwarders, to resolve a query.

For example, you might want to disable recursion when you have a public DNS server containing resource records for your publicly available servers (web, email, and so forth). The public DNS server is necessary to resolve iterative requests from other DNS servers for your public domain, but you don't want unauthorized Internet users using your DNS server to field recursive client requests.

Event and Debug Logging

When DNS is installed, a new event log is created to record informational, error, and warning events generated by the DNS server. You can configure which event types should be logged in the Event Logging tab of the server's Properties dialog box (shown in Figure 2-21). Events you're likely to find in the DNS Server log include zone serial number (referred to as *version number* in the DNS Server log) changes, zone transfer requests, and DNS server startup and shutdown events. The event log can help you diagnose problems, such as when an error causes the server to stop or keeps it from starting or when communication between servers for replication or zone transfers has failed. When DNS problems are evident and can't be traced easily to misconfiguration, the event log is the first place to look.

DNS Audit Events and Analytic Events

DNS audit events track changes to a DNS server such as when zone or resource changes are made. DNS audit events have an event ID in the range 513 to 582 and can be found in Event Viewer under Applications and Services Logs\Microsoft\Windows\DNS-Server\Audit. Audit events are enabled by

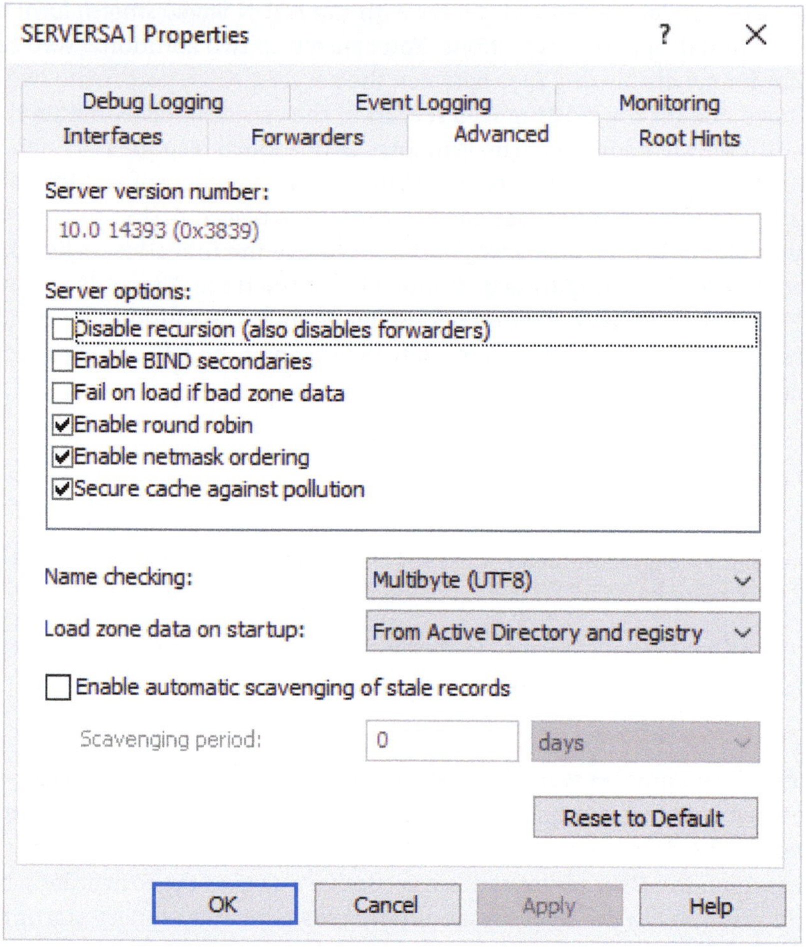

Figure 2-20 The Advanced tab of a DNS server's Properties dialog box

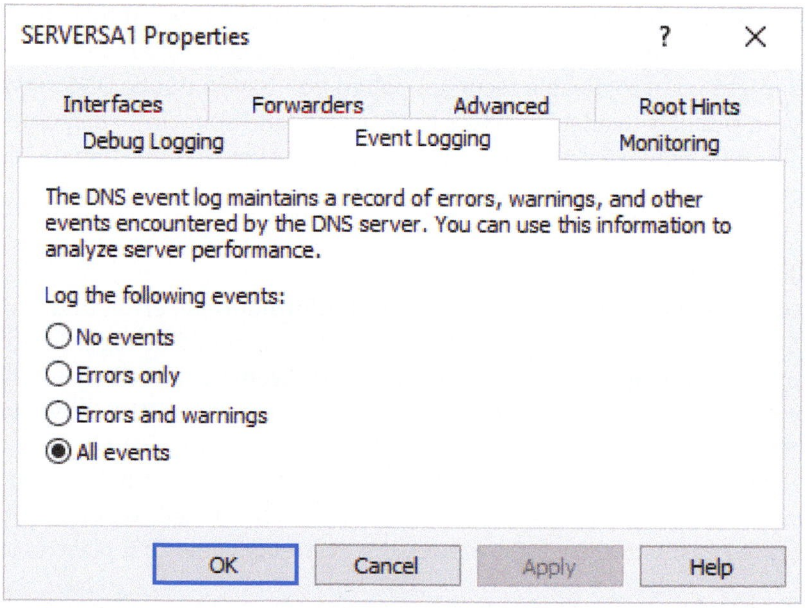

Figure 2-21 The Event Logging tab

default. **DNS analytic events** are created every time DNS sends and receives information. Analytic events are disabled by default, but they can be enabled by opening Event Viewer and navigating to Applications and Services Logs\Microsoft\Windows\DNS-Server. Right-click DNS-Server, point to View, and click Show Analytic and Debug Logs. The Analytical log is shown. Right-click the Analytical log, click Properties, and click Enable Logging. Analytic events have an event ID in the range 257 to 280.

Debug Logging

When serious DNS debugging is warranted, you can enable debug logging in the server's Properties dialog box. Debug logging records selected packets coming from and going to the DNS server in a text file. Figure 2-22 shows the packet-capturing options for debug logging.

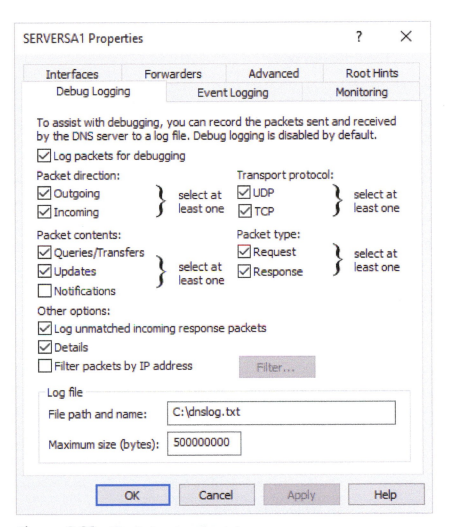

Figure 2-22   The Debug Logging tab

Figure 2-23 shows a sample of debug logging output. The first part of the file is a key to help you interpret the captured data. Each line of the file starting with date and time is a summary of a captured packet. If necessary, you can enable logging of detailed packet contents. The information from debug logging can help you solve problems related to "Web page not found" errors, zone transfer problems, redirect errors, and other DNS operational errors that aren't easy to find by examining the DNS configuration and event logs alone.

```
DNS Server log file creation at 2/16/2017 8:09:33 PM
Log file wrap at 2/16/2017 8:09:33 PM

Message logging key (for packets - other items use a subset of these fields):
        Field #  Information        Values
        -------  -----------        ------
           1     Date
           2     Time
           3     Thread ID
           4     Context
           5     Internal packet identifier
           6     UDP/TCP indicator
           7     Send/Receive indicator
           8     Remote IP
           9     Xid (hex)
          10     Query/Response     R = Response
                                    blank = Query
          11     Opcode             Q = Standard Query
                                    N = Notify
                                    U = Update
                                    ? = Unknown
          12     [ Flags (hex)
          13     Flags (char codes) A = Authoritative Answer
                                    T = Truncated Response
                                    D = Recursion Desired
                                    R = Recursion Available
          14     ResponseCode ]
          15     Question Type
          16     Question Name

2/16/2017 8:09:44 PM 13A8 PACKET  0000021B05EE2170 UDP Rcv 127.0.0.1      4cb0   Q [0001   D   NOERROR] A     (6)isatap(8)testdom1(5)local(0)

2/16/2017 8:09:44 PM 13A8 PACKET  0000021B05EE2170 UDP Snd 127.0.0.1      4cb0 R Q [8385 A DR NXDOMAIN] A     (6)isatap(8)testdom1(5)local(0)

2/16/2017 8:10:10 PM 13A8 PACKET  0000021B067A6170 UDP Rcv 127.0.0.1      0001   Q [0001   D   NOERROR] PTR   (1)1(1)0(1)0(3)127(7)in-addr(4)arpa(

2/16/2017 8:10:10 PM 13A8 PACKET  0000021B067A6170 UDP Snd 127.0.0.1      0001 R Q [8085 A DR NOERROR] PTR   (1)1(1)0(1)0(3)127(7)in-addr(4)arpa(

2/16/2017 8:10:10 PM 13A8 PACKET  0000021B0483B0C0 UDP Rcv 127.0.0.1      0002   Q [0001   D   NOERROR] A     (9)serverdm1(8)mcsa2016(5)local(0)

2/16/2017 8:10:10 PM 13A8 PACKET  0000021B0483B0C0 UDP Snd 127.0.0.1      0002 R Q [8085 A DR NOERROR] A     (9)serverdm1(8)mcsa2016(5)local(0)

2/16/2017 8:10:10 PM 13A8 PACKET  0000021B05EE2170 UDP Rcv 127.0.0.1      0003   Q [0001   D   NOERROR] AAAA  (9)serverdm1(8)mcsa2016(5)local(0)
```

Figure 2-23   Debug logging output

PowerShell Commands for Advanced DNS Server Settings

Table 2-3 lists PowerShell cmdlets you can use to configure some DNS server settings discussed in the preceding sections.

Table 2-3   PowerShell cmdlets for DNS server settings

PowerShell cmdlet	Description	Example
Add-DnsServerForwarder	Adds forwarders to the DNS server's forwarders list	Add-DnsServerForwarder -IPAddress 192.168.0.4
Set-DnsServerForwarder	Changes the settings of an existing forwarder or overwrites the existing list of forwarders	Set-DnsServerForwarder -IPAddress 192.168.0.4
Add-DnsServerRootHint	Adds a root hint to the DNS server	Add-DnsServerRootHint root.mydomain.local -IPAddress 192.168.0.10
Import-DnsServerRootHint	Imports root hints from another DNS server	Import-DnsServerRootHint serverdm1.testdom1.local
Set-DnsServerRecursion	Sets the recursion settings for the DNS server	Set-DnsServerRecursion -Enable $true
Set-DnsServerDiagnostics	Sets debugging and logging parameters	Set-DnsServerDiagnostics -All $true

Activity 2-7: Configuring and Testing Forwarders

Time Required: 10 minutes

Objective: Create and test a conditional forwarder and a regular forwarder.

Required Tools and Equipment: ServerDC1 and ServerSA1

Description: In this activity, you create a conditional forwarder on ServerSA1 that forwards queries for the MCSA2016.local domain. Then you remove the conditional forwarder and configure a standard forwarder.

1. Make sure ServerDC1 is running. On ServerSA1, open the DNS Manager console, if necessary. First, delete the secondary zone you created earlier by right-clicking **MCSA2016.local**, clicking **Delete**, and then clicking **Yes** to confirm.

2. At a PowerShell prompt, type **nslookup ServerDC1.MCSA2016.local** and press **Enter**. The lookup is not successful.

3. In DNS Manager, right-click **Conditional Forwarders** and click **New Conditional Forwarder**. The New Conditional Forwarder dialog box opens. In the DNS Domain text box, type **MCSA2016.local**. Click in the *IP addresses of the master servers* list box, type **192.168.0.1**, and press **Enter** (see Figure 2-24). If you see a red circle with an X, this should not be a problem as long as the name resolves to ServerDC1. Click **OK**.

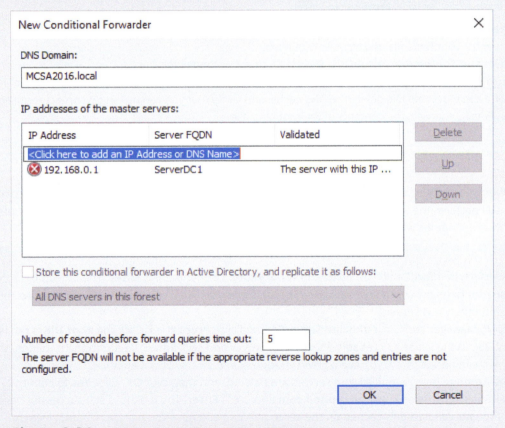

Figure 2-24 Adding a conditional forwarder

4. At the PowerShell prompt, type **nslookup ServerDC1.MCSA2016.local** and press **Enter**. The lookup is successful.

5. Next, you remove the conditional forwarder using PowerShell. Type **Remove-DnsServerZone MCSA2016.local** and press **Enter**. Press **Enter** to confirm. (*Note:* A conditional forwarder is considered a zone, which is why you used a zone cmdlet to delete it.)

6. Type **nslookup ServerDC1.MCSA2016.local** and press **Enter**. The lookup is still successful because the local DNS server cached the information for ServerDC1 from the previous successful lookup. Eventually, the cached information expires, but you delete it in the next step.

7. Type **Clear-DnsServerCache** and press **Enter**. Press **Enter** to confirm. Type **nslookup ServerDC1. MCSA2016.local** and press **Enter**. The lookup is no longer successful.

8. To create a standard forwarder, type **Add-DnsServerForwarder 192.168.0.1** and press **Enter**.

9. In DNS Manager, right-click **ServerSA1** in the left pane and click **Properties**. Click the **Forwarders** tab. You see the forwarder you created in Step 8. (If you don't see the forwarder, close the Properties dialog box, click **ServerSA1**, click the **Refresh** icon, and repeat this step.) Click **Cancel**.

10. Type **nslookup ServerDC1.MCSA2016.local** and press **Enter**. The lookup is successful. If the lookup is not successful, repeat the lookup several times; it can take a while before the forwarder takes effect. (If the lookup is still not successful, in DNS Manager, right-click **ServerSA1**, point to **All Tasks**, and click **Restart**.)

11. To remove the forwarder, type **Remove-DnsServerForwarder 192.168.0.1** and press **Enter** and press **Enter** again to confirm.

12. Stay signed in and continue to the next activity.

Activity 2-8: Working with Root Hints

Time Required: 15 minutes
Objective: View the root hints file and transfer root hints.
Required Tools and Equipment: ServerDC1, ServerSA1, Internet connection
Description: In this activity, you work with the root hints file. Verify that you can contact root servers for DNS lookups, and then delete the root hints file, delete the DNS cache, and verify that you can no longer contact root servers for DNS lookups. Finally, you view the contents of the root hints file.

> **Note** 📎
>
> Your server must be able to access the internet to perform this activity. If you don't have Internet access, you can still perform the steps of this activity so you are familiar with the root hints file, but attempts to look up Internet names will fail.

1. On ServerSA1, in PowerShell type **nslookup www.yahoo.com** and press **Enter**. The lookup is successful because root hints are configured on ServerSA1, and it performed a recursive lookup by contacting root servers and then TLD servers.

2. In the DNS Manager console, right-click **ServerSA1** and click **Properties**. Click the **Root Hints** tab (see Figure 2-25). In the list of 13 root servers, click any server and click **Edit**. DNS attempts to validate the root server. If it can be validated, you see a green check box and an OK. Click **Cancel**.

3. Click the **Remove** button until all root servers are deleted, and then click **OK**. Click **Yes** to confirm.

4. In PowerShell, type **nslookup www.yahoo.com** and press **Enter**. The lookup is still successful because the record for *www.yahoo.com* is cached on the server.

5. Type **Clear-DnsServerCache** and press **Enter**. Press Enter to confirm.

6. Type **nslookup www.yahoo.com** and press **Enter**. The lookup is no longer successful because your server can't contact the root servers.

7. In the DNS Manager console, right-click **ServerSA1** and click **Properties**. Click the **Root Hints** tab, and then click the **Copy from Server** button. In the IP address or DNS name text box, type **192.168.0.1** (the address of ServerDC1), and then click **OK** to repopulate the root server list. Click **OK**.

8. In PowerShell, type **nslookup www.yahoo.com** and press **Enter**. The lookup is successful. (If the lookup times out, try again; DNS must perform the entire recursive lookup process, including loading TLD servers, and this takes some time.)

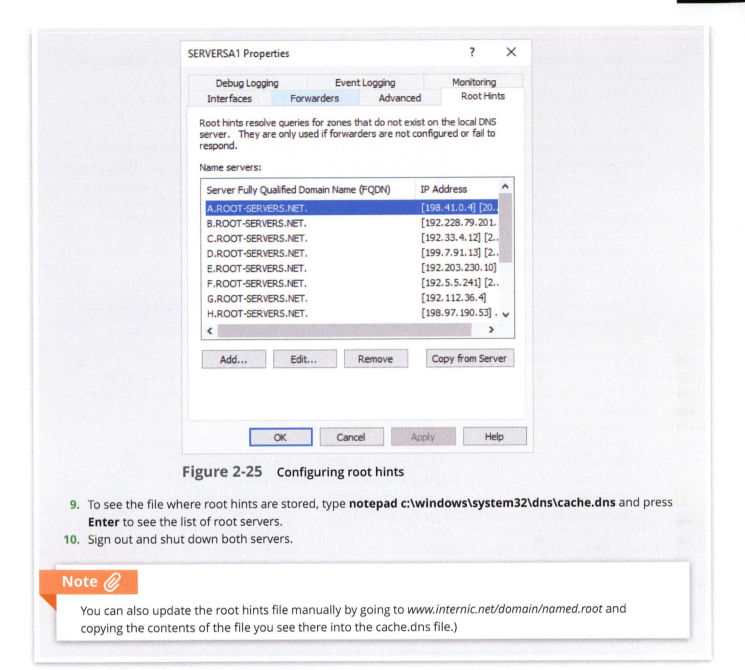

Figure 2-25   Configuring root hints

9. To see the file where root hints are stored, type **notepad c:\windows\system32\dns\cache.dns** and press **Enter** to see the list of root servers.
10. Sign out and shut down both servers.

Note

You can also update the root hints file manually by going to *www.internic.net/domain/named.root* and copying the contents of the file you see there into the cache.dns file.)

Monitoring and Troubleshooting DNS

Q | Certification

- 70-741 – Implement Domain Name System (DNS):
  Create and configure DNS zones and records

A network's DNS structure can range from a basic single-domain, single-server scheme to a complex multidomain scheme with subdomains, secondary zones, forwarders, and stub zones. In addition, many environments use more than one name resolution service; for example, some Windows applications and services depend on WINS and NetBIOS lookups. To troubleshoot a DNS problem, such as a failed name resolution, first you need to know that DNS is actually used for name resolution. After determining that DNS is part of the process, you can begin monitoring DNS if the problem is performance related or troubleshooting DNS queries and zone activities when there are query failures.

DNS Troubleshooting

Windows has several tools to administer, monitor, and troubleshoot DNS server operation, including the following commonly used tools:

- *DNS Manager*—The main DNS configuration tool used to perform most DNS configuration tasks, monitor zone data and the DNS cache's contents, and configure event logging and debug logging.
- `dcdiag /test:dns`—Tests DNS operation on domain controllers and solves problems with DNS forwarders, delegation, dynamic updates, and record registration. particularly useful for checking that SRV resource records are registered by using `dcdiag /test:dns /DnsRecordRegistration`.
- `dnscmd.exe`—A command-line tool that enables administrators to perform basic to advanced configuration and monitoring. Although `dnscmd` is still available in Windows Server 2016, Microsoft recommends transitioning to PowerShell. Some available command options are as follows:
  - `/info`: Displays server information
  - `/statistics`: Displays or clears server statistics
  - `/clearcache`: Clears the server cache
  - `/zoneinfo`: Displays zone information
  - `/directorypartitioninfo`: Lists information about the DNS application directory partition
  - `/enumrecords`: Lists all resource records for a zone
  - `/enumzones`: Lists all zones on the server
  - `/ipvalidate`: Validates a remote DNS server
- *PowerShell*—Dozens of PowerShell commands available for managing DNS. To see a list of all cmdlets for working with DNS, type `Get-Command -Module DnsServer` at a PowerShell prompt. Here are a few cmdlets that are useful for DNS troubleshooting:
  - `Clear-DnsServerCache`: Clears the DNS server cache
  - `Get-DnsServer`: Displays the DNS server configuration
  - `Get-DnsServerDiagnostics`: Displays details about DNS event logging
  - `Get-DnsServerForwarder`: Displays DNS forwarder configuration
  - `Get-DnsServerStatistics`: Shows statistics for the server or a specified zone
  - `Show-DnsServerCache`: Shows the cache records
  - `Test-DnsServer`: Tests the specified DNS server
- *Event Viewer*—Used to view the DNS Server event log (can also be viewed in the Global Logs node in DNS Manager).
- `dnslint`—A command-line program used to check for resource records on a server, verify delegations, verify resource records needed for Active Directory replication, and perform email connectivity tests. You can download `dnslint` from the Microsoft website and find information on using it at *http://support.microsoft.com/kb/321045*.
- `nslookup`—Used to test DNS queries with the default DNS server or a specific DNS server.
- `ipconfig`—Used to check DNS client configuration and the DNS suffix search list; also used to cause a client to register its DNS name and display and delete locally cached DNS records.
- *Performance Monitor*—Found in the Tools menu of Server Manager that allows you to monitor more than 60 performance counters related to DNS. It's used to create a baseline of performance data that you can use for comparison with future readings if DNS performance degrades.
- *Protocol analyzer*—Provides information similar to debug logging but with more flexibility. You can download Network Monitor or its successor Microsoft Message Analyzer from the Microsoft Download Center. An excellent free protocol analyzer, Wireshark, can be downloaded from *www.wireshark.org*.

Before you can begin troubleshooting DNS queries efficiently, you need a clear picture in your mind of the DNS lookup process. Earlier in the chapter, an example was given but didn't factor in variables such as the `Hosts` file, cache, and forwarders. Taking these factors into account, a DNS lookup involves the following steps, starting with the DNS client:

1. Check the local DNS cache, which contains the contents of the `Hosts` file.
2. Query the DNS server with a recursive lookup.

If the address is resolved in Step 1, it's returned to the requesting application, and the process is completed. After Step 2 has been initiated, the query is in the hands of the DNS server being queried, and the following steps occur on this server:

3. Check local zone data.
4. Check locally cached data.
5. Query root server or configured forwarders.

Remember that Step 3 can include primary zones, secondary zones, and stub zones as well as delegated zones. At Step 5, the recursive query process continues until the name is resolved or a "lookup failed" message is returned. At this point, however, the lookup process is largely out of the local administrator's hands.

When troubleshooting a query, you want to eliminate the easy things first, which usually means verifying the client configuration. To verify DNS configuration, use these `ipconfig` options:

- `/all`—Displays IP addresses of the configured DNS servers as well as the DNS suffix search list.
- `/displaydns`—Displays the local DNS cache, which also has the contents of the `Hosts` file.
- `/flushdns`—Deletes the local DNS cache. Sometimes the local cache is big, and spotting a problem could be difficult. Deleting the cache is harmless and can save you from wading through dozens of cached entries.

After these steps, double-check the Hosts file to make sure you didn't miss something when you displayed the local cache.

If everything checks out on the client, your job just got tougher. You'll probably want to proceed with analyzing the DNS server the client uses, including examining the following:

- *Locally cached data*—Stale records can return incorrect results. If you suspect records are stale, delete the cache or the suspect domains in the cache.
- *DNS Server log*—Use Event Viewer to view the DNS Server log or use DNS Manager to view the DNS Events node under the Global Logs node. Both applications record the same information. Look for warning or error messages indicating service failures or zone transfer or replication failures.
- *Verify Active Directory replication*—You can use `dcdiag` or `dnslint` to verify that the correct resource records exist for Active Directory replication. The `dnslint /ad /s localhost /v` command generates a report in HTML format and opens the report in Internet Explorer. Warnings and errors are color coded in the report.
- *Verify SRV records*—Use `dcdiag /test:dns /dnsrecordregistration` to be sure that SRV and other resource records are registered correctly. If SRV records for a DC aren't registered, start and stop the Netlogon service by entering `net stop netlogon` and then `net start netlogon` on the DC. Registered SRV records are stored in %*systemroot*%\System32\Config\netlogon.dns.
- *Verify zone transfers*—The `nslookup` command can request records from an entire zone. On a server hosting secondary zones, use `nslookup` in interactive mode by typing `nslookup` and pressing Enter. Change the server to the primary DNS server for the zone with the `server servername` command, and then use `ls -d domain` (substituting the name of the zone you want to verify for `domain`). If zone transfers aren't working, you get a "query refused" message. Otherwise, the zone data is displayed. Also, verify the settings in the Zone Transfer tab on the primary server to make sure the secondary server is in the server list or that any server can request zone transfers.
- *Verify zone delegations*—Use the `dnslint /d delegatedzone /s IP_of_authoritative_server` command to produce a report to verify the delegation.
- `ping`—Use `ping` to verify connectivity to remote DNS servers that might be part of the lookup process.
- *Verify PTR records*—It's easy to forget to create the zones needed for PTR records and make sure that PTR records are created when entering a new A record manually. Certain processes require reverse

lookups, so make sure that critical servers have PTR records as well as A records. To do this, check for the reverse lookup zone in DNS Manager, or use `nslookup` to do a forward lookup for the host's IP address first, and then do a reverse lookup using the returned IP address. If the lookup fails, the PTR record doesn't exist.

The procedures and tools described in this section should provide you with the knowledge you need to start the DNS troubleshooting process and solve at least minor problems. More complex problems take some perseverance with these tools and perhaps debug logging and protocol analysis. The better you understand the DNS process, the more quickly you can solve problems. Use debug logging and a protocol analyzer periodically to examine DNS operation when it's working correctly, and save these results. This way, you have something to compare with troubleshooting output when problems happen.

Chapter Summary

- DNS is based on a hierarchical naming structure and a distributed database. DNS names use the structure *host.domain.top-level-domain* or perhaps *host. subdomain.domain.top-level-domain*. This naming structure is the fully qualified domain name (FQDN).

- DNS can be described as an inverted tree with the root domain at the top, top-level domains branching off the root, and domains and subdomains branching off top-level domains. The entire DNS tree is called the *DNS namespace*. Every domain has one or more authoritative name servers.

- Hostnames are associated with an IP address, so when a client looks up the name *www.microsoft. com*, the DNS server returns an IP address. Second-level domains can also have subdomains, such as the technet in *technet.microsoft.com*.

- DNS lookups involve iterative and recursive queries. Most lookups start from the DNS resolver with a recursive query to a DNS server. The DNS server satisfies the query or performs a series of iterative queries, starting with a root server.

- DNS servers can perform one or more of the following roles: authoritative server, forwarder, conditional forwarder, and caching-only server.

- A *forwarder* is a DNS server to which other DNS servers send requests they can't resolve themselves. A conditional forwarder is a DNS server to which other DNS servers send requests targeted for a specific domain.

- DNS is an integral part of most network communication sessions between computers. A properly configured and efficiently functioning DNS, therefore, is essential for a well-functioning network. DNS can be installed automatically during Active Directory installation or as a separate server role.

- You might need to install a new zone manually if the DNS server isn't a DC when you create a stub zone, when you create a secondary zone, and when you create a zone for an Internet domain.

- A zone can be a forward lookup zone or a reverse lookup zone. FLZs contain host records primarily. Reverse lookup zones contain PTR records.

- DNS databases consist of the following zone types: primary zone, secondary zone, and stub zone. Primary and stub zones can also be Active Directory–integrated zones.

- Resource records can be static or dynamic. There are A, AAAA, CNAME, PTR, MX, NS, SRV, and SOA records.

- Dynamic records are often created with a DHCP server. Static records can be created by using DNS Manager or PowerShell cmdlets.

- SOA records contain information about a zone, including its serial number and timers used for zone transfers. NS records specify the name of a server that's authoritative for the zone.

- NS records specify FQDNs and IP addresses of authoritative servers for a zone. Each zone that's created has an NS record, which points to an authoritative server for that zone.

- There are two types of zone transfer: full zone transfers and incremental zone transfers. A full zone transfer was the only transfer method in older DNS versions prior to Windows Server 2003. Both the master and slave DNS servers must support incremental zone transfers to use them.

- Windows Internet Name Service (WINS) is a legacy name service used to resolve NetBIOS names, sometimes referred to as *single-label names*. You should configure your DNS server to use WINS only if you have older Windows clients, such as Windows 9x, and non-Windows clients that use only DNS.

- Advanced DNS settings include configuring forwarders, root hints, round robin, recursive queries, and logging.

- Tools for monitoring and troubleshooting DNS include `dcdiag`, `dnscmd`, `dnslint`, `nslookup`, `ipconfig`, PowerShell cmdlets, Performance Monitor, and protocol analyzers. You need to understand the DNS query process to troubleshoot DNS problems efficiently.

Key Terms

A record
AAAA record
authoritative server
caching-only DNS server
CNAME record
conditional forwarder
DNS analytic event
DNS audit event
DNS client
DNS namespace
DNS resolver
Domain Name System (DNS)
Dynamic DNS (DDNS)

forward lookup zone (FLZ)
forwarder
fully qualified domain name (FQDN)
GlobalNames zone (GNZ)
glue A record
hostname
host record
iterative query
MX record
primary zone
PTR record
recursive query

referral
resource records
reverse lookup zone (RLZ)
root hints
root server
round robin
secondary zone
stub zone
top-level domain (TLD) server
zone
zone transfer

Review Questions

1. Which of the following best describes DNS? (Choose all that apply.)
   a. Hierarchical database
   b. Flat database
   c. Monolithic database
   d. Distributed database

2. Which of the following accurately represents an FQDN?
   a. host.top-level-domain.subdomain.domain
   b. domain.host.top-level-domain
   c. host.subdomain.domain.top-level-domain
   d. host.domain.top-level-domain.subdomain

3. What specific type of DNS query instructs a DNS server to process the query until the server replies with an address that satisfies the query or with an "I don't know" message?
   a. Recursive
   b. Referral
   c. Iterative
   d. Resolver

4. What type of zone should you create that contains records allowing a computer name to be resolved from its IP address?
   a. RLZ
   b. FLZ
   c. Stub
   d. TLD

5. A resource record containing an alias for another record is which of the following record types?
   a. A
   b. CNAME
   c. NS
   d. PTR

6. What type of resource record is necessary to get a positive response from the command `nslookup 192.168.100.10`?
   a. A
   b. CNAME
   c. NS
   d. PTR

7. When a DNS server responds to a query with a list of name servers, what is the response called?
   a. Iterative
   b. Recursive
   c. Referral
   d. Resolver

8. You're scanning the local cache on a DNS client, and you come across the notation ::1. What does it mean?
   a. The cache is corrupt.
   b. It's the IPv6 localhost address.
   c. It's the link-local address.
   d. It's a reverse lookup record.

9. You have decided to install the DNS server role on Nano Server. What specific type of zone configuration is not supported when using the DNS on Nano Server?
   a. Standard directory-based
   b. Active Directory–integrated
   c. Replication-integrated
   d. Standard file-based

10. Your company just opened a small branch office where 10 computer users will work. You have installed a single Windows Server 2016 computer configured as a member server for basic file and print server needs. Users require DNS to access the Internet and to resolve names of company resources. You decide to install DNS on the existing server. Which of the following types of installations makes the most sense?
    a. A primary server hosting a standard zone
    b. An Active Directory–integrated zone hosting the zone in which the server is a member
    c. A caching-only DNS server
    d. A server that's a forwarder

11. You have a DNS server outside your corporate firewall that's a standalone Windows Server 2016 server. It hosts a primary zone for your public Internet domain name, which is different from your internal Active Directory domain names. You want one or more of your internal servers to be able to handle DNS queries for your public domain and to serve as a backup for the primary DNS server outside the firewall. Which configuration should you choose for internal DNS servers?
    a. A standard secondary zone
    b. A standard stub zone
    c. A forwarder to point to the primary DNS server
    d. An Active Directory–integrated stub zone

12. Which of the following is true about stub zones? (Choose all that apply.)
    a. They're authoritative for the zone.
    b. Their records are updated by the primary server automatically.
    c. They can't be Active Directory integrated.
    d. They contain SOA and NS records.

13. The DNS server at your headquarters holds a standard primary zone for the abc.com domain. A branch office connected by a slow WAN link holds a secondary zone for abc.com. Updates to the zone aren't frequent. How can you decrease the amount of WAN traffic caused by the secondary zone checking for zone updates?

   a. In the SOA tab of the zone's Properties dialog box, increase the minimum (default) TTL.
   b. In the Advanced tab of the DNS server's Properties dialog box, increase the expire interval.
   c. In the SOA tab of the zone's Properties dialog box, increase the refresh interval.
   d. In the Zone Transfers tab of the SOA Properties dialog box, decrease the retry interval.

14. What type of record does DNS create automatically to resolve the FQDN of an NS record?
    a. PTR   c. Glue A
    b. CNAME   d. Auto SRV

15. You want a DNS server to handle queries for a domain with a standard primary zone hosted on another DNS server, and you don't want the server to be authoritative for that zone. How should you configure the server? (Choose all that apply.)
    a. As a secondary zone on the DNS server
    b. As a stub zone on the DNS server
    c. As a forwarder on the DNS server
    d. As zone hints for the primary zone

16. You're in charge of a standard primary zone for a large network with frequent changes to the DNS database. You want changes to the zone to be transmitted as quickly as possible to all secondary servers. What should you configure and on which server?
    a. Configure DNS notifications on the primary zone server
    b. Configure DNS recursion on the secondary zone servers
    c. Configure round robin on the primary zone server
    d. Configure a smaller default TTL for the primary zone server

17. You have several hundred client computers using WINS to resolve names of some enterprise servers. Many of the client computers are laptops used to connect to the network remotely. You're trying to eliminate WINS from your network to reduce the number of protocols and services you must support. With the least administrative effort, what can you do that allows you to stop using WINS yet still allows clients' computers to use a single-label name for accessing enterprise servers?
    a. Create a GlobalNames zone and add CNAME records for enterprise servers
    b. Create a Hosts file containing servers' names and addresses and upload this file to each client that needs it

c. Configure each client computer with the correct domain suffix

d. Create a stub zone and add CNAME records for each enterprise server

18. You manage the DNS structure on your network. The network security group has decided that only one DNS server should contact the Internet. Under no circumstances should other servers contact the Internet for DNS queries even if the designated server is down. You have decided that the DNS server named DNS-Int should be the server allowed to contact the Internet. How should you configure your DNS structure to accommodate these requirements?

a. On each DNS server except DNS-Int, configure a forwarder pointing to DNS-Int. Configure DNS-Int as a forwarder by enabling forwarded requests in the Forwarders tab of the server's Properties dialog box.

b. On each DNS server except DNS-Int, configure a root hint to point to DNS-Int and delete all other root hints. Configure a root zone on DNS-Int.

c. On each DNS server except DNS-Int, configure a forwarder pointing to DNS-Int. Disable the use of root hints if no forwarders are available. No changes are necessary on DNS-Int.

d. On each DNS server except DNS-Int, in the Advanced tab of the server's Properties dialog box, disable recursion. No changes are necessary for DNS-Int.

19. You have a zone containing two A records for the same hostname, but each A record has a different IP address configured. The host records point to two servers hosting a high-traffic website, and you want the servers to share the load. After some testing, you find that you're always accessing the same web server, so load sharing isn't occurring. What can you do to solve the problem?

a. Enable the load sharing option on the zone

b. Enable the round robin option on both A records

c. Enable the load sharing option on both A records

d. Enable the round robin option on the server

20. Which is the correct order in which a DNS client tries to resolve a name?

a. Cache, DNS server, Hosts file

b. Hosts file, cache, DNS server

c. Cache, Hosts file, DNS server

d. DNS server, cache, Hosts file

21. You want to verify whether a PTR record exists for the server1.csmtech.local host, but you don't know

the server's IP address. Which of the following commands should you use to see whether a PTR record exists for server1.csmtech.local?

a. `ping -a server1.csmtech.local` and then `ping IPAddress` returned from the first `ping`

b. `nslookup server1.csmtech.local` and then `nslookup IPAddress` returned from the first `nslookup`

c. `dnscmd /PTR server1.csmtech.local`

d. `dnslint /PTR server1.csmtech.local`

22. You have two DCs, each with three Active Directory–integrated zones. You're getting inconsistent DNS lookup results and suspect there is a problem with Active Directory replication. What tool can you use to investigate the problem? (Choose all that apply.)

a. `nslookup`

b. `dnscmd`

c. `dcdiag`

d. `ipconfig`

23. You have just finished setting up your DNS infrastructure, and the DNS process seems to be working well. You want to be able to create a baseline of performance data so that if slowdowns occur later, you have information for comparison purposes. Which tool should you use?

a. dnscmd.exe

b. Debug logging

c. Performance Monitor

d. Event logging

24. You're having trouble with logons and other domain operations in your domain named *csmtech.local*. You want to verify that your domain clients can find domain controllers. Which of the following can you do? (Choose all that apply.)

a. Use the `dcdiag /test:dns / DnsRecordRegistration` command

b. Look at the *%systemroot%*\System32\Config\ netlogon.dns file

c. Look at the *%systemroot%*\System32\dns\ cache.dns file

d. Use the `nslookup -type = CNAME -domain=csmtech.local` command

25. You have decided that you need to change the setting of an existing DNS forwarder. Which of the following PowerShell cmdlets will allow you to accomplish this task?

a. `Add-DnsServerForwarder`

b. `Import-DnsServerForwarder`

c. `Set-DnsServerRecursion`

d. `Set-DnsServerForwarder`

Critical Thinking

The following activities give you critical thinking challenges. Case Projects offer a scenario with a problem to solve for which you supply a written solution.

Case Project 2-1: Resolving Names of Internet Resources

You have an Active Directory–integrated domain named. csmtech.local, with two DCs that are DNS servers. You also have an Internet presence with its own domain name, csmpub.com, and a DNS server that's not part of an Active Directory domain. You want the DCs to be able to resolve the names of csmpub.com resources and to act as backup for the csmpub.com DNS database. What can you do to achieve these goals? Describe the steps you would take.

Case Project 2-2: Restricting Registration

You manage an Active Directory domain named csmtech.local. The DNS server is a DC for csmtech.local and hosts a standard primary DNS zone for csmtech.local. You have noticed resource records in the zone from computers that aren't domain members. What can you do to ensure that only domain members can update resource records in the zone?

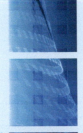

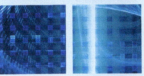

CHAPTER 3

CONFIGURING ADVANCED DNS

After reading this chapter and completing the exercises, you will be able to:

Manage DNS zones

Configure DNS zone storage

Implement DNS policies

Configure DNS security

Manage and monitor the DNS server

Domain Name System (DNS) is a critical part of every network today. It translates computer and domain names to addresses, allowing network users to access network resources by name rather than by address. In this chapter, you learn how to manage DNS zones, the main structural component of DNS. Zones hold resource records, which are the data component of DNS. Because DNS in an Active Directory environment can be stored in a traditional text file or in an Active Directory partition, you learn the advantages of using an Active Directory-integrated zone and how to tune replication between DNS servers. DNS is a popular target for attacks. If DNS is compromised, the results can range from denial of service to redirection of DNS clients to rogue servers. In this chapter, you explore several methods to secure and protect DNS. In addition, you learn about managing DNS with DNS policies, delegated administration, and performance monitoring and tuning.

Table 3-1 summarizes what you need for the hands-on activities in this chapter.

Table 3-1	Activity requirements	
Activity	**Requirements**	**Notes**
Activity 3-1: Resetting Your Virtual Environment	ServerDC1, ServerDM1	
Activity 3-2: Using Zone Delegation	ServerDC1, ServerDM1	
Activity 3-3: Configuring DNS Aging and Scavenging	ServerDC1	
Activity 3-4: Creating a Standard Stub Zone	ServerDC1, ServerDM1	
Activity 3-5: Converting a Standard Zone to an Active Directory-Integrated Zone	ServerDC1	
Activity 3-6: Configuring DNSSEC	ServerDC1	
Activity 3-7: Displaying DNS Zone Level Statistics	ServerDC1	

Managing DNS Zones

 Certification

- 70-741 – Implement Domain Name System (DNS):
  Install and configure DNS servers

After you create a zone and some resource records, you might want to configure some management settings, depending on the type of zone. You might want to configure zone delegation to spread the DNS load if you have domains and subdomains defined in a zone, for example. If your network has frequent changes to IP addresses and hosts coming online and going offline often, you might need to configure zone scavenging to delete stale resource records. These settings and others are discussed in the following sections.

Zone Delegation

Zone delegation is the transfer of authority for a subdomain to a new zone, which can be on the same server or another server. Typically, you use zone delegation when a business unit in an organization is large enough to warrant its own subdomain and has the personnel to manage its own DNS server for the subdomain. Even if the business unit won't be managing the subdomain, delegating the handling of the subdomain to other servers might make sense for performance reasons.

When a subdomain has been delegated to a zone on another server, the DNS server hosting the parent zone maintains only an NS record pointing to the DNS server hosting the delegated zone. When the parent DNS server receives a query for the subdomain, it refers the query to the DNS server hosting the subdomain.

Note

If IP address changes are made to the name servers hosting the delegated zone, the NS records on the server hosting the parent domain must be updated manually.

Automatically Delegated Zones on Domain Controllers

You might have noticed a zone called msdcs.MCSA2016.local on the domain controller ServerDC1. Every Windows domain zone has an _msdcs subdomain, which holds all the SRV records for Microsoft-hosted services, such as the global catalog, LDAP, and Kerberos. In the forest root domain, this subdomain is delegated to a new zone on the same server, not on a different server. For example, in DNS Manager in Figure 3-1, the msdcs.MCSA2016.local zone is under Forward Lookup Zones, and you also see _msdcs under the MCSA2016.local folder (highlighted in the figure). The _msdcs zone under the MCSA2016.local folder is grayed out, indicating that it has been delegated. It contains a single NS record pointing to the server it has been delegated to.

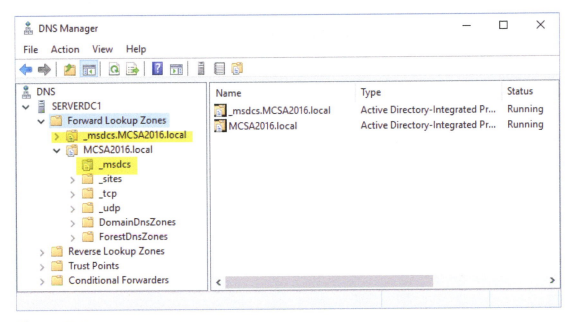

Figure 3-1   The delegated _msdcs zone

The reason _msdcs is created as a subdomain is so that Windows clients and other clients specifically looking for a Microsoft service can query DNS for the service in the _msdcs subdomain. Remember: It's possible for non-Microsoft OSs to be operating in the same domain, and they might offer some of the same services, such as Kerberos and LDAP. The reason _msdcs is delegated to a separate zone in the forest root domain is to change the zone's replication scope from domain-wide to forest-wide. Because the forest root contains specialized functions, such as global catalog servers, replication of this domain's SRV records to the entire forest is critical. If the _msdcs subdomain isn't delegated to its own zone, the records it contains are replicated according to the parent zone's setting, which is often only domain-wide, not forest-wide. Zone replication scope is discussed later in this chapter in the section "Active Directory Zone Replication Scope."

Aside from using zone delegation in Active Directory, you can use it when you have a domain with several subdomains. The burden of handling the primary domain and subdomains could be substantial for both the server and administrator. You can delegate some or all of the subdomains to other servers (and perhaps administrators, too) to share the overall DNS load.

For example, suppose you have a zone for your primary domain named mybigcorp.local. Within mybigcorp.local, you have a subdomain named *widgets*. The widgets.mybigcorp.local zone is hosted by default under mybigcorp.local. Suppose you have many resources such as websites, online apps, and so forth in the widgets subdomain and the DNS server hosting mybigcorp.local is suffering performance problems because of the many queries for resources in the widgets subdomain. You can delegate the widgets subdomain to a different server so in the future, all queries to widgets.mybigcorp.local are referred to the delegated server, thereby offloading the mybigcorp.local DNS server.

Configuring Zone Scavenging

When a dynamic resource record is created in a DNS zone, the record receives a time stamp based on the server's time and date. A static record can also be time-stamped if you enable the option to delete the record when it becomes stale. When a resource using dynamic DNS goes offline, it should contact the DNS server to delete its resource records. Unfortunately, this process doesn't always occur, and records that are no longer valid are left in the database. In fact, Windows clients usually delete their DNS records only when they release or renew their IP addresses, not when they shut down.

Over time, these stale resource records can degrade server performance, provide incorrect information to DNS queries, and generally make DNS less reliable and efficient. A **stale resource record** is a DNS record that is no longer valid either because the resource is offline for an extended period or permanently or because the resource's name or address has changed. To prevent stale resource records from accumulating in the DNS database, you need to enable scavenging. **Scavenging** is the process of periodically scanning the records in each zone and deleting stale records.

Enabling Scavenging

To occur, scavenging must be enabled in two places. First, it must be enabled on the server, which allows scavenging to occur on all zones where it's enabled. To do this, right-click the server icon in DNS Manager, click Properties, and click the Advanced tab. Then click the *Enable automatic scavenging of stale records* check box (highlighted in Figure 3-2). You set the scavenging period in units of days or hours. The default value is 7 days. The scavenging period determines how often the server scans the zones on which scavenging is enabled and deletes stale records.

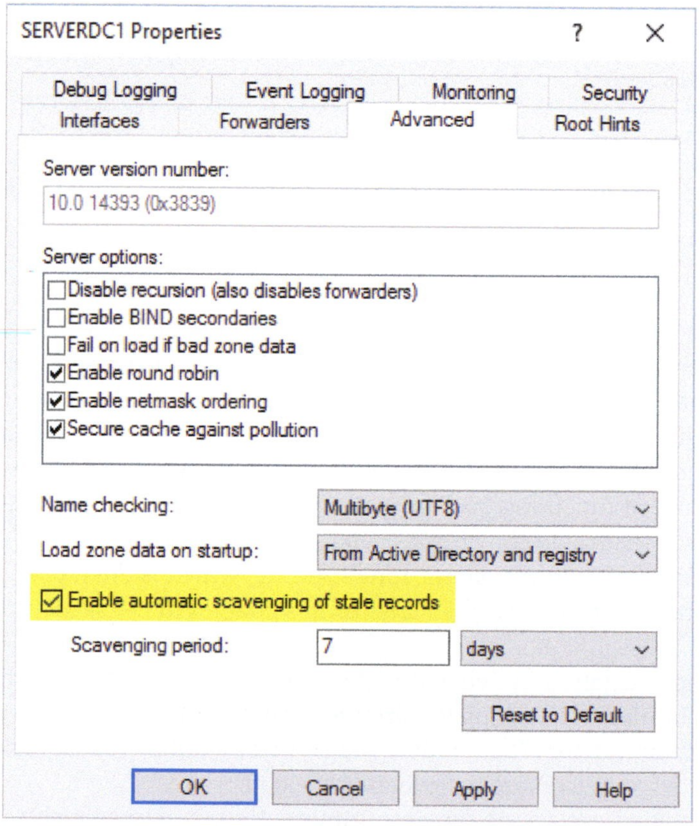

Figure 3-2   Enabling scavenging on the server

After you have enabled scavenging on the server, you enable it on zones. You can do this for all zones at once in DNS Manager by right-clicking the server icon and clicking Set Aging/Scavenging for All Zones. If you choose this option, you can set scavenging parameters for all zones at once. Scavenging parameters include No-refresh interval and Refresh interval, discussed in the following list.

You can also enable scavenging for specific zones. Scavenging parameters set at the zone level override those set at the server level. The dialog box for setting scavenging parameters for a particular zone is the same as for setting them at the server level for all zones. To open this dialog box for a particular zone, right-click a zone and click Properties, click the General tab, and then click the Aging button. By default, scavenging is disabled. When it's enabled (see Figure 3-3), the server checks the zone file for stale records periodically and deletes those meeting the criteria for a stale record.

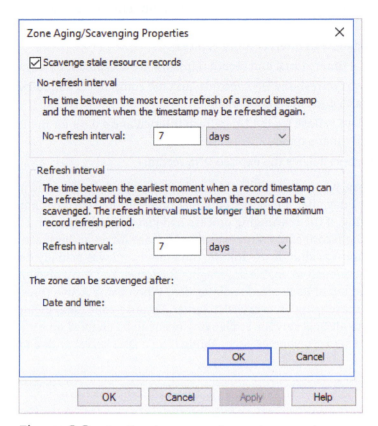

Figure 3-3   Configuring zone aging and scavenging

The options in the Zone Aging/Scavenging Properties dialog box are as follows:

- *Scavenge stale resource records*—When this check box is selected, scavenging is enabled for the zone or for all zones if you are setting it at the server level. Remember that scavenging must be enabled on the server in the Advanced tab of the DNS server's Properties dialog box. By default, scavenging on the server isn't enabled.
- *No-refresh interval*—To prevent DNS record time stamps from being updated too often, the No-refresh interval timer starts when a DNS record has been updated (refreshed). During this interval, DNS doesn't accept a time stamp change to the record. Time stamp changes can occur, for example, when a computer renews its IP address lease from DHCP, but no actual changes to DNS data occur. The No-refresh interval prevents excessive replication of DNS data because even a time stamp change requires record replication. The default No-refresh interval setting is 7 days.
- *Refresh interval*—After the No-refresh interval expires, the Refresh interval timer begins. During this interval, time stamp changes are accepted. If the Refresh interval timer expires, the record is considered stale and available for scavenging. If the record is refreshed during this period, the No-refresh interval timer begins again. The default Refresh interval setting is 7 days.
- *The zone can be scavenged after*—This setting is the earliest time and date that zone data can be scavenged. It's based on the current time and date plus the refresh interval. To see this information, you must have the Advanced View setting enabled in DNS Manager. This value is not shown when configuring aging and scavenging properties as the server level.

The process by which DNS records are aged and scavenged isn't obvious from reading descriptions of the No-refresh interval and Refresh interval timers, so a step-by-step example is in order, in which these timers are set to their default 7 days:

1. A DNS client computer gets a new IP address from a DHCP server and registers an A and a PTR record with the DNS server. Each record has its own set of timers, but because the records were created at the same time, the interval timers in this example apply to both the A and PTR records.

2. The No-refresh interval timer starts, and no time stamp refreshes are accepted for the record for 7 days.

3. After 7 days, the No-refresh interval timer expires.

4. The Refresh interval timer starts, and record refreshes are accepted for 7 days.

5. The computer doesn't refresh the DNS records, and the computer is shut down 1 day after the Refresh interval starts and isn't started again.

6. After a total of 14 days (7 days for the No-refresh interval and 7 days for the Refresh interval), the Refresh interval timer expires.

7. The scavenging process deletes the expired DNS record.

The scavenging process, when enabled, is also set for 7 days by default. In the preceding example, the computer was shut down 1 day after the Refresh interval timer began, so 6 days elapsed before the record was available for scavenging. If the scavenging process had just finished a scavenging run before the refresh interval expired, the record could remain in the database for an additional 7 days, totaling 13 days from the time the computer was shut down and the time the record was actually deleted.

As mentioned, it's not enough to enable scavenging for zones. You must also enable scavenging on the server in the Advanced tab of its Properties dialog box. When using Active Directory-integrated zones, you don't need to enable scavenging on every DNS server. Because zone data, including aging/scavenging parameters, is replicated to all DNS servers, scavenging needs to be enabled on only one server. Scavenging does consume server resources, so enabling it on a DNS server with a fairly light workload is best.

Using Stub Zones

A **stub zone** is a special type of zone containing only one SOA record, one or more NS records, and the necessary glue A records to resolve NS records. A stub zone isn't authoritative for the zone. Essentially, a stub zone points to another DNS server that is authoritative for the zone. A stub zone can be an Active Directory-integrated or a standard zone. If it's Active Directory integrated, its records, as in other Active Directory-integrated zones, are updated regularly through Active Directory replication. If the stub zone is a standard zone, the SOA and NS records are updated through zone transfers. The reasons for using stub zones include the following:

- *Maintenance of zone delegation information*—If changes are made to addresses of the name servers hosting a delegated zone, the NS records on the parent DNS server must be updated manually. If a stub zone is created for the delegated zone on the parent DNS server, the NS records are updated automatically. The use of a stub zone effectively eliminates manual maintenance of the delegated zone's NS records.

- *In lieu of conditional forwarders*—If changes are made to addresses of domain name servers that are conditionally forwarded, the IP addresses for the conditional forwarder records must be changed manually. If a stub zone is created instead of using a conditional forwarder, the NS records in the stub zone are updated automatically. In addition, because stub zones can be Active Directory integrated, you need to create the stub zone only once on a DC and it's replicated to all other DNS servers running on DCs.

- *Faster recursive queries for frequently used zones*—When a DNS server receives a query for a resource record in the stub zone, it can make a recursive query by using the stub zone's NS records instead of accessing a root server. So, if a zone is frequently queried, for example, for resources in the network of a corporate partner, using a stub zone will provide faster access to those resource records.

- *Distribution of zone information*—When a network consists of many zones, distribution of these zones is necessary to make the entire DNS namespace accessible throughout the network. Typically, this distribution requires secondary zones or Active Directory–integrated zones. Stub zones can be used strategically to reduce the number of secondary zones or full Active Directory–integrated zones; reducing the number of these zones cuts down network traffic caused by zone transfers and replication.

Activity 3-1: Resetting Your Virtual Environment

Time Required: 5 minutes
Objective: Reset your virtual environment by applying the InitialConfig checkpoint or snapshot.
Required Tools and Equipment: ServerDC1, ServerDM1, ServerSA1
Description: Apply the InitialConfig checkpoint or snapshot to ServerDC1, ServerDM1, and ServerSA1.

1. Be sure all three servers are shut down. In your virtualization program, apply the InitialConfig checkpoint or snapshot to both servers.
2. When the snapshot or checkpoint has finished being applied, continue to the next activity.

Activity 3-2: Using Zone Delegation

Time Required: 10 minutes
Objective: Create a zone and a delegation for the new zone.
Required Tools and Equipment: ServerDC, ServerDM1
Description: You create a zone on ServerDC1 named csmtech.local, then install DNS on ServerDM1. Then, you create a zone on ServerDM1 named pub.csmtech.local, which is a subdomain of csmtech.local located on ServerDC1. Next, on ServerDC1, you delegate the pub subdomain to ServerDC1.

1. Sign in to ServerDC1 as **Administrator** and open a PowerShell window.
2. Type **Add-DnsServerPrimaryZone csmtech.local -ZoneFile csmtech.local.dns** and press **Enter**.
3. Sign in to ServerDM1 as the domain **Administrator** and open a PowerShell window.
4. Type **Install-WindowsFeature DNS -IncludeManagementTools** and press **Enter**.
5. Type **Add-DnsServerPrimaryZone pub.csmtech.local -ZoneFile pub.csmtech.local.dns** and press **Enter**. This creates the subdomain that you will delegate from ServerDC1 to ServerDM1.
6. For testing purposes, create a host (A) record in the pub.csmtech.local zone **server1** with IP address 192.168.0.160. Type **Add-DnsServerResourceRecord -A -ZoneName pub.csmtech.local -Name server1 -Ipv4Address 192.168.0.160** and press **Enter**.
7. On ServerDC1, open DNS Manager. Click to expand **Forward Lookup Zones**. Click to select **csmtech.local**, then right-click **csmtech.local**, and click **New Delegation**. In the New Delegation Wizard, click **Next**.
8. In the Delegated Domain Name window, type **pub** in the Delegated domain text box. (The fully qualified domain name (FQDN) pub.csmtech.local is filled in for you.) Click **Next**.
9. In the Name Servers window, click **Add**. In the New Name Server Record dialog box, type **ServerDM1. MCSA2016.local**, and click **Resolve**. The IP address is shown as resolved in the Validated column. Click **OK**. Click **Next**, and then **Finish**.
10. The pub subdomain is displayed with a gray folder icon under csmtech.local to indicate that it has been delegated. Click the **pub** folder, if necessary. You see an NS record that points to ServerDM1.
11. On ServerDC1, in the PowerShell windows type **nslookup** and press **Enter**, then type **server1.pub.csmtech.local**, and press **Enter**. An address is returned. ServerDC1 sees that the pub subdomain is delegated to ServerDM1 and uses the NS record to contact ServerDM1 to retrieve the queried record. Close the PowerShell window.
12. Stay signed in to both servers, and leave DNS Manager open for the next activity.

Activity 3-3: Configuring DNS Aging and Scavenging

Time Required: 10 minutes

Objective: Configure aging and scavenging.

Required Tools and Equipment: ServerDC1

Description: In this activity, you enable and configure aging and scavenging to reduce the number of stale resource records.

1. On ServerDC1, open DNS Manager. Click **View**, and then click **Advanced** to enable advanced view settings.

2. In the left pane of DNS Manager, right-click **ServerDC1** and click **Properties**. Click the **Advanced** tab, and click the **Enable automatic scavenging of stale records** check box, which enables scavenging on the server. Leave the scavenging period set to **7 days**, and then click **OK**.

3. Right-click **ServerDC1** in the left pane and click **Set Aging/Scavenging for All Zones**. Click the **Scavenge stale resource records** check box to enable scavenging on all zones. Leave the No-refresh and Refresh interval timers set at **7 days**, and then click **OK**.

4. In the Server Aging/Scavenging Confirmation dialog box, click **Apply these settings to the existing Active Directory-integrated zones**, and then click **OK**. Click the **Refresh** icon in DNS Manager so that the information you look at next reflects the change you just made.

5. Right-click the **MCSA2016.local** zone and click **Properties**. Click the **Aging** button. The settings for the zone are the same as you set in Step 3. Notice also that the Date and time text box is filled in with a value approximately 7 days from now, which is the earliest any records will be scavenged (see Figure 3-4). Click **OK** twice.

6. Stay signed in to ServerDC1 and continue to the next activity.

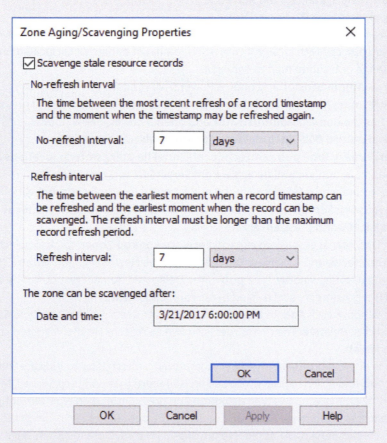

Figure 3-4   Zone Aging/Scavenging Properties dialog box

Activity 3-4: Creating a Standard Stub Zone

Time Required: 10 minutes
Objective: Create a standard stub zone.
Required Tools and Equipment: ServerDC1, ServerDM1
Description: In this activity, you create a stub zone on ServerDM1 that points to the MCSA2016.local zone on ServerDC1.

1. Make sure that ServerDC1 is running. On ServerDM1, open DNS Manager.
2. In DNS Manager, right-click **Forward Lookup Zones** and click **New Zone**.
3. In the Welcome to the New Zone Wizard window, click **Next**.
4. In the Zone Type window, click the **Stub zone** option button, and read the description. Click **Next**.
5. In the Zone Name window, type **MCSA2016.local**, and then click **Next**.
6. In the Zone File window, accept the default filename, **MCSA2016.local.dns**, and then click **Next**.
7. In the Master DNS Servers window, type **192.168.0.1** in the Master Servers text box, and press **Enter**. The address is resolved to ServerDC1. Click **Next**.
8. In the Completing the New Zone Wizard window, click **Finish**. The new zone is displayed in the right pane of DNS Manager, with the Type column set to Stub.
9. In the right pane, double-click **MCSA2016.local** to see the SOA, NS, and the glue A record (see Figure 3-5). In the Data column, the SOA and NS records contain the FQDN for ServerDC1. The A record contains the IP address of ServerDC1.

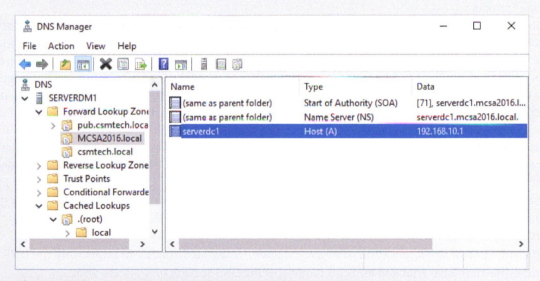

Figure 3-5   A stub zone with SOA, NS, and glue A records

10. Now, you'll test the stub zone. On ServerDM1 in a PowerShell window, type **nslookup** and press **Enter**. Type **server 127.0.0.1** and press **Enter** so ServerDM1 uses itself for DNS lookups.
11. Type **serverdm2.mcsa2016.local** and press **Enter**. The name is resolved because the stub zone for mcsa2016.local points to ServerDC1, which has the A record for ServerDM2.
12. Stay signed in to both servers and continue to the next activity.

Configuring DNS Zone Storage

Certification

- 70-741 – Implement Domain Name System (DNS):
  Create and configure DNS zones and records

As you have learned, standard zones are stored in text files, and Active Directory–integrated zones are stored in the Active Directory database. With standard zones, there aren't many options for how zone data is stored, except perhaps the path and the filename. Active Directory–integrated zones, however, do have some storage configuration options.

Zone replication is the transfer of zone changes from one DNS server to another. For a standard zone, you've learned that zone replication is called *zone transfer*. When DNS is installed on a domain controller, zone data is replicated automatically to other DCs. With standard zones, you need to create secondary zones on each DNS server that will host the zone. With Active Directory–integrated zones, a zone is created only once on a DC, and the zone is created and replicated automatically on every other DC in the zone replication scope.

For the purposes of zone replication, review the advantages that an Active Directory–integrated zone has over a standard zone:

- *Automatic zone replication*—When DNS is installed on a new domain controller, zones are replicated to the new DNS server automatically. Standard zones require manual configuration of zone transfers.
- *Multimaster replication and update*—Multiple domain controllers can be configured as primary DNS servers, and changes can be made on any of these domain controllers. Multimaster replication provides fault tolerance because no single server is relied on to make DNS changes. Changes to DNS are replicated to all other DCs in the domain configured as DNS servers. In contrast, a standard zone has a single primary DNS server (and possibly one or more secondary servers), which is the only server where changes to the database can be made. If a standard primary server fails, DNS changes can't be made until another primary server is brought online.
- *Secure updates*—DNS can be configured to allow dynamic DNS updates only from DNS clients that are authenticated to Active Directory. This option prevents rogue clients from introducing false information into the DNS database.
- *Use permissions to restrict which users can modify zone data*—You can control which users or groups can change zone data by changing the permissions to the zone in the Security tab of the zone's Properties dialog box.
- *Efficient replication*—Replication of Active Directory-integrated zones can target only the DNS record properties that have changed and can target specific DNS servers to replicate with.

Active Directory Zone Replication Scope

The **zone replication scope** determines which Active Directory partition the zone is stored in and to which DCs the zone information is replicated (see Figure 3-6). An **Active Directory partition** is a special file that Active Directory uses to store domain information. You can change the replication scope, if necessary, after a zone is created by selecting one of these options:

- *To all DNS servers running on domain controllers in this forest*—Stores the zone in the forest-wide DNS application directory partition called ForestDNSZones. This partition is created when DNS is installed on the first DC in the forest.
- *To all DNS servers running on domain controllers in this domain*—Stores the zone in the domain-wide DNS application directory partition DomainDNSZones. It's the default option for new zones.

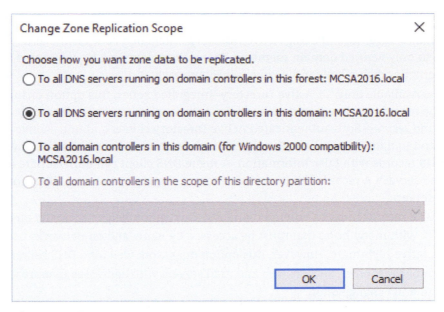

Figure 3-6   Selecting a zone replication scope

- *To all domain controllers in this domain (for Windows 2000 compatibility)*—Stores the zone in the domain partition, which is used to store most Active Directory objects. DNS zone information is replicated to all other DCs in the domain regardless of whether the DNS Server role is installed. This option is the only one available for Windows 2000 DCs and should be selected if DNS information must be replicated to Windows 2000 DNS servers.
- *To all domain controllers in the scope of this directory partition*—A custom DNS application partition must be created before selecting this option, and the partition must use the same name on each DC hosting DNS that should participate in replication. Use this option to limit which DNS servers receive zone data to control replication traffic. By default, this option is grayed out and disabled until you have created a custom DNS application directory partition, discussed next.

Controlling Replication to Specific Domain Controllers

The *To all domain controllers in the scope of this directory partition* option for configuring the zone replication scope requires additional explanation and configuration. Normally, you want zones to be replicated to all other DCs that are DNS servers, but in some circumstances, you might want to limit replication to specific DCs. For example, you have set up a zone for testing purposes to be used by only a few departments in an Active Directory site that has three DCs. You can limit replication to just these three DCs so that zone data doesn't have to travel across WAN links because the zones aren't needed by users in other sites.

To limit replication to specific DCs, create a custom DNS application directory partition on each DC to which the zone should be replicated. The partition must have the same name on each DC. After you create the custom partition, the option to replicate to specific domain controllers in the Change Zone Replication Scope dialog box is enabled. To create a custom DNS application directory partition, use one of the following commands:

- At a PowerShell prompt, run the `Add-DnsServerDirectoryPartition` cmdlet.
- At a command prompt, enter the `dnscmd.exe /CreateDirectoryPartition` command. (Be aware that `dnscmd.exe` might be deprecated in future versions of Windows Server).

Dynamic Updates

As mentioned, a major advantage of using Active Directory–integrated zones is the ability to limit dynamic updates to only verified domain members. Dynamic updates can be configured in one of three ways from the Properties dialog box for the zone (see Figure 3-7):

- *Secure only*—Available only for Active Directory–integrated zones, this option ensures that the host initiating the record creation or update has been authenticated by Active Directory.
- *Nonsecure and secure*—Both authenticated Active Directory clients and non–Active Directory clients can create and update DNS records. This option isn't recommended because it allows rogue clients to create DNS records with false information. A rogue DNS client can impersonate a server by updating the server's A record with its own IP address, thereby redirecting client computers to a fraudulent server.
- *None*—All DNS records must be entered manually. This option helps secure the environment, but on a network with many hosts that must be accessed by name and on networks using DHCP, it's an administrative nightmare. However, this option does work well for a DNS server that manages names for public resources, such as web and mail servers with addresses that are usually assigned statically and don't change often.

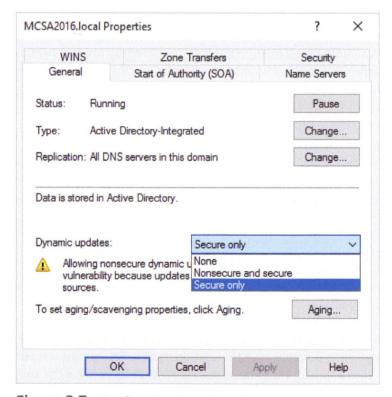

Figure 3-7   Configuring dynamic updates

What if you have a standard primary zone and want to ensure that dynamic updates are made only by known clients? The only option is to change the zone to an Active Directory–integrated zone. To do so, right-click the zone, click Properties, and in the General tab, click the Change button next to Type. Click the *Store the zone in Active Directory* check box. This option is available only on DNS servers that are domain controllers. The General tab also includes the option to disallow dynamic updates altogether so that all records are created manually.

Note 📎

Another form of DNS security, Domain Name System Security Extension (DNSSEC), is mostly intended to protect DNS clients from invalid DNS data supplied by rogue or poisoned DNS servers. DNSSEC is covered later in this chapter.

Configuring Unknown Record Support

A new feature of DNS in Windows Server 2016 is the ability to support resource records of a type unknown to the DNS server on Windows Server 2016. This feature, referred to simply enough as **unknown record support**, allows you to create resource records that are in a format unknown to Windows DNS server but that the Windows DNS server will return in response to client queries. However, the DNS server will not perform any record-specific processing such as scavenging. Unknown record types are defined by RFC 3597. You can add an unknown record to a zone using the `Add-DnsServerResourceRecord` PowerShell cmdlet with the `-Unknown` option.

Note 📎

Unknown record types are defined by RFC 3597, which you can learn more about at *https://tools.ietf.org/html/rfc3597*.

Activity 3-5: Converting a Standard Zone to an Active Directory-Integrated Zone

Time Required: 5 minutes
Objective: Convert a standard zone to an Active Directory-integrated zone.
Required Tools and Equipment: ServerDC1
Description: In this activity, you convert csmtech.local from a standard zone to an Active Directory-integrated zone and configure secure dynamic updates.

1. On ServerDC1, open DNS Manager.
2. In the left pane of DNS Manager, right-click **csmtech.local** and click **Properties**.
3. In the General tab of the csmtech.local Properties dialog box, click the **Dynamic updates** list arrow. You see only two options: *Nonsecure and secure* and *None*. There's no option to specify only secure updates until the zone is stored in Active Directory.
4. Click the **Change** button next to Type. Click the **Store the zone in Active Directory** check box, and then click **OK**. Click **Yes** to confirm.
5. Click the **Dynamic updates** list arrow. Click the **Secure only** option that's available now, and then click **OK**. Now only secure dynamic updates (and manual changes by an administrator) are allowed to the csmtech.local zone.
6. Continue to the next activity.

Implementing DNS Policies

Certification

- 70-741 – Implement Domain Name System (DNS):
  Install and configure DNS servers

Windows Server 2016 adds a feature called **DNS Policy** that allows you to manage DNS traffic, filter queries, and load balance your applications based on a number of criteria. The following list describes some of the ways you can use DNS policies:

- *Create query filters*—Create filters that configure the DNS server response based on the type and source of the query, including the ability to filter malicious queries.
- *Manage subnet-based traffic*—Create policies that respond to queries based on the client's IP address, for example, responding with the address of the host nearest to the client.
- *Balance the load of applications*—Create policies to balance the load among multiple instances of an application based on factors such as the subnet of the client or the time of day.
- *Specify split-brain DNS*—Create Zone Scopes to configure the DNS server to respond to clients based on whether the client is on the internal network or the external network (Internet).

DNS policies can be applied at the server level or zone level, depending on the type of policy and your requirements. There are two primary types of policy: query resolution policies and zone transfer policies. A **query resolution policy** specifies how DNS queries are handled by the DNS server. For example, you can specify whether the server should allow or deny a query based on the source IP address of the query. A **zone transfer policy** specifies whether a zone transfer is allowed. For example, you can allow or deny zone transfers to particular subnets.

As mentioned, DNS policies can be applied at the server level or zone level. In either case, you are likely to need to work with some new DNS objects that you can create and manage using PowerShell cmdlets:

- *Client subnet*—A **client subnet** is just what it sounds like, a named subnet that has a value in the format a.b.c.d/y, for example, 192.168.0.0/24. A client subnet can be assigned a name such as PhoenixSubnet, for example, `Add-DnsServerClientSubnet -Name Phoenix -IPv4Subnet "192.168.0.0/24"`. The PhoenixSubnet can then be used in other DNS policy cmdlets that use the subnet as a parameter.
- *Zone scope*—A **zone scope** is a subset of a zone where a zone can contain multiple zone scopes and each zone scope has its own set of resource records. In addition, a resource record can be in multiple zone scopes. Zone scopes are discussed in more detail later in this section.
- *Recursion scope*—A **recursion scope** defines which queries will use DNS recursion. For example, on a multihomed server, you can specify that only queries received on the interface connected to the internal network will use recursion. Recursion scopes are discussed in more detail later in this section.

Note

Although this chapter provides a few examples of using DNS policies for traffic management and recursion control, there are several different criteria that can be used to configure DNS policies. The objectives of Microsoft Exam 70-744 cover the use of DNS policies to manage and secure network traffic in more depth. Also, please refer to *https://technet.microsoft.com/en-us/windows-server-docs/networking/dns/deploy/dns-policies-overview* for a detailed description of the commands and criteria that can be used to create DNS policies.

Configuring Zone Scopes

For zone-level policies, you need to create one or more zone scopes. One use of DNS policies is to ensure that resource records of resources close to the client are returned by the DNS server. By doing so, clients use resources that are physically closer to them. For example, suppose you have two datacenters, one in Phoenix and one in Boston. You want to ensure that Phoenix users are directed to the resources in the Phoenix datacenter and Boston users are directed to resources in the Boston datacenter, but you don't want to have different names specified for these resources. The following example PowerShell cmdlets create two subnets and then add two zone scopes to the MCSA2016.local zone. Next, a host resource record named "www" is added to each zone scope. Finally, a policy for each location is created:

1. Create the client subnets.

```
Add-DnsServerClientSubnet -Name Phoenix -Ipv4Subnet 192.168.0.0/24
Add-DnsServerClientSubnet -Name Boston -Ipv4Subnet 192.168.1.0/24
```

2. Create the zone scopes.

```
Add-DnsServerZoneScope -ZoneName MCSA2016.local -Name PhoenixZScope
Add-DnsServerZoneScope -ZoneName MCSA2016.local -Name BostonZScope
```

3. Add a resource record to each zone scope; note the name of the record, "www," is the same in both zone scopes, but the IP address is different.

```
Add-DnsServerResourceRecordA -ZoneName MCSA2016.local -ZoneScope
   PhoenixZScope -Name www -Ipv4Address 192.168.0.200
Add-DnsServerResourceRecordA -ZoneName MCSA2016.local -ZoneScope
   BostonZScope -Name www -Ipv4Address 192.168.1.200
```

4. Create the DNS policies for each location. In the `-ClientSubnet` parameter, the first argument is the operator that can be either `"eq"` for "equal" or `"ne"` for "not equal." In the ZoneScope parameter, the value 1 indicates the weight for the Zone Scope. The weight can be used for load balancing. For example, if you want to load balance between the Phoenix and Boston locations, you could use: `-ZoneScope "PhoenixZScope,4;BostonZScope,1"`, which causes the records in the Phoenix Zone Scope to be returned 4 times for every 1 time for the Boston Zone Scope.

```
Add-DnsServerQueryResolutionPolicy -Name PhoenixPol -ZoneName
   MCSA2016.local -Action Allow -ClientSubnet "eq,Phoenix"
   -ZoneScope "PhoenixZScope,1"
Add-DnsServerQueryResolutionPolicy -Name BostonPol -ZoneName
   MCSA2016.local -Action Allow -ClientSubnet "eq,Boston" -ZoneScope
   "BostonZScope,1"
```

Note

DNS policies, zone scopes, and client subnets can be configured and viewed only using PowerShell.

Configuring DNS Recursion Scopes

If you enable or disable recursion from the Advanced tab of the DNS server Properties dialog as discussed in Chapter 2, you are enabling or disabling recursion for the entire server. However, if you have a DNS server that has an internal interface and an external, Internet-facing interface, you may want to enable recursion for your internal DNS clients while disabling it for external (Internet) clients. You can accomplish this using DNS recursion scopes. A **DNS recursion scope** is a DNS feature that allows you to specify which DNS queries will use recursion and which will not.

In the following example, the first cmdlet turns off recursion for the entire server by specifying the root (.) domain, which is the same as clicking the Disable recursion (also disables forwarders) option in the Advanced tab. The second cmdlet creates a new recursion scope, InternalNetwork, and enables recursion for that scope. The third cmdlet creates a DNS query resolution policy that associates the InternalNetwork scope with queries received on the network interface with IP address 192.168.0.2.

```
Set-DnsServerRecursionScope -Name . -EnableRecursion $false
Add-DnsServerRecursionScope -Name "InternalNetwork"
  -EnableRecursion $true
Add-DnsServerQueryResolutionPolicy -Name "RecursionPolicy"
  -Action Allow -ApplyOnRecursion -RecursionScope "InternalNetwork"
  -ServerInterfaceIP  "eq,192.168.0.2"
```

Note 📎

You can also base the recursion policy on the subnet address of the clients by using the `ClientSubnet` parameter instead of the `-ServerInterfaceIP` parameter.

Configuring DNS Security

Ⓠ **Certification**

- **70-741 – Implement Domain Name System (DNS):**
  Install and configure DNS servers

DNS is a common target for attacks because it figures so prominently in network transactions. The types of attacks on DNS include spoofing, DNS cache poisoning, denial of service, domain registration hijacking, and man-in-the-middle attacks, to name a few. The goal of most of these attacks is to compromise DNS so that users are unable to access network resources or are redirected to a different resource than was intended, often one with nefarious intentions. The techniques discussed in the following sections are steps that most DNS administrators should take to help prevent or at least mitigate the effectiveness of many DNS attacks.

Domain Name System Security Extension

Domain Name System Security Extension (DNSSEC) is a suite of features and protocols for validating DNS server responses. DNSSEC provides DNS clients with three critical methods to ensure that data they receive from DNS queries is accurate and secure:

- *Origin authentication of DNS data*—Verifies that the DNS server replying to a query is authentic
- *Authenticated denial of existence*—Allows verifying that a resource record couldn't be found
- *Data integrity*—Verifies that data hasn't been tampered with in transit

With DNSSEC in place, DNS is much less susceptible to spoofing and DNS cache poisoning. DNSSEC can secure zones by using a process called **zone signing** that uses digital signatures in DNSSEC-related resource records to verify DNS responses. Verifying the digital signature assures a DNS client that the DNS response is identical to the information published by the authoritative zone server. Zones that are signed using DNSSEC have the following additional resource records:

- *DNSKEY*—The **DNSKEY** record is the public key for the zone that DNS resolvers use to verify the digital signature in Resource Record Signature records.

- *RRSIG*—A **Resource Record Signature (RRSIG)** key contains the signature for a single resource record, such as an A or an MX record. RRSIG records are returned with the requested resource records so that each returned record can be validated.
- *NSEC*—**Next Secure (NSEC)** A DNSSEC record returned when the requested resource record doesn't exist. Used to fulfill the authenticated denial of existence security feature of DNSSEC.
- *NSEC3*—**Next Secure 3 (NSEC3)** records are alternatives to NSEC records. NSEC3 can prevent zone-walking, which is a technique of repeating NSEC queries to get all the names in a zone. Zones can use NSEC or NSEC3 records but not both.
- *NSEC3PARAM*—**Next Secure 3 (NSEC3) Parameter** records are used to determine which NSEC3 records should be included in responses to queries for nonexistent records.
- *DS*—**Delegation Signer (DS)** records hold the name of a delegated zone and are used to verify delegated child zones.

Zone signing uses public key cryptography. To secure a zone with a digital signature, a key master must be designated. It can be a Windows DNS server that's authoritative for the zone. Two keys must be generated:

- *Key-signing key*—A **key-signing key (KSK)** has a private and public key associated with it. The private key is used to sign all DNSKEY records, and the public key is used as a trust anchor for validating DNS responses. A **trust anchor** is usually the DNSKEY for the zone but can also be a DS key for a delegated zone.
- *Zone-signing key*—A **zone-signing key (ZSK)** is a public and private key combination stored in a certificate used to sign the zone. The KSK is used to sign the ZSK to validate it.

Trust anchors are distributed from authoritative DNS servers to nonauthoritative DNS servers that request DNSSEC validation. For example, when a client queries its local DNS server for a record in a zone not held by the local DNS server, the local DNS server must query the authoritative DNS server for that zone. When it does so, if the zone is protected by DNSSEC, the returned record contains the trust anchor (the DNSKEY or DS record) with the necessary public key to validate the record.

Note

DNSSEC doesn't provide confidentiality of data; that is, data isn't encrypted, only authenticated.

Validating DNS Responses

When a client requests a resource record from a zone secured with DNSSEC, the following steps take place:

1. A DNS client sends a query to the local DNS server configured in its network interface settings. If the client is DNSSEC aware, that information is included in the query message.
2. The local DNS server sends a query to a root server and top-level domain (TLD) server, as necessary. The message contains information indicating that the DNS server is DNSSEC aware.
3. The local DNS server receives a response containing the IP address of a DNS server authoritative for the zone.
4. The local DNS server sends a query to the authoritative DNS server. The message indicates that the DNS server is DNSSEC aware and the server can validate signed resource records.
5. The authoritative DNS server returns the resource record information requested plus the RRSIG records needed to validate the response.
6. The local DNS server returns the response to the DNS client with an indication of whether the response was validated.

Configuring DNSSEC

To configure DNSSEC in Windows Server 2016, use the following procedure:

1. In DNS Manager, right-click the zone you want to configure, point to DNSSEC, and click Sign the Zone to start the Zone Signing Wizard. Click Next to begin.

2. You have three options for signing a zone (see Figure 3-8):

   - Customize zone-signing parameters: Allows you to choose the details for signing the zone, including the DNS server that will serve as the key master and the KSK and ZSK parameters.
   - Sign the zone with parameters of an existing zone: Use the zone-signing parameters from an existing signed zone. If you choose this option, click Next and then Finish, and zone signing is completed.
   - Use default settings to sign the zone: Default values are configured for zone signing, and you can review them before continuing. If you choose this option, click Next and then Finish.

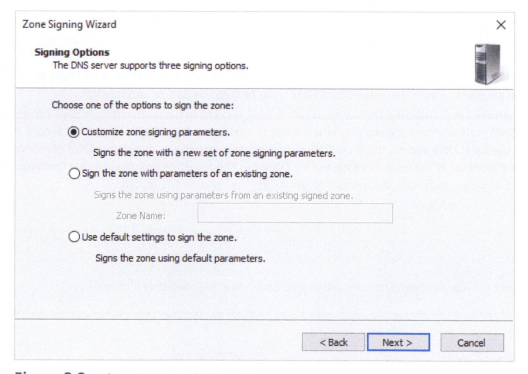

Figure 3-8   Choosing zone-signing options

3. If you selected *Customize zone-signing parameters* in Step 2, continue with the wizard; otherwise DNSSEC configuration is complete for this zone. The next step is to choose the Key Master. By default, the current DNS server is chosen as the key master, but you can choose another primary server for the zone.

4. Next, you configure parameters for the KSK (see Figure 3-9). You can use the default values or select new values. A globally unique ID (GUID) is generated automatically. You can configure between one and three KSKs.

5. Next, you configure the parameters for the ZSK; the window looks similar to the one for configuring the KSK.

6. The next step is to select NSEC or NSEC3 for authenticated denial of existence. NSEC3 is the default option.

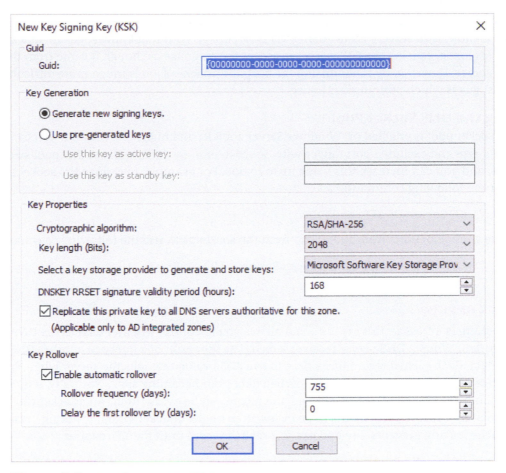

Figure 3-9   Configuring the KSK

7. Next, you specify how trust anchors are distributed. Trust anchors aren't required on authoritative DNS servers. You should distribute trust anchors only if other DCs provide nonauthoritative responses for the zone.

8. Last, you configure signing and polling parameters. You can accept the defaults for most situations. If you don't need to change any default values in the wizard, you could have selected the option to use the default settings in Step 2.

The DNS Socket Pool

The **DNS socket pool** is a pool of port numbers used by a DNS server for DNS queries. It protects against DNS cache poisoning by enabling a DNS server to randomize the source port when performing DNS queries. **DNS cache poisoning** is an attack on DNS servers in which false data is introduced into the DNS server cache, causing the server to return incorrect IP addresses. At best, this attack keeps clients from accessing requested network resources; at worst, clients are redirected to an attacker's server. By using a random source port chosen from the socket pool, an attacker must successfully guess the source port of a query issued by the server along with a random transaction ID.

As you've learned, DNS uses recursive queries. A client issues a query for a network resource, such as the www.cengage.com host record. The DNS server first looks in its local zone database or cache. If the record can't be found, the DNS server queries other DNS servers until it finds a DNS server that's authoritative for the cengage.com zone. This is where DNS cache poisoning comes in. If an attacker knows that the DNS server has requested the record for www.cengage.com, it can issue its own response to the query first, providing false information. The DNS server caches the information for www.cengage.com, and the current client query and future queries are resolved to the IP address supplied by the attacker.

However, to issue a valid response, the attacker must know what port the DNS server used to issue the query. By default, DNS servers issue queries via UDP port 53. With that knowledge, an attacker can send the response, causing the DNS server to accept the response as though it came from the authoritative server. However, by randomizing the port, the attacker's job is much more difficult because he or she must guess which port number to use.

Configuring the DNS Socket Pool

By default, a socket pool is enabled on Windows Server 2008 R2 and higher servers, but you can configure the socket pool size and excluded port ranges with `dnscmd.exe`. By default, the socket pool size is 2500 port numbers, and you can increase this value up to 10,000. For example, to change the socket pool size to 5000, enter the following command:

```
dnscmd /Config /SocketPoolSize 5000
```

To exclude a range of ports from 100 to 500 from the socket pool, use the following command:

```
dnscmd /Config /SocketPoolExcludedPortRanges 100-500
```

DNS Cache Locking

DNS cache locking is a DNS security feature that allows you to control whether data in the DNS cache can be overwritten. When a DNS server receives a record as the result of a query to another DNS server, it caches the data. Each cached record has a time to live (TTL) value that tells the server when the record should be deleted from the cache, preventing cached data from becoming stale. Normally, if updated information about the cached record is received, the record can be overwritten. An attacker can falsify update information, causing cached data to be overwritten by the attacker's data, resulting in cache poisoning. Cache locking prevents any updates to a cached record until the TTL expires.

Configuring DNS Cache Locking

DNS cache locking is configured as a percentage of the TTL. For example, if the cache locking value is set to 50, the cached data can be overwritten when the TTL is 50% expired. If the cache locking value is 100, the data can never be overwritten. Starting with Windows Server 2008 R2, cache locking is enabled and set at 100% by default. To change the cache locking value, use `dnscmd.exe`. For example, to change the value so that records can be overwritten when the TTL is 75% expired, use one of the two commands; the second command is a PowerShell cmdlet:

```
dnscmd /Config /CacheLockingPercent 75

Set-DnsServerCache -LockingPercent 75
```

> **Tip** ⓘ
>
> To see the current cache locking percentage, replace `/Config` with `/Info` in the preceding `dnscmd` command. In PowerShell, use `Get-DnsServerCache`.

Enabling Response Rate Limiting

A new DNS Server role feature in Windows Server 2016, **Response Rate Limiting (RRL)**, mitigates a type of distributed denial of service (DDoS) attack called a *DNS amplification attack*. A **DNS amplification attack** uses public DNS servers to overwhelm a target with DNS responses by sending DNS queries with spoofed IP addresses. The attacker sends DNS queries to multiple public DNS servers with the spoofed address of the target's system. The DNS servers send the responses to the queries to the target system. Because the query responses look like legitimate data, these types of attacks can be difficult to prevent with firewalls.

Response Rate Limiting examines queries to the DNS server and flags them when many queries received in a short period of time have a similar source address and query parameters. RRL will cause the DNS server to limit the number of responses sent to the same subnet when certain parameters have been met. By default, RRL is disabled, but it can be enabled with the following PowerShell cmdlet with the default parameters:

```
Set-DNSServerRRL
```

There are a number of parameters that can be set to change when RRL flags queries as suspect and begins limiting responses. To see the default values and the status of RRL, use the following PowerShell cmdlet (see Figure 3-10):

```
Get-DNSServerRRL
```

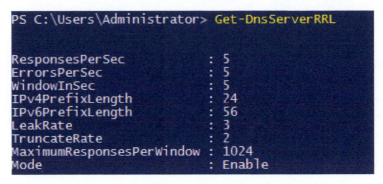

Figure 3-10   Viewing the status of Response Rate Limiting

Here are descriptions of some of the RRL parameters you can configure:

- *ResponsesPerSec*—Sets the maximum number of identical responses the DNS server will send a client in 1 second. The default value is 5.
- *ErrorsPerSec*— Sets the maximum number of error responses the DNS server will send a client in 1 second. The default value is 5.
- *WindowInSec*— Sets the time period in seconds over which RRL measures and averages queries from the same subnet. If queries from the same subnet occur more frequently, RRL is applied. The default value is 5.
- *IPv4PrefixLength*—Used to determine the number of bits to match in the IP address of the query to determine whether queries are from the same subnet. The default is 24. For example, with a value of 24, IP addresses 172.16.1.10 and 172.16.1.100 are considered to be from the same subnet because the first 24 bits of the address match. However, 172.16.1.10 and 172.16.2.10 are considered to be from different subnets. The same description applies to IPv6 addresses, but the default value is 56.
- *LeakRate*—When RRL is in effect for a particular query, the value that determines how many queries should be dropped before sending a response anyway. This allows the coincidental legitimate query to be responded to amid a flood of spoofed queries. The default is 3 and can range from 2 to 10. A value of 0 disables this feature.
- *Mode*—Possible values are Enable, Disable, and LogOnly. When this parameter is omitted with the `Set-DNSServerRRL` cmdlet, RRL is enabled. Use `-Mode Disable` to disable RRL. Use `-Mode LogOnly` if you want to log RRL information but do not want to prevent DNS from responding when RRL is triggered.

DNS-Based Authentication of Named Entities

DNS-based Authentication of Named Entities (DANE) is a new feature in Windows Server 2016 that is used to provide information about the certification authority (CA) used by your domain when a client is requesting DNS information for your domain. This feature prevents man-in-the-middle attacks in which a cached DNS entry for your domain is altered by an attacker, pointing the client to a server run by the attacker. If the attacker sends a forged certificate from a different CA, the client will reject it. DANE uses Transport Layer Security Authentication (TLSA) records, which you can add to a DNS zone using the `Add-DnsServerResourceRecord` cmdlet with the following syntax:

```
Add-DnsServerResourceRecord -ZoneName MCSA2016.local -TLSA
  -CertificateUsage DomainIssuedCertificate
```

This command is not complete, as you also need to include certificate data and additional parameters, but those aspects of DANE are beyond the scope of this book. DANE is just another security measure available in Windows Server 2016 to protect your data and your identity.

Activity 3-6: Configuring DNSSEC

Time Required: 10 minutes
Objective: Configure DNSSEC.
Required Tools and Equipment: ServerDC1
Description: In this activity, you configure DNSSEC and test it.

1. On ServerDC1, open DNS Manager.
2. Click to expand **Forward Lookup Zones**, and click to select **MCSA2016.local**. Then, right-click **MCSA2016.local**, point to **DNSSEC**, and click **Sign the Zone** to start the Zone Signing Wizard. In the welcome window, click **Next**.
3. In the Signing Options window, leave the default option **Customize zone signing parameters** selected. (Note that you aren't changing any default options, so you could select the *Use the default settings* option to sign the zone, but this way you can see the configurable options.) Click **Next**.
4. In the Key Master window, leave the default option that selects ServerDC1 as the key master, and click **Next**.
5. In the Key Signing Key (KSK) window, read the information about the KSK, and then click **Next**. Click **Add**. In the New Key Signing Key (KSK) dialog box, accept the defaults, and click **OK**. Click **Next**.
6. In the Zone Signing Key (ZSK) window, read the information about the ZSK, and then click **Next**. Click **Add**. In the New Zone Signing Key (ZSK) dialog box, accept the defaults, and click **OK**. Click **Next**.
7. In the Next Secure (NSEC) window, accept the default option **Use NSEC3**, and then click **Next**.
8. In the Trust Anchors (TAs) window, accept the default **Enable automatic update of trust anchors on key rollover**, and then click **Next**.
9. In the Signing and Polling Parameters window, accept the default settings, and click Next. Review the selected options, and then click **Next** and **Finish**.
10. In DNS Manager, click the **Refresh** icon to see the RRSIG, DNSKEY, and NSEC3 resource records that were created.
11. Now you remove DNSSEC. In DNS Manager, right-click **MCSA2016.local**, point to **DNSSEC**, and click **Unsign the Zone**. Click **Next** and then **Finish**. Click the **Refresh** icon in DNS Manager to see that the DNSSEC-related records are gone.
12. Continue to the next activity.

Managing and Monitoring the DNS Server

 **Certification**

- 70-741 – Implement Domain Name System (DNS):
  Install and configure DNS servers

As you have learned, DNS plays a vital role in almost all network transactions. This chapter wraps up the coverage of DNS by discussing some additional management tasks including delegated administration as well as performance monitoring and tuning.

Delegated Administration

In a large network, there might be several zones, both Active Directory-integrated and standard zones, and dozens of DNS servers. As you have learned, there's a lot to keep up with to make sure DNS is running well on your network. Members of the Domain Admins or Enterprise Admins group have full access to manage the DNS service, but you might want to delegate DNS administration to an employee without allowing the broader domain administrative rights that these groups afford. To that end, the DnsAdmins group in Active Directory enables its members to manage the DNS server without giving them broader administrative rights. The DnsAdmins group has Read, Write, Create all child objects, and Delete all child objects permissions on the DNS server and DNS zones, and it has Read and Write permission on DNS resource records. DnsAdmins is a domain local group and has no members by default. If you want users to have this group's rights and permissions, you should follow best practices by creating a global group, adding user accounts to it, and adding the global group to the DnsAdmins group.

DNS Performance Tuning

Good DNS performance is critical to overall good network performance because DNS lookups are part of most network transactions. One of the primary tools for monitoring your server in general is Performance Monitor, discussed in *MCSA Guide to Installation, Storage, and Compute with Windows Server 2016, Exam 70-740* (Cengage, 2018). Performance Monitor has several DNS-specific counters, only a few of which you can see in Figure 3-11.

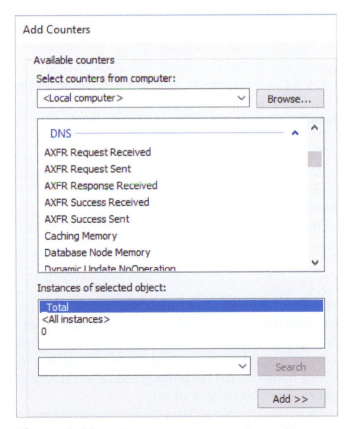

Figure 3-11   DNS Performance Monitor counters

You can also monitor CPU and memory usage by DNS right from Server Manager by clicking DNS in the left pane and scrolling down to Performance. Click Tasks, and click Configure Performance Alerts to set alerts when CPU or memory usage by DNS exceeds specified thresholds (see Figure 3-12).

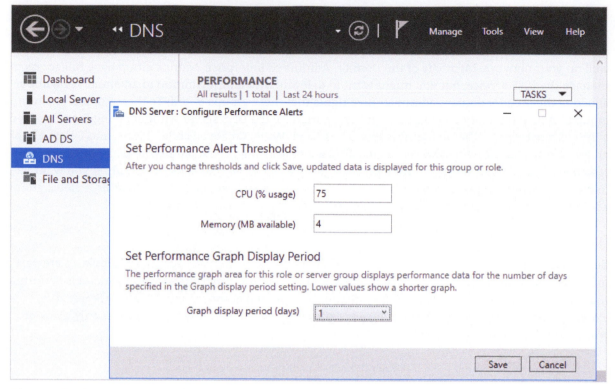

Figure 3-12   Monitoring DNS from Server Manager

There are a few system-specific settings you can configure to optimize DNS performance:

- *System configuration*—Dedicate the system to DNS; do not run other services or install DNS on Server Core or Nano Server. If DNS is running on a virtual machine (VM), dedicate CPU cores to the VM.
- *NIC settings*—Set the receive buffer to the maximum using the `Set-NetAdapterAdvancedProperty` cmdlet. Enable Receive Side Scaling (RSS) on the NIC using the `Enable-NetAdapterRSS` cmdlet. Use `Set-NetAdapterRSS` to fine-tune RSS.
- *Network settings*—Bind multiple IP addresses to your NIC cards.
- *Recursion settings*—Set the recursion timeout value and retry an interval higher if the DNS server must contact other servers over slow WAN links.

Analyzing Zone-Level Statistics

The feature **zone-level statistics** provides a detailed look at how a DNS server is used with respect to queries, zone transfers, and zone updates. The following types of statistics are available for each authoritative zone on a DNS server:

- *Zone queries*—Show queries received and responded to successfully as well as query failures.
- *Zone transfers*—Show zone transfers between primary and secondary zone servers. If a zone is Active Directory integrated, no information is shown.
- *Zone updates*—Show how many dynamic updates the server received and rejected.

You can view zone-level statistics with the PowerShell cmdlet `Get-DnsServerStatistics`. Statistics are returned as a list that can be stored in a variable. The data can then be retrieved based on the category of statistic you want to examine. The following PowerShell commands show how to access zone level statistics. To store zone level statistics for the MCSA2016.local zone in the variable `$zonestatistics`, enter the following command:

```
$zonestatistics = Get-DnsServerStatistics -ZoneName MCSA2016.local
```

To retrieve zone query statistics and display them onscreen, enter this command:

```
$zonestatistics.ZoneQueryStatistics
```

To retrieve zone transfer statistics and display them onscreen, use this command:

```
$zonestatistics.ZoneTransferStatistics
```

To retrieve zone update statistics and display them onscreen, enter this command:

```
$zonestatistics.ZoneUpdateStatistics
```

PowerShell Cmdlets for Working with DNS

Table 3-2 describes some of the many PowerShell cmdlets for working with DNS. The last entry in the table lists all DNS-related cmdlets. As with all PowerShell cmdlets, to get help on using one, type `Get-help cmdletName -detailed` at a PowerShell prompt (replacing *cmdletName* with the name of the cmdlet).

Table 3-2 PowerShell cmdlets for working with DNS

Cmdlet	Function	Example
`Add-DnsServerClientSubnet`	Creates a client subnet for use in DNS policies	`Add-DnsServerClientSubnet -Name Phoenix -Ipv4Subnet 192.168.0.0/24`
`Add-DnsServerZoneScope`	Creates a zone scope for use in DNS policies	`Add-DnsServerZoneScope -ZoneName MCSA2016.local -Name PhoenixZScope`
`Add-DnsServerQueryResolutionPolicy`	Creates a DNS policy using a client subnet and zone scope	`Add-DnsServerQueryResolutionPolicy -Name PhoenixPol -ZoneName MCSA2016.local -Action Allow ClientSubnet "eq,Phoenix" ZoneScope "PhoenixZScope,1"`
`Add-DnsServerConditionalForwarderZone`	Adds a conditional forwarder	`Add-DnsServerConditionalForwarderZone -Name "csmpub.local" -MasterServers 10.11.1.2`
`Add-DnsServerDirectoryPartition`	Creates a custom DNS application directory partition	`Add-DnsServerDirectoryPartition -Name csmpart`
`Add-DnsServerForwarder`	Adds a traditional forwarder	`Add-DnsServerForwarder -IPAddress 10.11.1.2`
`Add-DnsServerPrimaryZone`	Creates a primary zone	`Add-DnsServerPrimaryZone -Name "csmpub.local" -ZoneFile "csmpub.local.dns"`
`Add-DnsServerResourceRecord`	Creates a resource record of a specified type	`Add-DnsServerResourceRecord -ZoneName "csmpub.local" -A -Name "www" -IPv4Address "10.11.1.150"`
`Add-DnsServerSecondaryZone`	Creates a secondary zone	`Add-DnsServerSecondaryZone -Name "csmpub.local" -ZoneFile "csmpub.local.dns" -MasterServers 10.11.1.5`

(continues)

Table 3-2 PowerShell cmdlets for working with DNS *(continued)*

Cmdlet	Function	Example
`Add-DnsServerStubZone`	Creates a stub zone	`Add-DnsServerStubZone -Name "csmtech.local" -MasterServers 10.11.1.1 -ReplicationScope "Domain"`
`Add-DnsServerZoneDelegation`	Creates a zone delegation	`Add-DnsServerZoneDelegation -Name "csmpub.local" -ChildZoneName "tech" -NameServer "serv1.tech.csmpub.local" -IPAddress 10.11.1.5`
`Set-DnsServerRecursionScope`	Sets a recursion scope for use in a DNS resolution policy	`Set-DnsServerRecursionScope -Name . -EnableRecursion $false`
`Add-DnsServerRecursionScope`	Creates a DNS recursion scope	`Add-DnsServerRecursionScope -Name "InternalNetwork" EnableRecursion $true`
`Add-DnsServerQueryResolutionPolicy`	Creates a DNS resolution policy	`Add-DnsServerQueryResolutionPolicy Name "RecursionPolicy" Action Allow -ApplyOnRecursion RecursionScope "InternalNetwork" -ServerInterfaceIP "eq,192.168.0.2"`
`Set-DnsServerResourceRecordAging`	Starts aging of resource records in a specified zone	`Set-DnsServerResourceRecordAging -ZoneName "csmtech.local"`
`Set-DnsServerScavenging`	Sets scavenging settings	`Set-DnsServerScavenging RefreshInterval 3.00:00:00`
`Show-DnsServerCache`	Shows the records in the DNS server cache, including the name, record type, timestamp, TTL, and record data	`Show-DnsServerCache -ComputerName serv1.csmpub.local`
`Start-DnsServerScavenging`	Starts the scavenging process to look for stale resource records	`Start-DnsServerScavenging`
`Get-DNSServerRRL`	Displays the default values and status of DNS RRL	`Get-DNSServerRRL`
`Set-DNSServerRRL`	Sets DNS response rate limiting with the default values	`Set-DNSServerRRL`
`Get-DnsServerStatistics -ZoneName MCSA2016.local`	Gets zone-level statistics	`$zonestatistics = Get-DnsServerStatistics -ZoneName MCSA2016.local $zonestatistics.ZoneQueryStatistics`
`Get-Command -module DNSServer`	Displays a list of all DNS-related cmdlets	

Activity 3-7: Displaying DNS Zone-Level Statistics

Time Required: 10 minutes
Objective: Display DNS zone-level statistics.
Required Tools and Equipment: ServerDC1
Description: In this activity, you use the `Get-DnsServerStatistics` PowerShell cmdlet to display DNS statistics.

1. On ServerDC1, open a PowerShell window.
2. Type **$zonestats = Get-DnsServerStatistics -ZoneName MCSA2016.local** and press **Enter**.
3. Type **$zonestats.ZoneQueryStatistics** and press **Enter**. You see a list of statistics for queries received and sent by the DNS server.
4. Type **$zonestats.ZoneTransferStatistics** and press **Enter**. Because this zone is Active Directory integrated and this statistic shows information only for zone transfers between primary and secondary zones, all the statistics are 0.
5. Type **$zonestats.ZoneUpdateStatistics** and press **Enter**. You see a list of statistics for dynamic updates the server has received and rejected.
6. Close the PowerShell prompt, and sign out of or shut down ServerDC1 and ServerDM1.

Chapter Summary

- Zone delegation transfers authority for a subdomain to a new zone, which can be on the same server or another server. When a subdomain has been delegated to a zone on another server, the DNS server hosting the parent zone maintains only an NS record pointing to the DNS server hosting the delegated zone.

- Every Windows domain zone has an _msdcs subdomain, which holds all the SRV records for Microsoft-hosted services, such as the global catalog, LDAP, and Kerberos. In the forest root domain, this subdomain is delegated to a new zone on the same server, not on a different server.

- When a dynamic resource record is created in a DNS zone, the record receives a time stamp based on the server's time and date. A static record can also be time-stamped if you enable the option to delete the record when it becomes stale.

- Scavenging is the process of scanning the records in each zone and deleting stale records. Scavenging must be enabled in two places to occur. After you have enabled scavenging on the server, you enable it on zones. You can also enable scavenging for specific zones.

- A stub zone is a special type of zone containing only an SOA record, one or more NS records, and the necessary glue A records to resolve NS records. A stub zone isn't authoritative for the zone. Essentially, a stub zone points to another DNS server that is authoritative for the zone.

- Zone replication is the transfer of zone changes from one DNS server to another. When DNS is installed on a domain controller, zone data is replicated automatically to other DCs. With standard zones, you need to create secondary zones on each DNS server that will host the zone. With Active Directory–integrated zones, a zone is created only once on a DC, and the zone is created and replicated automatically on every other DC in the zone replication scope.

- A major advantage of using Active Directory–integrated zones is the ability to limit dynamic updates to only verified domain members. Dynamic updates can be configured in one of three ways; allow only secure dynamic updates, allow both nonsecure and secure dynamic updates, and do not allow dynamic updates.

- A new feature of DNS in Windows Server 2016 is the ability to support resource records of a type unknown to the DNS server on Windows Server 2016. This feature, referred to simply enough as *unknown record support*, allows you to create resource records that are in a format unknown to Windows DNS server but that the Windows DNS server will return in response to client queries.

- Windows Server 2016 adds a feature called DNS Policy that allows you to manage DNS traffic, filter queries, and load balance your applications based on several criteria. DNS policies can be applied at the server level or zone level, depending on the type of policy and your requirements. There are two primary types of policy: query resolution policies and zone transfer policies.

- Domain Name System Security Extension (DNSSEC) is a suite of features and protocols for validating DNS server responses. DNSSEC provides DNS clients with three critical methods to ensure that data they receive from DNS queries is accurate and secure; origin authentication of DNS data, authenticated denial of existence, and data integrity.

- DNS socket pool is a pool of port numbers used by a DNS server for DNS queries. It protects against DNS cache poisoning by enabling a DNS server to randomize the source port when performing DNS queries.

- DNS cache locking is a DNS security feature that allows you to control whether data in the DNS cache can be overwritten. When a DNS server receives a record as the result of a query to another DNS server, it caches the data.

- A new DNS Server role feature in Windows Server 2016, Response Rate Limiting (RRL), mitigates a type of distributed denial of service (DDoS) attack called a DNS amplification attack. RRL examines queries to the DNS server and flags them when many queries received in a short period of time have a similar source address and query parameters.

- DNS-based Authentication of Named Entities (DANE) is a new feature in Windows Server 2016 used to provide information about the certification authority (CA) used by your domain when a client is requesting DNS information for your domain. This feature prevents man-in-the-middle attacks.

- DNS performance is critical to overall good network performance because DNS lookups are part of most network transactions. One of the primary tools for monitoring your server is Performance Monitor. You can also monitor CPU and memory usage by DNS right from Server Manager.

Key Terms

Active Directory partition	Domain Name System Security	stale resource record
client subnet	Extension (DNSSEC)	stub zone
Delegation Signer (DS)	key-signing key (KSK)	trust anchor
DNS amplification attack	Next Secure (NSEC)	unknown record support
DNS-based Authentication of	Next Secure 3 (NSEC3)	zone delegation
Named Entities (DANE)	Next Secure 3 (NSEC3) Parameter	zone-level statistics
DNS cache locking	query resolution policy	zone replication
DNS cache poisoning	recursion scope	zone replication scope
DNS Policy	Resource Record Signature	zone scope
DNS recursion scope	(RRSIG)	zone signing
DNS socket pool	Response Rate Limiting (RRL)	zone-signing key (ZSK)
DNSKEY	scavenging	zone transfer policy

Review Questions

1. You have delegated a subdomain to a zone on another server. Several months later, you hear that DNS clients can't resolve host records in the subdomain. You discover that the IP address scheme was changed recently in the building where the server hosting the subdomain is located. What can you do to make sure DNS clients can resolve hostnames in the subdomain?

   a. Configure a forwarder pointing to the server hosting the subdomain.

   b. Edit the NS record in the delegated zone on the parent DNS server.

   c. Edit the NS record in the delegated zone on the DNS server hosting the subdomain.

   d. Configure a root hint pointing to the server hosting the subdomain.

2. You have an Active Directory–integrated zone named csmtech.local on the DNS1 server. The forest root Active Directory domain is csmtech.local. Why is the _msdcs subdomain zone delegated on the DNS1 server?
   a. To offload the DNS processing required of DNS1
   b. To change the replication scope of _msdcs
   c. To allow Windows clients to access Microsoft services
   d. To allow dynamic updates to the _msdcs zone

3. You have a DNS server running Windows Server 2016 named DNS1 that contains a primary zone named csmtech.local. You have discovered a static A record for the server DB1 in the zone, but you know that DB1 was taken offline several months ago. Aging and scavenging are enabled on the server and the zone. What should you do first to ensure that stale static records are removed from the zone?
   a. Change the default TTL on static records.
   b. Enable the Advanced View setting in DNS Manager.
   c. Configure the "Expires after" value in the SOA.
   d. Change the "No-refresh interval" timer to a lower number.

4. Which of the following are true about a stub zone? (Choose all that apply.)
   a. It's not authoritative for the zone.
   b. It holds mostly A records.
   c. It can't be Active Directory integrated.
   d. It contains SOA and NS records.

5. You have seven DNS servers that hold an Active Directory–integrated zone named csmpub.local. Three of the DNS servers are in the Chicago site, which is connected to three other sites through a WAN link with limited bandwidth. Only users in the Chicago site need access to resources in the csmpub.local zone. Where should you store the csmpub.local zone?
   a. ForestDNSZones partition
   b. csmpub.local.dns
   c. DomainDNSZones partition
   d. Custom application partition

6. You have a primary zone stored in the myzone.local.dns file. Some devices that aren't domain members are creating dynamic DNS records in the zone. You want to make sure only domain members can create dynamic records in the zone. What should you do first?
   a. Configure the *Secure only* option for dynamic updates.
   b. Configure permissions in the Security tab of the zone's Properties dialog box.
   c. Configure the *Store the zone in Active Directory* option.
   d. Configure the *None* option for dynamic updates.

7. Which of the following is *not* an advantage of using Active Directory–integrated zones?
   a. Provides automatic zone replication
   b. Gives multimaster updates
   c. Can be stored on member servers
   d. Is able to configure secure updates

8. You have a DNS server running Windows Server 2016. You would like to configure the DNS server to respond to requests based on the source of the query and include the capability to filter malicious queries. Which feature should you enable?
   a. DNS Policy and Security
   b. DNS Policy
   c. DNS Security
   d. DNS Zone Policy

9. You have a DNS server that has multiple network interface cards; one is an internal interface and the second is an external interface that faces the Internet. You would like to enable recursion for your internal DNS clients and disable it for any Internet clients. Which Windows Server 2016 DNS feature will allow you to specify which DNS queries will use recursion and which DNS queries will not?
   a. DNS recursion scope
   b. DNS recursion rules
   c. Recursion permissions
   d. DNS recursion zones

10. You have decided to create multiple zone scopes to configure your DNS server to respond to clients based on whether the client is on your internal network or an external network. What specific configuration can you use to implement this policy?
    a. Selected DNS
    b. Query filters
    c. Subnet-based DNS
    d. Split-brain DNS

11. If you disable the option to use root hints when no forwarders are available, what are you doing?
    a. Enabling the socket pool
    b. Locking the cache
    c. Disabling recursion
    d. Configuring the netmask

12. Domain Name System Security Extension (DNSSEC) provides specific features and protocols for validating server responses. Which of the following methods are used by DNSSEC to ensure that the data they receive from DNS queries is accurate and secure? (Choose all that apply.)
    a. Data integrity
    b. Authenticated zone signing
    c. Authenticated denial of existence
    d. Origin authentication of DNS data

13. Which of the following records is returned when the requested resource record doesn't exist and is used to fulfill the authenticated denial of existence security feature of DNSSEC?
    a. DNSKEY
    b. Delegation Signer
    c. Next Secure
    d. zone-signing key

14. Which of the following uses digital signatures contained in DNSSEC-related resource records to verify DNS responses?
    a. Zone signing
    b. Data integrity
    c. Socket pool
    d. Cache locking

15. Which of the following protects against DNS cache poisoning by enabling a DNS server to randomize the source port when performing DNS queries?
    a. Zone signing
    b. Data integrity
    c. Socket pool
    d. Cache locking

16. You have noticed that your server's DNS cache locking value is configured to 100. What effect does this have on the DNS server's cached data?
    a. The data cannot be overwritten.
    b. All data will be completely overwritten.
    c. All data will be overwritten after it is cached.
    d. The data will be partially overwritten.

17. You're in charge of a small group of DNS servers running Windows Server 2016. After careful review of your current security policies, you

have decided you need to protect your servers from DNS amplification attacks. What specific feature can be used in Windows Server 2016 to provide you the resources to complete this task?
    a. DNS Cache Locking
    b. DNS Rate Limiting
    c. Response Rate Limiting
    d. DDoS mitigation

18. You have noticed that one of your DNS servers has possibly been compromised. You believe that a cached DNS entry for your domain is being targeted by an attacker. What new feature in Windows Server 2016 could you use on your DNS server to help prevent a man-in-the-middle attack in which your cached DNS entry for your domain is altered by an attacker?
    a. DNS-based Authentication of Named Entities
    b. DNS-Expiration
    c. DNS Cache Locking
    d. Authenticated-DNS

19. You want to give a junior administrator access to DNS servers so that he can configure zones and resource records, but you don't want to give him broader administrative rights in the domain. What should you do?
    a. Make his account a member of DnsAdmins.
    b. Add his account to the Administrators group on all DNS servers.
    c. Delegate control for the OU where the DNS computer accounts are.
    d. Add his account to the Administer DNS Servers policy.

20. After utilizing Performance Monitor to analyze your DNS server, you have decided to optimize your server's performance. After investigating the possible system settings you can configure, you decide to set the receive buffer to the maximum and enable RSS. Which type of setting will allow you to accomplish this task?
    a. Zone settings
    b. Recursion settings
    c. System configuration
    d. NIC Settings

Critical Thinking

The following activities give you critical thinking challenges. Case Projects offer a scenario with a problem to solve and for which you supply a written solution.

Case Project 3-1: Configuring Zones

You have an Active Directory forest named csmtech.local and two Active Directory domains in the forest named csmpub.local and csmsales.local. You want the DNS servers in each domain to be able to handle DNS queries from client computers for any of the other domains. DNS servers in the csmtech.local and csmpub.local domains should be authoritative for their own domains and the csmsales.local domain. However, DNS servers in csmsales.local should be authoritative only for csmsales.local.

How should you set up the DNS servers and zones to handle this situation? Explain how the DNS servers in each domain should be configured with zones. Be sure to include information about replication scope and zone types.

Case Project 3-2: Configuring DNS Policies

The CSM Tech organization has a substantial web presence with several publicly accessible web and application servers. You have DNS servers that handle Internet queries for all your publicly accessible resources. However, after doing some statistics analysis on your public DNS servers, you find that your servers are handling recursive lookups for clients that are not within your organization. Your public DNS servers should handle recursive queries only for your internal clients, but the servers should handle iterative (nonrecursive) queries from external sources. What do you recommend? What are the commands needed to implement the solution?

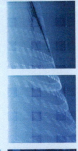

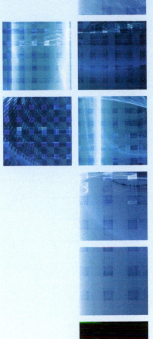

CHAPTER 4

IMPLEMENTING DHCP

After reading this chapter and completing the exercises, you will be able to:

Describe the DHCP protocol and process

Install and configure a DHCP server

Configure a DHCP server

Implement DHCPv6

Configure DHCP high availability

Transmission Control Protocol/Internet Protocol (TCP/IP) is the standard networking protocol for all types and sizes of networks. As you know, every device on a TCP/IP network needs an IP address to communicate with other devices. Two methods are available for IP address assignment: static and dynamic. Although static IP addressing has its merits, managing static addresses on networks of more than a few dozen computers can descend into chaos quickly.

After Dynamic Host Configuration Protocol (DHCP) has been configured, it relieves many of the administrative headaches of managing static IP addressing on large networks. Small office and home networks typically use a Wi-Fi-enabled router, which is configured to assign an IP address via DHCP to devices that connect to the network. These routers might require little to no configuration because they come configured as a DHCP server. On a larger Windows-based network, however, you want more control over IP addressing and the ability to use features such as authorization and filters to enhance security, reservations, exclusions, IPv6 compatibility, and server policies. Windows Server 2016 has the DHCP Server role with these features and others to give you an enterprise-scale dynamic IP addressing solution.

This chapter discusses how DHCP works, and you learn how to install and configure DHCP, including server authorization, scopes, and DHCP options. You also learn about some advanced features, such as reservations, exclusions, server policies, and filters. IPv6 is increasing in importance, and although IPv6 is autoconfiguring, you may still want to use DHCPv6 to maintain tighter control over your IPv6 addresses and to configure address options. You'll learn how DHCPv6 works and how to configure a DHCPv6 scope and options. In addition, you learn how to configure DHCP to work with DNS, DHCP relay, and DHCP high availability. Finally, you'll get some tips for troubleshooting DHCP deployments.

Table 4-1 describes what you need for the hands-on activities in this chapter.

Table 4-1 Activity requirements

Activity	Requirements	Notes
Activity 4-1: Resetting Your Virtual Environment	ServerDC1, ServerDM1, ServerSA1	
Activity 4-2: Installing and Authorizing a DHCP Server	ServerDC1, ServerDM1, ServerSA1	
Activity 4-3: Working with Exclusions and Reservations	ServerDC1, ServerDM1, ServerSA1	
Activity 4-4: Configuring DHCP Options	ServerDC1, ServerDM1, ServerSA1	
Activity 4-5: Creating a Superscope	ServerDC1, ServerDM1, ServerSA1	
Activity 4-6: Creating a Multicast Scope	ServerDC1, ServerDM1	
Activity 4-7: Creating a DHCP Policy	ServerDC1, ServerDM1, ServerSA1	
Activity 4-8: Creating a DHCP Filter	ServerDC1, ServerDM1, ServerSA1	
Activity 4-9: Creating and Testing a DHCPv6 Scope	ServerDC1, ServerDM1, ServerSA1	
Activity 4-10: Working with Split Scopes	ServerDC1, ServerDM1, ServerSA1	
Activity 4-11: Configuring DHCP Failover	ServerDC1, ServerDM1, ServerSA1	
Activity 4-12: Uninstalling the DHCP Server Role	ServerDC1, ServerDM1, ServerSA1	

An Overview of Dynamic Host Configuration Protocol

 **Certification**

- **70-741 – Implement DHCP:**
  Install and configure DHCP

Dynamic Host Configuration Protocol (DHCP) is a component of the TCP/IP protocol suite, which is used to assign an IP address to a host automatically from a defined pool of addresses. IP addresses assigned via DHCP are leased, not permanently assigned. When a client receives an IP address from a server, it can keep the address until the lease expires at which point the client can request a new IP address. However, to prevent a disruption in communication, the client attempts to renew the lease when the lease interval is 50% expired. DHCP is based on broadcast packets, so there must be a DHCP server or DHCP relay agent (discussed later in "DHCP Relay Agents") in the same subnet as the client. Recall that broadcast packets are forwarded by switches but not by routers, so they're heard only by devices on the same LAN. DHCP is a fairly simple protocol consisting of just eight message types. These message types, the DHCP address assignment, and renewal processes are discussed in the following sections.

The DHCP Address Assignment Process

Like most TCP/IP protocols, DHCP is a client/server protocol. A client makes a request for an IP address, and the server responds. The process of a DHCP client requesting an IP address and a DHCP server fulfilling the request is actually a four-packet sequence. All four packets are broadcast packets. DHCP was designed to use broadcast packets because a client that doesn't have an IP address can't be sent a unicast packet; it can, however, receive and respond to a broadcast packet. DHCP uses the UDP Transport-layer protocol on ports 67 and 68. Port 67 is for sending data from the client to the server, and port 68 is for sending data from the server to the client. The four-packet sequence is explained in the following list and illustrated in Figure 4-1:

1. *DHCPDISCOVER*—The client transmits a broadcast packet via UDP source port 68 and UDP destination port 67 to the network, asking for an IP address from an available DHCP server. The client can request its last known IP address and other IP address parameters, such as the subnet mask, router (default gateway), domain name, and DNS server.

2. *DHCPOFFER*—A DHCP server receives the DHCPDISCOVER packet and responds with an offer of an IP address and subnet mask from the pool of addresses along with the lease duration. The broadcast packet is transmitted via UDP source port 67 and UDP destination port 68. Because the packet is a broadcast, all devices on the subnet get it. The packet contains the MAC address of the client computer that sent the DHCPDISCOVER packet, so other devices disregard it.

3. *DHCPREQUEST*—The client responds by requesting the offered address. Because it's possible that multiple DHCP servers responded to the DHCPDISCOVER, the client might get multiple offers but accepts only one offer. The DHCPREQUEST packet includes a server identifier, which is the IP address of the server from which the offer is accepted. Any other DHCP servers that made an offer see the server identifier and return the offered, but not accepted, IP address to the pool.

4. *DHCPACK*—The server the offer was accepted from acknowledges the transaction and sends any other requested IP parameters, such as default gateway and DNS server address, to the client. The transaction is now complete, and the client binds the IP address and other parameters to its network interface.

Figure 4-1   The packet sequence for DHCP address assignment

DHCP Address Renewal

The DHCPDISCOVER broadcast packet is sent only when the client currently has no IP address configured on the interface from which the packet is transmitted or after its current address has expired. As mentioned, a client attempts to renew the address lease when it's 50% expired. The **lease renewal** process is somewhat different, and because the client already has an IP address and the address of the DHCP server, the client uses unicast packets rather than broadcast packets. A successful renewal is a two-packet sequence:

1. *DHCPREQUEST*—When the lease is 50% expired, the client sends a unicast packet to the DHCP server, requesting a renewal lease for its current IP address. If the server doesn't respond, the client retries the renewal request up to three more times occurring at 4, 8, and 16 seconds after the first renewal request.

2. *DHCPACK*—If the server responds and can honor the renewal request, the server sends a unicast packet to the client granting and acknowledging the renewal request.

The two-packet sequence for a lease renewal occurs when a server is available to service the request and the server can honor the renewal request. The renewal request might fail in these common situations:

- The server responds but can't honor the renewal. This situation can occur if the requested address has been deleted or deactivated from the scope or the address has been excluded from the scope since the time the client received it. The server sends a DHCPNAK to the client, the client unbinds the address from its network interface and begins the process anew with a broadcast DHCPDISCOVER packet.

- The server doesn't respond. If the server has been taken offline, moved to another subnet, or can't communicate (perhaps because of a hardware failure), the DHCPREQUEST packet can't be serviced. In this case, the following steps occur:

  1. The client keeps its current address until 87.5% of the lease interval has expired. At that time, the client sends a broadcast DHCPREQUEST requesting a lease renewal from any available DHCP server.

  2. There are two possible results from the DHCPREQUEST broadcast:
     - A DHCP server responds to the request. If it can provide the requested address, it replies with a DHCPACK and the address is renewed; otherwise, it replies with a DHCPNAK (negative acknowledgement) indicating that it can't supply the requested address. In this case, the client immediately unbinds the address from the network interface and starts the DHCP sequence over, beginning with a DHCPDISCOVER broadcast packet.
     - No DHCP server responds. In this case, the client waits until the lease period is over, unbinds the IP address, and starts the sequence over with a DHCPDISCOVER broadcast packet. If no server responds, a Windows client (other client OSs might behave differently) binds an Automatic Private IP Addressing (APIPA) address to the network interface and sends a DHCPDISCOVER every 5 minutes in an attempt to get a DHCP-assigned address. If an alternate IP address configuration has been configured on the interface, it's used instead of an APIPA address, and no further attempts are made to get a DHCP-assigned address until the interface is reset or the computer restarts.

DHCP Messages

Table 4-2 describes all the message types exchanged between a DHCP server and a client. The first column includes the message type number found in the DHCP packet. Message types that have been covered already are described briefly.

Table 4-2 DHCP message types

Message number	Message name	Description
1	DHCPDISCOVER	Sent by a client to discover an available DHCP server and request a new IP address.
2	DHCPOFFER	Sent by the server in response to a DHCPDISCOVER with an offer of an IP address.
3	DHCPREQUEST	Sent by a client to request a lease on an offered IP address in response to a DHCPOFFER or to renew an existing lease.
4	DHCPDECLINE	Sent by a client in response to a DHCPOFFER to decline an offered IP address. Usually occurs when the client has determined that the offered address is already in use on the network.
5	DHCPACK	Sent by the server to acknowledge a DHCPREQUEST or DHCPINFORM. This message also contains DHCP options requested by the client.
6	DHCPNAK	Sent by the server in response to a DHCPREQUEST. Indicates that the server can't fulfill the request. Usually occurs when a client is attempting a renewal and the requested address is no longer available for lease.
7	DHCPRELEASE	Sent by a client to release a leased address. Usually occurs when a user runs the `ipconfig /release` command or a command of a similar function. However, it can also occur if a client is configured to release its address when the computer is shut down. (By default, Windows clients don't release an address when they are shut down.)
8	DHCPINFORM	Sent by a client to request additional configuration. The client must already have an IP address and a subnet mask. Message can be used by a client that has a static IP address but has been configured to get a DNS address or router address via DHCP.

Installing and Configuring a DHCP Server

- **70-741 – Implement DHCP:**
  Install and configure DHCP

The DHCP service is installed as a server role, aptly named DHCP Server. There are no role service components for this server role; the DHCP management tool is the only additional component installed. DHCP Server can be installed by using the Add Roles and Features Wizard via Server Manager or the following PowerShell cmdlet:

```
Install-WindowsFeature DHCP -IncludeManagementTools
```

After you install this role, the DHCP console (see Figure 4-2) is available on the Tools menu in Server Manager. The red down arrow on the IPv4 and IPv6 nodes indicates that the server isn't currently providing services. In a Windows domain network, the DHCP server must be authorized, and a scope must be created before the server can begin providing DHCP services. In a workgroup network, authorization is automatic.

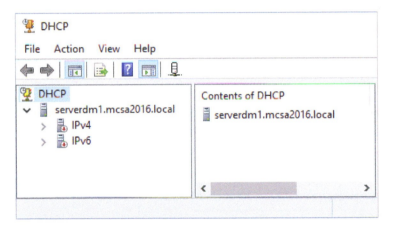

Figure 4-2   The DHCP console

DHCP Server Authorization

A DHCP server must be authorized on a domain network before it can begin providing services. **DHCP server authorization** is the process of enabling a DHCP server in a domain environment to prevent rogue DHCP servers from operating on the network. DHCP clients have no way to determine whether a DHCP server is valid. When a client transmits a DHCPDISCOVER packet, any DHCP server receiving the broadcast can respond. The client accepts the first offer it gets that meets the requirements in the DHCPDISCOVER packet. If a rogue DHCP server is installed on a network, whether accidentally or on purpose, incorrect IP address settings could be configured on client computers. These settings likely include the DNS server and default gateway the client uses in addition to the IP address and subnet mask. At best, incorrect IP address settings cause the client to stop communicating correctly. At worst, servers set up by an attacker to masquerade as legitimate network resources can capture passwords and other sensitive information.

On a domain network, a DHCP server can be installed on a domain controller, a member server, or a standalone server. However, for authorization to work correctly, installing DHCP on a standalone server in a domain network isn't recommended. If you use this setup in a network that already has an authorized server, the standalone server can't lease addresses.

After a DHCP server is installed, you authorize it by right-clicking the server name in the DHCP console and clicking Authorize. DHCP server authorization requires Enterprise Administrator credentials, so if you aren't signed in as an Enterprise Administrator (the Administrator account in the forest root domain or a member of the Enterprise Administrators universal group), you're prompted for credentials. To authorize a DHCP server with PowerShell, use the `Add-DhcpServerInDC` cmdlet.

DHCP Scopes

A **DHCP scope** is a pool of IP addresses and other IP configuration parameters that a DHCP server uses to lease addresses to DHCP clients. A scope consists of the following required parameters:

- *Scope name*—A descriptive name for the scope. You can define multiple scopes on a DHCP server, so you might name the scope based on the range of IP addresses in it. For example, a scope that services the 192.168.0/24 network might be named "192.168.0-subnet."
- *Start and end IP addresses*—The start and end IP addresses define the address pool. You can't specify a start address that's the network ID or an end address that's the broadcast address for the subnet.
- *Prefix length or subnet mask*—Specify a prefix length or subnet mask that's assigned with each IP address. For example, you can specify 16 for the prefix length or 255.255.0.0 for the subnet mask. Windows fills in the prefix and subnet mask automatically based on the class of the start and end IP addresses, but you can change this information (see Figure 4-3).

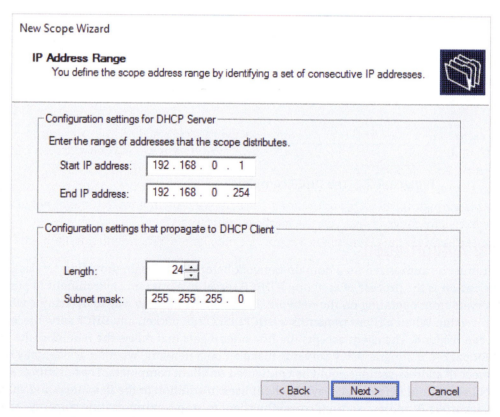

Figure 4-3   Setting the IP address range for a scope

- *Lease duration*—The **lease duration** specifies how long a DHCP client can keep an address. As discussed, a client tries to renew the address long before the lease expires but must release the address if it can't renew it before it expires. The lease duration is specified in days, hours, and minutes with a minimum lease of 1 minute and a maximum lease of 999 days, 23 hours, and 59 minutes. The default lease duration is 8 days. The lease can also be set to unlimited, but this setting isn't recommended because if the client is removed from the network or its NIC is replaced, the address is never returned to the pool for lease to other clients. An unlimited duration can also cause DNS records to become stale when DHCP is configured to update DNS records on behalf of the client.

> **Note** 📎
>
> These four items are the required DHCP scope options. You can configure other options when you create a scope with the New Scope Wizard or PowerShell or change the scope's properties after it's created.

After a scope is created, you must activate the scope before it can begin serving IP addresses. Until the scope is activated, the scope will be shown in the DHCP console with a red down arrow. To activate a scope with the DHCP console, simply right-click the scope and click Activate. To activate a scope with PowerShell, use the `Set-DhcpServerv4Scope` cmdlet with the `-State Active` parameter.

Exclusion Ranges

A DHCP scope contains a continuous range of IP addresses that are leased to DHCP clients. You might want to exclude certain addresses or a range of addresses from the scope for use in static address assignments. Static addresses are usually assigned to servers, routers, and other critical infrastructure devices to make sure they always have an address that never changes. So to avoid IP address conflicts, you need to exclude addresses that are assigned statically. Addresses can be excluded in two ways:

- *De facto exclusion*—You don't actually create an exclusion with this method; you simply set the start and end IP addresses in the scope so that several addresses in the subnet fall outside the scope's range. For example, if you set a scope's start address to 192.168.0.10 and end address to 192.168.0.240 with a 24-bit prefix, you have addresses 192.168.0.1 through 192.168.0.9 and addresses 192.168.0.241 through 192.168.0.254 to use for static address assignments. You might not need to create an exclusion range unless you use all these addresses.

- *Create an exclusion range*—Sometimes a scope is created after static address assignments have been made, and the static addresses occupy several ranges of addresses throughout the subnet (instead of at the beginning or end). For example, if your subnet is 192.168.0.0/24 and you have devices with static addresses in the range 192.168.0.100 through 192.168.0.110, you probably need to create one or more exclusion ranges because these addresses fall right in the middle of the subnet. An **exclusion range** consists of one or more addresses in the scope that the DHCP server doesn't lease to clients. They can be created when the scope is created with the New Scope Wizard or afterward by right-clicking the Address Pool node under the scope and clicking New Exclusion Range. In the Add Exclusion dialog box, type the start and end IP addresses. You can exclude a single IP address by specifying only the start address. You can create as many exclusion ranges as you need.

Reservations

A **reservation** is an IP address associated with the MAC address of a DHCP client to ensure that when the client requests an IP address, it always gets the same one along with any configured options. The IP address in the reservation must fall within the same subnet as the scope and uses the same subnet mask that's configured for the scope. If options are configured for the reservation, they take precedence over options configured at the scope or server level (discussed later in "DHCP Options"). A reservation address can be any address in the subnet defined by the scope's address range and can even be within an exclusion range.

If the IP address you want to use in the reservation is already in use by another DHCP client, the client using the address continues to use it until it attempts to renew it. You can force the client to release the address and get a different address by entering `ipconfig /release` and `ipconfig /renew` at a command prompt. The client the reservation is made for can be forced to start using the reserved address by entering `ipconfig /renew` at the command prompt, or you can wait until it attempts to renew its current address.

Multiple Subnets, Multiple Scopes

A DHCP scope can service a single subnet. When a DHCP server receives a DHCPDISCOVER message on an interface, it offers an IP address from the scope in which the address pool is in the same subnet as the interface's address. For example, suppose that a DHCP server has a single network interface configured for address 192.168.0.1/24. When a DHCPDISCOVER is received on that interface, the server offers an address from the scope containing addresses in the 192.168.0.0/24 network. Likewise, if the DHCP server receives a DHCPREQUEST for a particular IP address, as when a client renews a lease, the server can fulfill the request only if the requested address is on the same subnet as the server's interface and there's a matching scope.

> **Note** 📎
>
> You can't create overlapping scopes. In other words, you can't create multiple scopes with address pools in the same subnet. For example, suppose that you create a scope with the start address 192.168.0.1, end address 192.168.0.100, and prefix length 24. You can't create another scope with the start address 192.168.0.150 and end address 192.168.0.200 because both address pools are in the 192.168.0.0 subnet.

What do you do when your network has multiple subnets? Because DHCP is based on broadcasts, which can't traverse routers, there are three main methods for handling a network with multiple subnets:

- Configure a DHCP server in each subnet, each configured with a scope to service that subnet.
- Configure a single DHCP server with network interfaces connected to each subnet and scopes defined for each subnet. This setup is shown in Figure 4-4. This method obviously becomes untenable when the number of subnets increases because you need an interface for each subnet.
- Configure DHCP relay agents on subnets that don't have a DHCP server. DHCP relay agents forward DHCP requests to a central DHCP server configured with scopes for each subnet. DHCP relay agents are discussed later in "DHCP Relay Agents."

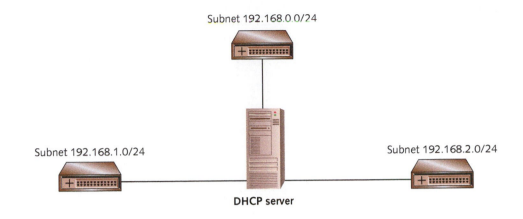

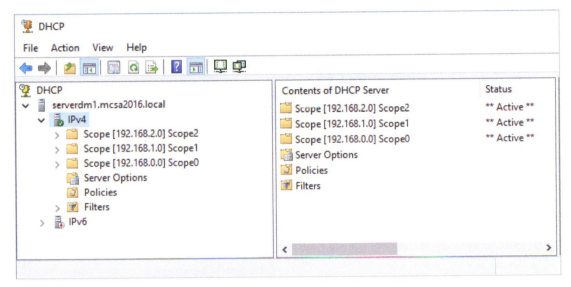

Figure 4-4   A server configured with three scopes

Configuring Superscopes and Multicast Scopes

A **superscope** is a special type of scope consisting of one or more member scopes that allows a DHCP server to service multiple IPv4 subnets on a single physical network. (Superscopes aren't supported in IPv6.) Although it isn't a common configuration for a network, it can and does occur. A superscope directs the DHCP server to draw addresses from both scopes, even though it has only a single interface configured for one of the IP subnets. This configuration can be useful if the number of computers on a physical network exceeds the original subnet's size or when a second subnet has been added to a physical network for testing purposes. To configure a superscope, first configure two or more scopes to include in the superscope; each scope that's part of a superscope is referred to as a *member scope*. Then create the superscope and add the member scopes. Superscopes don't have any DHCP options of their own, and you can't create an IP address pool for a superscope. All IP address pools and options are configured in member scopes. However, you can deactivate a superscope, which deactivates all member scopes as well.

Figure 4-5 is an example of a network with a superscope. Two subnets are configured: 192.168.0.0/24 and 192.168.1.0/24. The router interface is configured with two IP addresses and can route between the two subnets. The DHCP server is configured with a superscope named Superscope1 that has two member scopes, one for each subnet.

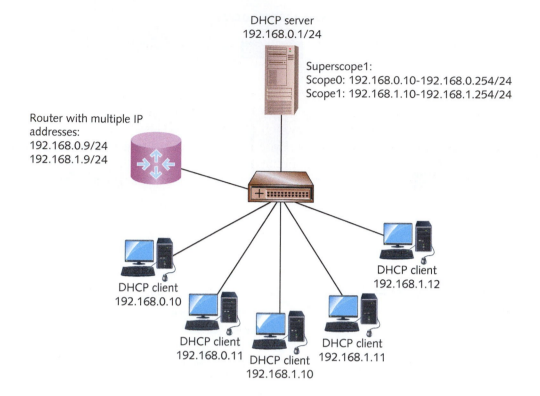

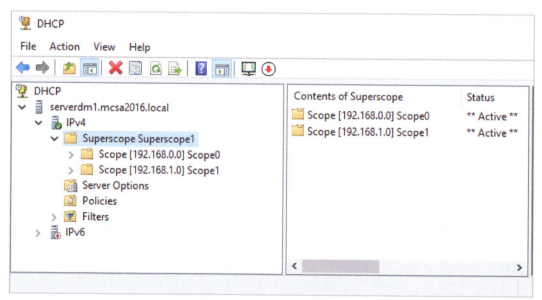

Figure 4-5 A network that uses a superscope

You create superscopes in the DHCP console by right-clicking the IPv4 node and clicking New Superscope, and then following the New Superscope Wizard. You can also create a superscope with PowerShell, as in the following example:

```
Add-DhcpServerv4SuperScope -SuperscopeName "NewSuperScope"
  -ScopeID 192.168.0.0,192.168.1.0
```

The IP addresses that follow the `-ScopeID` option are the subnet addresses of the two scopes you want to add to the superscope.

Configuring Multicast Scopes

Most network packets are addressed as unicast packets, meaning that a single host is the intended recipient, or as broadcast packets, meaning that all hosts on the network should process them. An IPv4 multicast packet is a network packet addressed to a group of hosts listening on a particular multicast IP address. These hosts listening for multicast packets receive and process them while other hosts ignore them. A multicast address doesn't replace a host's regular IP address assignment. Recall that the first octet of IPv4 multicast addresses is in the range 224 to 239 and is classified as a class D IP address. Multicast addresses can't be assigned as a host's IP address; instead, a network service or application informs the IP protocol that it wants to "join" a multicast group. By doing so, the network software listens for the specified multicast address in the destination field of packets and processes them rather than ignores them.

> **Note** 📎
>
> Although IPv6 does support multicasting and uses it much more than IPv4 does, there's no support for IPv6 DHCP multicast scopes.

Most multicast applications use a reserved multicast address known by the server running the multicast service and by the clients that might join the multicast group, and there's no need for dynamic multicast address allocation. For example, several routing protocols use multicast addresses to exchange information. Routing Information Protocol version 2 (RIPv2) uses the reserved multicast address 224.0.0.9, and Open Shortest Path First (OSPF) uses addresses 224.0.0.5 and 224.0.0.6. All routers supporting these protocols have these addresses statically assigned, so there's no need to use DHCP for multicast address assignment in these cases. However, if you're using an application that doesn't use a reserved multicast address, you might want to use DHCP to assign multicast addresses temporarily on your network. If you want to reserve an address permanently, you must register it with the Internet Assigned Numbers Authority (IANA).

> **Note** 📎
>
> You can find a list of multicast addresses reserved by the IANA for designated purposes at *www.networksorcery .com/enp/protocol/ip/multicast.htm*.

A **multicast scope** allows assigning multicast addresses dynamically to multicast servers and clients with the Multicast Address Dynamic Client Allocation Protocol (MADCAP). Typically, a multicast server (MCS) is allocated a multicast address, and multicast clients register or join the multicast group, which allows them to receive multicast traffic from the MCS.

> **Note** 📎
>
> All devices using TCP/IP must be assigned a unicast IP address before they can be assigned and begin using multicast addresses.

There are two common ranges of multicast addresses that you can use to create a multicast scope:

- *Administrative scopes*—An administrative scope is composed of multicast addresses intended to be used in a private network. This range of addresses is similar to the private unicast IP address ranges beginning with 10, 172.16-172.31, and 192.168. The range most recommended for this purpose is 239.192.0.0/14, which has plenty of addresses for a large enterprise. The range you specify when configuring the multicast scope must contain at least 256 addresses.
- *Global scopes*—In a global scope, the multicast application is used across the public Internet and has the recommended range of 233.0.0.0/24. There's no minimum number of addresses in a global scope.

Note

The preceding ranges are recommended. You can use any range of multicast addresses for creating a scope, as long as it doesn't include any addresses reserved by the IANA.

You configure multicast scopes in the DHCP console or with PowerShell cmdlets. You don't configure options for a multicast scope, but you can configure exclusions, and you must specify a lease time. (The default value is 30 days.) The multicast scope consists of start and end IP addresses in the multicast address range along with a time to live (TTL) value that specifies how many routers a multicast packet can pass through before being discarded. No subnet mask is specified in the scope because multicast addresses are considered secondary addresses and a host already has a subnet mask assigned along with its unicast IP address.

DHCP Options

An IP address and subnet mask are the minimum settings needed for a computer to communicate on a network. However, almost every network requires a DNS server IP address for name resolution and a default gateway to communicate with other subnets and the Internet. The DHCP server can be configured to send both these addresses to DHCP clients along with the IP address and subnet mask. Many other options can be configured and might be necessary, depending on the network environment. DHCP options can be assigned at the following levels:

- *Server options*—Options configured at the server level affect all scopes but can be overridden by a scope, policy, or reservation option.
- *Scope options*—Scope options affect clients that get a lease from the scope in which the option is configured. Scope options can be overridden by reservation options or DHCP policies.
- *Policy options*—DHCP policies allow an administrator to assign IP address options to clients based on client properties, such as device type, MAC address, or OS. DHCP policies are discussed later in "Configuring Policies." Options specified at the policy level can be overridden only by reservation options.
- *Reservation options*—As discussed, a reservation is an address associated with a computer's MAC address. When the computer with the specified MAC address requests an IP address, the DHCP server offers the reserved address and any configured options, thus ensuring that the computer is always assigned the same IP address settings. Options set on a reservation take precedence over any conflicting options set at any other level.

Common DHCP Options

DHCP options are specified in the format *NNNOptionName* with *NNN* representing a three-digit number that uniquely identifies the option in the DHCP packet, and *OptionName* being the option's user-friendly name. Some of the most common options include the following:

- *003 Router*—This option is almost always requested by the DHCP client and supplied by the DHCP server because it configures the client's default gateway setting, which is needed for the client to communicate with other networks. This option is usually configured at the scope level because each scope has a different default gateway associated with it. If you have only one scope, you can configure it at the server level. If you use policies or reservations, you can configure the router option at these levels so that selected computers can use a different default gateway than the rest of the scope does, if needed.

- *006 DNS Servers*—This option is often configured as a server option that applies to all scopes because DNS servers often provide services for an entire internetwork. However, if the option is configured on a scope, the scope option takes precedence. The DNS Servers option consists of a list of IP addresses of DNS servers the client can use for name resolution.

- *015 DNS Domain Name*—This option can also be configured as a server or scope option. It provides a domain name, such as csmtech.local, to DHCP clients. The DNS Domain Name option configures the client domain name, which a client needs when performing a DNS query with a single-label name. For example, if a user types \\Server1 in the Run dialog box, the DNS client attempts to resolve Server1 to an IP address. If no domain name is configured, the client sends the query to the DNS server as just Server1. Without a domain name, the lookup fails. However, if a domain name is configured, the DNS client software adds the domain name to the query so that the actual DNS query is sent as Server1.csmtech.local. The domain name is also used by the client when registering its computer name with the DNS server. Without a domain name that matches a zone name on the server, the registration fails. Domain members configure their DNS domain names automatically with the name of the domain they're a member of, so this option is unnecessary if all computers receiving DHCP addresses are domain members.

- *044 WINS/NBNS Servers*—This option is used only on networks with Windows Internet Name Service (WINS) servers.

- *046 WINS/NBT node type*—This option is used with option 044 to specify the WINS node type.

Configuring Options

Server options are configured in the DHCP console by right-clicking Server Options under the IPv4 or IPv6 node and clicking Configure Options. The Server Options dialog box has two tabs. The General tab has a list of available options in the upper pane. If you click the check box for an option, the lower pane is enabled so that you can enter information for the selected option. For example, in Figure 4-6, the 003 Router option is selected. For this option, you add one or more router addresses that clients use for their default gateway configuration.

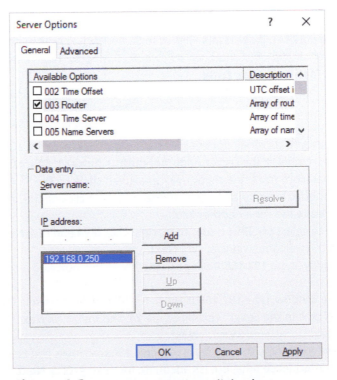

Figure 4-6   The Server Options dialog box

The Advanced tab of the Server Options dialog box has the same list of options as well as a list box to choose the **Vendor Class**, a field in the DHCP packet that device manufacturers or OS vendors use to identify a device model or an OS version. You can use this field to set different DHCP options. Starting with Windows Server 2012, the Vendor Class options should be used only when creating DHCP policies, discussed later in "Configuring Policies."

Scope and reservation options are set the same way as server options. To configure scope options, click the scope in the DHCP console, and then right-click Scope Options in the right pane and click Configure Options. To configure reservation options, right-click a reservation and click Configure Options. You can configure different options for each reservation.

Activity 4-1: Resetting Your Virtual Environment

Time Required: 5 minutes
Objective: Reset your virtual environment by applying the InitialConfig checkpoint or snapshot.
Required Tools and Equipment: ServerDC1, ServerDM1, ServerSA1
Description: Apply the InitialConfig checkpoint or snapshot to ServerDC1, ServerDM1, ServerDM2, and ServerSA1.

1. Be sure all servers are shut down. In your virtualization program, apply the InitialConfig checkpoint or snapshot to all servers.
2. When the snapshot or checkpoint has finished being applied, continue to the next activity.

Activity 4-2: Installing and Authorizing a DHCP Server

Time Required: 10 minutes
Objective: Install and authorize a DHCP server.
Required Tools and Equipment: ServerDC1, ServerDM1, ServerSA1
Description: In this activity, you install the DHCP Server role on a domain member server and authorize it. Then, you create and configure a DHCP scope.

1. Start ServerDC1 and ServerDM1, if necessary. Sign in to ServerDM1 as **Administrator**.
2. On ServerDM1, open Server Manager and open a PowerShell window. Type **Install-WindowsFeature DHCP -IncludeManagementTools** and press **Enter**.
3. When the DHCP Server installation finishes, click **Tools, DHCP** from the Server Manager menu to open the DHCP console.
4. Click to expand the server node in the left pane. Notice that both the IPv4 and IPv6 nodes show red down arrows, indicating that they're currently not enabled because the server is not authorized.
5. To authorize the server, right-click the server node (**serverdm1.mcsa2016.local**) and click **Authorize**.
6. Click the **Refresh** toolbar icon. You see a check mark in a green circle on the IPv4 and IPv6 nodes. If you need to, you can unauthorize a server after it's authorized by right-clicking the server node and clicking Unauthorize. For now, leave the server authorized.
7. To create a scope, click to select the **IPv4** node. Then, right-click **IPv4** and click New Scope to start the **New Scope** Wizard. In the welcome window, click **Next**.
8. In the Scope Name window, type **192.168.0-Scope** in the Name text box, add a description, if you like, and then click **Next**.
9. In the IP Address Range window, type **192.168.0.100** in the Start IP address text box and **192.168.0.200** in the End IP address text box. In the Length text box, type **24**, and then click **Next**.
10. In the Add Exclusions and Delay window, click **Next**.
11. In the Lease Duration window, type **0** in the Days text box, **1** in the Hours text box, and **0** in the Minutes text box. One hour is a short lease time, but it's adequate for testing. Click **Next**.

12. In the Configure DHCP Options window, click **No, I will configure these options later**, and then click **Next**.

13. In the Completing the New Scope Wizard window, click **Finish**.

14. In the DHCP console, you see the new scope, but a red down arrow indicates that it's not activated. Click the scope you just created. You see additional folders under it, which you work with later. Right-click the scope and click **Activate**. The scope is now activated.

15. Start ServerSA1, and sign in as **Administrator**.

16. On ServerSA1, open a PowerShell window and type **Set-NetIPInterface -InterfaceAlias Ethernet Dhcp Enabled** and press **Enter**. To set the DNS server address for DHCP, type **Set-DnsClientServerAddress -InterfaceAlias Ethernet -ResetServerAddresses** and press **Enter**.

17. Type **ipconfig /all** and press **Enter**. You see that the address 192.168.0.100 with subnet mask 255.255.255.0 was assigned. Look for the line starting with DHCP Server; the address is 192.168.0.2, the address of ServerDM1.

18. On ServerDM1 in the DHCP console, click **Address Leases**. You see the address leased to ServerSA1 (see Figure 4-7). If necessary, click the Refresh icon to see the address lease.

19. Stay signed in to ServerDM1 and ServerSA1 if you're continuing to the next activity.

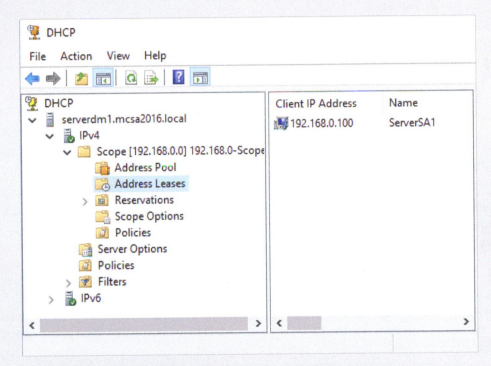

Figure 4-7   **Viewing address leases**

Activity 4-3: Working with Exclusions and Reservations

Time Required: 20 minutes

Objective: Create exclusion ranges and reservations and test them.

Required Tools and Equipment: ServerDC1, ServerDM1, ServerSA1

Description: In this activity, you create an exclusion range and verify that the address can't be leased. You also create a reservation for ServerSA1 and verify that the reserved address is leased by ServerSA1.

1. On ServerSA1 in a PowerShell window, type **ipconfig /renew** and press **Enter** to get a fresh lease on the IP address. The leased address should still be 192.168.0.100.

2. On ServerDM1 in the DHCP console, click to expand the **192.168.0-Scope** scope that you created earlier. Click to select Address Pool, and then right-click **Address Pool** and click **New Exclusion Range**.

3. In the Start IP address text box, type **192.168.0.100**, and in the End IP address text box, type **192.168.0.105**. Click **Add** and then **Close**. You see the exclusion range in the middle pane with a red × (highlighted in Figure 4-8).

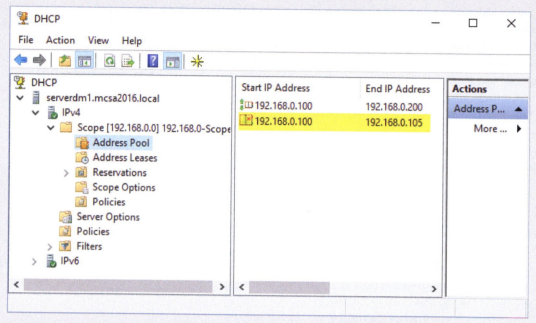

Figure 4-8   An exclusion range

4. On ServerSA1 in the PowerShell window, type **ipconfig /all** and press **Enter**. In the output, look for the Lease Obtained and Lease Expires lines under the Ethernet connection to see your lease information.

5. Type **ipconfig /renew** and press **Enter**. You'll probably see an error message indicating that an error occurred while renewing the interface. Because you excluded the address that ServerSA1 was using, it was unable to renew the address, but it leased a new one. Type **ipconfig** and press **Enter**. You should see that you now have the address 192.168.0.106.

6. On ServerDM1, click **Address Leases** in the DHCP console. Click the **Refresh** icon to see the new address lease in the middle pane. You see the lease for ServerSA1. In the middle pane, scroll to the right until you see the Unique ID column, which is the MAC address of ServerSA1.

7. You can create a reservation manually or from an existing lease. To create a reservation from ServerSA1's existing lease, right-click the lease in the middle pane and click **Add to Reservation**. You see a message stating that the lease was converted to a reservation successfully. Click **OK**.

8. In the left pane, click **Reservations**. Right-click the new reservation in the middle pane and click **Properties**. You can change the name of the reservation and the MAC address and add a description, but you can't change the IP address. If you need to change the IP address, you must delete the reservation and create a new one. Click **Cancel**.

9. To delete this reservation, right-click the reservation and click **Delete**. Click **Yes** to confirm.

10. To create a reservation manually, you need the MAC address of the computer for which you're creating the reservation. In the PowerShell window, type **ping 192.168.0.106** and press **Enter**. Don't worry if the ping times out.

11. Type **arp –a** and press **Enter** to list the MAC addresses known by ServerDM1. Use your mouse to select the MAC address next to the entry starting with **192.168.0.106** and press **Control+C** to copy it.

12. In the DHCP console, right-click **Reservations** and click **New Reservation**. In the Reservation name text box, type **ServerSA1**. (The reservation name is just a label and doesn't affect a reservation's function.)

13. In the IP address text box, Windows starts the address. Finish it by typing **0.100**. Right-click the MAC address text box and click **Paste** to paste the MAC address of ServerSA1 that you copied in Step 11 (see Figure 4-9, although your address will be different from the one in the figure). Click **Add**, and then **Close**. Remember that 192.168.0.100 is in the excluded range you created earlier, but as you see in the next step, reservations still work even if they're in the excluded range.

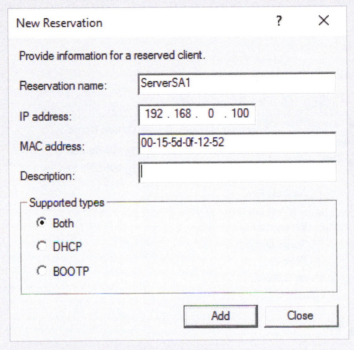

Figure 4-9   Creating a reservation

14. On ServerSA1, type **ipconfig /renew** in the PowerShell window and press **Enter**. An error message is displayed. Type **ipconfig** and press **Enter**. ServerSA1 now has the address 192.168.0.100.

15. Stay signed in to ServerDM1 and ServerSA1 and continue to the next activity.

Activity 4-4: Configuring DHCP Options

Time Required: 10 minutes

Objective: Configure router and DNS server options.

Required Tools and Equipment: ServerDC1, ServerDM1, ServerSA1

Description: You have the scope configured and tested. Now, you need to add router and DNS server options so that clients are fully functional. First, you configure the 003 Router and 006 DNS Servers options in the scope, and then you configure a different value for the 006 DNS Servers option in the reservation so that you can see reservation options take precedence over scope options.

1. On ServerDM1 in the DHCP console, click the **192.168.0** scope. In the left pane, right-click **Scope Options** and click **Configure Options**.

2. In the Scope Options dialog box, click the **003 Router** check box. In the lower pane, type **192.168.0.250** (or another value if required for your network) in the IP address text box and click **Add**.

3. In the upper pane, click the **006 DNS Servers** check box. Type **192.168.0.1** in the IP address text box, and click **Add**. Windows attempts to validate the address. (If ServerDC1 isn't running, you see a message stating that the address is not a valid DNS address and asking whether you still want to add it. Click **Yes**.) Click **OK**.

4. In the DHCP console, double-click **Scope Options** in the middle pane. You see the two options you just configured (see Figure 4-10).

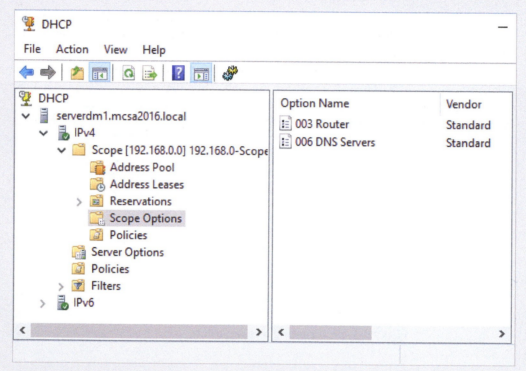

Figure 4-10 Scope options

5. On ServerSA1 in a PowerShell window, type **ipconfig /renew** and press **Enter**. You see that the default gateway is set to 192.168.0.250. Type **ipconfig /all** and press **Enter**. The DNS Servers line under the Ethernet connection should be set to 192.168.0.1.

6. Next, you configure options for the reservation. On ServerDM1, click to expand **Reservations**. Click then right-click the **ServerSA1** reservation, and click **Configure Options**.

7. Click the **006 DNS Servers** check box. Type **192.168.0.2** in the IP address text box and click **Add**. Click **Yes** in the message box and click **OK**.

8. On ServerSA1, type **ipconfig /renew** and press **Enter**, and then type **ipconfig /all** and press **Enter**. The DNS Servers line under the Ethernet connection should be set to 192.168.0.2 because the reservation option takes precedence over the scope option.

9. On ServerDM1, click **Reservations** in the left pane. Right-click the reservation and click **Delete**. Close the DHCP console.

10. Stay signed in to ServerDM1 and ServerSA1 and continue to the next activity.

Activity 4-5: Creating a Superscope

Time Required: 15 minutes
Objective: Create a superscope and test it.
Required Tools and Equipment: ServerDC1, ServerDM1, ServerSA1
Description: You want to see how to use superscopes. You already have one scope, so you create a new scope, and then create a superscope and add both scopes to it.

1. On ServerDM1 at the PowerShell prompt, type **Add-DhcpServerV4Scope -Name 192.168.1-Scope StartRange 192.168.1.100 -EndRange 192.168.1.200 -SubnetMask 255.255.255.0** and press **Enter**.
2. To create the new superscope, type **Add-DhcpServerv4SuperScope -SuperscopeName SuperScope-1 -ScopeID 192.168.0.0,192.168.1.0** and press **Enter**. Close the PowerShell prompt.
3. Open the DHCP console. Click to expand the server node and the **IPv4** node to see the new superscope. If you don't see it, click the **Refresh** icon on the DHCP console. Click **Superscope SuperScope-1** to see the two scopes that are members of the superscope.
4. On ServerSA1 in the PowerShell window, type **ipconfig /release** and press **Enter**, then type **ipconfig /renew**, and press **Enter**. The ServerSA1 computer will probably be assigned the same address it had before you created the superscope.
5. On ServerDM1, click to expand **Scope [192.168.0.0] 192.168.0-Scope** and click **Address Leases**. You see the address leased by ServerSA1.
6. Right-click **Scope [192.168.0.0] 192.168.0-Scope** and click **Deactivate**. Click **Yes** to confirm.
7. On ServerSA1 at the command prompt, type **ipconfig /renew** and press **Enter**. You might see an error message, but an address from the 192.168.1.0 scope should be leased. Type **ipconfig** and press **Enter** to see the address to which the computer was leased, which should be 192.168.1.100.
8. On ServerDM1, right-click **Scope [192.168.0.0] 192.168.0-Scope** and click **Activate**. You're finished with the 192.168.1.0 scope, so right-click **Scope [192.168.1.0] 192.168.1-Scope** and click **Delete**. Click **Yes** to confirm, and then click **Yes** again. Now right-click **Superscope SuperScope-1** and click **Delete**. Click **Yes** to confirm. Deleting the superscope doesn't delete the member scopes, so 192.168.0-Scope remains.
9. On ServerSA1, type **ipconfig /release**, press **Enter**, and then type **ipconfig /renew** and press **Enter**. You might see an error message. Type **ipconfig** and press **Enter** to verify that you have an address from the 192.168.0.0 subnet again.
10. Stay signed in to ServerDM1 and ServerSA1 and continue to the next activity.

Activity 4-6: Creating a Multicast Scope

Time Required: 10 minutes
Objective: Create a multicast scope.
Required Tools and Equipment: ServerDC1, ServerDM1
Description: You want to see how to create a multicast scope, so you create an administrative multicast scope with the minimum required 256 addresses.

1. On ServerDM1 in the DHCP console, right-click the **IPv4** node and click **New Multicast Scope** to start the New Multicast Scope Wizard. In the welcome window, click **Next**.
2. Type **Admin1** in the Name text box (because you're creating an administrative scope), and then click **Next**.
3. In the Start IP address text box, type **239.192.0.0**, and in the End IP address text box, type **239.192.0.255**, which provides the minimum 256 addresses required for an administrative scope. Leave the TTL at the default value, **32**, and then click **Next**.
4. In the Add Exclusions window, click **Next**. In the Lease Duration window, note that the default lease time is 30 days compared with 8 days for a unicast scope. Click **Next**.

5. In the Activate Multicast Scope window, accept the default value **Yes**, and click **Next**. Click **Finish**.
6. In the DHCP console, click to expand **Multicast Scope [Admin1]**. You see an Address Pool node and an Address Leases node. Click the **Address Pool** node to see the scope (Figure 4-11).

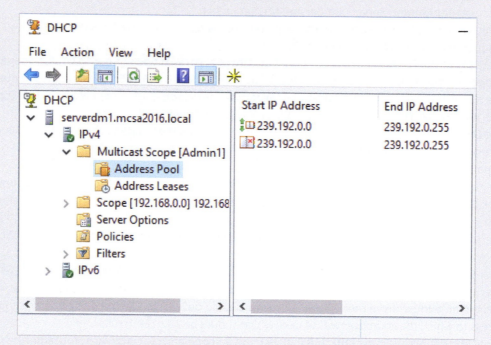

Figure 4-11 A multicast scope

7. Continue to the next activity.

 Tip ⓘ

For a good tutorial on IPv4 multicasting, see *https://technet.microsoft.com/en-us/library/cc772041(v=ws.10).aspx*.

DHCP Server Configuration

 **Certification**

- **70-741 – Implement DHCP:**
  Manage and maintain DHCP

You can perform several DHCP server configuration tasks in the DHCP console. The options you can change depend on whether you right-click the topmost node with the server name or the IPv4 or IPv6 nodes. If you right-click the server node, you see a menu listing the tasks you can perform, most of which are described in the following list:

- *Add/Remove Bindings*—This option is useful on multihomed servers. If the DHCP server has two or more network connections, you might not always want it to respond to DHCP packets from all networks, as when one network is connected to the Internet. You can enable or disable the binding for each interface (see Figure 4-12). When a binding is disabled, it prevents the server from listening for DHCP messages on port UDP 67.

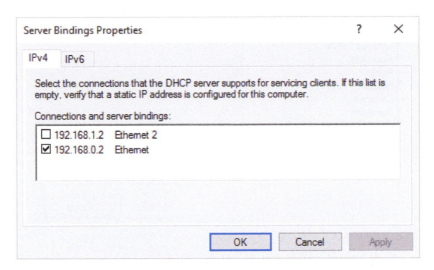

Figure 4-12   The Server Bindings Properties dialog box

- *Backup*—You can back up the DHCP database, which is stored in %*systemroot*%\System32\dhcp\ dhcp.mdb. The backup is stored in %*systemroot*%\System32\dhcp\backup\DhcpCfg by default, but you're prompted to change the path if needed. After you select a path, the DHCP database is backed up, including all scopes, options, exclusion ranges, reservations, and leases.
- *Restore*—If you need to restore a backup of the DHCP database, perhaps after database corruption caused by a system crash, choose this option and the path to the most current backup. When you restore the database, the DHCP server is stopped and restarted after the restore is finished. You should then reconcile the scopes, which you do by right-clicking the IPv4 or IPv6 node in the DHCP console and clicking Reconcile All Scopes. You can also reconcile a scope separately by right-clicking it and clicking Reconcile.
- *All Tasks*—If you point to All Tasks, you have the option to start, stop, pause, resume, or restart the DHCP server service.
- *Delete*—Deletes the server from the console but doesn't actually uninstall the DHCP Server role.
- *Refresh*—Refreshes the view.
- *Properties*—Opens the Properties dialog box for the DHCP server where you can change the default database path and backup path.

The IPv4 and IPv6 nodes have many of the same options, but several are found only in the IPv4 mode. Right-click the IPv4 node to see the menu options described in the following list:

- *Display Statistics*—This option displays statistics about the server and DHCP transactions (see Figure 4-13) that can be useful in troubleshooting problems. For example, a lot of Nacks can indicate an incorrect configuration, such as a corrupt or deactivated scope. A lot of Declines can indicate IP address conflicts. If a DHCP client finds that the leased IP address is in use, it sends a DHCPDECLINE and requests another address.
- *New Scope*—Starts the New Scope Wizard.
- *New Superscope*—Starts the New Superscope Wizard. This option is available only under the IPv4 node because IPv6 doesn't support superscopes.
- *New Multicast Scope*—Starts the New Multicast Scope Wizard.
- *Configure Failover and Replicate Failover Scopes*—These options configure high availability for DHCP services. You can configure fault tolerance and load balancing of DHCP services by allowing two DHCP servers to provide IP address and DHCP option information for the same scopes. The servers

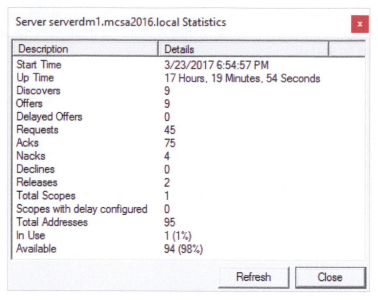

Figure 4-13 Server statistics

replicate configuration and lease information with each other to ensure that both servers have current data for leasing IP addresses to clients. Configuring high availability for DHCP is covered later in this chapter. Failover isn't an option in IPv6.

- *Define User Classes and Define Vendor Classes*—These options are used to define User Class and Vendor Class values that can be used in DHCP policies.

- *Reconcile All Scopes*—If the lease information shown in the DHCP console doesn't seem to reflect the actual client leases or if the database appears corrupted, use this option to try to solve the problem. It attempts to fix inconsistencies between DHCP summary lease information stored in the Registry and detailed lease information stored in the DHCP database. If no problems are found, DHCP reports that the database is consistent. If inconsistencies are found, the inconsistent addresses are listed in the Reconcile All Scopes dialog box. Select the addresses listed and click Reconcile. The reconcile process restores an inconsistent address to the original DHCP client or creates a temporary reservation for the address. With a temporary reservation, when the lease time expires or a renewal attempt is made, the address is returned to the scope. This option isn't available for IPv6 scopes.

- *Set Predefined Options*—Using this selection, you can create custom DHCP options. One use is to create the 060 PXEClient option required for some configurations of Windows Deployment Services (WDS) discussed later in "Configuring DHCP for PXE Boot." Some specialized IP devices, such as Voice over IP (VoIP) phones, might also require custom options.

- *Properties*—This option opens the Properties dialog box for the IPv4 server discussed next.

Configuring IPv4 Server Properties

The IPv4 Properties dialog box has these six tabs:

- *General*—Specify statistics and logging parameters (see Figure 4-14). In addition, if you enable the *Show the BOOTP table folder* option, a new folder is added under the IPv4 node in the DHCP console so that you can configure BOOTP support. BOOTP is a remote boot protocol that devices use to boot from an image stored on a server.

- *DNS*—Configure how DHCP interacts with a DNS server for making dynamic updates on behalf of DHCP clients (see Figure 4-15). You can configure the following settings:
  - Dynamically update DNS records only if requested by the DHCP clients: This option is the default. When a client leases an IP address or renews a lease and sends option 81 in the DHCPREQUEST packet, the DHCP server attempts to register records dynamically with the DNS server on behalf of

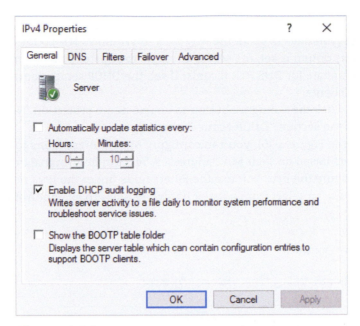

Figure 4-14   The General tab for IPv4 Properties

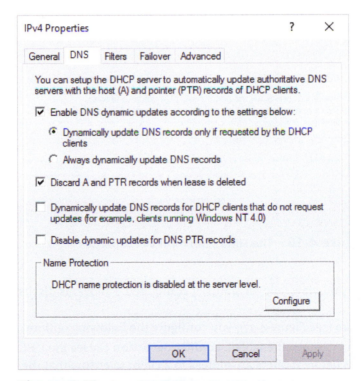

Figure 4-15   The DNS tab for IPv4 Properties

the client. Option 81 in the DHCPREQUEST packet contains the client's FQDN. By default, Windows clients configure option 81 so that the client updates its own A record and requests that the server update the PTR record.

- Always dynamically update DNS records: If this option is set, the DHCP server always attempts to register A and PTR records for the client as long as the client supports option 81.
- Discard A and PTR records when lease is deleted: If a lease is deleted and this option is selected (the default), the DHCP server attempts to contact the DNS server to delete the A and PTR records associated with the lease.

- Dynamically update DNS records for DHCP clients that do not request updates: If a client doesn't support option 81 (you have to go all the way back to Windows NT 4.0 for Windows clients that don't support it) and this option is set, the server attempts to register DNS records on the client's behalf.
    - Disable dynamic update for DNS PTR records: If set, the DHCP server doesn't attempt to register PTR records for DHCP clients.
    - Name Protection: Click the Configure button to enable name protection. Name protection is discussed later in the section "DHCP Name Protection."
- *Filters*—In this tab (see Figure 4-16), you can configure MAC address filters to allow or deny DHCP services to computers based on their MAC addresses. You can only enable or disable the allow or deny list. To configure the lists, you use the Filters node under the IPv4 node. If you click the Advanced button, you can select from a list of hardware types to exempt from filtering.

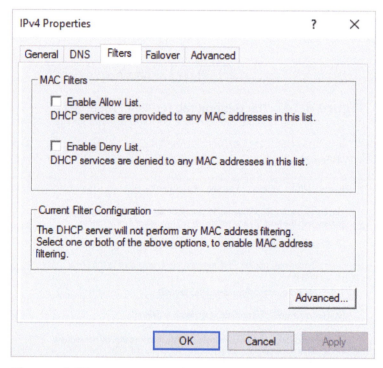

Figure 4-16   The Filters tab for IPv4 Properties

- *Failover*—Configure and view failover status, if configured. Failover is discussed later in this chapter.
- *Advanced*—In this tab (see Figure 4-17), you configure the following options:
    - Conflict detection attempts: If enabled, **conflict detection** causes the DHCP server to attempt to ping an IP address before it offers an address to a client to ensure that the address isn't already in use. Conflict detection attempts can be set between 0 and 5, which specifies how many `ping` packets the server should send before assuming the address isn't in use. By default, conflict detection attempts are set to 0, which disables conflict detection. In most cases, the server never sends a `ping` packet because it must first send an ARP to get a MAC address unless the server has an entry for the IP address in its ARP cache already. In any case, the DHCP server must time out between attempts before trying another attempt or proceeding with the lease, which slows down the DHCP lease process. Because most client computers do conflict detection before accepting an offered address, conflict detection should be enabled on the DHCP server only if the server is receiving many DHCPDECLINE messages. After the problem is remedied, conflict detection should be disabled.
    - Audit log file path: You can change the default path for the audit log file.

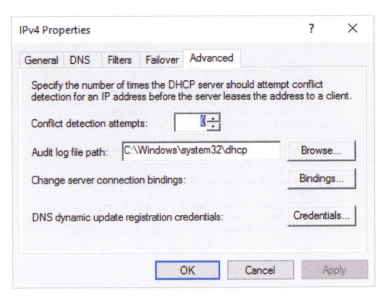

Figure 4-17 The Advanced tab for IPv4 Properties

- Change server connection bindings: Clicking the Bindings button performs the same function as the Add/Remove Bindings option you see when you right-click the server node as discussed earlier.
- DNS dynamic update registration credentials: If you click the Credentials button, you can enter the username, domain name, and password for a domain account that has permission to send dynamic updates. Configuring credentials is needed only if the DHCP service is running on a domain controller and secure dynamic DNS update is enabled.

> **Note**
>
> The IPv6 Properties dialog box has only the General, DNS, and Advanced tabs with largely the same configuration options as these tabs in the IPv4 Properties dialog box.

DHCP Name Protection

On networks with both Windows and non-Windows computers, a problem known as **name squatting** can occur when a non-Windows computer registers its name with a DNS server, but the name has already been registered by a Windows computer. Name squatting isn't a problem on networks where all computers are members of a Windows domain because Active Directory ensures that all computer names are unique.

DHCP name protection prevents name squatting by non-Windows computers by using a DHCP resource record called Dynamic Host Configuration Identifier (DHCID). It's a resource record used by DHCP and DNS to verify that a name being registered in DNS is from the original computer that registered it if the name already exists. DHCP name protection can be configured at the scope level or the IPv4 and IPv6 server node levels. If it's configured at the IPv4 or IPv6 server level, all the corresponding scopes are configured. Name protection configured at the scope level doesn't affect other scopes.

Configuring DHCP Name Protection

To configure name protection, right-click the scope, IPv4, or IPv6 node in the DHCP console and click Properties. Click the DNS tab, and then click the Configure button in the Name Protection section. In the Name Protection dialog box, click the Enable Name Protection check box to enable or disable name protection (see Figure 4-18).

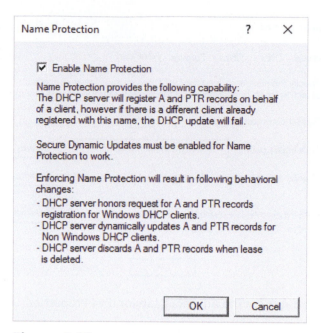

Figure 4-18   Configuring name protection

Configuring Scope Properties

To access a scope's properties, right-click it and click Properties. The Scope Properties dialog box has three tabs:

- *General*—In the General tab (see Figure 4-19), you can change the scope name and the start and end IP addresses, but you can't change the subnet mask (prefix length). You can also change the lease duration, which by default is 8 days. This duration is fine for a typical office environment where

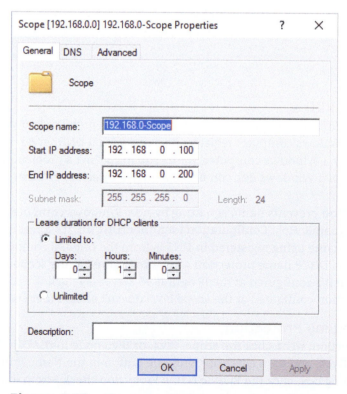

Figure 4-19   The General tab for scope properties

the same computers are used each day. Having a long lease duration prevents unnecessary traffic from frequent lease renewals. However, you might want a shorter lease time in a less predictable environment where many computers are used for brief periods and then not used again for long periods or ever as in a testing or training environment that uses a lot of virtual machines. Another example is a wireless network in a public setting where mobile devices come and go constantly. Another reason to set a short lease duration is if you're planning to make changes to the IP addressing scheme that requires a major scope change. As the time for the change approaches, you can make the lease time shorter and shorter until it's less than a day. You can make the scope change overnight or over a weekend, and the short lease time ensures that all clients need to renew their lease in a short period. Renewal requests are denied; instead, clients are assigned addresses from the new scope.

- *DNS*—This tab contains the same dynamic DNS configuration options as the DNS tab in the IPv4 Properties dialog box discussed earlier, but it pertains to only a single scope rather than all scopes.
- *Advanced*—Configure which type of clients the server responds to (see Figure 4-20):

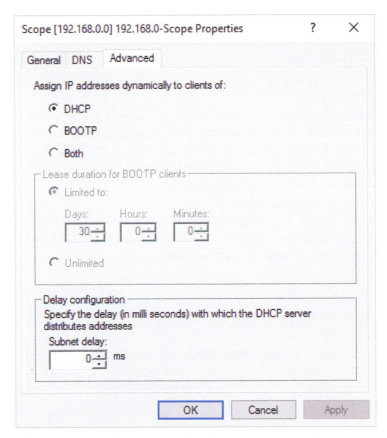

Figure 4-20   The Advanced tab for scope properties

- DHCP: The default setting; the server responds only to DHCP client requests.
- BOOTP: The server responds to BOOTP clients.

Note 📎

If BOOTP or DHCP is selected, you can choose a maximum lease duration for BOOTP clients.

- Both: The server responds to DHCP and BOOTP clients.
- Delay configuration: You can set a delay specified in milliseconds before the server responds to DHCPDISCOVER messages. This option is useful in split scope configurations as discussed later in the chapter and is configured automatically by the split scope wizard.

Configuring Filters

DHCP filters allow administrators to restrict which computers on a network are leased IP addresses. Filters use MAC addresses as the filtering criteria, so it's a simple allow or deny permission based on a client's MAC address. Filters are configured under the IPv4 node and aren't available for IPv6 DHCP. To set a filter, click Filters under the IPv4 node, and then right-click Allow or Deny and click New Filter. In the New Filter dialog box, you add each MAC address you want to allow or deny, along with an optional description for each address. After the addresses are added, you enable the filter.

If you create an allow filter, only a device with a MAC address in the filter list can lease an IP address from the DHCP server. All other devices are denied. If you create a deny filter, all devices except those with a MAC address in the filter list can lease an address from the DHCP server.

You can add addresses to the allow or deny filter from the list of current address leases instead of manually adding each address. To do so, click Address Leases under a scope, select one or more addresses you want to add to a filter, right-click a selected address, point to Add to Filter, and click Allow or Deny to add the selected addresses to the filter.

Configuring Policies

DHCP policies, a new feature starting in Windows Server 2012, give administrators more fine-tuned control over address lease options with conditions. A policy contains conditions that specify one or more clients to which IP address settings should be delivered. Conditions can be based on a number of criteria, and more than one criterion can be used in a condition with AND and OR operators. You can create policy conditions with any combination of the following criteria:

- *Vendor Class*—Defined earlier, the Vendor Class is most often used by device or OS manufacturers to identify a type of device or OS. Vendor Classes can be used to identify VoIP phones, printers, mobile devices, and so forth. For example, you can create the condition "Vendor Class equals Hewlett-Packard JetDirect" to identify all HP printers.

> **Tip** ⓘ
>
> Finding the Vendor Class in a device's documentation can be difficult. One way to discover this information is to set up the device on the network, configure it to use DHCP, and then capture the DHCP packets it transmits with a protocol analyzer, such as Wireshark. The Vendor Class is in the DHCPDISCOVER packet in the Option 60 field.

- *User Class*—This is similar to the Vendor Class except that a **User Class** can be a custom value you create on the DHCP server and then configure on a DHCP client. For example, if you have special settings that you want the DHCP server to deliver to all computers in the Engineering Department, you can create a User Class named Engineering and then configure the network interface on the relevant computers with this User Class. To configure a User Class on a Windows computer, type `ipconfig /setclassid Ethernet "Engineering"`, which sets the User Class on the Ethernet network connection to Engineering.
- *MAC address*—You can use wildcards with a list of MAC addresses so that you can use the organizationally unique identifier (OUI) part of the MAC address to specify a manufacturer. The OUI is the first 24 bits of a MAC address. For example, you can create the condition "MAC address equals 000F34*" to identify certain types of Cisco routers.

- *Client identifier*—The client identifier (ClientID) is usually the MAC address but can also be the globally unique ID (GUID) of the NIC on a PXE client.
- *Fully qualified domain name*—You can use a fully qualified domain name (FQDN) in a condition starting with Windows Server 2012 R2. An FQDN can be used only to configure DNS-related configuration information, such as dynamic DNS registration. You can use this criterion to match computers based on their FQDNs and use wildcards to group computers based on their hostnames or DNS suffixes. For example, you can create a condition such as "Fully qualified domain name equals *.csmtech.local," which matches computers with an FQDN ending with csmtech.local. You can also use this criterion to identify workgroup computers (computers that aren't domain members).
- *Relay agent information*—This criterion is useful when a wireless access point acts as a DHCP relay, sending DHCP requests to the DHCP server on behalf of wireless clients. You can assign wireless clients' IP addresses with a shorter lease time and perhaps a different default gateway and DNS server. To create a condition based on relay agent information (DHCP option 82), you enter a hexadecimal code provided by the relay agent's manufacturer.

Policies can be configured at the server level or the scope level. Scope-level policies take precedence over server-level policies if both are configured and there's a conflict. Server-level policies are limited to assigning DHCP options and lease duration to clients matching the policy conditions. Scope-level policies can also issue IP addresses from a specified range to matching clients. For example, if the scope has the start address 192.168.0.1 and end address 192.168.0.254 with the prefix length 24, the policy can specify that all matching clients are issued an address in the range 192.168.0.100 through 192.168.0.150. To create a policy, just right-click the Policies node under the IPv4 node or the scope and click New Policy to start the DHCP Policy Configuration Wizard. Then follow these steps:

1. Give the policy a name and optionally a description.
2. Create one or more conditions that identify devices.
3. Configure settings for the policy, such as router and DNS servers.
4. Configure additional settings in the policy's Properties dialog box. You can configure lease time and DNS settings and make changes to other settings that were configured in the wizard.

Configuring DHCP for PXE Boot

If you're using Windows Deployment Services (WDS) to install Windows OSs on computers, you might need to configure DHCP to respond to **Preboot Execution Environment (PXE)** network interfaces. PXE is a network environment built into many network interface cards (NICs) that allows a computer to boot from an image stored on a network server. WDS uses this feature to install the Windows OS remotely. In many cases, when you configure the WDS role service, the DHCP configuration is handled by the WDS configuration wizard, but in some circumstances, you need to configure DHCP options manually.

If a Microsoft DHCP server and WDS are on the same server and all potential WDS clients are on the same network as the WDS server, you don't have to change any DHCP settings. However, if the DHCP server is on a different server or a different subnet, you do. Here are the most commons setups that require special DHCP configuration:

- *The DHCP server is on a different server or a different subnet from the WDS server*—You must configure two DHCP server options. For Option 066 Boot Server Host Name, you can supply the WDS server's IP address or server name. Option 067 Bootfile Name is the name and path of the boot file WDS clients need to start remote OS installation.
- *DHCP is installed on the same server as WDS, but it's not a Microsoft DHCP server, or the Microsoft DHCP server is installed after WDS was installed*—In this case, you need to configure a predefined DHCP option (discussed earlier in "DHCP Server Configuration") with code 060. Add the 060 PXEClient option to the DHCP server by right-clicking the IPv4 node in the DHCP console and clicking Set Predefined Options. Click Add, and then fill in the dialog box as shown in Figure 4-21. Type the WDS server's IP address or name in the String text box and click OK. Under the IPv4 node, right-click

Server Options, click Configure Options, and then click o60 PXEClient. When PXE clients request an IP address, this option instructs them to contact the specified WDS server to get their boot configuration.

Option Type		?	×
Class:	Global		
Name:	PXEClient		
Data type:	String ▼	☐ Array	
Code:	060		
Description:	PXE Client options		
		OK	Cancel

Figure 4-21   Creating the PXEClient option

DHCP Relay Agents

A **DHCP relay agent** is a device that listens for broadcast DHCPDISCOVER and DHCPREQUEST messages and forwards them to a DHCP server on another subnet. You configure a DHCP relay agent on a subnet that doesn't have a DHCP server so that you can still manage DHCP addresses from a central server without having to configure the DHCP server with network interfaces in each subnet. In this setup, a DHCP server is configured on one subnet and has multiple scopes configured, one for each subnet in the internetwork that has DHCP clients (as shown in Figure 4-22). This figure shows three subnets. The DHCP server in the 10.1.1.0/24 subnet has three scopes configured, one for each of the three subnets. When a DHCP client in the 10.1.2.0 or 10.1.3.0 subnet requests an IP address, the DHCP relay agent in the same subnet forwards the request to the DHCP server on the 10.1.1.0 subnet.

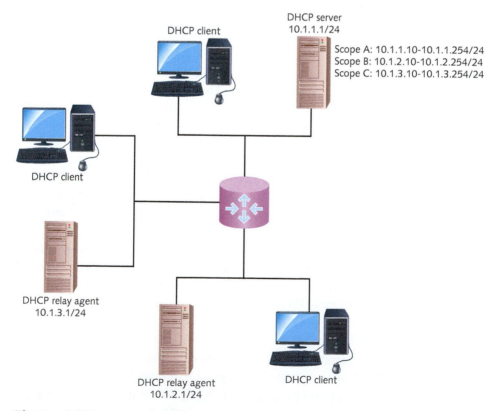

DHCP client

DHCP server
10.1.1.1/24

Scope A: 10.1.1.10-10.1.1.254/24
Scope B: 10.1.2.10-10.1.2.254/24
Scope C: 10.1.3.10-10.1.3.254/24

DHCP client

DHCP relay agent
10.1.3.1/24

DHCP relay agent
10.1.2.1/24

DHCP client

Figure 4-22   DHCP relay agents

The details of the DHCP relay process are as follows:

1. A client on the same subnet as the DHCP relay agent sends a DHCPDISCOVER broadcast requesting an IP address.

2. The relay agent forwards the message to the DHCP server's IP address as a unicast.

3. The DHCP server receives the unicast DHCPDISCOVER. The relay agent's address is contained in the message, so the DHCP server knows to draw an address from the scope matching the relay agent's IP address. For example, if the relay agent has the address 10.1.2.10, the DHCP server looks for a scope containing a range of addresses that includes 10.1.2.10.

4. The DHCP server sends a unicast DHCPOFFER message to the relay agent.

5. The relay agent forwards the DHCPOFFER as a broadcast to the subnet from which the DHCPDISCOVER was received. Because the client doesn't yet have an IP address, the agent must forward the DHCPOFFER as a broadcast message.

6. The DHCP client broadcasts a DHCPREQUEST.

7. The relay agent receives the DHCPREQUEST and forwards it to the DHCP server.

8. The DHCP server replies with a DHCPACK to the relay agent.

9. The relay agent forwards the DHCPACK to the client, and the client binds the address to its interface.

10. Renewal requests are unicast packets, so the DHCP client can communicate directly with the DHCP server for renewals.

Installing a DHCP Relay Agent

The DHCP relay agent function is configured as part of the Routing role service under the Remote Access server role. To make a Windows Server 2016 server a DHCP relay agent, follow these steps:

1. Install the Remote Access server role and include the Routing role service.

2. In the Routing and Remote Access console, right-click the server node and click Configure and Enable Routing and Remote Access.

3. In the Routing and Remote Access Server Setup Wizard, click Next, and then click Custom configuration.

4. In the Custom Configuration window, click the LAN routing check box (see Figure 4-23). Click Next and then Finish. Click Start service when prompted.

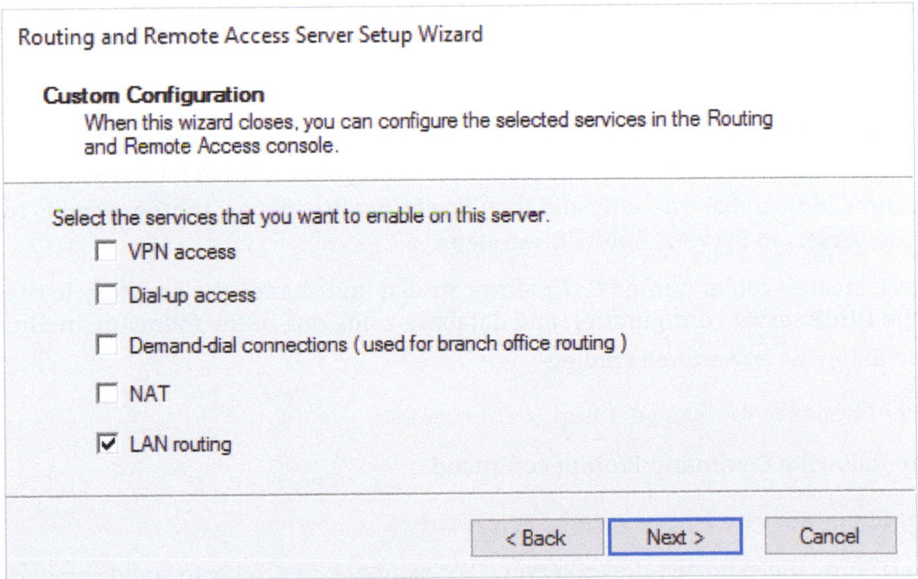

Figure 4-23   **The Custom Configuration window**

5. In the Routing and Remote Access console, expand the IPv4 node, and then right-click the General node and click New Routing Protocol. Click DHCP Relay Agent. If you have more than one interface, you see other options in addition to DHCP Relay Agent. Click OK.

6. In the Routing and Remote Access console, right-click DHCP Relay Agent and click New Interface. Click the interface you want the server to provide relay services on, and click OK. If the server has more than one network connection, you can add interfaces.

7. In the DHCP Relay Properties dialog box, accept the default settings (see Figure 4-24) and click OK.

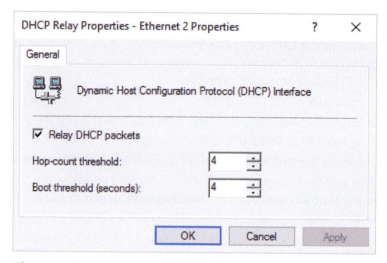

Figure 4-24   Setting DHCP relay properties

8. In the Routing and Remote Access console, right-click DHCP Relay Agent and click Properties. Type the address of the DHCP server to which the relay agent should forward DHCP messages and then click Add. You can add more than one address if you're using load balancing. Click OK. The relay agent is configured to send DHCP messages to the specified IP address.

Note

A DHCP server can't be configured as a DHCP relay agent.

Server Migration, Export, and Import

If you need to migrate the DHCP server role to another server, you can do so fairly easily by exporting the server configuration and database to a file and then importing that file on another server. To migrate a DHCP server from Server1 to Server2, follow these steps:

1. On Server1, create a folder named *C:\Export* or similar and change the directory to that folder. Export the DHCP server configuration and database using one of the following methods:
   - Use the following PowerShell cmdlet:

     ```
     Export-DhcpServer -File Dhcp.xml -Leases
     ```

   - Use the following Command Prompt command:

     ```
     netsh dhcp server export Dhcp.txt all
     ```

2. On Server1, copy the exported file to Server2. For example, use the command `copy dhcp.xml \\server2\c$` to copy the file to the root of the C: drive on Server2.

3. Unauthorize the DHCP server, stop the DHCP service, or uninstall the DHCP Server role on Server1.

4. On Server2, install the DHCP server role and authorize it, if necessary.

5. On Server2, import the exported file using one of the following methods:

   • Use the following PowerShell cmdlet:

   ```
   Import-DhcpServer -File C:\Dhcp.xml -Leases -BackupPath C:\dhcpback
   ```

   • Use the following Command Prompt command:

   ```
   netsh dhcp server import C:\Dhcp.txt all
   ```

6. On Server2, verify that the scope and existing leases were imported and that the DHCP service is running.

In the preceding procedure, the `-Leases` option of the PowerShell cmdlet specifies that current lease data should be exported and imported. If you want to migrate only the configuration and scopes, you can omit that option.

Troubleshooting DHCP

DHCP is a generally reliable protocol, but things can and do go wrong from time to time. The following is a list of possible problems, symptoms, and solutions for troubleshooting DHCP:

• *A client is not receiving a DHCP address*—A Windows DHCP client assigns itself an APIPA address in the range 169.254.0.0/16 if no DHCP server responds to its DHCPDISCOVER message. Verify that the DHCP service is running and authorized, that the scope is activated, and that addresses are available in the scope. If the client was recently moved to a different subnet and a reservation exists for the client from the old subnet, its request for an address will be denied because the reservation is for an address in the wrong subnet. In this case, delete the reservation and create a new one.

• *A client is receiving an incorrect DHCP address*—Another DHCP server might be operating on the subnet. Check the IP address of the DHCP server from which the client received the address (run `ipconfig /all` from a command prompt) and verify its identity.

• *IP address conflicts are occurring*—This can happen if there is a rogue DHCP server on the network or if the DHCP database needs to be reconciled. Check server statistics for a high number of Declines, which can be an indication of address conflicts resulting from rogue DHCP servers. Verify the identity of DHCP servers on the network and reconcile all scopes. In addition, look for addresses that are assigned statically. Be sure to create exclusions for statically assigned addresses.

• *The DHCP server service is not starting*—Verify that the server is authorized. Check for a corrupt scope. Reconcile the scope, if necessary. Restore the database from a backup if the scope data appears to be corrupted.

• *No addresses are being leased*— Verify that the DHCP service is running and authorized and that the scope is activated. Verify that addresses are available in the scope. For single-subnet deployments, verify that the scope is in the same subnet as the server's IP address. For DHCPv6, make sure the server has been assigned an IPv6 address with the same prefix as the scope. In multi-subnet deployments, make sure that the DHCP relay is configured with the correct IP address of the DHCP server. Also, verify the server bindings from the Server Bindings Properties dialog (shown earlier in Figure 4-12).

DHCP Troubleshooting Tools

There are a number of tools you can use to troubleshoot DHCP. We've discussed some of them including reviewing DHCP server statistics and reconciling scopes. If you need to see what's really happening between your DHCP server and clients, use a third-party protocol analyzer such as Wireshark. Configure the protocol analyzer to capture packets on UDP ports 67 and 68, and then from a client station, issue the `ipconfig /release` and `ipconfig /renew` commands to generate DHCP messages.

Another troubleshooting tool is the built-in DHCP audit logging feature that is enabled by default (recall Figure 4-14). The logging file shows information about when addresses were leased, renewed, and released as well as information about DNS updates attempted by the DHCP server. The log also shows when the server was authorized and when the service started and stopped. The log file is a simple text file you can open with Notepad or any text editor, and it can be found by default in C:\Windows\System32\dhcp.

Activity 4-7: Creating a DHCP Policy

Time Required: 10 minutes

Objective: Create a DHCP policy.

Required Tools and Equipment: ServerDC1, ServerDM1, ServerSA1

Description: Suppose you have new Cisco VoIP phones that require different IP address settings than the rest of the devices on the network. You decide to create a policy to deliver different options to these phones. In this activity, you create a new User Class so that you can test the policy with your ServerSA1 computer. In a real situation, the phones would have a defined Vendor Class, so if you were doing this for actual Cisco IP phones, you would replace User Class with Vendor Class wherever you see it in this activity.

1. On ServerDM1 in the DHCP console, click to expand the server node and the **IPv4** node, if necessary.
2. To create a new User Class, right-click the **IPv4** node and click **Define User Classes.** In the DHCP User Classes dialog box, click **Add**. In the New Class dialog box, type **Cisco IP Phone** in the Display name text box and **Cisco Voice over IP phones** in the Description text box.
3. In the lower pane of the New Class dialog box, click in the box under ASCII and type **Cisco IP Phone** (see Figure 4-25). This is the actual Vendor Class ID used by DHCP; the display name might not be the same. Click **OK**, and then **Close**.

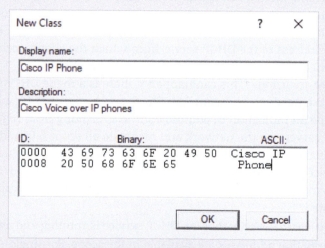

Figure 4-25 The New Class dialog box

4. Under the IPv4 node, right-click **Policies** and click **New Policy**. In the DHCP Policy Configuration Wizard, type **Cisco VoIP Policy** and click **Next**.
5. In the Configure Conditions for the policy window, click **Add**.
6. In the Add/Edit Condition dialog box, click the arrow to see the available criteria in the Criteria list box, and click **User Class**. In the Operator list box, you have the choice of Equals or Not Equals. Leave the default setting **Equals**.
7. In the Value(s) section, click the **Value** list arrow and click **Cisco IP Phone**. Because there might be different models of Cisco IP phones, click the **Append wildcard** check box so that the condition is "User Class Equals Cisco IP Phone*," meaning that any string can come after "Phone," and the User Class will match. Click **Add** (see Figure 4-26), and then click **Ok**.

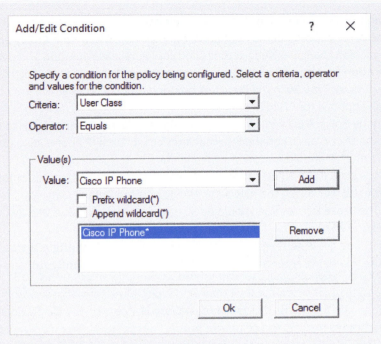

Figure 4-26   Adding a condition

8. In the Configure Conditions for the policy window, you see the line "User Class Equals Cisco IP Phone*." You can add conditions, if needed (see Figure 4-27). Leave the **OR** option button selected, and click **Next**.

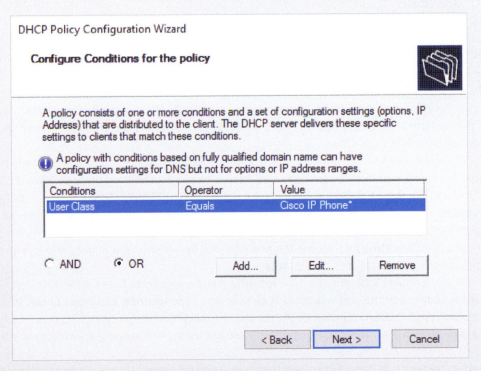

Figure 4-27   Configure Conditions for the policy

9. In the Configure settings for the policy window, you select the DHCP options you want to apply to the selected devices. You might want a different default gateway for these devices, so click the **003 Router** check box. Type **192.168.0.251** in the IP address text box, and click **Add**. Click **Next**.

10. In the Summary window, check your settings and click **Finish**.

11. Click **Policies** in the DHCP console. In the right pane, right-click the **Cisco VoIP Policy** and click **Properties**. In this dialog box, you can change existing settings and configure lease duration and dynamic DNS settings. Click **Set lease duration for the policy**. Because phones are on all the time, you might want a longer lease duration for these devices. Type **30** in the Days text box, and click **OK**. Policies are enabled by default, so it's ready to start serving options for Cisco IP phones.

12. On ServerSA1 from the PowerShell window, type **ipconfig /setclassid Ethernet "Cisco IP Phone 2640"** and press **Enter** to set the User Class ID on the Ethernet interface to Cisco IP Phone 2640. Because the policy says to match Cisco IP Phone*, it should match.

13. When you change the class ID on a PC, it attempts to renew IP address settings automatically, so type **ipconfig /all** and press **Enter** to see the new settings. Look for the Default Gateway line, which should now be 192.168.0.251. The Lease Expires line should be 30 days from now, and the DHCPv4 Class ID line should be set to Cisco IP Phone 2640.

14. To delete the class ID and get IP settings from the regular scope, type **ipconfig /setclassid Ethernet** and press **Enter**. Because you didn't enter a class ID, it's set to blank. Type **ipconfig /all** and press **Enter** to see that your settings are back to normal.

15. Continue to the next activity.

Activity 4-8: Creating a DHCP Filter

Time Required: 10 minutes
Objective: Create a DHCP filter.
Required Tools and Equipment: ServerDC1, ServerDM1, ServerSA1
Description: In this activity, you configure DHCP Allow and Deny filters. First, you create an Allow filter manually, and then you create a Deny filter from an existing lease.

1. On ServerDM1 in the DHCP console, click to expand the server node and the **IPv4** node, if necessary.

2. In the left pane, click to expand **Filters**. In the left pane, right-click **Allow** and click **New Filter.** In the New Filter dialog box, type **123456789012** in the MAC address text box. In the Description text box, type **Sample filter**, and then click **Add**. Click **Close**.

3. In the left pane, click **Allow** to see the new filter in the middle pane. Notice that the Allow node has a red down arrow, indicating that the filter isn't enabled. You won't test this filter, so you can leave it disabled.

4. Now, you'll add a filter from an existing lease. Click to expand the **192.168.0-Scope** scope, and then click **Address Leases**. In the middle pane, right-click the lease for ServerSA1, point to **Add to Filter**, and click **Deny** to add ServerSA1's MAC address to the Deny filter.

5. In the left pane, click the **Deny** filter to see the new entry for ServerSA1. (You might need to click the Refresh icon.) Right-click the **Deny** filter and click **Enable**.

6. On ServerSA1 in the PowerShell window, type **ipconfig /renew** and press **Enter**. After a while, you see an error message stating that the address couldn't be renewed. Type **ipconfig** and press **Enter**. Because the lease hasn't expired, ServerSA1 still has its IP address. The deny filter keeps clients from getting a new address or renewing an address, but it doesn't prevent them from keeping an address already leased.

7. Type **ipconfig /release** and press **Enter**, and then type **ipconfig /renew** and press **Enter**. ServerSA1 is unable to lease an IP address.

8. On ServerDM1 in the DHCP console, right-click the **Deny** filter and click **Disable**.

9. On ServerSA1, type **ipconfig /renew** and press **Enter**. ServerSA1 can lease an address again.

10. Continue to the next activity.

Implementing DHCPv6

- **70-741 – Implement DHCP:**
  Install and configure DHCP

Up to now, you have learned how to use DHCP in an IPv4 environment. Although IPv6 provides automatic address assignment without using a DHCP server, you might still want to use DHCPv6 for IPv6 address assignment. DHCPv6 enables you to manage IPv6 address assignment better, see which addresses are being used on the network, and control IPv6 address options. Before you get into configuring DHCPv6, the following sections review some IPv6 concepts.

IPv6 Address Structure

An IPv6 address is a 128-bit number written as eight 16-bit hexadecimal numbers separated by colons. There's no official name for each part of the address, so each 16-bit value is simply called a *field*. A valid IPv6 address looks like this:

```
fe80:0:0:0:18ff:0024:8e5a:60
```

IPv6 addresses often have several 0 values. One or more consecutive 0 values can be written as a double colon (`::`), so the preceding address can be written as `fe80::18ff:0024:8e5a:60`. However, you can have only one double colon in an IPv6 address. Leading 0s are optional. The value `0024` in the previous example could just as easily have been written as `24`, and the value `60` could have been written as `0060`. The hexadecimal numbering system was chosen to represent IPv6 addresses largely because it's much easier to convert to binary than decimal is. Each hexadecimal digit represents 4 bits, so to convert an IPv6 address to binary, simply convert each hexadecimal digit (accounting for leading 0s) to its binary equivalent.

The IPv6 Interface ID

The prefix length (network ID) of an IPv6 host address is always 64 bits. Therefore, the interface ID of an IPv6 address is 64 bits, too. For this reason, you can identify the network ID of an IPv6 address easily by looking at the first 64 bits (16 hex digits or four fields) and the interface ID by looking at the last 64 bits. For example, in the address `fe80:0:0:0:18ff:0024:8e5a:60`, the network ID is `fe80:0:0:0`, and the interface ID is `18ff:0024:8e5a:60`.

Because the prefix isn't a variable length, working with IPv6 addresses is somewhat easier because you don't have to do a binary calculation with a subnet mask to determine the network and interface IDs.

An IPv6 interface ID can be assigned to a host in these ways:

- *Using the 48-bit MAC address*—Because a MAC address is only 48 bits, the other 16 bits come from the value `fffe` inserted after the first 24 bits of the MAC address. In addition, the first two zeros that compose most MAC addresses are replaced with 02. For example, given the MAC address 00-0C-29-7C-F9-C4, the host ID of an IPv6 address is `020c:29ff:fe7c:f9c4`. This autoconfigured 64-bit host ID is an Extended Unique Identifier (EUI)-64 interface ID defined in RFC 4291.
- *A randomly generated permanent interface identifier*—The interface ID is generated randomly but is a permanent assignment maintained through system restarts. Windows Server 2008 and later versions use this method by default for permanent interfaces, such as Ethernet ports. However, you can specify that Windows use EUI-64 addresses with the `netsh` command or a PowerShell cmdlet.
- *A temporary interface identifier*—Some connections, such as dial-up Point-to-Point Protocol (PPP) connections, might use this method for interface IPv6 address assignment, defined in RFC 4941, by which the interface ID is assigned randomly and changes each time IPv6 is initialized to maintain anonymity.

- *Via DHCPv6*—Addresses are assigned via a DHCPv6 server to IPv6 interfaces when they're initialized.
- *Manually*—Similar to IPv4 configuration, the IPv6 address is entered manually in the interface's Properties dialog box.

IPv6 Autoconfiguration

IPv6 autoconfiguration occurs by two methods: stateless and stateful. With Windows Vista/Windows Server 2008 and later computers, these methods can actually be used together.

- *Stateless autoconfiguration*—With **stateless autoconfiguration**, the node listens for router advertisement messages from a local router. If the Autonomous flag in the router advertisement message is set, the node uses the prefix information contained in the message. In this case, the node uses the advertised prefix and its 64-bit interface ID to generate the IPv6 address. If the Autonomous flag isn't set, the prefix information is ignored, and the node can attempt to use DHCPv6 for address configuration or an automatically generated link-local address.
- *Stateful autoconfiguration*—With **stateful autoconfiguration**, the node uses an autoconfiguration protocol, such as DHCPv6, to get its IPv6 address and other configuration information. A node attempts to use DHCPv6 to get IPv6 address configuration information if there are no routers on the network providing router advertisements or if the Autonomous flag in router advertisements isn't set.

How Autoconfiguration Works on Windows Hosts

The Windows autoconfiguration process in Windows hosts involves the following steps:

1. At initialization, a link-local address is determined.
2. The link-local address is verified as unique by using duplicate address detection.
3. If the address is verified as unique, the address is assigned to the interface; otherwise, a new address is generated and Step 2 is repeated.
4. The host transmits a router solicitation message. This message is addressed to the *all-routers* multicast address.
5. If no router advertisement messages are received in response to the solicitation message, the host attempts to use DHCPv6 to get an address.
6. If a router advertisement message is received and has an Autonomous flag set, the prefix in the router advertisement is used along with the interface ID to configure the IPv6 address on the interface. The host can also use a DHCPv6 server to acquire other IPv6 configuration parameters if specified in the router advertisement. If the Autonomous flag isn't set, the host uses DHCPv6 to acquire the address.

Note that the IPv6 client maintains its link-local address even if it successfully gets an address via autoconfiguration or DHCPv6. Also, it's possible for the router advertisement to have the Autonomous flag set, causing the IPv6 client to autoconfigure an address *and* specify that the client should use DHCPv6 to get an address. In this case, the client does both and ends up with two addresses. It's also possible for more than one router to advertise an IPv6 prefix, causing the client to autoconfigure multiple addresses.

Configuring DHCPv6 Scopes

You configure a DHCPv6 scope in the DHCP console or with the `Add-DhcpServerV6Scope` PowerShell cmdlet. To configure a DHCPv6 scope, you need to provide the following information:

- *Scope name*—A name for your scope that identifies its purpose.
- *Prefix*—The 64-bit prefix value for the scope. The **prefix** is the part of the IPv6 address that's the network identifier. For example, a valid prefix is `2001:db8:2016::/64`. You can use the standard abbreviated methods for entering each field, including omitting leading zeroes. You must terminate the prefix with a double colon (see Figure 4-28). You don't specify start and end addresses for the range as you do with an IPv4 scope. The entire address range is used based on the prefix you enter. To exclude servers and other devices with static IPv6 addresses, use exclusions.

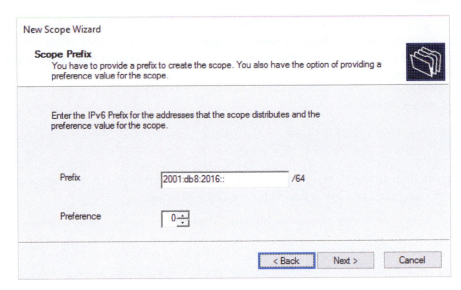

Figure 4-28   Specifying the IPv6 scope prefix and preference

- *Preference*—The **preference** value is used to indicate priority when there are multiple DHCPv6 servers. It's an optional value in the DHCPv6 message. A higher preference value indicates a higher priority. The default value is 0, meaning no preference value should be included in the message. If the preference option is included and a DHCPv6 client receives replies from more than one server, it chooses the reply with the highest priority (highest preference value). If the preference values are the same, the client chooses the reply with the best configuration options.
- *Exclusions*—You add exclusions just as you do for an IPv4 scope. You can specify a range of addresses, a single address, or no exclusions.
- *Scope lease*—The lease duration has two values: Preferred Life Time and Valid Life Time. The Preferred Life Time is the initial lease time, but when the time expires, the address remains valid until the Valid Life Time expires. The Valid Life Time must be equal to or greater than the Preferred Life Time. The default Preferred Life Time is 8 days, and the default Valid Life Time is 12 days (see Figure 4-29).

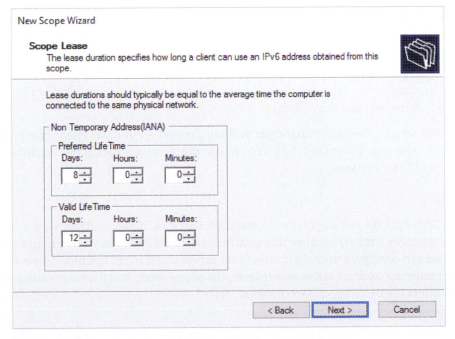

Figure 4-29   IPv6 scope lease preferred and valid life time

As with IPv4 scopes, you can create reservations and include options for DNS servers and other services; however, you can't assign a default gateway (router) with DHCPv6. IPv6 relies on router advertisements to get the address of its default gateway, or it can be assigned manually in the network interface's Properties dialog box.

> **Caution** ⚠
>
> Before Windows Server 2016 can begin assigning IPv6 addresses via DHCPv6, you must assign a static IPv6 address to the server, using the same prefix you do for the DHCPv6 scope.

DHCPv6 Operation

Unlike DHCPv4, the client's MAC address isn't used to lease an address and create reservations. DHCPv6 uses a **DHCP Unique Identifier (DUID)**. In Windows, a DUID is a hexadecimal number usually derived from the network interface's MAC address. It's created when Windows is installed and doesn't change even if the NIC changes. The DUID is stored in the HKLM\System\CurrentControlSet\Services\TCPIP6\ Parameters Registry key. If you delete this key, the DUID is created when the system is restarted. You can see it by using the `ipconfig /all` command. In the output of the command, look for the line that begins with DHCPv6 Client DUID.

After a DHCPv6 scope is created and activated, the DHCPv6 server is ready to begin assigning IPv6 addresses. The dynamic assignment of IPv6 addresses is similar to the process for IPv4 addresses. It consists of a series of four packets between the client and the server using UDP ports 546 and 547. The DHCPv6 client listens on port 546, and the DHCPv6 server listens on port 547. The four-message exchange is as follows:

1. The DHCPv6 client sends a Solicit message from its link-local address via UDP source port 546 to the IPv6 multicast address `ff02::1:2` on destination port 547.

2. The DHCPv6 server replies with an Advertise message to the link-local address of the client on destination port 546. This message contains the IPv6 address offered to the client.

3. The DHCPv6 client replies with a Request message from its link-local address, accepting the offered address. The message is still addressed to the IPv6 multicast address `ff02::1:2` at UDP port 547.

4. The DHCPv6 server responds with a Reply message confirming the address assignment. At this point, the client binds the assigned IPv6 address to its interface, the server adds the address to its list of leased addresses, and the process is completed.

To test a DHCPv6 scope, open a command prompt window on a Windows client computer, and enter the `ipconfig /renew6` command. You need to use the `/renew6` parameter because the `/renew` parameter is only for IPv4 addresses.

DHCPv6 Options

You configure DHCPv6 options just as you do for standard DHCPv4. However, there's no option in DHCPv6 to assign a default gateway (router) because this task is handled by router advertisements sent by routers on the network. You can configure domain names, DNS servers, and other options, however. As with DHCPv4, you can configure options at the server level, the scope level, and the reservation level, but there are no policies or filters for DHCPv6, unlike DHCPv4.

Activity 4-9: Creating and Testing a DHCPv6 Scope

Time Required: 10 minutes

Objective: Create and test a DHCPv6 scope.

Required Tools and Equipment: ServerDC1, ServerDM1, ServerSA1

Description: In this activity, you create a DHCPv6 scope and then test it.

1. On ServerDM1 in the DHCP console, click to expand the server node, if necessary, and then click to select **IPv6**. Right-click the **IPv6** node and click **New Scope** to start the New Scope Wizard. In the welcome window, click **Next**.

2. Type **IPv6-Scope** in the Name text box, and then click **Next**.

3. In the Prefix text box, type **2001:db8:2016::**. Recall that addresses starting with 2001:db8 are reserved for testing and documentation purposes. Leave the Preference setting at the default value **0**, and then click **Next**.

4. In the Add Exclusions window, type **1** in the Start IPv6 Address text box, and type **10** in the End IPv6 Address text box, to exclude the first 10 addresses. Click **Add** and then **Next**.

5. In the Scope Lease window, accept the defaults, and click **Next**.

6. In the final window, accept the default **Yes** to activate the scope now, and then click **Finish**.

7. On ServerSA1 in the PowerShell window, type **ipconfig /renew6 Ethernet** and press **Enter**. You might see an error message, and you won't be leased an IPv6 address on the Ethernet interface until you assign the server an address within the scope you created. If you don't specify the interface to renew, Windows takes longer because it is trying to configure ISATAP and Teredo interfaces.

8. On ServerDM1, right-click **Start** and click **Network Connections**. Right-click **Ethernet** and click **Properties**. Double-click **Internet Protocol Version 6 (TCP/IPv6)** and click the **Use the following IPv6 address** option button. In the IPv6 address text box, type **2001:db8:2016::1**, and in the Subnet prefix length text box, type **64**, if necessary. Click **OK** twice, and close Network Connections.

9. On ServerSA1, type **ipconfig /renew6 Ethernet** and press **Enter**. You should see that your Ethernet interface was assigned an address starting with 2001:db8:2016.

10. On ServerDM1, click **Address Leases** in the DHCP console under the scope you created. You should see the leased address and the name of the client, ServerSA1.

11. Continue to the next activity.

DHCP High Availability

 **Certification**

- **70-741 – Implement DHCP:**
  Manage and maintain DHCP

DHCP is a crucial service in networks that use it. If the DHCP server fails to respond to client requests, clients can't communicate on the network. Microsoft offers the following ways to achieve high availability for DHCP:

- Split scopes
- DHCP failover
- DHCP server cluster
- Hot standby

Using a DHCP server cluster requires a complex network setup, including shared storage for the DHCP database that multiple DHCP servers access. This method works well, but setup and configuration can be difficult, and the shared storage can be a single point of failure. The hot standby method consists of two DHCP servers configured with identical scopes and options. If the primary DHCP server fails, an administrator must manually restore the DHCP database from backup to the standby server, which might not have the most recent lease data. The following sections cover the most recommended methods for providing DHCP high availability and fault tolerance: split scopes and DHCP failover.

DHCP Split Scopes

A **split scope** is a fault-tolerant DHCP configuration in which two DHCP servers share the same scope information, allowing both servers to offer DHCP services to clients. One server is configured as the primary DHCP server and the other as the secondary. In most cases, the secondary server leases addresses only if the primary server is unavailable. The DHCP Server role has the Dhcp Split-Scope Configuration Wizard to automate the process of configuring a split scope. You create a split scope by using the wizard as follows:

1.   Install the DHCP Server role on two servers designated DHCP1 and DHCP2 for this example. DHCP1 is the primary DHCP server, and DHCP2 is the secondary.

2.   Create a scope on DHCP1, including any options, and activate it.

3.   Run the DHCP Split-Scope Wizard on DHCP1. To do so, right-click the scope in the DHCP console, point to Advanced, and then click Split-Scope. The wizard prompts you for the following information:

   • The name or address of the secondary DHCP server.

   • The percentage of split (see Figure 4-30). A typical split percentage is 80/20, meaning the primary server can lease 80% of the addresses and the secondary server has 20%, but you can configure the split as needed for your environment. If you're configuring the split scope for load balancing rather than fault tolerance, you can set the split to 50%.

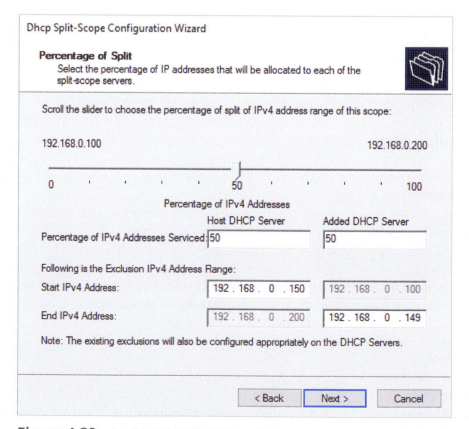

Figure 4-30   Setting the percentage of split

- Delay in DHCP offer. Specify the number of milliseconds that each server should delay between receiving a DHCPDISCOVER and sending a DHCPOFFER. You usually set the primary server for a 0 delay. You want the secondary server to delay long enough that the primary server services most client requests. You might have to adjust this value until you get the intended results. A value of 1000 is a good place to start. If you're configuring a split scope for load balancing, leave the delay at 0 for both servers. Both servers will respond to all requests, but the client will accept only the first response. With the delay set at 0 for both servers and assuming similar load and network conditions, each server should be the first to respond about half the time, which is what you want in a load-balancing arrangement.

4. The wizard creates the scope on the secondary server and creates the necessary exclusion range, according to the split percentage on both servers, to ensure that IP addresses aren't duplicated.

5. Create reservations on both servers. If you're using reservations, you need to create them manually on both servers so that either server can offer reserved addresses; the split scope function doesn't replicate reservations.

One problem with split scopes is that if one DHCP server fails, the lease information it stores is lost. In addition, because the second server has only a portion of the IP addresses available to lease, it could run out of IP addresses before the failed server is back up and running. Both these problems are solved by DHCP failover, discussed next.

> **Note** 📎
>
> Split scopes are an option only on IPv4 scopes, not on IPv6 scopes.

DHCP Failover

DHCP failover allows two DHCP servers to share the pool of addresses in a scope, giving both servers access to all the addresses in the pool. Lease information is replicated between the servers, so if one server goes down, the other server maintains the lease information. Like split scopes, DHCP failover is available only in IPv4 scopes; if you need fault tolerance for IPv6 scopes, you have to use traditional server clustering or hot standby servers. There are two modes for DHCP failover:

- *Load-balancing mode*—With **load-balancing mode**, which is the default, both DHCP servers participate in address leasing at the same time. You can configure the load-balancing priority if you want one server to service the majority of DHCP clients. If one server fails, the other server takes over all leasing duties, and because the DHCP database is replicated between the servers, no lease information is lost.

- *Hot standby mode*—With **hot standby mode**, one server is assigned as the active server that provides DHCP services to clients while the other server is placed in standby mode. The standby server begins providing DHCP services if the primary server becomes unresponsive.

Because DHCP failover is configured per scope, not per server, you can configure load balancing for one scope and hot standby for another. In addition, with hot standby mode, you can configure one server as the primary server for one scope and the secondary server for another scope.

> **Caution** ⚠
>
> DHCP failover requires close time synchronization between servers. Server clocks should be synchronized within 1 minute of each other, so make certain all servers use the same reliable time source.

Configuring Load-Balancing Modes

You configure DHCP failover in the DHCP console by right-clicking the IPv4 node or the target scope and then clicking Configure Failover. The Configure Failover Wizard guides you through the process, including whether you want to use load sharing or hot standby mode. In the first window, you choose the scope or scopes on which you want to configure failover. If you configure failover from the IPv4 node, all scopes are listed and selected by default.

 Note

You can configure DHCP failover with the `Add-DhcpServerV4Failover` PowerShell cmdlet.

Next, you choose the partner server, which must be an authorized server that already has the DHCP Server service configured. If any servers have an existing failover configuration, you can select one from a list.

In the next window, you name the failover relationship and choose whether the failover configuration will be load balancing or hot standby. By default, the relationship name is composed of the names of the servers. Load balancing is the default configuration mode, and you configure the following additional parameters (see Figure 4-31):

- *Maximum Client Lead Time*—The **maximum client lead time (MCLT)** defines the maximum amount of time that a DHCP server can extend a lease for a DHCP client without the partner server's knowledge. It also defines the amount of time a server waits before assuming control over all DHCP

```
Configure Failover

  Create a new failover relationship


    Create a new failover relationship with partner serverdc1

    Relationship Name:            serverdm1.mcsa2016.local-serverdc1

    Maximum Client Lead Time:          1 ⬍ hours   0 ⬍ minutes

    Mode:                         Load balance                ▼
    ┌ Load Balance Percentage ────────────────────────────────────┐
    │ Local Server:                    50 ⬍ %                       │
    │                                                              │
    │ Partner Server:                  50 ⬍ %                       │
    └──────────────────────────────────────────────────────────────┘

    ☐ State Switchover Interval:       60 ⬍ minutes

    ☑ Enable Message Authentication

    Shared Secret:               [                                  ]


                              < Back      Next >       Cancel
```

Figure 4-31   Configuring failover parameters

services if its partner is in Partner Down state. In Partner Down state, the DHCP server assumes that its failover partner is no longer operational.

- *Load Balance Percentage*—Define the percentage of client requests serviced by each server. The default value is 50% for each server.
- *State Switchover Interval*—When a DHCP server loses communication with its partner, it enters the Communication Interrupted state, whereby each server operates independently but assumes the other server is still operational. If the State Switchover Interval option is enabled, you can define the time in which a server transitions from Communication Interrupted state to Partner Down state. By default, this option isn't enabled, and an administrator must manually configure Partner Down state.
- *Enable Message Authentication*—To increase security, you can enable authentication between failover partners, an option that is configured by default. If you do, you must enter a shared secret on both DHCP servers.

Finally, review the selected options and click Finish to create the failover relationship. After the failover relationship is established, both inbound and outbound rules for TCP port 647 (DHCP Server Failover) are configured on the Windows firewall to allow communication between the two servers.

Configuring Hot Standby Mode

The process for configuring hot standby mode is almost identical to configuring load-balancing mode with the following exceptions:

- Select the *Hot standby* option for the failover mode.
- Instead of choosing a load-balancing percentage, specify whether the failover partner is the active server or the standby server, and assign a percentage of addresses reserved for the standby server (see Figure 4-32).

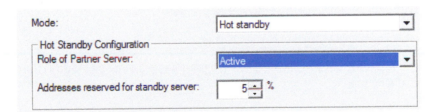

Figure 4-32   Configuring hot standby mode

In hot standby mode, the standby server doesn't normally lease IP addresses. However, if communication between the servers is interrupted, the standby server leases the addresses defined in the *Addresses reserved for standby server* option. If these addresses are exhausted before the MCLT timer has expired, the standby server no longer leases new addresses, but it can continue to renew existing address leases. If the MCLT timer expires and the primary server is in Partner Down state, the standby server takes full control of the address pool.

Editing and Deleting a Failover Configuration

If you need to edit or delete a failover configuration, right-click the IPv4 node in the DHCP console and click Properties. Click the Failover tab (see Figure 4-33). Select the name of the failover relationship, and click Edit to edit the failover parameters or Delete to delete the failover relationship. If you delete the failover relationship in a hot standby configuration, the scope is deleted from the standby server but retained on the active server. If you delete a load-balancing configuration, the scope is deleted from the partner server, and all addresses are available to the local server.

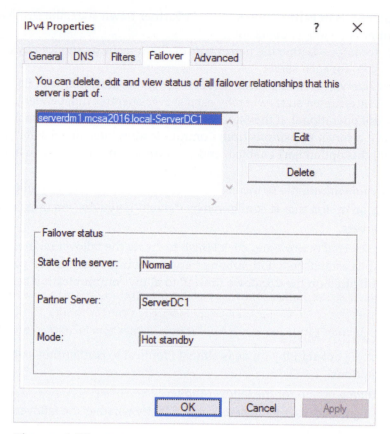

Figure 4-33   Editing or deleting a failover configuration

> If you view the Failover tab in the Properties dialog box for a scope, you see information about the failover relationship (if any) of that scope, but you can't make changes. Changes must be made in the Failover tab of the IPv4 node's Properties dialog box.

Activity 4-10: Working with Split Scopes

Time Required: 10 minutes

Objective: Install a second DHCP server and configure a split scope.

Required Tools and Equipment: ServerDC1, ServerDM1, ServerSA1

Description: You want to work with split scopes, so you install the DHCP Server role on ServerDC1, configure a split scope between ServerDM1 and ServerDC1, and then test it.

1. On ServerDC1, sign in as **Administrator**. Open a PowerShell window. Type **Install-WindowsFeature DHCP -IncludeManagementTools** and press **Enter**.

2. When the DHCP Server installation finishes, in Server Manager, click **Tools, DHCP** to open the DHCP console. Click to select **ServerDC1.mcsa2016.local** (the server node), then right-click it, and click **Authorize**.

3. On ServerDM1, click to select **Scope [192.168.0.0] 192.168.0-Scope**. Then right-click it, point to **Advanced**, and click **Split-Scope** to start the Dhcp Split-Scope Configuration Wizard. Click **Next**.

4. In the Additional DHCP Server window, type **ServerDC1** in the Additional DHCP Server text box, and then click **Next**.

5. In the Percentage of Split window, move the slider so that both the Host DHCP Server and Added DHCP Server text boxes show **50** (see Figure 4-30 shown earlier). You use this kind of configuration for load-balancing DHCP. Click **Next**.

6. In the Delay in DHCP Offer window, leave both values at **0** for a load-balancing arrangement. (If you were more concerned with having a secondary DHCP server in case the primary server failed, you would set the delay for Added DHCP Server to about 1000.) Click **Next**, and then Click **Finish**. Click **Close**.

7. Click **Address Pool** to see that an exclusion range has been added to exclude addresses 192.160.0.150 to 192.168.0.200, which are the addresses that ServerDC1 will allocate. (*Note*: You might need to click **Refresh** to see the exclusion range.) Right-click the scope and click **Deactivate** so that ServerDM1 can no longer allocate IP addresses. Click **Yes** to confirm.

8. On ServerDC1, open the DHCP console, if necessary. Right-click **192.168.0-Scope** and click **Activate**. Click **Address Pool** to see the exclusion range of 192.168.0.100 through 192.168.0.149, the addresses that ServerDM1 is configured to allocate.

9. On ServerSA1 from a PowerShell window, type **ipconfig /release** and press **Enter**, and then type **ipconfig /renew** and press **Enter**. You'll see that an address from ServerDC1 was assigned.

10. On ServerDC1, right-click **192.168.0-Scope** and click **Delete**. Click **Yes** twice to confirm the deletion. On ServerDM1, delete the exclusion in 192.168.0-Scope and reactivate the scope.

11. On ServerSA1, type **ipconfig /release** and press **Enter**, and then type **ipconfig /renew** and press **Enter** so its address is again leased from ServerDM1.

12. Continue to the next activity.

Activity 4-11: Configuring DHCP Failover

Time Required: 10 minutes
Objective: Configure DHCP failover.
Required Tools and Equipment: ServerDC1, ServerDM1, ServerSA1
Description: In this activity, you configure DHCP failover in hot standby mode.

1. On ServerDM1 in the DHCP console, right-click **192.168.0-Scope** and click **Configure Failover** to start the Configure Failover Wizard. In the welcome window, click **Next**.

2. In the Partner Server text box, type **ServerDC1**, and click **Next**. The partnership is validated.

3. In the Create a new failover relationship window, type **ServerDM1-ServerDC1-HotStandby** in the Relationship Name text box. Leave the Maximum Client Lead Time set at the default **1 hour**. In the Mode list box, click **Hot standby**.

4. In the Role of Partner Server list box, leave the default **Standby**, and leave the default **5%** for the Addresses reserved for standby server setting.

5. Click the **State Switchover Interval** check box, and leave the default value **60** in the minutes text box. Click to clear the **Enable Message Authentication** check box (see Figure 4-34), and then click **Next**.

6. Confirm the configuration, and then click **Finish**. The failover configuration might take several seconds. After it's finished, click **Close**.

7. On ServerDC1 in the DHCP console, click the **Refresh** icon. Click **Address Leases** under 192.168.0-Scope. You should see the current address lease for ServerSA1. (If you don't, click the **Refresh** icon.)

8. On ServerSA1 from a PowerShell window, type **ipconfig /release** and press **Enter**. Verify that the lease is no longer shown on ServerDM1 and ServerDC1. (You probably need to click the **Refresh** icon in the DHCP console on both servers.)

9. On ServerSA1, type **ipconfig /renew** and press **Enter** to lease an address. Verify that the address lease can be seen on both servers, and then close the DHCP console on both servers.

10. Continue to the next activity.

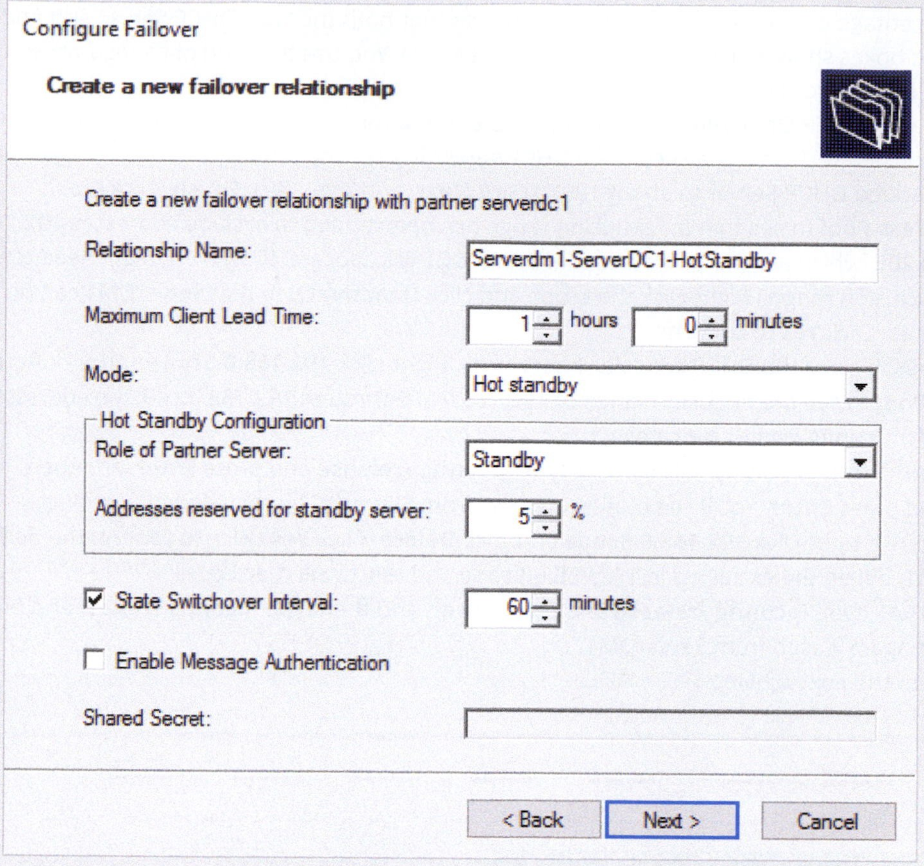

Configure Failover

Create a new failover relationship

Create a new failover relationship with partner serverdc1

Relationship Name:	Serverdm1-ServerDC1-HotStandby
Maximum Client Lead Time:	1 hours 0 minutes
Mode:	Hot standby

Hot Standby Configuration

Role of Partner Server:	Standby
Addresses reserved for standby server:	5 %

☑ State Switchover Interval: 60 minutes

☐ Enable Message Authentication

Shared Secret:

< Back   Next >   Cancel

Figure 4-34 Configuring failover

Activity 4-12: Uninstalling the DHCP Server Role

Time Required: 5 minutes
Objective: Uninstall the DHCP server role.
Required Tools and Equipment: ServerDC1, ServerDM1, ServerSA1
Description: You've finished working with DHCP, so you uninstall the role on ServerDC1 and Server DM1 and set ServerSA1's IP address back to a static address.

1. On ServerDC1 from a PowerShell window, type **Uninstall-WindowsFeature DHCP** and press **Enter**. On ServerDM1, from a PowerShell window, type **Uninstall-WindowsFeature DHCP** and press **Enter**.
2. Shut down ServerDM1 and ServerDC1.
3. On ServerSA1, open Network Connections and change the IPv4 address settings for the Ethernet connection as follows:
   IP address: 192.168.0.4
   Subnet mask: 255.255.255.0
   Default gateway: 192.168.0.250
   Primary DNS server: 192.168.0.1
4. Shut down ServerSA1.

Chapter Summary

- Dynamic Host Configuration Protocol (DHCP) is a component of the TCP/IP protocol suite that's used to assign an IP address to a host automatically from a defined pool of addresses. IP addresses assigned via DHCP are usually leased, not permanently assigned. DHCP is a client/server protocol.

- The process of a DHCP client requesting an IP address and a DHCP server fulfilling the request is actually a four-packet sequence of broadcasts: DHCPDISCOVER, DHCPOFFER, DHCPREQUEST, and DHCPACK. DHCP uses the UDP Transport-layer protocol on ports 67 and 68. Port 67 is used for sending data from the client to the server, and port 68 is for sending data from the server to the client. There are eight DHCP message types.

- The DHCP service is installed as a server role named DHCP Server; it has no role service components. A DHCP server must be authorized on a domain network before it can begin providing services.

- A DHCP scope is a pool of IP addresses and other IP configuration parameters that a DHCP server uses to lease addresses to DHCP clients. An exclusion range consists of one or more addresses in the scope that the DHCP server doesn't lease to clients. A reservation is an IP address associated with the MAC address of a DHCP client to ensure that when the client requests an IP address, it always gets the same one, along with any configured options.

- A split scope is a fault-tolerant DHCP configuration in which two DHCP servers share the same scope information, allowing both servers to offer DHCP services to clients.

- A superscope is a special type of scope consisting of one or more member scopes that allow a DHCP server to service multiple IPv4 subnets on a single physical network. It directs the DHCP server to draw addresses from both scopes, even though it has only a single interface configured for one of the IP subnets.

- An IPv4 multicast packet is a network packet addressed to a group of hosts listening on a particular multicast IP address. Multicast DHCP scopes allow assigning multicast addresses dynamically to multicast servers and clients by using Multicast Address Dynamic Client Allocation Protocol (MADCAP).

- Almost every network requires a DNS server's IP address for name resolution and a default gateway to communicate with other subnets and the Internet. The DHCP server can be configured to send both these addresses to DHCP clients along with the IP address and subnet mask. DHCP options can be assigned at these levels: server, scope, policy, and reservation.

- You can perform several DHCP server configuration tasks in the DHCP console. The options you can change depend on whether you right-click the topmost node with the server name or the IPv4 or IPv6 nodes. Server configuration tasks include adding or removing bindings, backing up and restoring, creating scopes, configuring failover, reconciling scopes, setting predefined options, and configuring properties.

- The IPv4 server properties include statistics and logging parameters, dynamic DNS configuration, NAP configuration, filters, conflict detection, and configuration of DNS registration credentials. Configuring scope properties includes scope name and address range, dynamic DNS configuration, and DHCP/BOOTP configuration.

- On networks with both Windows and non-Windows computers, a problem known as name squatting can occur when a non-Windows computer registers its name with a DNS server, but the name has already been registered by a Windows computer. DHCP name protection prevents name squatting by non-Windows computers by using the DHCP resource record Dynamic Host Configuration Identifier (DHCID).

- DHCP filters allow administrators to restrict which computers on a network are leased an IP address based on the client MAC address.

- DHCP policies allow you more fine-tuned control of address lease options than you have with server, scope, and reservation options. Policies can be configured based on criteria such as Vendor Class, User Class, MAC address, client identifier, FQDN, and relay agent information.

- If you're using Windows Deployment Services to install Windows OSs on computers, you might need to configure DHCP to respond to Preboot Execution Environment (PXE) network interfaces. It is a network environment built into many NICs to allow a computer to boot from an image stored on a network server.

- A DHCP relay agent is a device that listens for broadcast DHCPDISCOVER and DHCPREQUEST messages and forwards them to a DHCP server on another subnet. It's configured as part of the Routing role service under the Remote Access server role.

- Windows Server 2016 allows you to migrate the DHCP server role to another server; you can do so easily by exporting the server configuration and database to a file and then importing that file on another server.

- DHCP is a fairly reliable protocol, but at times, you may encounter some basic problems. These problems may include: a client is not receiving a DHCP address, a client is receiving an incorrect DHCP address, IP address conflicts are occurring, the DHCP server service is not starting, and no addresses are being leased.

- The DHCP audit logging feature, which is enabled by default, provides a logging file that shows information about when addresses were leased, renewed, and released as well as information about DNS updates attempted by the DHCP server. The log also shows when the server was authorized and when the service started and stopped.

- Microsoft has several ways to achieve high availability for DHCP: split scopes, DHCP failover, DHCP server cluster, and hot standby. A split scope is a fault-tolerant DHCP configuration in which two DHCP servers share the same scope information, allowing both servers to offer DHCP services to clients.

- DHCP failover allows two DHCP servers to share the pool of addresses in a scope, giving both servers access to all addresses in the pool. There are two modes for DHCP failover: load-balancing mode and hot standby mode.

Key Terms

conflict detection	exclusion range	preference
DHCP failover	hot standby mode	prefix
DHCP filter	lease duration	reservation
DHCP name protection	lease renewal	split scope
DHCP policies	load-balancing mode	stateful autoconfiguration
DHCP relay agent	maximum client lead time	stateless autoconfiguration
DHCP scope	(MCLT)	superscope
DHCP server authorization	multicast scope	User Class
DHCP Unique Identifier (DUID)	name squatting	Vendor Class
Dynamic Host Configuration	Preboot Execution Environment	
Protocol (DHCP)	(PXE)	

Review Questions

1. Which of the following are true about the DHCP protocol? (Choose all that apply.)
   a. There are eight message types.
   b. DHCPDISCOVER messages sent by clients traverse routers.
   c. It uses the UDP Transport-layer protocol.
   d. An initial address lease involves three packets.

2. You have a DHCP server set up on your network and no DHCP relay agents. You're capturing DHCP packets with a protocol analyzer and see a broadcast packet with UDP source port 68 and UDP destination port 67. Which of the following DHCP message types can the packet be?
   a. A DHCPREQUEST to renew an IP address lease
   b. A DHCPACK to acknowledge an IP address lease request
   c. A DHCPDISCOVER to request an IP address
   d. A DHCPOFFER to offer an IP address lease

3. In the DHCP server's statistics, you notice that a lot of DHCPNAK packets have been transmitted. What's the most likely reason?
   a. You changed the range of addresses in a scope recently.
   b. The DHCP server has been taken offline.
   c. The server is offering a lot of addresses that are already in use.
   d. Client computers are getting multiple offers when they request an address.

4. You have configured your computers with static IP addresses but want them to get the DNS server and default gateway settings via DHCP. What type of DHCP message do you see as a result?

   a. DHCPREQUEST
   b. DHCPRELEASE
   c. DHCPNAK
   d. DHCPINFORM

5. After you install the DHCP Server role on a member server, what must you do before the server can begin providing DHCP services?

   a. Configure options.
   b. Activate the server.
   c. Authorize the server.
   d. Create a filter.

6. Which of the following are required elements of a DHCP scope? (Choose all that apply.)

   a. Subnet mask
   b. Scope name
   c. Router address
   d. Lease duration

7. What's the default lease duration on a Windows DHCP server?

   a. 8 hours
   b. 16 minutes
   c. 8 days
   d. 16 hours

8. What should you define in a scope to prevent the DHCP server from leasing addresses that are already assigned to devices statically?

   a. Reservation scope
   b. Exclusion range
   c. Deny filters
   d. DHCP policy

9. You have four printers that are accessed via their IP addresses. You want to be able to use DHCP to assign addresses to the printers, but you want to make sure they always have the same address. What's the best option?

   a. Create reservations.
   b. Create exclusions.
   c. Configure filters.
   d. Configure policies.

10. You have defined a scope on your DHCP server with the start address 172.16.1.1, end address 172.16.1.200, and prefix length 16. You want to create another scope on the server. Which of the following is a valid scope you can create on this server?

    a. Start address 172.19.1.1, end address 172.19.1.255, prefix length 24
    b. Start address 172.17.1.1, end address 172.17.1.200, prefix length 16
    c. Start address 172.16.2.1, end address 172.19.2.100, prefix length 16
    d. Start address 172.31.0.1, end address 172.31.1.254, prefix length 8

11. What should you create if you need to service multiple IPv4 subnets on a single physical network?

    a. Split scope
    b. Relay agent
    c. Superscope
    d. Multicast server

12. What do you configure if you need to assign addresses dynamically to applications or services that need a class D IP address?

    a. IPv6 relay
    b. Multicast scope
    c. Dynamic scope
    d. Autoconfiguration

13. You want high availability for DHCP services, a primary server to handle most DHCP requests, and a secondary server to respond to client requests only if the primary server fails to in about a second. The primary server has about 85% of the IP addresses to lease, leaving the secondary server with about 15%. You don't want the servers to replicate with each other. What should you configure?

    a. Multicast scope
    b. Failover
    c. Superscope
    d. Split scope

14. A subnet on your network uses DHCP for address assignment. The current scope has a start address 192.168.1.1 and an end address of 192.168.1.200 with the subnet mask 255.255.255.0. Because of network expansion, you have added computers, bringing the total number that need DHCP for address assignment to 300. You don't want to change the IP addressing scheme or the subnet mask for computers already on the network. What should you do?

    a. Create a new scope with the start address 192.168.2.1 and an end address 192.168.2.200 with prefix length 24 and add the existing scope and a new scope to a superscope.
    b. Add a scope with the start address 192.168.1.1 and an end address 192.168.2.200 with the subnet mask 255.255.255.0. Then delete the existing scope.
    c. Create a new scope with the start address 192.168.1.1, an end address 192.168.2.200, and a prefix length 16.
    d. Add another DHCP server. Using the split scope wizard, split the existing scope with the new server and assign each server 100% of the addresses.

15. You want mobile devices on your network to have a shorter lease time than other devices without having a different scope. You don't have detailed information about the mobile devices, such as MAC addresses, because they are employees' personal devices. What DHCP feature might you use to assign a shorter lease to these mobile devices?
    a. Reservation options
    b. Scope options
    c. Policy options
    d. Filter options

16. You have DHCP clients on the network that aren't domain members. You want to be sure these computers can register their hostnames with your DNS servers. Which option should you configure?
    a. 003 Router
    b. 044 WINS/NBNS Servers
    c. 006 DNS Servers
    d. 015 DNS Domain name

17. You want all computers in the Management Department to use a default gateway that's different from computers in other departments. All departments are on the same subnet. What should you do first on the server?
    a. Create a User Class.
    b. Create a new scope.
    c. Create an allow filter.
    d. Create a Vendor Class.

18. You have a DHCP server with two NICs: NIC1 and NIC2. NIC1 is connected to a subnet with computers that use DHCP for address assignment. NIC2 is connected to the data center subnet where all computers should use static addressing. You want to prevent the DHCP server from listening for DHCP packets on NIC2. What should you do?
    a. Configure bindings.
    b. Disable the scope.
    c. Create a filter for NIC2.
    d. Configure failover.

19. You notice that some information shown in the DHCP console for DHCP leases doesn't agree with lease information you see on some client computers where you used `ipconfig /all`. What should you do to make DHCP information consistent?
    a. Back up and restore the database.
    b. Reconcile the scopes.
    c. Create a deny filter for the leases that look wrong.
    d. Delete the dhcp.mdb file and click Refresh.

20. Some of your non-Windows clients aren't registering their hostnames with the DNS server. You don't require secure updates on the DNS server. What option should you configure on the DHCP server so that non-Windows clients names are registered?
    a. Update DNS records dynamically only if requested by the DHCP clients.
    b. Always dynamically update DNS records.
    c. Update DNS records dynamically for DHCP clients that don't request updates.
    d. Configure name protection.

21. You're reviewing DHCP server statistics and notice that the server has received many DHCPDECLINE messages. What should you configure on the server to reduce the number of DHCPDECLINE messages?
    a. DHCP policies
    b. Conflict detection
    c. Connection bindings
    d. DNS credentials

22. You have a network of 150 computers and notice that a computer you don't recognize has been leasing an IP address. You want to make sure this computer can't lease an address from your server. What's the best solution that takes the least administrative effort?
    a. Create an allow filter.
    b. Create a new policy.
    c. Create a deny filter.
    d. Create a Vendor Class.

23. Which of the following are criteria you can use with conditions in DHCP policies? (Choose all that apply.)
    a. Vendor Class
    b. MAC address
    c. OS version
    d. SSID

24. Why might you need to create predefined options with code 060?
    a. To support WSUS clients
    b. To support Linux clients
    c. To support WDS clients
    d. To support mobile clients

25. You have been assigned the task of migrating the DHCP server role to another server. Which of the following PowerShell cmdlets will allow you to transfer the DHCP server configuration and database?
    a. `Import-Dhcp -File C:\Dhcp.xml -Leases`
    b. `netsh dhcp server export Dhcp.txt all`
    c. `netsh dhcp server import C:\Dhcp.txt all`
    d. `Export-DhcpServer -File Dhcp.xml -Leases`

26. You have noticed that your DHCP service is not starting. You must immediately troubleshoot your DHCP server and determine the cause of the problem as quickly as possible. Which of the following DHCP troubleshooting steps should you perform? (Choose all that apply.)
    a. Reconcile all scopes.
    b. Verify that the scope is not corrupted.
    c. Power cycle the DHCP Server immediately.
    d. Verify that the DHCP server is authorized.

27. What type of IPv6 address configuration uses DHCPv6?
    a. Unicast allocation
    b. Stateless autoconfiguration
    c. Dynamic allocation
    d. Stateful autoconfiguration

28. Which of the following is *not* part of a DHCPv6 scope configuration?
    a. Default gateway
    b. Prefix
    c. Preference
    d. Scope lease

29. Which of the following is a DHCP high-availability option that includes hot standby mode?
    a. DHCP load balancing
    b. Superscopes
    c. DHCP split scope
    d. DHCP failover

Critical Thinking

The following activities give you critical thinking challenges. Case Projects offer a scenario with a problem to solve and for which you supply a written solution.

Case Project 4-1: Configuring DHCP for a New Subnet

CSM Tech Publishing has expanded its network from one subnet to two subnets and is putting 200 computers on the new subnet with plans for adding up to 100 more computers over the next few years. Currently, it's using DHCP for the existing subnet and has a scope configured with start address 172.16.1.1 and end address 172.16.1.200 with a prefix length of 24. The DHCP server is in the main distribution facility where the router is placed to route between the subnets. The current DHCP server runs Windows Server 2016, is performing well, and has plenty of unused computing resources (CPU, memory, and so forth). You need to configure DHCP for the new subnet at the lowest cost possible. What do you recommend for adding DHCP services to the new subnet? Propose a DHCP configuration, the scope's start and end addresses, and the prefix length for the new subnet.

Case Project 4-2: Supporting New Mobile Devices

You're called in to consult for a company that's issuing about 100 new wireless mobile devices to selected employees. There are two subnets, each with a DHCP scope that has about 150 unused addresses and an access point that relays DHCP requests from wireless clients to the DHCP server. The mobile devices will be equally distributed between the subnets. Both scopes are served by a dual-homed server. You want these mobile devices to be issued IP addresses, using the last 75 addresses of both scopes, and have a shorter lease time for addresses. What do you propose? What information do you need to carry out the proposal?

CHAPTER 5

IMPLEMENTING IPAM

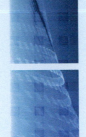

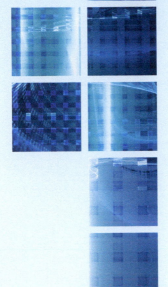

After reading this chapter and completing the exercises, you will be able to:

Describe the purpose and infrastructure options of Internet Protocol Address Management (IPAM)

Deploy an IPAM solution

Administer IPAM

Audit IPAM

In Chapter 4, you learned about advanced DHCP configurations. In this chapter, you learn how to use a DHCP management tool, the Internet Protocol Address Management (IPAM), to centrally manage DHCP servers and IP address spaces and DNS servers and zones. You learn how to install and provision an IPAM server and to select servers to manage and collect server data. Because management of DHCP and DNS in a large enterprise can be a big but focused job, you also learn how to delegate IPAM administration without granting broader administrative rights to users or groups. Finally, you see how you can audit IPAM server configuration and address lease events.

Table 5-1 lists what you need for the hands-on activities in this chapter.

Table 5-1	Activity requirements	
Activity	**Requirements**	**Notes**
Activity 5-1: Resetting Your Virtual Environment	ServerDC1, ServerDM1, ServerDM2, ServerSA1	
Activity 5-2: Installing DHCP Roles on Managed Servers	ServerDC1, ServerDM2	
Activity 5-3: Installing and Provisioning the IPAM Server	ServerDC1, ServerDM1, ServerDM2	
Activity 5-4: Discovering and Selecting Servers	ServerDC1, ServerDM1, ServerDM2	
Activity 5-5: Using IPAM	ServerDC1, ServerDM1, ServerDM2	
Activity 5-6: Configuring Access Control in IPAM	ServerDC1, ServerDM1, ServerDM2	

Introduction to IP Address Management

 **Certification**

- **70-741 – Implement IP Address Management (IPAM):**
  Install and configure IP Address Management (IPAM)

A large enterprise network has thousands of IP addresses in use, usually configured by several DHCP servers, and thousands of hostnames maintained by DNS servers. With so many addresses, hostnames, and servers to manage, IP address management can become unwieldy. **IP Address Management (IPAM)** is a feature in Windows Server 2016 that enables an administrator to manage the IP address space. IPAM has monitoring, auditing, and reporting functions to help you manage key server components in an IP network. IPAM handles forest-wide discovery and management of all Microsoft DHCP, DNS, NPS, and DC servers and monitors DHCP scopes and DNS zones throughout the network. The following problems are some you might be able to solve with IPAM:

- Manual address management with spreadsheets or another custom solution
- Inefficiency in keeping track of and managing multiple DNS and DHCP servers
- Difficulties keeping track of address use across multiple domains and sites
- Global changes to all DHCP scopes across several servers, such as changing a DNS server address
- Problems identifying available IP addresses quickly

This chapter describes the IPAM infrastructure and shows you how to set up an IPAM solution, including IPAM requirements and installation, server provisioning, server discovery and selection, IP address block management and monitoring, migrating to IPAM, and configuring IPAM storage.

The IPAM Infrastructure

The IPAM infrastructure consists of IPAM servers and managed servers. You can also install the IPAM management console on another server, called an **IPAM client**, so that you can manage the IPAM server remotely. The IPAM client can also be on a computer running a Windows client OS with remote server administration tools installed.

The **IPAM server** discovers servers you want to manage and collects and stores data from IPAM-managed servers in the IPAM database. A **managed server** is a Windows server running one or more of these Microsoft services: DHCP, DNS, Active Directory, and NPS. You can install more than one IPAM server on your network, particularly when it includes multiple sites, domains, or forests, and select which servers each IPAM server manages. An IPAM deployment has three topology options:

- *Centralized*—In a **centralized topology**, a single IPAM server is deployed for the entire enterprise (see Figure 5-1). The central server collects information from all managed servers. With this type of topology, the IPAM server should be centrally located with a reliable and high-performance connection to the network. A variation on this topology is to have multiple IPAM servers centrally located with each IPAM server dedicated to managing a particular type of server. For example, one IPAM server can manage DHCP servers, another can manage DNS servers, and a third can manage DCs and NPS servers.
- *Distributed*—In a **distributed topology**, an IPAM server is deployed at every site in the network. Each server is assigned a group of managed servers in the same site. There's no communication between IPAM servers.

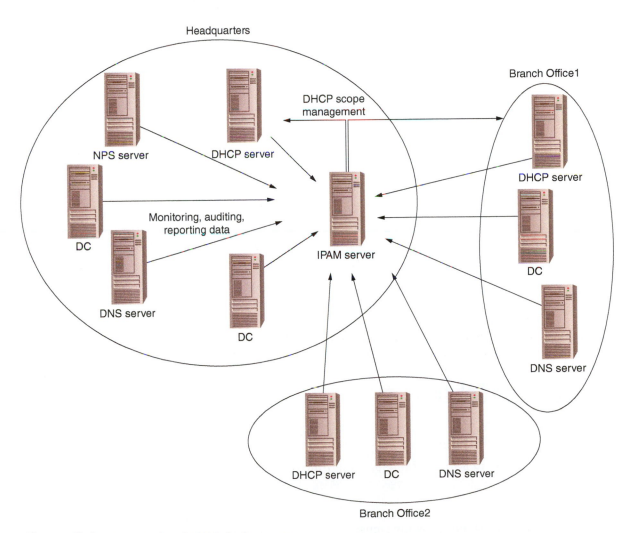

Figure 5-1   A centralized IPAM deployment

• *Hybrid*—Like the centralized topology, in a **hybrid topology**, a single IPAM server collects information from all managed servers in the enterprise; however, an IPAM server is also deployed at key branch locations. You might use this method when you have some large branch locations with IT staff so that they can easily manage servers in their locations. Figure 5-2 shows a hybrid IPAM deployment with an IPAM server in the headquarters and the larger branch office locations as well as an IPAM client running the IPAM management console at the headquarters location. In this topology, the IPAM server in the headquarters collects data from servers in all three locations. The IPAM server in the branch office collects data from servers only in that location.

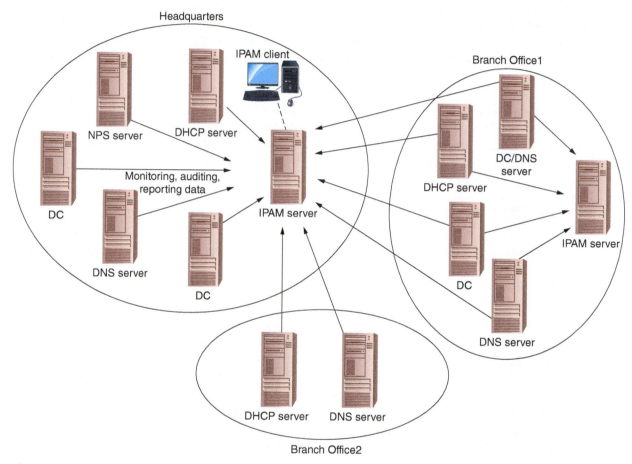

Figure 5-2   A hybrid IPAM deployment

Deploying an IPAM Solution

• **70-741 – Implement IP Address Management (IPAM):**
  Install and configure IP Address Management (IPAM)

IPAM deployment involves the following steps:

1. Determining the requirements for an IPAM deployment
2. Installing the IPAM Server feature
3. Provisioning the IPAM server

4. Performing server discovery
5. Provisioning IPAM Group Policy Objects (GPOs)
6. Selecting servers and services to manage
7. Collecting data from managed servers

The following sections discuss each of the steps necessary to deploy IPAM.

Meeting IPAM Requirements

Before you deploy IPAM, you should have a good understanding of its requirements and limitations. The following list describes the requirements for the IPAM server, client, and managed servers:

- *IPAM server*—The IPAM server must be running the Standard or Datacenter Edition of Windows Server 2012 or later and must be a domain member. The IPAM server can't be a domain controller. IPAM should be the sole server role installed on the server, although IPAM can coexist with other server roles. However, if IPAM is installed on a DHCP server, DHCP server discovery is disabled, which defeats one of the primary purposes of using IPAM.
- *IPAM client*—An IPAM client isn't a necessary component in an IPAM deployment because you can manage IPAM from the IPAM server. However, if you want to manage IPAM from a different computer, you can install the IPAM management console on a computer running Windows Server 2012 or later or a Windows client computer with the Remote Server Administration Tools (RSAT) installed.
- *IPAM managed server*—All servers managed by IPAM must be running Windows Server 2008 or later. In previous versions of IPAM, the IPAM server could manage domain member servers only in the same Active Directory forest. Starting with Windows Server 2016, the managed servers can be members of other forests if a two-way trust relationship between the forests exists. As mentioned, IPAM can collect monitoring, reporting, and auditing data from the following services: Active Directory, DHCP, DNS, and NPS. IPAM can manage DHCP scopes.

Installing the IPAM Server Feature

IPAM Server is a feature that you install with the Add Roles and Features Wizard or the `Install-WindowsFeature` PowerShell cmdlet. To install IPAM Server, run the Add Roles and Features Wizard from Server Manager, and in the Select Features window, select IP Address Management (IPAM) Server. Group Policy Management and the Windows Internal Database are also required, and you're prompted to include these features in the installation. By default, the IPAM management console is also installed. To use PowerShell, enter the following command at a PowerShell prompt:

```
Install-WindowsFeature IPAM -IncludeManagementTools
```

If you just want to install the IPAM client feature on a server to manage an IPAM server remotely, in the Select Features window, expand Remote Server Administration Tools and then expand Feature Administration Tools and select IP Address Management (IPAM) Client. Enter the following command at a PowerShell prompt:

```
Install-WindowsFeature IPAM-Client-Feature
```

To install the IPAM feature in a Windows client OS such as Windows 8/8.1 or Windows 10, download the Remote Server Administration Tools from the Microsoft Download Center and follow the installation instructions. Then add the IPAM server to Server Manager, and the IPAM console is installed on your Windows client computer.

After IPAM Server is installed, IPAM is added to the left pane in Server Manager. To get started, click IPAM in the left pane of Server Manager, and you see a list of IPAM server tasks you can perform (see Figure 5-3). If you're running the management console on the server, the first task, Connect to IPAM server, takes place automatically. Now you're ready to provision the IPAM server.

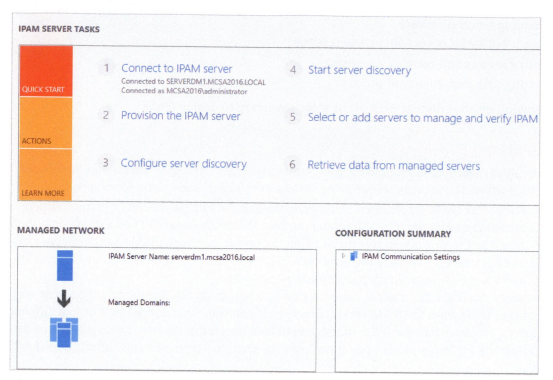

Figure 5-3   The IPAM server management console

Provisioning the IPAM Server

The next step is to provision the IPAM server. In the IPAM Server Tasks window (shown in Figure 5-3), click Provision the IPAM server to start the Provision IPAM Wizard. The first window gives you information about IPAM and the provisioning process. In the next window, you select the type of IPAM database you want to use (see Figure 5-4). The default option is to use the Windows Internal Database (WID), which stores the database on the Windows system drive by default in C:\Windows\System32\ IPAM\database. Starting in Windows Server 2012 R2, you can use a Microsoft SQL Server database, which must already be installed and running. If you choose to use the WID and later want to migrate the IPAM database to a Microsoft SQL server, you can move the IPAM database with the Move-IpamDatabase PowerShell cmdlet.

In the next window, you select the method to provision managed servers. The default and recommended method is to use Group Policy provisioning. **Group Policy provisioning** uses group policies to perform tasks such as creating security groups, setting firewall rules, and creating shares for each IPAM-managed server. **Manual provisioning** requires manually configuring each IPAM server task and managed server. If you choose Group Policy provisioning, you must enter a GPO name prefix, which is used to name the GPOs that are created. For example, if you enter the name prefix IPAMmcsa (see Figure 5-5), the following GPOs are created and linked to the domain object:

- *IPAMmcsa_DC_NPS*—This GPO sets the firewall rules and other policies needed for the IPAM server to collect data from domain controllers and NPS servers.
- *IPAMmcsa_DHCP*—This GPO sets the firewall rules and other policies needed to collect data from and manage DHCP servers.
- *IPAMmcsa_DNS*—This GPO sets the firewall rules and other policies needed for the IPAM server to collect data from DNS servers.

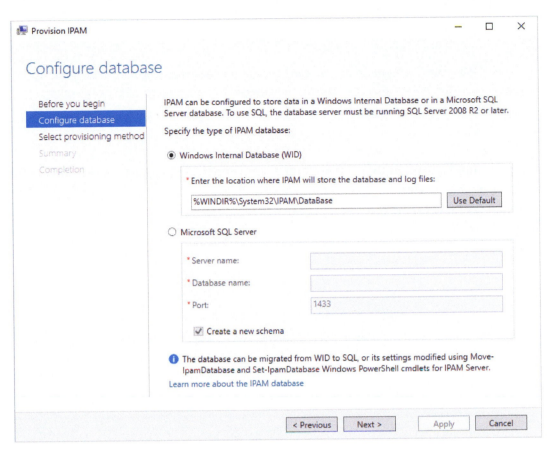

Figure 5-4   Configuring the IPAM database

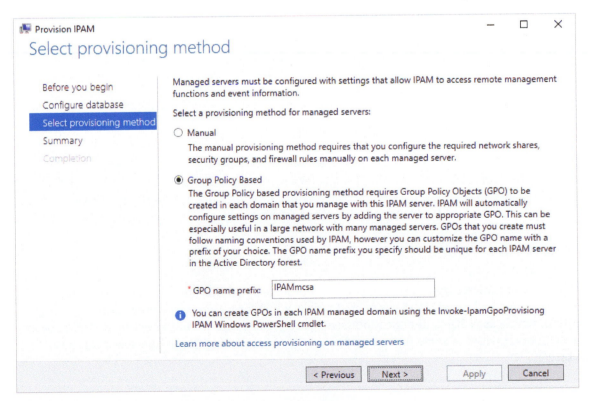

Figure 5-5   Selecting the IPAM provisioning method

Caution ⚠

If you choose the GPO provisioning method, you can't change to manual provisioning. However, using the `Set-IpamConfiguration` PowerShell cmdlet, you can change from manual to GPO provisioning.

Manual provisioning requires that you perform a number of tasks manually on each managed server:

- Configure security groups
- Create and configure shares
- Set firewall rules

Note 📎

For detailed steps on manually configuring a DHCP managed server, see *https://technet.microsoft.com/en-us/library/jj878311(v=ws.11).aspx*. For a DNS managed server, see *https://technet.microsoft.com/en-us/library/jj878346(v=ws.11).aspx*. For DC and NPS servers, see *https://technet.microsoft.com/en-us/library/jj878317(v=ws.11).aspx*.

GPO-based provisioning performs those tasks using the GPOs created by the provisioning wizard. Clicking Next in the wizard shows a summary of tasks performed by the provisioning process:

- Prepares GPO settings (if GPO-based provisioning was selected) so that an administrator can deploy the IPAM GPOs discussed earlier. GPOs must be deployed by running the `Invoke-IpamGPOProvisioning` PowerShell cmdlet after servers have been discovered and selected.
- Creates the specified database to store IPAM server configuration parameters and collected data.
- Creates scheduled tasks on the IPAM server to discover servers and collect data from managed servers.
- Creates local security groups used to assign IPAM administrator permission.
- Enables the IPAM server to track IP addressing.

Using Microsoft SQL Server for IPAM Database Storage

You can use Microsoft SQL Server for the IPAM database instead of the default WID. The SQL server can be on the same server as the IPAM feature or on a different server. To use Microsoft SQL Server during IPAM provisioning, select Microsoft SQL Server and provide the following information (see Figure 5-6):

- SQL server name
- Database name
- Port number

When you use Microsoft SQL Server, you must provide credentials to connect to the database. You have the option of using IPAM server credentials, which uses Windows authentication, or SQL credentials, which uses SQL authentication (see Figure 5-7). Be sure to configure the IPAM database on the SQL server with the same type of credentials (IPAM server or SQL) as you select for the IPAM server.

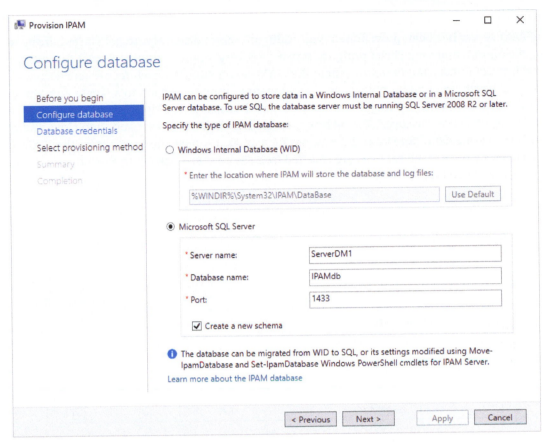

Figure 5-6   Selecting Microsoft SQL Server for the IPAM database

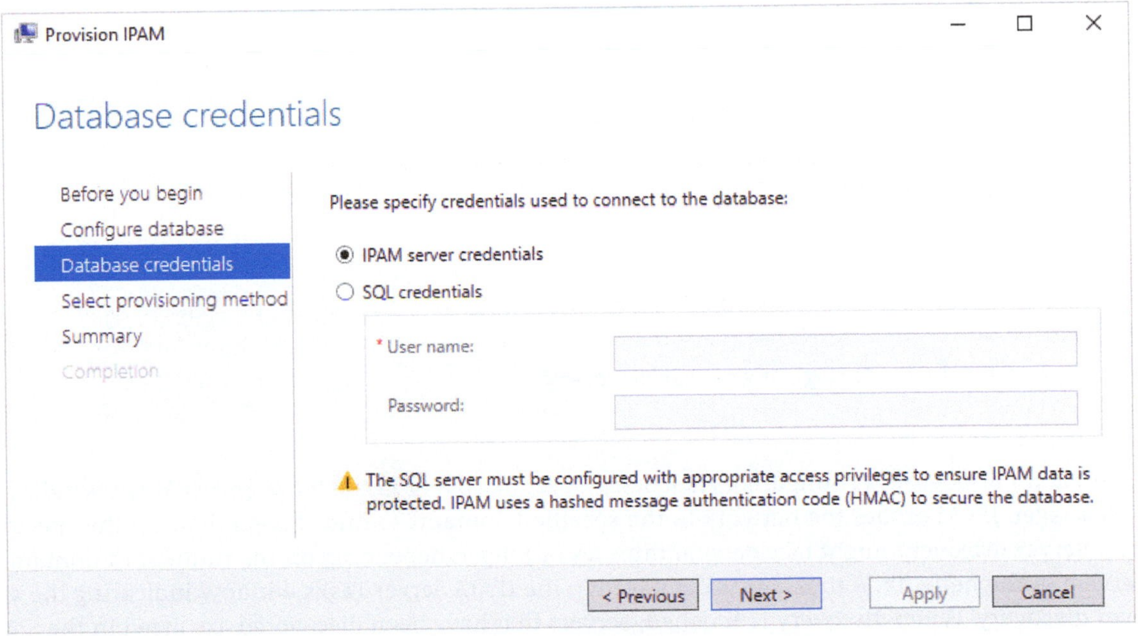

Figure 5-7   Specifying database connection credentials

Configuring Server Discovery

After the IPAM server has been provisioned, you configure server discovery. To get started, from Server Manager, click IPAM, and then click Configure server discovery. In the Configure Server Discovery dialog box, you select the forests and domains where the IPAM server should search for servers to manage. If you're using a distributed IPAM topology, you might want to limit the search to a single domain, but with a central or hybrid topology, you might want to select all domains in multiple forests. When you first open the Configure Server Discovery dialog box, you need to click Get forests and then close and reopen the dialog box to see a list of forests and domains. You can also choose the server roles the IPAM server should discover. By default, all services are selected (see Figure 5-8). Click OK to close the Configure Server Discovery dialog box.

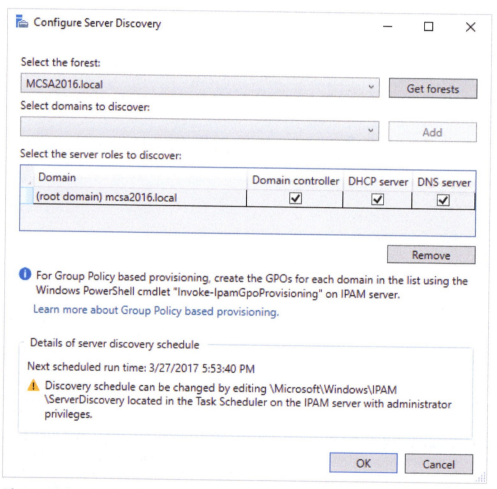

Figure 5-8   Configuring server discovery

After server discovery is configured, click Start server discovery in the IPAM Server Tasks window in Server Manager. IPAM probes the network in the specified domains to find servers that run the specified services. Server discovery might take several minutes or longer, depending on the number of domains and servers in the network. A message is displayed in the IPAM Server Tasks window indicating the status of server discovery. When discovery is finished, servers that have been discovered are listed in the Server Inventory window (see Figure 5-9). Server discovery is scheduled to occur once per day by default and any new servers are added to the database. DHCP servers must have at least one scope defined and DNS servers must be authoritative for an Active Directory domain that is included in server discovery.

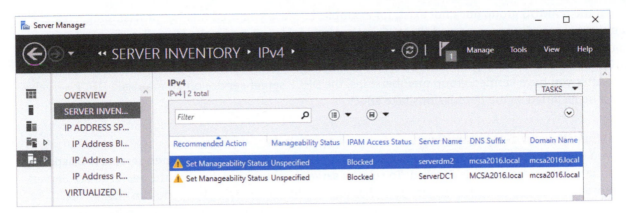

Figure 5-9   The Server Inventory window

Provisioning GPOs

The IPAM server provisioning process doesn't actually create and link the IPAM GPOs to the domain. After the managed servers have been identified, run the following PowerShell cmdlet to provision the GPOs:

```
Invoke-IpamGpoProvisioning -domain yourdomain -GpoPrefixName
   GPOprefix -DelegatedGpoUser IPAMUser
```

In this command, replace *yourdomain* with your domain name. If you're managing multiple domains, run the command for each domain. Replace *GPOprefix* with the prefix specified in the Provision IPAM Wizard. The account running the cmdlet requires domain administrator privileges to create and link the GPOs. The `IPAMUser` specified in the command is a list of users who have been delegated permissions to edit the IPAM GPOs later. The `DelegatedGpoUser` parameter isn't required. After running the cmdlet, the three GPOs are created and linked to the domain node of the specified domain.

After provisioning the GPOs, you can open the Group Policy Management console on a DC in the domain to see the IPAM GPOs that have been linked to the domain. You'll see that the security filtering on each GPO is blank, which means that the GPOs aren't applied to any servers. The next step in the process, selecting servers to manage, adds the managed server to the security filtering on the GPOs. The `Invoke-IpamGpoProvisioning` cmdlet also creates the universal security group IPAMUG and adds the computer account of the IPAM server to the group.

Verifying IPAM Server Group Membership

Before the IPAM server can perform management tasks, the following security group memberships should be verified:

- The IPAMUG universal group is created on a domain controller in the domain, and the server computer account that the IPAM feature is installed on is a member of the group. For example, if you installed the IPAM feature on ServerDM1, the ServerDM1 computer account must be a member of the IPAMUG universal group in Active Directory.
- The IPAMUG universal group is a member of DHCP Users local group on all managed DHCP servers.
- The IPAMUG universal group should be a member of the Event Log Readers local group on all managed DHCP servers and DNS servers. For managed domain controllers, the IPAMUG should be a member of the Event Log Readers Builtin Local group.

Note

If the DHCP Users group does not exist, you can create it from an elevated command prompt using the `netsh dhcp add securitygroups` command or using the PowerShell cmdlet: `Add-DhcpServerSecurityGroup`.

If the IPAMUG group does not exist, for example, because you used manual provisioning, create a universal security group named IPAMUG in the Users folder on a domain controller. Then, add the computer account that is running IPAM to the group. Next, add the IPAMUG group as a member of the DHCP Users and Event Log Readers groups of the managed servers.

After you have verified group memberships, the DHCP server service on all managed DHCP servers must be restarted so the permissions take effect.

Selecting Servers to Manage

As you can see in Figure 5-9, shown earlier, the manageability status of discovered servers is Unspecified, and the IPAM access status is Blocked. To select a server to manage, right-click the server in the Server Inventory window and click Edit Server. In the Add or Edit Server dialog box, you can change the manageability status to Managed if you want this IPAM server to manage the server; otherwise, it should be Unmanaged. You can also choose the services you want to manage on the selected server (see Figure 5-10).

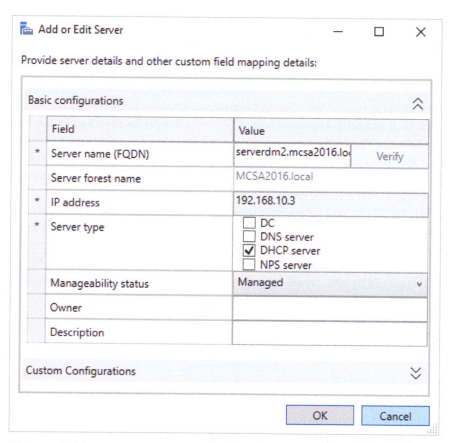

Figure 5-10   Changing the manageability status to Managed

When you set a server's manageability status to Managed, the server account is added to the security filter of the corresponding GPOs (depending on which services the server is running). However, you'll see that the IPAM access status remains in the Blocked state because the GPOs must be applied to each server. You can wait until the servers refresh their computer policies or run `gpupdate /force` at a command prompt on each managed server. After the policies are updated, right-click a server in the Server Inventory window, click Refresh Server Access Status, and then click the Server Manager refresh icon. The IPAM access status should then be Unblocked (see Figure 5-11). Alternatively, you can wait until the IPAM scheduled task automatically refreshes the access status, which is every 15 minutes. IPAM can then collect data from servers and manage DHCP addressing.

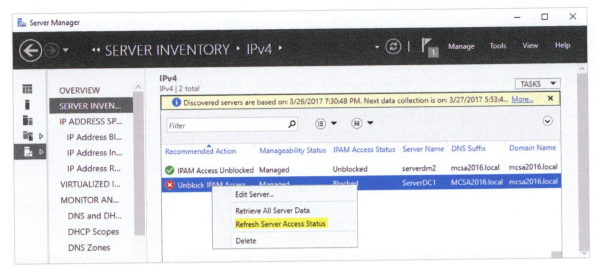

Figure 5-11   Unblocking servers

Note

After running `gpupdate` on servers, you might need to refresh the access status and the Server Manager window more than one time to see servers' Unblocked status.

Retrieving Server Data

The next step is to retrieve data from the managed servers. In the IPAM Server Tasks window, click *Retrieve data from managed servers* to begin the process, or in the Server Inventory window, right-click a server and click *Retrieve All Server Data*. When data retrieval is finished, you see a message at the top indicating the date and time of the last data collection and the schedule for the next data collection. You're now ready to start using the IPAM server and administering the IP address space.

Activity 5-1: Resetting Your Virtual Environment

Time Required: 5 minutes
Objective: Reset your virtual environment by applying the InitialConfig checkpoint or snapshot.
Required Tools and Equipment: ServerDC1, ServerDM1, ServerDM2, ServerSA1
Description: Apply the InitialConfig checkpoint or snapshot to ServerDC1, ServerDM1, ServerDM2, and ServerSA1.

1. Be sure all servers are shut down. In your virtualization program, apply the InitialConfig checkpoint or snapshot to all servers.
2. When the snapshot or checkpoint has finished being applied, continue to the next activity.

Activity 5-2: Installing DHCP Roles on Managed Servers

Time Required: 10 minutes

Objective: Install DHCP on ServerDC1 and ServerDM2 for management by IPAM.

Required Tools and Equipment: ServerDC1 and ServerDM2

Description: In this activity, you install DHCP on ServerDC1 and ServerDM1. Then, you authorize the server and create and activate a scope on each server. The DHCP servers are only for the purpose of working with IPAM.

1. Start ServerDC1 and ServerDM2. Sign in to both servers as the domain administrator.
2. On ServerDC1, open a PowerShell window and type **Install-WindowsFeature DHCP -IncludeManagementTools** and press **Enter**. To authorize the server, type **Add-DhcpServerInDC** and press **Enter**.
3. To create a new scope and activate it, type **Add-DhcpServerV4Scope -Name 192.168.0-Scope -StartRange 192.168.0.100 -EndRange 192.168.0.200 -SubnetMask 255.255.255.0 -State Active** and press **Enter**.
4. Create the necessary DHCP security groups. Type **Add-DhcpServerSecurityGroup** and press **Enter**.
5. On ServerDM2, from the command prompt, type **powershell** and press **Enter**. Type **Install-WindowsFeature DHCP** and press **Enter**. To authorize the server, type **Add-DhcpServerInDC** and press **Enter**.
6. To create a new scope and activate it, type **Add-DhcpServerV4Scope -Name 192.168.1-Scope -StartRange 192.168.1.100 -EndRange 192.168.1.200 -SubnetMask 255.255.255.0 -State Active** and press **Enter**.
7. Create the necessary DHCP security groups. Type **Add-DhcpServerSecurityGroup** and press **Enter**.
8. Continue to the next activity.

Activity 5-3: Installing and Provisioning the IPAM Server

Time Required: 10 minutes

Objective: Install the IPAM Server feature and provision the IPAM server.

Required Tools and Equipment: ServerDC1, ServerDM1, ServerDM2

Description: In this activity, you install the IPAM Server feature on ServerDM1 and provision the IPAM server using Group Policy–based provisioning.

1. Make sure ServerDC1 and ServerDM2 are running. Start ServerDM1, and sign in to the domain as **Administrator**.
2. On ServerDM1, open Server Manager, and click **Manage, Add Roles and Features** from the menu. Click **Next** until you get to the Features window. Click to select **IP Address Management (IPAM) Server** and click **Add Features**. Click **Next**, and then click **Install**. When the installation is finished, click **Close**.
3. In Server Manager, click the **IPAM** node in the left pane.
4. In the IPAM Server Tasks window, verify that you see the server name under Connect to IPAM server. Click **Provision the IPAM server** to start the Provision IPAM Wizard.
5. In the Before you begin window, read the information about IPAM provisioning, and then click **Next**.
6. In the Configure database window, accept the default option of **Windows Internal Database** and click **Next**.
7. In the Select provisioning method window, accept the default option, **Group Policy Based**, and type **IPAMmcsa** in the GPO name prefix text box. Click **Next**.
8. In the Summary window, verify the settings. Read the information describing what tasks are performed with Group Policy provisioning. Click **Apply**. When provisioning is finished, read the information under Next steps. You're performing these steps in the next activity. Click **Close**.
9. In the IPAM Server Tasks window, under Configuration Summary, click to expand **Access Provisioning Method** to see a summary of how IPAM is provisioned, including the names of GPOs to be created. Click the other configuration categories to see IPAM scheduled tasks, IPAM security groups, and IPAM communication settings.
10. Open a PowerShell window. Type **Invoke-IpamGpoProvisioning -Domain mcsa2016.local -GpoPrefixName IPAMmcsa** and press **Enter**. You see a message stating that you didn't specify the `-DelegatedGpoUser` parameter, but it's needed only if you want non-administrator users to be able to edit the IPAM GPOs. Press **Enter** to confirm. After the command is finished running, close the PowerShell window.

11. On ServerDC1, open **Active Directory Users and Computers** and click **Users**. In the right pane, double-click the **IPAMUG** group that was created. Click the **Members** tab and verify that ServerDM1 is a member. Click **Cancel**. Next, you'll configure group memberships for the managed servers ServerDC1 and ServerDM2.

12. Double-click the **DHCP Users** group. Click the **Members** tab, click **Add**, type **IPAMUG**, and click **Check Names**. Click **OK**. Click **OK** again.

13. In the left pane, click the **Builtin** folder and double-click the **Event Log Readers** group. Click the **Members** tab, click **Add**, type **IPAMUG**, and click **Check Names**. Click **OK**. Click **OK** again.

14. In the left pane, click the **Computers** folder, right-click **SERVERDM2**, and click **Manage**.

15. Click to expand **Local Users and Groups** and click **Groups**. In the right pane, double-click the **DHCP Users** group. Click **Add**, type **IPAMUG**, and click **Check Names**. Click **OK**. Click **OK** again.

16. Double-click the **Event Log Readers** group. Click **Add**, type **IPAMUG**, and click **Check Names**. Click **OK**. Click **OK** again.

17. You need to restart the DHCP service for the new permissions to take effect. Click to expand the **Services and Applications** node and click **Services**. In the right pane, right-click **DHCP Server** and click **Restart**. Close the Computer Management console.

18. Now restart the DHCP service on ServerDC1. Right-click **Start** and click **Computer Management**. Repeat the previous step to restart the DHCP service and close the Computer Management console.

19. Continue to the next activity.

Activity 5-4: Discovering and Selecting Servers

Time Required: 15 minutes
Objective: Discover and select servers to manage.
Required Tools and Equipment: ServerDC1, ServerDM1, ServerDM2
Description: With IPAM installed and provisioned, you can start server discovery and then select servers to manage. Because you have only one other server, IPAM discovers it, and you select ServerDC1 to manage.

1. On ServerDM1, in Server Manager, click **IPAM**, if necessary. In the IPAM Server Tasks window, click **Configure server discovery**. In the Configure Server Discovery dialog box, the forest MCSA2016.local is listed. If it's not listed, click **Get forests**, click **OK**, and then close Configure Server Discovery and then open it again. If it is listed already, continue to the next step.

2. Next to the Select domains to discover box, click **Add** (see Figure 5-12). By default, the server discovery process will discover servers running the following roles: Domain controller, DHCP server, and DNS server. Click **OK**.

3. In the IPAM Server Tasks window, click **Start server discovery**. You see a message near the top of the window indicating that an IPAM task is running. After a while, you see the message "Discovered servers are based on: *date and time*" (with *date and time* representing the current date and time). When you see this message, click **Select or add servers to manage and verify IPAM access**. You see ServerDC1 and Serverdm2 in the inventory window. The manageability status is Unspecified, and the IPAM access status is Blocked (see Figure 5-13).

4. Right-click **ServerDC1** and click **Edit Server**. In the Add or Edit Server dialog box, in the Server type section, The DC, DNS server, and DHCP server check boxes are selected in the Add or Edit Server dialog box, in the Server type section. Click the **Manageability status** list arrow and click **Managed** (see Figure 5-14). Click **OK**. You see the manageability status is set to Managed, but the IPAM access status is still set to Blocked.

5. Repeat Step 4 for ServerDM1 (only ServerDM1 has the DHCP Server check box selected).

6. On ServerDC1, click **Tools** and click **Group Policy Management** to open the Group Policy Management console. Click to expand the **Forest** and **Domains** node and click to expand **MCSA2016.local**. Click the **Linked Group Policy Objects** tab to see the IPAM GPOs (see Figure 5-15). In the left pane, under MCSA2016.local, click each of the IPAM GPOs. You should see that ServerDC1 has been added to the security filtering for each GPO and that ServerDM1 has been added to the Security Filtering for the DHCP GPO. This means that the policies specified in those GPOs can be applied to those servers. The policies that are applied are primarily firewall settings that allow the IPAM server (ServerDM1) to manage the selected services.

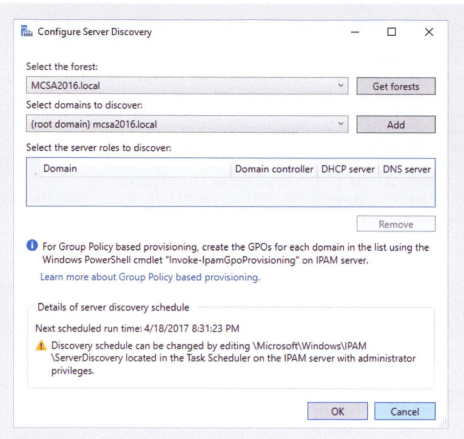

Figure 5-12   Configuring server discovery

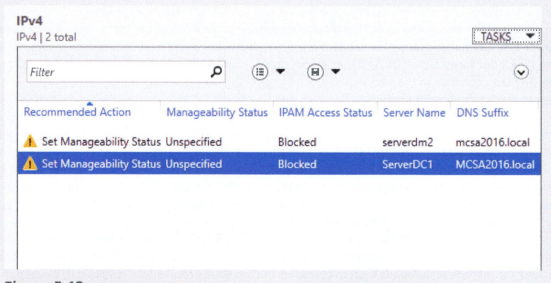

Figure 5-13   Server inventory

7. Group policies are applied to a computer when the computer starts and every 90 minutes. To make sure that the policies are applied immediately, open a command prompt window, and then type **gpupdate /force** and press **Enter**. Close the command prompt. Repeat this step for ServerDM2.

8. On ServerDM1 in the IPAM Server Inventory window, right-click **ServerDC1** and click **Refresh Server Access Status**. You see a message that IPAM tasks are running. After you see the Discovered servers message, click

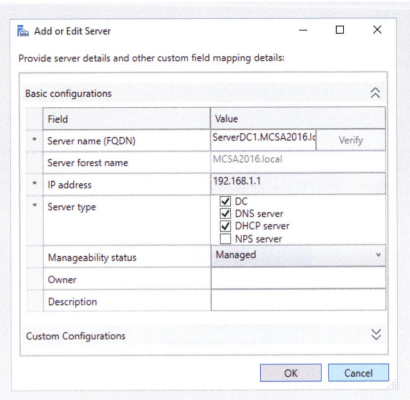

Figure 5-14   Setting the manageability status

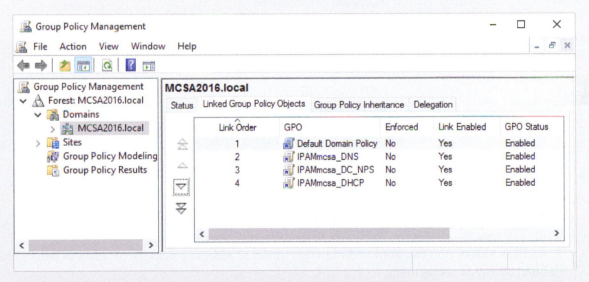

Figure 5-15   Viewing the IPAM GPOs in Group Policy Management

the **Refresh** icon in Server Manager to refresh the view. If all went well, you should see that the IPAM access status is set to Unblocked, and you'll see a white check mark in a green circle next to the ServerDC1 entry. Repeat this step for ServerDM2.

9. Click **ServerDC1** in the IPAM Server Inventory window, scroll down to the Details View. You see detailed status information for the server. If access to the IPAM server is blocked, you can see which service is causing IPAM access to be blocked. For example, if Event Log Access is blocked, the IPAM server needs to be added to the Event Log Readers group on the managed server.

10. Continue to the next activity.

Administering IPAM

 **Certification**

- **70-741 – Implement IP Address Management (IPAM):**
  Install and configure IP Address Management (IPAM)

After the IPAM server has collected data from selected servers and services, you can start working with IPAM. The IPAM console's navigation pane (see Figure 5-16) contains links to several monitoring and management views of your IP address space and DNS zone data:

Figure 5-16 The IPAM console's navigation pane

- *OVERVIEW*—Shows the IPAM Server Tasks window.
- *SERVER INVENTORY*—Lists the servers the IPAM server has discovered.
- *IP ADDRESS SPACE*—Allows you to choose three different views:
  - IP Address Blocks: You can view and manage current IP address blocks. No IP address blocks are defined until you create them.
  - IP Address Inventory: Displays the IP address range group that's organized by device type.
  - IP Address Range Groups: Displays the IP address ranges organized by IP address range groups. You can organize IP address ranges into logical groups such as geographic location or business unit.
- *VIRTUALIZED IP ADDRESS SPACE*—An IPAM feature that enables you to manage virtual IP address spaces created with Microsoft System Center Virtual Machine Manager.
- *MONITOR AND MANAGE*—Enables you to monitor and manage DNS and DHCP server status, DHCP scopes, DNS zones, and server groups with the following views:
  - DNS and DHCP Servers: Lists managed servers by service type along with their current status (see Figure 5-17). You can right-click a DHCP server to edit its properties and options and create a scope. You can define MAC address filters and manage DHCP policies. You can also open the DHCP management console (MMC) for the selected server. If you right-click a DNS server, you can open the DNS management console for that server.

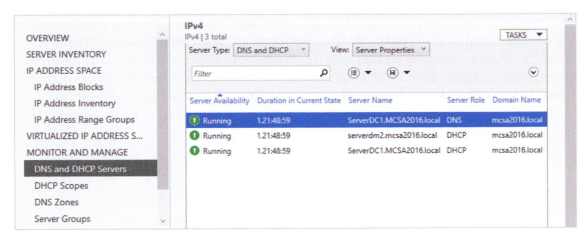

Figure 5-17   Monitoring and managing DNS and DHCP servers

- DHCP Scopes: Lists available scopes on all managed servers and allows you to edit, delete, duplicate, and activate or deactivate the scope. You can create a reservation or superscope, configure DHCP failover, configure DHCP policies, and set the access scope. You use the access scope to customize which objects on a managed server a user can access. The default access scope is Global, and all IPAM objects are a member of it.
- DNS Zones: Displays the status of all DNS server zones. New for Windows Server 2016, you can add DNS resource records and edit and delete a zone. In previous IPAM versions, you could only set the access scope.
- Server Groups: Servers can be grouped by using custom criteria, much as you do with IP address ranges. For example, you might want to group servers by region or country.
- *EVENT CATALOG*—Displays information about IPAM and DHCP configuration and operational events (see Figure 5-18) and allows you to track IP addresses by address, client ID, host name, and user name.

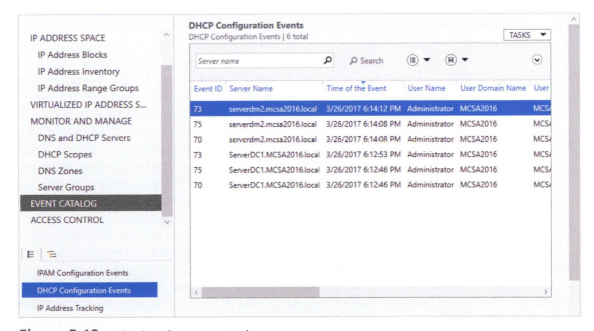

Figure 5-18   Viewing the event catalog

- *ACCESS CONTROL*—Shows the defined roles for IPAM administration, allowing you to configure **role-based access control (RBAC)**. RBAC allows you to define different IPAM administrative roles. There are a number of built-in roles (see Figure 5-19), such as IPAM Administrator, DNS Record Administrator, IPAM DHCP Administrator, and so forth. Each built-in role has permissions assigned to it. For example, the IP Address Record Administrator role can create, edit, and delete IP addresses. You can't change the permissions of built-in roles, but you can create custom roles and define custom permissions for them.

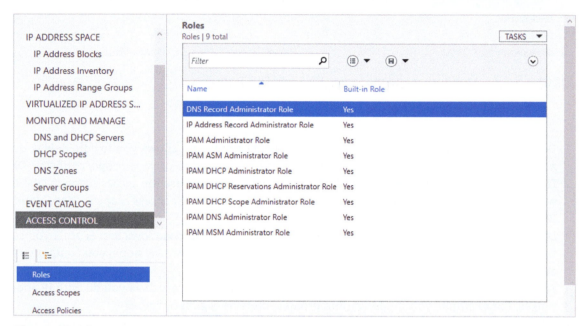

Figure 5-19   Viewing built-in roles

Creating and Managing IP Address Blocks and Ranges

Before you start using IPAM, it's helpful to understand how IPAM views the IP address space, which is divided into the following units:

- *IP address block*—An **IP address block** is the largest unit used to refer to the IP address space. It consists of a contiguous range of IP addresses with a corresponding subnet mask. Each IP address block is categorized as a public or private block as defined by the Internet Assigned Numbers Authority (IANA). For example, 192.168.0.0/24 is a private address block. IP address blocks are divided into IP address ranges. By default, no IP address blocks are defined until you create them. One of the first things you do with IPAM is to create one or more IP address blocks to be the parent block to IP address ranges.
- *IP address range*—An **IP address range** is a pool of continuous addresses in an IP address block and usually corresponds to a DHCP scope. Every IP address range is a member of a parent IP address block. There can be one or more IP address ranges in an IP address block. For example, you might have IP address ranges of 192.168.0.0/24 and 192.168.1.0/24 in the 192.168.0.0/16 IP address block. IP address ranges contain IP addresses that are used to assign to host IP devices.
- *IP address range group*—An **IP address range group** consists of one or more IP address ranges that are logically grouped by some criteria. The default group called Managed by Service contains all address ranges. You can create new IP address range groups based on criteria that you assign to IP address ranges, such as the Active Directory site, country or region or the device type in which the IP address range is used. For example, you can assign two IP address ranges to the Active Directory

site named Site100. You can then create a custom group named SiteGroup that groups IP address ranges by Active Directory site. Then you can view information and statistics about both ranges as a group instead of individually.

- *Unmapped address space*—**Unmapped address space** is any IP address or IP address range that hasn't been assigned to an IP address block. By default, all IP address ranges are unmapped until you create IP address blocks.

Each IP address range should be a member of an IP address block. To create an IP address block, click IP Address Blocks in the IPAM console's navigation pane, and in the right pane, click Tasks and then Add IP Address Block. The address block requires a network ID and prefix length. The Start and End IP address is filled in automatically, but you can change these values as long as they fall within the range specified by the network ID and prefix length (see Figure 5-20). If you're creating a public IP address range, you need to select the Regional Internet Registry (RIR) that issued IP addresses to your organization. After you have created one or more IP address blocks, your existing IP address ranges are listed when you click IP Address Blocks in the navigation pane. From the IP Address Blocks view, click Tasks to see other tasks you can perform, which include adding and importing IP address ranges, IP address subnets, and IP addresses.

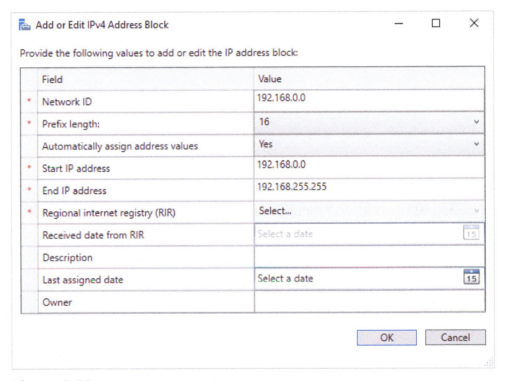

Figure 5-20   Creating an IPv4 address block

You can also create IPv6 address blocks. To create an IPv6 address block, click Address Blocks in the IPAM console's navigation pane and in the bottom half of the pane, click IPv6. Then click Tasks and Add IP Address Block. Specify the network ID for the IPv6 address block and then the prefix length (see Figure 5-21).

After you have created address blocks, existing address ranges are mapped to the address block. For example, if you create an address block with network ID and prefix length of 192.168.0.0/16, any existing address ranges that fall in that scope will be automatically mapped to that address block. So, for example, address ranges 192.168.0.0/24 and 192.168.1.0/16 will be mapped to the 192.168.0.0/16 address block. An address range can be mapped to a single address block, and the address ranges mapped to a block cannot overlap.

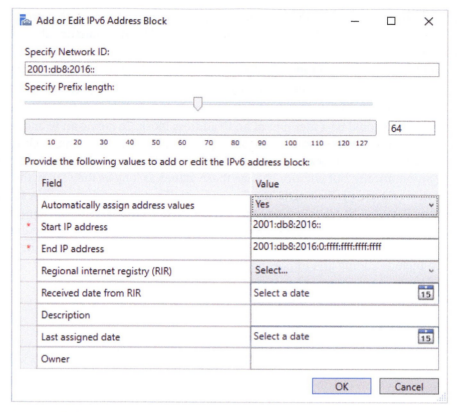

Figure 5-21 Creating an IPv6 address block

Creating New Address Ranges

After IPAM has collected server data, any DHCP address scopes that it discovers are added to the list of IP address ranges. You can view IP address ranges by clicking IP Address Blocks in the IPAM console's navigation pane, and in the right pane, clicking IP Address Ranges in the Current view list box (see Figure 5-22).

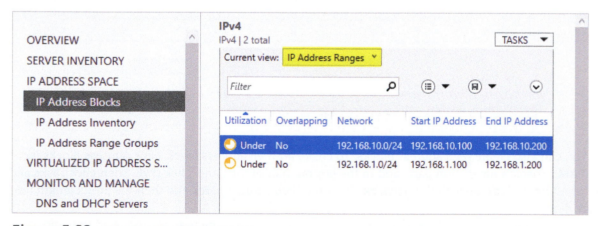

Figure 5-22 Viewing IP address ranges

You can create new address ranges by clicking Tasks and then Add IP Address Range. In the IP Address Range Properties dialog box, type the network ID and prefix length and then change the other parameters as necessary (see Figure 5-23). If the IP address subnet doesn't already exist, click the *Automatically create IP address subnet* check box. You create IPv6 address ranges in a similar fashion. If the address range doesn't fall within the scope of an existing address block, the address range will fall

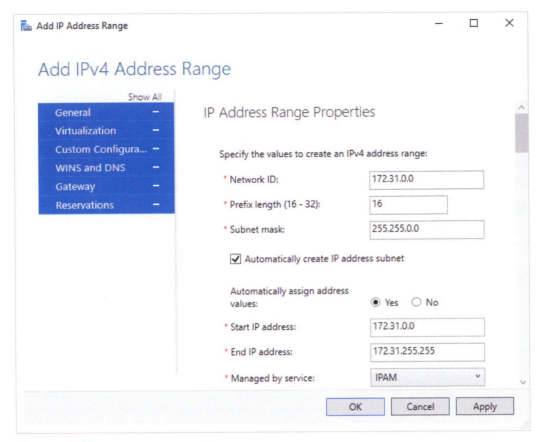

Figure 5-23   Creating an IP address range

under the category of unmapped address space. If that's the case, create a new address block that will encompass the address range.

Address ranges that are created manually are managed by IPAM by default. Address ranges that are added to IPAM from discovered DHCP scopes on DHCP servers are managed by the Microsoft DHCP (MS DHCP) server service. When you create a new address range, you can choose which service manages the range from the choices IPAM, Non-MS DHCP, Others, or VMM (Virtual Machine Manager). You should choose the service that provides IP addresses in the specified range.

Monitoring IP Address Space Utilization

With IPAM, you can monitor IP address space utilization by IP address block, IP address range, and IP address subnet. To do so, click IP Address Blocks in the IPAM console's navigation pane. In the Current view list box, select IP Address Ranges, IP Address Blocks, or IP Address Subnets. In the Utilization column, you'll see one of the following values:

- *Under*—This indicates that IP address usage is under the specified threshold. By default, the Under threshold means that utilization is less than 20%.
- *Over*—This indicates that IP address usage is over the specified threshold. By default, the Over threshold means that utilization is higher than 80%.
- *Optimal*—This indicates that IP address usage is between the Under and Over utilization thresholds.

You can change the utilization thresholds by clicking Overview in the IPAM console's navigation pane, then click Manage in the upper right of Server Manager, and click IPAM Settings. Then click Configure Utilization Threshold. Type the Under utilized and Over utilized threshold values as shown in Figure 5-24.

You can also view address utilization trends in a graph format. You can select the period over which to view utilization trends from 1 day to 5 years. To see utilization trends, click an address range, block, or subnet, and scroll down to the Details view and click Utilization Trend (see Figure 5-25).

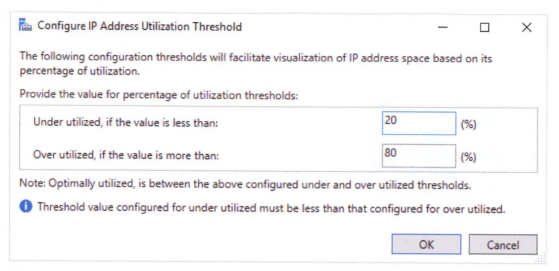

Figure 5-24 Setting utilization thresholds

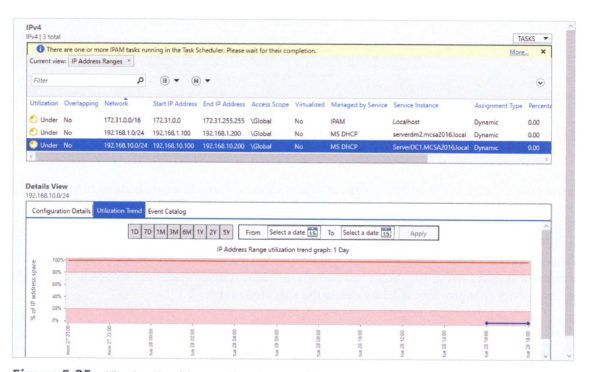

Figure 5-25 Viewing IP address utilization trends

Managing DHCP with IPAM

Managing the IP address space is a key feature of IPAM, but you can also fully manage DHCP servers from within IPAM. To manage DHCP servers, click Monitor and Manage in the IPAM console's navigation pane, and click DNS and DHCP Servers. The servers managed by IPAM are listed in the right pane. Right-click a server running the DHCP server role to see the management options (see Figure 5-26).

The top two choices in Figure 5-26 allow you to edit the properties of the DHCP server and DHCP server options as described in the following list. Note that you can also open the DHCP management console from this menu.

- *Edit DHCP Server Properties*—From the Edit DHCP Server Properties dialog box, you can enable DHCP audit logging, configure dynamic DNS updates and DNS update credentials, and configure MAC address filtering (see Figure 5-27).

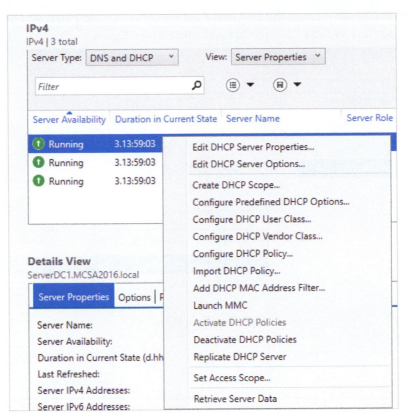

Figure 5-26   DHCP Server Management options

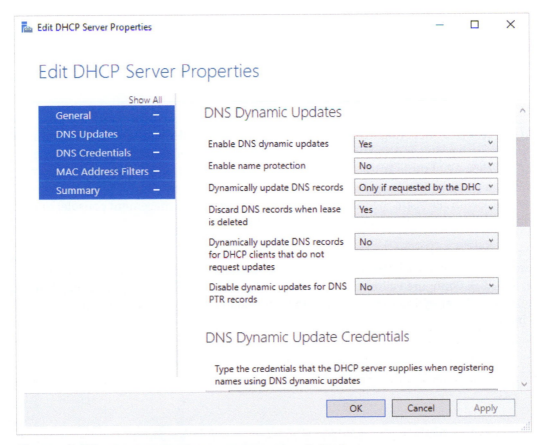

Figure 5-27   The Edit DHCP Server Properties dialog box

- *Edit DHCP Server Options*—From the Edit DHCP Server Options dialog box, you can configure global configuration options such as DNS servers and routers (see Figure 5-28).

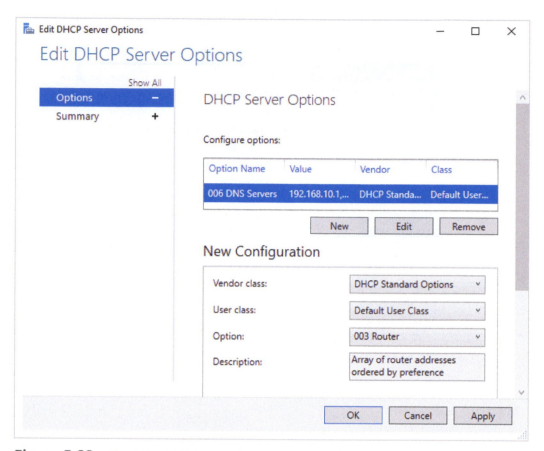

Figure 5-28   The Edit DHCP Server Options dialog box

As you can see, you can configure most everything about your DHCP servers directly from within IPAM, including configuring and creating DHCP scopes, setting user and vendor class values, and configuring policies. All of these DHCP configuration tasks were discussed in Chapter 4; however, in Chapter 4, you used the DHCP console or PowerShell to perform these tasks. The procedures for configuring DHCP with IPAM are the same as when using the DHCP management console; only the user interface differs.

Configuring DHCP Failover with IPAM

To configure DHCP failover, click DHCP Scopes in the IPAM navigation pane, right-click a scope in the right pane, and click Configure Failover to open the Configure Failover Relationship dialog box (see Figure 5-29). The failover options are similar to those found in the DHCP management console as discussed in Chapter 4.

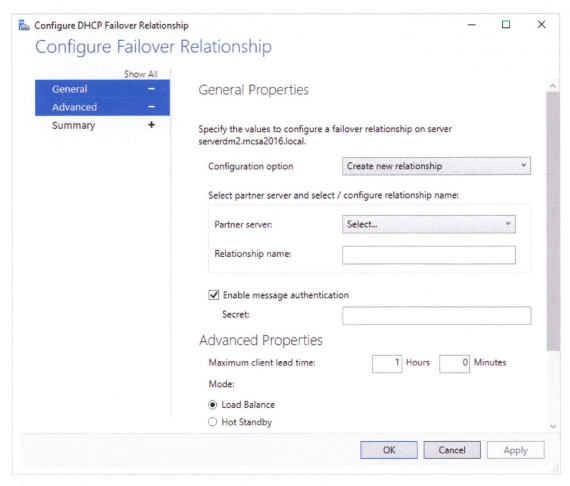

Figure 5-29   The Configure Failover Relationship dialog box

Managing DNS with IPAM

Although you can configure all aspects of DHCP using IPAM, the management of DNS using IPAM is more limited, but you can launch the DNS MMC from within IPAM to have full management capabilities of the target DNS server. From within IPAM, you can perform the following DNS server management tasks:

- Launch the DNS MMC for a selected server
- Create a DNS zone
- Create a conditional forwarder

To perform any of these tasks, in the IPAM navigation console under Monitor and Manage, click DNS and DHCP Servers and then right-click the DNS server you wish to manage. You can perform the following DNS zone configuration tasks from within IPAM:

- Add a DNS resource record
- Configure a preferred DNS server
- Edit a DNS zone
- Delete a DNS zone

To perform these tasks, click DNS Zones in the IPAM navigation console under Monitor and Manage, and then right-click the DNS zone you wish to configure. The only task that is unique in the task list is Configure a preferred DNS server. This options allows you to select the authoritative DNS server from which IPAM should collect zone data.

Managing DNS and DHCP Servers in Multiple Forests

As mentioned, starting with Windows Server 2016, IPAM allows you to manage DHCP and DNS servers across multiple forests. To do so, a two-way trust relationship must exist between all the forests that are being managed. If you have multiple forests in your Active Directory environment, create a two-way forest trust between the forests using the Active Directory Domains and Trusts management console. Then, from the IPAM Server Tasks window, click Configure server discovery. In the Configure Server Discovery dialog box (see Figure 5-30), click Get forests. You may need to close and re-open the Configure Server Discovery dialog box.

Select the forest you wish to manage and add each domain that is found in each forest to the dialog box. You must run the `Invoke-IpamGpoProvisioning` PowerShell cmdlet in each domain of each forest you wish to manage.

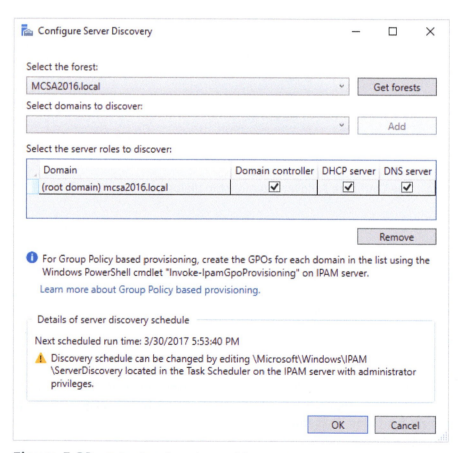

Figure 5-30   Selecting domains and forests to manage

IPAM Administration Delegation

As mentioned, IPAM supports role-based access control (RBAC). As you have seen, a number of IPAM-related groups are created to allow delegation of IPAM administration. You add users to these groups to allow them to manage and monitor aspects of IPAM without giving them broader administrative authority. There are no users in these groups by default; however, the Administrator account has full administrative permissions on the IPAM server. The IPAM groups that are created and their capabilities are as follows:

- *IPAM Administrators*—Members can view all IPAM data and perform all IPAM administrative tasks.
- *IPAM ASM Administrators*—Members can perform IP address space management (ASM) tasks.
- *IPAM IP Audit Administrators*—Members can view IP address tracking data.
- *IPAM MSM Administrators*—Members can monitor and manage IPAM tasks.
- *IPAM Users*—Members can view server inventory information and IP address space data (but not IP address tracking data) and access the MONITOR AND MANAGE view in the IPAM console. They can also view the event catalog. All the other groups in this list have the same access that this group does and the additional capabilities described.

There are also a number of built-in access controls that define administrative roles, scopes, and policies that allow you to assign fine-grained access controls over IPAM administration. In the IPAM navigation console, click ACCESS CONTROL. To see the available roles and the operations that each role can perform, click Roles in the lower pane of the navigation console. Click any of the listed roles to see the what actions the role can perform (see Figure 5-31).

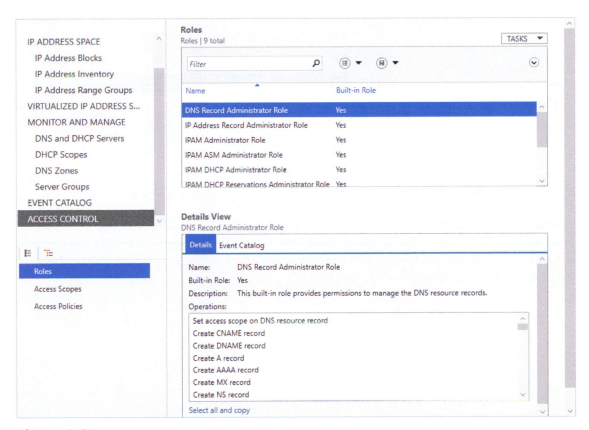

Figure 5-31   IPAM roles

Access scopes allow you to define which IPAM objects an administrative role can access. For example, you can create scopes based on location or business unit, or both. Access scopes are hierarchical, and the predefined scope Global already exists. The Global scope includes all discovered IPAM objects. Any scope you create will have Global as its parent scope. For example, you can create a new scope named US, which will have Global as its parent scope and two other scopes, WestCoast and EastCoast, which will have US as their parent scope.

Access policies assign users or groups to specific roles and access scopes. For example, you can create a group named US-IPAMAdmins and assign the group to the IPAM Administrator Role with scope Global \US, which allows the members of the group to perform IPAM administrative tasks only on objects that are assigned the US scope (see Figure 5-32).

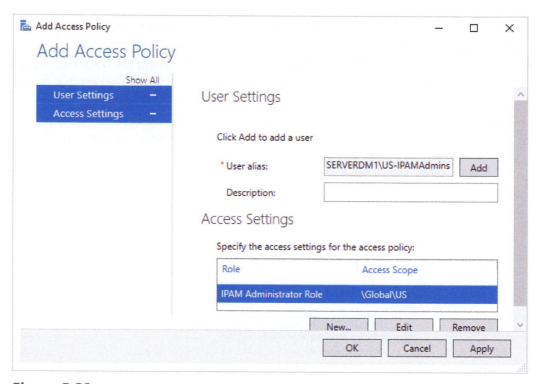

Figure 5-32   Creating an access policy

After you have created scopes and policies, you need to assign various IPAM objects to the scopes. For example, to assign a DHCP server to the Global \US scope, right-click the server in the IPAM console, and click Set Access Scope. In the Set Access Scope, uncheck the Inherit access scope from parent check box and click the desired access scope (see Figure 5-33).

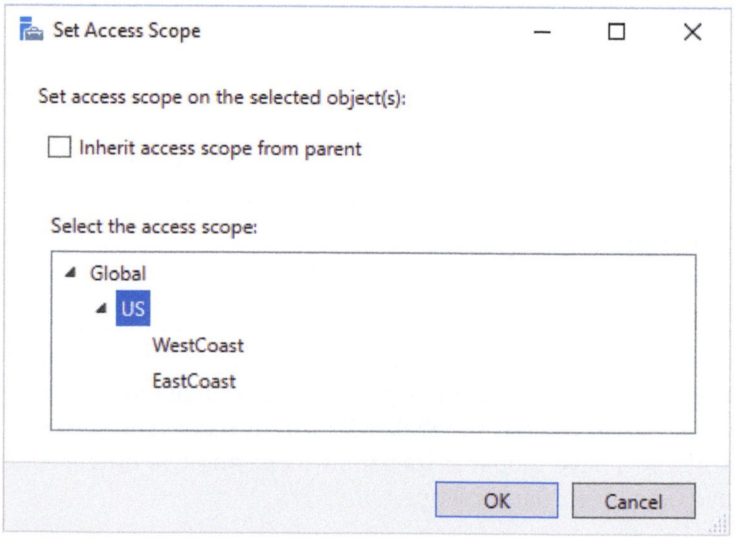

Figure 5-33   Setting the access scope

Note 📎

For a user to manage a remote IPAM server in Server Manager, the user must also be a member of the winRMRemoteWMIUsers group on the target IPAM server as well as a member of one of the groups in the preceding list.

Managing IPAM Data Collection Tasks

A number of IPAM scheduled tasks are created when you provision an IPAM server. Open the Task Scheduler on the IPAM server to see the list of scheduled tasks and, if necessary, change their frequency (see Figure 5-34). Table 5-2 lists the tasks along with their purpose and default frequency.

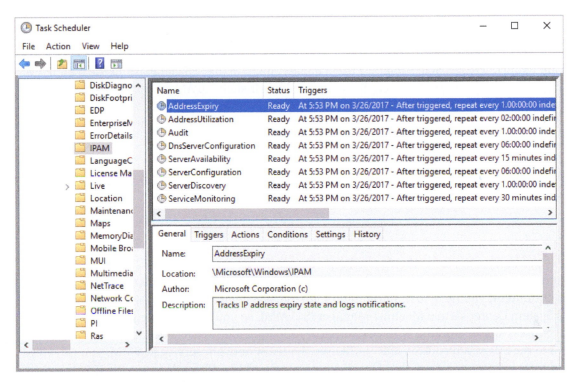

Figure 5-34   IPAM scheduled tasks

Table 5-2   IPAM scheduled tasks

Task name	Purpose	Default frequency
AddressExpiry	Tracks IP address lease expiration states and logs notifications	1 day
AddressUtilization	Collects IP address space use from DHCP servers	2 hours
Audit	Collects DHCP and IPAM operational events and events from DCs and NPS servers plus IP address tracking events from DHCP servers	1 day
DnsServerConfiguration	Gets DNS server information	6 hours
ServerAvailability	Gets status information from managed DNS and DHCP servers	15 minutes
ServerConfiguration	Get DHCP and DNS server configuration information	6 hours
ServerDiscovery	Discovers DCs and DHCP and DNS servers in the selected domains	1 day
ServiceMonitoring	Gets DNS zone status event information	30 minutes

Migrate IPAM to a New Server

If you are migrating IPAM from Windows Server 2012 or to another server, you can migrate the IPAM database and update the IPAM schema, if necessary. If you are using the built-in Windows Internal Database (WID), follow these steps:

1. Stop the WID service on the existing IPAM server using the Services console.
2. Make a copy the IPAM database files ipam.mdf and ipam_log.ldf located at C:\Windows\System32\ipam\Database.
3. Install IPAM on the destination server to which you wish to migrate IPAM.
4. Stop the WID service on the destination server.
5. Copy the database files from the existing IPAM server to C:\Windows\System32\ipam\Database.
6. Start the WID service on the new IPAM server.
7. If you are migrating IPAM to a new OS version, for example, from Windows Server 2012 R2 to Windows Server 2016, run the `Update-IpamServer` PowerShell cmdlet on the new IPAM server.

If you are using Microsoft SQL Server for the database, migrate the SQL database to the new IPAM server using the `Move-IpamDatabase` cmdlet after you have installed IPAM on the new server.

Note

If you are simply doing an in-place upgrade of the IPAM server from Windows Server 2012 R2 to Windows Server 2016, you need to run the `Update-IpamServer` cmdlet after the OS upgrade is completed.

IPAM and System Center Virtual Machine Manager

Most large enterprises today use virtualization, and just as you need to manage IP addresses in the physical environment, you need to manage them in the virtual environment. IPAM integrates with Microsoft's System Center Virtual Machine Manager (SCVMM), so you can manage your entire physical and virtual address space. Working with SCVMM is beyond the scope of this book, but once you have added IPAM to the SCVMM resources and configured the IPAM network service in VMM, you can view virtual IP address information from IPAM by clicking Virtualized IP Address Space in the IPAM navigation console. Logical networks in VMM are shown in IPAM, and you can create logical networks in IPAM, and they are added to the VMM.

Integrating IPAM with SCVMM is recommended in the following scenarios:

- You have multiple Hyper-V servers that you want to manage with SCVMM. SCVMM provides management of all your Hyper-V servers from a single console. With IPAM integration, you can manage all your physical and virtual networks and IP addresses from a single console.
- You are a cloud provider and need a centralized location to manage all your client networks, IP address spaces, and DNS servers and zones.

Activity 5-5: Using IPAM

Time Required: 10 minutes
Objective: Retrieve server data and create an IP address block.
Required Tools and Equipment: ServerDC1, ServerDM1, ServerDM2
Description: In this activity, you start using IPAM by retrieving server data and creating an IP address block.

1. On ServerDM1, open Server Manager, and click **IPAM**, if necessary. Click **OVERVIEW** in the IPAM console's navigation pane. In the IPAM Server Tasks window, click **Retrieve data from managed servers**.

2. After a while, you see the message "Server data is based on *date and time*." In the navigation pane, click **IP ADDRESS SPACE**. Read the information displayed. Click to expand the following items and read more about each: **IP Address Blocks, IP Address Inventory**, and **IP Address Range Groups**.

3. In the navigation pane, click **IP Address Blocks**. In the Current view list box, click **IP Address Blocks**. There are no IP address blocks at first. Click the **TASKS** list arrow, and click **Add IP Address Block**.

4. In the Add or Edit IPv4 Address Block dialog box, type **192.168.0.0** in the Network ID text box, and in the Prefix length list box, click **16**. The Start IP address and End IP address text boxes are filled in automatically. Click **OK**. In the Current view list box, click **IP Address Ranges**. You should see the IP address range 192.168.0.0/24 and 192.168.1.0/24 from the scopes defined on ServerDC1 and ServerDM2. If you don't see the address ranges, click the **Refresh** icon in Server Manager.

5. Click **DNS and DHCP Servers** under MONITOR AND MANAGE in the IPAM console's navigation pane. You see one entry for each DNS and DHCP server you're managing. Right-click the **DHCP** entry for **ServerDC1** and click **Edit DHCP Server Properties**. Browse through the settings in the Edit DHCP Server Properties dialog box. You can manage all your DHCP servers in this console. Click **Cancel** when finished.

6. Right-click the **DNS** entry for **ServerDC1** and review the options available for managing DNS servers.

7. Click **DHCP Scopes** in the navigation pane. You see the scopes defined on ServerDC1 and ServerDM2. Scroll down to the Details view. You can view details about the scope and see the current scope utilization. Scroll up and right-click the scope to see the management tasks you can perform.

8. Click **DNS Zones** in the navigation pane to see the DNS zones defined on ServerDC1. Right-click one of the zones to see the zone configuration options available.

9. Continue to the next activity.

Activity 5-6: Configuring Access Control in IPAM

Time Required: 15 minutes
Objective: Configure access control in IPAM.
Required Tools and Equipment: ServerDC, ServerDM1, ServerDM2
Description: In this activity, you configure an access scope and policy and configure an IPAM object with the access controls.

1. First, create a group that will be used to create an IPAM policy. On ServerDC1, open a PowerShell window. Type **New-ADGroup US-IPAMAdmins -GroupScope Global** and press **Enter**.

2. On ServerDM1, click **ACCESS CONTROL** in the IPAM console's navigation pane.

3. In the lower half of the navigation pane, click **Access Scopes**. Notice that a default scope of Global already exists. Click **Tasks** and click **Add Access Scopes**.

4. In the Add Access Scope dialog box, click **New** and type **US** in the **Name** box and click **Add**. Click **OK**. Notice that US is placed under the Global scope. You can then create additional scopes under the Global scope, or you can create additional scopes under the US scope, if desired.

5. In the lower half of the navigation pane, click **Access Policies**. Click **Tasks** and click **Add Access Policy**.

6. In the Add Access Policy window, click **Add**. In the Select user or group dialog box, type **mcsa2016 \ US-IPAMAdmins** and click **Check Names**. Click **OK**.

7. In the Access Settings section of the Add Access Policy dialog box, click **New**.

8. In the New Setting section, click **IPAM Administrator Role** in the Select role list box, and then click **US** in the Select the access scope for the role check box (see Figure 5-35).

9. Click **Add Setting**. Click **OK**. You see the new policy in the Access Polices window.

10. Next, you'll set the access scope on an IPAM object. Click **DNS and DHCP Servers** in the IPAM console's navigation pane.

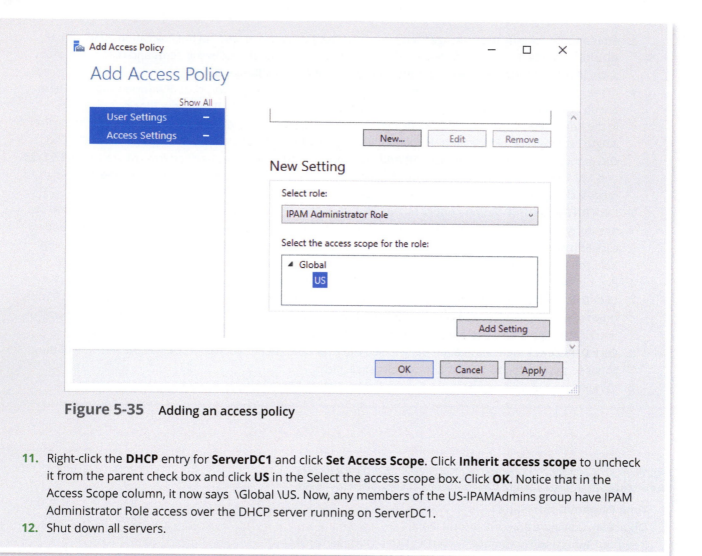

Figure 5-35   Adding an access policy

11. Right-click the **DHCP** entry for **ServerDC1** and click **Set Access Scope**. Click **Inherit access scope** to uncheck it from the parent check box and click **US** in the Select the access scope box. Click **OK**. Notice that in the Access Scope column, it now says \Global \US. Now, any members of the US-IPAMAdmins group have IPAM Administrator Role access over the DHCP server running on ServerDC1.

12. Shut down all servers.

Auditing IPAM

 **Certification**

- 70-741 – Implement IP Address Management (IPAM):
  Audit IPAM

In a large enterprise with dozens of DHCP servers and DNS servers as well as both physical and virtual networks, aside from central management and monitoring of your address space and servers, IPAM provides extensive auditing features. With IPAM auditing, you can audit the following types of events:

- Changes performed on the DNS and DHCP servers
- DHCP lease events and user logon events
- IPAM address usage trail

Before IPAM can successfully perform all the auditing events, you must ensure the following:

- The IPAMUG group must be a member of the Event Log Readers local group on all managed servers.
- To audit user logon events, the Account Logon Events policy must be enabled on domain controllers and NPS servers.

Auditing DNS and DHCP Server Changes

When something goes wrong, the problem can often be traced to a configuration change that was made. IPAM lets you easily review events related to IPAM and DHCP server configuration changes. In the IPAM navigation console, click EVENTS CATALOG, and then click IPAM Configuration Events in the lower pane of the navigation console. All events related to configuration changes made to the IPAM server and of the managed DHCP or DNS servers are listed. Click an event to see more information in the Details pane (see Figure 5-36). For example, in Figure 5-36, you can see that a DNS zone was created by the Administrator. You can also see that an access policy was added and that access control was modified on the DHCP server.

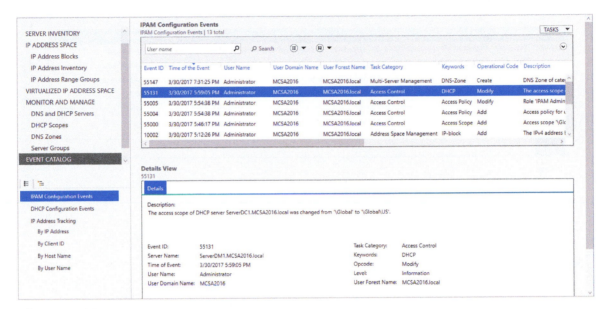

Figure 5-36   Viewing IPAM configuration events

To see events related to changes in DHCP scopes or policies, click DHCP Configuration Events in the lower pane of the navigation console.

> **Tip ⓘ**
>
> Be aware that events are not visible in real time. The IPAM server periodically collects data from the managed servers, including event data. If you want to see recent events, you need to click Retrieve data from managed servers from the IPAM Server Tasks windows and wait until the task is complete. After collecting data from servers, be sure to click the Refresh button in Server Manager.

Auditing DHCP Lease Events and Logon Events

You can audit IP address leases by IP address, client ID, or host name. And you can audit logon events by user name. To see lease information, with the EVENTS CATALOG option selected, click By IP Address in the lower pane of the navigation console. Type the IP address for which you wish to see lease information, including the start and end dates, and then click Search. You see event lease information as shown in Figure 5-37. To see user logon events, click By User Name in the lower pane of the navigation console. The displays show the user name of the account that logged on, the domain and forest name, the name of the server that authenticated the user, and the IP address of the station from which the user logged on.

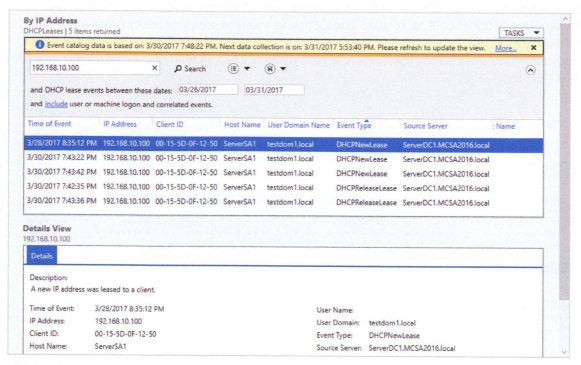

Figure 5-37　IP address lease events

Auditing IP Address Usage

As discussed earlier, IP address usage can be monitored and trends analyzed by IP address blocks, ranges, and subnets. Click IP ADDRESS SPACE in the navigation console and click IP Address Blocks. Select what you want to view in the Current view selection box. You can view utilization by percentage, total number of addresses and threshold value (Over, Under, or Optimal). In the Details View pane, you can view usage trends over varying periods of time and by start and end dates (refer back to Figure 5-25).

Chapter Summary

- IP Address Management (IPAM) is a Windows Server 2016 feature for managing the IP address space. IPAM has monitoring, auditing, and reporting functions to help manage key server components in an IP network.

- The IPAM infrastructure consists of IPAM servers and managed devices. The IPAM server discovers servers that you want to manage and collects and stores data from IPAM-managed devices in the IPAM database. Managed devices are Windows servers running DHCP, DNS, Active Directory, or NPS.

- An IPAM deployment has three topology options: centralized, distributed, and hybrid. IPAM deployment includes installing the IPAM Server feature, conducting IPAM server provisioning, performing server discovery, provisioning GPOs, selecting servers, and collecting data.

- Before you deploy IPAM, you should understand the requirements and limitations relating to an IPAM server, IPAM client, and an IPAM managed server. The IPAM Server is a feature you install with the Add Roles and Features Wizard or the `Install-WindowsFeature` PowerShell cmdlet.

- To provision the IPAM server, you use the IPAM Server Tasks window and click *Provision the IPAM server* to start the Provision IPAM Wizard. You can then select the method to provision managed servers. The default and recommended method is to use Group Policy provisioning.

- When the IPAM server has been provisioned, you configure server discovery. After server discovery has been configured, click *Start server discovery* in the IPAM Server Tasks window in Server Manager. IPAM probes the network in the specified domains to find servers that run the specified services.

- The IPAM server provisioning process doesn't create and link the IPAM GPOs to the domain, but you can utilize PowerShell to provision the GPOs. After provisioning the GPOs, you can open the Group Policy Management console on a DC in the domain to see the IPAM GPOs that have been linked to the domain.

- When selecting a server to manage, right-click the server in the Server Inventory window and click Edit Server. In the Add or Edit Server dialog box, you can change the manageability status to Managed if you want this IPAM server to manage the server.

- Once the IPAM server has collected data from selected servers and services, you can start working with IPAM. The IPAM console's navigation pane contains links to several monitoring and management views of your IP address space and DNS zone data.

- An IP address block is the largest unit for referring to an IP address space. It consists of a contiguous range of IP addresses with a corresponding subnet mask. An IP address range is a pool of continuous addresses in an IP address block and usually corresponds to a DHCP scope. An IP address range group consists of one or more IP address ranges that are logically grouped by some criteria.

- The IPAM console's navigation pane contains links to several monitoring and management views of the IP address space and DNS zone data. Each IP address range should be a member of an IP address block.

- After IPAM has collected server data, any DHCP address scopes that IPAM discovered are added to the list of IP address ranges. Address ranges that are created manually are managed by IPAM by default.

- IPAM can monitor IP address space utilization by IP address block, IP address range, and IP address subnet. You can change the utilization thresholds and view address utilization trends in a graph format.

- Managing the IP address space is a key feature of IPAM, but you can also fully manage DHCP servers from within IPAM. The procedures for configuring DHCP with IPAM are the same as when using the DHCP management console except that the user interface differs.

- You can manage a limited number of DNS options within IPAM. However, you can launch the DNS MMC from within IPAM to have full management capabilities of the target DNS server.

- In order to allow IPAM to manage DHCP and DNS servers across multiple forests, a two-way trust relationship must exist between all the forests that are being managed.

- IPAM-related groups can be created to allow delegation of IPAM administration, and IPAM scheduled tasks are created when you provision an IPAM server.

- There are several built-in access controls that define administrative roles, scopes, and policies that allow you to assign fine-grained access controls over IPAM administration. Access scopes allow you to define which IPAM objects an administrative role can access, and access policies assign users or groups to specific roles and access scopes.

- IPAM can integrate with Microsoft's System Center Virtual Machine Manager (SCVMM) so you can manage the enterprise's entire physical and virtual address space. Integrating IPAM with SCVMM is recommended when you have multiple Hyper-V servers that you want to manage with SCVMM or you are a cloud provider and need a centralized location to manage all your client networks, IP address spaces, and DNS servers and zones.

- IPAM provides extensive auditing features. You can audit changes performed on the DNS and DHCP servers, DHCP lease events and user logon events, and IPAM address usage trail.

- IPAM lets you easily review events related to IPAM and DHCP server configuration changes. You can also audit IP address leases by IP address, client ID, or host name.

Key Terms

access policy

access scope

centralized topology

distributed topology

Group Policy provisioning

hybrid topology

IP address block

IP Address Management
(IPAM)

IP address range

IP address range group

IPAM client

IPAM server

managed server

manual provisioning

role-based access control
(RBAC)

unmapped address space

Review Questions

1. You want to deploy IPAM in your network. You have four servers running and need to decide on which server you should install the IPAM Server feature. Which of the following server configurations is the best solution?

   a. Windows Server 2016 domain controller

   b. Windows Server 2016 standalone server running DHCP

   c. Windows Server 2016 member server running Web Server

   d. Windows Server 2016 member server running DHCP

2. Your company has a main office with four branch offices; each has about 30 computers and a single server running file and print services, DNS, and DHCP. There are no IT personnel at branch offices. You want to set up IPAM in your network. Which IPAM topology makes the most sense?

   a. Centralized

   b. Distributed

   c. Unified

   d. Hybrid

3. You recently configured IPAM in your Windows Server 2016 domain. When you view the Server Inventory window, you notice that one DHCP server isn't displayed. This missing server runs Windows Server 2012 R2 in a workgroup configuration and is located in the Engineering Department. Which of the following actions is most likely to display the missing server in the Server Inventory window?

   a. Upgrade the server to Windows Server 2016.

   b. Join the server to the domain.

   c. Configure the server's firewall.

   d. Uninstall DHCP from the server.

4. You have recently installed IPAM on a server running Windows Server 2016. Your network has four DHCP servers, six DNS servers, and three DCs. All the DHCP and DNS servers are domain members. When you look at the Server Inventory window,

you don't see any of the DHCP servers, but you do see the DNS servers and DCs. What should you do to solve this problem?

   a. Reinstall IPAM on a server that isn't a DC.

   b. Configure the DHCP servers as workgroup servers.

   c. Demote the IPAM server.

   d. On the IPAM server, uninstall DHCP.

5. You have recently installed the IPAM Server feature on a server running Windows Server 2016. You chose manual provisioning during installation. You have 15 servers to be managed by IPAM and have decided that the manual provisioning tasks are too much work. You want to use Group Policy provisioning instead. What should you do?

   a. Delete any GPOs you have created. In the Overview window of the IPAM console, enable Group Policy provisioning.

   b. Uninstall IPAM and reinstall it, making sure to select Group Policy provisioning in the Provision the IPAM server step.

   c. Run the `Invoke-IpamGpoProvisioning -GroupPolicy` PowerShell cmdlet.

   d. Create a GPO, configure the IPAM-Provisioning setting, and link the GPO to an OU containing the IPAM server account.

6. You have just installed a Microsoft SQL server and want to use it to store IPAM data, which is currently using the WID. What should you do?

   a. Copy the files from C:\Windows\System32\ ipam\database folder to the SQL server and import the files.

   b. Uninstall IPAM and reinstall it, making sure to choose Microsoft SQL Server during server provisioning.

   c. In the IPAM Overview window, run the Change Database Storage Method Wizard.

   d. Run the `Move-IpamDatabase` PowerShell cmdlet from the IPAM server.

7. You have just finished the Add Roles and Features Wizard and clicked the IPAM node in Server Manager. The IPAM Server Tasks window indicates that you're connected to the IPAM server. What should you do next?
   a. Provision the IPAM server.
   b. Configure server discovery.
   c. Start server discovery.
   d. Select servers to manage.

8. You have been assigned the task of installing the IPAM feature on a Windows client computer running Windows 10. What specific set of tools should you acquire from the Microsoft Download Center to facilitate this task?
   a. Remote Administration Console
   b. Remote Server Administration
   c. IPAM client
   d. IPAM Manager

9. You have decided to use Microsoft SQL Server for your IPAM database. When you are provisioning IPAM, what information will you need to provide after selecting the Microsoft SQL Server option for your IPAM database? (Choose all that apply.)
   a. Port number
   b. Database name
   c. SQL Server IP address
   d. SQL Server name

10. You have just provisioned an IPAM server and are ready to configure server discovery. During this process while working in the Configure Server Discovery dialog box, you have clicked Get forests to view the list of forests and domains. However, after clicking Get forests, no forests or domains are listed. What must you do to see the list of forests and domains?
    a. Close and reopen the Configure Server Discovery dialog box.
    b. Close the Configure Server Discovery dialog box and refresh Server Manager.
    c. Restart the IPAM server.
    d. Repeat the process of provisioning the IPAM server.

11. You have just set a server's manageability status to Managed. However, you have observed that the IPAM access status remains in the Blocked state. Which of the following commands can be run on the server to avoid waiting for the server to refresh its computer policies?
    a. `gpupdate /forceupdate`
    b. `gpupdate /apply`
    c. `gpupdate /force`
    d. `netsh /add`

12. Which of the following specific views under the IPAM console's navigation IP Address Space pane link allows you to display the IP address range group that's organized by device type?
    a. IP Address Range Groups
    b. IP Address Inventory
    c. IP Address Blocks
    d. IP Address Range Groups

13. When using IPAM, it is critical for a system administrator to understand how IPAM views the IP address space. Which of the following units best represents an IP space that consists of one or more IP address ranges that are logically grouped by some criteria?
    a. IP address range
    b. IP address block
    c. Unmapped address space
    d. IP address range group

14. What specific options are available to a system administrator to monitor IP address space utilization? (Choose all that apply.)
    a. IP address block
    b. IP address type
    c. IP address subnet
    d. IP address range

15. A system administrator who utilizes IPAM may decide to use IPAM to manage their DHCP servers. Which of the following DHCP options can be configured within IPAM? (Choose all that apply.)
    a. Configure group policy DHCP preference.
    b. Create and configure DHCP scopes.
    c. Configuring DHCP policies.
    d. Set user and vendor class values.

16. When using Windows Server 2106, you can manage DHCP and DNS servers across multiple domains. However, what specific type of relationship must exist between all forests that you wish to manage?
    a. Two-way limited trust
    b. One-way incoming trust
    c. One-way outgoing trust
    d. Two-way trust

17. You are a senior system administrator and have decided to delegate specific IPAM administration tasks to some of your junior system administrators. What IPAM group should you use to allow members to view IP address tracking data?
    a. IPAM Users
    b. IPAM MSM Administrators
    c. IPAM IP Audit Administrators
    d. IPAM ASM Administrators

18. When you provision an IPAM server, several IPAM scheduled tasks are created by default. Which of the following default tasks allows you to collect DHCP and IPAM operational events?
    a. ServerDiscovery
    b. Audit
    c. ServiceMonitoring
    d. AddressUtilization

19. You want to migrate IPAM from a server using Microsoft SQL to a new server on which you have just installed IPAM. Which of the following PowerShell cmdlets should you use to migrate the SQL database to the new IPAM server?
    a. `Move-IpamDatabase`
    b. `Copy-IpamSQLDatabase`
    c. `Move-IpamSQLDatabase`
    d. `Migrate-IpamDatabase`

20. IPAM can provide a system administrator to manage a large enterprise environment with the ability to perform extensive auditing of its DHCP and DNS servers. What specific configurations must be in place before you can fully perform all the available auditing events IPAM offers? (Choose all that apply.)
    a. Account Event policies must be disabled on all domain controllers and NPS servers.
    b. IPAMUG group must be a member of the Event Log Readers local group on all managed servers.
    c. Audit User Logon Events must be enabled on all member servers.
    d. Account Logon Events policy must be enabled on domain controllers and NPS servers.

Critical Thinking

The following activity gives you a critical thinking challenge. Case Projects offer a scenario with a problem to solve and for which you supply a written solution.

Case Project 5-1: Implementing IPAM

You're a consultant for a large enterprise that needs a comprehensive IP addressing and DNS management solution for its physical and virtual networks. The enterprise has a primary office in Pittsburgh and three branch offices in Los Angeles, New York, and Miami. It has IT support staff only in the branch offices. The enterprise's server specialists are located in Pittsburgh. The IT directory in Pittsburgh wants to offload some of the IPAM management functions to some of the IT staff without giving them broader domain or forest administrative right. Which type of IPAM architecture do you recommend? Which features of IPAM are you likely to recommend using to address the requirements?

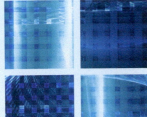

CHAPTER 6

IMPLEMENTING REMOTE ACCESS

After reading this chapter and completing the exercises, you will be able to:

Describe remote access

Install and configure the Remote Access server role

Configure the DirectAccess role service

The old work model of throngs of workers going to an office and staying there from 9 to 5 no longer applies to many businesses. With remote access technology, employees can work from home or on the road and still have access to all the resources and applications they would have sitting at a desk in the company office. With the Remote Access server role, network administrators can offer options to employees for accessing network resources remotely. The Remote Access server role also has features that enable you to configure a Windows server as a local area network (LAN) router or Network Address Translation device. In this chapter, you learn how to install and configure the Remote Access server role and its three role services. This chapter also focuses on configuring virtual private networks (VPNs) and the DirectAccess role service.

Table 6-1 describes what you need for the hands-on activities in this chapter.

Table 6-1	Activity requirements	
Activity	**Requirements**	**Notes**
Activity 6-1: Resetting Your Virtual Environment	ServerDC1, ServerDM1, ServerSA1	
Activity 6-2: Installing and Configuring the Remote Access Role	ServerDC1, Server DM1	
Activity 6-3: Creating a VPN Connection and Testing the VPN	ServerDC1, ServerDM1, ServerSA1	
Activity 6-4: Configuring Routing	ServerDC1, ServerDM1	

An Overview of Remote Access

 **Certification**

- 70-741 – Implement network connectivity and remote access solutions:
  Implement network connectivity solutions

Remote Access is a server role that provides services to keep a mobile workforce and branch offices securely connected to resources at the main office. Some reasons that businesses, large and small, use a remote access solution include the following:

- *Work from home employees*—Employees' physical locations might not be as important as their ability to produce the required work. In addition, teleconferencing applications can often meet the need for personal interactions with other employees and team members.
- *Frequent travelers*—Employees who are on the road a lot, such as salespeople and product support specialists, and people who need to make contact with customers or the product in the field need up-to-date access to company resources.
- *Business partners*—You might need to provide limited access to the company network (intranet) for partners who need real-time information on inventory and product delivery.
- *Branch offices*—With the widespread availability of high-speed Internet connections, branch offices can often use less expensive, but still secure, VPNs to connect to the main office.

No matter how remote access is set up, the goal is usually the same: giving remote users access to network resources in a way that's much like being on the network premises. The Remote Access server role has several services and tools to help achieve this goal, including the following:

- *Virtual private network*—A VPN uses the Internet to create a secure connection from a client computer or branch office to the company's intranet. It has largely replaced remote dial-in for client computers.
- *Remote dial-in*—This technology is less common but still used when broadband Internet isn't available. It uses the phone system and modems to connect remotely.
- *Routing*—This service configures a Windows server as a router with support for static and dynamic routing.
- *Network Address Translation (NAT)*—This is used with routing to translate private IP addresses to public IP addresses to facilitate hosts accessing the Internet in a private network.
- *DirectAccess*—Similar to VPNs, DirectAccess provides a more convenient and manageable secure remote connection using features available in IPv6.

The Remote Access server role has some additional features, but the ones in the preceding list are the core services for most remote access needs and are discussed in the following sections.

Installing and Configuring the Remote Access Role

 **Certification**

- **70-741 – Implement network connectivity and remote access solutions:**
  Implement virtual private network (VPN) and DirectAccess Solutions

The Remote Access server role is installed by using Server Manager or the `Install-WindowsFeature` PowerShell cmdlet. Under the main Remote Access server role, there are three role services to choose from:

- *DirectAccess and VPN (RAS)*—This role service has the features needed for dial-in, VPN, and DirectAccess remote access.
- *Routing*—This role service provides routing and NAT. The Routing role service requires the DirectAccess and VPN (RAS) role service.
- *Web Application Proxy*—This allows publishing web-based applications for use by clients outside the network. This role service is discussed in more detail in *MCSA Guide to Identity with Windows Server 2016, Exam 70–742* (Cengage, 2018).

Virtual Private Networks

A **virtual private network (VPN)** is a network connection that uses the Internet to give mobile users or branch offices secure access to a company's network resources on a private network. VPNs use encryption and authentication to ensure that communication is secure and legitimate, so while data travels through the public Internet, the connection remains private—hence, the name virtual private network.

Privacy is achieved by creating a "tunnel" between the VPN client and VPN server. A **tunnel** is a method of transferring data across an unsecured network in such a way that the actual data in the transmission is hidden from all but the sender and the receiver. Tunnels are created by encapsulation in which the inner packet containing the data is encrypted, and the outer headers contain the unencapsulated addresses that Internet devices need to route packets correctly. To use a mail delivery analogy, suppose you have an ultra-secure package to deliver, but you must use a courier. In a separate transaction, you deliver a key to the office manager at the package recipient's location. Next, you place the secret package containing the recipient's name in a lockbox. You put the lockbox inside an envelope and address the envelope to the office manager of the company where the recipient works. The courier can read the addressing on the envelope, but if the envelope is opened, the package contents can't be accessed without the key to the lockbox. The envelope is delivered, and the office manager removes the lockbox from the envelope and opens it with the key delivered earlier. The office manager can then deliver the package to the final recipient. In this analogy, the lockbox and outer envelope make up the VPN tunnel, and the office manager is the VPN server to which messages are delivered.

Figure 6-1 shows a VPN tunnel between a client computer and an intranet. The tunnel connection is made between the client computer and the VPN server. After the VPN server opens the packet, the inner packet is decrypted (unlocked) and delivered to the resource the client requested. From the client computer's standpoint, access to network resources is little different than if the client were physically connected to the company network. In fact, the VPN network connection on the client OS is assigned an IP address on the network.

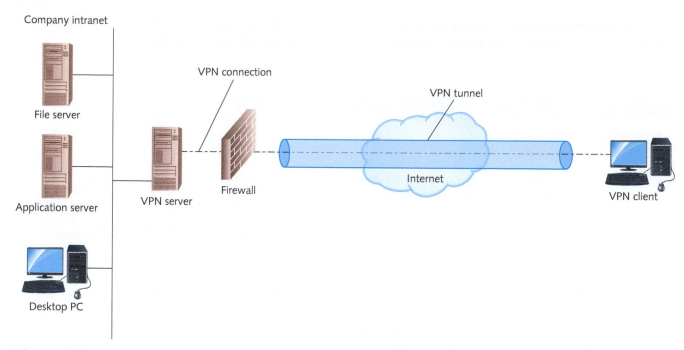

Figure 6-1   A typical VPN connection

VPN Tunnel Types

Windows Server 2016 has a VPN server solution with Routing and Remote Access Service (RRAS), a component of the Remote Access server role, that supports three types of VPN tunnels:

- *Point-to-Point Tunneling Protocol (PPTP)*—A commonly used VPN protocol that encapsulates Point-to-Point Protocol (PPP), using a modified version of Generic Routing Encapsulation (GRE). The data in encapsulated PPP frames is compressed, encrypted, or both. Frames are encrypted with Microsoft Point-to-Point Encryption (MPPE) by using encryption keys from the authentication process. Authentication uses Microsoft Challenge Handshake Authentication Protocol version 2 (MS-CHAP v2) or Extensible Authentication Protocol-Transport Layer Security (EAP-TLS) (described later). An advantage of using PPTP is that it's well supported by most OSs and network devices and doesn't require exchanging a preshared key or certificates. Because of its widespread support, this tunnel type is often used when a variety of clients are used to connect to the VPN.

- *Layer 2 Tunneling Protocol with Internet Protocol Security (L2TP/IPsec)*—Developed in cooperation with Cisco Systems and Microsoft, L2TP/IPsec generally provides a higher level of security than PPTP. L2TP doesn't use MPPE for encryption; instead, it uses the encryption technology built into IPsec. IPsec uses Data Encryption Standard (DES) or Triple DES (3DES), using encryption keys generated by the Internet Key Exchange (IKE) process. L2TP/IPsec requires certificates or preshared keys for authentication. Certificates issued to both client and server computers from a public key infrastructure (PKI) is recommended. In addition to securing data through encryption, L2TP/IPsec provides data integrity and identity verification. This tunnel type is most often used when an organization has an established PKI and client computers are members of the organization's network (as opposed to being employee home computers).

- *Secure Socket Tunneling Protocol (SSTP)*—SSTP has the advantage of working behind most firewalls without firewall administrators needing to configure the firewall to allow VPN. It uses the standard TCP port 443 used for Secure Sockets Layer (SSL) communication (HTTPS). SSTP is supported only on Windows clients, starting with Vista SP1, and as a VPN server, starting with Windows Server 2008. It requires the VPN server to have a valid digital certificate issued by a certification authority (CA) for server identification. This tunnel type is gaining in popularity because of its ease of use and compatibility with firewalls but only when client computers run Windows Vista SP1 and later.

All three types are enabled by default when you configure Windows Server 2016 as a VPN server, so any type of client that tries to connect will be successful, as long as each tunnel type is configured correctly. VPN server configuration in Windows Server 2016 is fairly straightforward. After the Remote Access server role is installed, you configure it in the Routing and Remote Access console, accessed from the Tools menu in Server Manager.

VPN Requirements

Before you can configure a VPN with RRAS, your server and network must meet the following requirements for the type of VPN you want to set up:

- *Two or more NICs installed on a server*—One NIC is connected to the private network you're allowing remote access to, and the other is connected to the Internet. The VPN server acts as a kind of router, receiving traffic on the interface connected to the Internet from VPN clients and routing it to the private network. The VPN server decrypts, authenticates, and validates the traffic as required by the tunnel type before sending it to the private network. Traffic from the private network is received on one or more other NICs and routed to the Internet-connected NIC, where it's made secure for transmission to the VPN client.
- *Correctly configured firewall*—The network firewall must be configured according to the requirements of the VPN tunnel type. When the VPN is configured on the Windows server, Windows configures Windows Firewall for the VPN tunnel type, but the firewall protecting the network must also be configured to allow VPN traffic to reach the VPN server. Firewall configurations are discussed later in this section.
- *Authentication*—Depending on which tunnel types your VPN supports, you might need to configure one or more authentication methods, such as a Remote Authentication Dial In User Service (RADIUS) server to handle user authentication. RADIUS is a service that's part of the Network Policy Server (NPS) server role, which provides centralized authentication for remote access and wireless clients. (NPS and RADIUS are discussed in Chapter 7.) If the VPN supports SSTP connections, the server must have a digital certificate assigned by a public CA, such as VeriSign. L2TP/IPsec tunnels that don't use preshared keys need both client and server certificates, which can be issued from a Windows-based PKI with Windows Certificate Services.
- *DHCP configuration*—Clients that connect to the VPN server are usually assigned an IP address dynamically. Although the server can be configured with a pool of addresses to assign to clients, a Dynamic Host Configuration Protocol (DHCP) server is recommended for centralized IP address management. When a DHCP server is used, the VPN server requests a small pool of 10 addresses from the DHCP server and then allocates these addresses to clients when they connect. If the VPN server runs out of addresses, it requests another small pool of addresses to lease to clients.

Network Firewall Configuration for a VPN

Configuring the perimeter network firewall is critical for VPN operation. A **perimeter network** is a boundary between the private network and the public Internet that is where most resources available to the Internet, such as mail, web, DNS, and VPN servers, are located. Although these resources can be accessed from the Internet, they're still guarded by a firewall to prevent malicious packets from entering the network.

Most firewalls are configured to allow only limited types of incoming traffic. For example, if you have a company web server, the firewall must allow TCP port 80 for incoming web traffic to reach the web server. If you're running a DNS server for Internet resources, the firewall must allow UDP port 53 for DNS queries. For VPNs, the firewall must be configured to allow the following types of traffic to the VPN server, according to the VPN tunnel type:

- *PPTP tunnels*
  - Inbound destination TCP port 1723 for PPTP maintenance traffic from VPN client to server
  - Inbound destination IP protocol ID 47 (GRE) for tunneled data transfers from VPN client to server
  - Outbound source TCP port 1723 for PPTP maintenance traffic from VPN server to client
  - Outbound source IP protocol ID 47 (GRE) for tunneled data transfers from VPN server to client

- *L2TP/IPsec tunnels*
  - Inbound destination User Datagram Protocol (UDP) port 500 for IKE traffic from VPN client to server
  - Inbound destination UDP port 4500 for IPsec NAT traversal traffic from VPN client to server
  - Inbound destination IP protocol ID 50 for IPsec Encapsulating Security Payload (ESP) traffic from VPN client to server
  - Outbound source UDP port 500 for IKE traffic from VPN server to client
  - Outbound source UDP port 4500 for IPsec NAT traversal traffic from VPN server to client
  - Outbound source IP protocol ID 50 for IPsec ESP traffic from VPN server to client
- *SSTP tunnels*
  - Inbound destination TCP port 443 for HTTPS traffic from VPN client to server
  - Outbound source TCP port 443 for HTTPS traffic from VPN server to client

VPN Configuration

After meeting the requirements for a VPN server and network, it's time to configure a VPN. If the VPN server is a domain member, its computer account must first be added to the RAS and IAS Servers group in Active Directory. (IAS stands for Internet Authentication Service.) The RAS and IAS Servers group is in the Users folder. When you install the Remote Access server role, the computer on which you are installing it should automatically be added to this group, but it's a good idea to verify it.

Although you can use PowerShell cmdlets to configure RRAS, the following steps use the Routing and Remote Access console. By default, all remote access functions are disabled, indicated by a red down arrow on the server icon. To enable these functions, right-click the server icon and click Configure and Enable Routing and Remote Access. After the Welcome window, the Configuration window gives you the following options for the type of remote access server you want to configure (see Figure 6-2):

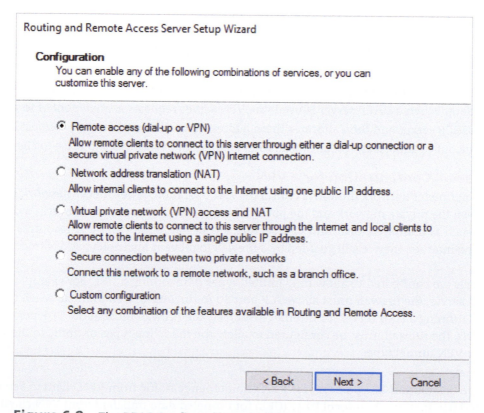

Figure 6-2   The RRAS Configuration window

- *Remote access (dial-up or VPN)*—Configures the server as a VPN server, a dial-up server, or both. Select this option if the server will provide incoming VPN or dial-up services for remote clients but will not act as a NAT device for outgoing Internet connections.
- *Network address translation (NAT)*—Configures the server as a NAT router to allow computers on the private network to access the Internet with a public IP address.
- *Virtual private network (VPN) access and NAT*—Configures the server as both a remote access (VPN or dial-up) server and a NAT router. This option combines the first two options.
- *Secure connection between two private networks*—Configures the server as a VPN router between two networks, such as between a main office and a branch office. With this configuration, all traffic between the two networks is secure, but the server doesn't accept client connections.
- *Custom configuration*—Allows you to manually configure the routing and remote access features you need if one of the standard options doesn't meet your requirements.

For a standard VPN server, select the *Remote access (dial-up or VPN)* option. In the next window, you can choose VPN, dial-up, or both. For a VPN server without dial-up support, select the VPN option. In the VPN Connection window, select the network interface that connects the server to the Internet (see Figure 6-3). This interface must be connected to the Internet and the correct firewall ports must be open to allow VPN traffic to this interface's IP address.

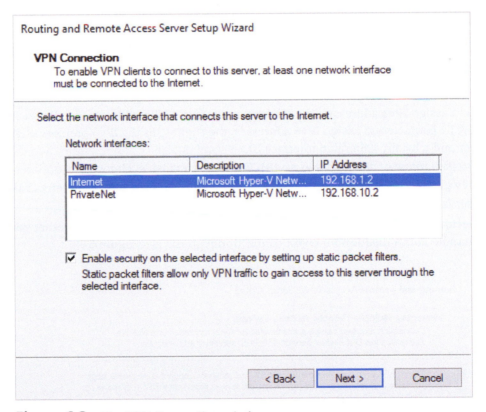

Figure 6-3   The VPN Connection window

In Figure 6-3, the network connections are named descriptively; although this naming convention isn't required, it's a good idea on any computer with multiple network connections. You can rename network connections in the Network Connections window. The *Enable security on the selected interface by setting up static packet filters* option is enabled by default. It prevents the interface connected to the Internet from accepting any traffic that isn't part of a VPN connection. For example, even if the firewall is configured to allow ping packets into the network, the packet filters created by this option deny these packets unless they originate from a VPN client. Next, you decide how VPN client connections are assigned an IP address when they connect to the VPN (see Figure 6-4):

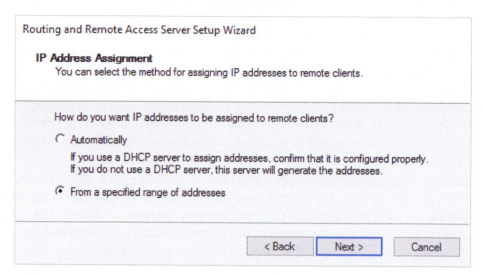

Figure 6-4 The IP Address Assignment window

- *Automatically*—This option is preferred and requires a correctly configured DHCP server on the network. The VPN server gets a pool of 10 addresses at a time to allocate to VPN clients. If the DHCP server is on a different subnet from the VPN client, the DHCP relay agent must be configured. Both IPv4 and IPv6 addresses can be assigned. If you select this option and no DHCP server can be contacted to assign IPv4 addresses, the VPN server assigns APIPA addresses to clients. If a DHCP server can't be contacted to assign IPv6 addresses, the client uses the IPv6 prefix configured on the VPN server and a locally generated interface ID.
- *From a specified range of addresses*—If no DHCP server is available, choose this option to specify a range of IPv4 addresses for allocation to clients. For IPv6 addresses, only the prefix is assigned by the VPN server; the client uses a locally generated interface ID.

Next, you decide how clients are authenticated to the VPN server and specify whether you want to use RADIUS to handle authentication for client connection requests (see Figure 6-5):

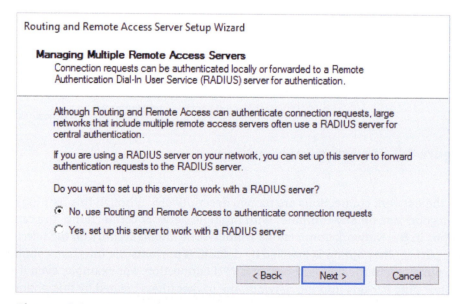

Figure 6-5 Configuring authentication

- *No, use Routing and Remote Access to authenticate connection requests*—With this option, the VPN server authenticates connection requests by contacting a domain controller if the server is a domain member. If it isn't a domain member, it uses accounts from the local SAM database. For security reasons, a domain-joined VPN server isn't recommended.
- *Yes, set up this server to work with a RADIUS server*—Choose this option when there are multiple remote access servers that aren't joined to a domain. A RADIUS server performs centralized authentication, as you will learn in Chapter 7.

After you click Finish in the summary window, you see a message stating that you must configure the DHCP relay agent. You need to do this only if you configured automatic IP address assignment and the DHCP server isn't on the same subnet as the server's private network connection.

Finishing VPN Configuration

After you have finished the RRAS Setup Wizard, the VPN server is ready to start accepting VPN client connections. However, first you need to define who's allowed to connect via remote access. By default, all users are denied remote access. There are two ways to allow users to connect via remote access: configuring dial-in settings in user accounts and configuring a network policy in the Network Policy Server (NPS) console.

Configuring Dial-in Settings in User Accounts

If you have only a few users who should be able to access the network remotely, you can configure each user's account properties in Active Directory or Local Users and Groups to allow remote access. In the account's Properties dialog box, click the Dial-in tab (see Figure 6-6). By default, the Network Access Permission attribute is set to *Control access through NPS Network Policy*. The NPS Network Policy is configured to deny access to all users by default, so select the *Allow access* option (highlighted in the figure) to give the user permission to connect remotely via dial-in, VPN, and DirectAccess.

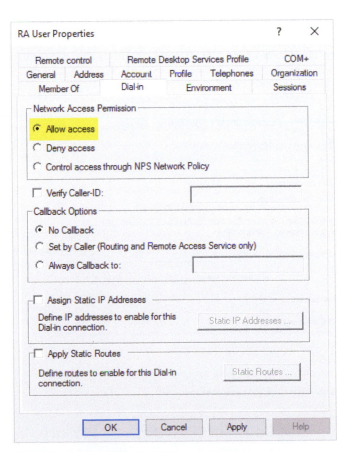

Figure 6-6   Configuring the Network Access Permission attribute for a user account

The remaining settings on the Dial-in tab are as follows:

- *Verify Caller-ID*—This option is used only for dial-in remote access. When the user attempts to log on, the phone number attempting the remote connection is verified against the phone number entered in the text box by using caller ID. If the number doesn't match or caller ID isn't supported, the connection is denied.
- *Callback Options*—This option is used only for dial-in remote access and by default is set to No Callback. If Set by Caller is selected, the remote access client enters a number, and the server calls the client back to make the connection, thereby saving client phone charges. If the *Always Callback to* option is selected, the server attempts to call the number specified to make the connection.
- *Assign Static IP Addresses*—Use this option to assign static IPv4 and IPv6 addresses the client uses for remote access connections rather than dynamic addresses assigned by the VPN server.
- *Apply Static Routes*—Select this option to configure routes that the client's connection uses when accessing certain network resources.

VPN Client Configuration

The VPN client is configured by setting up a new connection in the Network and Sharing Center. When you set up a new connection, you choose *Connect to a workplace* option, and then you have the option to use your existing connection to the Internet, if you have one, or to create a dial-up connection. After you choose the connection, you enter the address of the VPN server you'll connect to and enter a name for the connection. You can also create a VPN connection by using the following PowerShell cmdlet in Windows 10 and Windows Server 2012 R2 and later:

```
Add-VpnConnection -Name "VPN to Work" -ServerAddress
    "203.0.113.1"
```

If you need to set up a VPN connection to several computers in your network, you can do so with group policy preferences. Open a GPO in Group Policy Management Editor and navigate to Computer Configuration, Preferences, and Control Panel Settings. Right-click Network Options, point to New, and click VPN Connection. In the New VPN Properties dialog box, fill in the information shown in Figure 6-7.

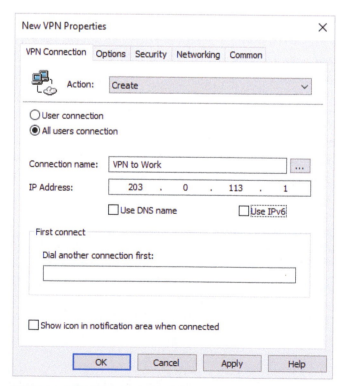

Figure 6-7 Creating a VPN connection with group policy preferences

When you create a VPN connection, the default tunnel type is Automatic. This means that the VPN client attempts to make the connection by using each tunneling method until it's successful or the connection fails. You can configure the client to use a particular tunnel type in the connection's properties.

Configuring Remote Dial-in

As discussed, remote dial-in (called *dial-up networking* in the past) uses the phone system to connect a computer with a remote network. Each connection requires a modem and a phone line on both ends of the connection. So, a server supporting remote dial-in must have one modem connected to a phone line for each simultaneous remote access user. It's not a very efficient system, which is why it has been largely replaced by VPN and, more recently, DirectAccess in Windows environments. Nevertheless, it might be the only option available for some clients in remote locations who don't have access to reliable Internet connections.

Remote dial-in is configured almost the same way as VPN configuration, but in the Network Selection window, you choose the private network from which dial-in clients are assigned an IP address. After the Routing and Remote Access Server Setup Wizard is finished, you need to configure the modems used for servicing dial-in connections. This configuration is beyond the scope of this book, however.

Note

Remote dial-in supports both plain old telephone service (POTS) and ISDN connections.

Configuring Remote Access Options

The default settings for VPN and dial-up might be adequate in many circumstances, but you might need to support different OSs and VPN clients over a variety of tunneling methods, which could require security settings different from the default. In addition, although RRAS allows multiple tunneling types by default for VPN connections, you might want to restrict connections to a particular tunneling method.

As you've learned, you can configure remote access settings in the properties of a user account, but this method can prove inefficient when many users need remote access permission. Instead, you can allow or disallow remote access to users based on connection-related group policies. The following sections cover tasks you might need to perform after configuring RRAS.

Configuring Remote Access Security

To configure security settings for remote access, right-click the server in the Routing and Remote Access console and click Properties. In the Security tab (see Figure 6-8), you can configure the following settings:

- *Authentication provider*—Choose Windows Authentication or RADIUS Authentication. If you choose Windows Authentication, Windows tries to authenticate users attempting to log on via VPN or dial-in from the local SAM account database or a DC. If you choose RADIUS, you must specify which RADIUS servers the RRAS server should use.
- *Authentication Methods*—Whether you're using Windows Authentication or RADIUS Authentication, you can select the authentication methods available to the user account trying to log on. Authentication is attempted by using the enabled methods in the order you see in Figure 6-9:
  - Extensible authentication protocol (EAP): Selected by default, it's the most flexible authentication method because it works with non-Windows clients, and third-party providers can develop custom authentication schemes. EAP is required for the use of smart cards and can be used for biometric authentication.

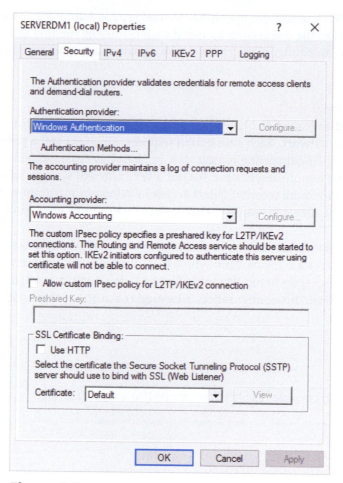

Figure 6-8 Security settings for remote access

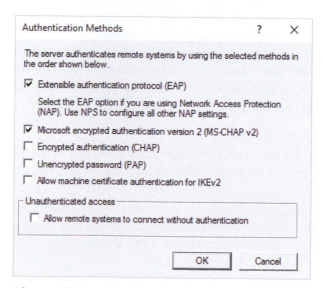

Figure 6-9 Authentication methods

• Microsoft encrypted authentication version 2 (MS-CHAP v2): This mutual authentication protocol encrypts both authentication information and data. A different encryption key is used each time a connection is made and on both ends of the connection. MS-CHAP v2 is compatible with most Windows clients, going back to Windows 98. This method has the advantage of being able to prompt the user to change an expired password.

- Encrypted authentication (CHAP): This method provides compatibility with non-Windows clients and encrypts authentication data but not connection data.
- Unencrypted password (PAP): This method has no encryption of user credentials or data, so it's not recommended for most applications.
- Allow machine certificate authentication for IKEv2: This method authenticates the client computer with a digital certificate and can be used only when the tunnel type is L2TP/IPsec.
- Allow remote systems to connect without authentication: This method allows anonymous authentication, meaning no user credentials are required. It should be used only to test other aspects of the remote access connection.
- *Accounting provider*—Options are Windows Accounting, RADIUS Accounting, and none. If you leave Windows Accounting (the default) selected, the server logs information about remote access connections in the log files configured in the Logging tab. If you select RADIUS Accounting, connection information is sent to a RADIUS server for logging.
- *Allow custom IPsec policy for L2TP/IKEv2 connection*—If you select this option, you must supply a preshared key for all connections using the custom IPsec policy.
- *SSL Certificate Binding*—If you're using the SSTP tunneling type, you can click the HTTP check box to specify that SSTP should use the same certificate as the HTTP server. Otherwise, you select the certificate in the Certificate drop-down list. The certificate must already be installed.

Configuring Available Tunnel Types

When a VPN client attempts to connect to a VPN, it tries to use each of the tunneling types until it's successful or the connection fails. By default, each tunneling type is enabled in the RRAS service when you configure a VPN, and each type allows up to 128 connections or ports. You can configure the number of ports in the Routing and Remote Access console by right-clicking Ports and clicking Properties. In the Ports Properties dialog box, double-click a tunnel type to see the Configure Device dialog box, where you can change the maximum number of ports (see Figure 6-10). Changing the number of ports to 0 effectively disables the tunnel type. You can also disable inbound remote access connections for that tunnel type, which also disables the tunnel type.

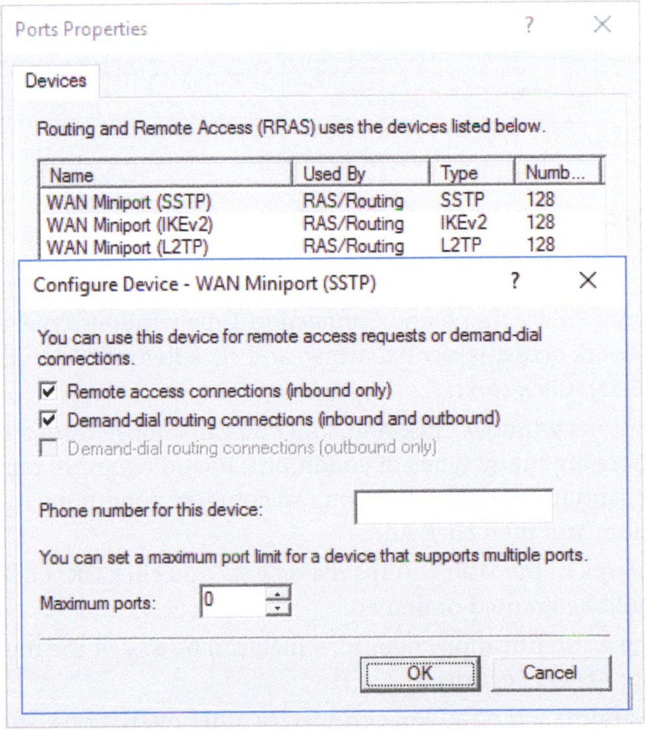

Figure 6-10   Configuring port properties

Configuring Network Policies

As discussed, you can configure a user's account to allow connecting to the network via remote access, but controlling remote access permissions with network policies is more efficient. Network policies are discussed more in Chapter 7, but this section gives you a brief introduction. By default, a user account's Network Access Permission attribute is set to *Control access through NPS Network Policy* in the Dial-in tab of the user account's Properties dialog box, and the default NPS Network Policy disallows all remote access. So, to make a remote access server useful, you must change the Network Access Permission attribute to *Allow access* on user accounts or configure an NPS network policy.

You configure a network policy in the Network Policy Server console (accessed via the Tools menu in Server Manager). Follow these steps to configure a remote access policy for RRAS:

1. In the Network Policy Server console, click to expand Policies in the left pane (see Figure 6-11). Right-click Network Policies and click New to start the New Network Policy Wizard.

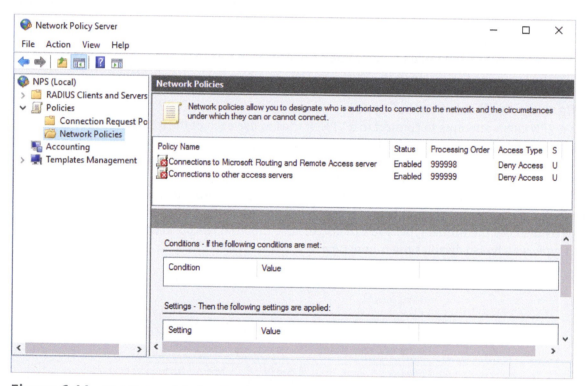

Figure 6-11   The Network Policy Server console

2. In the Specify Network Policy Name and Connection Type window, type a name for the policy. Click the *Type of network access server* list arrow, and click Remote Access Server(VPN-Dial up) in the list (see Figure 6-12). Click Next.

3. In the Specify Conditions window, click Add, and you can choose from a list of conditions (see Figure 6-13). There are many types of conditions, including group membership, IP address, authentication type, and tunnel type, and you can combine conditions in a single policy. Click the User Groups condition, and then click Add.

4. Add the group or groups in the User Groups dialog box, and click OK. Click Next, and then specify whether access should be granted or denied.

5. Next, you specify the authentication method, which can be any of the methods discussed earlier in "Configuring Remote Access Security."

6. In the Configure Restraints window, you can specify other restrictions, such as day and time restrictions and timeouts.

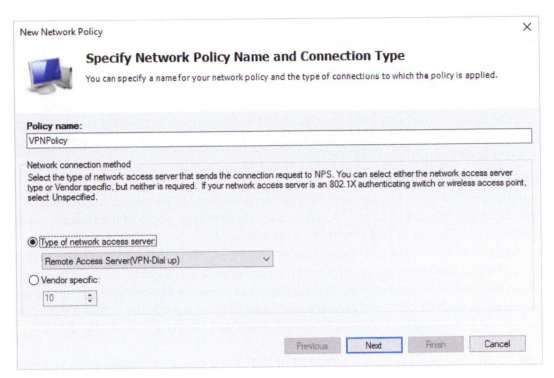

Figure 6-12   Specifying a name and connection type

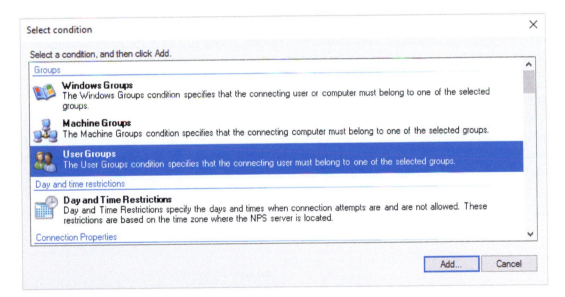

Figure 6-13   Selecting a condition

7. In the Configure Settings window, you can configure RADIUS attributes, filters, and encryption settings.

8. After reviewing your settings, click Finish in the last window to create the policy.

After you create network policies and make an attempt to connect via remote access, the policies are evaluated to determine whether the connection should be permitted. If the connection attempt doesn't match any of the policies that allow a connection or if it matches a policy that denies the connection, the connection is denied. Policies are evaluated in the order you see them in the Network Policy Server console, so it's always a good idea to list the most specific policies first (those specifying a single user or very specific conditions, for example). You can change a policy's order in the list by right-clicking it and clicking Move Up or Move Down. Don't delete the default policies, but leave them at the bottom of the list because they're a safeguard: Any policies you create that don't match a connection attempt are matched by the default policies, and the connection is denied.

Configuring VPN Reconnect

VPN reconnect is a feature that automatically re-establishes a VPN connection that is temporarily lost with no intervention from the user. For example, if a user is using a mobile device to connect with the VPN and the device temporarily loses the signal, VPN will reconnect to the VPN when the signal is resumed. The feature is supported only on IKEv2-based VPNs on Windows 7 and newer clients and Windows Server 2008 R2 and newer VPN servers.

Creating Connection Profiles

VPN connection profiles allow you to create VPN connections that can be distributed to users' computers so that VPN clients do not have to be configured on each client station. Some of the features available with VPN profiles in Windows 10 and later include the following:

- *App trigger*—The VPN client will connect automatically when the specified applications are started.
- *Always on*—The VPN client will connect automatically when a user signs in, when a change in network status is detected (such as connecting to the Internet), or when the device's screen is turned on.
- *Name-based*—The VPN client will connect automatically when a particular domain name is accessed.
- *LockDown VPN*—Allows only VPN traffic on the device and attempts to maintain the VPN connection at all times.
- *Traffic Filters*—You can configure filters to allow VPN traffic only from certain apps, protocols, ports, or addresses.

Connection profiles are created with Microsoft InTune, System Center Configuration Manager, or the Configuration Manager Administration Kit (CMAK), which can be downloaded and installed from the Microsoft Download Center. To create VPN connections with CMAK, run the CMAK Wizard, which walks you through the steps for creating a VPN connection profile. When you have finished with the wizard, an executable (.exe) file is created that can be distributed to users through image deployment, network shares, or software deployment tools such as System Center Configuration Manager.

Configuring a Site-to-Site VPN

A site-to-site (S2S) VPN securely connects two networks, for example, a branch office and a main office. The VPN tunnel is established between two network devices such as routers or Windows servers configured as VPN servers (see Figure 6-14). Client computers do not run a VPN client, so traffic between the client computers and the router/VPN server is not encrypted; only traffic between the router/VPN servers is encrypted.

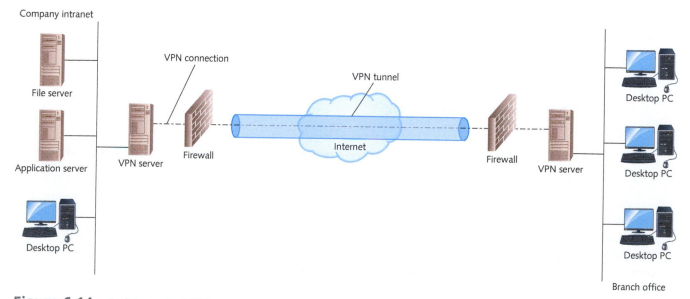

Figure 6-14 A site-to-site VPN

To configure a S2S VPN with Windows Server 2016, configure Routing and Remote Access using the Secure connection between two private networks option in the Configuration window. In the Demand-Dial Connections window, choose Yes. You will configure the demand-dial connection after the wizard finishes. After the wizard has finished, the Demand-Dial Wizard starts. A **demand-dial interface** is a network connection that is used to establish the VPN connection when network traffic from the internal network has a destination address of the other network to which you are connecting. To configure the demand-dial interface, follow the Demand-Dial Interface Wizard that is started automatically:

1. On the first screen of the Demand-Dial Interface Wizard, you are prompted to enter the name of the interface. The interface name is usually the name of the router or device to which you are connecting. For example, if you are configuring the main office server, you might name the connection BranchOffice (see Figure 6-15), and if you are configuring the branch office server, you might name the connection MainOffice.

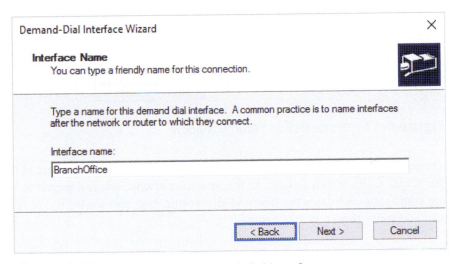

Figure 6-15   Specifying the demand-dial interface name

2. Next, you specify the connection type. You have the option of VPN or PPoE. Choose VPN and click Next.

3. Specify the connection type. You can select Automatic, PPTP, L2TP, or IKEv2 (see Figure 6-16).

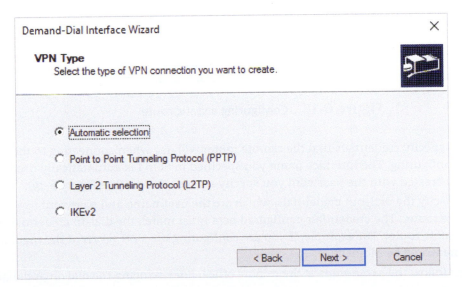

Figure 6-16   Selecting the VPN type

4. Next, you enter the host name or IP address of the remote router to which you are connecting.

5. On the Protocols and Security window (see Figure 6-17), select *Route IP packets on this interface* and *Add a user account so a remote router can dial in*. These options allow the VPN server to act as a router and require authentication with the other network.

Figure 6-17   Protocols and Security window

6. Next, you configure static routes. A static route specifies the IP network address of the remote network (see Figure 6-18). When a client on the internal network sends a packet to the remote network, the static route activates the demand-dial connection and routes the packet over the VPN. You can add more than one static route.

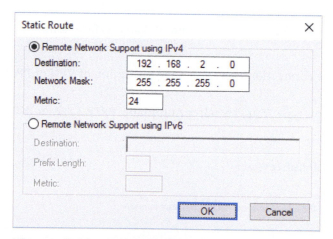

Figure 6-18   Configuring a static route

7. Next, you specify credentials that the remote router will use when connecting to the VPN server you are configuring. The interface name you specified in Step 1 is automatically used and a user account is created with the password you specify in this window (see Figure 6-19).

8. Finally, specify the dial-out credentials, which are the user name and password used to connect to the remote router. The credentials configured here must match the dial-in credentials configured on the remote router. For example, if you are configuring the VPN server at the main office, your user name would be MainOffice.

9. You must follow the same steps at the remote office, interchanging the dial-in and dial-out credentials.

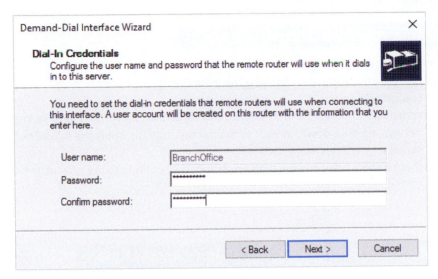

Figure 6-19   Setting the dial-in credentials

After you have configured the demand-dial interface, you can further configure it by clicking Network Interfaces in Routing and Remote Access and right-clicking the demand-dial interface. You can configure the credentials, set the demand-dial filter to allow only certain types of traffic to activate the demand-dial interface, and set dial-out hours to restrict when the VPN connection can be used (see Figure 6-20).

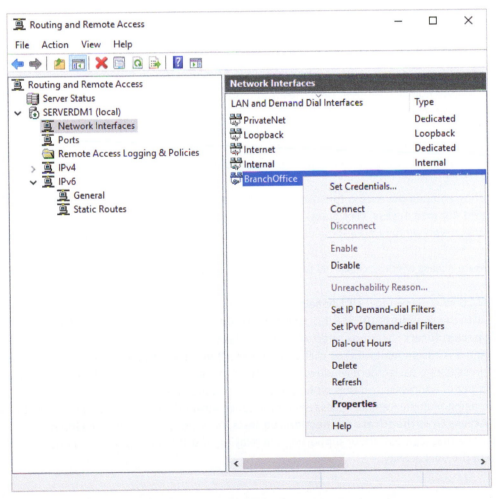

Figure 6-20   Configuring the demand-dial interface

Activity 6-1: Resetting your Virtual Environment

Time Required: 5 minutes
Objective: Reset your virtual environment by applying the InitialConfig checkpoint or snapshot.
Required Tools and Equipment: ServerDC1, ServerDM1, ServerSA1
Description: Apply the InitialConfig checkpoint or snapshot to ServerDC1, ServerDM1, and ServerSA1.

1. Be sure that all servers are shut down. In your virtualization program, apply the InitialConfig checkpoint or snapshot to all servers.
2. When the snapshot or checkpoint has finished being applied, continue to the next activity.

Activity 6-2: Installing and Configuring the Remote Access Role

Time Required: 20 minutes
Objective: Install the Remote Access role and role services and configure a VPN server.
Required Tools and Equipment: ServerDC1, ServerDM1
Description: In this activity, you install the Remote Access server role and associated role services. Then you will configure a VPN server.

1. Start ServerDC1 and ServerDM1. On ServerDM1, sign in as **Administrator**.
2. Open Server Manager, and click **Manage, Add Roles and Features** from the menu. In the Add Roles and Features Wizard, click **Next** until you get to the Server Roles window.
3. Click **Remote Access**, and then click **Next** twice. In the Remote Access window, read the information describing the features of the Remote Access role, and then click **Next**.
4. In the Role Services window, click to select **DirectAccess and VPN (RAS)**. When prompted, click the **Add Features** button. Click **Routing**, and then click **Next**.
5. In the Web Server Role (IIS) window, read the information, and click **Next**. Accept the default role services for the Web Server role, and then click **Next**.
6. Click **Install**. The installation might take a while. When it's finished, click **Close**.
7. The next step is to configure routing and remote access in the Routing and Remote Access console accessed via Server Manager. In Server Manager, click **Tools**, **Routing and Remote Access** from the menu.
8. In the Routing and Remote Access console, right-click **SERVERDM1 (local)** and click **Configure and Enable Routing and Remote Access**. Click **Next**.
9. In the Configuration window, accept the default setting **Remote access (dial-up or VPN)**, and click **Next**.
10. In the Remote Access window, click **VPN** to configure the server to accept VPN connections, and then click **Next**.
11. In the VPN Connection window, click to select the interface that connects to the Internet. In this case, it's the interface with the IP address 192.168.1.2. Leave the **Enable security on the selected interface by setting up static packet filters** check box selected and click **Next**.
12. In the IP Address Assignment window, click **From a specified range of addresses**, and click **Next**.
13. In the Address Range Assignment window, click **New**. In the Start IP address text box, type **192.168.0.100**, and in the Number of addresses text box, type **10**. Click **OK**, and then click **Next**.
14. In the Managing Multiple Remote Access Servers window, accept the default setting **No, use Routing and Remote Access to authenticate connection requests**. Click **Next**, and then click **Finish**.
15. Click **OK** in the message box about supporting the relaying of DHCP messages. Click **Finish**.
16. Continue to the next activity.

Activity 6-3: Creating a VPN Connection and Testing the VPN

Time Required: 15 minutes

Objective: Create and test a VPN connection.

Required Tools and Equipment: ServerDC1, ServerDM1, ServerSA1

Description: Test the VPN configuration by creating a VPN client connection on ServerSA1 and attempting to connect to the VPN server. For this activity, you'll disable the network interface on ServerSA1 that is connected to the 192.168.0.0/24 network. The second network interface on ServerSA1 with address 192.168.1.4/24 will be used to make the VPN connection as in Figure 6-21.

> **Note** 🖉
>
> In a real VPN scenario, the VPN client and server would be on different subnets; however, the arrangement in this activity is meant only to illustrate and test a VPN connection.

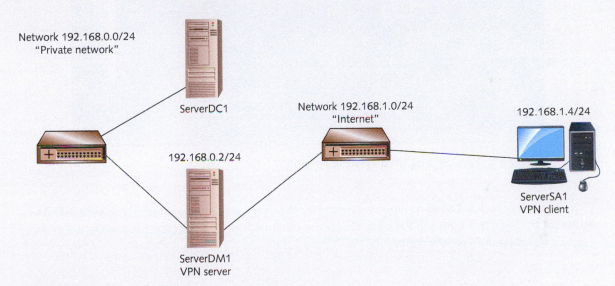

Figure 6-21   Network setup for Activity 6-3

1. On ServerDM1, right-click **Start** and click **Computer Management**. Click to expand **Local Users and Groups**, right-click **Users**, and click **New User**.
2. In the User name text box, type **VPNTest1** and type **Password01** in the Password and Confirm password text box. Click to clear the **User must change password at next logon** box and click to select the **Password never expires** box. Click **Create** and click **Close**.
3. Double-click **VPNTest1** to open the Properties dialog box. Click the **Dial-in** tab, click **Allow access** in the Network Access Permission section, and then click **OK**. Close Computer Management.
4. On ServerSA1, sign in as **Administrator**. Right-click Start and click **Network Connections**. Right-click **Ethernet** and click **Disable**. Verify that Ethernet 2 has an IP address of 192.168.1.4 by right-clicking **Ethernet 2**, clicking **Status**, and clicking **Details**. Click **Close** twice and close the Network Connections window.
5. Click the network icon in the right side of the taskbar and click **Network Settings**. Click **VPN** and then click **Add a VPN connection**.
6. In the Add a VPN connection window, fill out the form as in Figure 6-22. Click **Save**.

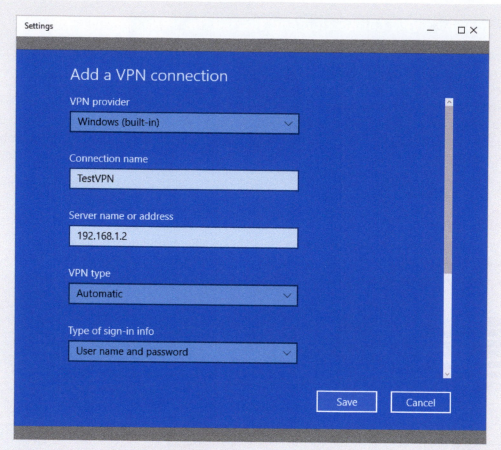

Figure 6-22   Setting up a VPN connection

7. Click **TestVPN** and click **Connect**. When prompted for the user name and password, type **serverdm1\vpntest1** for the user name and **Password01** for the password and click **OK**. You will see the word Connected under the TestVPN connection (see Figure 6-23).

Figure 6-23   Connected to a VPN

8. Click **Change adapter options.** Right-click **TestVPN** and click **Status.** Click **Details** to see the IPv4 address assigned, which should be 192.168.0.101. Click **Close** twice.

9. Right-click **TestVPN** and click **Connect/Disconnect.** In the Networks panel, click **TestVPN** and click **Disconnect.** Right-click **Ethernet** and click **Enable** to re-enable the network interface connected to the 192.168.0.0/24 network.

10. Close the Network Connections window and continue to the next activity.

Configuring IPv4 and IPv6 Routing

 **Certification**

- **70-741 – Implement network connectivity and remote access solutions:**
  Implement network connectivity solutions

Using RRAS, a Windows server can be configured as a router to connect multiple subnets (see Figure 6-24) in a network or connect the network to the Internet. Windows Server 2012/R2 supports static routing and dynamic routing with Routing Information Protocol Version 2 (RIPv2). To configure a server as a router, select the Custom configuration option in the Configuration window (shown earlier in Figure 6-2) of the Routing and Remote Access Server Setup Wizard, and then select the LAN routing option. If the server has two or more interfaces, packets are routed between the networks to which the interfaces are connected.

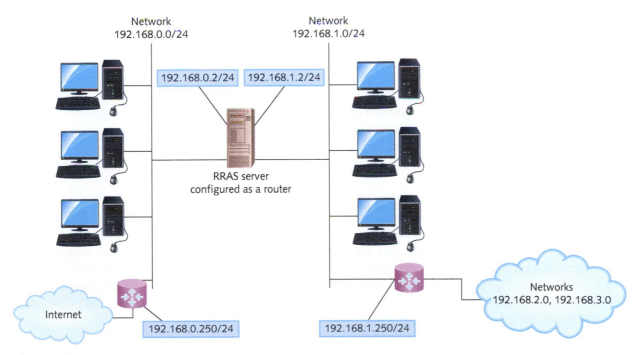

Figure 6-24   **An RRAS server configured as a router**

By default, only IPv4 routing is enabled. If you want to route IPv6 packets, right-click the server in the Routing and Remote Access console and click Properties. In the General tab, click the IPv6 Router check box.

Routing Tables

A router determines where to send packets it receives by consulting a routing table. A **routing table** is a list of network destinations along with information on which interface can be used to reach the destination (see Figure 6-25). The routing table in this figure matches the drawing in Figure 6-24. The routing table has the following columns of information:

SERVERDM1 - IP Routing Table

Destination	Network mask	Gateway	Interface	Metric	Protocol
0.0.0.0	0.0.0.0	192.168.0.250	Ethernet	271	Network management
127.0.0.0	255.0.0.0	127.0.0.1	Loopback	76	Local
127.0.0.1	255.255.255.255	127.0.0.1	Loopback	331	Local
192.168.0.0	255.255.255.0	0.0.0.0	Ethernet	271	Local
192.168.0.2	255.255.255.255	0.0.0.0	Ethernet	271	Local
192.168.0.255	255.255.255.255	0.0.0.0	Ethernet	271	Local
192.168.1.0	255.255.255.0	0.0.0.0	Ethernet 2	271	Local
192.168.1.2	255.255.255.255	0.0.0.0	Ethernet 2	271	Local
192.168.1.255	255.255.255.255	0.0.0.0	Ethernet 2	271	Local
224.0.0.0	240.0.0.0	0.0.0.0	Ethernet	271	Local
255.255.255.255	255.255.255.255	0.0.0.0	Ethernet	271	Local

Figure 6-25   A routing table

- *Destination*—The destination network or host address. In most cases, this column is a network address but can also be a host or broadcast address. A value of 0.0.0.0 indicates a default route or default gateway. The **default route** destination is the network where the router sends all packets that don't match any other destinations in the routing table. If there's no default route, the router discards packets that don't match a destination in the table. The destination 255.255.255.255 is the local broadcast address. Destination 224.0.0.0 is for multicast packets, and entries beginning with 127 are for the loopback address.
- *Network mask*—The subnet mask for the corresponding address in the Destination column. A mask of 0.0.0.0 is used for the default route, and a mask of 255.255.255.255 indicates a host address rather than a network address; it's sometimes referred to as a *host route*.
- *Gateway*—The address to which packets are forwarded that matches the destination address/ network mask; also referred to as the *next hop address*. If there are two or more identical Destination and Network mask columns, the Metric column is used to decide which gateway address to use. If the Gateway column is 0.0.0.0, the destination address is connected directly to an interface.
- *Interface*—The interface used to reach the destination address.
- *Metric*—The value assigned to the route. Lower metrics take precedence when there are two or more routes to the same destination.
- *Protocol*—The report on how the route was derived. The value *Local* indicates the route is connected directly to an interface. The value *Network management* means that the route was derived internally, usually by a default gateway assignment in the interface's IP address configuration. Other values include *Static*, which indicates that an administrator added the route to the table, and *RIP*, which means the route was derived from the RIPv2 routing protocol.

Configuring Static Routes

After routing is enabled, you can add routing protocols and configure static routes. When a router receives packets on one interface, it consults its routing table to determine where to send the packet to get the packet to its destination. If there's no entry in the routing table that matches the destination network in the packet, the router forwards the packet via the default route if it's configured. If no default route is configured, the router discards the packet. Examine Figures 6-24 and 6-25 again. The RRAS server can route packets between the 192.168.0.0 and 192.168.1.0 networks because it has an interface configured in both networks. It can also route packets to the Internet because it has a default route configured for the router at 192.168.0.250. However, it can't route packets to 192.168.2.0 or 192.168.3.0 because it doesn't have a route to those networks. In fact, the RRAS server attempts to send packets to the 192.168.0.250 router to get packets to the 192.168.2.0 or 192.168.3.0 network. The solution to this problem is to use **static routes**, which instruct the router where to send packets destined for particular networks. An IPv4 static route has the following pieces of information, as shown in Figure 6-26:

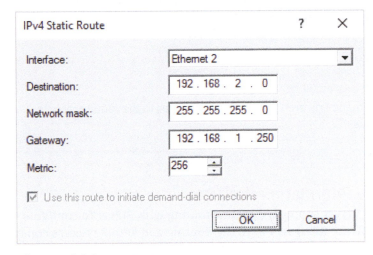

Figure 6-26   An IPv4 static route

- *Interface*—The place to select which interface should be used to reach the destination network.
- *Destination*—The network address. If you're creating a default route, use 0.0.0.0 as the destination network.
- *Network mask*—The subnet mask for the destination network. For a default route, use 0.0.0.0 as the subnet mask.
- *Gateway*—The address of the router to which packets should be sent to reach the destination network.
- *Metric*—A value assigned to the route; used by the router to determine which gateway to use if there are identical routes.

In Figure 6-26, a static route is created for network 192.168.2.0, shown previously in Figure 6-24. A similar route should be added to reach network 192.168.3.0 to arrive at the routing table shown in Figure 6-27.

SERVERDM1 - IP Routing Table

Destination	Network mask	Gateway	Interface	Metric	Protocol
0.0.0.0	0.0.0.0	192.168.0.250	Ethernet	271	Network management
127.0.0.0	255.0.0.0	127.0.0.1	Loopback	76	Local
127.0.0.1	255.255.255.255	127.0.0.1	Loopback	331	Local
192.168.0.0	255.255.255.0	0.0.0.0	Ethernet	271	Local
192.168.0.2	255.255.255.255	0.0.0.0	Ethernet	271	Local
192.168.0.255	255.255.255.255	0.0.0.0	Ethernet	271	Local
192.168.1.0	255.255.255.0	0.0.0.0	Ethernet 2	271	Local
192.168.1.2	255.255.255.255	0.0.0.0	Ethernet 2	271	Local
192.168.1.255	255.255.255.255	0.0.0.0	Ethernet 2	271	Local
192.168.2.0	255.255.255.0	192.168.1.250	Ethernet 2	271	Static (non demand-dial)
192.168.3.0	255.255.255.0	192.168.1.250	Ethernet 2	271	Static (non demand-dial)
224.0.0.0	240.0.0.0	0.0.0.0	Ethernet	271	Local
255.255.255.255	255.255.255.255	0.0.0.0	Ethernet	271	Local

Figure 6-27   A routing table with static routes

Static routes can be configured at the command line, too. The following command adds a route to network 192.168.2.0, using gateway 192.168.1.250. The interface doesn't need to be included because the interface connected to the gateway network is used by default. The metric uses the default value for the interface:

```
route add 192.168.2.0 mask 255.255.255.0 192.168.1.250
```

Here's the PowerShell cmdlet to add a static route:

```
New-NetRoute -DestinationPrefix 192.168.2.0/24 -InterfaceAlias
   "Ethernet 2" -NextHop 192.168.1.250
```

Note 📎

Routes created at the command line aren't listed as static routes in the routing table in RRAS; they're listed as network management routes.

Configuring Routing Information Protocol

As mentioned, Windows Server supports dynamic routing with RIPv2. To configure RIPv2, you must have first configured routing on the RRAS server. In the Routing and Remote Access console, under the IPv4 node, right-click General and click New Routing Protocol. Select RIP Version 2 for Internet Protocol in the New Routing Protocol dialog box, and then RIP is added under the IPv4 node.

Next, you need to configure RIP by enabling it on interfaces that RIP uses to send and receive routing information. Right-click the RIP node and click New Interface, and then select the interface. Repeat this step for each interface RIP uses. RIP should be enabled only on interfaces connected to the internal network, not interfaces connected to the Internet.

RIPv2 works by communicating with other routers on the internetwork. Each router that uses RIPv2 sends a copy of its routing table to other RIPv2 routers on the same network; these routers are called *neighbors*. Routing table information is passed along from neighbor to neighbor until all routers on the internetwork know about each network and how to get there. RIPv2 uses the **hop count**, a metric for determining the best path to a network by counting the number of routers a packet must go through to reach the destination network.

Note 📎

Several other routing protocols are used by commercial routers in large internetworks; they're more complex and more efficient than Routing Information Protocol (RIP). One example is Open Shortest Path First (OSPF), a routing protocol that determines the best path by using the speed (or cost) of each link in the path from source network to destination network.

Configuring IPv6 Routing

Up to now, the discussion about routing has focused on IPv4 routing. Windows Server 2016 also supports IPv6 routing. IPv6 routing is configured largely the same way as IPv4 routing; however, there is no version of RIPv2 for IPv6, so dynamic routing is supported using Border Gateway Protocol (BGP), discussed next. You can create IPv6 static routes in a manner similar to creating IPv4 static routes as shown in Figure 6-28. You can also use the `route add` command using the `-6` option and the `New-NetRoute` PowerShell cmdlet using the `-AddressFamily IPv6` option to create IPv6 static routes.

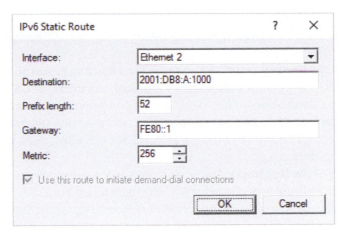

Figure 6-28   Configuring an IPv6 static route

Configure Border Gateway Protocol (BGP)

Border Gateway Protocol (BGP) is an advanced dynamic routing protocol that can be used to route between remote networks, including site-to-site VPNs, and between physical and virtual networks. Like RIPv2, BGP learns about the networks in an enterprise by communicating with other routers; however, BGP is much more complex than RIPv2.

BGP can be configured on a computer running the Remote Access server role using the remote access PowerShell cmdlets. To see a list of remote access PowerShell cmdlets, type `Get-Command -Module RemoteAccess` in a PowerShell window. To see commands specific to BGP, type `Get-Command *-BGP*`. BGP is most often used in virtual environments where BGP is deployed on a virtual machine acting as a gateway for large enterprises and cloud providers. This configuration is referred to as Windows Server Gateway, and it allows a cloud service provider (CSP) to use a virtual machine (VM) configured as a gateway to route multiple tenants using the same physical network.

Activity 6-4: Configuring Routing

Time Required: 15 minutes
Objective: Configure routing in the Routing and Remote Access console.
Required Tools and Equipment: ServerDC1, ServerDM1
Description: In this activity, you disable RRAS, and then you enable and configure routing. You also create a static route and configure the RIPv2 routing protocol.

1. On ServerDM1, open the Routing and Remote Access console. Right-click **ServerDM1** and click **Disable Routing and Remote Access**. When prompted, click **Yes**. The RRAS service stops, and you see the red down arrow on the ServerDM1 icon to indicate that the service is disabled.
2. Right-click ServerDM1 and click **Configure and Enable Routing and Remote Access**. Click **Next** in the Welcome window.
3. In the Configuration window, click **Custom configuration**, and then click **Next**.
4. In the Custom Configuration window, click **LAN routing**, and then click **Next**.
5. Click **Finish**. When prompted, click **Start service**.
6. The server routes between known networks in its routing table by default. Click to expand the **IPv4** node, and then right-click **Static Routes** and click **Show IP Routing Table**. You see entries for the default route, the 192.168.0.0 network, the 192.168.1.0 network, the loopback network, and other host and broadcast routes. Close the routing table.
7. To create a static route, right-click **Static Routes** and click **New Static Route**. In the Destination text box, type **192.168.2.0**, and in the Network mask text box, type **255.255.255.0**. In the Gateway text box, type **192.168.1.250**, and then click **OK**. The route is added to the list of static routes.

8. Right-click **Static Routes** and click **Show IP Routing Table** to verify that the route is in the routing table. Close the routing table.

9. To enable RIPv2, right-click **General** under IPv4 and click **New Routing Protocol**. In the **New Routing Protocol** dialog box, click **RIP version 2 for Internet Protocol**, and then click **OK**.

10. By default, no interfaces are enabled for RIP. In the Routing and Remote Access console, right-click **RIP** under IPv4 and click **New Interface**. Click the first interface listed, and then click **OK**. In the RIP Properties dialog box, you can change settings for the RIPv2 routing protocol. For this activity, just click **OK**. Repeat this step, selecting the second interface.

11. Right-click **RIP** and click **Show Neighbors**. Any other routers in the networks connected to either of ServerDM1's interfaces are listed here. Close the RIP Neighbors dialog box.

12. Disable Routing and Remote Access. To reset your network interfaces, restart ServerDM1.

Configuring Network Address Translation

 Certification

- 70-741 – Implement network connectivity and remote access solutions:
  Implement network connectivity solutions

Network Address Translation (NAT) is a process by which a router or other type of gateway device replaces the source or destination IP addresses in a packet before forwarding the packet. It's used mainly to allow networks to use private IP addressing while connected to the Internet. It does this by replacing private IP addresses with public IP addresses in outgoing packets and replacing public IP addresses with private IP addresses in incoming packets.

This process allows companies to use private IP addresses in their own internal network, requiring a public IP address only when a workstation attempts to access the Internet. Therefore, NAT reduces the number of public IP addresses needed. A drawback of NAT is that one public address is required for every computer with an active connection to the Internet. However, it's usually used only for web servers and other devices that must be accessed through the Internet.

An extension of NAT, called **Port Address Translation (PAT),** allows several hundred workstations to access the Internet with a single public Internet address. This process relies on each packet containing not only source and destination IP addresses but also source and destination TCP or UDP port numbers. With PAT, the address is translated into a single public IP address for all workstations, but a different source port number (which can be any value from 1024 to 65,535) is used for each communication session, allowing a NAT device to differentiate between workstations. The device configured as a NAT router keeps track of the active translations using a NAT table. When you configure Windows RRAS for NAT, you're actually configuring PAT. To configure NAT in the Routing and Remote Access Server Setup Wizard, select the *Network address translation (NAT)* option in the Configuration window. For LAN-based Internet access, choose the interface connected to the Internet in the NAT Internet Connection window, just as you did when you configured a VPN server. If the Internet connection uses a demand-dial interface, you can choose the option to create a new demand-dial interface to the Internet. A demand-dial interface is activated when a client attempts to connect to the Internet, such as with a dial-up modem or Point-to-Point Protocol over Ethernet (PPPoE) connection. The IP address of the interface you choose is used for all address translations.

Figure 6-29 shows what a NAT configuration might look like along with the NAT table. In this figure, when a computer on the private network tries to access the Internet, the source address and source port number in the packet are translated into the public address of the NAT router's Internet interface and a port number before being delivered to the Internet. The port number may or may not stay the same in the private and public addresses. When a device on the Internet responds, the destination public address and port number are translated back to the private address and port number before being delivered to the host on the private network.

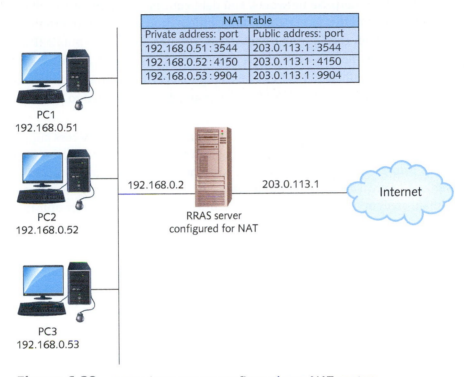

NAT Table	
Private address: port	Public address: port
192.168.0.51 : 3544	203.0.113.1 : 3544
192.168.0.52 : 4150	203.0.113.1 : 4150
192.168.0.53 : 9904	203.0.113.1 : 9904

PC1
192.168.0.51

PC2
192.168.0.52

192.168.0.2

RRAS server
configured for NAT

203.0.113.1

Internet

PC3
192.168.0.53

Figure 6-29   A Windows server configured as a NAT router

The DirectAccess Role Service

 **Certification**

- **70-741 – Implement network connectivity and remote access solutions:**
  Implement virtual private network (VPN) and DirectAccess solutions

The **DirectAccess** role service is part of the DirectAccess and VPN role service under the Remote Access server role. DirectAccess provides many of the same features as a VPN but adds client management and always-connected capability. DirectAccess uses IPv6 and IPsec to create secure connections to the network and almost eliminates client connection problems caused by firewall settings. On networks that don't yet fully support IPv6, transition technologies such as 6to4, Teredo, and IP-HTTPS are used to allow IPv6 clients to access IPv6 resources across an IPv4 Internet or intranet.

DirectAccess Requirements

The following sections list requirements for the DirectAccess server and clients. These requirements are for a basic configuration using Windows Server 2016 and a Windows 10 or Windows Server 2016 client and the Getting Started Wizard in the Remote Access Management console. Optional configurations are listed, too.

DirectAccess Server Requirements

The following are requirements for DirectAccess in Windows Server 2016:

- *Two NICs as for a VPN server*—Although a single-NIC setup is possible, the two-NIC solution is preferred. Like a VPN server, one NIC is connected to the private network, and the other is connected to the Internet.
- *Server as a domain member*—The server must be a domain member. DirectAccess is a remote access solution best suited for enterprise networks, and tight control over servers and clients is one of the goals. In addition, much of the server and client configuration is done with group policies.
- *A public IP address*—When configuring DirectAccess, you need to enter a public IP address or a fully qualified domain name (FQDN) that can be resolved to a public IP address associated with the DirectAccess server. The public address can be configured on the interface connected to the Internet or on an address that's translated by a NAT router to an address assigned to the DirectAccess Internet-connected interface.

You might be asking "What about encryption and authentication?" DirectAccess supports the option for the DirectAccess server to use self-signed certificates and Kerberos proxy for authentication and encryption. **Kerberos proxy** allows a client computer to authenticate to a domain controller, using the DirectAccess server as a proxy. The client computer is issued a certificate through Kerberos, which is used with the user's domain credentials to establish an authenticated and secure communication session with IPsec and IPv6.

Optional Server Configurations

The preceding server requirements are for a basic DirectAccess configuration. The following is a list of recommended enhancements for production environments or when there are multiple DirectAccess servers providing remote access connectivity.

- *An internal PKI*—A public key infrastructure (PKI) is a system for managing digital certificates for use in public key cryptography. At the heart of a PKI is a certification authority (CA) that issues certificates. It can be a public entity, such as VeriSign, that issues certificates to organizations for use in public key encryption applications, such as HTTPS, or you can set up an internal PKI with Active Directory Certificate Services.
- *SSL certificate issued by a public CA for IP-HTTPS*—**Internet Protocol-Hypertext Transfer Protocol Secure (IP-HTTPS)** is a tunneling protocol used to transport IPv6 packets over an HTTPS connection. The DirectAccess Getting Started Wizard issues a self-signed certificate if you don't install one issued by a CA. Self-signed certificates are okay for testing, but they can be spoofed easily and generally shouldn't be used for production networks.
- *SSL certificate issued by an internal PKI for Network Location Server*—A **Network Location Server (NLS)** is a basic web server used by DirectAccess client computers to determine whether they're on the intranet or a remote network. If the client determines that a computer is on the intranet, the client turns off the connection to the DirectAccess server. The DirectAccess Getting Started Wizard installs NLS on the DirectAccess server and issues a self-signed certificate by default; however, a separate server with a certificate issued by an internal PKI is recommended.
- *Computer certificate issued by an internal PKI for IPsec authentication*—DirectAccess uses IPsec for secure packet transport and computer authentication. Both the client computer and the server must have a certificate for authentication and encryption. However, because Kerberos proxy is used, there's no need for computer certificates issued by a PKI. This solution works only with a single DirectAccess server, however, meaning that you can't have multisite DirectAccess or use DirectAccess in a server cluster.
- *Two consecutive public IP addresses*—This configuration is recommended for optimal operation. It was a strict requirement with Windows Server 2008 R2, but starting with Windows Server 2012, the DirectAccess server needs only one public IP address or even none if the server will be behind a NAT router because it can use IP-HTTPS.

DirectAccess Client Requirements

There's nothing special about the client configuration because no special software needs to be installed on clients. DirectAccess works by using standard Windows client software and IPv6 technology built into current Windows OSs. The following is a list of requirements for DirectAccess clients:

- *Must be running at least Windows 7 Enterprise or Ultimate, or Windows Server 2008 R2*—To use the basic configuration generated by the Getting Started Wizard, you need at least Windows 8 Enterprise or Windows Server 2012 clients.
- *Must be a domain member* —Client configuration is done strictly with the Group Policy tool, so the client must be a member of a domain so that it can download group policy settings from a DC.
- *Must have IPv6 enabled*—By default, IPv6 is enabled on the supported client OSs, so this is a concern only if IPv6 was disabled or unbound from the NIC.

How DirectAccess Connections Work

Before you learn more about deploying DirectAccess, take a look at how a DirectAccess connection is established from a client to a DirectAccess server. As mentioned, users don't have to do anything to initiate a DirectAccess connection. The built-in Windows software with IPv6 attempts to connect whenever the computer is connected to the Internet rather than the company's intranet. The following steps explain this process:

1. The DirectAccess client computer detects that it has a valid network connection.
2. Using an NLS server, the client determines whether it's connected to the Internet or the intranet by attempting to connect to the URL of the NLS server using HTTPS (this URL is configured in a group policy), which is available only on the intranet. If it can connect to the NLS, the computer knows it's on the intranet. In this case, no DirectAccess connection is made, and the process stops. If it isn't connected to the intranet, the process continues to the next step.
3. The DirectAccess client attempts to connect to the DirectAccess server via IPv6 and IPsec. Depending on the server configuration, the client uses 6to4, Teredo, or IP-HTTPS, in that order, to try to connect over an IPv4 Internet connection. If a native IPv6 connection to the DirectAccess server is available, no transition technology is needed. The 6to4 or Teredeo technology is preferred but can be blocked by a firewall or if the client is using a proxy server to connect to the Internet. 6to4 is used only if the client is using a public IPv4 address. Teredo is used only if the DirectAccess server has two consecutive public IP addresses.
4. The DirectAccess client and server authenticate with each other by using computer certificates issued by a PKI or Kerberos proxy.

All these steps take place when the client computer is turned on or connected to a new network. A user doesn't need to be signed in. At this point, the **infrastructure tunnel** has been created between the client computer and the DirectAccess server. When a user signs in, the DirectAccess client establishes the **intranet tunnel** with user account credentials, which provides access to resources on the network. When a client requests access to a network resource, traffic is forwarded from the DirectAccess server to the resource.

Installing and Configuring DirectAccess

This section describes a basic DirectAccess configuration, which requires only a domain controller, a member server for installing the DirectAccess role service, and a client computer. For this basic test configuration, the network is configured similar to Figure 6-30. The Internet is simulated by a router with connections to two interfaces: one for the network the DirectAccess client is on and one for the network the DirectAccess server's public interface is on. The DirectAccess server has two interfaces, one connected to the intranet and the other to the Internet with a public IP address. The DirectAccess server is not behind a NAT router.

> **Caution** ⚠️
>
> These steps use the Getting Started Wizard, which is fine for a test environment. However, this wizard configures DirectAccess in a very basic way, using self-signed certificates for authentication and disabling Teredo. For security and the most flexible client configuration, it's recommended that you run the Remote Access Setup Wizard and use certificates issued by a CA.

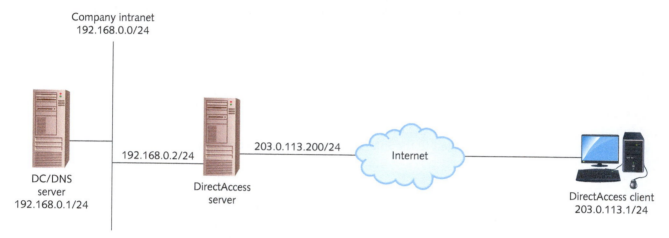

Figure 6-30 A DirectAccess test network

Here are the steps for configuring DirectAccess with the Getting Started Wizard, using the network configuration in Figure 6-30:

1. On the domain controller, create a global security group named DA-Computers (or a similar name). Add to this group the computer accounts you want to be able to connect to the network via DirectAccess. This step isn't required, but it's recommended because the default settings apply DirectAccess client settings to all mobile computers in the domain.

2. Install the DirectAccess role service, if necessary. If the Remote Access server role is installed for VPN connections, the DirectAccess role service is already installed.

3. Open the Remote Access Management console from the Tools menu in Server Manager. Under Configuration in the left pane, click DirectAccess and VPN. Click the Run the Getting Started Wizard link in the right pane.

4. In the Configure Remote Access window (see Figure 6-31), click *Deploy DirectAccess only*. The wizard verifies that your server meets the prerequisites for deployment.

5. In the Remote Access Server Setup window, you choose the network topology and enter the server's name or IPv4 address. The default option, Edge, is similar to the one in Figure 6-30 where one interface of the DirectAccess server is connected to the network and the other directly to the Internet. The next option, *Behind an edge device (with two network adapters)*, is similar, but one adapter is connected to a perimeter network behind a firewall and the other to the intranet. For the last option, *Behind an edge device (with a single network adapter)*, the DirectAccess server is connected only to the intranet, and NAT is used to translate a public address to the private address assigned to the interface. For the purposes of this example, we'll choose Edge. In the text box, type the DirectAccess server's public IPv4 address, which is 203.0.113.200 for this example (see Figure 6-32).

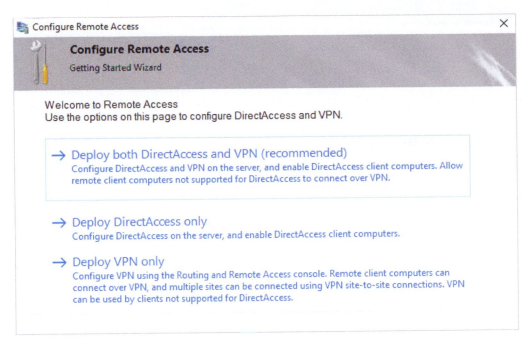

Figure 6-31   The Configure Remote Access window

Figure 6-32   The Remote Access Server Setup window

6. In the next window, click the link to edit the wizard settings. You see a summary of the configuration settings (see Figure 6-33).

7. Click the Change link next to Remote Clients. In the DirectAccess Client Setup window, you can change the default group. Click the Remove button to remove the Domain Computers group, click Add, type DA-Computers, and click OK. Then click to clear the Enable *DirectAccess for mobile computers only* check box (see Figure 6-34). This setting changes the scope of the group policy so that only computers in the DA-Computers group are affected by the DirectAccess Client Settings GPO. If you leave this check box selected, a Windows Management Instrumentation (WMI) filter is applied to the GPO so that only computers identified as laptops are enabled for DirectAccess. This setting might be what you want for a production deployment but not for testing. Click Next, and then click Finish.

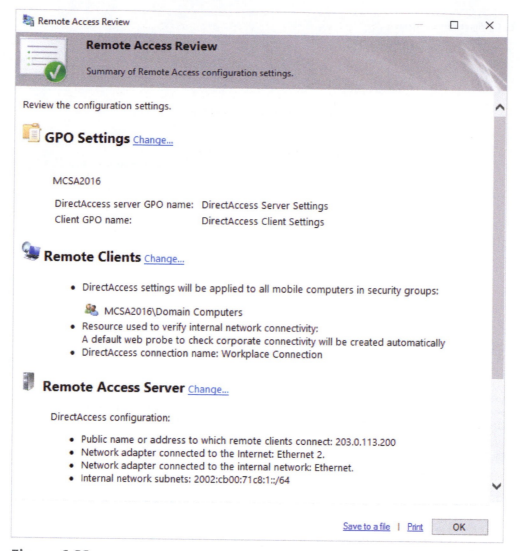

Figure 6-33 The Remote Access Review window

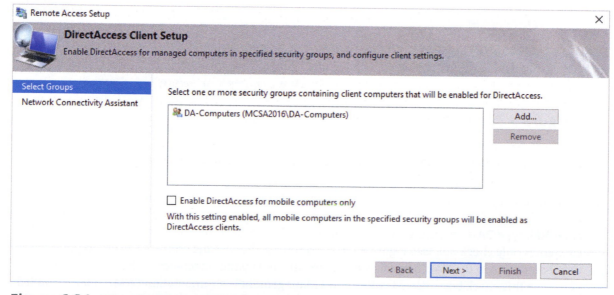

Figure 6-34 The DirectAccess Client Setup window

8. Back in the Remote Access Review window, click OK, and then click Finish. The necessary GPOs are created, and settings for the DirectAccess server are applied. The NLS server is configured, and self-signed certificates are generated for IP-HTTPS and the NLS server. Click Close, and you're back in the Remote Access Management console (see Figure 6-35). If necessary, you can click the Edit button to change any settings for DirectAccess components.

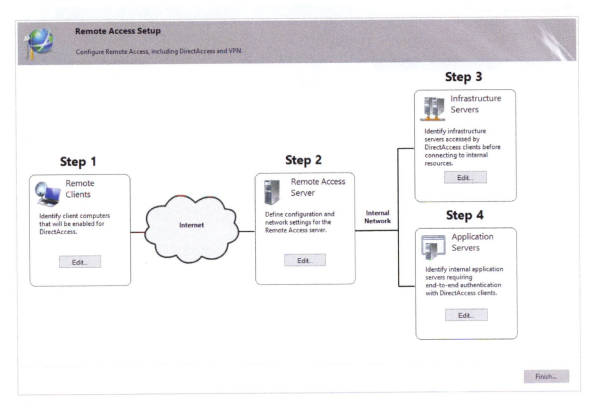

Figure 6-35   Options for editing DirectAccess components

9. The only step left is verifying and testing the configuration. If you click Operations Status in the left pane of the Remote Access Management Console, you see the window shown in Figure 6-36, assuming that everything is working as planned. If any component doesn't show a check mark in a green circle, you can click it to see additional information and troubleshooting suggestions. A question mark in a blue circle means that the status can't yet be determined. Press F5 or click Refresh in the Tasks pane to refresh the screen; it might take a while for DirectAccess to determine a component's status.

To test the DirectAccess configuration with a client computer, follow these steps:

1. Use domain credentials to sign in to a domain member Windows 10 Enterprise or Windows Server 2016 computer. The client computer needs to be connected to the intranet at this point.

2. If the client computer is already on, open a command prompt window and enter the `gpupdate` command to be sure that the computer gets the client configuration settings from group policies.

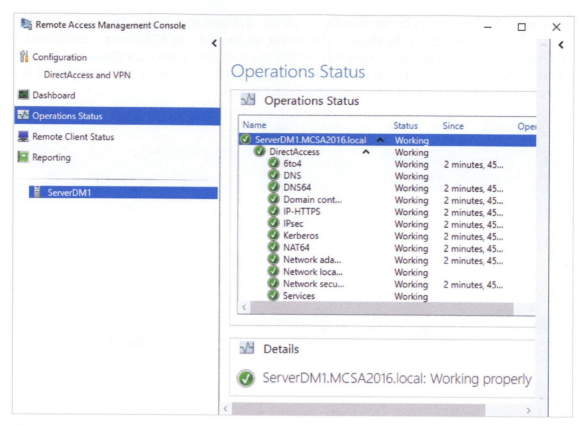

Figure 6-36   Viewing the status of DirectAccess operation

3. Open a PowerShell prompt, type `Get-DAConnectionStatus`, and press Enter. You should see output similar to that in Figure 6-37 showing that the DirectAccess Connection Assistant (DCA) has determined that you're on the intranet (connected locally).

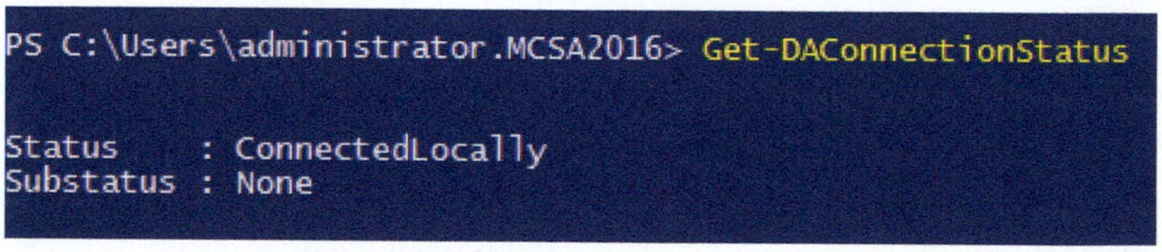

```
PS C:\Users\administrator.MCSA2016> Get-DAConnectionStatus

Status    : ConnectedLocally
Substatus : None
```

Figure 6-37   Results of the `Get-DAConnectionStatus` cmdlet

4. Shut down the client computer, and connect it to the public (Internet) side of the network. Make sure it can get an IP address configuration via DHCP or has a static IP address and can communicate with the public interface on the DirectAccess server.

5. Turn on the client computer, and sign in with domain credentials. Open a PowerShell prompt, type `Get-DAConnectionStatus`, and press Enter to see that you are now connected remotely. To verify that you can access local resources, ping the domain controller. You will see that IPv6 is used to communicate with local resources (see Figure 6-38).

6. Last, click the network icon in the notification tray. You see the list of connected networks (see Figure 6-39). The Workplace Connection is the DirectAccess connection. If your test client is not connected to the Internet or does not have access to a DNS server on the external network, you'll see a message stating No Internet under the Workplace Connection icon.

```
PS C:\Users\administrator.MCSA2016> Get-DAConnectionStatus

Status    : ConnectedRemotely
Substatus : None


PS C:\Users\administrator.MCSA2016> ping serverdc1

Pinging serverdc1.MCSA2016.local [fd5a:e9d7:8275:7777::c0a8:a01] with 32 bytes of data:
Reply from fd5a:e9d7:8275:7777::c0a8:a01: time=1ms
Reply from fd5a:e9d7:8275:7777::c0a8:a01: time=1ms
Reply from fd5a:e9d7:8275:7777::c0a8:a01: time=1ms
Reply from fd5a:e9d7:8275:7777::c0a8:a01: time=1ms
```

Figure 6-38   The DirectAccess connection status and ping results

Figure 6-39   List of connected networks

Advanced DirectAccess Deployment Options

After you have established a basic DirectAccess configuration, you might want to add some features for security or convenience. Some options discussed in the following sections include the following:

- Setting up a PKI
- Configuring NLS on a separate web server
- Configuring the NRPT
- Configuring forced tunneling
- Configuring Intra-Site Automatic Tunnel Addressing Protocol (ISATAP)

Setting Up a PKI

You can configure a DirectAccess server without using a PKI if you're using a Windows Server 2012 or newer DirectAccess server and all your clients are Windows 8 or newer. As you've learned, self-signed certificates present a security risk in production environments, and if you want to use multiple DirectAccess servers, a PKI is required because Kerberos proxy doesn't work with multiple DirectAccess servers. This section doesn't go into the details of setting up a PKI, but here are the basic steps to follow:

1. On a server separate from the DirectAccess server, install Active Directory Certificate Services configured as an Enterprise Certificate Authority.

2. Issue an SSL certificate to the NLS server set up on a server separate from the DirectAccess server (discussed in the next section).

3. Issue machine certificates to the DirectAccess server and each DirectAccess client computer. It's best to configure autoenrollment so that each client computer can automatically request and be issued a machine certificate.

An internal PKI is highly recommended for a production DirectAccess deployment because it widens your configuration options, offering the following:

- Support for Windows 7 clients.
- Better security than self-signed certificates.
- Support for multisite DirectAccess and DirectAccess server clusters. **Multisite DirectAccess** just means that there are two or more DirectAccess servers, each providing a secure entry point into the network. For example, companies with multiple locations can have a DirectAccess server in each one. A DirectAccess cluster uses Windows clustering technology for fault tolerance and load balancing.
- Support for two-factor authentication, such as smart cards.

Configuring NLS on a Separate Web Server

Even the Getting Started Wizard suggests that the NLS server should be on a separate machine from the DirectAccess server. You need only IIS installed on any server in the network. DirectAccess clients connect to it with HTTPS, so it requires an SSL certificate. The certificate can be issued by an internal PKI because it won't be publicly accessible. You also need to make sure that a DNS record that points to the NLS server is created on internal DNS servers, using a name such as nls.csmtech.local. The name is published to DirectAccess clients with a group policy. Creating a simple `Default.htm` file instead of using the IIS default home page is recommended but not necessary. You can change the NLS server in the Remote Access Management console by clicking DirectAccess and VPN under the Configuration node, and then clicking the Edit button in the Step 3 box for infrastructure servers in the Remote Access Setup window (refer back to Figure 6-35).

Configuring the Name Resolution Policy Table

When DirectAccess clients are connected to the Internet, the **name resolution policy table (NRPT)** makes sure that DNS requests for intranet resources are directed to internal DNS servers, not Internet DNS servers. For example, if the internal DNS domain name is csmtech.local, a DNS query for server1.csmtech.local is directed to the intranet DNS servers. A DNS query for www.google.com, however, is sent to the DNS servers configured in the client's IP settings, usually on the ISP's network. All these settings are configured by default. However, some companies have an Internet and an intranet version of certain resources, such as web servers. For example, internal DNS servers might return the address 192.168.0.25 when www.csmtech.local is queried, and Internet DNS servers return 203.0.113.100 for the same URL. If you want DirectAccess clients to use the Internet address, you create an exemption rule in the NRPT on client computers. Creating NRPT exemptions is referred to as *split-brain DNS*. You create exemptions by following these steps:

1. On a domain controller, open the Group Policy Management console.
2. To edit the DirectAccess Client Settings GPO, expand Computer Configuration, Policies, and Windows Settings, and click Name Resolution Policy. In the right pane, click the DNS Settings for DirectAccess tab, and then click the *Enable DNS Settings for DirectAccess in this rule* check box.
3. Add one or more rules or edit existing rules. To create a new rule, you specify which part of the DNS namespace the rule applies to (suffix, subnet, prefix, FQDN, or any other), fill in information for the type of rule, and click Create. To edit an existing rule, click the rule in the Name Resolution Policy Table section, and click the Edit Rule button.
4. Run `gpupdate` on the clients, or wait until the client downloads any new computer group policies.

Configuring Force Tunneling

The default DirectAccess client configuration is **split tunneling**, a remote access method in which only requests for resources on the intranet are sent over the DirectAccess tunnel. Requests for Internet resources are sent out through the regular Internet connection. Split tunneling is usually preferred from the client and network administrator's standpoint because the client's Internet traffic doesn't have to traverse the network. It usually means faster response times for clients and less consumption of network bandwidth. If you configure **force tunneling**, all traffic from the client goes over the DirectAccess tunnel. When using force tunneling, the only tunnel option is IP-HTTPS. Because the connection from the client to the DirectAccess server uses IPv6, clients using force tunneling can access only IPv6 resources on the Internet unless an IPv6-to-IPv4 proxy is configured on the intranet that provides IPv4 Internet access. Therefore, force tunneling is usually used only when you want to limit DirectAccess clients' access to the Internet.

You configure force tunneling by using group policies with the same procedure for configuring NRPT exemptions but expand Computer Configuration, Administrative Templates, Network, and Network Connections, and enable the *Route all traffic through the internal network* policy.

> **Note** 📎
>
> You can also enable force tunneling during DirectAccess setup if you use the Remote Access Setup Wizard instead of the Getting Started Wizard.

Configuring ISATAP

Intra-Site Automatic Tunnel Addressing Protocol (ISATAP) allows computers on the network to access DirectAccess clients that are connected via the Internet. For example, suppose a user on a DirectAccess client computer is having problems with an application on her laptop. The help desk personnel can open a Remote Desktop Protocol (RDP) session with the client and help solve the problem. For this situation to occur on an IPv4 network, ISATAP must be in place. The tunnels created by DirectAccess work only when a client connects to the DirectAccess server and establishes the communication session. The IPv6 IPsec tunnel created between the client and DirectAccess server is used by devices on the network to respond to the client. However, if a computer inside the network tries to initiate communication with the DirectAccess client, it will likely fail because there's no existing tunnel for the communication session to use. This is where ISATAP comes in. ISATAP is discussed in more detail in Chapter 1, but here are two ways to enable it on the network:

- *Enable ISATAP for all computers on the network*—Create a DNS A record with the hostname ISATAP and the IP address of the DirectAccess server's internal interface. This record sets up the DirectAccess server as an ISATAP router and attempts to connect to clients connected to the DirectAccess server by going through the DirectAccess server. If you use this method, you also need to configure DNS by entering `dnscmd /config /globalqueryblocklist wpad` at a command prompt. By default, DNS ignores queries to resolve the name `isatap`, and this command removes `isatap` from the list of names that are blocked by default.

- *Enable ISATAP for only certain computers*—The problem with the preceding method for enabling ISATAP is that all computers on the network are ISATAP enabled, which can put a strain on the DirectAccess server. To prevent this problem, you can select which computers to initiate communication with DirectAccess clients.

To selectively enable ISATAP, follow these steps:

1. Create a DNS A record with a hostname something like "DA-ISATAP," using the IP address of the DirectAccess server's internal interface.

2. Create a security group and add the computer accounts for which you want to enable ISATAP.

3. Create a GPO and enable this policy: Computer Configuration, Policies, Administrative Templates, Network, TCPIP Settings, IPv6 Transition Technologies, Set ISATAP Router Name. In the *Enter a router or relay name* text box, type the name of the DNS record you created in Step 1.

4. Enable the ISATAP State policy setting (in the same path as the Set ISATAP Router Name policy in Step 3).

ISATAP is a good solution on networks that don't support IPv6 by default if you need to initiate communication with DirectAccess clients. You probably also need to set policies to configure the Windows firewall on client computers to allow the particular types of communication you configured ISATAP for in the first place. For example, if you want network computers to connect via RDP to DirectAccess clients, you need to open port 3389 on the client firewall and allow edge traversal if the client is using Teredo.

Note 📎

ISATAP doesn't work reliably with multisite DirectAccess because computers on the network don't know to which DirectAccess server a particular client is connected.

Chapter Summary

- Remote Access is a server role that provides services to keep a mobile workforce and branch offices securely connected to the main office. Services include virtual private network (VPN), remote dial-in, routing, NAT, Web Application Proxy, and DirectAccess.

- When you install the Remote Access server role, you can install three role services: DirectAccess and VPN, Routing, and Web Application Proxy.

- A VPN is a network connection that uses the Internet to give users or branch offices secure access to a company's network resources on a private network. VPNs use encryption and authentication to ensure that communication is secure and legitimate, so although data travels through the public Internet, the connection remains private.

- Windows Server 2016 supports three tunnel types: PPTP, L2TP/IPsec, and SSTP. After you finish the VPN server configuration, you need to define who's allowed to connect via remote access. You can do this with a user's account settings or by configuring a network policy in the Network Policy Server (NPS) console.

- Remote dial-in uses the telephone system to connect a computer to a remote network. Each connection requires a modem and a phone line on both ends of the connection. Remote dial-in is not a very efficient system, which is why it has been largely replaced by VPN and, more recently, DirectAccess in Windows environments.

- The default settings for VPN and dial-up might be enough in many circumstances, but you also might need to support different OSs and different VPN clients over different tunneling methods, which could require security settings different from the defaults.

- Using Routing and Remote Access Service (RRAS), a Windows server can be configured as a router to connect multiple subnets in the network or connect the network to the Internet. After routing is enabled, you can add routing protocols and configure static routes.

- Windows Server 2016 supports IPv6 routing. IPv6 routing is configured largely the same way as IPv4 routing is; however, there is no version of RIPv2 for IPv6, so dynamic routing is supported in IPv6 using Border Gateway Protocol (BGP).

- BGP is an advanced dynamic routing protocol that can be used to route between remote networks and is most often used in virtual environments where BGP is deployed on a virtual machine acting as a gateway for large enterprises and cloud providers.

- Network Address Translation (NAT) is a process whereby a router or other type of gateway device replaces the source or destination IP addresses in a packet before forwarding the packet. An extension of NAT, called Port Address Translation (PAT), allows several hundred workstations to access the Internet with a single public Internet address.

- The DirectAccess role service is part of the DirectAccess and VPN role service under the Remote Access server role. It provides many of the same features as a VPN but adds client management and always-connected capability.
- A basic DirectAccess deployment requires only a domain controller, a member server to install the DirectAccess role service, and a client computer. After basic DirectAccess configuration, you might want to add some features for security or convenience, such as setting up a PKI, configuring NLS on a separate web server, configuring the name resolution policy table (NRPT), configuring force tunneling, and configuring Intra-Site Automatic Tunnel Addressing Protocol (ISATAP).

Key Terms

Border Gateway Protocol (BGP)
default route
demand-dial interface
DirectAccess
force tunneling
hop count
infrastructure tunnel
Internet Protocol-Hypertext
    Transfer Protocol Secure
    (IP-HTTPS)

intranet tunnel
Kerberos proxy
multisite DirectAccess
name resolution policy table
    (NRPT)
Network Address Translation
    (NAT)
Network Location Server
    (NLS)
perimeter network

Port Address Translation (PAT)
Remote Access
routing table
split tunneling
static route
tunnel
virtual private network
    (VPN)
VPN connection profile
VPN reconnect

Review Questions

1. Which of the following are services provided by the Remote Access server role? (Choose all that apply.)
   a. Network Address Translation
   b. Web Application Proxy
   c. Windows Server Update Services
   d. Internet Information Services

2. Which role service should you install if you want client computers to be able to authenticate an IPsec connection with Kerberos proxy?
   a. DirectAccess and VPN
   b. Web Application Proxy
   c. Routing
   d. Remote dial-in

3. Which VPN tunnel type requires the firewall to allow TCP port 443?
   a. PPTP
   b. SSTP
   c. L2TP/IPsec
   d. PPP

4. Which VPN tunnel type uses an Internet Key Exchange?
   a. PPP
   b. PPTP
   c. SSTP
   d. L2TP/IPsec

5. Which tunnel type needs to authenticate client and server computers with a preshared key or a digital certificate?
   a. PPTP
   b. SSTP
   c. L2TP/IPsec
   d. PPP

6. Which of the following need to be configured on the firewall to allow PPTP VPN connections? (Choose all that apply.)
   a. UDP port 4500
   b. TCP port 1723
   c. IP protocol ID 50
   d. IP protocol ID 47

7. Which remote access configuration option should you choose if you want mobile users to be able to make a secure connection to the main network and allow computers on the private network to access the Internet with a public IP address?
   a. Remote access (dial-up or VPN)
   b. NAT
   c. VPN access and NAT
   d. Secure connection between two private networks

8. The Network Access Permission attribute for a user account is set to which of the following by default?
   a. Control access through NPS Network Policy
   b. Allow access
   c. Deny access
   d. Control access through Group Policy

9. When you create a VPN connection on a client computer, what is the default tunnel type?
   a. SSTP
   b. PPTP
   c. Automatic
   d. L2TP/IPsec

10. Which authentication method should you choose if users authenticate with smart cards?
    a. MS-CHAPv2
    b. PAP
    c. EAP
    d. RADIUS

11. What should you configure if you want only users who are members of particular groups to be able to connect to the VPN?
    a. Connection Request Policy
    b. Network Policy
    c. Remote Authentication Rule
    d. Network Access Rule

12. What do you configure in Routing and Remote Access that specifies the server should send its routing table to its neighbors?
    a. Static routing
    b. L2TP
    c. RIPv2
    d. Default route

13. What is the metric used by the dynamic routing protocol you configure in Routing and Remote Access?
    a. Least cost
    b. Bandwidth
    c. Ping time
    d. Hop count

14. What should you configure in Routing and Remote Access if you want computers using a private IP address to access the public Internet?
    a. Demand-dial interface
    b. NAT
    c. Dynamic routing
    d. Web Application Proxy

15. Which of the following routing protocols would you choose when using dynamic routing with IPv6?
    a. RIPv2
    b. IGRP
    c. IS-IS
    d. BGP

16. What specific type of Windows Server 2016 configuration allows a cloud service provider to use a virtual machine configured as a gateway to route multiple tenants using the same physical network?
    a. Windows Server Gateway
    b. RADIUS Server
    c. Cloud Services Gateway
    d. Hybrid Gateway

17. Which of the following does a router do if it receives a packet for a destination network that's not in its routing table and no default route is configured?
    a. Broadcasts the packet
    b. Discards the packet
    c. Returns the packet to the sender
    d. Sends a route query to the next router

18. Remote access is denied to users by default. Which of the following must you do to allow users to connect via remote access? (Choose all that apply.)
    a. Configure settings in the Routing and Remote Access console
    b. Configure dial-in settings in user accounts
    c. Configure a network policy in the Network Policy Server console
    d. Set up a VPN

19. Which DirectAccess IPv6 transition technology uses Secure Sockets Layer over port 443?
    a. 6to4
    b. Teredo
    c. IP-HTTPS
    d. ISATAP

20. Which DirectAccess component allows clients to determine whether they're on the company network or a remote network?
    a. NLS
    b. PKI
    c. Kerberos proxy
    d. ISATAP

21. Which of the following are benefits of using a PKI instead of self-signed certificates when configuring DirectAccess? (Choose all that apply.)
    a. Better security
    b. Support for multisite configurations
    c. Two-factor authentication support
    d. Simpler DirectAccess client deployment

22. Which of the following should you configure if you want DirectAccess clients to access the Internet through the company network?
    a. Split tunneling
    b. NLS
    c. Force tunneling
    d. Intranet tunnel

Critical Thinking

The following activities give you critical thinking challenges. Case Projects offer a scenario with a problem to solve and for which you supply a written solution.

Case Project 6-1: Deploying Remote Access

You are consulting for a company that uses Windows Server 2016 servers in a domain environment. All desktop computers are running Windows 10. You have been told to come up with a remote access solution for the company's mobile workforce. Employees will be using company-issued laptops that they also can use when they're on the premises. The solution should provide access to the intranet when employees have an Internet connection without them having to specifically initiate a connection. The solution should be secure and allow IT staff to perform maintenance tasks via Remote Desktop sessions on the laptops when they're connected locally or remotely. What remote access solution do you recommend, and why? Are there any configuration options you should consider for this solution?

Case Project 6-2: Solving a Router Problem

CSM Tech Publishing has four buildings connected by fiber-optic cabling and 12 subnets connected by several routers running RIPv2. One building has flooded, so employees and their equipment have moved to a temporary building on the same site. A router with three interfaces in the flooded building was also damaged. There are no spare routers, and the router can't be replaced for several days. Five servers running Windows Server 2016 have been moved to the temporary building. One of these servers is available as a spare or for other purposes. What can you do to solve your routing problem? Be specific about how you would carry out your solution, and state whether you would use static or dynamic routing.

CHAPTER 7

IMPLEMENTING NETWORK POLICY SERVER

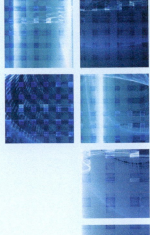

After reading this chapter and completing the exercises, you will be able to:

Describe the components and flow of Network Policy Server (NPS) and RADIUS

Install and configure NPS and RADIUS

Configure NPS Policies

Although good internal security policies are a must, ensuring that unauthorized access to the network is blocked is the first line of defense, so you should pay particular attention to this task. Knowing who is allowed access and by what methods can help limit network attacks and make creating and monitoring security policies easier. Incorporating industry standards for authentication and authorization, Windows Server 2016 includes ways to protect a network at the gate. With Network Policy Server, for example, you can create policies to determine who can access your network and how they can connect. In this chapter, you learn how to configure centralized authentication and authorization policies using Network Policy Server and Remote Authentication Dial In User Service (RADIUS).

Table 7-1 summarizes what you need for the hands-on activities in this chapter.

Table 7-1	Activity requirements	
Activity	**Requirements**	**Notes**
Activity 7-1: Resetting Your Virtual Environment	ServerDC1, ServerDM1, ServerSA1	
Activity 7-2: Installing the NPS and RRAS	ServerDC1, ServerDM1	
Activity 7-3: Configuring a RADIUS Server	ServerDC1, ServerDM1, ServerSA1	
Activity 7-4: Creating a VPN Connection and Testing RADIUS	ServerDC1, ServerDM1, ServerSA1	
Activity 7-5: Configuring a RADIUS Proxy	ServerDC1, ServerDM1, ServerSA1	
Activity 7-6: Configuring RADIUS Accounting	ServerDC1, ServerDM1, ServerSA1	
Activity 7-7: Creating a Connection Request Policy	ServerDC1	
Activity 7-8: Creating a VPN Client Network Policy	ServerDC1	
Activity 7-9: Creating a Shared Secret Template	ServerDC1	

Network Policy Server Overview

 Certification

- **70-741 – Implement network connectivity and remote access solutions:**
  Implement Network Policy Server (NPS)

With Network Policy Server (NPS), a role service of the Network Policy and Access Services (NPAS) server role, you can define and enforce rules that determine who can access your network and how they can access it (via VPN, dial-up, and so forth). Access attempts, both successful and unsuccessful, can be logged, so NPS has authentication, authorization, and auditing capabilities. The NPS architecture includes three features: RADIUS server, RADIUS proxy, and RADIUS accounting.

The RADIUS Infrastructure

Network Policy Server is Microsoft's implementation of the **Remote Authentication Dial In User Service (RADIUS)** protocol, a proposed IETF standard that's widely used to centralize authentication, authorization, and accounting to network services. To use NPS, you need to understand the types of messages used in a RADIUS infrastructure carried out in an NPS environment. The following list describes the process and what types of messages are sent:

1. An **access client** (for example, a user on a laptop) makes a connection request to a **network access server (NAS)**, which handles access to a network. An NAS can be, for example, a wireless access point, a VPN server, or a dial-up server. In the RADIUS infrastructure, an NAS is configured as a RADIUS client.

 Note

The term *client* can be a bit confusing. Only an NAS that's already part of the network can be a RADIUS client. Devices such as users' desktops, laptops, or mobile devices that are requesting access to the network are called *access clients* in this context, not RADIUS clients.

2. The RADIUS client sends an Access-Request message, including a user name/password combination or a certificate from the user, to an NPS server acting as a RADIUS server. This message can include other information about the user, such as the network address.

3. The NPS server evaluates the Access-Request message. This process can include authenticating the user name and password (along with other user information) via a domain controller or client certificate.

4. The NPS server can respond with one of three types of messages:

   • Access-Reject: The request is rejected, and access is denied to the network or resources.
   • Access-Challenge: More information is requested, such as a secondary password or other access code or credential.
   • Access-Accept: Access is granted, and authorization is given to certain resources based on defined network policies.

5. The connection is completed, and the NAS sends an Accounting-Request message to the NPS server to be logged. This message is sent to collect information about the user, such as the IP address, method of connecting to the network, and a session identifier so that additional information that's sent can be attributed to this user's connection.

6. The NPS server sends an Accounting-Response message, which acknowledges that the request was received, to the NAS.

7. During the session, additional Accounting-Request messages containing information about the current session are sent. Each Accounting-Request message is acknowledged by an Accounting-Response message.

8. When the user's connection ends, one last Accounting-Request message with information about the overall use during the session is sent. This final message is acknowledged by an Accounting-Response message.

A RADIUS proxy can be inserted between Network Access Servers and NPS servers to help manage the load on the NPS servers. The proxy receives the Access-Request and Accounting-Request messages from an NAS and directs them on to the NPS server. Figure 7-1 shows the overall RADIUS message flow between access clients, RADIUS clients, and RADIUS servers, and access clients, RADIUS clients, RADIUS proxies, and RADIUS servers.

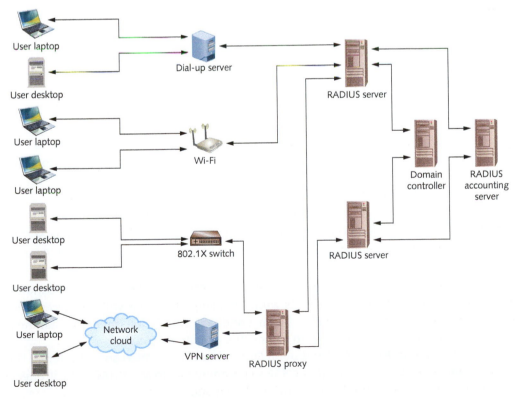

Figure 7-1   RADIUS infrastructure

Installing and Configuring NPS and RADIUS

Certification

- 70-741 – Implement network connectivity and remote access solutions:
Implement Network Policy Server (NPS)

There are two main reasons you should set up an NPS architecture with RADIUS when you have different connection paths to your network. First, RADIUS centralizes control over authentication and authorization. No matter which path a user uses to access the network, a single point of contact—the NPS server acting as a RADIUS server—handles authenticating the user and determining the level of authorization. Next, standardizing on RADIUS requires all NAS devices to be RADIUS clients so that only one protocol performs authentication and authorization and only one standard configuration process is used, regardless of the kind of device connecting to the network. To begin configuring an NPS/RADIUS environment, you must install the NPS role. To do so, install the Network Policy and Access Services server role from Server Manager or with the following PowerShell cmdlet:

```
Install-WindowsFeature NPAS -IncludeManagementTools
```

After NPS is installed, you can configure the server to be a RADIUS server, RADIUS proxy, or both. In a small environment with few network logon requests, a single RADIUS server is usually sufficient. After you have installed the NPS Server role, you can manage NPS in the Network Policy Server console. You need to configure a couple of settings: which NASs can connect and the authentication method that each one uses. NPS gives you the choice of standard or advanced configuration options. The advanced configuration option requires you to set up the components for a RADIUS server or proxy. The standard configuration has wizards to walk you through these policy settings:

- *RADIUS server for Dial-Up or VPN Connections*—This option defines network policies for authenticating and authorizing connections from these RADIUS clients: dial-up or VPN network access servers.
- *RADIUS server for 802.1X Wireless or Wired Connections*—This option defines network policies for authenticating and authorizing connections from these RADIUS clients: wireless access points and authenticating switches.

A policy must be defined for each type of RADIUS client, such as VPN NAS, in the NPS console. To create these policies, you need to consider several factors. Just as you want to authenticate clients attempting to access the network, you need to validate communication between a RADIUS client and a RADIUS server or proxy with a **shared secret**, a text string that acts as a password between RADIUS clients, servers, and proxies. Here are a few guidelines for creating shared secrets:

- A shared secret should be at least 22 characters to make guessing or using brute-force techniques more difficult. It should include uppercase and lowercase letters, numbers from 0 to 9, and symbols such as !, &, and @.
- A shared secret can be up to 128 characters.
- Use a random combination of letters, numbers, and symbols rather than a phrase.

The credentials that the NAS passes need to be authenticated. Depending on the type of NAS, two general types of authentication methods are used: password based and certificate based. Four password-based methods are supported:

- *Microsoft Challenge Handshake Authentication Protocol*—**Microsoft Challenge Handshake Authentication Protocol (MS-CHAP)** starts with a challenge-response with the access client and then sends the user name and a password with a one-way encryption (meaning that the password can't be unencrypted) to be authenticated against the stored credentials.
- *Microsoft Challenge Handshake Authentication Protocol version 2*—**Microsoft Challenge Handshake Authentication Protocol version 2 (MS-CHAP v2)** is an update to MS-CHAP with stronger security. Of the four password-based methods, it's the preferred one.

- *Challenge Handshake Authentication Protocol*—**Challenge Handshake Authentication Protocol (CHAP)** is similar to MS-CHAP, but the password must be able to be unencrypted, making it less secure than MS-CHAP.
- *Password Authentication Protocol*—**Password Authentication Protocol (PAP)** is the least secure method. The password is sent in plaintext, and there's no challenge and response. Because the password could be captured easily, PAP isn't recommended.

The certificate-based authentication method is **Extensible Authentication Protocol (EAP)**. Certificate-based authentication is more secure than password-based methods. Depending on the method you choose, there are two authentication types. The authentication type for EAP is **Transport Layer Security (TLS)**, which is a cryptographic protocol used to encrypt network messages. TLS provides privacy (data encryption), data integrity (detection of unauthorized changes in the data), and authentication. Certificates and options for using certificates are discussed later in "Using Certificates for Authentication."

Protected Extensible Authentication Protocol (PEAP) is a special way to encrypt a password being sent via MS-CHAP v2. With PEAP, you can check the server's certificate, but user authentication is still done through passwords.

The groups to which a user belongs can control access based on the network policy's access permission setting. With user groups and IP filters, you can create policies that restrict users to specific protocols and specific servers. For example, you could restrict a VPN user to have access only to the FTP servers via using the FTP protocol. Several other authentication settings can be configured. If the client is encrypting its messages to the NAS, you can specify what level of encryption is supported. For example, with a Routing and Remote Access Service (RRAS) server such as VPN or dial-up, Encryption, Strong Encryption, and Strongest Encryption are all supported.

Another part of the network policy is the **realm**, the Active Directory domain where the RADIUS server is located. By default, it's the domain where the NPS server is located. If connection requests require authentication from another domain controller, they can be sent to an NPS server acting as a RADIUS proxy, and the realm determines to which server the request is routed.

Although a basic RADIUS infrastructure is adequate for most cases, a simple configuration has a few drawbacks. Lack of fault tolerance is the biggest disadvantage. If the one and only RADIUS server goes down, no network connection requests can be authenticated, which makes the network inaccessible to users. To eliminate this single point of failure, you can deploy multiple RADIUS servers. RADIUS clients can be configured to use a primary server and alternates, so if the primary isn't available, the client tries the alternates in turn.

Another concern is the server's load. In a network with hundreds or thousands of requests in extremely short periods, a single RADIUS server could be overwhelmed. One solution is to use RADIUS proxies (having only one proxy reintroduces the single-point-of-failure problem) with multiple RADIUS servers. Requests received by a proxy are forwarded to a **RADIUS server group** composed of one or more RADIUS servers for handling. In a server group of two or more RADIUS servers, the load can be balanced based on these properties:

- *Priority*—Tells the NPS proxy the order of importance of this server group member when passing on requests. This setting is a non-zero integer number (such as 1, 2, 3). The lower the number, the higher the priority, so servers assigned a priority of 1 get requests first. If the Priority 1 server is unavailable, the request is sent to the Priority 2 server, and so on. Setting just the priority doesn't result in load balancing because the lowest-priority server continues getting requests unless it becomes unavailable. However, a priority of 1 can be assigned to multiple servers, and the Weight setting can be used to force load balancing.
- *Weight*—Determines what percentage of connection requests are sent to a server group member when the priority is the same as other members. This setting is also a non-zero integer number between 1 and 100. For example, to distribute the load between two servers evenly, you could assign each a priority of 1 and a weight of 50 so that each server gets 50% of the connection requests. The sum of all weights in the server group must be 100.

- *Advanced settings*—Determines whether a server group member is unavailable and whether connection requests need to be routed to another server in the group. The settings include the number of seconds a proxy should wait for a response before deciding that the request is dropped, the maximum number of requests dropped before the group server is considered unavailable, and the number of seconds between requests before the group server is considered unavailable.

Configuring RADIUS Accounting

RADIUS accounting is essentially a log of the different access and accounting requests and responses sent between RADIUS clients and RADIUS servers that were outlined previously in "The RADIUS Infrastructure." NPS logs requests and responses by using one of these methods:

- *Event logging*—Events that occur while NPS is running are written to event logs.
- *Local text file*—Each user authentication and accounting request is logged to a text file.
- *Microsoft SQL Server XML-compliant database*—Logged data is written to a SQL Server database. Multiple servers can write to a single database. One advantage of this method is that the accounting data is stored in an easily accessible container (a SQL Server database), and the data for multiple systems is combined in this container, which makes reporting more flexible.

The default setting is to log accounting information in a local text file in C:\Windows\System32\LogFiles. You can change this setting in the Network Policy Server console.

Using Certificates for Authentication

The easiest authentication method to set up is password based. Unfortunately, easy authentication methods often have less security. For stronger security, **certificate-based authentication** is recommended; it uses a certificate (a digital document) containing information that establishes an entity's identity, such as an NPS server or an access client. With this authentication method, a server's or client's identity can be verified. You have seen this type of authentication in action on the Internet. When you connect to a website by using https:// in the URL instead of http://, the server is asked for the website certificate to prove that you're connecting to the site you requested. If the server doesn't present the certificate, the connection fails. If the certificate has expired or information such as the requested URL doesn't match what's on the certificate, the connection fails. With NPS, the certificate is presented when the client is attempting to connect, and the server, the client, or both are asked to prove their identity.

Certificates are created and distributed by a **certification authority (CA)**, which is given information that can uniquely identify the server or client. There are two types of CAs: public and private. Examples of public CAs are VeriSign and Thawte. You purchase certificates from these companies and give them information to prove that you are who you say you are. A private CA, such as Active Directory Certificate Services, allows you to produce as many certificates as you want.

For a certificate to be used for authentication, the CA must be trusted by the client or server, and to be trusted, it must have a **root certificate** (also called a *CA certificate*) in the Trusted Root Certification Authorities certificate store. Think of the root certificate as the master certificate for a CA. After the root certificate is installed, all other certificates from this CA are trusted automatically by the client or server. The process of requesting a certificate, having it approved, and downloading it is called *enrollment*. Clients can be enrolled automatically for some certificates in a domain. For example, if the client is a member of the same domain as the CA, the CA certificate is autoenrolled. In addition to the root certificate, there are three other important certificate types:

- *Client computer certificate*—This certificate verifies a client computer's identity to an NPS server. It's enrolled automatically for domain members and imported manually for non-domain members.
- *Server certificate*—This certificate verifies a server's identity to a client. It can be set for autoenrollment in Active Directory.
- *User certificate*—This certificate can be put on a smart card to verify a user's identity, and the smart card reader is attached to the client computer. If you're using smart cards, you don't autoenroll client computer certificates.

When a certificate is presented for authentication, it must meet these three criteria for authentication to succeed:

- It must be valid (for example, hasn't expired).
- It must be configured for the purpose for which it's presented.
- It must be issued by a trusted CA.

For a client to accept a certificate from an NPS server, the certificate must meet these requirements:

- The subject name can't be blank.
- The certificate is linked to a trusted root CA.
- The purpose of the certificate is server authentication.
- The algorithm name is RSA, and the minimum key size is at least 2048.
- If the subject alternative name (SubjectAltName) extension is used, which allows multiple servers to use the certificate, the certificate must contain the NPS server's DNS name.

You can select certificate-based authentication—EAP—when you're setting the authentication method. EAP requires both the server and the access client to present valid certificates, which is the most secure authentication method. However, in a large organization, maintaining potentially thousands of client certificates can be a daunting administrative job even with autoenrollment for new access clients. Selecting PEAP as the authentication method doesn't involve using a client certificate; instead, it uses MS-CHAP v2 for client authentication. It's not as secure, however, as a pure certificate-based authentication method (such as EAP) because users still enter passwords, which can be guessed or stolen. However, PEAP can be configured to require a server certificate. This method protects clients from connecting to a server that's pretending to be the server they want to connect to, and PEAP encrypts the information it's passing.

Activity 7-1: Resetting your Virtual Environment

Time Required: 5 minutes
Objective: Reset your virtual environment by applying the InitialConfig checkpoint or snapshot.
Required Tools and Equipment: ServerDC1, ServerDM1, ServerSA1
Description: Apply the InitialConfig checkpoint or snapshot to ServerDC1, ServerDM1, and ServerSA1.

1. Be sure all servers are shut down. In your virtualization program, apply the InitialConfig checkpoint or snapshot to all servers.
2. When the snapshot or checkpoint has finished being applied, continue to the next activity.

Activity 7-2: Installing the NPS and RRAS

Time Required: 10 minutes
Objective: Install Network Policy Server and Remote Access.
Required Tools and Equipment: ServerDC1, ServerDM1
Description: In this activity, you install the Network Policy Server role service as well as the DirectAccess and VPN Routing and Remote Access role services. Then you configure a VPN server so you can test RADIUS.

1. Start ServerDC1 and ServerDM1. On ServerDC1, sign in as **Administrator**, if necessary. Open a PowerShell window.
2. Type **Install-WindowsFeature NPAS -IncludeManagementTools** and press **Enter**. Close the PowerShell window.
3. On ServerDM1, sign in as **Administrator**, if necessary. Open a PowerShell window. Type **Install-WindowsFeature DirectAccess-VPN -IncludeManagementTools** and press **Enter**. Close the PowerShell window.

4. In Server Manager, click **Tools, Routing and Remote Access** to start the RRAS console.
5. In the Routing and Remote Access console, right-click **ServerDM1** and click **Configure and Enable Routing and Remote Access**. Continue with the Routing and Remote Access Server Setup Wizard, making sure to configure a VPN using the network connection with address **192.168.0.2** as the Internet connection (if necessary, review the steps in Activity 6-2 from Chapter 6). For IP Address Assignment, specify the range **192.168.0.100** to **192.168.0.109**. Accept the default selections for the rest of the settings.
6. Continue to the next activity.

Activity 7-3: Configuring a RADIUS Server

Time Required: 15 minutes
Objective: Configure a RADIUS server to authenticate VPN access requests.
Required Tools and Equipment: ServerDC1, ServerDM1, ServerSA1
Description: You want to authenticate and authorize VPN traffic coming into the network, so you need to configure a RADIUS server to accept access requests from VPN clients.

1. On ServerDC1, in Server Manager click **Tools**, **Network Policy Server** from the menu to open the Network Policy Server console.
2. In the Standard Configuration section of the Getting Started window shown in Figure 7-2, be sure that **RADIUS server for Dial-Up or VPN Connections** is selected in the list box and then click the **Configure VPN or Dial-Up** link to start the corresponding wizard.

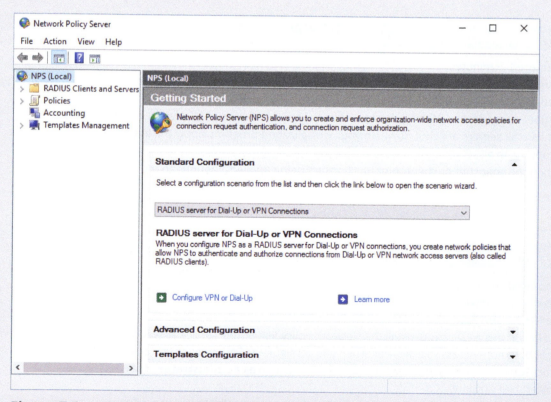

Figure 7-2   Selecting a configuration option for the RADIUS server

3. In the Select Dial-up or Virtual Private Network Connections Type window, click the **Virtual Private Network (VPN) Connections** option button. This option adds text to the Virtual Private Network (VPN) Connections text box that's used as part of the name of all policies created with the wizard. Leave this text as is, and click **Next**.

4. In the Specify Dial-Up or VPN Server window, click **Add** to open the New RADIUS Client dialog box. In the Friendly name text box, type **ServerDM1**, and in the Address (IP or DNS) text box, type **192.168.0.2** (see Figure 7-3). You can click the **Verify** button to make sure you entered the correct address. Type **Password01** in the Shared secret and Confirm shared secret text boxes.

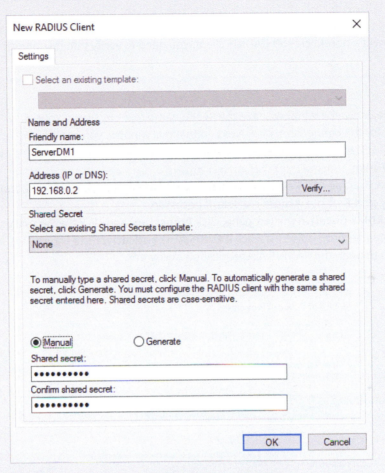

Figure 7-3   The New RADIUS Client dialog box

Tip ⓘ

For the purposes of this activity, you're using a simple password. For a production server, you should use a password that has at least 22 characters and contains a random mix of uppercase and lowercase letters, numbers, and symbols.

5. Click **OK**, and then click **Next** to continue. In the Configure Authentication Methods window, click **Microsoft Encrypted Authentication version 2 (MS-CHAP v2)**, if necessary, and then click **Next**.
6. In the Specify User Groups window, you can add Active Directory user groups that the policy affects. You want this policy to apply to all users, so leave this window blank and click **Next** to continue.
7. In the Specify IP Filters window, you can add IPv4 and IPv6 inbound and outbound filters or select from a template you have created. Filters allow you to restrict remote access to specific source and destination IP addresses and protocols. You do not need to add filters for this activity. Click **Next** to continue.

8. Because Routing and Remote Access Service supports all three types of encryption (Basic, Strong, and Strongest), all are selected in the Specify Encryption Settings window. The VPN will use the strongest encryption supported by both the client and server. Leave them selected, and click **Next** to continue.

> **Note** 🔗
>
> If you want to connect a non-Microsoft RADIUS client, you need to verify that it supports the encryption type you select.

9. In the Specify a Realm Name window, leave the Realm name text box blank. Your ISP will tell you if a realm name is required for the connection. Click **Next**. In the final window, you see a summary of the settings, including the RADIUS clients and the names of the connection request policy and the network policies to be generated. Click **Finish**.

10. Now you configure Routing and Remote Access to use RADIUS authentication and accounting. On ServerDM1, open the **Routing and Remote Access** console, if necessary.

11. Right-click **SERVERDM1 (local)** in the left pane, click **Properties**, and click the **Security** tab. In the Authentication provider drop-down list, click **RADIUS Authentication** (see Figure 7-4), and then click the **Configure** button to open the RADIUS Authentication dialog box.

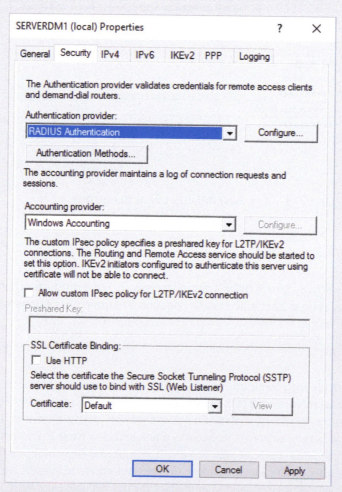

Figure 7-4   Selecting RADIUS Authentication on the Security tab

12. Click **Add** to open the Add RADIUS Server dialog box. Type **ServerDC1** in the Server name text box, click the **Change** button (see Figure 7-5), and type **Password01** in the New secret and Confirm new secret text boxes. Click **OK**.

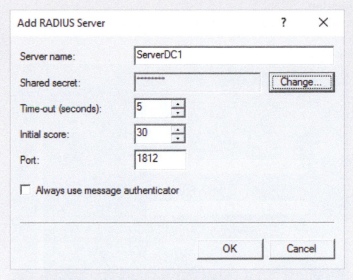

Figure 7-5   The Add RADIUS Server dialog box

13. Click **OK** twice to return to the Properties dialog box. In the Accounting provider drop-down list, click **RADIUS Accounting**, and then click the **Configure** button to open the RADIUS Accounting dialog box. Repeat Step 12 to add ServerDC1 as the RADIUS Accounting provider. Click **OK** to close the Properties dialog box.
14. You need to restart the RRAS service for the changes to take effect. To do so, in the Routing and Remote Access console, right-click **SERVERDM1 (local)**, point to **All Tasks**, and click **Restart**.
15. Continue to the next activity, where you'll connect to the VPN server to verify that the authentication is working.

Activity 7-4: Creating a VPN Connection and Testing RADIUS

Time Required: 15 minutes
Objective: Create a VPN connection to test RADIUS.
Required Tools and Equipment: ServerDC1, ServerDM1, ServerSA1
Description: Test the VPN and RADIUS configuration by creating a VPN client connection on ServerSA1 and attempting to connect to the VPN server. For this activity, you disable the network interface on ServerSA1 that is connected to the 192.168.0.0/24 network. The second network interface on ServerSA1 with address 192.168.1.4 is used to make the VPN connection.

1. First, create a user on ServerDC1 that will be used to authenticate to the VPN. On ServerDC1, in Server Manager, click **Tools, Active Directory Users and Computers**.
2. Click the **Users** folder and click the User icon on the toolbar. Use the following criteria to create the user:
   Full Name: VPN Test1
   User logon name: VPNTest1
   Password: Password01
   Password never expires: Checked
3. Double-click **VPNTest1** to open the Properties dialog box. Click the **Dial-in** tab, click **Allow access** in the Network Access Permission section, and then click **OK**. Close Active Directory Users and Computers.

4. On ServerSA1, sign in as **Administrator**. Right-click **Start** and click **Network Connections**. Right-click **Ethernet** and click **Disable**. Verify that Ethernet 2 has an IP address of 192.168.1.4 by right-clicking **Ethernet 2**, clicking **Status**, and clicking **Details**. Click **Close** twice and close the Network Connections window.

5. Click the network icon in the right side of the taskbar and click **Network Settings**. Click **VPN**, and then click **Add a VPN connection**.

6. In the Add a VPN connection window, fill out the form as in Figure 7-6. Click **Save**.

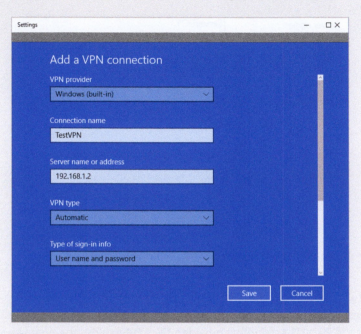

Figure 7-6   Setting up a VPN connection

7. To verify the authentication type, click **Change adapter options**. Right-click **TestVPN** and click **Properties**. Click the **Security** tab. Click **Allow these protocols** and click to select **Microsoft CHAP Version 2**, if necessary (see Figure 7-7). Click **OK**.

Figure 7-7   Setting the authentication type on the VPN client

8. Right-click **TestVPN** and click **Connect/Disconnect**. In the Networks panel, click **TestVPN** and click **Connect**. When prompted for the user name and password, type **mcsa2016\vpntest1** for the user name and **Password01** for the password and click **OK**. You will see the word Connected under the TestVPN connection.

9. On ServerDC1, right-click **Start** and click **Event Viewer**. Click to expand **Windows Logs** and click **Security**. In the right pane, look for an event with **Event ID 6272** and double-click it. You will see that the event says *Network Policy Server granted access to a user*. Scroll down to view more of the event. You'll see that the NAS shows that RADIUS Client is shown as ServerDM1 (see Figure 7-8). Click **Close** and then close Event Viewer.

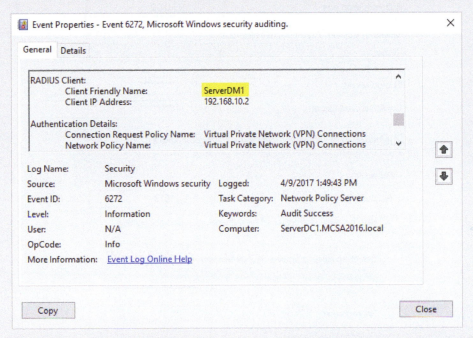

Figure 7-8   Viewing an NPS event

10. On ServerSA1, in Network Connections, right-click **TestVPN** and click **Connect/Disconnect**. In the Networks panel, click **TestVPN** and click **Disconnect**.

11. Close the Network Connections window and continue to the next activity.

Activity 7-5: Configuring a RADIUS Proxy

Time Required: 25 minutes
Objective: Configure a RADIUS proxy.
Required Tools and Equipment: ServerDC1, ServerDM1, ServerSA1
Description: In this activity, you configure a RADIUS proxy. Because there are is only one authentication server (ServerDC1), this activity has no bearing on how the client is authenticated. The power of a RADIUS proxy is when you have multiple authentication servers.

1. On ServerDC1, open **Network Policy Server**, if necessary.

2. Expand **NPS (Local)**, if necessary, and **RADIUS Clients and Servers** in the left pane. Right-click **Remote RADIUS Server Groups** and click **New**.

3. Type **Test Server Group** for the group name, and then click **Add** to open the Add RADIUS Server dialog box.

4. Type **192.168.0.1** (the IP address of ServerDC1), and then click the **Authentication/Accounting** tab.

5. Type **Password01** in the Shared secret and Confirm shared secret box, and click the **Request must contain the message authenticator attribute** check box (see Figure 7-9).

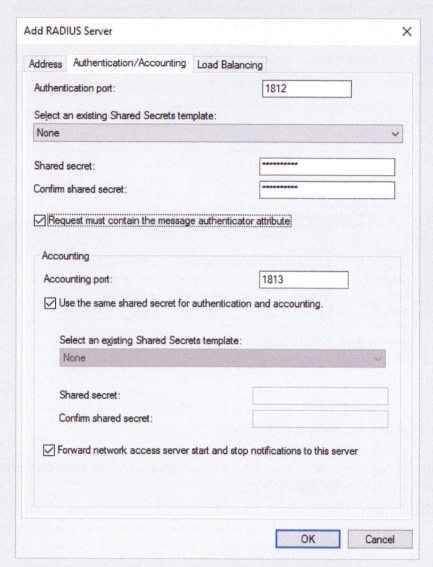

Figure 7-9   Configuring authentication and accounting for a RADIUS proxy

6. Because you haven't changed the default ports, you can leave them as they are. Make sure the **Use the same shared secret for authentication and accounting** check box is selected.
7. Click the **Load Balancing** tab. Leave the default values as shown in Figure 7-10, and then click **OK** twice to finish.
8. Using the VPN client on ServerSA1, connect using the VPN connection again using the same credentials used in the previous activity (you may not need to enter credentials because the computer caches them locally). You won't see any difference connecting when a proxy is configured. The difference would come if you had multiple RADIUS servers to handle the authentication. In that case, a different RADIUS server might be shown in the event that is created.
9. Disconnect the VPN connection and continue to the next activity.

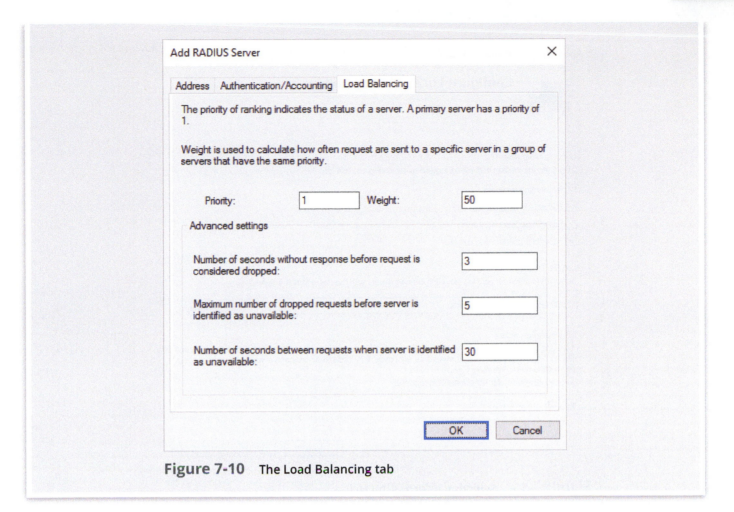

Figure 7-10   The Load Balancing tab

Activity 7-6: Configuring RADIUS Accounting

Time Required: 5 minutes
Objective: Configure RADIUS accounting to write to an XML-formatted text file.
Required Tools and Equipment: ServerDC1, ServerDM1, ServerSA1
Description: In this activity, you set up RADIUS accounting to have it write information to a standard XML-formatted text file.

1. On ServerDC1, open the **Network Policy Server** console, and click **Accounting** in the left pane.
2. Click **Configure Accounting** in the right pane to start the Accounting Configuration Wizard.
3. Read the information in the first window, and then click **Next**.
4. In the Select Accounting Options window, click the **Log to a text file on the local computer** option, and then click **Next**.
5. In the Configure Local File Logging window, be sure that the **Accounting requests, Authentication requests, Periodic accounting status**, and **Periodic authentication status** check boxes are all selected (see Figure 7-11), and then click **Next** twice. Click **Close** in the Conclusion window.
6. Using the VPN client on ServerSA1, connect using the VPN connection again. On ServerDC1, open File Explorer and navigate to **C:\Windows\System32\LogFiles**. You should see the in $yymm$ file with yy representing the year and mm representing the month, such as IN1704. You can open it to see a record of your connection attempts in XML format.
7. On ServerSA1, disconnect the VPN connection. Continue to the next activity.

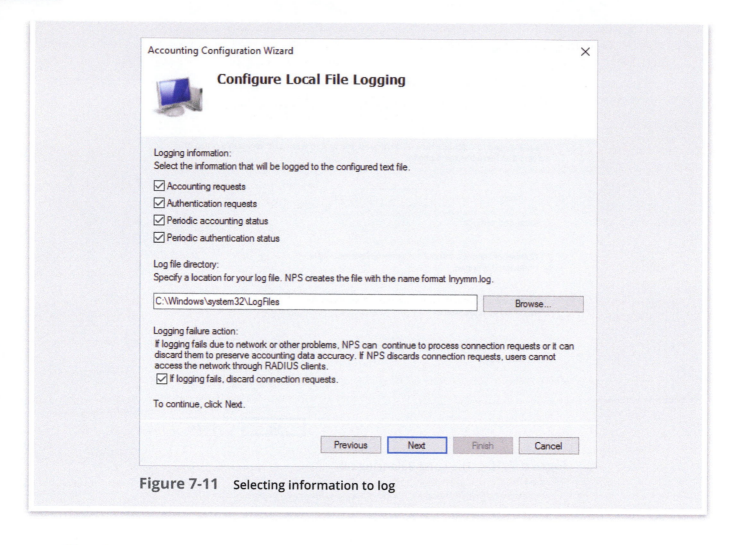

Figure 7-11   Selecting information to log

Configuring NPS Policies

 **Certification**

- 70-741 – Implement network connectivity and remote access solutions:
  Implement Network Policy Server (NPS)

NPS policies define who can connect, when they can connect, and how they can connect to the network. Two policy types are available:

- *Connection request policies*—Specify which RADIUS servers handle connection requests from RADIUS clients.
- *Network policies*—Specify which users and groups have access, the times they can access the network, and any conditions that apply.

Configuring Connection Request Policies

Connection request policies are used to specify which RADIUS servers perform authentication and authorization of RADIUS clients' connection requests. These policies can also specify to which servers RADIUS accounting requests are sent. They're applied to NPS servers configured as RADIUS servers or RADIUS proxies. Requests are authenticated and authorized by NPS acting as a RADIUS server or forwarded by NPS acting as a RADIUS proxy for authentication and authorization by another RADIUS server only if settings in the Access-Request message match at least one of the connection request policies that have been configured. You can define connection request policies for the following NAS types:

- *Unspecified*—Process or forward connection requests from any type of NAS, depending on whether the server receiving the message is configured as a RADIUS server or RADIUS proxy.
- *Remote Desktop Gateway*—Process or forward connection requests from an NAS that's managing connections from Remote Desktop clients.
- *Remote access server (VPN-dial up)*—Process or forward requests from an NAS that's managing dial-up and VPN connections.
- *Vendor specific*—Process or forward requests from an NAS with proprietary RADIUS attributes not included in RFC 2865 and 2866, which list the standard RADIUS attributes.

Note

For a policy to apply to an 802.1x authenticating switch (such as several types of Cisco switches that can act as RADIUS clients) or a wireless access point, the NAS type must be Unspecified.

When a RADIUS server receives a RADIUS Access-Request message from a RADIUS client, the client's attributes are checked against the connection request policy's conditions. The attributes in the Access-Request message must match at least one of the conditions in the policy before the NPS server acts as a RADIUS server (authenticating and authorizing the connection request) or a RADIUS proxy (passing the request on to a RADIUS server for authentication and authorization). Creating conditions allows you to control who can access the network, how they can access it, and when they can access it based on the NAS that the client is using to request access. For example, you might decide that dial-in users should be allowed to connect anytime on Sunday but only during certain times on other days of the week. The condition you set up would specify that users can connect on Monday through Saturday, 7:00 a.m. to 6:00 p.m., and from midnight Saturday to midnight Sunday. You could also limit access to certain user names or user names starting with certain characters (such as an abbreviation for a project group or a company).

The following groups of condition attributes can be used in a connection request policy to compare with the attributes of the RADIUS Access-Request message:

- *User name*—Restricts access to certain user names, which can be partial names or a pattern to match
- *Connection properties*—Restrict access to certain IPv4 or IPv6 addresses, service types, such as PPP or Telnet, and tunnel types such as Point-to-Point Tunneling Protocol (PPTP) or Layer Two Tunneling Protocol (L2TP)
- *Day and time restrictions*—Restrict access to specific days and times
- *RADIUS client properties*—Specifies information about the RADIUS client such as phone number, IP address, RADIUS client computer name, and RADIUS client vendor name
- *Gateway properties*—Specify where a client is connecting from, such as the NAS IP address, or port type (for example, VPN, Ethernet, or cable)

Note

In Activity 7-3, you created a connection request policy automatically when you were setting up and configuring a RADIUS server, but you can also add policies after a server has been configured.

Configuring Network Policies

After you have configured RADIUS servers and clients defined in connection request policies, you need to specify who can connect to the network and under what conditions. To do this, you create network policies. Connection request policies are specific to an NAS type, but network polices affect all clients who are trying to connect. For these policies, you must configure at least one condition. As with connection request policies, there are groups of conditions for determining access, each with attributes to compare to the incoming request:

- *Groups*—Specify user or computer groups created in Active Directory Domain Services that the client must be a member of to match the policy. Using this condition, you can restrict access to users or computers belonging to a particular Windows group, computers belonging to a particular machine group, or users who are members of a particular user group.
- *Day and time restrictions*—Specify days and times clients can or can't access the network.
- *Connection properties*—Specify attributes for how the access client is connecting to the network. This condition compares attributes such as the access client's (not the RADIUS client's) IP address, the authentication method being used, the framing protocol (for example, PPP), the service being used (such as Telnet or PPTP), and the tunnel type (PPTP or L2TP). This condition could be used to restrict access for clients with a particular IP address yet allow access for other clients using the same NAS.
- *RADIUS client properties*—Specify RADIUS attributes the client must have to match the policy. For example, you could restrict access to RADIUS clients that have a certain IP address or fall in a specified range of addresses.

> **Note** 📎
>
> A RADIUS client's IP address isn't the same as an access client's IP address. This condition applies to all access clients connecting via a particular NAS type, such as a VPN server.

- *Gateway*—Specify NAS attributes, such as the phone number, name, IP address, and port type. For example, this condition can limit access to connection requests from an NAS with a particular IP address or clients requesting access via a wireless connection.

In addition to network policy conditions, you can specify network policy constraints. Constraints are similar to conditions with one major difference. If a condition in a policy isn't met, NPS continues trying to find a match in the remaining conditions. If a constraint doesn't match the connection request, however, no further policies are checked, the request is rejected, and access to the network is denied. You can configure the following constraints found in the Constraints tab of a network policy's Properties dialog box:

- *Authentication method*—The authentication method used when requesting access
- *Idle timeout*—The maximum number of minutes an NAS can be idle before dropping the connection
- *Session timeout*—The maximum number of minutes a user can remain connected to the network
- *Called station ID*—The phone number of the dial-up server (NAS) that access clients use
- *Day and time restrictions*—The schedule of days and times access is allowed
- *NAS port type*—The allowed access client's media type (such as phone lines or VPNs)

Configuring Network Policies for Virtual Private Networks

VPNs are common methods of accessing networks remotely and securely. Because VPNs access a network remotely, using a network policy to control how they can access your network is a natural choice. The authentication type for a VPN can be password based or certificate based. Certificate-based methods are more secure, but you must have a valid CA certificate installed on every computer connecting via the VPN and client certificates installed on each computer. Some of the settings made in the Routing and Remote Access console when you configure a network policy are particularly applicable to VPNs:

- *Multilink and Bandwidth Allocation Protocol (BAP)*—Handle connection types that include multiple channels (for example, ISDN). You can adjust how multilink connections are handled and modify BAP parameters to specify when to drop the extra connections.
- *IP filters*—Filter access based on the client computer's IP address. You can permit or disallow packets from a particular address or network and restrict access to certain ports and protocols.
- *Encryption settings*—Specify which encryption strengths you allow. The choices are Basic, Strong, Strongest, and No encryption (not recommended). All are supported by RRAS, but some third-party clients might not support them. The connection tries the strongest type first and then moves to the weaker choices, if needed.
- *IP settings*—Adjust how IP addresses are assigned to the access client. The choices are Server must supply an IP address, Client may request an IP address, Server settings determine IP address assignment (the default), and Assign a static IPv4 address.

Managing NPS and RADIUS Templates

Templates can reduce the amount of work and minimize the chance of error, especially when many RADIUS servers and clients need to be configured. You can use NPS or RADIUS templates to reuse settings on the local server or export settings to other NPS servers. If you have many NPS servers and proxies to manage, templates can save time and prevent configuration errors when you're replacing a server or adding a new one.

Note

Template settings apply only when the template is selected and actually applied in a RADIUS configuration; merely creating a template has no effect on a server's configuration.

Templates are in the Network Policy Server console under the Templates Management node. There are four template types:

- *Shared Secrets*—Specify a reusable password for validating a connection between RADIUS servers and proxies and NAS servers.
- *RADIUS Clients*—Specify reusable RADIUS client settings.
- *Remote RADIUS Servers*—Specify reusable RADIUS server settings.
- *IP Filters*—Specify reusable lists of the IPv4 and IPv6 addresses of allowed destinations.

Exporting and Importing Templates

NPS can export templates to an XML file that can then be imported to another NPS server, which is particularly useful when you're setting up multiple NPS servers that should be configured the same way (for example, a server group). To export a template, open the Network Policy Server console. Right-click Templates Management and click Export Templates to a File. Select a location for the file, enter a name, and click Save.

To import a template, open the Network Policy Server console. Right-click Templates Management and click Import Templates from a File. Navigate to and select the XML file, and click Open. You can also click Import Templates from a Computer and enter the name of another NPS server on your network.

Importing and Exporting NPS Policies

After configuring policies and templates, you can back up the entire NPS configuration by exporting it to an XML file. You can keep it to restore the configuration, if needed, or use it to configure other NPS servers in your network. To export an NPS backup file, follow these steps in the Network Policy Server console:

1. In the left pane, right-click the NPS (Local) node and click Export Configuration. In the message box about exporting shared secrets, click the *I am aware that I am exporting all shared secrets* check box, and then click OK.

2. Choose a name and location to save the XML file, and click Save.

3. To restore the configuration, right-click the NPS (Local) node and click Import Configuration. Navigate to the XML file, and click Open.

To perform this same task from the command line, follow these steps:

1. Open a command prompt window. Type `netsh` and press Enter. At the `netsh` prompt, type `nps` and press Enter.

2. Type `export filename=`*path*`\NPSconfig.xml exportPSK=YES`, replacing *path* with the location you specified and `NPSconfig.xml` with a name of your choosing, and press Enter.

3. To import the file on this server or another server, type `netsh` and press Enter.

4. Type `nps` and press Enter, and then type `import filename="`*path*`\`*filename*`.xml"` and press Enter.

5. You get a message stating that the import was successful. Close the command prompt window.

Activity 7-7: Creating a Connection Request Policy

Time Required: 10 minutes
Objective: Create a connection request policy.
Required Tools and Equipment: ServerDC1
Description: In a previous activity, you created a connection request policy by configuring a RADIUS server with a wizard, but in this activity, you create a connection request policy manually.

1. On ServerDC1, open **Network Policy Server**.

2. In the left pane, expand **Policies**, and then right-click **Connection Request Policies** and click **New** to start the New Connection Request Policy wizard. Enter **TestCRP** for the name of the policy. Leave **Unspecified** selected in the *Type of network access server* drop-down list and click **Next**.

3. In the Specify Condition window, click **Add** to open the Select condition dialog box (see Figure 7-12).

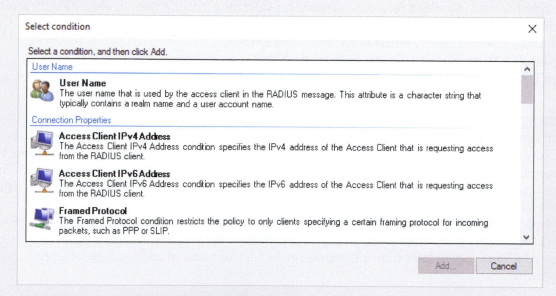

Figure 7-12 The Select condition dialog box

4. Scroll down and click **Tunnel Type**, and then click **Add** to open the Tunnel Type dialog box. Click **GRE, L2TP, PPTP**, and **SSTP** to allow a wide variety of VPN tunnels, and then click **OK**. Click **Next**.

5. In the Specify Connection Request Forwarding window, leave the **Authenticate requests on this server** option selected, and leave the default accounting settings (see Figure 7-13). You can also use this window to forward requests to a RADIUS server group if you want these functions to be performed elsewhere. Click **Next**.

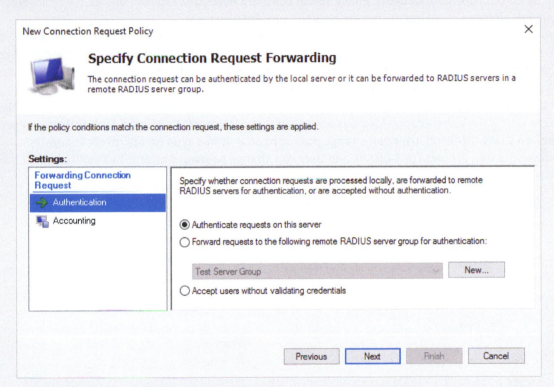

Figure 7-13   The Specify Connection Request Forwarding window

6. In the Specify Authentication Methods window, you can override the authentication methods specified in the network policy, if needed. For this activity, leave the **Override network policy authentication settings** check box cleared, and click **Next**.

7. In the Configure Settings window, you can enter a realm name or a RADIUS attribute, if needed. Click **Next**, and then click **Finish** in the Completing Connection Request Policy Wizard window.

8. Continue to the next activity.

Tip (i)

Policies are processed until a matching one is found. To make sure more specific policies are evaluated, place them higher in the list than general policies.

Activity 7-8: Creating a VPN Client Network Policy

Time Required: 10 minutes

Objective: Create a network policy for VPN clients.

Required Tools and Equipment: ServerDC1

Description: Network policies help determine what resources a client can access in the network. In this activity, you set up a network policy for VPN clients to give only domain users access to network resources.

1. On ServerDC1, open the **Network Policy Server** console if necessary, expand **Policies**, right-click **Network Policies**, and then click **New** to start the New Network Policy wizard.

2. Type **Test VPN Policy** in the Policy name text box, click **Remote Access Server (VPN-Dial up)**, and then click **Next**.

3. In the Specify Conditions window, click **Add** to open the Select condition dialog box. Click **Windows Groups**, and then click **Add** to open the Windows Groups dialog box. Click **Add Groups**, type **Domain Users**, click **Check Names**, and click **OK** twice. Click **Next**.

4. In the Specify Access Permission window, leave the default **Access granted** selected, and then click **Next**.

5. In the Configure Authentication Methods window, click the **Microsoft Encrypted Authentication Protocol version 2 (MS-CHAP v2), User can change password after it has expired, Microsoft Encrypted Authentication Protocol (MS-CHAP)**, and **User can change password after it has expired** check boxes, if necessary (see Figure 7-14), and then click **Next**.

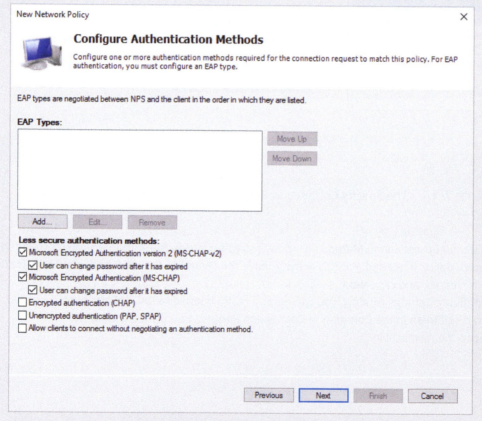

Figure 7-14   Configuring authentication methods

6. In the Configure Constraints window, review the possible options, and click **Next** to go to the Configure Settings window where you can specify settings such as standard and vendor-specific RADIUS attributes, NAP settings, and RRAS settings. Click **Next**.

7. In the Completing New Network Policy window, click **Finish**.

8. Continue to the next activity.

Activity 7-9: Creating a Shared Secret Template

Time Required: 5 minutes

Objective: Create and apply a shared secret template.

Required Tools and Equipment: ServerDC1

Description: In this activity, you create a template to set the shared secret between ServerDC1 (the RADIUS server) and ServerDM1 (the RADIUS client).

1. On ServerDC1, open the Network Policy Server console, if necessary.
2. In the left pane, expand **Templates Management**, right-click **Shared Secrets**, and then click **New**.
3. Type **Test Shared Secret** as the template's name and **Password01** in the Shared secret and Confirm shared secret boxes, and then click **OK**.
4. In the left pane, expand **RADIUS Clients and Servers**, and click **RADIUS Clients**. In the right pane, right-click **ServerDM1** (the RADIUS client) and click **Properties**. In the Shared Secret section, click **Test Shared Secret** in the drop-down list (see Figure 7-15), and then click **OK**.
5. Shut down all servers.

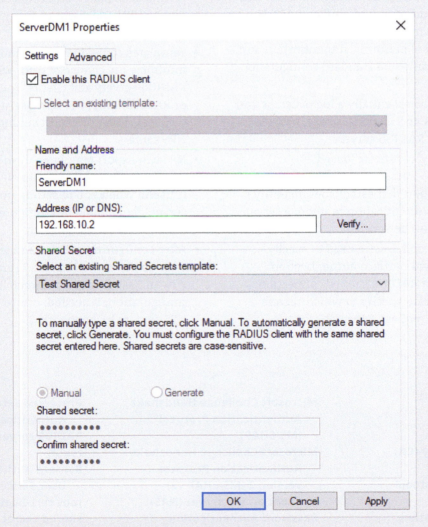

Figure 7-15   Setting the Shared Secret template

Chapter Summary

- Ensuring that unauthorized access to the network is blocked is the first line of defense. Knowing who is allowed access and by what methods can help limit attacks on the network and make creating and monitoring security policies easier.

- Network Policy Server (NPS) is Microsoft's implementation of the RADIUS protocol, a proposed IETF standard that's widely used to centralize authentication, authorization, and accounting.

- There are two main reasons you should set up an NPS architecture with RADIUS when you have different connection paths to your network. First, RADIUS centralizes control over authentication and authorization. Second, standardizing on RADIUS requires all NAS devices to be RADIUS clients so that only one protocol performs authentication and authorization, and only one standard configuration process is used.

- RADIUS accounting is essentially a log of access and accounting requests and responses sent between RADIUS clients and RADIUS servers.

- For stronger security, certificate-based authentication is recommended; it uses a certificate containing information that establishes an entity's identity. With this authentication method, a server's or client's identity can be verified.

- Connection request policies are used to specify which RADIUS servers perform authentication and authorization of RADIUS clients' connection requests. They can also specify to which servers RADIUS accounting requests are sent.

- After configuring RADIUS servers and clients defined in connection request policies, you need to specify who can connect to the network and under what conditions by creating a network policy.

- VPNs are common methods of accessing networks remotely and securely. A network policy should be used to control how VPN clients can access a network.

- The authentication type for a VPN can be password based or certificate based. Certificate-based methods are more secure, but you must have a valid CA certificate installed on every computer connecting via the VPN and client certificates installed on each computer.

- Templates can reduce the amount of work and minimize the chance of error when configuring RADIUS servers and clients. You can use NPS or RADIUS templates to reuse settings on the local server or export settings to other NPS servers.

- NPS can export templates to an XML file that can then be imported to another NPS server, which is useful when you're setting up multiple NPS servers that should be configured the same way (for example, a server group).

- After configuring policies and templates, you can back up the entire NPS configuration by exporting it to an XML file. You can keep it to restore the configuration, if needed, or use it to configure other NPS servers in a network.

Key Terms

access client
certificate-based authentication
certification authority (CA)
Challenge Handshake Authentication Protocol (CHAP)
Extensible Authentication Protocol (EAP)

Microsoft Challenge Handshake Authentication Protocol (MS-CHAP)
Microsoft Challenge Handshake Authentication Protocol version 2 (MS-CHAP v2)
network access server (NAS)
Password Authentication Protocol (PAP)

Protected Extensible Authentication Protocol (PEAP)
RADIUS server group
realm
Remote Authentication Dial In User Service (RADIUS)
root certificate
shared secret
Transport Layer Security (TLS)

Review Questions

1. Which of the following can function as a RADIUS client? (Choose all that apply.)
   a. A VPN server
   b. An unmanaged switch
   c. A wireless access point
   d. A dial-in server

2. Which authentication methods does NPS use? (Choose all that apply.)
   a. Passwords
   b. Smart cards
   c. Certificates
   d. Biometrics

3. What is the maximum size of a shared secret?
   a. 128 characters
   b. 64 characters
   c. 32 characters
   d. 256 characters

4. What client authentication method can PEAP use? (Choose all that apply.)
   a. Passwords
   b. Certificates
   c. Biometrics
   d. None of the above

5. What criteria can a RADIUS proxy use to determine where to forward a request? (Choose all that apply.)
   a. The priority assigned the server
   b. The weight assigned the server
   c. The availability of the server
   d. The IP address of the server

6. To what formats does RADIUS accounting write? (Choose all that apply.)
   a. Event log
   b. SQL Server
   c. RADIUS accounting format
   d. Text file

7. What do connection request policies specify?
   a. Which RADIUS servers handle connection requests from RADIUS clients
   b. Which users and groups can connect, what times they can access the network, and what conditions apply
   c. a and b
   d. None of the above

8. What do network policies specify?
   a. Which RADIUS servers handle connection requests from RADIUS clients
   b. Which users and groups can connect, what times they can access the network, and what conditions apply

   c. a and b
   d. None of the above

9. To make a connection request policy apply to a wireless access point, the NAS type must be set to which of the following?
   a. Wireless access point
   b. 802.11
   c. Unspecified
   d. None of the above

10. Which of the following is *not* a template type?
    a. Certificates
    b. Shared secrets
    c. RADIUS clients
    d. Remote RADIUS servers

11. Authentication methods can be overridden by using which of the following?
    a. Connection Request Policies
    b. Network Policy node
    c. Override policy
    d. Templates

12. When all NPS policies on an NPS server are exported, what else is exported?
    a. The RADIUS accounting log
    b. Physical device names
    c. Shared secrets
    d. A list of client access devices

13. RADIUS proxies distribute requests equally between servers when which of the following is true?
    a. The load balancing attribute is set.
    b. The servers have the same priority.
    c. Each server has a different weight.
    d. The servers have the same weight.

14. Which of the following are possible responses from an NPS server when evaluating an Access-Request message? (Choose all that apply.)
    a. Access-Reject
    b. Access-Deny
    c. Access-Accept
    d. Access-Challenge

15. Which of the following is an authentication type for EAP and is a cryptographic protocol used to encrypt network messages?
    a. System Extensible Protocol
    b. Transport Layer Security
    c. Protected Extensible Authentication Protocol
    d. Password Authentication Protocol

16. When a connection request requires authentication from another domain controller and is sent to an NPS server acting as a RADIUS proxy, what specific part of the network policy determines the server to which the request is routed?
    a. Realm
    b. PEAP
    c. Priority
    d. Weight

17. When a certificate is used for authentication, the certification authority must be trusted by the client or server. To be trusted, it must have which of the following in the Trusted Root Certification Authorities certificate store?
    a. Trusted CA
    b. CA certificate
    c. Client certificate
    d. Authenticated certificate

18. Which of the following NPS template types can specify a reusable password for validating a connection between RADIUS servers and proxies and NAS servers?
    a. System health agent
    b. NPS agent
    c. System health validator
    d. Shared Secrets

19. When configuring network policies, after you have configured your RADIUS servers and clients, which specific policy allows you to specify attributes for how the access client is connecting to the network?
    a. Day and time restrictions
    b. Connection properties
    c. RADIUS client properties
    d. Gateway properties

20. When a RADIUS server receives a RADIUS Access-Request message from a RADIUS client, which of the following are checked against the connection request policy's conditions?
    a. Client's permissions
    b. Radius server's attributes
    c. Group policies
    d. Client's attributes

Critical Thinking

The following activities give you critical thinking challenges. Case Projects offer a scenario with a problem to solve and for which you supply a written solution.

Case Project 7-1: Adding a RADIUS Infrastructure

CSM Tech Publishing is growing. To keep building costs down, it's allowing more people to work from home and connect to the network via a VPN. For this reason, the CIO has asked you to propose a RADIUS infrastructure. The resources users access are about the same as though they were logged on at the office. The only external access to the network is through a VPN, and the internal infrastructure uses switches that don't perform any kind of authentication. Although not many people are currently working from home, the number is expected to grow quickly if things work out well. Given these considerations, what suggestions should you give the CIO?

Case Project 7-2: Setting Up Remote Access for Contractors

Several new projects are being staffed by outside contractors who will be working on servers in the contractors' office, not in the company building, and will have their own VPN server. The contracting company has informed your company that none of its people will be working weekends. What VPN controls can you set up to minimize contract employees' access to your network?

CHAPTER 8

CONFIGURING DISTRIBUTED FILE SYSTEM AND BRANCHCACHE

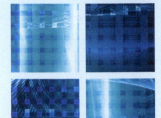

After reading this chapter and completing the exercises, you will be able to:

Describe the Distributed File System (DFS) architecture

Configure DFS servers

Create DFS replication groups

Describe the BranchCache role service

Configure BranchCache

As networks continue to grow and the need for easy access to documents and other types of files increases, making sure your users have the access they need becomes more challenging. In addition, you must ensure the security and availability of their files. The Distributed File System (DFS) is a tool for meeting all these challenges. In this chapter, you learn how to configure DFS namespaces and replication, two of the main components of the DFS role service. You also learn about BranchCache, a file-sharing technology that allows computers at a branch office to cache files retrieved from a central server across a WAN link. Using BranchCache improves file-sharing performance for branch office users and reduces WAN link usage. This chapter discusses the requirements and configuration steps for deploying BranchCache in a multisite network.

Table 8-1 summarizes what you need for the hands-on activities in this chapter.

Activity	Requirements	Notes
Table 8-1 — Activity requirements		
Activity 8-1: Resetting Your Virtual Environment	ServerDC1, ServerDM1, ServerDM2	
Activity 8-2: Installing the DFS Namespace and DFS Replication Role Services	ServerDC1, ServerDM1, ServerDM2	
Activity 8-3: Creating a Domain-Based Namespace	ServerDC1, ServerDM1, ServerDM2	
Activity 8-4: Creating a Replication Group	ServerDC1, ServerDM1, ServerDM2	
Activity 8-5: Configuring BranchCache on a File Server	ServerDC1, ServerDM1	
Activity 8-6: Configuring BranchCache on a Client	ServerDC1, ServerDM1, ServerDM2	

An Overview of the Distributed File System

Certification

- **70-741 – Implement core and distributed network solutions:**
  Implement Distributed File System (DFS) and Branch Office solutions

A network can have any number of file servers, each with its own storage. Shares make it easy for users to access parts of this storage, but as the number of servers increases, so do the number of shares, and productivity suffers when users must try to navigate a complex maze of server names and share names. **Distributed File System (DFS)** is a role service under the File and Storage Services role that enables you to group shares from different servers into a single logical share called a **namespace**. Users see each namespace as a share with subfolders, giving them access to files that are actually stored on different servers. The DFS Namespaces role service is used to create and manage these logical shares.

DFS has four main components as shown in Figure 8-1:

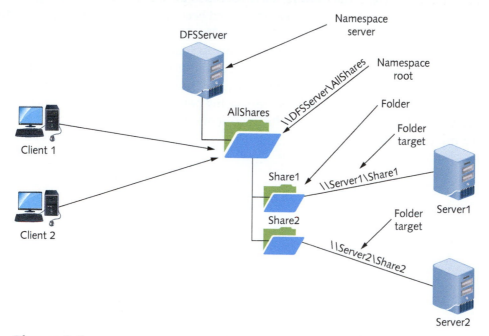

Figure 8-1 Namespace organization

- *Namespace server*—A **namespace server** is a Windows server with the DFS Namespaces role service installed.
- *Namespace root*—The **namespace root** is a folder that's the logical starting point for a namespace. It contains one or more folders or folder targets but no files. To access it, you use a UNC path, such as \\Domain1\AllShares or \\DFSServer\AllShares. In Figure 8-1, AllShares is the name of the namespace root. The domain name is used in the UNC path for a domain-based namespace; the server name is used for a stand-alone namespace. (Domain-based and stand-alone namespaces are discussed later in "Creating a Namespace.")
- *Folder*—A folder can be used to organize the namespace without containing any actual files, or a folder can contain one or more folder targets. A folder without folder targets simply adds structure to the namespace hierarchy. For example, a folder named Marketing Docs might contain one or more folders with folder targets that are shared folders containing files for the Marketing Department. In Figure 8-1, Share1 and Share2 are folders, and both contain folder targets.
- *Folder target*—A **folder target** is a UNC path that points to a shared folder hosted on a server. A folder can have one or more folder targets. If there's more than one folder target, the files are usually replicated between servers to provide fault tolerance. In Figure 8-1, the folder target for Share 1 is \\Server1\Share1, and for Share2, it's \\Server2\Share2. The folder names can be the same as the share name, but they don't have to be.

In Figure 8-1, the two client computers need to know only the name of the namespace server (or the domain name) and the DFS root folder to access Share1 and Share2 even though the shares are actually hosted on Server1 and Server2.

Increasing ease of access, however, increases the consequences of file loss (because more users have access to files) and means that files must be more available throughout an organization. Increased loads mean servers might go down, which could make the files stored on them inaccessible to users. One way to help ensure reliable access to files is to use **replication** to make copies of files in different locations as shown in Figure 8-2. In this figure, the shares are replicated between the two file servers, so if either server becomes unavailable, the files in the shares are still accessible through the other server. There are several ways to use DFS replication, including replicating the entire DFS namespace. In this example, the DFS Replication role service must be installed on Server1 and Server2.

Combining these two server roles makes it possible to set up access to files in easy-to-access logical groups and maintain copies of critical files to minimize loss and downtime in case of a server failure. You can also configure them to work together to provide failover to help ensure continuous access for users.

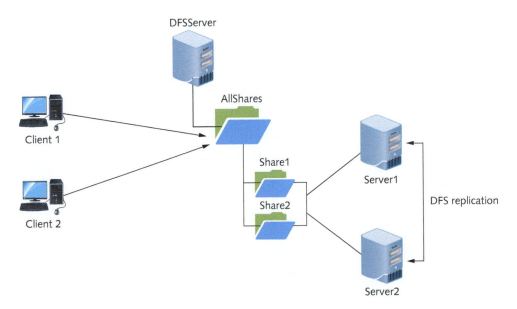

Figure 8-2   DFS replication

> **Note**
>
> DFS replication isn't designed to be a substitute for regular backups, but it can be used to enhance backup effectiveness and efficiency. For example, files can be replicated to a central location where a single backup can be done.

Installing and Configuring DFS

 **Certification**

- **70-741 – Implement core and distributed network solutions:**
  Implement Distributed File System (DFS) and Branch Office solutions

To use DFS namespaces and replication, you must install the DFS Namespaces and DFS Replication role services. In the Add Roles and Features Wizard, these role services are under the File and Storage Services role and the File and iSCSI Services role service. To install DFS Namespaces and DFS Replication using PowerShell, run the following cmdlets in a PowerShell window:

```
Install-WindowsFeature FS-DFS-Namespace -IncludeManagementTools
Install-WindowsFeature FS-DFS-Replication -IncludeManagementTools
```

After installing the two role services, you can manage your namespaces and replication using the DFS Management console (see Figure 8-3) or using a number PowerShell cmdlets. To see a list of PowerShell cmdlets for managing the DFS namespace, use the cmdlet `Get-Command -Module DFSN`. To see a list of PowerShell cmdlets for managing DFS replication, use the cmdlet `Get-Command -Module DFSR`.

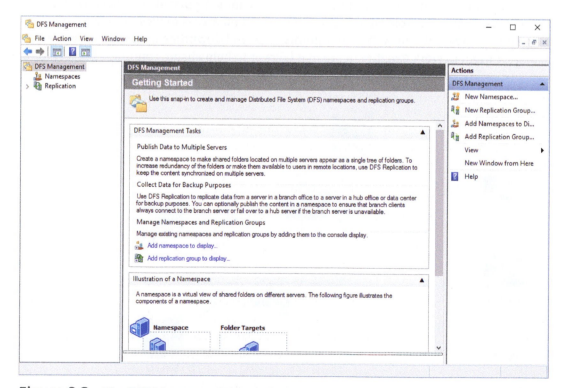

Figure 8-3   The DFS Management console

Creating a Namespace

After the DFS Namespace role service is installed, you can begin creating namespaces. Remember that a namespace doesn't actually contain the shares (and the files in them); instead, it's a list of pointers to the shares referred to in the namespace. Review Figure 8-1; the Namespace server doesn't actually host the shares but contains pointers to the shares residing on other servers; to users, however, the shares appear to all reside in one place.

> **Note** 📎
>
> The server that hosts the namespace can host some of the shares contained in the namespace.

There are two types of namespaces: domain based and stand-alone. The type you choose depends on several factors: whether you're using Active Directory, the availability requirements of the namespace, the number of folders needed in a namespace, and the need for access-based enumeration. **Access-based enumeration** is a feature of the Windows file system that allows users to see only files and folders in a File Explorer window or in a list of files from the `dir` command to which they have been given at least read (or equivalent) permission.

A namespace must be stored somewhere on the network, and the type of namespace determines the storage location. A domain-based namespace enables you to increase its availability by using multiple namespace servers in the same domain. This namespace type doesn't include the server name in the namespace, making it easier to replace a namespace server or move the namespace to a different server. A stand-alone namespace stores information only on the server where it's created and includes the server name in the namespace. If this server becomes unavailable, the namespace becomes unavailable, too. However, you can improve the availability of a stand-alone namespace by creating it on a failover cluster.

In organizations with different types of users (for example, mobile and guest users in addition to regular users) and a wide variety of documents and media with varying degrees of sensitivity, being able to control file permissions is crucial. File security in DFS namespaces is managed via the same permissions as for standard files and folders: share permissions and NTFS permissions. As a general rule, adjusting permissions on shares before configuring DFS is best. However, if multiple servers and folder targets are used with DFS replication, permissions on files and folders are replicated by DFS. During namespace creation, you can specify basic permission settings or set custom permissions that apply to the entire namespace (see Figure 8-4).

Stand-alone namespaces in Windows Server 2016 can support up to 50,000 folders and access-based enumeration. The maximum number of folders and whether access-based enumeration is supported depend on whether you choose Windows Server 2008 mode or Windows 2000 Server mode. Windows Server 2008 mode is available if the domain uses the Windows Server 2008 (or higher) functional level, and all the namespace servers are running Windows Server 2008 or newer. If you choose Windows 2000 Server mode, domain-based namespaces are limited to 5000 folders and don't support access-based enumeration. During namespace creation, you choose the type of namespace you wish to create and whether Windows Server 2008 mode is enabled, which is the default option (see Figure 8-5).

After a namespace is created, you add folders to the namespace. The folders can be existing shares, or you can create new folders and shares from the DFS Management console. To create new folders, click New Folder in the Actions pane to open the New Folder dialog box. You give the folder a name and add one or more folder targets (see Figure 8-6). A folder target is specified using UNC path syntax. You can select an existing share as the folder target or create new shares on remote servers or the local server. In Figure 8-6 a new folder named Marketing was created with a target of \\ServerDM2\MktgDocs. If you specify multiple folder targets for a folder, you would do so for fault tolerance or load sharing, and you would want to have the folder targets residing on different servers.

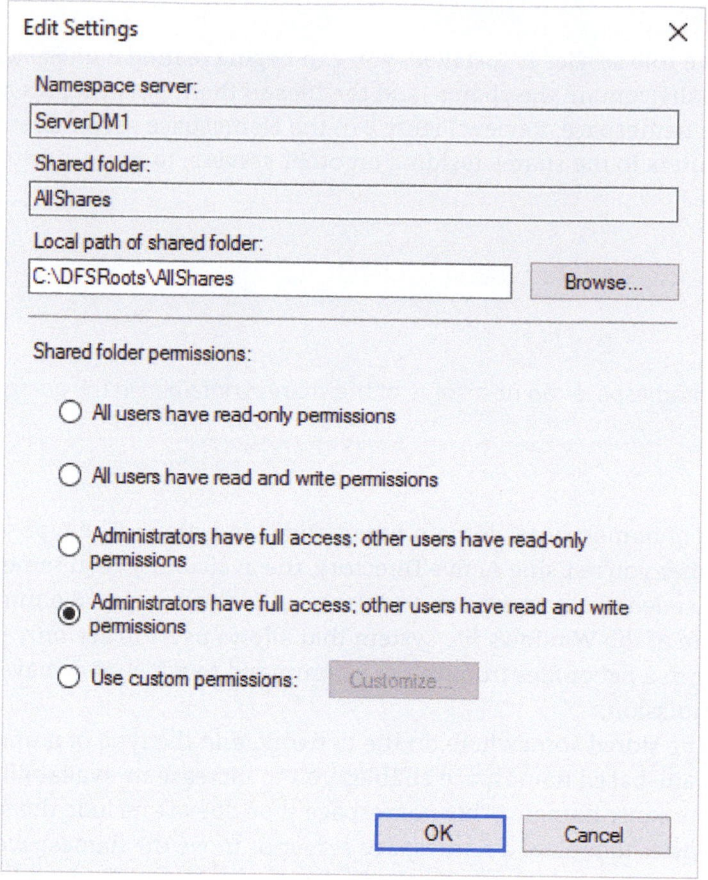

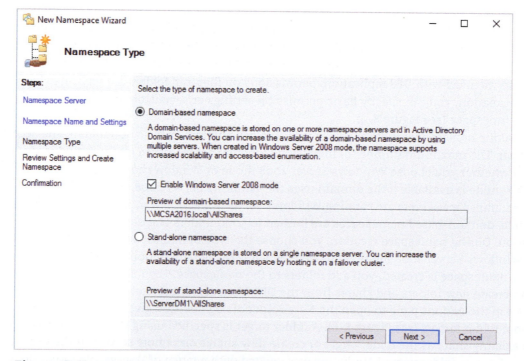

Figure 8-4 Setting namespace permissions

Figure 8-5 Selecting the namespace type

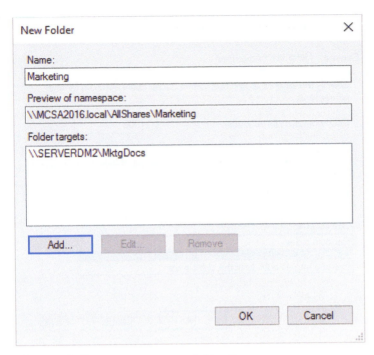

Figure 8-6   Creating a new folder for a namespace

Configuring Referrals and Advanced Namespace Settings

A simple DFS namespace with a single server for hosting the namespace and a single folder target for each folder might not require more configuration. However, if you want to add fault tolerance and load sharing to a DFS namespace, you might want to configure the namespace's properties. To do so, right-click the namespace in DFS Management and click Properties. The namespace Properties dialog box has three tabs: General, Referrals, and Advanced.

The General tab just supplies information about the namespace, such as name, type (Windows Server 2008 or Windows 2000 Server), an optional description, and the number of folders in the namespace.

You use the Referrals tab (shown in Figure 8-7) to configure how DFS works when there are multiple servers for a namespace root or folder target. Recall that the namespace root can have multiple servers hosting it, and each folder can have multiple targets. When a client attempts to access a namespace root or the underlying folders, it receives a *referral*, which is a prioritized list of servers (targets) that host the namespace or folder. The client then attempts to access the first server in the referral list. If the first server is unavailable, the client attempts to access the second server in the referral list and so forth. The first option in the Referrals tab is the cache duration, which is the time (300 seconds by default) a client keeps a referral before requesting it again. By caching the referral, the client doesn't have to request the referral list each time it accesses the namespace, thereby maximizing access speed and reducing the bandwidth needed to access the namespace.

The next option is the ordering method, which determines the order in which servers are listed in a referral and can be set to the following values:

- *Lowest cost*—Lists servers in the same Active Directory site as the client first. If there's more than one server in the site, servers in the same site as the client are listed in random order. Servers outside the client's site are listed from lowest cost to highest cost. Cost is based on the cost value assigned to a site in Active Directory Sites and Services.
- *Random order*—Similar to the "Lowest cost" option, servers in the same Active Directory site as the client are listed first. However, servers outside the client's site are ordered randomly, ignoring cost.
- *Exclude targets outside of the client's site*—The referral contains only servers in the same site as the client. If there are no servers in the client's site, the client can't access the requested part of the namespace. This method can be used to ensure that low-bandwidth connections, such as virtual private networks (VPNs), can't access shares containing large files.

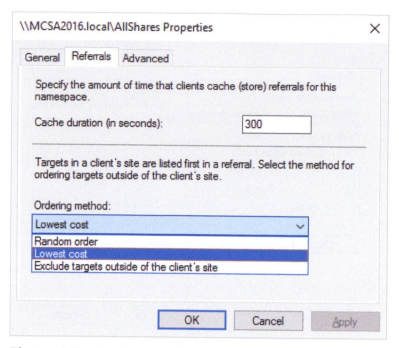

Figure 8-7   Configuring referral settings for a namespace

The last option in the Referrals tab under the Ordering method list box is *Clients fail back to preferred targets* (not shown in Figure 8-7 because it is covered by the Ordering method list). This option is important only if referral order has been overridden in the properties of the namespace server or folder target, which essentially configures a preferred target. If the option is selected and the preferred server fails, the client chooses another server from the referral list. If the preferred server comes back online, the client begins using it again.

The Advanced tab has options for configuring polling and access-based enumeration (see Figure 8-8). When namespaces change, changes are reflected instantly in a stand-alone namespace. If a domain-based namespace changes, however, information must be relayed to all the namespace servers. Namespace changes are first reported to the server in the domain holding the PDC emulator Flexible Single Master Operation (FSMO) role. The PDC emulator then replicates this information to all other domain controllers.

By default, namespace servers poll the PDC emulator to get the most current information for a namespace. In DFS configurations with many namespace servers, polling can place a considerable load on the PDC emulator. The more namespace servers in a domain, the larger the load on the PDC emulator because of increased polling. If necessary, you can configure polling options to reduce the load on the PDC emulator:

- *Optimize for consistency*—This setting is the default. In a domain with 16 or fewer namespace servers, this method is preferred because namespace servers poll the PDC emulator, which is the first DC updated after a namespace change.

- *Optimize for scalability*—This setting causes namespace servers to poll the nearest DC for namespace changes. This setting reduces the load on the PDC emulator but should be used only when there are more than the recommended 16 namespace servers in the domain. Because there's a delay between the PDC emulator getting a namespace update and the other DCs receiving it, users might have an inconsistent view of a namespace.

The last option in the Advanced tab is for enabling access-based enumeration for the namespace. Making sure only authorized users have access to sensitive data is a concern in most organizations. Restricting permissions on files and folders certainly helps, but to improve security, you can enable access-based enumeration to prevent users from even seeing files and folders they don't have permission to access.

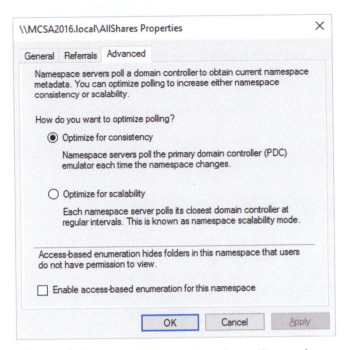

Figure 8-8   Namespace settings for polling and access-based enumeration

Overriding Referral Order

You can use the namespace Properties dialog box to configure referral settings that affect all folder targets in the namespace. However, you might want to override these settings for a particular folder target. For example, suppose that you have a folder in the namespace with two folder targets. One target is a high-performance file server, and the other server has lower performance. In this example, you might want the high-performance server to be the preferred server that clients use when accessing the folder instead of using the normal referral order.

To make changes to specific targets, you configure the properties of folder targets. In the DFS Management console, click the folder you want to change, and then right-click the folder target and click Properties. In the folder's Properties dialog box, click the Advanced tab and select the *Override referral ordering* check box (see Figure 8-9). Then select one of the following target priorities:

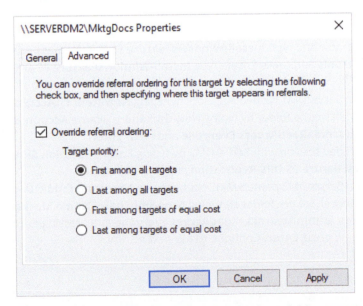

Figure 8-9   Configuring referral order for a folder target

- *First among all targets*—This server is the default target if it's available. Use this option if you want clients to always use this target to access the folder.
- *Last among all targets*—You want clients to use this target only if no other targets are available.
- *First among targets of equal cost*—If more than one target exists in a site, this target is always listed first in the referral list.
- *Last among targets of equal cost*—If more than one target exists in a site, this target is always listed last in the referral list.

Activity 8-1: Resetting Your Virtual Environment

Time Required: 5 minutes

Objective: Reset your virtual environment by applying the InitialConfig checkpoint or snapshot.

Required Tools and Equipment: ServerDC1, ServerDM1, ServerDM2

Description: Apply the InitialConfig checkpoint or snapshot to ServerDC1, ServerDM1, and ServerDM2.

1. Be sure all servers are shut down. In your virtualization program, apply the InitialConfig checkpoint or snapshot to all servers.
2. When the snapshot or checkpoint has finished being applied, continue to the next activity.

Activity 8-2: Installing the DFS Namespace and DFS Replication Role Services

Time Required: 10 minutes

Objective: Install the DFS Namespace and DFS Replication role services.

Required Tools and Equipment: ServerDC1, ServerDM1, ServerDM2

Description: Install the DFS Namespace and DFS Replication role services on ServerDM1, which will maintain the namespace, and install just the DFS Replication role service on ServerDM2. Then you create shares on both servers to be used in the next activity.

1. Make sure that ServerDC1 is running because you will be creating a domain-based namespace. Start ServerDM1 and ServerDM2 and sign in to ServerDM1 as the domain **Administrator**, if necessary.
2. Open a PowerShell window and type **Install-WindowsFeature FS-DFS-Namespace-IncludeManagementTools** and press **Enter**. Type **Install-WindowsFeature FS-DFS-Replication** and press **Enter**.
3. Create a new folder on ServerDM1 named AcctDocs by typing **New-Item C:\AcctDocs -Type Directory** and press **Enter**. Now, share the folder by typing **New-SmbShare -Name Accounting -Path c:\AcctDocs -FullAccess Administrators -ReadAccess Everyone** and press **Enter**.
4. Open a remote PowerShell session with ServerDM2 by typing **Enter-PSSession ServerDM2** and press **Enter**. Type **Install-WindowsFeature FS-DFS-Replication** and press **Enter**.
5. Create a new folder on ServerDM2 named MktDocs by typing **New-Item C:\MktDocs -Type Directory** and pressing **Enter**. Now, share the folder by typing **New-SmbShare -Name Marketing -Path c:\MktDocs -FullAccess Administrators -ReadAccess Everyone** and pressing **Enter**.
6. Type **Exit-PSSession** and press **Enter**. Continue to the next activity.

Activity 8-3: Creating a Domain-Based Namespace

Time Required: 15 minutes
Objective: Create a domain-based namespace and add shares to it.
Required Tools and Equipment: ServerDC1, ServerDM1, ServerDM2
Description: Use DFS to create a domain-based namespace, and then add several shares from ServerDM1 and ServerDM2 to this namespace. This new namespace allows users to access shared folders from a single location without needing to know on which server the files are stored.

1. Start ServerDM1, and sign in to ServerDC1 as **Administrator**, if necessary. Open Server Manager, and click **Tools**, **DFS Management** from the menu to open the DFS Management console.

2. On ServerDM1, in Server Manager, click **Tools**, **DFS Management** to open the DFS Management console. In the Actions pane, click **New Namespace** to start the New Namespace Wizard.

3. In the Namespace Server window, type **ServerDM1** to specify the server hosting the new namespace, and then click **Next**.

4. In the Namespace Name and Settings window, you specify the name of the namespace you're creating. Type **AllShares** in the Name text box. Users will access the namespace by using the UNC path \\MCSA2016\AllShares or \\ServerDM1\AllShares. Click the **Edit Settings** button to change the shared folder location and permissions. By default, the namespace is located at C:\DFSRoots*Namespace* (with *Namespace* representing the name of the namespace). All users have read-only permission by default. You can choose any of the predefined permission settings or create custom permissions. Leave the defaults and click **OK** to close the Edit Settings dialog box. Click **Next** to continue.

5. In the Namespace Type window, you choose a domain-based or stand-alone namespace. Both types show a preview of the namespace's full name. Notice that for a domain-based type, the name starts with the domain name, and for a stand-alone type, it starts with the server name. Leave the default settings *Domain-based namespace* and *Enable Windows Server 2008 mode*, and then click **Next**.

6. Verify the settings in the Review Settings and Create Namespace window. (If necessary, you can click the Previous button to change a setting.) If everything is correct, click **Create**.

7. In the Confirmation window, you should see a message indicating success. Click **Close**.

8. In the DFS Management console, click to expand **Namespaces** in the left pane, and then click the **MCSA2016.local\AllShares** namespace you created. In the middle pane, you see four tabs. The Namespace tab shows the shares that are members of the new namespace. Because you haven't added any shares, it's empty. Click the **Namespace Servers** tab to see the servers configured with the namespace (see Figure 8-10). As you learn later, more than one server can be configured with the same namespace to provide fault tolerance and load balancing.

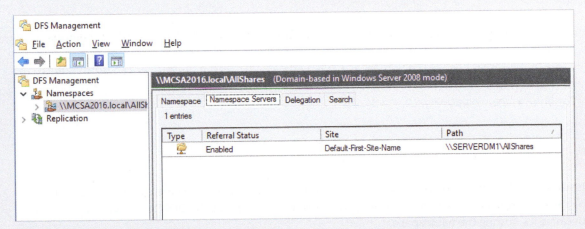

Figure 8-10   The Namespace Servers tab

9. Now it's time to add some folders to the namespace. You can add existing folders and shares or create new ones. Click the **Namespace** tab. In the Actions pane, click **New Folder**. In the New Folder dialog box, type **Accounting** in the Name text box. This name is what users see when they connect to the namespace, and it can be different from the actual share name. Click **Add**.

10. In the Add Folder Target dialog box, you can enter the folder target with its UNC name or click the Browse button and select the folder target. Click **Browse**.

11. In the Browse for Shared Folders dialog box, the shares on the current server are listed. You can click **Browse** to choose a different server, select an existing share on the current server, or create a new shared folder. Click **Accounting**, the share that you created in the previous activity, and click **OK**. Click **OK** again.

12. Back in the New Folder dialog box, notice that the UNC path to the Accounting share is added to the Folder targets list. You can add folder targets to provide fault tolerance. Click **OK**.

13. Now add the share from ServerDM2. Click **New Folder** again in the Actions pane of the DFS Management console. Type **Marketing** in the Name text box, and click **Add**. Click **Browse**. In the Browse for Shared Folders dialog box, type **ServerDM2** and click **Show Shared Folders**.

14. In the Shared Folders box, click **Marketing**, if necessary, and then click **OK**. Click **OK** twice more to return to the DFS Management console, which should now look like Figure 8-11 with both shares listed in the Namespace tab.

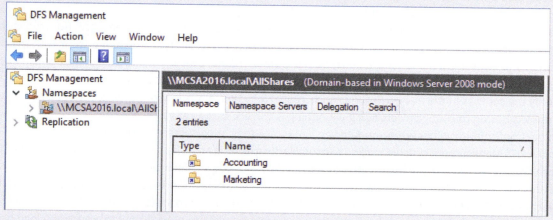

Figure 8-11 A namespace with two shares

15. To see how users would use this feature, right-click **Start**, click **Run**, type **MCSA2016\AllShares**, and press **Enter**. You see both shares, Accounting and Marketing, in File Explorer. Users could also enter the name of the server hosting the namespace, \\ServerDM1\AllShares. A drive letter can be mapped to the namespace, too.

16. Continue to the next activity.

Note 📎

Installing the DFS Namespace role service on ServerDM2 isn't required; a share can be added to a namespace from any server in the domain. Only ServerDM1 requires the DFS Namespace role service because it's hosting the namespace.

Creating DFS Replication Groups

 **Certification**

- 70-741 – Implement core and distributed network solutions:
  Implement Distributed File System (DFS) and Branch Office solutions

A **replication group** consists of servers, known as *members*, that synchronize data in folders so that when a change occurs, all replication group members are updated at once. To create a replication group, you must have a minimum of two servers. One server is designated as the primary and the other as the secondary. After a replication group is defined, you add folders to it. Files in replicated folders on the secondary server, if any, are overwritten. There are several maximums to take into account when creating a replication group:

- A single file to be replicated must be less than 250 GB.
- The number of files to be replicated on a volume must be less than 70 million.
- The total size of all replicated files on a server must be less than 100 TB.

There are two types of replication groups: a multipurpose replication group and a replication group for data collection. A multipurpose replication group contains two or more servers and is used for content sharing and document publication when you want to provide fault tolerance and load balancing for file shares. A replication group for data collection consists of only two servers and is used mainly to transfer data from one server to another for backup purposes. For example, a server in a branch office that hosts a shared folder can use this type of replication group to transfer the share's contents to a server in the main office for centralized backups.

The folders specified in replication groups need not be shared folders or part of a DFS namespace, but they often are. You can create a replication group for folders that are already part of a DFS namespace to provide fault tolerance, or you can create a replication group on shared or nonshared folders and add them to a DFS namespace later, if needed.

 Note

All servers participating in a DFS replication group must have the DFS Replication role service installed.

Optimizing DFS Replication

In many situations, simply using the default settings when creating a replication group could cause problems by overusing network bandwidth. For example, accepting the default replication schedule between servers in a replication group that communicate over a low-bandwidth WAN link could create excessive network traffic. Several features, discussed in the following sections, can be configured to meet special bandwidth, network configuration, and server load needs:

- Replication topology
- Replication scheduling
- Remote differential compression

Replication Topology

A **replication topology** describes the connections used to replicate files between servers. Three topologies are available for replication groups: Hub and spoke, Full mesh, and No topology (see Figure 8-12). With *Hub and spoke*, all members of the group synchronize with the hub only. So, a change on one member is updated on the hub, and then the hub replicates the change to all other members. This topology is available only if the group has three or more servers. You can specify a primary hub and a secondary hub for each spoke member. With a secondary hub in place, if one of the hubs goes down, members are configured to recognize the secondary hub, and replication occurs with it. The two hubs synchronize with each other. This topology reduces the overall network load because the spokes don't synchronize with each other, only with the hub. However, there can be a slight delay in propagating changes throughout the group because the hub must distribute all the changes.

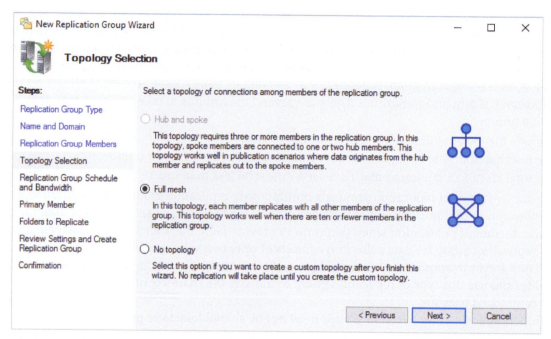

Figure 8-12   Replication topology selection

With a *Full mesh* topology, which is the default, synchronization is bidirectional, meaning that all members synchronize with each other. It's ideal when you have just a few servers. In a larger network with 10 or more members or when you have a main office connected to several branch offices, switching to a hub and spoke topology might be best to reduce network traffic. With large replication groups, the network load of communicating between all servers could become severe, depending on the replication schedule (discussed in the next section), the total number of files, the number of changes, and the overall size of files.

The *No topology* option is exactly what it sounds like: There are no initial connections, so you must define them. When would defining your own connections be useful? Say that you have a central server where changes are being made and several other servers where you want files to be available locally, but they should be read-only. You could configure a Hub and spoke topology with the central server as the hub where files are updated and the other servers as spokes with read-only copies of files (which is an option when configuring a replication group). The hub synchronizes changes with the spokes, but it's a one-way synchronization: The members never change the files, so they never replicate them back to the hub or to other members.

DFS Replication Scheduling

Scheduling can help manage peak bandwidth needs by forcing replication to occur during off hours. This option can be particularly good when you have large files that need to be replicated across lower bandwidth connections. However, keep in mind that changes made on one end of a connection usually aren't available to the other end until the next day. If the information is time sensitive, scheduling replication during off hours could cause problems if a file is changed in one location and someone uses it at another location before it is synchronized. The trade-off for the delay is more bandwidth available for other functions during peak hours.

By default, DFS replication tries to use the connection's full bandwidth when replicating files, which might not be what you want. Luckily, you can throttle (reduce) the bandwidth so that replication uses a specified maximum percentage of available bandwidth. To configure this scheduling, follow these steps in the DFS Management console:

1. In the left pane, select the replication group you want to adjust. In the Actions pane, click Edit Replication Group Schedule.

2. The Edit Schedule dialog box opens (see Figure 8-13), showing the existing schedule and bandwidth use setting. You can select a maximum percentage in the Bandwidth usage drop-down list box. If you want to adjust the schedule, click Details. Select a day and click Edit, and you can adjust the times as needed.

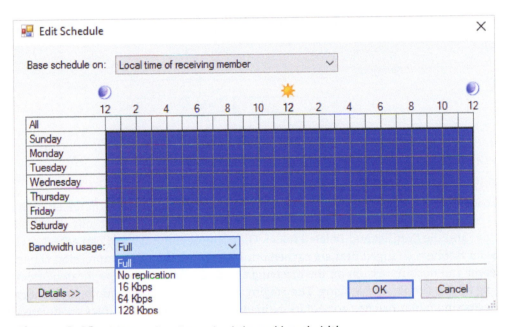

Figure 8-13   Edit replication schedule and bandwidth

Remote Differential Compression

Copying the contents of hundreds or thousands of files across a network can waste bandwidth, especially when the amount of data that actually changed is fairly small. DFS replication uses an algorithm known as **remote differential compression (RDC)**, which replicates only the changes made in files. By default, RDC is used during replication. Because only pieces of files are transmitted across the network, the use of network bandwidth is reduced. The trade-off is increased CPU and disk I/O overhead on servers because they do extra work to update files with the replicated changes. When you have a good combination of enough bandwidth and fewer files to synchronize, you might want to disable RDC. To configure RDC, follow these general steps:

1. In the DFS Management console, click the replication group in the left pane, and in the center pane, click the Connections tab.

2. Right-click a member server and click Properties. Next, clear the *Use remote differential compression (RDC)* check box, and then click Apply (see Figure 8-14).

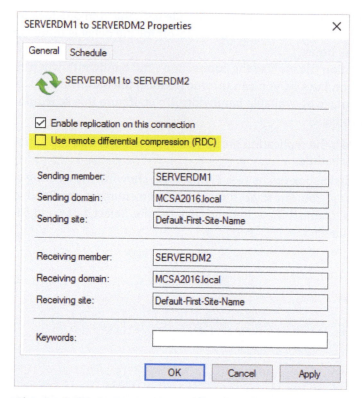

Figure 8-14 Disabling remote differential compression

Managing the Staging Folder and the Conflict and Deleted Folder

An important consideration when configuring replication groups is making sure there's enough space on each drive that hosts a replicated folder. Each drive must have space to house not only the files but also the Staging folder and the Conflict and Deleted folder. Only a local administrator can access these folders. The Staging folder is where changed files are cached until they're replicated; compression is performed on the sending server and decompression on the receiving server. By default, each replicated folder contains a hidden Staging folder: DfsrPrivate\Staging. The Staging folder's size acts as a quota, and its default size is 4 GB. When the Staging folder reaches 90% of its defined size, the oldest staged files are deleted until it's at 60%. Depending on the type of files to be replicated, its size might need to be adjusted, especially if you have extremely large files, such as multimedia files. For initial replication, which occurs from the primary server to other servers in the group when the group is created, the Staging folder should be at least as big as the combined size of the largest 32 files in the replicated folder on the primary member. If the folder is read-only, you can use the combined size of the largest 16 files. To improve replication performance or if you need more space for caching changed files, you can move the Staging folder to a different volume.

The Conflict and Deleted folder stores files that were deleted and files that have a conflict. If both copies of a file—the main copy and the replicated copy—were modified during a replication cycle, it results in a conflict between which copy to use and which one to cache. When a conflict occurs, DFS replication uses a "last-writer-wins" model to make this determination. The losing file is cached in the Conflict and Deleted folder, a hidden folder in the replicated folder named DfsrPrivate\ConflictAndDeleted. Its default size is 4 GB. The log of the original names of files stored in this folder is written to the `ConflictandDeletedManifest.xml` file, which is also in the DFSRPrivate folder. Like the Staging folder, the Conflict and Deleted folder's size can be changed, and the path can be changed to move the folder to another volume.

To manage these settings in the DFS Management console, select the replication group. In the Memberships tab, open the properties for the replicated folder and replication member you want to change. The Staging folder's settings can be changed in the Staging tab (see Figure 8-15), and the Conflict and Deleted folder can be changed in the Advanced tab (see Figure 8-16).

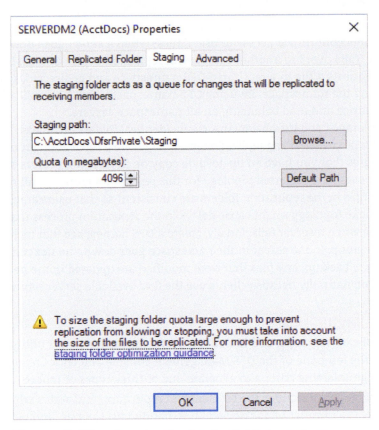

Figure 8-15   Changing the Staging folder's settings

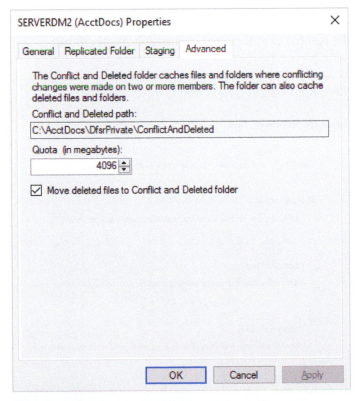

Figure 8-16   Changing the Conflict and Deleted folder's settings

DFS Fault Tolerance and Load Balancing

DFS fault tolerance ensures continuous access to users' files; when a server goes down, DFS fault tolerance automatically "fails over" to another server with replicated copies of files. Load balancing is achieved when a user requests a file in a replicated DFS namespace and is directed, via a referral, to one of the DFS servers hosting the namespace. By using DFS namespaces and DFS replication together, you can have both fault tolerance and load balancing on all namespace servers.

To configure fault tolerance and load balancing, create identical folders on at least two servers and share them. Add the folders to an existing replication group or create a replication group for this purpose. Replicating the files ensures that you have an up-to-date copy on at least two servers for fault-tolerance and load-balancing purposes. The preferred topology for this replication group is Full mesh because it makes sure all copies of files in the replication folders are consistent so that users aren't using outdated files. Using a Hub and spoke topology might cause delays in the replication process that could result in inconsistent file contents when a server fails. Finally, create a DFS namespace that includes targets of all folders in the replication group. If one server in the namespace goes down, the next target server is selected. When the original server is back up, any files that were modified are updated in the next replication cycle. Load balancing is achieved naturally because clients use the first available server returned in the referral list.

Using Replication Diagnostics

To help troubleshoot replication groups, DFS includes a useful diagnostic report utility. To use it, right-click the replication group in the left pane of the DFS Management console and click Create Diagnostic Report. A wizard guides you through selecting criteria to generate one of three types of reports (see Figure 8-17):

- *Health report*—This report describes the efficiency of replication and states whether there are any problems. It shows the number of backlogged files, bandwidth savings, and whether any servers in the group have reported errors or warnings.
- *Propagation test*—This option conducts a propagation test but doesn't actually produce a report. The test creates a test file in a replicated folder and then tests the replication (propagation) of that file to other servers in the replication group.
- *Propagation report*—This report generated from the results of the propagation test shows how long it took to replicate the test file to each server in the replication group.

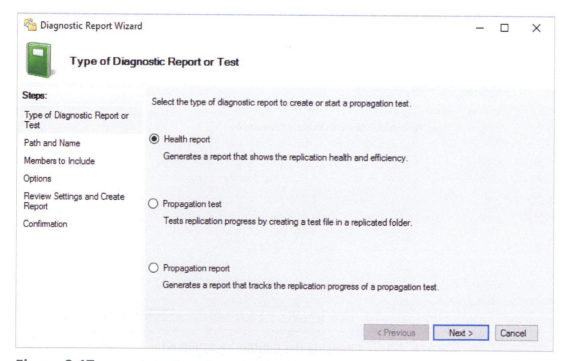

Figure 8-17 Creating DFS replication diagnostic reports

Cloning and Recovering a DFS Replication Database

One of the most resource-heavy parts of replication is the setup that the system must perform when adding replication targets, replacing a server, or recovering from the loss or corruption of a DFS replication database. The files and file metadata must be copied and set up. Much of this work can be eliminated by cloning the DFS replication database. Importing a clone of the replication database can substantially reduce this synchronization time—up to 99%, depending on the number of changes to the database that occur between exporting the clone and importing it. To create a clone, use the `Export-DfsrClone` command at a PowerShell prompt:

```
Export-DfsrClone -Volume D: -Path D:\DFSRclone
```

In this command, `D:` is the drive letter of the volume containing the DFS database you want to export, and `D:\DFSRclone` is the destination folder to which the exported replication database files are written. You then copy the folder with the exported files to a destination server for import. Next, you use the following command at a PowerShell prompt to import the clone:

```
Import-DfsrClone -Volume D: -Path D:\DFSRclone
```

A DFS replication database could become corrupted. Although Windows has features to automatically rebuild a corrupted database, this rebuilding might not work and could take a lot of time. Importing a clone can save more time than allowing the system to do the recovery automatically. There are a few factors to consider when recovering a replication database with a clone:

- Make sure there's no replicated folder on the destination volume. You can't merge a clone with an existing replication database.
- Make sure there's no write access to shares on the destination replication folders.
- Remove the destination server from the affected replication group before importing the clone.

Tip

For more on DFS replication cloning, see *http://technet.microsoft.com/library/dn482443.aspx*.

Activity 8-4: Creating a Replication Group

Time Required: 15 minutes
Objective: Configure a replication group.
Required Tools and Equipment: ServerDC1, ServerDM1, ServerDM2
Description: In this activity, you create a multipurpose replication group, which allows replicating a share on one server to another server for fault tolerance and load balancing. If one server becomes unavailable, users can access files from the other server. You use a Full mesh topology so that changes made to either server are synchronized and replicated on the other.

1. On ServerDM1, in a PowerShell window, type **New-Item C:\ReplDocs -Type Directory** and press **Enter**. Now, share the folder by typing **New-SmbShare -Name Replicated -Path c:\ReplDocs FullAccess Administrators -ReadAccess Everyone** and pressing **Enter**.
2. Create a new file in the ReplDocs folder by typing **New-Item C:\ReplDocs\testfile1.txt** and pressing **Enter**.
3. Start a PowerShell session with ServerDM2 and repeat the commands from Step 1. Then type **New-Item C:\ReplDocs\testfile2.txt** and press **Enter**. Exit the PowerShell session with ServerDM2.
4. On ServerDM1, open the DFS Management console. In the left pane, click to expand **Replication**.
5. Right-click **Replication** and click **New Replication Group** to start the New Replication Group Wizard.
6. In the Replication Group Type window, accept the default type *Multipurpose replication group*, and then click **Next**.

7. In the Name and Domain window, type **ReplGroup1** in the *Name of replication group* text box. Leave the domain set at *MCSA2016.local*, and then click **Next**.

8. In the Replication Group Members window, you add servers to participate in the group. Click **Add**, and in the Select Computers dialog box, type **ServerDM1;ServerDM2**, click **Check Names**, and click **OK**. You see a progress indicator while Windows verifies that the DFS Replication service is running on the specified servers. After the servers have been added (see Figure 8-18), click **Next**.

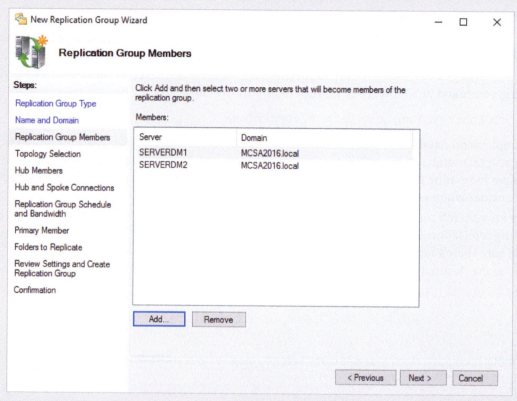

Figure 8-18   The Replication Group Members window

9. In the Topology Selection window, leave the default option **Full mesh**. Notice that the *Hub and spoke* option is grayed out because you have fewer than three servers. If you wanted to configure a custom replication topology, you would select the *No topology* option. Click **Next**.

10. In the Replication Group Schedule and Bandwidth window (see Figure 8-19), you configure scheduling and bandwidth throttling. Leave the default option *Replicate continuously using the specified bandwidth* and *Full* for the Bandwidth setting. If you select *Replicate during the specified days and times*, you can configure the replication schedule by clicking the Edit Schedule button. Click **Next**.

11. In the Primary Member window, click **ServerDM1** in the Primary member list box to make this server's contents authoritative for the replication, which means files are copied from ServerDM1 to ServerDM2, and any existing files on ServerDM2 are overwritten. Click **Next**.

12. In the Folders to Replicate window, click **Add**. In the Add Folder to Replicate dialog box, click **Browse**. In the Browse For Folder dialog box, click **ReplDocs**, and then click **OK**. Any folder, whether it's shared or not, can be in the replication group, but in this activity, you replicate the ReplDocs folder you just created (see Figure 8-20). You can change the folder name by clicking the *Use custom name* option button or leave the default folder name. You can also change permissions for the folder, if needed. Leave the default option *Existing permissions*, click **OK**, and then click **Next**.

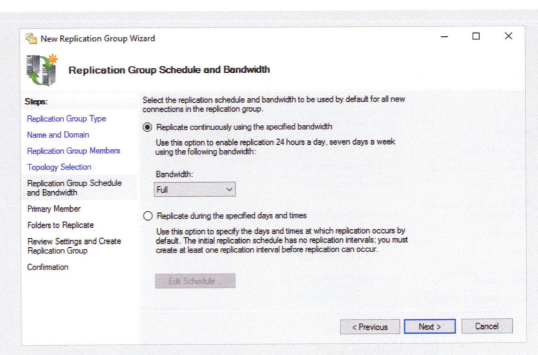

Figure 8-19   The Replication Group Schedule and Bandwidth window

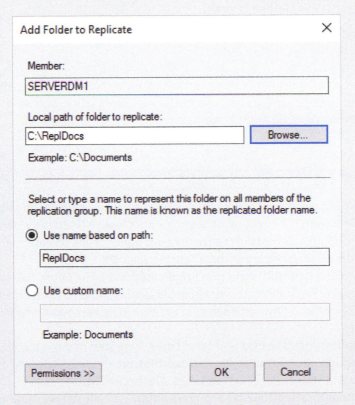

Figure 8-20   The Add Folder to Replicate dialog box

13. In the Local Path of ReplDocs on Other Members window, click **ServerDM2**, if necessary, and click **Edit**. In the Edit dialog box, click **Enabled** to enable replication on ServerDM2. Click **Browse** to select the path where data will be replicated. Click the **ReplDocs** folder, and then click **OK**. Because ServerDM1 is the primary member, files in the ReplDocs folder on ServerDM2 will be overwritten. Click **Next**.

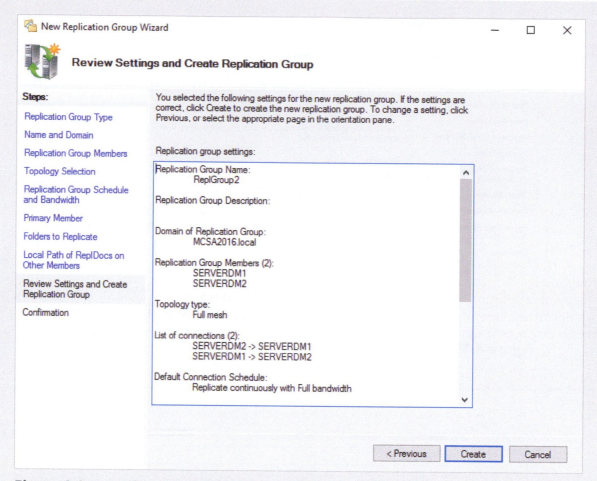

Figure 8-21 Reviewing replication group settings

14. In the Review Settings and Create Replication Group window (see Figure 8-21), verify your choices, and then click **Create**.

15. In the Confirmation window, you see the results as well as a link to a help file on staging folder optimization that has important information on replication staging. Click **Close** to finish the wizard. You see a message explaining that the replication process isn't instantaneous but depends on each member server's picking up the configuration from Active Directory Domain Services. Click **OK**.

16. In the PowerShell window, type **dir \\serverdm2\replicated** and press **Enter**. You should see only `testfile1.txt` because replication occurred from ServerDM1 to ServerDM2, erasing the `testfile2.txt` file you created on ServerDM2. (If you still see `testfile2.txt`, give replication a minute to work, and then repeat the command.)

17. Type **notepad c:\repldocs\testfile1.txt** and press **Enter**. Type your name in the file, save it, and close Notepad. Type **notepad \\serverdm2\replicated\testfile1.txt** and press **Enter** to open the file on ServerDM2. You see that your change was replicated. Close Notepad.

18. Type **New-Item C:\ReplDocs\testfile2.txt** and press **Enter**. Type **dir \\serverdm2\replicated** and press **Enter** to see that the file has been replicated to ServerDM2. If needed, you could add the replicated folder to the DFS namespace that you created earlier by selecting the replication group in the DFS Management console, clicking the Replicated Folders tab, then right-clicking ReplDocs, and clicking Share and Publish in Namespace.

19. Continue to the next activity.

An Overview of BranchCache

- **70-741 – Implement core and distributed network solutions:**
  Implement Distributed File System (DFS) and Branch Office solutions

Sharing files across a WAN link can be slow and sometimes expensive. Organizations with branch offices can solve some problems of sharing files across WAN links by placing traditional file servers in branch offices and using file replication to synchronize files between branch offices and the main office. However, this solution requires servers and someone to maintain servers and file shares, which isn't always practical or economical. **BranchCache** is a file-sharing technology that allows computers at a branch office to cache files retrieved from a central server across a WAN link. When a computer in the branch office requests a file for the first time, it's retrieved from a server in the main office and then cached locally. When a subsequent request for the file is made, only content information, not actual file contents, is transferred. This **content information** indicates to the client where the file can be retrieved from the cache in the branch office. The content information that's transferred is very small compared with the original file contents and can also be used by clients to secure cached information so that it can be accessed only by authorized users.

BranchCache supports content stored on Windows Server 2008 R2 and later servers running the following roles and protocols:

- *File Server role*—A file server sharing files by using the Server Message Block (SMB) protocol
- *Web Server (IIS) role*—A web server using the HTTP or HTTPS protocol
- *Background Intelligent Transfer Service (BITS) feature*—An application server running on a Windows server with BITS installed

BranchCache has two modes of operation, so you can configure it depending on the resources available at a branch office:

- *Distributed*—With **distributed cache mode**, cached data is distributed among client computers in the branch office. Client computers must be running Windows 7 or later.
- *Hosted*—With **hosted cache mode**, cached data is stored on one or more file servers in the branch office. Servers operating in this mode must be running Windows Server 2008 R2 or later, and clients must be running Windows 7 or later.

If you have more than one branch office, you can choose the mode that's suitable for each office, but only one mode can be used at each branch office. Figure 8-22 shows a central office with a connection to two branch offices using different BranchCache modes. In the figure, Branch office1 uses hosted cache mode in which client PCs access a central BranchCache server to retrieve cached files. Branch office2 uses distributed cache mode in which cached files are distributed among all client computers that retrieve the files from one another. In this case, the content information retrieved from servers in the main office specifies which computer hosts a requested file.

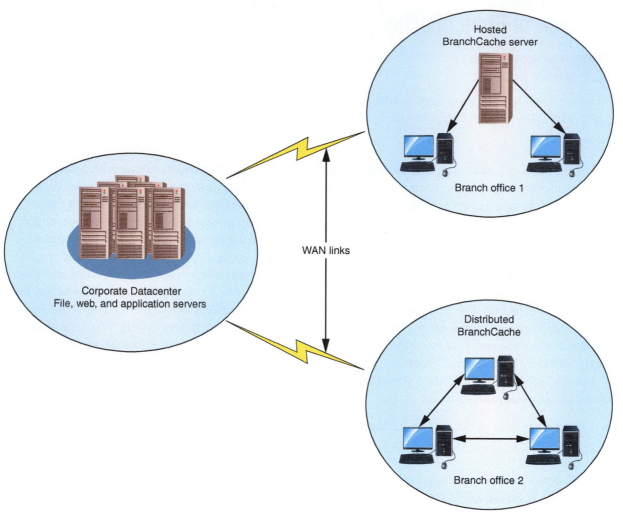

Figure 8-22   BranchCache modes of operation

Benefits of Distributed Cache Mode

Distributed cache mode is the best solution for small branch offices when having a dedicated server is neither practical nor desirable. Servers require more expertise to maintain and secure and have a higher cost than client computers. No extra equipment and no additional resources or personnel for server maintenance are necessary when using BranchCache in distributed cache mode.

Benefits of Hosted Cache Mode

Hosted cache mode is best for branch offices that already have servers performing other functions, such as a domain controller or a DHCP server. Using hosted cache mode has the following advantages over distributed cache mode:

- *Increased availability of cached files*—In distributed cache mode, if the client that cached the file is turned off, the file is unavailable to other clients. With hosted cache mode, all cached files are stored on servers, which are rarely turned off.
- *Support for multiple subnets*—A large branch office might have more than one IP subnet. Distributed cache mode works only in a single subnet, so files cached by computers on one subnet aren't available to computers on another subnet. Hosted cached mode works across subnets, so files cached by a server on one subnet are available to client computers on all subnets. You can also deploy multiple servers operating in hosted cache mode, and clients are directed to the server hosting the requested file, even if it's on a different subnet from the client.

How BranchCache Handles Changes to Cached Files

When a change is made to a cached file, clients accessing the file after the change has occurred must have a way to access the changed content. The fact that a file has changed is reflected in the content information clients retrieve from the server hosting the original file. There are two versions of the content information. Version 1 content information is the original version supported by Windows Server 2008 R2 and later and Windows 7 and later. Version 2 content information is supported by Windows Server 2012 and later and Windows 8 and later.

When a file is changed, some or all of it must be retrieved from the server hosting the original content. With version 1 content information, changes made to a file require the client to retrieve the entire file, starting with the part that changed. With version 2, only the changed part of the file must be retrieved, saving bandwidth because fewer bytes must be transferred across the WAN link. Version 2 content information can be used only when all devices involved in BranchCache support version 2; otherwise, version 1 is used. This means that the client requesting the file, the local hosted cache server, and the server hosting the original content must all be Windows 8 or Windows Server 2012 or later to use version 2 content information.

> **Note**
>
> With distributed cache mode, clients using different content information versions can't share cached files with each other.

Installing and Configuring BranchCache

 **Certification**

- **70-741 – Implement core and distributed network solutions:**
  Implement Distributed File System (DFS) and Branch Office solutions

The procedure to install and configure BranchCache depends on the type of content you want to cache and whether you're using hosted or distributed cache mode, as shown in Table 8-2.

Table 8-2   BranchCache installation

Content type	Installed on content server	Hosted cache mode	Distributed cache mode
File server using the SMB protocol	BranchCache for Network Files role service	BranchCache feature on hosting server	Enable BranchCache on client
Web server using HTTP or HTTPS	BranchCache feature	BranchCache feature on hosting server	Enable BranchCache on client
Application server using BITS	BranchCache feature	BranchCache feature on hosting server	Enable BranchCache on client

Note

In all cases, BranchCache must be enabled on client computers whether you're using hosted or distributed cache mode. After you enable BranchCache, you select the cache mode you want the client to use. If no mode is selected, the client uses only locally cached files. BranchCache is supported only in Windows 7 Ultimate and Enterprise editions, Windows 8/8.1 Enterprise editions, and Windows 10 Education and Enterprise editions.

Installing BranchCache on a File Server

To install BranchCache to cache files in shared folders, take the following steps:

1. Install the File Server role service and the BranchCache for Network Files role service on all servers that will host shared folders by using BranchCache. You can use Server Manager or the PowerShell cmdlet:

   ```
   Install-WindowsFeature FS-BranchCache
   ```

2. Configure the Hash Publication for BranchCache group policy (see Figure 8-23), located under Computer Configuration, Policies, Administrative Templates, Network, Lanman Server. In most cases, you should place the computer accounts for servers using BranchCache for shared folders in a separate OU in Active Directory and link a GPO with this policy configured to this OU. The hash publication is part of the content information that allows BranchCache servers to find a file that has been cached on the local servers.

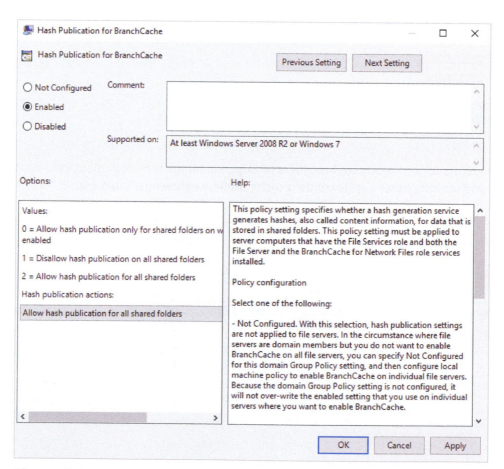

Figure 8-23   Configuring the Hash Publication for BranchCache policy

3. Set the BranchCache support tag on each shared folder that should be cached. Click File and Storage Services in Server Manager and click Shares. Right-click the share and click Properties. Click to expand Settings, and click the *Enable BranchCache on the file share* option (highlighted in Figure 8-24). You can also enable BranchCache in the Shared Folders snap-in in the Computer Management MMC. The share is now ready to be cached with hosted or distributed cache mode.

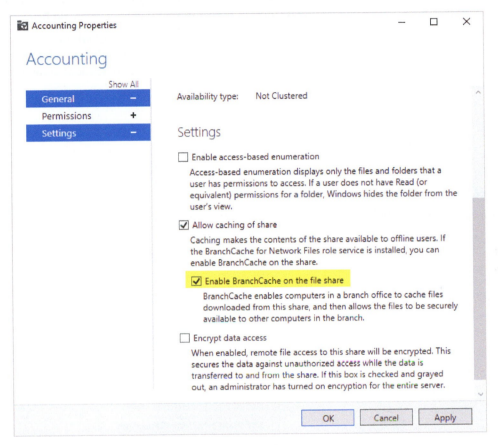

Figure 8-24   Enabling BranchCache on a share

Installing BranchCache on a Web Server or an Application Server

To install BranchCache on a web server or an application server, you just need to install the BranchCache feature in Add Roles and Features or use the PowerShell cmdlet `Install-WindowsFeature BranchCache`. The Web Server role or an application using BITS takes advantage of the BranchCache service automatically, so no additional configuration on the content server is needed.

Configuring a Server for Hosted Cache Mode

If you're using BranchCache in hosted cache mode, you need to configure a server running Windows Server 2008 R2 or later. The hosted cache server must be trusted by BranchCache clients, so part of the process involves installing a certificate on the server that's trusted by the BranchCache client computers. This requires issuing a certificate from a Windows server configured as a certification authority (CA) or installing a certificate issued by a third-party CA. The details of working with a CA and issuing a certificate are beyond the scope of this book, but *MCSA Guide to Identity with Windows Server 2016, Exam 70–742* (Cengage, 2018) discusses Active Directory Certificate Services in detail. The following steps outline the process for installing a hosted cache server:

1. Install the BranchCache feature by using Add Roles and Features or the PowerShell cmdlet `Install-WindowsFeature BranchCache`.

2. Import a certificate that's trusted by the branch office client computers.

3. Link the certificate to BranchCache with the `netsh HTTP ADD SSLCERT` command.

4. Configure BranchCache clients to use BranchCache in hosted cache mode.

Configuring Clients to Use BranchCache

The BranchCache client feature is built into Windows client operating systems that support BranchCache, so no installation is needed. Enabling client computers to use BranchCache is a simple three-step process:

1. To enable BranchCache with a group policy, open a GPO linked to the OU where the branch office computer accounts are located. Navigate to Computer Configuration, Policies, Administrative Templates, Network, BranchCache, and then double-click the Turn on BranchCache policy. Click the Enabled option button (see Figure 8-25).

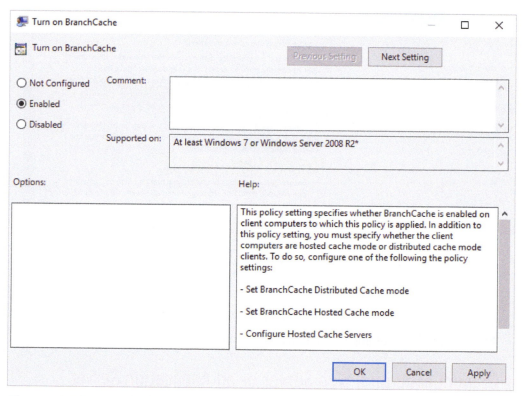

Figure 8-25 Enabling BranchCache on clients with a group policy

2. To configure BranchCache clients to use BranchCache in hosted cache mode, open the GPO you used in Step 1 and navigate to the same location. Double-click Set BranchCache Hosted Cache mode, and click the Enabled option button. Type the name of the hosted cache server under Options, as shown in Figure 8-26. The name must match the name on the certificate installed on the hosted cache server. If you're using distributed cache mode, enable the Set BranchCache Distributed Cache mode policy instead.

3. To configure Windows Firewall on client computers, use a group policy or the Windows Firewall with Advanced Security console to configure inbound rules that allow the following predefined rules:

   • BranchCache: Content Retrieval (uses HTTP)
   • BranchCache: Hosted Cache Server (uses HTTPS)
   • BranchCache: Peer Discovery (uses WSD): This rule is required only for distributed cache mode.

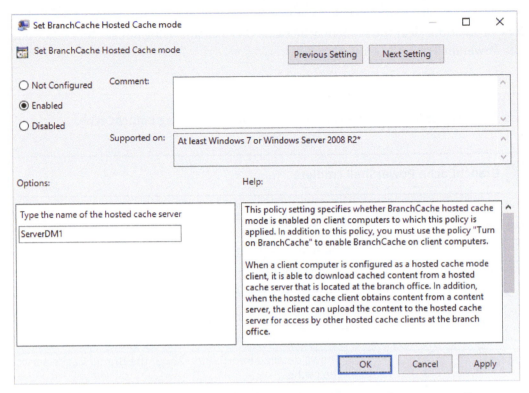

Figure 8-26   Setting BranchCache hosted mode on clients with a group policy

 Tip

All three steps of the client configuration process can be done with a single `netsh` command: `netsh branchcache set service mode=hostedclient location=ServerName`. For distributed cache mode, use `netsh branchcache set service mode=distributed`. The `netsh` command configures the client firewall for the specified mode or with PowerShell cmdlets: `Enable-BCDistributed or Enable-BCHostedClient`.

Troubleshooting BranchCache

BranchCache is usually reliable if the underlying network infrastructure is working well and configured correctly. However, configuration errors can occur, especially when it comes to correctly configuring Group Policy. Here are some of the issues to look out for and some of the commands you can use to verify BranchCache operation:

- Some of the BranchCache configuration relies on Windows Active Directory and Group Policy. Ensure that the policies are correctly configured and the GPOs are linked to the correct organizational units where the BranchCache server and client accounts are located.
- Verify correct certificate distribution when using hosted cache mode.
- Verify the firewall settings.
- Verify that all clients are on the same subnet as the BranchCache server.
- Ensure that the `peerdistsvc` is running on clients and servers when running in distributed caching mode. Check using `Get-Service peerdistsvc` in PowerShell.
- Make sure all clients are using the same caching mode and that caching is enabled and the cache is not full. Check these items and general status of BranchCache using `netsh branchcache show status all`, or the PowerShell cmdlets `Get-BCStatus` and `Get-BCDataCache`.

- Be sure to clear application caches such as web browser caches and the Offline Files cache on file servers. In addition, clear the BranchCache cache on all clients using `netsh branchcache flush` or with PowerShell using `Clear-BCCache`.

Configuring BranchCache with PowerShell

Table 8-3 lists some PowerShell cmdlets commonly used for configuring BranchCache.

Table 8-3   BranchCache PowerShell cmdlets

Cmdlet	Description
Clear-BCCache	Deletes all cached data
Disable-BC	Disables BranchCache
Enable-BCDistributed	Configures BranchCache in distributed cache mode
Enable-BCHostedClient	Configures a BranchCache client to operate in hosted cache mode
Enable-BCHostedServer	Configures a BranchCache server to operate in hosted cache mode
Get-BCDataCache	Shows information about the cache
Get-BCStatus	Shows detailed information about the BranchCache service and the cache
Reset-BC	Resets the configuration of BranchCache
Set-BCCache	Configures the cache parameters
Set-BCDataCacheEntryMaxAge	Configures the maximum time data remains in the cache
Set-BCMinSMBLatency	Sets the minimum latency between the client and server before caching can take place
Get-Command -Module BranchCache	Displays all cmdlets related to the BranchCache service

Activity 8-5: Configuring BranchCache on a File Server

Time Required: 15 minutes
Objective: Configure BranchCache on a file server.
Required Tools and Equipment: ServerDC1, ServerDM1
Description: In this activity, you configure BranchCache on ServerDM1 and enable it on a share.

1. On ServerDM1, open a PowerShell window and type **Install-WindowsFeature FS-BranchCache** and press **Enter**.
2. On ServerDC1, open a PowerShell window. Create an OU for BranchCache servers by typing **New-ADOrganizationalUnit BCServers** and pressing **Enter**. Move ServerDM1 to the BCServers OU by typing **Get-ADComputer ServerDM1 | Move-ADObject -TargetPath "ou=BCServers,dc=mcsa2016,dc=local"** and pressing **Enter**.
3. In Server Manager, click **Tools, Group Policy Management**. Click to expand the forest and domain nodes and then right-click the **BCServers** OU and click **Create a GPO in this domain, and Link it here**.
4. In the New GPO dialog box, type **BranchCache Server** in the Name text box, and click **OK**.
5. Click the **BCServers** OU, if necessary, and in the right pane, right-click the **BranchCache Server** GPO, and click **Edit**. In the Group Policy Management Editor, navigate to **Computer Configuration, Policies, Administrative Templates, Network, Lanman Server**.

6. In the right pane, double-click **Hash Publication for BranchCache**. Click the **Enabled** option button, and leave the default option *Allow hash publication for all shared folders*. Click **OK**. Close the Group Policy Management Editor and Group Policy Management console.

7. On ServerDM1, in Server Manager, click **File and Storage Services** in the left pane, and then click **Shares**. Right-click **Accounting** and click **Properties** (you created the Accounting share in Activity 8-2). Click to expand **Settings**. Click the **Enable BranchCache on the file share** check box, and then click **OK**. Click the **back arrow** in Server Manager twice to return to the Dashboard. BranchCache is now enabled on the server.

8. Continue to the next activity.

Activity 8-6: Configuring BranchCache on a Client

> **Note**
>
> Configuring BranchCache in hosted cache mode requires a certificate, so this activity configures your ServerDM1 computer to use distributed mode. There's only one computer, but you'll see how to check the status of BranchCache to know if it's working.

Time Required: 20 minutes
Objective: Configure BranchCache on a client computer with `netsh`.
Required Tools and Equipment: ServerDC1, ServerDM1, ServerDM2
Description: In this activity, you configure BranchCache on a client computer in distributed mode and test it.

1. First, you'll copy some files to the share enabled for BranchCache. On ServerDM1, from a PowerShell window, type **copy c:\windows*.exe c:\acctdocs** and press **Enter**. It doesn't matter which files you copy; you just need some files large enough to test the cache.

2. Sign in to ServerDM2 as **Administrator**. Because ServerDM2 is a server, not a client OS, you'll first need to install the BranchCache feature. The feature is already installed on Windows clients like Windows 10 Enterprise. Open a PowerShell window and type **Install-WindowsFeature BranchCache** and press **Enter**.

3. Verify that the BranchCache service, named peerdistsvc, is running by typing **Get-Service peerdistsvc** and pressing **Enter**. The Status column should say Running. Type **Enable-BCDistributed** and press **Enter** to set the mode to distributed.

4. Type **Get-BCStatus** and press **Enter**. You should see output similar to Figure 8-27. Type **Set-BCMinSMBLatency 0** and press **Enter** to have BranchCache cache all files, even if there's no delay in retrieving them from the file server. The default latency value is set to 80 ms.

```
PS C:\Users\Administrator> Get-BCStatus

BranchCacheIsEnabled        : True
BranchCacheServiceStatus    : Running
BranchCacheServiceStartType : Automatic


ClientConfiguration:

    CurrentClientMode         : DistributedCache
    HostedCacheServerList     :
    HostedCacheDiscoveryEnabled : False


ContentServerConfiguration:

    ContentServerIsEnabled : True
```

Figure 8-27   Checking the status of BranchCache on a client

5. Type **copy \\ServerDM1\accounting*.exe** and press **Enter**.
6. Type **Get-BCStatus** and press **Enter**. You should see that the line beginning with "CurrentActiveCache Size" shows a number of bytes in use by the cache. If the value is still 0, wait a while and try the command again. Sometimes it takes a while for the statistics to update. Review the command output to verify that the current status is running and the firewall rules are enabled.
7. Type **PowerShell** and press **Enter**. Type **Get-BCDataCache** and press **Enter**. You see information about the cache, such as the maximum percent of the volume used by the cache and the current use of the cache.
8. Shut down all servers.

Chapter Summary

- Distributed File System is a role service under the File and Storage Services role that enables you to group shares from different servers into a single logical share called a namespace. Users see each namespace as a share with subfolders, giving them access to files that are actually stored on different servers.

- DFS namespaces create a hierarchy of shared folders to provide access to shared files from a single logical reference point across an organization.

- The DFS Namespaces role service is used to create and manage these logical shares. DFS has four main components: namespace server, namespace root, folder, and folder target.

- There are two types of DFS namespaces: domain based and stand-alone. Domain-based information is stored in the Active Directory, and namespaces are available even if server names change. Stand-alone information is stored on the server where it was created.

- File security is managed with share permissions and NTFS permissions. Access-based enumeration allows users to see only files and folders they have permission to access.

- Stand-alone namespaces in Windows Server 2016 can support up to 50,000 folders and access-based enumeration. If Active Directory is at a Windows Server 2008 functional level, you can choose from Windows Server 2008 mode or Windows Server 2000 mode. Windows Server 2008 mode supports up to 50,000 folders and access-based enumeration. Windows 2000 Server mode supports 5000 folders.

- Referrals are prioritized lists of folder targets. They can be configured by using lowest cost and random order, and by excluding targets outside the client's site.

- There are two types of replication groups: a multipurpose replication group and a replication group for data collection.

- A replication topology describes the connections used to replicate files between servers. Three topologies are available for replication groups: Hub and spoke, Full mesh, and No topology.

- DFS replication scheduling can help manage peak bandwidth needs by forcing replication to occur in off hours. This option can be particularly good when you have large files that need to be replicated across lower bandwidth connections.

- DFS replication uses an algorithm known as remote differential compression (RDC), which replicates only the changes made in files. By default, RDC is used during replication.

- DFS fault tolerance ensures continuous access to users' files; when a server goes down, DFS fault tolerance automatically "fails over" to another server with replicated copies of files. Load balancing is achieved when a user requests a file in a replicated DFS namespace and is directed, via a referral, to one of the DFS servers hosting the namespace.

- DFS includes a useful diagnostic report utility. You can generate one of three types of reports: health report, propagation test, or a propagation report.

- BranchCache is a file-sharing technology that allows computers at a branch office to cache files retrieved from a central server across a WAN link. It supports content stored on Windows Server 2008 R2 and later servers running the File Server Role for SMB shares, the Web Server role, and the BITS feature.

- BranchCache has two modes of operation: distributed cache mode and hosted cache mode. Distributed cache mode is the best solution for small branch offices where having a dedicated server is neither practical nor desirable. Hosted cache mode is best for branch offices that already have servers performing other functions, such as a domain controller or a DHCP server.

- The procedure to install and configure BranchCache depends on the type of content you want to cache and whether you're using hosted or distributed cache mode.

- BranchCache is usually reliable if the underlying network infrastructure is working well and configured correctly. However, configuration errors can occur, especially when it comes to correctly configuring Group Policy.

Key Terms

access-based enumeration
BranchCache
content information
distributed cache mode
Distributed File System
  (DFS)

folder target
hosted cache mode
namespace
namespace root
namespace server
referral

remote differential
  compression (RDC)
replication
replication group
replication topology

Review Questions

1. The Distributed File System role service provides which of the following? (Choose all that apply.)
   a. Access to files across the network
   b. Replacement for regular backups
   c. Copies of files created automatically for redundancy
   d. Fault-tolerant access to files

2. Which of the following is true about the two types of namespaces?
   a. Stand-alone namespaces always use more bandwidth.
   b. Domain-based namespaces remain regardless of the server status where the share resides.
   c. Domain-based namespaces include the current server name for faster name resolution.
   d. Stand-alone namespaces can't be replicated.

3. Folders added to a namespace can be described as which of the following?
   a. Copies of existing folders
   b. Copies of existing folders that are initially empty
   c. Pointers to existing shared folders
   d. Copied to a staging area automatically

4. In DFS, what are the differences between Windows Server 2008 mode and Windows Server 2000 mode?

   a. Server 2008 mode supports 15,000 folders and access-based enumeration, and Server 2000 mode supports 5000 folders.
   b. Server 2008 mode supports 75,000 folders, and Server 2000 mode supports 10,000 folders.
   c. Nothing a user can see.
   d. Server 2008 mode supports 50,000 folders and access-based enumeration, and Server 2000 mode supports 5000 folders.

5. Where does a referral originate when a client accesses a DFS namespace?
   a. From the namespace server
   b. From the domain controller
   c. From the namespace server for a stand-alone type and from the domain controller for a domain-based type
   d. From a cached copy of referrals on the server where the share is located

6. Which of the following ordering methods lists servers in the same Active Directory site as the client first and does not ignore a site's cost?
   a. No default; you must choose an ordering method during initial configuration.
   b. Random order to ensure load balancing.
   c. Lowest cost, selecting the closest server first.
   d. The order in which the target servers were defined.

7. If a client is on the same site as a particular target, what will it do?
   a. Follow the referral ordering method
   b. Always go to that target
   c. Ignore the targets on the same site
   d. Go to a target randomly

8. How can the referral order be customized?
   a. There's no way to customize the referral order.
   b. Exclude targets in the client's site.
   c. Use the Override Referral Ordering option.
   d. Put in nonexistent targets, forcing the system to follow your custom order.

9. When should share permissions be set?
   a. Before DFS configuration.
   b. During DFS configuration.
   c. After DFS configuration is finished.
   d. Never; DFS handles all permissions.

10. DFS replication configuration requires a minimum of how many targets?
    a. One
    b. Two
    c. Three
    d. Four

11. Which is the best method of synchronization to reduce bandwidth with a DFS replication group made up of a main office and eight branch offices?
    a. Full mesh topology
    b. Hub and spoke topology
    c. Round robin topology
    d. Random synchronization

12. What's the algorithm used to replicate only changes made in files?
    a. Remote replication connection
    b. Remote change comparison
    c. Remote differential compression
    d. Remote change compression

13. Where are changed files cached until replication is finished?
    a. Caching folders in the C:\DFScache folder on the namespace server
    b. The Staging folder on the target server
    c. No caching is done
    d. The Staging folder for the folder being replicated

14. What's the model used when there's an update conflict?
    a. Last writer wins; losing file is cached.
    b. First writer wins; losing file is cached.
    c. First writer wins; losing file is deleted.
    d. Last writer wins; losing file is deleted.

15. Which of the following features or services should you install on Windows Server 2016 if you want to improve file-sharing performance in a remote office connected to the main office by a WAN link?
    a. Distributed cache mode
    b. Tiered cache mode
    c. Single cache mode
    d. Hosted cache mode

16. Which specific mode should you configure if you want to support multiple subnets?
    a. Hosted cache mode
    b. Distributed cache mode
    c. Branch cache mode
    d. Tiered cache mode

17. Which of the following roles or protocols can benefit from using the BranchCache role service? (Choose all that apply.)
    a. File Server
    b. Web Server
    c. Network File System
    d. BITS

18. Which of the following scenarios would benefit from selecting a distributed cache mode over a hosted cache mode? (Choose all that apply.)
    a. Small branch office with two dedicated servers
    b. Small branch office with no dedicated server
    c. Additional resources and personnel are not available
    d. Unlimited resources and multiple servers are available

19. Which of the following PowerShell cmdlets will allow you to install BranchCache on a file server?
    a. `Install-WindowsFeature -BranchCache`
    b. `Add-WindowsFeature -BranchCache`
    c. `Install-Windows FS-BranchCache`
    d. `Install-WindowsFeature FS-BranchCache`

20. When troubleshooting your BranchCache configurations, what specific commands allow you to verify that all your clients are using the same caching mode, caching is enabled, and the cache is not full? (Choose all that apply.)
    a. `Get-BCStatus`
    b. `Get-BCDataCache`
    c. `Show-BCDataCache`
    d. `netsh branchcache show status all`

Critical Thinking

The following activities give you critical thinking challenges. Case Projects offer a scenario with a problem to solve and for which you supply a written solution.

Case Project 8-1: Managing DFS Referrals

Your organization has expanded dramatically, and suddenly there's heavy file server use. All the file servers are fairly close to clients, and you're adding several more, creating a large group. The number of namespace servers has also expanded. Your initial configuration used default settings for the referral ordering method and polling. What changes should you consider?

Case Project 8-2: Optimizing DFS Replication

The Marketing Department for CSM Tech Publishing is busy producing videos and print materials (stored in PDF format) for distribution and use by the Sales Department. With new products being introduced and a good bit of marketing testing, marketing materials change often, and there's often a substantial delay before the Sales Department gets access to these changes. The Sales Department is in another site and wants access to the marketing materials, but given the size of files and the number of updates, you're reluctant to give the Sales Department direct access to files across the WAN link. What DFS replication group configuration could you consider for replication and frequency of access?

Case Project 8-3: Using Advanced File and Storage Features

You're the IT administrator for CSM Tech Publishing. You've just had a meeting with the general manager about a data storage problem the company has been having. You've been asked to find solutions for the following problem:

- Two satellite offices have been complaining about slow access to shared files on the servers at the company's headquarters. One office has about 25 client computers running Windows 10, and one server running Windows Server 2016 provides DHCP and DNS services but isn't heavily loaded. The other office has only four client machines running Windows 10. There's no budget for additional hardware at either location.

What solution do you propose for this problem? Include implementation details.

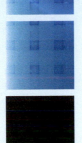

CHAPTER **9**

IMPLEMENTING ADVANCED NETWORK SOLUTIONS

After reading this chapter and completing the exercises, you will be able to:

Implement high-performance network solutions

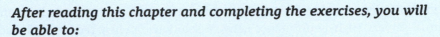

Determine scenarios and requirements for implementing software-defined networking

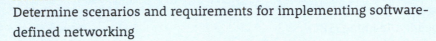

This chapter introduces you to several high-performance networking features that can be implemented on physical computers and virtual machines (VMs). Features such a QoS, RDMA, data center bridging, and virtual machine queue keep network traffic moving through your servers to keep up with today's demand for high-bandwidth network services. Next, in keeping with Windows Server 2016's focus on the software-defined datacenter (SDDC), you learn about software-defined networking (SDN) features available in Windows Server 2016 including Hyper-V Network Virtualization, Software Load Balancer, and Windows Server Gateways.

331

High-Performance Network Solutions

 Certification

- **70-741 – Implement an advanced network infrastructure:**
  Implement high performance network solutions

Windows Server 2016 includes several technologies to optimize network performance, both on physical servers and on virtual servers. High-performance network solutions can help reduce bottlenecks on both your physical servers and inside your virtual networks. This section looks at technologies you can implement to get the most out of your server's network interfaces and network services including the following:

- NIC teaming
- Switch Embedded Teaming (SET)
- Quality of Service (QoS) with data center bridging
- Virtual machine queue (VMQ)
- Receive side scaling (RSS)
- Virtual machine multi-queue (VMMQ)
- SMB Direct and SMB Multichannel
- Single-root IO virtualization (SR-IOV)

Configuring NIC Teaming

NIC teaming allows multiple network interfaces to work in tandem to provide increased bandwidth, load balancing, and fault tolerance. Another term for this is **load balancing and failover (LBFO)**. You can create a NIC team with a single network interface, but most of the utility of a NIC team comes from having more than one NIC in the team. Windows Server 2016 supports up to 32 NICs in a team.

Let's consider how NIC teaming provides load balancing. **Load balancing** distributes traffic between two or more interfaces, providing an increase in the overall network throughput that a server is able to maintain. A basic example illustrates the concept. Suppose two client stations are each transferring a 100 MB file to a share on a Windows server. A server with a single NIC operating at 100 Mbps could transfer both files in about 20 seconds (10 seconds for each file). A server with a two-NIC team would load balance the data from the two clients, with each NIC able to transfer data at 100 Mbps, totaling 200 Mbps, cutting the total transfer time in half.

Let's look at an example of how to use NIC teaming for fault tolerance, or failover. **Failover** in this context is the ability of a server to recover from network hardware failure by having redundant hardware that can immediately take over for a device failure. Suppose you have a server that must be highly available. A server with a single NIC that is connected to a switch becomes unavailable if the switch or the NIC fails. However, with a NIC team configured to provide failover, you can connect one NIC to one switch and the other NIC to another switch. If one NIC or switch fails, the other NIC takes over, maintaining server availability.

You configure NIC teaming using Server Manager or PowerShell. The process is the same whether you configure it on a physical computer or on a VM; however, there are additional considerations when you configure NIC teaming on a VM as described later. From Server Manager, click Local Server. In the left-hand column of the Properties page, you'll see a link for NIC Teaming, which is disabled by default. Clicking the link brings you to the NIC Teaming configuration page as shown in Figure 9-1.

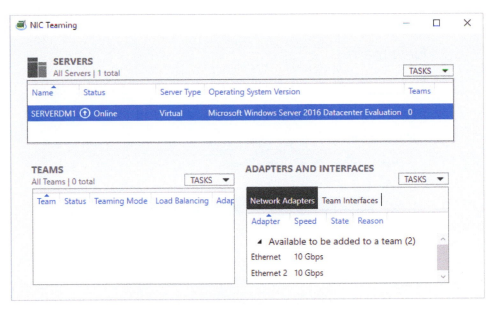

Figure 9-1   NIC Teaming configuration

In Figure 9-1, you see three panes that have the following functions:

- *Servers*—This pane shows the available servers for which you can manage NIC teaming. You add servers to this list in a manner similar to adding servers to Server Manager: by clicking Tasks and Add Servers. The Servers pane also shows you whether the server is a physical or virtual server and the number of NIC teams defined.
- *Teams*—This pane lists the current NIC teams, their mode, and status, and which network adapters are part of the team. You can create or delete a NIC team by clicking Tasks.
- *Adapters and interfaces*—This pane shows you the list of network adapters available to be added to a NIC team. You can add an interface to an existing team or add an adapter to a new team.

From PowerShell, you can list, create, remove, rename, and set properties of a team using the following commands:

- `Get-NetLbfoTeam`: Shows a list of NIC teams on the server.
- `New-NetLbfoTeam`: Creates a new NIC team and adds network adapters to the team; you can optionally set the properties of the team.
- `Remove-NetLbfoTeam`: Deletes a team.
- `Rename-NetLbfoTeam`: Renames a team.
- `Set-NetLbfoTeam`: Sets the properties of an existing team.

To get help on using any of these PowerShell commands from a PowerShell prompt, type `get-help` followed by the command.

NIC Teaming Modes

When you create a new NIC team, you can configure the teaming mode and the load balancing mode (see Figure 9-2):

- *Teaming mode*—There are three teaming modes:
  - Switch Independent: This is the default mode and the only mode available for VMs. Using Switch Independent mode, you connect the NICs in a team to separate switches for fault tolerance. The switches are unaware that a connected NIC is part of a team; the server provides all the teaming functions. You can also connect the NICs to the same switch. Switch Independent mode allows you to configure fault tolerance in one of two ways: Active or Standby. Active makes all NICs active, which means that you get the benefit of the bandwidth from all NICs in the team. If a NIC fails, the others continue to run. Standby lets you choose an adapter that remains in standby mode until there is a failure. Upon failure, the NIC in Standby mode switches to Active mode. The default setting is Active.

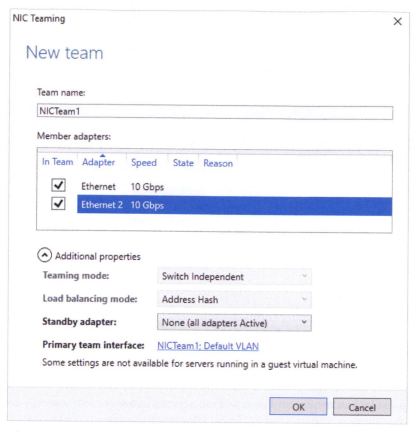

Figure 9-2 Configure NIC Teaming modes

- Static Teaming: This mode, also called *Switch Dependent mode*, is primarily used for load balancing. All NICs are connected to one switch, and the switch participates in the NIC teaming process. You must use a switch that supports IEEE 802.3ad, which is a standard that defines link aggregation. The switch must be manually configured to identify ports to which members of a switch team are connected. The switch load balances network traffic between the switches.
- LACP: Link Aggregation Control Protocol (LACP), defined in IEEE 802.1ax, allows a switch to automatically identify the ports to which a team member is connected and to dynamically create a team. You must use a switch that supports LACP and enable the protocol before it can be used.

- *Load balancing mode*—The load balancing mode determines how the server load balances outgoing data packets among the NICs in the team. There are three options:

- Address Hash: This mode uses an algorithm based on properties of the outgoing packet to create a hash value. The hash value is then used to assign the packet for delivery using one of the NICs in the team. This is the only load balancing mode available when configuring NIC teaming on a VM.
- Hyper-V Port: This method is used when the team members on a physical computer are connected to a Hyper-V switch. Each virtual NIC is associated with only one team member at system startup. This method works well to evenly distribute the load among NICs in the team if there are several VMs running.
- Dynamic: This is the default mode on physical computers. In this mode, traffic is evenly distributed among all team members, including from virtual NICs. A potential problem with the Address Hash and Hyper-V Port modes is that a NIC in the team could be overwhelmed when there are very large traffic flows involving a single NIC even when the other NICs have unused capacity. This mode balances large flows of traffic over multiple NICs, thereby providing even distribution of traffic among all team members.

NIC Teaming on Virtual Machines

As mentioned, you can configure NIC teaming on VMs as well as on physical computers. On VMs, you use the same procedure as on physical computers, but for the most reliability, you should enable the feature first in the network adapter's Advanced Features dialog box (shown in Figure 9-3). If you don't enable it, you can still create a NIC team in the VM's guest OS, but if one of the physical NICs in the team fails, the team stops working instead of providing failover protection. NIC teaming can be configured only on virtual NICs (vNICs) connected to an external virtual switch.

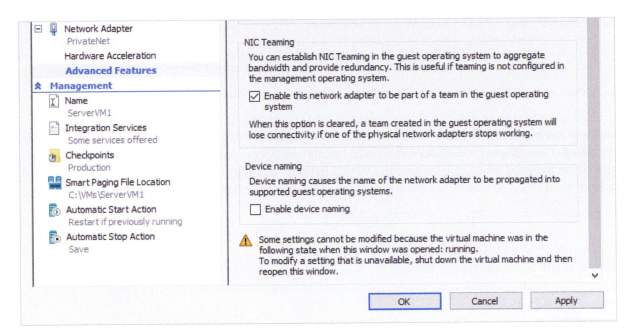

Figure 9-3   Enabling NIC teaming on a VM's network adapter

If you have already configured NIC teaming on the Hyper-V host server, configuring it on VMs running on the host isn't necessary. Any VM connected to an external virtual switch that's mapped to the host's NIC team gets the benefits of NIC teaming on the host. However, if you want a VM to have a dedicated NIC team, you should configure NIC teaming on the VM, too. In this case, NIC teaming must be enabled on each virtual network adapter that's part of the team, and each virtual network adapter must be connected to a separate external virtual switch. You can have NIC teams configured on the host computer and on VMs, but they must use separate physical NICs. That is, the NICs on the host that are part of a NIC team can't be used in a NIC team on a VM and vice versa. Likewise, an external virtual switch can be mapped only to a NIC team on the host or to a physical NIC on the host; it can't be mapped to a NIC that's a member of a NIC team. You must plan physical and virtual network configurations carefully to be sure you have enough physical NICs to accommodate the host's physical network needs and the virtual network needs.

Note

Although NIC teaming on physical computers can use up to 32 NICs in a team, Microsoft supports VM NIC teams with only two team members. You can create a team with more members, but it's not officially supported.

Implementing Switch Embedded Teaming

Switch Embedded Teaming (SET) is a new feature in Windows Server 2016 that allows up to eight identical physical adapters on the host system to be configured as a team and mapped to a virtual switch. The virtual switch can control all the physical adapters simultaneously, providing fault tolerance and load balancing. SET is targeted for enterprise servers with very fast NICs (10 Gb and faster). The physical NICs can be connected to the same or different physical switches providing additional fault tolerance. To configure SET, you simply create a new virtual switch and specify the network adapters that should be members as in the following cmdlet:

```
New-VMSwitch -Name SETSwitch1 -NetAdapter
  Ethernet1,Ethernet2 -EnableEmbeddedTeaming $true
```

Next, you add the virtual network adapters that will communicate through the SET-enabled switch:

```
Add-VMNetworkAdapter -SwitchName SETSwitch1 -Name Adapter1
```

SET supports remote direct memory access (RDMA) on virtual network adapters, which provides additional performance benefits. You must enable RDMA on the virtual network adapter created on the host system. The adapter will always be named "vEthernet (*VirtualAdaperName*)"; *VirtualAdapterName* is the name assigned when you created the virtual network adapter. The following cmdlet provides an example of enabling RDMA on a virtual network adapter named vEthernet (Adapter1).

```
Enable-NetAdapterRDMA "vEthernet (Adapter1)"
```

NIC Teaming versus SET

Traditional NIC teaming and SET provide similar functions, but there are important differences and limitations to each. The following list describes some of the differences to help you determine when to use each technology:

- SET is a feature that is bound to Hyper-V virtual switches, so you can't use it on physical servers connected to the physical network. For load balancing and failover on physical servers connected to the physical network, use traditional NIC teaming.
- Traditional NIC teaming is not compatible with RDMA or software defined networking (SDN) version 2, available in Windows Server 2016 and discussed later in this chapter. So, if you want to use RDMA or SDN, you should use SET instead of traditional NIC teaming.
- If you want a solution that provides active/standby operation, use NIC teaming; with SET, all NICs are always active, providing both load balancing and fault tolerance.
- SET requires all NICs to be identical and operate at the same speed; with NIC teaming, you can have NICs of different speeds as members of the same team.
- NIC teaming supports receive side scaling (RSS, discussed later in this chapter); SET does not.
- Switch independent mode is the only teaming mode available for SET whereas NIC teaming supports switch independent, static, and LACP modes.
- SET works best with 10 Gb adapters, which are expensive; NIC teaming works well with slower NICs.

Configuring Data Center Bridging

Data center bridging (DCB) is an enhancement to Ethernet that provides additional features for use in enterprise datacenters, in particular when server clustering and SANs are in use. As it pertains to SANs and iSCSI, Ethernet by itself has some problems. Ethernet is a "best-effort" delivery system that doesn't guarantee delivery of frames. Lost frames can be tolerated by many applications because network protocols, such as TCP, detect missing data and retransmit it. However, storage is less forgiving of lost data even if that data will eventually be retransmitted. Storage input/output cannot easily tolerate delays, so DCB was designed specifically to prevent delays in delivery of data in iSCSI applications and create what is referred to as a "lossless" environment, meaning a network environment in which data delivery is guaranteed without undue delays. DCB improves performance in iSCSI deployments in the following ways:

- *Quality of Service (QoS)*—Bandwidth can be allocated on a per-protocol basis ensuring that iSCSI traffic gets a minimum of network bandwidth.
- *Deterministic performance*—A feature called performance flow control (PFC) ensures a consistent stream of data providing a lossless Ethernet environment with no dropped frames or retransmissions.
- *DCB exchange*—This provides automatic configuration of iSCSI parameters between DCB-enabled network interfaces and DCB-enabled network switches.

Windows Server 2016 supports DCB as an installable feature using the Add Roles and Features Wizard in Server Manager or the `Install-WindowsFeature Data-Center-Bridging` PowerShell cmdlet. You can list the PowerShell cmdlets specific to configuring DCB using the `Get-Command -Module DCBQoS` cmdlet. Although there are a few configuration settings possible with DCB, it's important to understand that your network interface and the networks switches must support DCB. By default, network interfaces are set to allow DCB configuration to be managed by the switch the interface is connected to. If you want to manage DCB configuration from Windows Server, perform the following steps:

1. Turn the `DCBX Willing` parameter to false using `Set-NetQoSDcbxSetting -Willing $false`.
2. Enable DCB on the network adapter using `Enable-NetAdapterQoS Ethernet`, replacing "Ethernet" with the name of your network adapter.

Configuring QoS with DCB

Quality of Service (QoS) in a network allows you to configure priorities for different types of network traffic so that delay-sensitive data is prioritized over regular data. For example, real-time voice and video are sensitive to delays and dropped packets, but file transfers and webpage data are not, so voice and video can be given a higher priority to guarantee timely and reliable delivery. The DCB feature has built-in QoS capabilities to allow your server to handle different data priorities. To enable QoS with DCB, follow these steps:

1. Install the DCB feature and enable it on your NICs as described earlier.
2. Create QoS policies. QoS policies define the traffic types you wish to prioritize. When using QoS policies with DCB, you assign a priority value to each type of traffic.
3. Create QoS traffic classes that map traffic classes to the QoS policies and assign a bandwidth percentage value to each type of traffic. The combined bandwidth values should add up to 100.

Note

DCB must be enabled on the switches to which your network adapters are connected for QoS with DCB to work.

Creating QoS Policies

QoS policies are created using the `New-NetQosPolicy` cmdlet. A QoS policy includes a descriptive name and defines the type of traffic you wish to prioritize by specifying a destination port and a priority number based on IEEE 802.1p from 0 to 7.

Here are some examples of creating QoS policies with an IEEE 802.1p priority:

- This command creates a policy named SMBtraffic that assigns a priority value of 4 (see Figure 9-4).

```
New-NetQosPolicy SMBtraffic -SMB -Priority 4
```

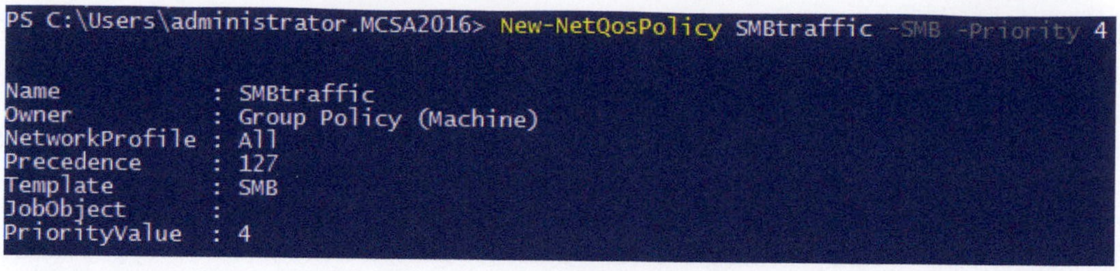

```
PS C:\Users\administrator.MCSA2016> New-NetQosPolicy SMBtraffic -SMB -Priority 4

Name           : SMBtraffic
Owner          : Group Policy (Machine)
NetworkProfile : All
Precedence     : 127
Template       : SMB
JobObject      :
PriorityValue  : 4
```

Figure 9-4 Output of the `New-NetQosPolicy` cmdlet

- This command creates a policy named Webtraffic that assigns a priority value of 6.

```
New-NetQosPolicy Webtraffic -IPPort 80 -IPProtocol TCP -Priority 6
```

- This command creates a policy named Livetraffic that assigns a priority value of 5.

```
New-NetQosPolicy Livetraffic -LiveMigration -Priority 5
```

- This command creates a default policy named Defaulttraffic that assigns a priority value of 2. A default policy matches all traffic that doesn't match another QoS policy.

```
New-NetQosPolicy Defaulttraffic -Default -Priority 2
```

> **Note** 📎
>
> There are many different criteria you can use to define QoS policies; these examples show only a very small sample. For more on creating QoS policies, see *https://technet.microsoft.com/en-us/itpro/powershell/windows/netqos/new-netqospolicy*.

Creating QoS Traffic Classes

Traffic classes map to QoS policies and assign bandwidth weight values to each policy. Although it is not required, it is best to create traffic classes in which the bandwidth values add up to 100 so that each bandwidth weight represents a percentage of total bandwidth. You assign a name to each traffic class that can but doesn't have to match the name assigned to a QoS rule. It is the priority value specified in the traffic class that ties the class to the QoS rule. The following are some examples of creating QoS traffic classes that map back to the QoS policies in the earlier examples:

- This command creates the traffic class SMBtraffic that ties back to a QoS policy with priority 4 and assigns a bandwidth weight of 25 as shown in Figure 9-5.

```
New-NetQosTrafficClass SMBtraffic -Priority 4 -Algorithm ETS -Bandwidth 25
```

```
PS C:\Users\administrator.MCSA2016> New-NetQosTrafficClass smbtraffic -Priority 4 -Algorithm ETS -Bandwidth 25

Name           Algorithm Bandwidth(%) Priority          PolicySet        IfIndex IfAlias
----           --------- ------------ --------          ---------        ------- -------
smbtraffic     ETS       25           4                 Global
```

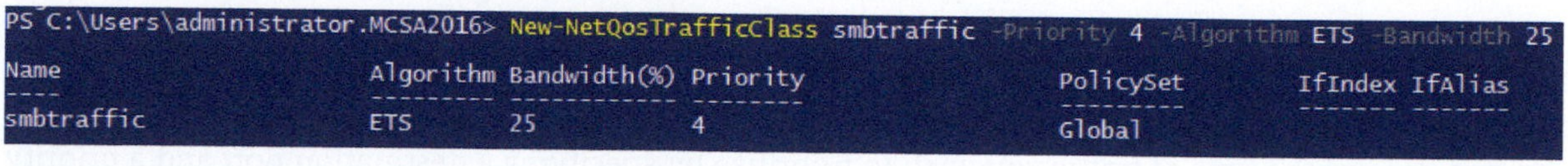

Figure 9-5 Output of the `New-NetQoSTrafficClass` cmdlet

- This command creates the traffic class Webtraffic that ties back to a QoS policy with priority 6 and assigns a bandwidth weight of 35.

```
New-NetQosTrafficClass Webtraffic -Priority 6 -Algorithm ETS -Bandwidth 35
```

- This command creates the traffic class Livetraffic that ties back to a QoS policy with priority 5 and assigns a bandwidth weight of 30.

```
New-NetQosTrafficClass Livetraffic -Priority 5 -Algorithm ETS -Bandwidth 30
```

- This command creates the traffic class Defaulttraffic that ties back to a QoS policy with priority 2 and assigns a bandwidth weight of 10.

```
New-NetQosTrafficClass Defaulttraffic -Priority 2 -Algorithm ETS -Bandwidth 10
```

In the preceding cmdlets, the `-Algorithm ETS` parameter is required and specifies that the priority scheduling algorithm should use the 802.1Qaz Enhanced Transmission Selection (ETS) algorithm. The other algorithm option is `Strict`. The Strict algorithm always selects packets with a higher-priority value that can completely block lower-priority packets if higher-priority packets overwhelm those of lower priority whereas ETS ensures that all priorities receive a minimum of bandwidth.

Virtual Machine Queue

Virtual machine queue (VMQ) accelerates vNIC performance by delivering packets from the external network directly to the vNIC, bypassing the management operating system. VMQ is enabled or disabled on each vNIC. When VMQ is enabled, a dedicated queue is created for the vNIC on the physical NIC. When packets arrive on the physical interface for the vNIC, they are delivered directly to the VM. In contrast, when VMQ is not enabled, packets are placed in a common queue and distributed to the destination vNIC on a first-come, first-served basis. Without VMQ, the common queue is serviced by a single CPU core, so all VM traffic is processed by a single CPU core on the host computer. With VMQ enabled, each queue can be serviced by a different CPU core on the host computer, reducing the potential for the host CPU to be a VM network traffic bottleneck. Figure 9-6 illustrates VM network communication with the host with VMQ disabled and with VME enabled. VMQ is enabled by default but must be supported by the physical NIC on the host computer.

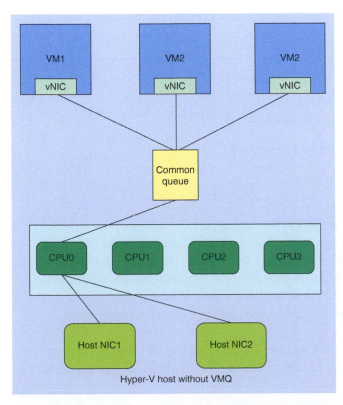
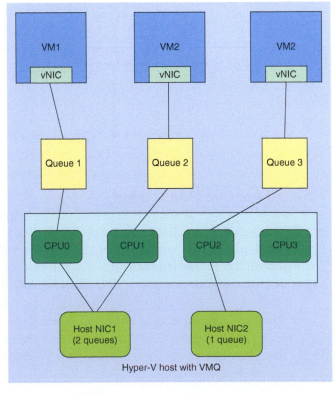

Figure 9-6   Hyper-V host without VMQ and with VMQ

Receive Side Scaling

Receive side scaling (RSS) is a feature for network drivers that efficiently distributes the processing of incoming network traffic among multiple CPU cores. On Windows, the feature is enabled by default, but you might need to enable it on individual network adapters. Without RSS, all incoming network data is processed on the CPU where the network interface card interrupt occurs, potentially leading to an imbalance in CPU usage on systems with multiple CPUs or multiple CPU cores.

We first discussed RSS in Chapter 3 in the context of improving DNS performance, but RSS can improve the performance of any network service. Enable RSS on the NIC using the `Enable-NetAdapterRSS` cmdlet. Use `Set-NetAdapterRSS` to fine-tune RSS. On systems with a GUI, you enable and configure RSS through the Properties dialog box of the network connection as shown in Figure 9-7. RSS may or may not be an option depending on the type of NIC installed and the driver. Some NIC drivers include many additional RSS-related options to fine-tune RSS as you can see in Figure 9-7. Check the documentation of your NIC for details on configuring each option.

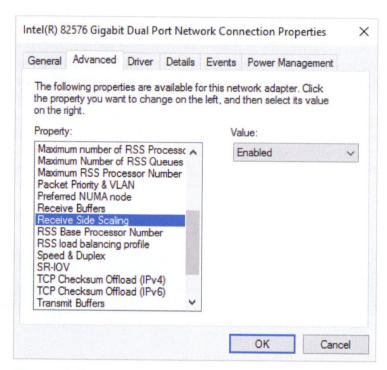

Figure 9-7   Enabling RSS on a network interface

Virtual Receive Side Scaling

Virtual receive side scaling (vRSS), as the name suggests, is RSS for virtual network adapters. Its purpose is the same as RSS—to distribute the processing load for incoming network traffic among multiple processors, in this case virtual processors in a VM. vRSS requires that the physical NIC to which the virtual switch is connected support VMQ. You can see whether your physical adapters that are connected to your virtual switches support VMQ using the following cmdlets on the Hyper-V host:

- `Get-VMSwitch`—This cmdlet lists the virtual switches and shows which network adapter, if any, they are connected to as shown in Figure 9-8.
- `Get-NetAdapterVmq`—This cmdlet lists the network adapters, if any, that support VMQ as shown in Figure 9-9. Notice that the feature is disabled on both adapters because neither adapter supports 10 Gb Ethernet.

```
PS C:\Users\Administrator> Get-VMSwitch

Name                    SwitchType NetAdapterInterfaceDescription
----                    ---------- ------------------------------
TestingNet1-192.168.10  Internal
Net1-192.168.0          Private
TestingNet2-192.168.1   Private
YC-CNT1                 External   Intel(R) PRO/1000 PT Dual Port Server
Net2-192.168.1          Private
HyperVNet               Private
Intern-192.168.0.1      Internal
```

Figure 9-8   Output of the `Get-VMSwitch` cmdlet

```
PS C:\Users\Administrator> Get-NetAdapterVmq

Name      InterfaceDescription           Enabled BaseVmqProcessor MaxProcessors

----      --------------------           ------- ---------------- -------------
HyperVMgt Intel(R) 82576 Gigabit Dual ...#2 False 0:0              8
YC-CNT2   Intel(R) 82576 Gigabit Dual Po... False 0:0              8
```

Figure 9-9   Output of the `Get-NetAdapterVmq` cmdlet

`Set-NetAdapterVmq Ethernet -Enabled $true`—This cmdlet enables VMQ on the network adapter named Ethernet if the adapter supports 10 Gb Ethernet.

Tip ⓘ

The properties of a network adapter might report that VMQ is enabled, but if the adapter isn't at least 10 Gb, the virtual switch will disable it. The `Get-NetAdapterVmq` cmdlet reports the setting more reliably.

VMQ is supported only on 10 Gb and higher network adapters, thus limiting vRSS to VMs running on hosts that have 10 Gb NICs. You enable and configure vRSS the same way you do RSS, using the network connection properties or using PowerShell.

Note 📎

RSS and vRSS distribute the load among multiple cores or multiple physical processors, but that does not include hyperthreading. Many systems report hyperthreaded cores as individual CPU cores; for example, a dual-core CPU with hyperthreading enabled will be reported as four CPU cores. RSS and vRSS distributes the load only across the actual CPU cores and ignores hyperthreading.

Virtual Machine Multi-Queue

Virtual machine multi-queue (VMMQ) is a new feature in Windows Server 2016 that reduces the overhead in getting packets from the physical network to a VM on the host. Before VMMQ, a VM was assigned a single queue on the host adapter and each queue was processed by a single virtual CPU (vCPU) core, creating a bottleneck between the host adapter and the VM. With VMMQ, a VM can be assigned multiple queues on the host adapter with each queue having a vCPU core to process its incoming data. Of course, this means that the VM must be assigned multiple cores to take advantage of this feature. To enable VMMQ on a VM, run the following PowerShell cmdlet on the host computer:

```
Set-VMNetworkAdapter VMName -VmmqEnable $true
```

The VM can be on or off when you enable VMMQ. To see the status of VMMQ, use the following cmdlet and scroll down to the `VmmqEnabled` row:

```
Get-VMNetworkAdapter VMName | fl
```

The physical NIC must support VMMQ and, like VMQ, requires a 10 Gb or faster Ethernet adapter.

SR-IOV

Single-root IO virtualization (SR-IOV) enhances a virtual network adapter's performance by allowing a virtual adapter to bypass the virtual switch software on the parent partition (the Hyper-V host) and communicate directly with the physical hardware, thereby lowering overhead and improving performance. The performance advantage is most obvious on high-speed NICs, such as 10 Gb and higher Ethernet. SR-IOV must be supported by a PCI Express NIC installed on the host, and installing drivers on the guest OS might be necessary. If you enable SR-IOV and resources to support it aren't available, the virtual network adapter connects by using the virtual switch as usual. You must also enable SR-IOV in the Virtual Switch Manager when you create the external virtual switch. If you enable SR-IOV and it's supported, you can check Device Manager on the VM and see the actual NIC make and model listed under network adapters. For adapters with SR-IOV not enabled or not supported, you see only the Microsoft Hyper-V network adapter. You enable SR-IOV during virtual switch creation (see Figure 9-10); it cannot be enabled after the switch has already been created. You can also use the `New-VMSwitch` cmdlet with the `-EnableIOV $true` parameter.

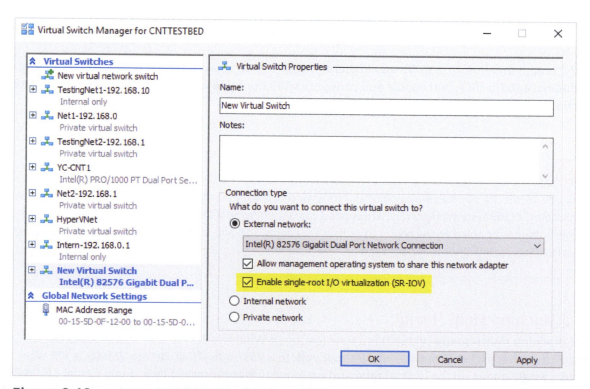

Figure 9-10   Creating a switch with SR-IOV enabled

SMB Direct and SMB Multichannel

Server Message Block (SMB), the primary Windows protocol for file sharing, can take advantage of some of the performance features already discussed, such as RSS and SR-IOV. **SMB Direct** is a performance technology designed specifically for the SMB protocol. SMB Direct uses the capabilities of an RDMA capable network adapter, nearly eliminating server processor utilization for data transfers. SMB Direct requires the host network adapter to be RDMA compatible, which you can check by running the `Get-NetAdapterRdma` cmdlet (see Figure 9-11). The command lists the adapters that support RDMA.

```
PS C:\Users\Administrator> Get-NetAdapterRdma

Name                        InterfaceDescription                      Enabled
----                        --------------------                      -------
vEthernet (Intern-192....   Hyper-V Virtual Ethernet Adapter #2       True
vEthernet (TestingNet1...   Hyper-V Virtual Ethernet Adapter          False
```

Figure 9-11   The results of the `Get-NetAdapterRdma` cmdlet

To enable RDMA on an adapter that supports it, use the following PowerShell cmdlet or enable it in the network adapter's properties:

```
Set-NetAdapterRdma "AdapterName" -Enabled $true
```

SMB Multichannel provides fault tolerance and improved performance in a connection between a client and a server providing an SMB share. SMB Multichannel is included in SMB 3.0 and works automatically without configuration on the client or server. When a connection with a share is established, SMB probes for additional paths to the server, and if found, the additional paths are used to increase performance and provide fault tolerance in the event that one of the paths is interrupted. To see whether a connection with an SMB share is using SMB Multichannel, establish a connection with an SMB share on a Windows server. View information about the connection using the `Get-SmbConnection` cmdlet. Then, see if multichannel can be used by running the following cmdlet (see Figure 9-12):

```
Get-SmbMultichannelConnection
```

The output of this command shows you the available paths that can be used to establish a connection with the server. To see if multiple paths are being used, use the `Get-NetTCPConnection -RemotePort 445` cmdlet. The output shows you all the connections to port 445, which is the port used by SMB. SMB Multichannel requires at least two computers running at least Windows Server 2012 or Windows 8, and both computers must have one of the following configurations: two network adapters, at least one adapter that supports RSS, NIC teaming configured, and support for RDMA. For optimal performance, these features can be combined. For example, you can have multiple NICs with RSS enabled or multiple NICs with RDMA support. However, you cannot have teamed NICs with RDMA enabled.

```
PS C:\Users\Administrator> Get-SmbConnection

ServerName    ShareName  UserName                   Credential      Dialect NumOpens
----------    ---------  --------                   ----------      ------- --------
cnt209-instr  c$         CNTTESTBED\Administrator    yc-cnt\gtomsho  3.1.1   1

PS C:\Users\Administrator> Get-SmbMultichannelConnection

Server Name   Selected Client IP      Server IP       Client Interface Index Server Interface Index
-----------   -------- ---------      ---------       ---------------------- ----------------------
cnt209-instr  True     172.31.220.102 172.31.209.100  15                     14
cnt209-instr  True     172.31.220.100 172.31.209.100  2                      14
```

Figure 9-12   Viewing information about SMB Multichannel

> **Note**
>
> As mentioned, SMB Multichannel is enabled by default, but if you wish to disable it, you can do so on either the SMB server, client, or both. To disable it on the server, use `Set-SmbServerConfiguration` `-EnableMultiChannel $false`, and on the client, use `Set-SmbClientConfiguration` `-EnableMultiChannel $false`. To re-enable it, just replace `$false` with `$true` in the earlier commands.

Software-Defined Networking

Certification

- **70-741 – Implement an advanced network infrastructure:**
  Determine scenarios and requirements for implementing software-defined networking (SDN)

Software-defined networking (SDN) is a collection of technologies designed to make the network infrastructure flexible and responsive to the ever-changing network requirements in today's enterprise and cloud networks. SDN extends the software-defined datacenter paradigm found in technologies such as Hyper-V virtualization, containers, and Storage Spaces.

SDN allows administrators to centrally manage aspects of key physical and virtual infrastructure devices such as routers, switches, and access gateways. The key components of SDN in Windows Server 2016 include Hyper-V virtual switches, Hyper-V Network Virtualization (HNV), and Network Controller. Hyper-V virtual switches are discussed at length in *MCSA Guide to Installation, Storage, and Compute with Windows Server 2016, Exam 70-740* (Cengage, 2018), so this chapter focuses on the other technologies that work along with Hyper-V virtual switches to provide SDN-specific features.

SDN is not an all-or-nothing proposition; traditional routers and switches will continue to be a part of the network for the foreseeable future. SDN can be employed in key areas of the network, especially those that require deep integration between the physical and virtual networks. And although many new physical routers and switches have built-in support for SDN technologies, you can use SDN with existing devices albeit with less integration.

To better understand what SDN is and how it can be utilized, it's valuable to understand the three network planes that define the functions of a network device:

- *Data plane*—The **data plane** is the component that processes data as it travels through the device. For a router, this means receiving an incoming packet, looking up the destination network in the routing table, and forwarding the packet to the outgoing interface to get it to the destination network. For a switch, this means receiving an incoming frame, looking up the destination MAC address in its switching table, and switching the frame to the outgoing interface to deliver it to the destination device.
- *Control plane*—The **control plane** is the component that determines how the device operates and how it learns about its network environment. For a router, the network environment consists of the routing protocols and discovery protocols that enable the router to learn the network topology and build the routing table. For a switch, the environment might include the software that builds the switching table and the spanning tree protocol that prevents switching loops.
- *Management plane*—The **management plane** is the component that allows the device to be configured through a user interface by a network administrator, and management software such as Simple Network Management Protocol (SNMP) that allows the device to be monitored and managed remotely.

On a traditional network device, these three planes are tightly integrated with the device and each device vendor may implement aspects of each plane with proprietary technologies. SDN with Windows Server 2016 is built on the concept that the control and management planes are decoupled from the device, allowing you to dynamically manage the network and provision network resources using tools built in to Windows Server 2016. Many of the technologies discussed in this chapter such as NIC teaming, SET, and RDMA, along with Hyper-V virtual switches are part of the SDN tool set, but this section focuses on some of the higher-level tools used to deploy an SDN solution.

SDN brings the following features and advantages to your enterprise network and datacenter:

- Manage virtual and physical devices with common tools from a central location
- Define and deploy systemwide control and network security policies including traffic flows between virtual and physical networks
- Define granular firewall policies to enhance network security
- Dynamically provision network resources to respond to changing network conditions
- Enhance network performance
- Reduce infrastructure and network management costs

Note

The 70-741 certification exam objectives pertaining to SDN focus on understanding the scenarios and requirements for deploying SDN. SDN implementation details are beyond the scope of the exam and this book.

SDN Deployment Requirements

The requirements to deploy a basic Windows Server 2016 SDN solution are modest, but to get the most out of SDN, your physical servers and network infrastructure should include some high-performance network features. Here is a list of recommendations for your physical network environment:

- Because much of SDN relies on network virtualization, Windows Server 2016 Datacenter edition with Hyper-V must be installed on one or more servers.
- At least one RDMA-compatible 1 Gbps network interface card. Two or more 10 Gbps cards are desirable if you wish to take advantage of advanced features such as VMQ and RSS.
- DCB-compatible switches.
- You should have administrative access to all physical network devices such as routers and switches.

Hyper-V Network Virtualization

Hyper-V Network Virtualization (HNV) is a key component of the Windows Server 2016 software-defined network (SDN) environment. HNV provides a virtual network infrastructure that decouples the virtual network topology from the physical network. A virtualized network allows a business to, for example, move some or all of its datacenter operations to a cloud provider while maintaining its existing topology and IP subnets. This functionality provides businesses with a seamless hybrid cloud, allowing workloads to operate on the physical network or anywhere in the cloud without having to alter addressing schemes or topologies.

HNV allows you to move a VM using live migration to a server on a different subnet without having to change the VM's address and with no down time. Let's say you have a datacenter in Miami and a datacenter in Chicago. Your Miami datacenter is in danger of an imminent hurricane. Virtual workloads of the entire Miami datacenter could be moved to the Chicago datacenter, which has a totally different addressing scheme, without much address and topology configuration because the virtual network is independent of the physical network.

Another scenario for using HNV is with cloud providers that offer Infrastructure as a Service (IaaS). Businesses can move some or all of their existing private cloud infrastructure or physical network to the cloud provider's network while maintaining their current subnet infrastructure. The cloud provider can manage any number of these customers (referred to as *tenants*) even if their addressing schemes conflict because each tenant has its own virtualized network. In fact, different tenants can use the same VM IP addressing scheme even if the VMs are running on the same host server.

Without network virtualization, cloud providers would have to carefully maintain isolated VLANs for customers to avoid address conflicts, a management-intensive activity potentially fraught with errors. With HNV, little configuration is necessary to maintain multiple tenants on the same hosts and the same underlying physical networks.

To summarize, HNV provides the following benefits:

- Provides network isolation and flexible placement of workloads without using VLANs and without concern for addressing conflicts between tenants.
- Supports cross-subnet live migration.
- Maintains existing infrastructure during moves and migrations.
- Supports policy-based configuration of virtual networks.
- Decouples server and network administration because the physical network is independent of the VM addressing scheme. VMs can be placed anywhere in the physical network without the need to change addresses or access policies.

Virtual Networks with HNV

An **HNV virtual network** can be described as an autonomous system, to use routing parlance. This means that the virtual network is "owned" by a single tenant and is therefore isolated from other virtual networks. Other terms used to describe a virtual network include a *routing domain* or a *VM network*. HNV uses the term **routing domain**, which is a virtual network with one or more subnets that are isolated from other virtual networks. With HNV, each routing domain is assigned a **routing domain ID (RDID)**, a number that uniquely identifies a virtual network within the datacenter. Note that the RDID is unique throughout the datacenter rather than the Hyper-V host because a routing domain can be spread across multiple Hyper-V hosts. Each routing domain can contain one or more virtual subnets, each of which is assigned a **virtual subnet ID (VSID)**. A VSID is a unique 24-bit number throughout the datacenter in the range 4096 to 16,777,214. Figure 9-13 depicts two virtual networks, each with two virtual subnets. Each virtual network is assigned an RDID, and each virtual subnet is assigned a VSID. Notice that both virtual networks have a 192.168.1.0/24 subnet. This is possible because they are in different routing domains and cannot communicate with one another, so there is no conflict.

Communication between virtual subnets within a single routing domain is handled by the HNV distributed router as shown in Figure 9-13. A **distributed router** is a feature of a Hyper-V virtual switch that forwards packets from one virtual subnet to another virtual subnet within the same routing domain. However, hosts within one routing domain cannot interact with hosts in another routing domain or with an external network such as the Internet unless a gateway is present. To communicate outside the routing domain requires a tunneling protocol such as Virtual Extensible LAN (VXLAN) or Network Virtualization using Generic Routing Encapsulation (NVGRE). In addition, these tunneling protocols are used to allow VMs to communicate within a virtual subnet that is spread between Hyper-V hosts. The Hyper-V hosts need not even be located on the same physical network subnet.

VXLAN and NVGRE are both encapsulation protocols that create a tunnel through which packets travel. The encapsulation hides the addressing scheme of the underlying network, which is how the virtual network is decoupled from the physical network. VXLAN is the default protocol. Figure 9-14 depicts a HNV implementation in which the virtual networks connect to physical networks using a tunneling protocol. In the figure, both virtual networks could be running on the same or different hosts using a single tunnel or multiple tunnels. The tunneling protocols use the VSID in their protocol headers to differentiate between virtual subnets.

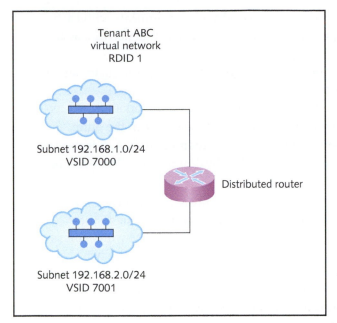
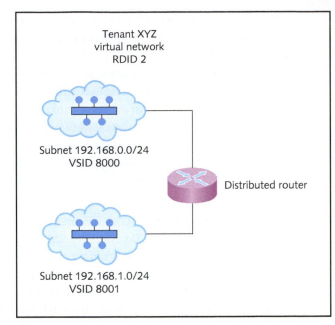

Hyper-V Network Virtualization (HNV)
running on Hyper-V hosts

Figure 9-13   Hyper-V Network Virtualization (HNV)

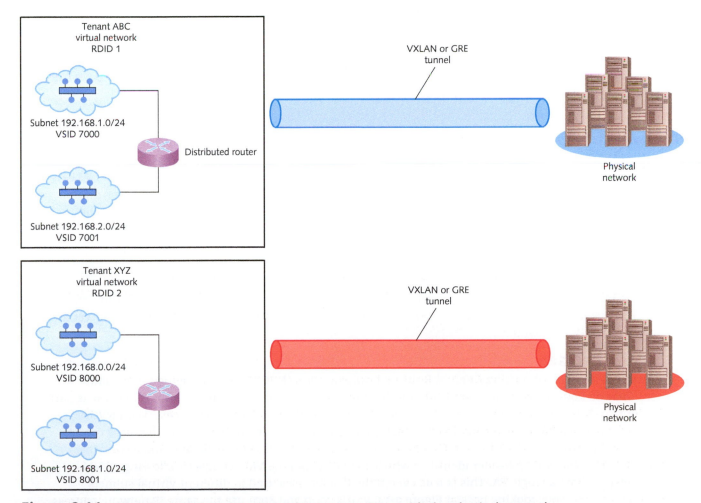

Figure 9-14   Virtual networks using a tunnel to communicate with the physical network

Tunneling protocols use packet encapsulation to allow virtual networks to communicate with each other and with the outside world. With HNV, tunneling works by associating each virtual network adapter with two IP addresses:

- *Customer address*—The **customer address (CA)** is the address assigned to VMs by the customer, or tenant, and reflects the customer's IP addressing scheme.
- *Provider address*—The **provider address (PA)** is the address used by the host network that reflects the hosting provider's physical network addressing scheme. It is the address used in the outer packet header of the tunneling protocol that encapsulates the frame containing the CA. It is used to transport packets between Hyper-V hosts and other devices on the physical network. The PA is not visible to the VMs on the virtual network.

Figure 9-15 illustrates how these addresses might be used to allow a VM hosted on one Hyper-V host to communicate with another VM hosted on another Hyper-V host where both VMs are in the same virtual subnet with VSID 7000. The VM with address 192.168.1.1 sends a packet to VM with address 192.168.1.2. The PAs 172.30.1.1 and 172.31.1.1 are the addresses used to communicate between the two Hyper-V hosts. Note that the two Hyper-V hosts are on two different subnets. When the packets reach the destination Hyper-V host at 172.31.1.1, they are de-encapsulated by the host and delivered to VM 192.168.1.2 in the virtual network. Communication in the reverse direction works the same way.

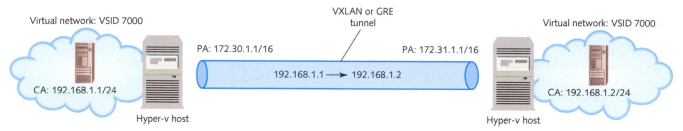

Figure 9-15 Use of the CA and PA in virtual network communication

HNV with VXLAN

Virtual Extensible LAN (VXLAN) is a standard and widely supported tunneling protocol that allows you to communicate between virtual networks and between virtual networks and the physical network. VXLAN is defined by RFC 7348 and operates over UDP port 4789. VXLAN encapsulates the original Layer 2 frame sent by a VM with a VXLAN header that includes a VXLAN Network Identifier field that specifies the VSID. The VXLAN header is in turn encapsulated by the UDP header and finally the outer IP header that includes the PAs.

VXLAN requires the installation of the Network Controller server role (a new feature in Windows Server 2016). Because VXLAN is a standard encapsulation protocol, it should be used for the widest compatibility with networking equipment vendors. However, because it requires Network Controller, which is available only in Windows Server 2016, you can't use it if earlier versions of Windows Server are part of the HNV deployment.

HNV with NVGRE

Network Virtualization using Generic Routing Encapsulation (NVGRE) is a tunneling protocol that uses Generic Routing Encapsulation (GRE) for the tunnel header. GRE, if you recall from Chapter 6, is part of Point-to-Point Tunneling Protocol (PPTP) used to implement VPNs for remote access. With NVGRE, a packet sent by a VM (which contains the CAs) is encapsulated inside another packet that uses the PA source and destination IP addresses. One of the NVGRE header fields is the GRE Key, which contains the VSID. The VSID in the header identifies which virtual subnet the VM belongs to, allowing all VMs on a host to share a single PA. This is true even if the IP addresses used in different virtual subnets overlap. For example, looking back at Figure 9-14, VSIDs 7000 and 8001 use the same IP network address (192.168.1.0/24). The figure shows two different tunnels for illustration purposes, but since the VSID is used to differentiate where the packets originated from, the VMs in the virtual networks could use the same NVGRE tunnel. In Windows Server 2012 R2, you needed one PA per VSID, but in Windows Server 2016, you can use one PA per NIC team member.

Network Controller

As mentioned, Network Controller is a new server role in Windows Server 2016 and is available only in the Datacenter edition. Network Controller is a necessary component for implementing what Microsoft refers to as *Software Defined Networking version 2 (SDNv2)*. Windows Server 2012/ R2 supported SDNv1 and required System Center Virtual Machine Manager (SCVMM) to manage network virtualization. With Network Controller, you can use PowerShell and Microsoft Azure for SDNv2 and network virtualization management if you are not using SCVMM in your enterprise (although, if you are currently using SCVMM to manage your Hyper-V environment, you can use it to manage SDNv2). Network Controller is installed like any server role, using Server Manager or the `Install-WindowsFeature` cmdlet.

Software Load Balancing

Software load balancing (SLB) is an SDN feature available in Windows Server 2016 that allows a hosting provider to distribute tenant network traffic across virtual network resources to increase virtual network performance and provide fault tolerance.

A datacenter has two types of network traffic:

- **East-West network traffic** is network traffic between virtual networks and between servers within the datacenter.
- **North-South network traffic** is network traffic traveling between the datacenter and external clients that need to access services provided by the datacenter.

SLB on Windows Server 2016 provides both East-West and North-South network traffic load balancing implemented in Layer 4 (TCP and UDP) protocols. To do so, SLB supports virtual IP address to dynamic IP address mapping and VLANs on virtual networks. A **virtual IP address (VIP)** is an IP address exposed to the public Internet that clients use to access resources on VMs in the datacenter. A **dynamic IP address (DIP)** is an address dynamically assigned to a VM that is a member of an SLB pool. SLB works by mapping VIPs to DIPs. For example, if an Internet client wants to access a webpage hosted on a VM in a datacenter that uses SLB, the process goes something like this:

1. A DNS lookup for the web server results in the client's receiving a VIP.
2. The client sends an HTTP request to the VIP.
3. The SLB process determines that there are two DIPs associated with the VIP. The DIPs are assigned to VMs hosted within the datacenter. The VMs are running on different Hyper-V hosts that are quite possibly on different physical subnets.
4. The SLB process selects one of the DIPs and sets the destination address of the packets using the DIP. VXLAN is then used to encapsulate the packet using the host server's physical address.
5. The host server receives the packet, de-encapsulates it, and delivers it to the VM that is assigned to the DIP.
6. When the VM replies to the HTTP request, the host server replaces the DIP source address with the VIP and sends the packet on to the requesting client.

This process is an example of East-West load balancing and allows a network service to be hosted on several VMs on any one of multiple hosts within a datacenter. The hosts could be on different subnets or even in multiple physical locations, allowing the VM closest to the requesting client to handle the request. With North-South load balancing, the network traffic stays within the datacenter, so there is no need for VIPs. As an example of North-South load balancing, suppose an application running on a VM within the datacenter uses a database running on multiple VMs within the datacenter. SLB can be used to load balance requests to the database.

SLB Components

SLB is composed of several components working together as described in the following list:

- *System Center Virtual Machine Manager (SCVMM)*—A system management product that must be purchased and installed on a Windows Server 2016 server. With SCVMM, you can manage all your Hyper-V hosts, Network Controller, and all SLB components. SCVMM is not required to deploy SLB because you can use PowerShell cmdlets, but it is highly recommended if you have an extensive Hyper-V environment.
- *Hyper-V hosts and SDN-enabled virtual switches*—Virtual networks and VMs used for SLB run on Windows Server 2016 Hyper-V hosts. Virtual switches can be created using Hyper-V Virtual Switch Manager or PowerShell and require the Virtual Filtering Platform (VFP), which can be enabled when the switch is created (see Figure 9-16). VFP provides SDN functionality on virtual switches by accepting SDN policies from Network Controller.

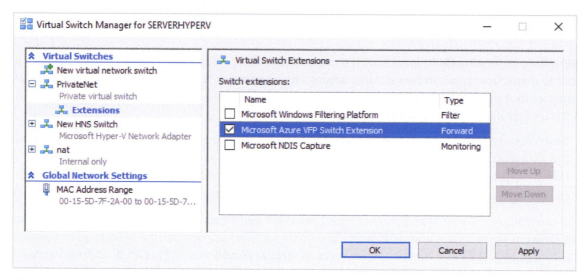

Figure 9-16   Enabling the Virtual Filtering Platform on a Hyper-V virtual switch

- *Network Controller*—Processes SLB commands and distributes SLB policies among Hyper-V hosts and other SLB components and monitors the SLB infrastructure to provide health status.
- *SLB MUX*—The **SLB MUX** maps VIPs to DIPs on incoming East-West traffic and forwards the traffic to the selected DIP.
- *SLB Host Agent*—The **SLB Host Agent** interfaces between Hyper-V hosts and Network Controller to distribute SLB policies and configure Hyper-V virtual switches for SLB.
- *BGP router*—Routes traffic to the SLB MUX; monitors SLB MUXs for availability; and receives route updates for VIPs from the SLB MUX.

Note

For more on SLB with Hyper-V Network Virtualization, see *https://docs.microsoft.com/en-us/windows-server/networking/sdn/technologies/network-function-virtualization/software-load-balancing-for-sdn*.

Windows Server Gateways

Hyper-V uses the distributed router function implemented on virtual switches to route traffic between virtual networks. To route traffic between virtual networks and the physical network requires a Windows Server Gateway. You have already seen an example of this with GRE tunneling. Windows Server Gateway, also known as *RAS Gateway*, is a software router that can be deployed in both single-tenant and multitenant datacenters. RAS Gateway can be implemented in a number of ways:

- *Layer 3 forwarder*—A **layer 3 (L3) forwarder** performs simple routing between virtual networks on a host and VLANs configured on the physical network.
- *GRE tunneling*—GRE tunneling was discussed earlier. It is used when using traditional VLANs to maintain subnet isolation becomes too unwieldy. GRE tunnels are established between two Hyper-V hosts or between a Hyper-V host and a router and can support multiple tenants on a single host.
- *Site-to-site VPN*—A site-to-site (S2S) VPN is frequently used to connect a tenant's virtual network residing in the cloud provider's datacenter to the tenant's own on-site datacenter. An S2S VPN typically uses IPsec to securely transfer data across the Internet.
- *NAT gateway*—A NAT gateway allows VMs on virtual networks to access the Internet by translating private IP addresses to public IP addresses.

All of the RAS Gateway implementations are multitenant aware so tenants that use overlapping IP address spaces can use the same gateway. **Multitenant aware** means that the gateway software supports multiple isolated virtual networks.

Distributed Firewall Policies and Security Groups

Distributed firewall policies, a new feature in Windows Server 2016, enable a network administrator to manage firewall policies for all of a datacenter's virtual networks. Distributed firewall policies are implemented using the Datacenter Firewall, a new service in Windows Server 2016. The Datacenter Firewall provides the following features:

- Scalable software-based firewall solution that a cloud provider can offer to multitenant virtual networks.
- Operating system independent protection of VMs because the firewall is implemented in the virtual switch.
- Flexible protection of VMs, allowing VMs to be moved among Hyper-V hosts without the need to reconfigure the firewall.
- Ability of tenants to define firewall rules specific to their requirements. Tenants can protect VMs from Internet threats and the service provider network as well as control traffic within and between virtual subnets.

Datacenter Firewall policies are distributed to virtual networks using Network Controller. Policies are created using PowerShell or SCVMM and are implemented on individual virtual switch ports, not on the host OS. Figure 9-17 illustrates how Distributed Firewall Manager works within Network Controller. The Northbound interface is the application programming interface (API) in Network Controller through which firewall policies are sent from SCVMM or PowerShell to Distributed Firewall Manager. The Southbound interface is used to distribute firewall policies to individual virtual switch ports. The terms *Northbound interface* and *Southbound interface* are common terms in SDN. The **Northbound interface** is an application programming interface through which commands and policies are sent to the SDN controller, in this case Network Controller. The **Southbound interface** is the interface through which policies are sent from the SDN controller to the network device or, in this case the virtual switch.

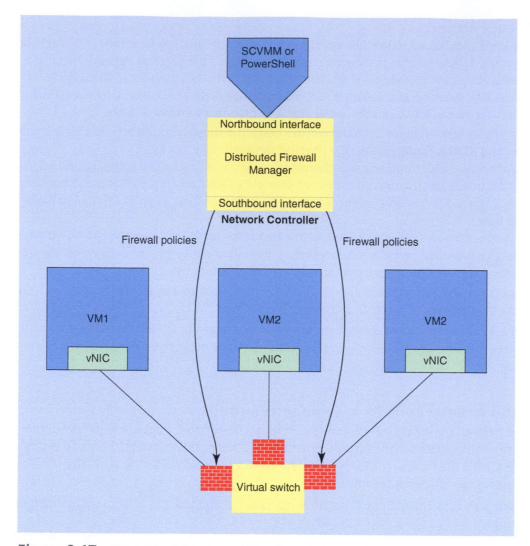

Figure 9-17   Conceptual diagram of Distributed Firewall Manager

Network Security Groups

A **Network Security Group (NSG)** is a named security policy based on access control lists. An **access control list (ACL)** is a set of rules that define what traffic is allowed to pass through a network interface. NSGs can be applied to host NICs attached to VMs, individual VMs, or entire virtual subnets. NSGs contain a list of inbound ACL rules that are applied to network traffic coming into the interface or subnet and outbound ACL rules that are applied to network traffic leaving the interface or subnet. ACL rules have the following properties:

- *Rule name*—For example, you may have a rule named WebIn to define inbound web traffic.
- *Protocol*—Can be TCP, UDP, or *. A * for the protocol matches TCP, UDP, and ICMP traffic.
- *Source port*—The source TCP or UDP port number or a range of port numbers.
- *Destination port*—The destination TCP or UDP port number or a range of port numbers.
- *Source address*—The source IP address or subnet. You can use * to include any address.
- *Destination address*—The destination IP address or subnet. You can use * to include any address.
- *Direction*—Inbound or outbound.

- *Priority*—A number between 100 and 4096 that determines the order in which the rules are processed. Rules with lower-priority values are processed first, and when a match is made, processing stops.
- *Access*—Options are Allow or Deny. If a packet matches an Allow rule, the packet is allowed in or out of the interface depending on the direction specified. If a packet matches a Deny rule, the packet is dropped. Packets that don't match any rules are dropped.

> **Note**
>
> NSGs are implemented in Resource Manager in Microsoft Azure or with PowerShell.

Chapter Summary

- NIC teaming allows multiple network interfaces to work together to provide increased bandwidth, load balancing, and fault tolerance. Another term for this is load balancing and failover (LBFO). Load balancing distributes traffic between two or more interfaces, providing an increase in a server's overall network throughput. Failover is the ability of a server to recover from network hardware failure by having redundant hardware that can immediately take over for a device failure.

- When creating a new NIC team, you can configure the teaming mode and the load balancing mode. The three teaming modes are Switch Independent, Static Teaming, or Link Aggregation Control Protocol (LACP). The three load balancing modes are Address Hash, Hyper-V Port, and Dynamic.

- You can configure NIC teaming on VMs as well as on physical computers. If you have already configured NIC teaming on the Hyper-V host server, configuring it on VMs running on the host isn't necessary.

- Switch Embedded Teaming (SET) is a new feature in Windows Server 2016 that allows up to eight identical physical adapters on the host system to be configured as a team and mapped to a virtual switch. The virtual switch can control all the physical adapters simultaneously.

- Data center bridging (DCB) is an enhancement to Ethernet that provides additional features for use in enterprise datacenters, in particular when server clustering and SANs are in use. Ethernet is a "best-effort" delivery system that doesn't guarantee delivery of frames. DCB improves performance in iSCSI deployments by utilizing Quality of Service, deterministic performance, and DCB Exchange.

- Quality of Service (QoS) in a network allows you to configure priorities for different types of network traffic so delay-sensitive data is prioritized over regular data. QoS policies are created using the `New-NetQoSPolicy` cmdlet. A QoS policy includes a descriptive name and defines the type of traffic you wish to prioritize by specifying a destination port and a priority number based on IEEE 802.1p from 0 to 7.

- Virtual machine queue (VMQ) accelerates virtual NIC (vNIC) performance by delivering packets from the external network directly to the vNIC, bypassing the management operating system. VMQ is enabled or disabled on each vNIC. When packets arrive on the physical interface for the vNIC, they are delivered directly to the VM.

- Receive side scaling (RSS) is a feature for network drivers that efficiently distributes the processing of incoming network traffic among multiple CPU cores. Without RSS, all incoming network data is processed on the CPU where the network interface card interrupt occurs.

- Virtual machine multi-queue (VMMQ) is a new feature in Windows Server 2016 that reduces the overhead in getting packets from the physical network to a VM on the host. With VMMQ, a VM can be assigned multiple queues on the host adapter with each queue having a vCPU core to process its incoming data.

- Server Message Block (SMB) is the primary Windows protocol for file sharing. SMB Direct is a performance technology designed specifically for the SMB protocol that nearly eliminates server processor utilization for data transfers. SMB Multichannel provides fault tolerance and improved performance in a connection between a client and a server providing an SMB share.

- Software-defined networking (SDN) is a collection of technologies designed to make the network infrastructure flexible and responsive to the ever-changing network requirements in today's enterprise and cloud networks.

- SDN is composed of three network planes: the data plane, the control plane, and the management plane.

- Hyper-V Network Virtualization (HNV) is a key component of the Windows Server 2016 SDN environment. HNV provides a virtual network infrastructure that decouples the virtual network topology from the physical network.

- Virtual Extensible LAN (VXLAN) is a standard and widely supported tunneling protocol that allows communication between virtual networks and between virtual networks and the physical network. VXLAN is defined by RFC 7348. Network Virtual using Generic Routing Encapsulation (NVGRE) is a tunneling protocol that uses Generic Routing Encapsulation for the tunnel header.

- Network Controller is a new server role in Windows Server 2016 and is available only in the Datacenter edition. Network Controller is a necessary component for implementing what Microsoft refers to as Software Defined Networking version 2 (SDNv2).

- Software load balancing (SLB) is an SDN feature available in Windows Server 2016 that allows a hosting provider to distribute tenant network traffic across virtual network resources to increase virtual network performance and provide fault tolerance.

- Windows Server Gateway, also known as RAS Gateway, is a software router than can be deployed in both single-tenant and multitenant datacenters. RAS Gateway can be implemented in the following ways: Layer 3 forwarder, GRE tunneling, site-to-site VPN, or a NAT gateway.

- Distributed firewall policies, a new feature in Windows Server 2016, enables a network administrator to manage firewall policies for all of a datacenter's virtual networks. Datacenter Firewall policies are distributed to virtual networks using Network Controller. Policies are created using PowerShell or SCVMM and are implemented on individual virtual switch ports, not on the host OS.

Key Terms

access control list (ACL)
control plane
customer address (CA)
data center bridging (DCB)
data plane
distributed firewall policies
distributed router
dynamic IP address (DIP)
East-West network traffic
failover
HNV virtual network
Hyper-V Network Virtualization (HNV)
layer 3 (L3) forwarder
load balancing
load balancing and failover (LBFO)

management plane
multitenant aware
Network Security Group (NSG)
Network Virtualization using Generic Routing Encapsulation (NVGRE)
NIC teaming
Northbound interface
North-South network traffic
provider address (PA)
Quality of Service (QoS)
receive side scaling (RSS)
routing domain
routing domain ID (RDID)
single-root IO virtualization (SR-IOV)

SLB Host Agent
SLB MUX
SMB Direct
SMB Multichannel
software-defined networking (SDN)
software load balancing (SLB)
Southbound interface
Switch Embedded Teaming (SET)
Virtual Extensible LAN (VXLAN)
virtual IP address (VIP)
virtual machine multi-queue (VMMQ)
virtual machine queue (VMQ)
virtual receive side scaling (vRSS)
virtual subnet ID (VSID)

Review Questions

1. What technology in Windows Server 2016 allows several network interfaces to work together in a coordinated effort to provide load balancing and fault tolerance?
   a. Load balancing
   b. QoS
   c. NIC teaming
   d. Failover

2. Which of the following terms best describes a server's ability to recover from a network hardware failure because additional network hardware can immediately take over when a device has malfunctioned?
   a. QoS
   b. Failover
   c. RSS
   d. Load balancing

3. You have been assigned the task of managing a group of Windows 2016 servers that are currently utilizing NIC teaming. You would like to view a list of the NIC teams that currently exist on a specific server. What PowerShell cmdlet should you use?
   a. `Set-LbfoTeam`
   b. `Show-NetLbfoTeam`
   c. `Get-NetLbfoTeam`
   d. `Get-LbfoTeam`

4. Which of the following load balancing modes is the default load balancing mode on physical machines, allows traffic to be distributed evenly among all team members, and can include virtual NICs?
   a. LACP
   b. Dynamic
   c. Hyper-V Port
   d. Address Hash

5. You are currently reviewing the capabilities of Switch Embedded Teaming (SET) available in Windows Server 2016. You have decided to implement SET into your current system. Which of the following requirements must be met to utilize SET in your network? (Choose all that apply.)
   a. Switch independent mode must be the teaming mode utilized.
   b. SET must use receive side scaling (RSS).

   c. SET requires all NICs to be identical and operate at the same speed.
   d. You must use only physical servers connected to the physical network.

6. Which of the following technologies was designed to avert delays in the delivery of data in iSCSI applications and create a "lossless" environment?
   a. Quality of Service
   b. Link Aggregation Control Protocol
   c. Data center bridging
   d. DCB Exchange

7. What technology can be implemented to allow you the ability to configure priorities for different types of network traffic so that delay-sensitive data is prioritized over regular data?
   a. Quality of Service
   b. DCB Exchange
   c. LACP
   d. SET

8. When a vNIC's performance is increased by delivering packets from the external network directly to the vNIC, bypassing the management operating system, what specific technology is being used?
   a. NIC acceleration
   b. Virtual machine queue
   c. Receive side scaling
   d. Quality of Service

9. What feature is designed for network drivers and used to efficiently distribute the processing of incoming network traffic among multiple CPU cores?
   a. Virtual machine queue
   b. QoS traffic classes
   c. Receive side scaling
   d. DCB Exchange

10. You are in the process of setting up a VM with multiple cores and wish to reduce the overhead in getting packets from the physical network to your VM. What Windows Server 2016 feature can be implemented to allow you to utilize more than one queue on the host adapter with each queue having a vCPU core to process data?
    a. Virtual machine multi-queue
    b. Data center bridging
    c. Virtual machine queue
    d. SMB Multichannel

11. Which of the following advantages would a virtual adapter gain by enabling single-root I/O virtualization when you create a virtual switch? (Choose all that apply.)
    a. A second virtual adapter would be created.
    b. It would have lower overhead.
    c. The virtual adapter would bypass the virtual switch software.
    d. The virtual adapter would not bypass the virtual switch software.

12. What requirement must be met on your host's network adapter if you are planning to implement SMB Direct to reduce server processor utilization for data transfers?
    a. SR-IOV enabled
    b. VMQ compatible
    c. QoS enabled
    d. RDMA compatible

13. What specific technology is included in SMB 3.0 that operates automatically and provides fault tolerance to improve performance in a connection between a client and a server providing an SMB share?
    a. SMB Direct
    b. SR-IOV
    c. SMB Multichannel
    d. SMB Connect

14. Which of the following key technologies, virtual or physical, are most likely to be centrally managed when using software-defined networking? (Choose all that apply.)
    a. Router
    b. Networked power supply
    c. Access gateway
    d. Switch

15. SDN utilizes three main network planes that define the functions of a network device. Which of the following is *not* an SDN plane?
    a. Hardware
    b. Management
    c. Control
    d. Data

16. Which SDN plane would dictate how a switch operates and discovers the network it operates within?

    a. Control
    b. Data
    c. Hardware
    d. Data

17. What features and advantages are added when you choose to utilize SDN in a datacenter or enterprise network? (Choose all that apply.)
    a. Enhances network performance
    b. Defines traffic flows between virtual and physical networks
    c. Increases network management costs
    d. Enhances network security

18. Your organization has decided to expand its infrastructure using a cloud provider's IaaS offerings. What Windows Server 2016 technology will allow your organization to move a share of its private cloud infrastructure to the cloud provider's network while maintaining the current subnet infrastructure?
    a. VSID
    b. Hyper-V Network Virtualization
    c. Software-defined networking
    d. Virtual Extensible LAN

19. Which of the following is a standard tunneling protocol, operating over UDP port 4789, that permits communication within virtual networks and between virtual networks and the physical network?
    a. NVGRE
    b. RDID
    c. VSID
    d. VXLAN

20. When utilizing the Windows Server 2016 distributed firewall policies, which of the following features are provided? (Choose all that apply.)
    a. Firewall solution for multitenant virtual networks
    b. VMs moved among Hyper-V hosts without reconfiguring the firewall
    c. Operating system dependent protection of VMs
    d. A scalable software-based firewall solution

Critical Thinking

The following activities give you critical thinking challenges. Case Projects offer a scenario with a problem to solve and for which you supply a written solution.

Case Project 9-1: Selecting a High-Performance Technology

You are experiencing network performance bottlenecks with your virtual networks and their access to the physical network on one of your server. Your server has four physical NICs, one 10 Gb NIC and three 1 Gb NICs. You are not sure if you want to use SET or traditional NIC teaming. What are some of the considerations you need to keep in mind as you make your decision?

Case Project 9-2: Working in the Clouds

You are asked to consult for a cloud services provider. It is reaching limitations with its virtual networks because virtual network to physical network access is managed by traditional VLANs. The provider has lost some customers because the customers' IP addressing scheme had to be changed to work in their environment without conflicting with other customers' networks. What do you suggest that this cloud provider do in order to maximize flexibility with its virtual network offerings? What problems does your proposed solution solve?

MCSA EXAM 70-741 OBJECTIVES

The table in this Appendix maps the exam objectives for Microsoft Certified Solutions Associate (MCSA) Exam 70-741, Networking with Windows Server 2016, to the corresponding chapter and section title where the objectives are covered in this book. After each main objective, the percentage of the exam that includes the objective is shown in parentheses.

MCSA Exam 70-741: Skill Measured	Chapter	Section
Implement Domain Name System (15–20%)		
Install and configure DNS servers	2, 3	
• Determine DNS installation requirements	2	Installing DNS
• Determine supported DNS deployment scenarios on Nano Server	2	Installing DNS
• Install DNS	2	Installing DNS
• Configure forwarders	2	Configuring DNS Server Settings
• Configure Root Hints	2	Configuring DNS Server Settings
• Configure delegation	3	Managing DNS Zones/Zone Delegation
• Implement DNS policies	3	Implementing DNS Policies
• Implement DNS global settings using Windows PowerShell	2	Configure DNS Server Settings/PowerShell Commands for Advanced DNS Server Settings
• Configure Domain Name System Security Extensions (DNSSEC)	3	Configuring DNS Security
• Configure DNS Socket Pool, configure cache locking	3	Configuring DNS Security
• Enable Response Rate Limiting	3	Configuring DNS Security
• Configure DNS-based Authentication of Named Entities (DANE)	3	Configuring DNS Security
• Configure DNS logging	2	Configuring DNS Server Settings
• Configure delegated administration	3	Managing and Monitoring the DNS Server
• Configure recursion settings	2	Configuring DNS Server Settings
• Implement DNS performance tuning	3	Managing and Monitoring the DNS Server
• Configure global settings using Windows PowerShell	2	Configure DNS Server Settings/PowerShell Commands for Advanced DNS Server Settings

MCSA Exam 70-741: Skill Measured	Chapter	Section
Create and configure DNS zones and records	2, 3	
• Create primary zones	2	Configuring DNS
• Configure Active Directory integration of primary zones	3	Configuring DNS Zone Storage
• Create and configure secondary zones	2	Configuring DNS Configuring DNS Zones
• Create and configure stub zones	3	Managing DNS Zones/Using Stub Zones
• Configure a GlobalNames zone	2	Configuring DNS Zones
• Analyze zone-level statistics	3	Managing and Monitoring the DNS Server/ Analyzing Zone-Level Statistics
• Create and configure DNS Resource Records (RR), including A, AAAA, PTR, SOA, NS, SRV, CNAME, and MX records	2	Creating DNS Resource Records Configuring DNS Zones
• Configure zone scavenging	3	Managing DNS Zones/Configuring Zone Scavenging
• Configure record options, including Time To Live (TTL) and weight	2	Creating DNS Resource Records
• Configure round robin	2	Configuring DNS Server Settings
• Configure secure dynamic updates	3	Configuring DNS Zone Storage
• Configure unknown record support	3	Configuring DNS Zone Storage
• Use DNS audit events and analytical (query) events for auditing and troubleshooting	2	Configuring DNS Server Settings/Event and Debug Logging
• Configure Zone Scopes	3	Implementing DNS Policies/Configuring Zone Scopes
• Configure records in Zone Scopes	3	Implementing DNS Policies/Configuring Zone Scopes
• Configure policies for zones	3	Implementing DNS Policies/Configuring Zone Scopes
Implement DHCP (15–20%)		
Install and configure DHCP	4	
• Install and configure DHCP servers	4	Installing and Configuring a DHCP Server
• Authorize a DHCP server	4	Installing and Configuring a DHCP Server
• Create and configure scopes	4	Installing and Configuring a DHCP Server
• Create and configure superscopes and multicast scopes	4	Installing and Configuring a DHCP Server
• Configure a DHCP reservation	4	Installing and Configuring a DHCP Server
• Configure DHCP options	4	Installing and Configuring a DHCP Server
• Configure DNS options from within DHCP	4	DHCP Server Configuration/Configuring IPv4 Server Properties
• Configure policies	4	DHCP Server Configuration/Configuring Policies
• Configure client and server for PXE boot	4	DHCP Server Configuration/Configuring DHCP for PXE Boot
• Configure DHCP Relay Agent	4	DHCP Server Configuration/DHCP Relay Agents
• Implement IPv6 addressing using DHCPv6	4	Implementing DHCPv6

MCSA Exam 70-741: Skill Measured	Chapter	Section
• Perform export and import of a DHCP server	4	DHCP Server Configuration/Server Migration, Export, and Import
• Perform DHCP server migration	4	DHCP Server Configuration/Server Migration, Export, and Import
Manage and maintain DHCP	4	
• Configure a lease period	4	DHCP Server Configuration
• Back up and restore the DHCP database	4	DHCP Server Configuration
• Configure high availability using DHCP failover	4	DHCP High Availability
• Configure DHCP name protection, troubleshoot DHCP	4	DHCP Server Configuration
Implement IP Address Management (15–20%)		
Install and configure IP Address Management (IPAM)	5	
• Provision IPAM manually or by using Group Policy	5	Deploying an IPAM Solution
• Configure server discovery	5	Deploying an IPAM Solution
• Create and manage IP blocks and ranges	5	Administering IPAM
• Monitor utilization of IP address space	5	Administering IPAM
• Migrate existing workloads to IPAM	5	Administering IPAM/Migrate IPAM to a New Server
• Configure IPAM database storage using SQL Server	5	Deploying an IPAM Solution
• Determine scenarios for using IPAM with System Center Virtual Machine Manager for physical and virtual IP address space management	5	Administering IPAM/IPAM and System Center Virtual Machine Manager
Manage DNS and DHCP using IPAM	5	
• Manage DHCP server properties using IPAM	5	Administering IPAM/Managing DHCP with IPAM
• Configure DHCP scopes and options	5	Administering IPAM/Managing DHCP with IPAM
• Configure DHCP policies and failover	5	Administering IPAM/Managing DHCP with IPAM
• Manage DNS server properties using IPAM	5	Administering IPAM/Managing DNS with IPAM
• Manage DNS zones and records	5	Administering IPAM/Managing DNS with IPAM
• Manage DNS and DHCP servers in multiple Active Directory forests	5	Administering IPAM/Managing DNS and DHCP Servers in Multiple Forests
• Delegate administration for DNS and DHCP using role-based access control (RBAC)	5	Administering IPAM/IPAM Administration Delegation
Audit IPAM	5	
• Audit the changes performed on the DNS and DHCP servers	5	Auditing IPAM
• Audit the IPAM address usage trail	5	Auditing IPAM
• Audit DHCP lease events and user logon events	5	Auditing IPAM
Implement network connectivity and remote access solutions (25–30%)		
Implement network connectivity solutions	6	
• Implement Network Address Translation (NAT)	6	Configure Network Address Translation
• Configure routing	6	Configure IPv4 and IPv6 Routing

MCSA Exam 70-741: Skill Measured	Chapter	Section
Implement virtual private network (VPN) and DirectAccess solutions	6	
• Implement remote access and site-to-site (S2S) VPN solutions using remote access gateway	6	Installing and Configuring the Remote Access Role/Configuring Remote Access Options
• Configure different VPN protocol options	6	Installing and Configuring the Remote Access Role/Configuring Remote Access Options
• Configure authentication options	6	Installing and Configuring the Remote Access Role/Configuring Remote Access Options
• Configure VPN reconnect	6	Installing and Configuring the Remote Access Role/Configuring Remote Access Options
• Create and configure connection profiles	6	Installing and Configuring the Remote Access Role/Configuring Remote Access Options
• Determine when to use remote access VPN and site-to-site VPN and configure appropriate protocols	6	Installing and Configuring the Remote Access Role/Configuring Remote Access Options
• Install and configure DirectAccess, implement server requirements, implement client configuration, troubleshoot DirectAccess	6	The DirectAccess Role Service
Implement Network Policy Server (NPS)	7	
• Configure a RADIUS server including RADIUS proxy	7	Installing and Configuring NPS and RADIUS
• Configure RADIUS clients	7	Installing and Configuring NPS and RADIUS
• Configure NPS templates	7	Configuring NPS Policies
• Configure RADIUS accounting	7	Installing and Configuring NPS and RADIUS
• Configure certificates	7	Installing and Configuring NPS and RADIUS
• Configure Connection Request Policies	7	Configuring NPS Policies
• Configure network policies for VPN and wireless and wired clients	7	Configuring NPS Policies
• Import and export NPS policies	7	Configuring NPS Policies
Implement core and distributed network solutions (10–15%)		
Implement IPv4 and IPv6 addressing	1, 6	
• Configure IPv4 addresses and options	1	Configuring IPv4 Addresses
• Determine and configure appropriate IPv6 addresses	1	Internet Protocol Version 6 Overview IPv6 Address Types
• Configure IPv4 or IPv6 subnetting	1	IPv4 Addresses IPv6 Address Types
• Implement IPv6 stateless addressing	1	IPv6 Autoconfiguration
• Configure interoperability between IPv4 and IPv6 by using ISATAP, 6to4, and Teredo scenarios	1	Transitioning from IPv4 to IPv6
• Configure Border Gateway Protocol (BGP)	6	Configuring IPv4 and IPv6 Routing
• Configure IPv4 and IPv6 routing	6	Configuring IPv4 and IPv6 Routing
Implement Distributed File System (DFS) and Branch Office solutions	8	
• Install and configure DFS namespaces	8	An Overview of the Distributed File System Installing and Configuring DFS

MCSA Exam 70-741: Skill Measured	Chapter	Section
• Configure DFS replication targets	8	Creating DFS Replication Groups
• Configure replication scheduling	8	Creating DFS Replication Groups
• Configure Remote Differential Compression (RDC) settings	8	Creating DFS Replication Groups
• Configure staging	8	Creating DFS Replication Groups
• Configure fault tolerance	8	Creating DFS Replication Groups
• Clone a Distributed File System Replication (DFSR) database	8	Creating DFS Replication Groups
• Recover DFSR databases	8	Creating DFS Replication Groups
• Optimize DFS Replication	8	Creating DFS Replication Groups
• Install and configure BranchCache	8	Installing and Configuring BranchCache
• Implement distributed and hosted cache modes	8	Installing and Configuring BranchCache
• Implement BranchCache for web, file, and application servers	8	Installing and Configuring BranchCache
• Troubleshoot BranchCache	8	Installing and Configuring BranchCache
Implement an advanced network infrastructure (10–15%)		
Implement high performance network solutions	9	
• Implement NIC Teaming or the Switch Embedded Teaming (SET) solution, and identify when to use each	9	High-Performance Network Solutions/Configuring NIC Teaming/High-Performance Network Solutions/Implementing Switch Embedded Teaming
• Enable and configure Receive Side Scaling (RSS)	9	High-Performance Network Solutions/Receive Side Scaling
• Enable and configure network Quality of Service (QoS) with Data Center Bridging (DCB)	9	High-Performance Network Solutions/Configuring QoS with DCB
• Enable and configure SMB Direct on Remote Direct Memory Access (RDMA) enabled network adapters	9	High-Performance Network Solutions/SMB Direct and SMB Multichannel
• Enable and configure SMB Multichannel	9	High-Performance Network Solutions/SMB Direct and SMB Multichannel
• Enable and configure virtual Receive Side Scaling (vRSS) on a Virtual Machine Queue (VMQ) capable network adapter	9	High-Performance Network Solutions/Receive Side Scaling
• Enable and configure Virtual Machine Multi-Queue (VMMQ)	9	High-Performance Network Solutions/Virtual Machine Multi-Queue
• Enable and configure Single-Root I/O Virtualization (SR-IOV) on a supported network adapter	9	High-Performance Network Solutions/SR-IOV
Determine scenarios and requirements for implementing software-defined networking (SDN)	9	
• Determine deployment scenarios and network requirements for deploying SDN	9	Software-Defined Networking
• Determine requirements and scenarios for implementing Hyper-V Network Virtualization (HNV) using Network Virtualization Generic Route Encapsulation (NVGRE) encapsulation or Virtual Extensible LAN (VXLAN) encapsulation	9	Software-Defined Networking/Hyper-V Network Virtualization

MCSA Exam 70-741: Skill Measured	Chapter	Section
• Determine scenarios for implementation of Software Load Balancer (SLB) for North-South and East-West load balancing	9	Software-Defined Networking/Software Load Balancing
• Determine implementation scenarios for various types of Windows Server Gateways, including L3, GRE, and S2S, and their use	9	Software-Defined Networking/Windows Server Gateways
• Determine requirements and scenarios for distributed firewall policies and network security groups	9	Software-Defined Networking/Distributed Firewall Policies and Security Groups

GLOSSARY

6to4 An IPv4-to-IPv6 transition protocol that provides automatic tunneling of IPv6 traffic over an IPv4 network. It can handle host-to-router or router-to-host tunneling but is most often used to create a router-to-router tunnel.

A

A record A resource record in a DNS zone that consists of a hostname and an IPv4 address. Also called a *host record*.

AAAA record A resource record in a DNS zone that consists of a hostname and an IPv6 address. Also called a *host record*.

access-based enumeration A feature of the Windows file system that allows users to see only files and folder in a File Explorer window or in a listing of files from the `dir` command to which they have been given at least read (or equivalent) permission.

access client A user or device attempting to access the network.

access control list (ACL) A set of rules that define what traffic is allowed to pass through a network interface.

access policy A policy that allows you to assign users or groups to specific roles and access scopes.

access scope A scope that allows you to define which IPAM objects an administrative role can access.

Active Directory partition A special file that Active Directory uses to store domain information.

authoritative server A DNS server that holds a complete copy of a zone's resource records (typically a primary or secondary zone).

Automatic Private IP Addressing (APIPA) A method of automatic IP address assignment that occurs when a computer can't contact a DHCP server; uses the range 169.254.1.0 through 169.254.254.255.

B

Border Gateway Protocol (BGP) An advanced dynamic routing protocol that can be used to route traffic between remote networks, including site-to-site VPNs, and between physical and virtual networks.

BranchCache A file-sharing technology that allows computers at a branch office to cache files retrieved from a central server across a WAN link.

broadcast A packet addressed to all computers on the network.

broadcast domain   The bounds of a network that defines which devices must receive a packet that's broadcast by any other device; usually an IP subnet.

C

caching-only DNS server   A DNS server with no zones. Its sole job is to field DNS queries, do recursive lookups to root servers, or send requests to forwarders and then cache the results.

centralized topology   An IPAM deployment option that has a single IPAM server for the entire enterprise. *See also* IP Address Management (IPAM).

certificate-based authentication   An authentication method that uses a certificate instead of a password to establish an entity's identity.

certification authority (CA)   An entity that issues digital certificates used for authentication.

Challenge Handshake Authentication Protocol (CHAP)   An authentication protocol that uses a series of challenges and responses to verify a client's identity.

CIDR notation   A method of expressing an IP address in the format A.B.C.D/n; n is the number of 1 bits in the subnet mask or the number of bits in the network ID. *See also* Classless Interdomain Routing (CIDR).

classful addressing   The use of IP addresses with their default subnet masks according to their address class: A, B, or C.

Classless Interdomain Routing (CIDR)   The use of IP addresses without requiring the default subnet mask. *See also* subnet mask.

client subnet   A named subnet that has a value in the format a.b.c.d/y, for example 192.168.0.0/24.

CNAME record   A record containing an alias for another record that enables you to refer to the same resource with different names yet maintain only one host record.

conditional forwarder   A DNS server to which other DNS servers send requests targeted for a specific domain.

conflict detection   A DHCP server property that causes the DHCP server to attempt to ping an IP address before it's offered to a client to make ensure that the address isn't already in use.

content information   A message transferred from a BranchCache server to a client that indicates to the client where the file can be retrieved from the cache in the branch office. *See also* BranchCache.

control plane   The software-defined networking (SDN) component that determines how the device operates and how it learns about its network environment.

customer address (CA)   The address assigned to virtual machines by the customer, or tenant, and it reflects the customer's IP addressing scheme.

D

data center bridging (DCB)   An enhancement to Ethernet that provides additional features for use in enterprise datacenters, in particular when server clustering and SANs are in use.

data plane   The software-defined networking (SDN) component that processes data as it travels through the device.

default gateway   Part of a computer's IP address configuration, it is the address of a device, usually a router, that tells the computer where packets destined for another network should be sent.

default route   The network where the router sends all packets that don't match any other destinations in the routing table.

Delegation Signer (DS)   A DNSSEC record that holds the name of a delegated zone and is used to verify delegated child zones. *See also* Domain Name System Security Extension (DNSSEC).

demand-dial interface   A network connection that is used to establish the VPN connection when network traffic from the internal network has a destination address of the other network to which you are connecting.

destination IP address   The IP address of the computer a packet is sent to.

DHCP failover   A feature in Windows Server 2016 that allows two DHCP servers to share the pool of IP addresses in a scope, giving both servers access to all addresses in the pool.

DHCP filter   A DHCP server feature that allows administrators to restrict which computers on a network are leased IP addresses.

DHCP name protection   A feature in DHCP that prevents name squatting by non-Windows computers by using the DHCP resource record Dynamic Host Configuration Identifier (DHCID). *See also* name squatting.

DHCP policies   A feature in Windows Server 2016 that gives administrators more fine-tuned control over IP address lease options with conditions based on criteria.

DHCP relay agent   A device that listens for broadcast DHCPDISCOVER and DHCPREQUEST messages and forwards them to a DHCP server on another subnet.

DHCP scope   A pool of IP addresses and optionally other IP configuration parameters from which a DHCP server leases addresses to DHCP clients.

DHCP server authorization   The process of enabling a DHCP server in a domain environment to prevent rogue DHCP servers from operating on the network.

DHCP Unique Identifier (DUID)   A hexadecimal number usually derived from the MAC address of the network interface used by DHCPv6 to identify clients for address leases and to create reservations.

DirectAccess   A role service that is part of the DirectAccess and VPN role service under the Remote Access server role that provides many of the same features as a VPN but adds client management and always-connected capability.

distributed cache mode   A BranchCache mode of operation in which cached data is distributed among client computers in the branch office. *See also* BranchCache.

Distributed File System (DFS)   A role service under the File and Storage Services role that enables you to group shares from different servers into a single logical share called a *namespace*.

distributed firewall policies   A new feature in Windows Server 2016 that enables a network administrator to manage firewall policies for all of a datacenter's virtual networks.

distributed router   A feature of a Hyper-V virtual switch that forwards packets from one virtual subnet to another virtual subnet within the same routing domain.

distributed topology   An IPAM deployment option that places an IPAM server at every site in a network. *See also* IP Address Management (IPAM).

DNS amplification attack   A type of DDoS attack that uses public DNS servers to overwhelm a target with DNS responses by sending DNS queries with spoofed IP addresses.

DNS analytic event   An event that is created every time DNS sends and receives information.

DNS audit event   An audit event that tracks changes to a DNS server, such as when zone or resource changes are made, and is enabled by default.

DNS-based Authentication of Named Entities (DANE)   A new feature in Windows Server 2016 that is used to provide information about the certification authority (CA) used by your domain when a client is requesting DNS information for your domain.

DNS cache locking   A DNS security feature that allows you to control whether data in the DNS cache can be overwritten.

DNS cache poisoning   An attack on DNS servers in which false data is introduced into the DNS server cache, causing the server to return incorrect IP addresses.

DNS client   A computer making a DNS query.

DNS namespace   The entire DNS tree that defines the structure of the names used to identify resources in network domains. It consists of a root name (defined as a period), top-level domains, second-level domains, optionally one or more subdomains, and hostnames separated by periods.

DNS Policy   A new feature in Windows Server 2016 that allows you to manage DNS traffic, filter queries, and load balance your applications based on a number of criteria.

DNS recursion scope   A DNS feature that allows you to specify which DNS queries will use recursion and which will not.

DNS resolver   *See* DNS client.

DNS socket pool   A pool of port numbers used by a DNS server for DNS queries to protect against DNS cache poisoning. *See also* DNS cache poisoning.

DNSKEY   The public key for the zone that DNS resolvers use to verify the digital signature in Resource Record Signature (RRSIG) records.

Domain Name System (DNS)   A distributed hierarchical database composed mainly of computer name and IP address pairs.

Domain Name System Security Extension (DNSSEC)   A suite of features and protocols for validating DNS server responses.

dual IP layer architecture   The current architecture of the IPv6 protocol in Windows, in which both IPv4 and IPv6 share the other components of the stack.

Dynamic DNS (DDNS)   A DNS name-registering process whereby computers in the domain can register or update their own DNS records.

Dynamic Host Configuration Protocol (DHCP)   A component of the TCP/IP protocol suite used to assign an IP address to a host automatically from a defined pool of addresses.

dynamic IP address (DIP)   An address dynamically assigned to a virtual machine that is a member of a software load balancing (SLB) pool.

East-West network traffic   The network traffic between virtual networks and between servers within the datacenter.

exclusion range   A range of IP addresses in the scope that the DHCP server doesn't lease to clients.

Extended Unique Identifier (EUI)-64 interface ID   An autoconfigured IPv6 host address that uses the MAC address of the host plus an additional 16 bits.

Extensible Authentication Protocol (EAP)   A certificate-based authentication method considered more secure than password-based methods.

failover   The ability of a server to recover from network hardware failure by having redundant hardware that can immediately take over for a device failure.

folder target   A UNC path configured on a DFS namespace folder that points to a shared folder hosted on a server.

force tunneling   A remote access method in which all traffic from the client, including traffic destined for the Internet, goes over the DirectAccess tunnel, in contrast to split tunneling in which only intranet traffic is sent over the DirectAccess tunnel. *See also* split tunneling.

forwarder   A DNS server to which other DNS servers send requests they can't resolve themselves.

forward lookup zone (FLZ)   A DNS zone containing records that translate names to IP addresses, such as A, AAAA, and MX records. It's named after the domain whose resource records it contains.

frame   A Data Link layer unit of data that contains a destination and source MAC address and an error-checking code that is ready to be transferred to the network medium.

fully qualified domain name (FQDN)   The full domain name for a host that specifically identifies it within the hierarchy of the Domain Name System.

G

GlobalNames zone (GNZ)   A feature that provides a way for IT administrators to add single-label names (computer names that don't use a domain suffix, such as NetBIOS names) to DNS, thereby allowing client computers to resolve these names without including a DNS suffix in the query.

glue A record   An A record used to resolve the name in an NS record to its IP address.

Group Policy provisioning   A method of provisioning IPAM that uses the Group Policy tool to perform tasks such as creating security groups, setting firewall rules, and creating shares for each IPAM-managed server. *See also* IP Address Management (IPAM).

H

HNV virtual network   An autonomous system in which a virtual network is "owned" by a single tenant and is therefore isolated from other virtual networks.

hop count   The number of routers a packet must go through to reach the destination network.

hosted cache mode   A BranchCache mode of operation in which cached data is stored on one or more file servers in the branch office. *See also* BranchCache.

hostname   An assigned name that is associated with an IP address, so when a client looks up the name www.microsoft.com, the DNS server returns an IP address.

host record   A resource record in a DNS zone that consists of a hostname and an IP address. Also called an *A record* or *AAAA record* depending on whether the IP address is IPv4 or IPv6.

hot standby mode   A DHCP failover mode in which one server is assigned as the active server to provide DHCP services to clients and the other server is placed in standby mode. *See also* DHCP failover.

hybrid topology   An IPAM deployment option that has a single IPAM server collecting information from all managed servers in the enterprise and IPAM servers at key branch locations. *See also* IP Address Management (IPAM).

Hyper-V Network Virtualization (HNV)   A key component of the Windows Server 2016 software-defined network (SDN) environment that provides a virtual network infrastructure that decouples the virtual network topology from the physical network.

I

infrastructure tunnel   A tunnel created between the client computer and the DirectAccess server used for control of the DirectAccess connection.

Internet Protocol-Hypertext Transfer Protocol Secure (IP-HTTPS)   A tunneling protocol used to transport IPv6 packets over an HTTPS connection.

intranet tunnel   The tunnel created when a user signs in to the DirectAccess client; it provides access to resources on the network.

Intra-Site Automatic Tunnel Addressing Protocol (ISATAP)   An automatic tunneling protocol used to transmit IPv6 packets between dual IP layer hosts across an IPv4 network. *See also* dual IP layer architecture.

IP address block   The largest unit for referring to an IP address space; consists of a contiguous range of IP addresses with a corresponding subnet mask.

IP Address Management (IPAM)   A feature in Windows Server 2016 that enables an administrator to manage the IP address space with monitoring, auditing, and reporting functions to help manage DHCP and DNS.

IP address range   A pool of continuous addresses in an IP address block; usually corresponds to a DHCP scope.

IP address range group   One or more IP address ranges that are logically grouped by some criteria.

IPAM client   A Windows computer with the IPAM management console installed that discovers servers that you want to manage and collects and stores data from IPAM-managed servers in the IPAM database; typically used for remote management. *See also* IP Address Management (IPAM).

IPAM server   A Windows Server member server with the IPAM Server feature installed. *See also* IP Address Management (IPAM).

iterative query   A type of DNS query to which a DNS server responds with the best information it has to satisfy the query. The DNS server doesn't query additional DNS servers in an attempt to resolve the query.

K

Kerberos proxy   An authentication method that allows a client computer to authenticate to a domain controller by using the DirectAccess server as a proxy.

key-signing key (KSK)   A DNSSEC key that has a private and public key associated with it. The private key is used to sign all DNSKEY records and the public key is used as a trust anchor for validating DNS responses. *See also* Domain Name System Security Extension (DNSSEC).

layer 3 (L3) forwarder   A forwarder that performs simple routing between virtual networks on a host and VLANs configured on the physical network.

lease duration   A parameter of a DHCP IP address lease that specifies how long a DHCP client can keep an address.

lease renewal   The process of a DHCP client renewing its IP address lease by using unicast DHCPREQUEST messages.

link-local   An address that can communicate only on the local LAN.

link-local IPv6 address   Similar in function to the IPv4 APIPA addresses, link-local IPv6 addresses begin with `fe80`, are self-configuring, and can't be routed. *See also* Automatic Private IP Addressing (APIPA).

load balancing   The distribution of traffic between two or more interfaces, providing an increase in overall network throughput that a server is able to maintain.

load balancing and failover (LBFO)   A technology that allows multiple network interfaces to work in tandem to provide increased bandwidth, load balancing, and fault tolerance. *See also* NIC teaming.

load-balancing mode   The default DHCP failover mode in which both DHCP servers participate in address leasing at the same time from a shared pool of addresses. *See also* DHCP failover.

localhost   A reserved name that corresponds to the loopback address, 127.0.0.1. *See also* loopback address.

logical AND operation   A binary operation in which there are two operands; the result is 0 if either operand is 0 and 1 if both operands are 1.

loopback address   The IP address 127.0.0.1, which always refers to the local computer and is used to test the functioning of TCP/IP.

M

MAC address   A physical-layer address that is an integral part of a network interface card (NIC).

managed server   A Windows server running one or more of these Microsoft services: DHCP, DNS, Active Directory, and NPS.

management plane   The SDN component that allows the device to be configured through a user interface by a network administrator utilizing management software.

manual provisioning   A method of provisioning IPAM that requires configuring each IPAM server task and managed server manually.

maximum client lead time (MCLT)   The maximum amount of time a DHCP server can extend a lease for a DHCP client without the partner server's knowledge. It also defines the amount of time a server waits before assuming control over all DHCP services if its partner is in Partner Down state.

metric   A value assigned to the gateway based on the speed of the interface used to access the gateway.

Microsoft Challenge Handshake Authentication Protocol (MS-CHAP)   Microsoft's implementation of CHAP used to authenticate an entity (for example, a user attempting access to the network). *See also* Challenge Handshake Authentication Protocol (CHAP).

Microsoft Challenge Handshake Authentication Protocol version 2 (MS-CHAP v2)   An authentication protocol used to authenticate a user or server. This newer version of MS-CHAP is more secure than MS-CHAP. *See also* Microsoft Challenge Handshake Authentication Protocol (MS-CHAP).

multicasting   A network communication in which a packet is addressed so that more than one destination can receive it.

multicast scope   A type of DHCP scope that allows assigning multicast addresses dynamically to multicast servers and clients by using Multicast Address Dynamic Client Allocation Protocol (MADCAP).

multisite DirectAccess   A DirectAccess configuration with two or more DirectAccess servers, each providing a secure entry point into a network.

multitenant aware   Gateway software that supports multiple isolated virtual networks.

MX record   A type of DNS resource record that is used to resolve a domain name in an email address to the IP address of a mail server for that domain.

N

name resolution policy table (NRPT)   A table configured on a DirectAccess client that makes sure DNS requests for network resources are directed to internal DNS servers, not Internet DNS servers.

namespace   A name given to a grouping of folders maintained on a DFS server that facilitates access to shares on multiple servers, using a single UNC path.

namespace root   A folder that's the logical starting point for a namespace.

namespace server   A server with the DFS Namespaces role service installed.

name squatting   A DNS problem that occurs when a non-Windows computer registers its name with a DNS server, but the name has already been registered by a Windows computer.

network access server (NAS)   A protocol-specific device that aids in connecting access clients to the network.

Network Address Translation (NAT)   A process by which a router or other type of gateway device replaces the source or destination IP addresses in a packet before forwarding the packet.

Network Location Server (NLS)   A basic web server used by DirectAccess client computers to determine whether they're on the intranet or a remote network.

Network Security Group (NSG)   A named security policy based on access control lists.

Network Virtualization using Generic Routing Encapsulation (NVGRE)   A tunneling protocol that uses Generic Routing Encapsulation for the tunnel header.

Next Secure (NSEC)   A DNSSEC record returned when the requested resource record does not exist. *See also* Domain Name System Security Extension (DNSSEC).

Next Secure 3 (NSEC3)   An alternative to NSEC records. NSEC3 can prevent zone-walking, which is a technique of repeating NSEC queries to get all the names in a zone. *See also* Next Secure (NSEC).

Next Secure 3 (NSEC3) Parameter   DNSSEC records used to determine which NSEC3 records should be included in responses to queries for nonexistent records. *See also* Next Secure 3 (NSEC3).

NIC teaming   A technology that allows multiple network interfaces to work in tandem to provide increased bandwidth, load balancing, and fault tolerance. *See also* load balancing and failover (LBFO).

Northbound interface   An application programming interface through which commands and policies are sent to the SDN controller, in this case the Network Controller.

North-South network traffic   The network traffic traveling between the datacenter and external clients that need to access services provided by the datacenter.

octet   An 8-bit value; a number from 0 to 255 that's one of the four numbers in a dotted decimal IP address.

packet   A Network-layer unit of data used by IPv4 and IPv6 that contains destination and source IP addresses along with other flags and parameters.

Password Authentication Protocol (PAP)   An authentication protocol that uses passwords sent in plaintext to authenticate an entity; not secure and therefore not recommended.

perimeter network   A boundary between the private network and the public Internet that is where most resources available to the Internet, such as mail, web, DNS, and VPN servers, are located.

Port Address Translation (PAT)   An extension of NAT that allows several hundred workstations to access the Internet with a single public Internet address.

Preboot Execution Environment (PXE)   A network environment built into many NICs that allows a computer to boot from an image stored on a network server.

preference   A value used to indicate priority when there are multiple DHCPv6 servers.

prefix   The part of the IPv6 address that's the network identifier.

primary zone   A DNS zone containing a read/write master copy of all resource records for the zone; this zone is authoritative for the zone.

Protected Extensible Authentication Protocol (PEAP)   A certificate-based and password-based authentication method designed to protect EAP messages by encapsulating them in a secure encrypted tunnel and using MS-CHAP v2 for user authentication. *See also* Extensible Authentication Protocol (EAP).

provider address (PA)   The address used by the host network that reflects the hosting provider's physical network addressing scheme.

PTR record   A type of DNS resource record that is used to resolve a known IP address to a hostname.

Q

Quality of Service (QoS)   A technology that allows you to configure priorities for different types of network traffic so that delay-sensitive data is prioritized over regular data.

query resolution policy   A DNS policy that specifies how DNS queries are handled by the DNS server.

R

RADIUS server group   A group of RADIUS servers configured to accept authentication and authorization requests from a RADIUS proxy. *See also* Remote Authentication Dial In User Service (RADIUS).

realm   The Active Directory domain where a RADIUS server is located.

receive side scaling (RSS)   A feature for network drivers that efficiently distributes the processing of incoming network traffic among multiple CPU cores.

recursion scope   A scope that defines which queries will use DNS recursion.

recursive query   A query in which the DNS server processes the query until it responds with an address that satisfies the query or with an "I don't know" message. The process might require the DNS server to query several additional DNS servers.

referral   (1) A response to an iterative query in which the address of another name server is returned to the requester. (2) A prioritized list of servers used to access files in a namespace.

Remote Access   A server role that provides services to keep a mobile workforce and branch offices securely connected to resources at the main office.

Remote Authentication Dial In User Service (RADIUS)   An industry-standard client/server protocol that centralizes authentication, authorization, and accounting for a network.

remote differential compression (RDC)   An algorithm used to determine changes that have been made to a file and replicate only those changes.

replication   The process of creating redundant copies of files on multiple servers.

replication group   Two or more servers, known as members, that synchronize data in folders so that when a change occurs, all replication group members are updated at once.

replication topology   A DFS replication setting that describes the connections used to replicate files between servers.

reservation   An IP address associated with a DHCP client's MAC address to ensure that when the client requests an IP address, it always gets the same one along with any configured options.

resource records   Data in a DNS database containing information about network resources, such as hostnames, other DNS servers, and services; each record is identified by a letter code.

Resource Record Signature (RRSIG)   A key containing the signature for a single resource record, such as an A or MX record.

Response Rate Limiting (RRL) A new DNS Server role feature in Windows Server 2016 that mitigates a type of distributed denial of service (DDoS) attack called a *DNS amplification attack*.

reverse lookup zone (RLZ) A DNS zone containing PTR records that map IP addresses to names; it's named with the IP network address (IPv4 or IPv6) of the computer whose records it contains.

role-based access control (RBAC) An access control option that allows you to define different IPAM administrative roles.

root certificate A certificate establishing that all other certificates from that CA are trusted; also called a *CA certificate*.

root hints A list of name servers preconfigured on Windows DNS servers that point to Internet root servers, which are DNS servers located on the Internet and managed by IANA.

root server A DNS server that keeps a database of addresses of other DNS servers managing top-level domain names.

round robin A method of responding to DNS queries when more than one IP address exists for the queried host. Each IP address is placed first in the list of returned addresses an equal number of times so that hosts are accessed alternately.

routing domain A virtual network with one or more subnets that are isolated from other virtual networks.

routing domain ID (RDID) A number that uniquely identifies a virtual network within the datacenter.

routing table A list of network destinations and information on which interface can be used to reach the destination.

S

scavenging The process whereby the DNS server periodically checks the zone file for stale records periodically and deletes those meeting the criteria for a stale record.

secondary zone A DNS zone containing a read-only copy of all resource records for the zone. Changes can't be made directly on a secondary DNS server, but because it contains an exact copy of the primary zone, it's considered authoritative for the zone.

segment A Transport-layer unit of data that is used by TCP and UDP; it contains the destination and source port numbers used to identify Application-layer protocols.

shared secret A text string known only to two systems trying to authenticate each other.

single-root IO virtualization (SR-IOV) A technology that enhances a virtual network adapter's performance by allowing a virtual adapter to bypass the virtual switch software on the parent partition (the Hyper-V host) and communicate directly with the physical hardware.

SLB Host Agent A software load balancing (SLB) component that interfaces between Hyper-V hosts and Network Controller to distribute SLB policies and configure Hyper-V virtual switches for SLB.

SLB MUX An SLB component that maps VIPs to DIPs on incoming East-West traffic and forwards the traffic to the selected DIP.

SMB Direct A performance technology designed specifically for the SMB protocol; SMB Direct protocol that uses the capabilities of an RDMA-capable network adapter, nearly eliminating server processor utilization for data transfers.

SMB Multichannel A technology that provides fault tolerance and improved performance in a connection between a client and a server providing an SMB share.

software-defined networking (SDN) A collection of technologies designed to make the network infrastructure flexible and responsive to the ever-changing network requirements in enterprise and cloud networks.

software load balancing (SLB)   A software-defined networking (SDN) feature available in Windows Server 2016 that allows a hosting provider to distribute tenant network traffic across virtual network resources to increase virtual network performance and provide fault tolerance.

source IP address   The IP address of a computer that's sending a packet.

Southbound interface   An interface through which policies are sent from the SDN controller to the network device, or in this case the virtual switch.

split scope   A fault-tolerant DHCP configuration in which two DHCP servers share the same scope information, allowing both servers to offer DHCP services to clients.

split tunneling   A remote access method in which only requests for resources on the intranet are sent over the DirectAccess tunnel; requests for Internet resources are sent out through the regular Internet connection.

stale resource record   A DNS record that is no longer valid, either because the resource is offline for an extended period or permanently, or because the resource's name or address has changed.

stateful autoconfiguration   A method of IPv6 autoconfiguration in which the node uses an autoconfiguration protocol, such as DHCPv6, to obtain its IPv6 address and other configuration information.

stateless autoconfiguration   A method of IPv6 autoconfiguration in which the node listens for router advertisement messages from a local router.

static route   A manually configured route in the routing table that instructs the router where to send packets destined for particular networks.

stub zone   A DNS zone containing a read-only copy of only the zone's SOA and NS records and the necessary A records to resolve NS records. A stub zone forwards queries to a primary DNS server for that zone and is not authoritative for the zone.

subnet mask   A 32-bit dotted decimal number consisting of an unbroken series of binary 1 digits followed by an unbroken series of binary 0 digits; used with an IP address to determine the network ID.

subnetting   A process that reallocates bits from an IP address's host portion to the network portion, creating multiple smaller address spaces.

supernetting   A process that reallocates bits from an IP address's network portion to the host portion, effectively combining smaller subnets into a larger supernet.

superscope   A special type of scope consisting of one or more member scopes; it allows a DHCP server to service multiple IP subnets on a single physical network.

Switch Embedded Teaming (SET)   A new feature in Windows Server 2016 that allows up to eight identical physical adapters on the host system to be configured as a team and mapped to a virtual switch.

Teredo   An automatic IPv6-over-IPv4 tunneling protocol that solves the problem of 6to4's requirement of a public IPv4 address and the inability to traverse NAT routers. *See also* 6to4.

Teredo client   A host device behind a NAT router that's running IPv4 and IPv6 and wants to use Teredo tunneling to access IPv6 devices or other Teredo clients across an IPv4 network.

Teredo relay   A router running IPv6 and IPv4 that forwards packets between Teredo clients and hosts on IPv6 networks. The Teredo relay advertises the 2001::/32 network to let hosts know that it provides Teredo relay services.

Teredo server   A host on the Internet running IPv4 and IPv6 that's connected to both IPv4 and IPv6 networks that facilitates communication between Teredo clients.

top-level domain (TLD) server   A DNS server that maintains addresses of other DNS servers that are authoritative for second-level domains.

Transmission Control Protocol/Internet Protocol (TCP/IP)   A network protocol suite designed to deliver data packets to computers on any scale of network from a small two-computer LAN to the worldwide Internet.

Transport Layer Security (TLS)   A cryptographic protocol used to encrypt messages over a network.

trust anchor   A DNSKEY that is usually for a zone but can also be a DS key for a delegated zone. Public keys are used as trust anchors for validating DNS responses.

tunnel   A method of transferring data across an unsecured network in such a way that the actual data is hidden from all but the sender and receiver.

tunneling   A common network protocol technique that allows transmitting a packet in a format that would otherwise be incompatible with the network architecture by encapsulating the packet in a compatible header format.

U

unicast address   An address in a unit of network data intended for a single destination computer.

unique local IPv6 address   An address for devices on a private network that can't be routed on the Internet.

unknown record support   A new feature of DNS in Windows Server 2016 that has the ability to support resource records of a type unknown to the DNS server on Windows Server 2016.

unmapped address space   Any IP address or IP address range that hasn't been assigned to an IP address block. By default, all IP address ranges are unmapped until you create IP address blocks.

User Class   A custom value you create on the DHCP server and then configure on a DHCP client; used much like the Vendor Class value.

V

Vendor Class   A field in the DHCP packet that device manufacturers or OS vendors can use to identify a device model or an OS version.

Virtual Extensible LAN (VXLAN)   A standard and widely supported tunneling protocol that allows you to communicate between virtual networks and between virtual networks and the physical network.

virtual IP address (VIP)   An IP address exposed to the public Internet that clients use to access resources on VMs in the datacenter.

virtual machine multi-queue (VMMQ)   A new feature in Windows Server 2016 that reduces the overhead in getting packets from the physical network to a virtual machine on the host.

virtual machine queue (VMQ)   A technology that accelerates vNIC performance by delivering packets from the external network directly to the vNIC, bypassing the management operating system.

virtual private network (VPN)   A network connection that uses the Internet to give mobile users or branch offices secure access to a company's network resources on a private network.

virtual receive side scaling (vRSS)   RSS for virtual adapters; its purpose is to distribute the processing load for incoming network traffic among multiple virtual processors in a VM.

virtual subnet ID (VSID)   A unique 24-bit number throughout the datacenter in the range 4096 to 16,777,214.

VPN connection profile   A connection profile that allows you to create VPN connections that can be distributed to user's computers so that VPN clients do not have to be configured on each client station.

VPN reconnect   A feature that automatically re-establishes a VPN connection that is temporarily lost with no intervention from the user.

Z

zone   A grouping of DNS information that represents one or more domains and possibly subdomains.

zone delegation   The transfer of authority for a subdomain to a new zone, which can be on the same server as the parent zone or another server.

zone id   A number that is used to distinguish which interface an IPv6 link-local address is bound to.

zone-level statistics   A feature in Windows Server 2016 that provides detailed statistics for each zone to show how a DNS server is used.

zone replication   The transfer of zone changes from one DNS server to another.

zone replication scope   A scope that determines which Active Directory partition the zone is stored in and which DCs the zone information is replicated to.

zone scope   A subset of a zone where a zone can contain multiple zone scopes and each zone scope has its own set of resource records.

zone signing   A DNSSEC feature that uses digital signatures contained in DNSSEC-related resource records to verify DNS responses. *See also* Domain Name System Security Extension (DNSSEC).

zone-signing key (ZSK)   A public and private key combination stored in a certificate used to sign the zone.

zone transfer   An operation that copies all or part of a zone from one DNS server to another and occurs as a result of a secondary server requesting the transfer from another server.

zone transfer policy   A DNS policy that specifies whether a zone transfer is allowed. For example, you can allow or deny zone transfers to particular subnets.

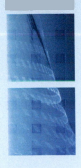

INDEX